The History of Islamic Political Thought

The History of Islamic Political Thought

From the Prophet to the Present

ANTONY BLACK

Routledge
New York

To Aileen, and Christopher

Published in 2001 by
Routledge
29 West 35th Street
New York, NY 10001

Routledge is an imprint of the Taylor and Francis Group

Copyright © 2001 by Antony Black

Originally published in Great Britain by
Edinburgh University Press, Edinburgh, in 2001

Typeset in Trump Medieval by Koinonia, Bury, and
printed and bound in Great Britain by
The University Press, Cambridge

*Library of Congress Cataloging-in-Publication data is available
from the Library of Congress*

Black, Antony
The history of Islamic political thought: from the prophet to
the present / by Antony Black
ISBN 0-415-93242-4 (hardback)
ISBN 0-415-93243-2 (paperback)
Includes bibliography and references.

Contents

Analytical Table of Contents

Abbreviations

Abbreviations in Roman type refer to entries in the Bibliography.

AS   Alam and Subrahmanyam (eds) (1998)
BL   Ashtiany et al. (eds) (1990)
BSOAS   *Bulletin of the School of Oriental and African Studies*
CH India *The New Cambridge History of India*
CH Iran   *The Cambridge History of Iran*
CH Islam *The Cambridge History of Islam*
EI   *Encyclopaedia of Islam*, 2nd edn
IC   *Islamic Culture*
IJMES   *International Journal of Middle Eastern Studies*
IS   *Islamic Studies*
JSAI   *Jerusalem Studies in Arabic and Islam*
LM   Lerner and Mahdi (eds) (1963)
NL   Nasr and Leaman (eds) (1996)
Q.   Qur'an
REI   *Revue d'Études Islamiques*
SI   *Studia Islamica*
VC   al-Farabi, *The Virtuous (or Excellent) City*, ed. R. Walzer (see p. 77, n. 14)
ZDMG   *Zeitschrift der Deutsche Morgenländische Gesellschaft*

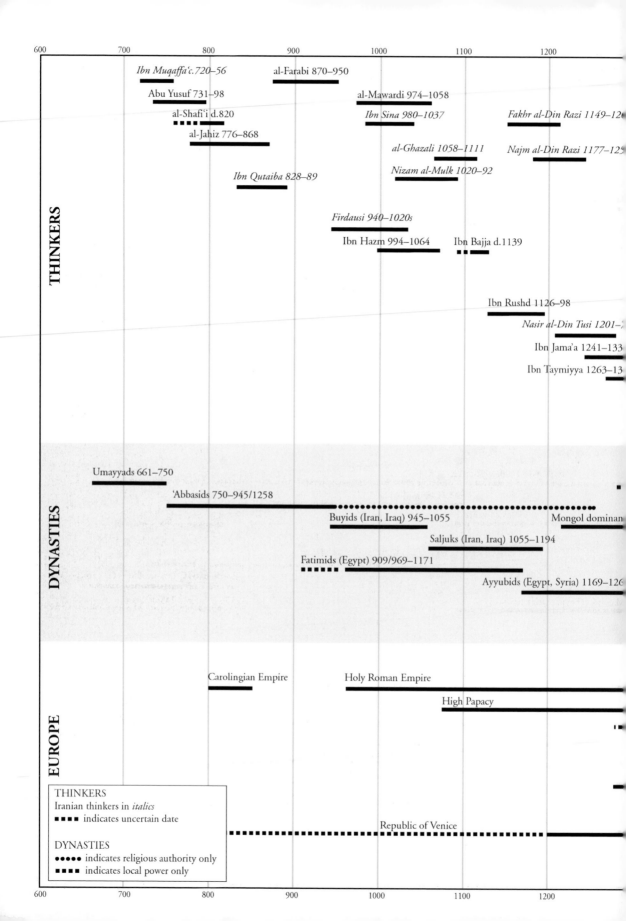

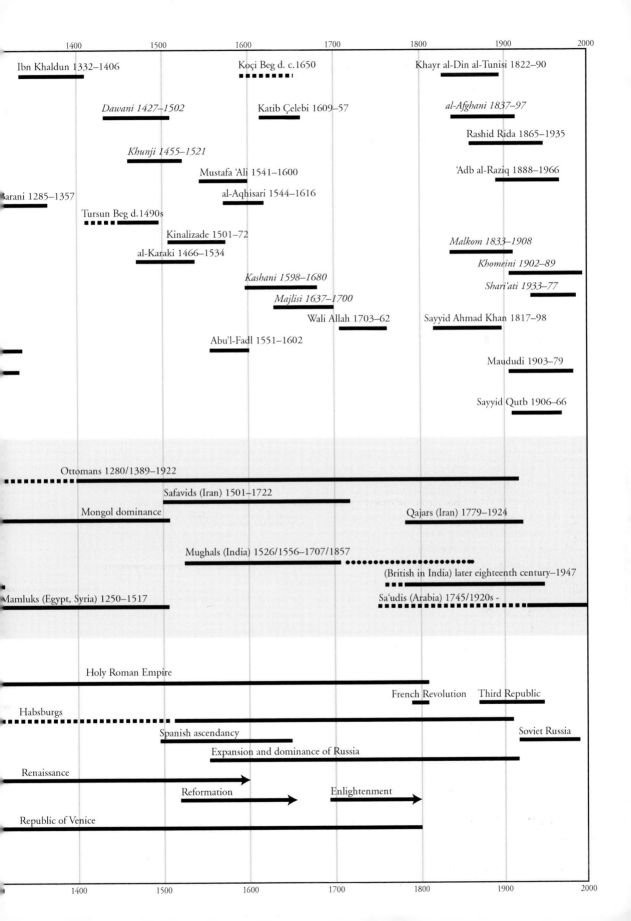

Preface

This is a complete history of Islamic political thought from early Islam (c.622–61) to the age of Fundamentalism (c.1922–2000). It is a description and an interpretation. I have explored the milieu, meaning and significance of thinkers, ideas and political cultures. This work encompasses religion, law, ethics, philosophy and statecraft. These were expressed in systematic treatises, occasional writings, official rhetoric and popular slogans.

This history of Islamic political thought is a gripping story in its own right. Up to now, it has been neglected by all but a few specialists. Islam was and is one of the most powerful means of explaining human life and giving meaning to our activity. As a political ideology, it has motivated and still does motivate individuals and groups. It is especially important today because, rightly or wrongly, it is perceived as the antagonist of Western values. Yet little attention has been paid to the *history* of Islamic political thought. One cannot understand political Islam today without understanding where it is coming from. Political and social movements within contemporary Islam are at least partly grounded on ideas based on historical precedents and earlier models. Not least, we can see both Western and Islamic political thought in a new light by setting the histories of each side by side. These were the reasons for writing this book. They will, I hope, prove reasons for reading it.

The book is divided into five parts: (1) the formative period, from early Islam to about 1000, (2) from the Saljuks to the Mongol invasions – the most prolific period, (3) from c.1220 to c.1500, a period of isolated giants and the decline of classical Islamic thought, (4) the early modern empires, (5) the period of Western influence, from c.1830 until today.

STYLE

I have attempted to present ideas remote from ourselves in time and place so far as possible in the idiom of those who expressed them and in the categories of their own culture. Many of the categories of European historiography (such as 'medieval', 'renaissance', 'feudalism' and 'class') are not directly applicable to the Islamic world,[1] and I have avoided them where possible. I have given the meaning of an original word or concept (for example, Shari'a) at its first mention and in the Glossary; I have subsequently used either the original term or the closest English equivalent (with a capital letter: Law, Code, Religious Law). Sometimes, terms like religio-political or moral-legal best describe what is being discussed. Dates are based on the (Western) Common Era (BC/AD).

BIBLIOGRAPHY AND REFERENCES

I have indicated further reading in notes at the beginnings of chapters or sections. Primary sources are given in a note at the beginning of the relevant passage, which is indicated in bold under the author's name in the Index, for example for al-Farabi in n. 14 indicated at p. 61. When a primary source is quoted from a secondary work, this is followed by, for example, (*in* Bloggs 1978: 144). In order to minimise notes without cluttering up the text, I have used the author–date system for frequently cited works, which are in the Bibliography, and conventional referencing for other works. Full accents of Arabic, Persian and Turkish words and names are given in the Glossary and Index.

ACKNOWLEDGEMENTS

My knowledge of original languages is confined to a limited acquaintance with Arabic. I have relied almost entirely on translations of original texts. I have tried to acquaint myself with the nuances of key terms so as to be able to grasp and convey the meaning of the originals. Since I do not read Arabic, Persian or Turkish, I am more than usually indebted to other scholars. I am grateful, first and foremost, to Islamicists who encouraged me as a novice when I set out on this venture despite my linguistic deficiencies, in the hope perhaps that division of labour may sometimes be fruitful. I am grateful to Patricia Crone, Sami Zubaida, Oliver Leaman, Richard Kimber, Ahmed Andrews and the late Salim Kemal for enlightening discussions. Patricia Crone has read and commented exhaustively on drafts of Chapters 1–5 and 12, and responded more than generously to my many queries about early Islam. Sami Zubaida has enlightened me in many conversations, and read and commented on Chapters 25 and 26. I am also very grateful to numerous scholars who have generously given their time to read and comment on various chapters: Michael Cook and Ira Lapidus on Chapters 1 to 3; Wilferd Madelung on Chapter 4; Oliver Leaman on Chapters 6 and 11; Carole Hillenbrand on Chapters 7–9; Kate Fleet on Chapters 20 and 21; Charles Melville on Chapter 22; Virginia Aksan on Chapters 24 and 25; Brian Baxter and Antony Wood on the Introduction. On Ottoman political thought, Metin Kunt gave me advice, and Rhoads Murphey clarified some textual points. These colleagues have saved me from many pitfalls and have indicated omissions, which, where possible, I have tried to make good. I have not always succeeded, and the errors which remain are entirely mine.

I owe a special debt of gratitude to Janet Coleman, and to the directors of the European Science Foundation project on The Origins of the Modern State (1989–92), Jean-Philippe Genet and Wim Blockmans, for including me in a working group on The Individual in Theory and Practice. It was through their intellectual hospitality, and the associated meeting with Turkish scholars in Istanbul (October 1991), that the present study was conceived.

I am grateful to The Nuffield Foundation for giving me a half-time research fellowship in 1993–4, which enabled me to continue research (though alas not to continue learning Arabic) despite being 'head of department'. I am also grateful to the British Academy for two small grants and to the University of Dundee for a small research grant, which have enabled me to travel to libraries. I would like to thank Nicola Carr of Edinburgh University Press for her patience in helping me steer this project towards publication.

My friends and family know how much I owe to them.

NOTE

1   See Antony Black, 'Decolonization of Concepts', *Journal of Early Modern History* 1 (1997), pp. 55–69.

Introduction

Islam comprises a distinct and self-contained cultural unit. Political thought is the study of the exercise of power, of who should exercise it, and how much power they should have; it is about justice in relationships between people, especially between those in power and those they rule, and the just distribution of goods in society. It enquires why states exist and what they should try to achieve.

Islamic political thought forms a significant part of the intellectual history of homo sapiens. It comprises a coherent, ongoing tradition, separate from the West and with a logic of its own. Within it are an array of sub-stories. The sources and data examined in this book are, therefore, an intrinsic part of human experience and achievement; the words and thoughts of generous spirits remain as vital as if they were still alive. Yet the history of Islamic political thought has been neglected by Western historians and political theorists alike.

In studying a subject like this, one is able to recognise and enjoy the diversity of human undertakings, the excitement of discovery, the kinship of the different. Since we are all members of one species, we should be able to understand each other's cultures, and recognise in them things which have some relevance to ourselves. Love of what is different is natural to an enquiring mind. The 'other' does not have to be an enemy; and indeed Edward Said's famed critique of the Western historiography of Islam[1] pales before the centuries of Islamic cultural imperialism, not only directed against Christendom and the West. In any case, history, insofar as it keeps alive the memory of past wrongs, is not helpful for the future. World history and comparative history are not tastes acquired from colonialism or globalisation. To reject them is to lock everyone into their own backyard.

Western political thought has been studied in great detail. Particular aspects of Islamic political thought have been studied, though there remains much scope for research. Attempts have been made to trace a continuous story for Western political thought, usually from the early Greeks to the present day; this 'history of political thought' has entered university curricula. Yet hardly any attempt has been made to look at Islamic political thought as a whole, to present its history from the origins to the present day. The only comprehensive study is Nagel (1981) (see Bibliography), but this is not very analytical and does not explore historical relationships. Erwin Rosenthal (1958) and Lambton (1981) survey wide ranges of thinkers; but neither seeks to be comprehensive or presents thinkers in their historical contexts. And what Islam achieved in this field has gone almost entirely unnoticed by pundits in political philosophy. How much better we would know Ibn Sina and Mawardi if they had written in Europe! This is particularly surprising in view of the recent surge of interest in political Islam.

A history of Western political thought can only claim to be 'the history of political thought' if we assume that what matters in history is what has led to the views we now hold and the consensus of which we approve (mostly, liberal democracy). In fact, some thinkers and movements in the present canon might not qualify on this ground, for example Thomas More or Karl Marx. Regardless of that, such an approach obviously omits much, perhaps most, of intellectual history. It prejudges the relevance that other thinkers or ideas may later be thought to have had to this development. Perhaps more seriously, it prejudges the relevance which other ideas in the past may have to some future consensus. (One may of course wish the present consensus to remain undisturbed, but that is unlikely and, in my view, undesirable.) Above all, ideas should not necessarily be treated in this teleological manner at all. It results in edited history. No botanist would dream of presenting a survey of flora based on what grows, or could grow, in a particular climate. Partial histories lead to a partial understanding of our species.

Further, I do not see how one can claim to understand the history of ideas even *in any single culture* without some awareness of what was going on in other cultures. One cannot explain any sequence of phenomena without reference to things outside it. This is generally acknowledged where there is interaction, as in the case of the histories of England and France, or of Rome and the Germans; though the need to know not only that an outside force made an impact, but also the mentality of those propelling it, is less often acknowledged, at least in practice.

But my point is, rather, that one can best isolate the causes of a phenomenon by examining different phenomena of the same class (in this case, different traditions of political thought) side by side. Comparison can be especially useful for causal explanation when one is able to examine two different sets of phenomena which emerged from the same or a similar starting point. One can then ask what it was that was present in the one but absent from the other, so that one can explain the differences. Comparison is as near as history gets to repeatable experiments. This was what first inspired the present study.

Thus an understanding of the history of Islamic political ideas may promote an understanding of the history of European political ideas. For it so happens that in their earlier phases the Islamic and European political cultures (as also the Byzantine) had more in common with each other than either had with other cultures: namely Abrahamic monotheism, the belief in a unique and final revelation by God to humankind, largely or wholly in textual form, and governing most or all of human conduct; plus the philosophies of Plato and

Aristotle. Islamdom and Christendom were moreover both part of a common Mediterranean world. Islamic intellectual history was the closest to Europe both geographically and in content. Any attempt to explain the uniqueness of Europe must therefore involve comparison with the Islamic world.

This is as true with regard to political institutions and ideology as it is with regard to economic life. What was it that caused modern states of the European type, and modern political ideas like sovereignty and representation, to develop here but not there? One can go some way towards explaining what it was that made European states and ideologies tick, by comparing them with states and ideologies in another political culture with a different outcome. One can best perceive both the historical and the human importance of an Aquinas or a Hobbes by considering how their counterparts elsewhere fared. The Islamic world offers the paradigmatic alternative to Europe.

The outcome of the impact of the Abrahamic and Platonic legacies upon the two cultures was indeed different in almost every respect. Moreover, we will find that, while there are some amazing similarities on certain points, the overall conceptual patterns were markedly different. This might make one reassess the importance sometimes attached to these traditions in histories of Western political thought. It may suggest that other factors (for example, the legacies of Rome and Iran) were of equal or greater importance.

In this book, I suggest some of the main similarities and differences between political ideas in the Islamic and European worlds; but, since this is a history of solely Islamic ideas, I do so only as a means of clarifying Islamic concepts. This may indicate where a systematic study of similarities and differences might go; and I would like to return to this on another occasion. I have not considered here the *influence* of Islamic thinkers upon the great European awakening from 1050; though I have of course considered the influence of European upon Islamic thought, especially from around 1800.

The importance of such comparison was clearly perceived by Max Weber (1864–1920), but it was lost sight of progressively during the twentieth century. This is partly because comparison is extraordinarily difficult. It requires mastery of two fields. Weber's understanding of the Islamic world was in some ways defective;[2] and the increase in knowledge since then makes the initial task much harder. One can see this in unsuccessful attempts by two outstanding Islamicists, Hodgson and Makdisi, both clearly out of their depth when speaking of the West.[3] Crone and Cook make a more convincing comparison between early Islam and early Calvinism.[4]

Another type of comparison could be conducted between intellectual traditions regardless of whether they came into contact or had similar origins. The purpose of this might be to discover, for example, whether these, or perhaps all, intellectual traditions share certain features and go through similar paths of change, or whether (equally illuminatingly) they have little or nothing in common. For this purpose, one could compare histories of political thought in China, India, Islam and Europe. While this is obviously far beyond the scope of the present study, I would be glad if this study helped provide the groundwork for such further comparison.

The ultimate point of all history (when it is not an expression of chauvinism) is to promote understanding of ourselves and our species. We cannot achieve this by looking only at one sub-species. Yet the history of Western political thought is taught and studied as if it were the only history of political thought.

Such imbalance is all the more surprising in an age (supposedly) of globalisation, and in a civilisation that professes belief in multi-cultural societies (of which Islamic history, as it happens, provides prototypes), and indeed in a multi-cultural international society. Is this because Islam (like other religions) is regarded as a personal creed, idiosyncratic perhaps (though with admittedly important social and political side-effects) rather than as a serious attempt to understand the universe? Yet even 'unbelieving' historians will not get far unless we appreciate that this is exactly what it is (and, still more, was); unless we recognise and respect the questions to which religions profess to be answers.

Turning to the history of Islam itself, I would suggest that one can only grasp the meaning, in either human or scientific terms, of *any one* tradition by seeing that tradition itself *as a whole* and at least trying to get all its parts into focus. In order to understand any topic or thinker within Islamic culture itself, it is necessary to have some grasp of the rest and be aware of the whole of which these are parts. It is heuristically necessary to correlate each object of historical study with what came before; and, if we are to grasp its long-term cultural function and influence, with what came after. Thus, for example, to understand what Ibn Khaldun was doing, you have to take account (as he certainly did) of Aristotle; and to grasp his historical significance you have to consider Durkheim.

In this way, one can begin to see how the various possible meanings of a belief-system have up to now been put into practice, developed, modified, reformulated or changed. One may, or may not, conclude that, after a given time, all the potentialities of a given belief-system have been expressed. History enables one to avoid misunderstandings which certain miscreants, inside or outside the Islamic world, have foisted on the world in order to obtain their moment in the clouds; here, readers must judge for themselves. In any case, the human story will only be known when we know, among other things, the Islamic story; and the Islamic story can only be known if we view it from the start to the present.

Nowadays the division of intellectual labour in the sciences has been taken to absurd lengths. History suffers especially from this because it is relatively easy to chop a bit off (the life of an individual, a period, a fashion) and make a story of it; these are the most marketable products of history. But it means that quite precisely more and more is known about less and less. This is encouraged by natural human possessiveness ('my subject'), shyness and the fear of making mistakes ('that's not my period'), and public policy (the British 'Research Assessment Exercise'). Large-scale topics take longer to complete, increase the likelihood of error, and are always contentious in their interpretation. But surely one of the joys of science is knowing when you are wrong. Such enterprises usually take one outside the tutelage of an academic patron into an area that is unlikely to be on today's curricula. Unless undertaken (as in the present case) late in life, they diminish the prospect of a career slot.

'Political thought' here refers not just to what is expressed in philosophical and legal treatises, but also to the way people and rulers thought, to the political convictions of individuals and groups, commoners and elites – that is, political culture. It includes systematic treatises, occasional writings, official rhetoric, popular slogans and other evidence of the way people thought about authority and order (Black 1984: 244–51). Ideas and attitudes may often be inferred from casual statements, from political practice itself, from policies and institutions – the types of solution people sought to political problems. This remains, nonetheless, a study of ideas and beliefs, not of institutions and regimes. Yet the two interact; you cannot understand one without the other.

There is no clear demarcation, either in pre-modern or modern times, in Islamdom or Christendom, between the political and the social. Moreover, in the Islamic world, as in pre-modern Europe, politics and the state were not conceived as a category separate from other forms of activity, but as an integral part of religion, morality, law or clan values. Thus our discussion will some-times include what the participants themselves conceived of as religion, law, ethics and statecraft. In particular, under Islam even more than under Christianity, a great deal of political ideology was conducted in terms of *Religionspolitik*.

There were of course, as in all cultures, immense gaps between practice and theory, in this case the ideas of religious Jurists (fuqaha), 'ulama (the Learned), Falasifa (Philosophers), or the Persianate 'Advice to Kings (nasihat al-muluk)' mode. To treat Ibn Sina, Ibn Khaldun and so on as 'Islamic political thought' would be like treating Hobbes, Rousseau and so on as 'European political thought' (as is often done), or (more absurd but more commonplace) Plato and Aristotle as 'Greek political thought'. One would have a study of only exceptional innovators. In fact, in the case of Islam, the (to us) famous 'Philosophers' turned out to be even more than elsewhere a sideshow; hardly anyone read them after 1300, and few before then.

Knowledge of another culture, and comparison with it, may make us see our own ideas in a new, more relative light, making us more aware how much they owe to specific historical conjunctures; and perhaps how fragmentary and even arbitrary they are. This does not compel us to conclude that all outcomes are of equally dubious value. Moral philosophy is a separate subject. Standing where I do, I prefer the Western outcome, but I would not have done so were I a Jew in Germany in the 1930s. If the Western outcome is 'better', it is better by very little. Both traditions have a lamentable record on poverty and the environ-ment. Comparative history may give one empirical reasons for thinking new thoughts.

NOTES

1. Edward W. Said, *Orientalism: Western Conceptions of Islam* (London: Routledge & Kegan Paul, 1978).
2. See Hodgson (1974: vol. 2, pp. 93–4).
3. Ibid., pp. 340–62; Makdisi (1981: 224–90); Makdisi (1990).
4. Crone and Cook (1977: 139–48).

Part I The Messenger and the Law
c.622–1000

The Mission of Muhammad

1

It began with the Qur'an, the 'recitation' by God to Muhammad (d.632). After early opposition and the Flight to Medina (hijra: 622, from which the Islamic calendar is dated), the new revelation fused the tribes of Arabia into a new unity. Nothing prepared Persia and East Rome for the explosion that followed. Between 634 and 656, Arab armies destroyed the one and dismembered the other. The heartlands of Eurasia – Palestine, Syria, Iraq, Egypt, Persia and beyond the Oxus – fell to them. Fifty years later, they had reached the Atlantic and the Indus. There were no reconquests. Such was the force of religion.[1]

This was based on a new religion and new ideas which uniquely combined faith and force. The Muslims organised the large societies fallen prey to them according to a programme, partly premeditated, partly worked out over time. The unique character of Muhammad's venture has amazed Muslims and Islamicists alike. However little we know of the Prophet himself and his original teaching, this was, compared with most revolutions, a success.

It was also a new beginning in the history of ideas; political thought under Islam was different from anything that had gone before. Muhammad was a *prophet* (rasul: messenger), claiming to recite whatever God told him to recite, with no human intermediary. Although he was influenced by Arab tribal custom, Judaism and Christianity, he rebelled against these, and recast their patterns in the furnace of his own revelation.

Thus the foundation of Islam was a decisive break in human thinking about politics and society. When Muhammad and his followers forged a new umma (People, nation), they brought into being at once a sense of Arab nationhood and a new kind of international community. For the first and only time in human history, the nation was transcended at the moment it was created. At the heart of the project was the transfer of power from empire to Prophet (and, later, religious community). The new community was to be based upon the Shari'a (Religious Law, or Code), which was designed to determine morals, law, religious belief and ritual, marriage, sex, trade and society.

What happened can only be explained by seeing it as something that was at the same time (in our language) spiritual and political. Muhammad's point was precisely that earlier theism, though humanitarian in principle, had failed to come to terms with the problem of power. The first conflicts within Islam, about who should lead and how the leader should be appointed, were about the exercise of power in a religious community.

It is clear, from the Constitution of Medina and the earliest phase of Muhammad's teaching there, that his purpose was to construct out of tribal confederacies a new people driven by his own sense of moral mission.[2] Judaism had preached an all-embracing (ethnic) law, while Christianity had preached spiritual (universal) brotherhood. But neither seriously addressed the problem of military power and political authority; both had accepted life under alien, pagan rule. Muhammad preached spiritual brotherhood *plus* an all-embracing law, *and* universal political control to be achieved, if necessary, by military power. Or at least he acted as if this was what he believed: for the irony was that the Muslims had little in the way of political theory to inform what they were doing.

The rise of Islam, and the subsequent shape of Islamic culture, can best be understood if we regard religion, whatever else it may do, as fulfilling identifiable social needs.[3] Muhammad created a new monotheism fitted to the contemporary needs of tribal society, *if* that society was to make something more of itself. To this end, he adapted ideas current in the Middle East. He gave a rationale for seeing the Arabs as the chosen people, *and* giving them a mission to convert or conquer the world. He enabled them to achieve the transition simultaneously from polytheism to monotheism, and from tribalism to nationhood to internationalism.

Thus Muhammad's teaching was applied by people whose way of thinking was suffused by a recent tribal past. Despite the claim to unmediated contact with the divine, Islam intertwined itself with traditional local cultures, especially, for most of its history, with Arab-bedouin tribalism and Iranian patrimonial monarchy. Tribes and tribal societies continued to exist and to flourish under Islamic rule; in mountainous and desert regions, they have persisted into the twentieth century. And we can see several ways in which tribal patterns, by a series of social-ethical mutations, moulded the new society. In revolt against the étatiste Roman and Persian empires, Islam developed a stateless praxis.

Tribal identity continued to have meaning within mainstream Islamic society. 'In the Arab-Muslim world, the social realities consisting of tribe, clan and lineage were characterised by a remarkable consistency and permanence.'[4] In the early army and garrison cities, and long afterwards in urban society, clan connections underlay social and political relationships. The early non-Arab converts had to be attached to an Arab tribe as clients (mawali) of one of its tribesmen. The space which Islam left for clans and tribes may help explain why it spread with such ease in central Asia and sub-Saharan Africa, absorbing newcomers (notably the Turco-Mongol peoples). Unlike the monarchical-feudal states of Christian Europe, the Islamic People linked segmental groups without destroying their internal structures. Observation of these phenomena inspired the greatest Islamic social theorist, Ibn Khaldun, much as observation of the Gaelic Highland clans – the only remaining tribal society in Europe – inspired the Scottish historical school and modern sociology.

Secondly, certain features of tribal society[5] were carried straight over into the new People; for example, there was a continued emphasis on genealogy and lineage in social relationships and cultural perceptions. Lineage conferred authority, and continued to be celebrated in poetry and historiography.[6] Leading positions among the 'ulama (Learned, Religious Experts) and Sufis were handed down in families.[7] One acquired special status if one could claim biological descent from Muhammad. Spiritual authority was personal, deriving from an individual's qualities, such as piety or learning. Sharif (lit. noble) referred primarily to ancestral nobility but became a general term for social and political leadership. This contrasted with the organisation of authority in Christianity in this period; the authority of bishops and clergy depended much more on their official position and less on personal merit.

Tribal values lived on in the moral order laid down in the Qur'an. 'Those that have kinship by blood are closer to one another in the book of God than the believers who are not kindred' (Q. 33:6). Good and bad were described in terms of personal relationships (trustfulness (iman), ingratitude/infidelity (kufr)). Members of the community were to possess personal honour, courage, manliness (muruwwa: *virtu*) and sidq (truthfulness, faithfulness, loyalty), and to practise hospitality.[8]

At the same time, these values were given a universalist meaning. The People, it was said, were bound together by faith and justice, not, like the Arab tribes, by kinship. Islam revolutionised tribal society by catapulting the individual into the centre of social responsibility; no longer could one shelter behind the group from God. Concern for justice must override clan ties. 'Asabiyya (clannishness, group spirit) in the sense of helping 'your own people in an unjust cause' was condemned.[9] What ultimately matters is not tribe, race or gender, but godliness:

> O believers, let not any people scoff at another people who may be better than they ... O mankind, we have created you male and female and appointed you races and tribes that you may know one another. Surely the noblest among you in the sight of God is the most God-fearing of you. (Q. 49:8–13)

Thirdly, certain tribal features were, again, sublimated onto the People as a whole.[10] The new religion and its Law instilled a social identity which bound members together and carved them off from outsiders. A strong sense of belonging and a 'clear-cut distinction between members and non-members' were transposed onto the religious umma. The Law achieved this partly because it covered most aspects of behaviour, often in great detail. It replaced tribal custom while retaining the immediacy of the group in the life of the individual. The Shari'a became the skeletal structure of Islamic society which was law-governed (nomocratic) to a peculiar degree.

All this was achieved by a variety of methods, not perhaps consciously designed for this end, but in some ways achieving social cohesion more successfully than the Judaic, Hellenic, Roman or Christian regimes. Many ritual parts of the Shari'a, rules about the body and its functions (such as circumcision, rules about defecation, menstruation, teeth-cleaning, dietary rules and the numerous details of sexual and familial etiquette), had the effect of making members instantly recognisable to one another, and of making relations between relative strangers predictable and manageable. Religious significance was attached to acts which were of no obvious utility but which achieved social bonding, such as communal prayer and pilgrimage. In the Pilgrimage, Islam brought together the universal and the particular with almost Hegelian genius, as believers from all over the world came together to revere, among other things, a black rock – once a focus of local tribal worship. The relationship between insiders and outsiders was not mitigated by a theory of values universal to human beings as such; Islam was an uncompromisingly pure form of revelationism. The boundaries of the People were the boundaries of the moral universe. This was symbolised and reinforced by the Arabic language.

All this was, as it were, neo-tribal.[11] The new society was in principle universal, and in practice commercial and 'citied' (Hodgson's phrase, meaning that cities were an integral part), but individuals were still removed from themselves and absorbed into the group. The result was a type of society generically different from Greek, Roman and also Euro-Christian civilisation.

Holy War (jihad) consummated the male fraternity and upheld the division between insiders and outsiders. The right to conquer and plunder were carried straight over from pre-Islamic nomadic tradition into Islam; 'Muhammad's God ... elevated tribal militance and rapaciousness into supreme religious virtues'.[12] Fighting unbelievers and killing idolaters, even if they were not the aggressors, were religious duties. Islam more than any other world religion made a virtue of war, but it also regulated it. A surprising proportion of hadith (Reports, narratives, 'traditions' about what the Prophet had said or done) were about the conduct of battle and division of spoils. The prospect of expansion and of exploitation of material and human resources was often decisive in creating and preserving Islamic dynasties. Absence of such opportunities usually resulted in their decline.

Neo-tribalism is evident in the relative informality and egalitarianism of early Islamic society.[13] The process by which the Shari'a itself (see below, Chapter 3) came into being was informal and personal, rather than institutional. In its formative period, it depended upon oral transmission and was implemented relatively informally. The Shari'a developed, rather like a language, by accretion from different sources spread by word of mouth – the Reports. The religious leaders were the 'ulama (lit. Learned, Experts, sing. 'alim), and their primary function was the transmission and application of the Code. Among the 'ulama, the relationship between teacher and pupil was personal. In contrast to the Christian clergy of this period, they were not a hierarchy; there was no formal organisation or even test of membership. They owed their position to a mutual acknowledgement of (religious) Learning ('ilm) and piety (Mottahedeh 1980: 137–40).

On the other hand, Muhammad and his followers did succeed in creating a society that was trans-tribal and trans-national. The religious rules governing inheritance and exchange facilitated long-distance commerce. The norms of the Shari'a provided a basis on which persons of different lineages, tribes and nations could interact, and on a relatively equal footing; they could recognise one another as members of the same People, without actually abandoning lineage, tribe or nationality. This was a new version of the monotheistic ideal of universal brotherhood.

The *political* pattern of Islam makes some sense if we identify it as a 'post-tribal' society, one which has recently emerged from tribalism. This helps explain why it never developed formal state structures or constitutions. There were political authorities, performing similar functions as in other societies. But these were individuals, usually a leading member of a dominant clan, and they tended to come to power not by a formal process of appointment, election or even hereditary succession but through their acknowledged prowess as individuals, and the military dominance of their clan. The impact of post-tribalism on political culture and political theory was incalculable. One consequence of this is that Westerners who study Islamic political thought are engaged upon a quest for which our political language equips us poorly.

Muhammad set out to replace both the tribe and the state with a religious community and a moral and legal order. And he did indeed found a unique type of community, face-to-face and worldwide, relating individual to group through a unique combination of rites and ethics which, in retrospect, could have been deliberately designed to forge interpersonal bonds on a global scale. Islam provided a specific path, quite different from that taken by Egypt, the Greek poleis and the feudal monarchies of Europe, from tribalism to a wider and more structured society. The space occupied in other cultures by relatively impersonal state officials was here occupied by the Shari'a and charismatic individuals. What all these societies had in common was dynasties.

A NEW KIND OF POLITICAL SOCIETY

Although the Qur'an is mostly concerned with religion and ethics and has rather little to say about law and less about government, it expresses a mood from which inferences can be taken. In particular, certain ideas cluster around its concept of Community (umma). The founding concept was *Islam*, meaning submission to God and 'entry into a covenant of peace'.[14] This was to be the fundamental relationship between God and humans. This very concept of *Islam* catches the fusion between religion and government, sacred and secular. 'Those who swear fealty to thee [Muhammad] swear fealty by that very act unto God. The hand of God is over their hands' (Q. 48:10). This was a metamorphosis of the Jewish idea of covenant.

First, the idea of the People was detached from nationhood. Non-Arabs are welcome; indeed they are as morally obliged to join as Arabs are. Humans 'were a single umma (people/nation) then they became disunited'. The Islamic community is supposed to be distinguished from the Christian (which also aspired to universalism) by its harmonious unity and absence of doctrinal disputes, ascribed partly to the simplicity of its teachings. The key internal function is the settlement of disputes peaceably among its members, and a united front against unbelievers. This was surely one reason for Muhammad's and his successors' legislative activity. The key external function was to spread the Message.

The unity of the People emerges as the fundamental social norm. Within the People, all adult males share the same rights and duties.[15] The only basis for human superiority is piety and Knowledge; even then (according to a hadith of uncertain date), 'a man shall not lead another man in prayer in a place where the latter is in authority, and no-one shall occupy the place of honour in another man's home except with his permission'.[16] There was a religious duty to provide for the needy (especially orphans) by charity (zakat: alms). This was the ideology which overthrew empires.

It was assumed, after Muhammad's death, that someone must succeed him in his role as Leader (Imam) of the community, as his Deputy (Caliph). Apart from that, there is almost nothing about political leadership or state structures. This may work for a Messenger in a tribal confederacy, inspired by God. Muhammad displayed special talents as a leader and military commander; but there was no provision for the succession. This had a disabling effect on Islamic dynasties. All we are told is: first, 'O believers, obey God, and obey the Messenger and those in authority among you. If you should quarrel on anything, refer it to God and the Messenger' (Q. 4:62, later known as 'the verse of the commanders'). (This sounds a bit like an adaptation of Luke 10:16.) Similarly, the Hadith (Reports: mostly compiled rather later, mainly 720–70) emphasised that 'He who obeys the commander has verily obeyed God'.[17] On the other hand, the principle of kingly domination (mulk) was bitterly attacked;[18] to call a human being king was to trespass upon the divine prerogative. (There was a faint parallel here with old Roman republicanism.) Rebellion was condemned but speaking out against injustice recommended ('The most excellent jihad is the uttering of truth in the presence of an unjust ruler').[19]

In the main, the Reports also seldom mention government or politics: this may be treated as a significant (indeed, a 'political') omission. Wensinck's concordance has fourteen columns on prayer, eight on barter (bai), six on war, six on marriage, three and a half on menstruation, two on community, two on imam (and three-quarters on the toothbrush).[20] Societies which emerged out of the Islamic faith tended to be strong on communal groups but to have weak or transient political structures.

THE WARS OF SUCCESSION

The problems of a Prophetic polity without an agreed way of organising itself became apparent in the divisions which tore the People apart from 656 to 661 (the first fitna: trial/civil war). Events of this period, or versions of them, acquired symbolic and credal significance for later Muslims and have partly shaped the identities and political thought of Islam ever since. Muhammad had left no known successor, and, on his death (632), before the conquests really began, his Companions chose as Leader (imam) and Deputy (caliph) of the Prophet, first Abu Bakr (r.632–4) – a colourless caretaker, then 'Umar (r.634–46), a respected figure, under whom the Muslims conquered what would ever after be their heartlands. He was to be the subject or source of many influential Reports. He was succeeded by 'Uthman (r.646–56). All three were chosen from Muhammad's tribe, the Quraysh, the latter two by a council of notables.

During 'Uthman's reign, a split developed between his family and associates and others, who believed they were being denied their fair share of wealth and other benefits accruing from the conquests. 'Uthman was assassinated, and his opponents rallied to 'Ali (Muhammad's cousin, married to his daughter, who had become a 'symbol of the party of protest')[21] as the new Deputy (r.656–61). They held that 'Uthman had 'forfeited his status as imam by his violations of the law'.[22] Those who thought that 'Uthman had remained the legitimate Leader, and had been unjustly killed, demanded a new election by consultation (shura).

In the ensuing war, 'Ali won the battle of 'the camel' (656: near Basra); but at the battle of Siffin (657: on the Euphrates) Mu'awiya, governor of Syria under 'Uthman, managed to obtain a truce. This alienated some of 'Ali's supporters, the Khariji (called seceders or rebels by their opponents); they condemned 'Ali for subjecting his entitlement to human arbitration, and elected their own Imam.[23] 'Ali was assassinated by a Khariji; his son recognised Mu'awiya (r.661–80). So began the Umayyad Caliphate (661–750). Islamic unity – of a kind – had been restored.

These divisions were about who was entitled to lead the Community and how he should be chosen. They were the origin not only of the two main rival branches of Islam throughout history to today, the Sunni and Shi'a, but also of other sects, some of which lasted for centuries, who also defined themselves by reference to these events. This further suggests the underlying political character of early Islam.

The Sunnis (Traditionals), who held that the Leader should be elected (in some sense) from within the Quraysh, would later look back to the Medina period and the first four 'rightly-guided' (rashidun) Deputies as a model and touchstone for Islamic political rectitude. The Shi'a would regard 'Ali as the sole legitimate successor of Muhammad on the ground that he had been chosen by the Prophet by 'designation (nass)'. In their view, the Leadership (Imama) belonged to whichever of Muhammad's direct biological descendants, from 'Ali's son Husayn onwards, had been designated by his predecessor.[24]

The question of the Leadership was related to the question of membership of the People: what qualifies a person to belong to the People and, therefore, to enter paradise? What kind of community is Islam? Under the Umayyads, some groups, the Mu'tazila (those neutral in the dispute between the claims of 'Uthman and 'Ali) and the Murji'a or Postponers (of a decision between 'Ali and 'Uthman) put a premium on unity and sought to prevent division by getting everyone to leave the claims of both parties to the judgement of God. These adopted a tolerant and inclusive view of membership; the Postponers held that even a sinner is still a Muslim, the Mu'tazilites that the serious sinner is in between believer and infidel.[25]

The Kharijites went in the opposite direction. Any lapse in faith or morals leads to instant exclusion from the People. They dropped the kinship requirement for the Leadership altogether, and insisted instead on very stringent moral conditions: the Leader must exceed all in justice and piety, and any lapse leads to instant deposition. Appointment is to be by election and oath of allegiance (bay'a), understood as a mutual pledge in which the Leader promises to implement the Qur'an and Tradition and nothing more, and the people pledge loyalty. The Najdiyya Kharijites of the late seventh century appear to have held the far more radical view that the Leadership can be dispensed with altogether: 'If (people) acted justly and cooperated and helped one another in piety', and if they fulfilled their legal obligations, 'then they could manage without the Imam'.[26]

The Kharijites were devotees of religious violence; for them, Holy War was the sixth pillar of Islam. They advocated indiscriminate killing (isti'rad) of all their opponents on the grounds that these must be polytheists and as such had no rights and should not exist.[27] Thus, while they denied lineage, they were neo-tribal in their ideal of equality and in their savage assertion of the division between insiders and outsiders.

NOTES

1. For what follows, see Hodgson (1974: vol. 1, pp. 154–217); Michael Cook, *Muhammad* (Oxford: Oxford University Press, 1983); Crone (1980), Crone and Cook (1977), Izutsu (1966).
2. Lewis (1988: 32); Crone (1980: 25); Izutsu (1966: 58); Patricia Crone, *Meccan Trade and the Rise of Islam* (Princeton: Princeton University Press, 1987), p. 237 ('there is a strong sense of ethnogenesis ... Muhammad [was] the creator of a people'), pp. 241, 246–7; G. E. von Grunebaum, 'The Nature of Arab Unity before Islam', *Arabica* 10 (1963), pp. 5–23; I. Lichtenstadter, 'From Particularism to Unity: Race, Nationality and Minorities in the Early Islamic Empire', *IC* 23 (1949), pp. 251–80.
3. Emile Durkheim, *The Elementary Forms of the Religious Life*, tr. J. W. Swain (London: Allen & Unwin, 1915); see Steven Lukes, *Emile Durkheim* (London: Allen Lane, 1973), pp. 463–6, 475–6.
4. Guichard (1977: 23) (in Spain there was a 'long continuance of contiguous human groups, constituting little ethnic entities, relatively closed to one another'); Reid (1983); Morony (1984: 515).
5. On the tribe, see M. H. Fried, 'On the Concept of Tribe', in J. Helm (ed.), *Essays on the Problem of Tribe* (University of Washington Press, 1967), pp. 1–24; Jean Baechler, *Democracies* (Paris: Calmann-Lévy, 1985), pp. 325–6, 568, 571; Patricia Crone, 'The Tribe and the State', in John A. Hall (ed.), *States in History* (Oxford: Blackwell, 1986), pp. 48–77.
6. Izutsu (1966: 62–3); Franz Rosenthal (1968: 29, 49, 100) ('the universal retention of the genealogical view of human relations as the driving force in history').
7. Lapidus (1988: 255, 428).
8. Izutsu (1966: 87, 252); *EI* 1: 325b. Quotations from the Qur'an are taken from *The Koran Interpreted*, trans. A. J. Arberry (Oxford: Oxford University Press, 1955 and 1964).

9. Izutsu (1966: 64, 155–6); Othman (1960: 100).
10. 'All Muslims were to be as one tribe': Hodgson (1974: vol. 1, p. 253); J.-O. Blickfeldt, *Early Mahdism: Politics and Religion in the Formative Period of Islam* (Leiden: Brill, 1985), p. 46.
11. The term used by Hodgson (1974: vol. 1, p. 229).
12. Crone, *Meccan Trade*, p. 245.
13. Marlow (1997: 4–5).
14. Crone and Cook (1977: 20); Izutsu (1966: 87–9).
15. Crone (1980: 62) and 'Tribe and State', pp. 84–6; Marlow (1997).
16. Maulana Muhammad Ali (ed.), *A Manual of Hadith* (Lahore: The Ahmadiyya Anjuman Ishaat Islam, n. d.).
17. Ibid., p. 396.
18. M. Rahimuddin (trans.), *Sahifah Hammam ibn Murrabih*, 5th edn (Paris: Publications du centre culturelle islamique, 1961), p. 82.
19. M. M. Ali (ed.), p. 398.
20. Wensinck (1971); Guillaume (1966).
21. Hodgson (1974: vol. 1, p. 213); Wilferd Madelung, *The Succession to Muhammad: A Study of the Early Caliphate* (Cambridge: Cambridge University Press, 1997).
22. Patricia Crone in *EI* s.v. 'Uthmaniyya.
23. *EI* 3: 1167–8 and on Kharidjites.
24. I am grateful to Patricia Crone for emphasising how remarkably little is known for certain about the exact positions adopted by various groups in the first century of Islam.
25. *EI* on Mu'tazila and on Murdji'a.
26. Patricia Crone, 'Ninth-century Muslim Anarchists', *Past and Present* 167 (2000), pp. 3–28.
27. *EI* on Kharidjites and on Isti'rad. I am grateful to Patricia Crone for this last point (personal communication).

The Idea of Monarchy under the Umayyads and 'Abbasids c.661–850   2

Under the Umayyads and early 'Abbasids, two forces – Islamic neo-tribalism (or communalism) and patrimonial bureaucracy – contended for ascendancy in political culture. The one drew on Arab sources and was expressed in fiqh (Religious Jurisprudence: lit. understanding); the other drew on Iranian sources, and was expressed in polite high culture (adab) and the Advice-to-Kings (nasihat al-muluk) genre. We will consider the latter first.[1]

By patrimonialism, we mean a system of government in which the ruler is permitted to regard the state as his and his family's benefice (from on high), and the people are regarded as clients under his protective and distributive patronage. His powers are subject not to the intervention of others (far less constitutional rules) but to the unwritten obligations of fatherly beneficence. This includes the duty-right to manage the economy for the benefit of the people ('estate-type domination').[2]

The continued threat of civil war encouraged absolutist notions. The Umayyads based their legitimacy, first, on kinship with 'Uthman; they were God's chosen lineage. 'Abd al-Malik (r.685–705) restored and expanded central authority on the basis of hereditary succession. Arabo-Islamic ways were being mingled with monarchical ideas and practice taken over from conquered Iran. The Sassanian appeal court became the 'redress of grievances' (mazalim) court. The Umayyads began to express a monarchical view of the Imamate in religious language. They tapped into the Middle Eastern rhetoric of monarchy (the majority of their subjects were not Muslims). The ruler is shepherd, the people his flock (ra'iyya). The Deputy fills the earth with light, mercy, justice and rain.[3] He is owed unconditional obedience.

They also began to use specifically Islamic ideas in support of monarchical authority. They called themselves the 'Deputy of *God*' as well as of the Prophet. It has been argued that this was not mere rhetoric, that it meant that the Caliph could claim the all-important function of overseeing and organising the Religious Law. This was certainly what Al-Walid II claimed (743):

> God deputed his caliphs over the path of his prophethood ... for the
> implementation of his decree, the establishment of his normative practice

(sunna) ... for the observance of his ordinances and his rights ... keeping people away from his forbidden things, providing for equity among his servants. (in Crone and Hinds 1986: 120)

Did they make the further claim that the Deputy can contribute to the actual development of the Shari'a, that is supplement the legislative role which the Prophet himself had fulfilled precisely as Deputy of God? In practice, certainly they 'concerned themselves with all aspects of the Shari'a ... they regularly laid down rules regarding marriage, succession, manumission and the like' (Crone and Hinds 1986: 53).

Such views found little support outside court circles. From the beginning, Umayyad rule was opposed from several quarters. Discontent was fanned by newly awakened religious enthusiasms. There was tension between informal tribal ideas of power as the perquisite of known outstanding individuals or families, and a massive empire which, in order to exist, had to rely on central authority and a defined chain of command (Marlow 1997: 4–5). Within the Muslim community, a wide variety of religious opinions emerged with different political implications. Competing schools held radically different views about government (imama) and society (umma). 'Ali's grandson, Husayn, rebelled and was killed (680: at Karbala, Iraq) in what Shi'ites came to see as the 'martyrdom' of the true Leader. Many Muslims, including proto-Sunni Religious Experts ('ulama; see below, Chapter 3) saw the Umayyads as deviating from the norms of Islam, because of their tyrannical method of government and the immorality/ illegality of their actions, for example unfairness in the distribution of revenues (Crone and Hinds 1986: 64). The Umayyads were resented by non-Arab converts to Islam precisely because of their reliance on Arab tribes and customs.

Yazid III (r.744) attempted to regain the support of the 'Piety-minded opposition' (as Hodgson terms it), offering a kind of political contract. In return for allegiance, he promised to rule 'according to Book and Tradition', as the 'ulama said he should (see below, p. 37), and to spend state revenues justly.

> If I keep my word in what I promise you here, you must obey me and support me, but if I do not you can remove me from office ... One ought not to obey a creature in disobedience to God ... Obey a man ... [only] as long as he remains obedient to God ... If [a human ruler] opposes God and summons you to disobedience, it is right to oppose him and to kill him. (in Lambton 1981: 35–6)

The right to depose a bad Deputy, then, was an issue.

The 'Abbasid clan came to power following the third civil war (744–50) as champions of Islamic justice against the corrupt Umayyads. Their chief, Abu-l-'Abbas al-Saffah (r.750–4), claimed descent from Muhammad's uncle; they appealed for loyalty to the Prophet's immediate family. They first gained support in Khurasan (eastern Iran) where they were known as 'the people of the dawla (that is, the providential dynasty)'. Kharijites rebelled in north-western Africa and Iraq; the Zaydis (see below, p. 39) gained power south of the Caspian and in the Lebanon; the proto-Sunnis were quietist and stood aside.[4]

At the very beginning of the 'Abbasid dynasty, an articulate tradition of centralised monarchy was transmitted from Iran by Ibn Muqaffa', at a time when the Islamic tradition was still not fully formed, its political drift not yet clear. This was linked to the cultural life of the court and its secretaries.

Patrimonial monarchy entered its classical phase under the 'Abbasids and their successors. This was at the very time when the notion of imperial monarchy was being revived in Europe under Charlemagne and the Ottonians. These twin ideological phenomena were not unconnected: Western Christendom was constructing itself politically in response to Muslim invasions. Both drew on Middle Eastern monarchical monotheism.

The 'Abbasids had begun as righteous revolutionaries, but they soon adopted patrimonial ideas of dynastic monarchy, tempered by Islamic post-tribalism. Soon after they came to power, they abandoned their sympathy for minority opposition groups, such as the various Shi'a ('Party') factions, and sought instead to accommodate the more numerous proto-Sunnis. But they still based their title to rule on their kinship with the Prophet. In his inaugural speech, al-Saffah referred to dawla, his dynasty's destined turn in power, a Qu'ranic and Hebrew idea of the divine transfer of power from one people to another (CH Iran 4: 57). This was to become the standard term for dynasty, regime and the state. In those times, it was dynastic clans who acquired, possessed and lost dawla. The implication was that success in seizing and holding power marked out an individual or house as the object of divine favour and, therefore (whatever the appearances), worthy and deserving of moral support. Those possessing the divine favour may act harshly, but their rule has to be endured; this lay behind later attitudes towards invaders and even the harshest of conquerors.

The House of Islam extended through the mountain systems of central Asia and north-western Africa and the highland grazing areas of central Iran and eastern Anatolia (which favoured a nomadic way of life), and agricultural systems largely based on irrigation, such as Iraq, Egypt and the Oxus region. The Islamic conquests opened up unprecedented opportunities for long-distance commerce, such as the east–west trade from China to Damascus and trade across the Indian Ocean and the Mediterranean; here, Egypt was a focal point. Craft manufacture flourished all over in urban centres, from Marv, Rayy and Bukhara to Baghdad, Damascus, Cairo (founded c.970) and Cordova.

The 'Abbasid victory sealed the destiny of Islam as a predominantly universalist faith with Arab moorings; it was also a victory for a multi-ethnic and multi-cultural society. Within Islamic territory, there was a steady stream of conversions from other faiths. Religious conversion came some time after conquest, and for a variety of reasons. In some places, such as Egypt and the Lebanon, very large Christian minorities led untroubled lives until the Crusades.

The 'Abbasids' main ideological initiative was to emphasise their position as Deputy of God and successor to the Prophet. Al-Mansur (r.754–75) said: 'I am simply the authority of God on this earth' (Crone and Hinds 1986: 84). Al-Ma'mun, when designating the eighth Shi'a Imam as his successor (817), reiterated al-Walid II's claim that the Deputy's leadership of the Community was based on divine authority: God has appointed the Deputies to continue the work of the Prophet. 'When the Prophethood came to an end ... God made the mainstay of the religion and the ordering of the government of the Muslims reside in the (Deputyship).' Al-Ma'mun has exhausted himself carrying out the Deputy's tasks – 'the subduing of polytheists, the well-being of the (People), the spreading of justice and the maintenance of the Book and the Tradition' (Crone and Hinds 1986: 135–7). Muslims must therefore help the Deputies to carry out their moral and political functions, 'to establish God's justice and His equity, to make the highways safe and prevent bloodshed, and to create a state of concord and unity of fellowship'. The Deputies must obey God; Muslims must obey the Deputies. Al-Ma'mun also stated that God had made the Deputies his heirs and entrusted them with 'the transmission of Knowledge which he has committed to their care' (Crone and Hinds 1986: 96). This implied a high sense of the Deputy's responsibilities, but it did not claim a monopoly of authority in the religious field. (Perhaps it implied executive rather than legislative power.) It is doubtful whether such statements had the kind of juridical precision claimed for otherwise not dissimilar ones by medieval popes.

IRANIAN INFLUENCES AND IBN MUQAFFA'

At the same time, the 'Abbasids introduced on a bigger scale Iranian ideas and practices of government. They developed a bureaucracy, a secret service, court culture and ritual. Baghdad was built (762) near the former Sassanian capital of Ctesiphon. 'Abbasid propaganda tended to imbue Irano-Sassanian concepts with Qur'anic meaning. 'The light of prophecy' shines from the Prince's forehead; 'the government (al-saltana) is God's shadow on earth, all those troubled find refuge in it' (in Goldziher 1971: 61, 67, 69). The caliph was a link with cosmic order. The Sassanian view of monarchy was transmitted in The Testament of Ardashir. This contained the famous statement that 'kingship and religion are twins ... religion is the foundation of kingship and kingship the protector of religion' (in Arjomand 1984: 93–4). This could of course be interpreted to imply a separation of spheres.

Islamo-Iranian political thought got off to a flying start with Ibn Muqaffa' (Fars c.720–Basra ?756). This uniquely gifted secretary, who served under both the Umayyads and then the 'Abbasids, undertook a massive programme of translation from Persian into Arabic; his works were 'the principal means of transmission to the Arabs of the epic history and institutions of Iran' (EI 3: 884a). Popular religion was poles apart from the polite culture of the court and the political class, the moral refinement (adab) which Ibn Muqaffa' did so much to promote. Many regarded the religious attitudes of the court with suspicion; some government officials were thought to be Manichees or sceptics. Ibn Muqaffa' may have defended Manichaeanism. In any case, he took a liberal view of religious truth, castigated pietism and dogmatism, condemned those who 'command you to believe in what you do not know', and advocated religious tolerance. The people he most admired were 'secretaries and doctors, people who (are) rich in experience ... circumspect, intelligent ... refined'.[5] But he wrote as a Muslim and took for granted an Islamic society.

Ibn Muqaffaʻ's *Message* (*Risala fi'l-sahaba*, written 754–6)[6] was a direct statement to the Deputy al-Mansur, who, Ibn Muqaffaʻ hoped, would be open to ideas for improving government, unlike some of his predecessors. Ibn Muqaffaʻ spoke as the self-confident representative of a superior culture. He did not hesitate to address the Caliph directly rather than through subordinates. In the *Risala*, he criticised former Deputies and subordinates of the present ruler. In fact, his plea for a pardon for the Deputy's brother probably led to his torture and execution.

The *Risala* had a clear programme: the application of the principles of patrimonial government developed in ancient Iran to the Caliphate. It was one of the most systematic and least rhetorical or reverential of early Islamic political writings. The narrative Report-culture was already established, but the Religious Jurists had not yet formulated a theory of government. There was therefore something of a gap in political theory and culture which Ibn Muqaffaʻ presumably thought he could fill. In fact, he quotes the Qur'an and not the Reports.

He covered, not in any particular order, the Leadership, the army, the bureaucracy, economics, interest groups, choice of counsellors, law and legislation, and how to manage one's subjects. The approach is prudential. To be successful, a Leader must have the allegiance of his people. But human experience shows (paras 55–7) that, for this to happen, people have to have a proper conception of the Leader's authority. Genuine allegiance requires that people understand what the Leadership (Imama) is for. Ibn Muqaffaʻ was especially concerned about the state of mind of the soldiery: what is needed is a clear set of army regulations spelling out their duties. But it is no good having troops who simply do whatever the Leader tells them; they must understand the reasoning behind their orders. What is needed is political theory.

Ibn Muqaffaʻ described two erroneous views of Caliphal authority. The first was that, because one must (as nearly everyone agreed) disobey a command to disobey God, anyone commanding obedience to God has the same right to be obeyed as does the Imam. This, he said, is to imply that all men are equal and that consequently we simply do not need a Leader. This may have been a reference to the views held by some Kharijites which may have been finding support within the army. The second error is that we should obey Leaders unconditionally (this may have referred to Shiʻite views).

According to Ibn Muqaffaʻ, the sensible view lies in between. The Leader must, indeed, be obeyed, but on the specific condition that he uphold the Law and its sanctions. And moderate Muslims will make a more formidable army. He observed that power based on a religion which prescribes the same duties for ruler and subjects is going to be more stable than power based on subordination or arbitrary force ('the play of an hour').

Ibn Muqaffaʻ linked the correct, middle-of-the-road conception of the legitimate authority of the Leader to a clear definition of the *scope* of the Leader's authority. Obedience is due to the Leader, and to him alone, in all measures, decrees and decisions which God has left to the discretion of the [Leaders] and concerning which no-one else has the right to issue orders and be obeyed: namely war, the appointment of officials, public income from tax and booty, and their distribution.

It would be difficult to disagree on religious grounds. But Ibn Muqaffa' then went on to link his view to an exalted view of the extent of the Leader's powers *over Islamic Law*. The Leader has the right not only to administer the Legal Penalties (as was generally agreed), but also to issue judgements on matters that the revealed texts do not clearly specify. Still more, he should clarify and systematise the whole framework of the Holy Law: he should produce his own authoritative codification. Thus Ibn Muqaffa' proposed that the development of the Law for Muslims should be taken out of the hands of the 'ulama and their conflicting Schools, and entrusted to the Commander of the Faithful.

> If the commander of the faithful should judge it opportune to give orders that these divergent decisions and practices should be submitted to him in the form of a dossier, accompanied by the [Traditions] and the solutions ... proffered by each School; if the commander of the faithful would then examine these documents and formulate on each question the opinion which God would inspire in him; if he would hold firmly to this opinion and forbid the Religious Judges to overturn it; if he would then make an exhaustive volume of these decisions – [then] we could have the hope that God would transform these judgements, in which (at present) error and truth are mixed up, into a *single just code*. We would be able to hope that the unification of judicial practices would be a means of harmonising justice according to the opinion, and through the mouth, of the Commander of the Faithful. (para. 34)

This project of codification echoed late Roman praxis. It was an invitation to the Deputy to assert his authority unequivocally.

Ibn Muqaffa' clearly saw the *religious* authority of the Deputy, at least in the legal sphere, as essential to his political power. The reason why Ibn Muqaffa' challenged head-on the 'ulama's prevailing perception of their role in Law (and so in society at large) was that he thought that it led to incompetent decisions and general confusion. The paradox was that the view he put forward, and so clearly spelled out, was bound to offend the very 'ulama whose support the 'Abbasid government knew it needed. In fact, Ibn Muqaffa' saw the claims currently voiced by the Learned as incompatible with stable political authority or even coherent social organisation. It was a distinctly Iranian perception. He came down firmly on the side of God's Deputy.

Ibn Muqaffa' based his argument on a view of religious Knowledge which would put him, and anyone who cared to support him, at odds with the basic premises of the 'ulama (those supposed to 'know'). The reason why Ibn Muqaffa' thought the *Leader* is entitled to make Judicial decisions and decide between conflicting interpretations of the Holy Law was that these depend, to some extent, upon personal opinion (ra'y) – that is, *reason*. And he held that people need reason as well as religion if they are to achieve happiness in this world or the next. For it was God who gave us reason; and, if every detail of conduct were prescribed by revelation, reason would be superfluous. The conclusion must be that 'God has left decisions and measures (not otherwise determined) to personal opinion'. He then simply *asserted* that God has reserved the use of personal opinion in legal matters to 'the holders of power (alone) … The people have, in this regard, no other (right) than to give counsel when consulted, to reply when appealed to, and to give sincere advice in secret' (para. 20). This was a strangely Hobbesian twist for which Ibn Muqaffa' gave no reason. Was it based on the need for political stability?

In all of this, Ibn Muqaffa' was writing as one thoroughly sympathetic to the Deputy's needs, but informing him that he ought to be much clearer about his relationship with his subjects and with the Islamic Law. In fact, a fundamental change was required in the Deputy's self-understanding.

So too with the methodology of government. The Leader's rule is necessary for the well-being of both common people and elite; but, if it is to achieve stability, certain moral and cultural reforms are needed. If the Caliphate is to retain popular support, the people must be correctly instructed, and their grievances must be redressed. Every district needs 'loyal men, versed in the knowledge of religious principles, the Tradition and history', who will teach the people, be aware of their problems, and nip sedition in the bud. In other words, the government must promote religious teaching, but on its own terms and as part of a two-way process, with information being fed back. The teacher will also be an informer.

Above all, the government needs the backing of the army. Khurasani troops are best, but they need more refinement. They must study the Qur'an and Tradition. The Leader must keep himself well informed about their mood. And the army must be put on a proper financial footing. Soldiers must be regularly paid – partly in kind, so as to maintain equivalence between the land-tax and army pay regardless of price fluctuations. They must be made aware that, like them, the Leader hates extravagance. Military control should be clearly separated from fiscal control.

Civil servants should be appointed on merit – the best are Iraqis. The ruler's entourage and bureaucratic elite must be carefully selected to avoid the misconduct of the past and to encourage the best people to enter government service: the ruler should promote Arabs of noble descent and men of intelligence, courage and religious knowledge, not upstarts. This marks an attempt to balance birth and merit.

Ibn Muqaffa''s tone was managerial. This brief, deceptively simple treatise stands at the gateway of Islamic monarchical thought; it set the tone for the Advice-to-Kings genre. Whether or not it caused his own downfall, Ibn Muqaffa''s recognition of the need for political legitimacy went to the heart of the 'Abbasid – and the Islamic – problem.

ABU YUSUF

Harun al-Rashid (r.781–809: he of the Arabian Nights) commissioned a review of taxation from the Chief Religious Judge (qadi al-qudat) – the first person to be appointed to the post, Ya'kub Abu Yusuf (731–98), a leading exponent of the Hanafi School, which gave more scope to individual reasoning. His *Book of Taxes* (*Kitab al-kharaj*) was the first known work on government by a Religious Jurist.[7]

Abu Yusuf's remit was to elucidate in terms of Right (Shari'a) the principles and methods behind the collection and distribution of the land-tax. In fact, he covered a wide variety of economic, military and social topics, including the treatment of Protected Peoples.

Taxation is placed in the context of ethics and the functions of government. Abu Yusuf emphasised, as one would expect from a Religious Jurist, equal justice for everybody: the Deputy must 'establish the order of God among the small and the great without distinction'; he must ensure that tax-collectors treat everyone alike; he must impose the Code impartially. He should err on the side of leniency; tax-collectors must be strict but gentle. The Deputy must treat the poor and prisoners with kindness.

Abu Yusuf made a suggestive remark about the relationship between the Deputy and the Shari'a: the Deputy's function is 'to illuminate for the subjects those of their affairs which are obscure to them and to clarify those duties about which they are in doubt'. But this probably did not mean he could interpret the Code: Abu Yusuf was probably referring to the Caliph's executive role in 'applying the Legal Penalties (hudud)' and 'giving to each his rights' (Crone and Hinds 1986: 82–3).

He addressed the Caliph reverently but emphasised the seriousness of his duties and his strict accountability to God. He must be conscientious (never postpone today's business until tomorrow; he who knows but acts not will have a 'serious audit' before God). Subjects are entrusted to the ruler as sheep to shepherd. Reports show that the fate of the ruler after death depends on his political conduct, for the Prophet will most love the just Leader, most hate the tyrant.

Abu Yusuf introduced one of the first references to political economy and its relationship to government. Justice in taxation increases prosperity; and in general economic well-being depends upon good government – another central Iranian idea. For if the rate of taxation is unjust, land will fall into disuse. Fair taxation and fair application of Shari'a Penalties will increase general prosperity and therefore government revenues. A Report is quoted as saying that prices should not be regulated, because 'high and low prices depend on God'; but it is the Deputy's duty to manage the irrigation of Iraq. The 'free-market' approach became standard Islamic doctrine, though price regulation was frequently practised, and advocated in the Advice-to-Kings literature. We find in Abu Yusuf the nucleus of a coherent attitude to political economy.

When the Deputyship was at its zenith, al-Rashid (not unlike Charlemagne in Europe) divided his inheritance by covenant between two sons; his death gave rise to the fourth civil war when different regions of the empire were ranged against each other.

THE CALIPH AL-MA'MUN

Of all the 'Abbasids, al-Ma'mun (r.813–33) emerges as the most determined to construct a high imperial ideal which would make the Deputyship independent of both the soldiery and popular religious leaders by appealing directly to the hearts and minds of his subjects. He adopted a cultural policy that was designed to boost high culture and the intellectual standing of the Caliphate. He was consistently opposed to the influence of the popularly-based Reporters and 'ulama (see below, Chapter 3). He allied himself with those schools of thought which were, for various reasons, opposed to literal-mindedness: the theologians (mutakallimun) (as opposed to Jurists), Hellenism and the Shi'a. He may have hoped thereby to promote the authority of the Deputyship; it probably also reflected his personal intellectual preferences. Al-Ma'mun pursued, consciously or otherwise, the programme set out by Ibn Muqaffa', who had precisely identified the need for the regime to have an ideological basis that would carry conviction in terms of the new religion.

The Shi'ite view of the Imam (Leader) would greatly enhance the Deputy's authority; and at one point al-Ma'mun designated the eighth Party Leader, 'Ali al-Rida, as his successor (Crone and Hinds 1986: 137–9). The work of translating Greek philosophical texts had gathered pace under al-Rashid and was strongly encouraged under al-Ma'mun. A House of Wisdom (library-cum-study-centre: Bayt al-hikma) was founded in Baghdad. The Alexander romance, now fully translated for the first time (815), became a popular tale and propelled Alexander, who had learned his wisdom under Aristotle himself, into the pantheon of wise and just rulers for the rest of the patrimonial era.[8] The Alexander myth reinforced the enlightened imperialism taken from other Greek as well as Persian sources. These legitimised conquest and the multi-ethnic society: they provided an argument and an inspiration for an ethical world government. This neo-Greek heritage also promoted the idea of a strong Deputy (see below, Chapter 6).

Above all, al-Ma'mun sought support from the Sunni religious group that, on intellectual grounds, was both opposed to the popularly-based Reporters and prepared to support a strong Deputyship: the theologians, and especially the Mu'tazilites, the school which emphasised the role of rational argument in religious discourse. The more that Religious Knowledge depended upon rational debate, the more credible were the claims of the Deputy, with an intellectual elite at his disposal, to govern a society dedicated to the pursuit of Religious Knowledge.

Certain of the Mu'tazilites were prepared to support the 'Abbasid dynasty on rational as well as religious grounds.[9] They may have been the first Muslim thinkers to present a reasoned argument for the state. The need for Leadership in human society can, they said, be deduced by reason, because humans are naturally contentious (see Qur'an 2:251). They combined an exalted view of the Leadership with strict conditions for its occupant. For the Mu'tazilites, the principal social and political value was justice. They stressed the Qur'anic duty to enjoin the good and restrain the evil as an obligation incumbent upon *every* Muslim, to be performed first by word, then by hand and, if necessary, by sword. It is justifiable, under certain conditions, to use armed resistance against an unjust ruler; guilty leaders can be deposed. The logic behind this was, presumably, that conscientious Muslims *could* accept legitimate political authority, provided it was open to correction on moral-religious grounds.

Al-Ma'mun promoted several Mu'tazilites. He intervened in their favour in doctrinal disputes, and tried to establish the createdness of the Qur'an (which they upheld against the proto-Sunni Reporters) as official doctrine. Finally, for the first and only time in Islamic history, he set up a state inquisition (mihna: 833). Its aim was to 'force government officials and religious leaders to accept his religious views and his authority in matters of religious ritual and doctrine' (Lapidus 1975: 379). 'Ulama and Judges were cross-examined; state officials were compelled to declare their acceptance of the Caliphal doctrine under pain of losing their posts. Anyone refusing to accept it was liable to the severest punishment.

It may have been about this time that a free rendering of the Pseudo-Aristotelian *Letter to Alexander* 'On the Government of Cities (Siyasat al-mudun)', deriving from a late Greek source with Persian touches (*EI* 7: 985a; NL 842), came into circulation (the actual date is quite uncertain).[10] This too included the germ of a theory of state legitimacy: our knowledge of human nature shows that humans will not obey the law without coercion (this seems close to the view of some Mu'tazilites); therefore the law needs someone to apply it; therefore a kingdom needs both a legislator (in the sense of someone who originally made the laws) *and* 'a coercive ruler' (an executive: pp. 58–60). The anonymous author repeated Ibn Muqaffa''s proposal for a middle way between anarchism and absolutism:

> In what concerns the sovereign men fall into error and occupy two positions. Some ... think that all men must be equal and that among them there should be neither sovereign nor subject. But these overlook that this would mean destruction of both the sovereign and justice; for there is no justice amongst people except by means of the sovereign. Others think that it does not matter if the sovereign is loathsome and departs from the law; that is clearly a form of corruption. (p. 63)

The same arguments were used to justify universal sovereignty on utilitarian grounds because it will bring peace and prosperity. Political ethics are emphasised for pragmatic reasons: the only kind of rule which will work is one that is 'legal and based on society and not on discord or tyranny'. The ruler must be loved by his people and combine clemency with severity.

AL-JAHIZ

The prominent Mu'tazilite al-Jahiz (Basra c.776–Baghdad 868/9)[11] also supported al-Ma'mun in his attempt to establish the primacy of the Deputy over the 'ulama. He was a philosophical literateur; he used witty anecdotes and vivid contemporary descriptions to convey moral teaching. He poured scorn on the literary pretensions of trendy government officials and admired the self-made tradesman (Pellat 1969: 272–5). A cosmopolitan (possibly of Abyssinian origin), al-Jahiz rejoiced in bringing together Persian, Arabic and Greek culture. But he warned against slavish imitation of Persian manners; and contemporary Greeks were no match for their illustrious predecessors. He shared the Mu'tazilite conviction that all opinions must be scrutinised by critical reason ('aql), 'a pilot and companion in good fortune and ill' (Goldziher 1981: 88). This ruled out Shi'i intuitionism. But he had no time for religious indifference or scepticism.

Al-Jahiz wrote several works, from 817–18 onwards, in support of al-Ma'mun and the 'Abbasid Deputyship. He shows us the Leadership from the viewpoint of a polished gentleman of the courtly milieu. Like many others, he expressed contempt for the common people; he was one of the first to emphasise the distinction between the elite and the masses (al-khassa wa 'l-'amma).[12] He attached considerable importance to this and used it in his discussions of the state and its constitution. Apropos the Reporters' doctrine of the uncreated Qur'an and their apparent anthropomorphism, he said: 'the people have organised all the elements of corruption [and] reached the limits of heresy [with] a fanaticism which has destroyed one world after another, and a party spirit which corrupts every religious benefit, and destroys every material benefit'.[13]

This attitude towards the masses went with a pessimistic view of human nature. He based the need for political authority and universal monarchy upon human nature as we know it:

> It is only by rigorous training, severe rebukes in this world, and the threat of terrible punishment in the next, that men are able to resist their own worst natures ... It is in men's nature ... to evade the enforcement of deserved penalties whenever they can. This is what causes general disorder and the non-enforcement of laws.

From this, al-Jahiz drew the conclusion that 'it is therefore our duty to establish a single Leader ... This is a fact confirmed by general observation and ... experience ... God so designed the world and its inhabitants ... that they are better off with a single Leader' (in Pellat 1969: 63–5).

Sound religion depends upon worldly order. This was an ancient Iranian theme, and it became a Sunni commonplace. Al-Jahiz rejected the anarchist view that 'it is more profitable for men to be left in liberty without a guardian ... This is more likely to bring them both salvation and booty' (in Pellat 1961: 38); this would make Prophecy itself redundant. Ibn Sina too would argue that our need for social control proves that religion is necessary (see below, p. 74). Like the Philosophers, al-Jahiz saw this as part of a wider pattern: people can only attend to spiritual needs if they have satisfied the material; Religious Knowledge derives from knowledge of worldly matters.

Unlike most Sunnis, al-Jahiz showed genuine concern for constitutional issues. How should the Leader be chosen? One cannot say 'by the people (al-nass)', because the elite are a separate entity from the masses (they don't even understand what the Leadership is for): differences between classes make it impossible for the community to undertake united political action. Rather, choice should lie with the elite (khassa); al-Jahiz does not define who they are.

What qualities must a Leader possess? Al-Jahiz singled out intelligence, erudition and good habits. Such qualities can be easily recognised, which ruled out the Shi'ite idea of a Leader known only to a few. Al-Jahiz emphasised, also against the Shi'a, the benefits of election rather than designation. Above all, it respects human choice; the Prophet 'did not choose for them … it was to their benefit that this choice was left with them, for he chose to leave them the choice'. Election may be by a variety of means. The right candidate may emerge from long consultations, or by being recognised by his family or in his home town; or someone may be chosen by testamentary will; or again from 'the noble title of his parentage or the privileges of a family' (in Pellat 1961: 45–6). Force should not be used. These wide-ranging alternatives were partly designed to accommodate 'Abbasid procedure. This could also have provided a text for democracy in Islam today.

Al-Jahiz, like some other Mu'tazilites, held that a tyrant *may* be deposed and a new Leader installed by force. He ridiculed the quietist views of the Traditionists, those 'innovators of our time … (who) pretend that to speak against bad government is tantamount to civil war, and that to curse tyrants is tantamount to heresy (bida')'.[14] Whether the obligation to depose a tyrant should be exercised, and how, depends upon circumstances. One possible situation was when injustice becomes so widespread that the elite (once again) begin to gather in groups, talk freely together, and then discover that they are not the only ones who think this way. Finally,

> They know that war is their only hope, and open revolt their one salvation … At that moment violence is a possibility and religious obligation becomes absolute. Thus the scope of action is a question of possibility.[15] If the possibility is lacking there is no obligation … In short, once it becomes possible for them to withstand and master their opponent, and a man worthy of the caliphate has appeared and is known to them, their duty is to put him in power, and defend him. (quoted in Pellat 1969: 80–1)

(Perhaps this was meant to include the process by which the 'Abbasids came to power.) All in all, al-Jahiz was one of the most original Sunni political thinkers.

THE FAILURE OF THE CALIPHATE

Al-Ma'mun's successor, al-Mu'tasim, continued his policies but with less conviction. Under al-Mu'tawakkil (r.847–61), the more literal-minded of Sunni 'people of Book-and-Tradition' gained in influence, and the role of the Mu'tazilites and neo-Greek philosophers declined. Al-Mu'tawakkil was assassinated by the Turkish slave-soldiers who had helped him to power. From now on, these dominated Baghdad politics, until the Shi'ite Buyids (945). One by one, just as the Carolingian empire was disintegrating, the provinces of the Caliphate became independent under new dynasties. These, none-the-less, continued to emulate the practice and ideology of patrimonial monarchy as it had developed through these remarkable syntheses of Islamic and Iranian moeurs under the 'Abbasids.

There was after all to be no Rome on the Tigris. The 'Abbasids remained a local power and a symbolic Sunni Caliphate. Whereas the Umayyads have ever since been regarded as deviant, the early 'Abbasid Deputyship became, in Sunni mythology, a silver age. The 'Abbasids lost political control; but they remained for future centuries a symbol of the People's unity. In theory, their tacit consent was still required for the application of Penalties and the validity of contracts.

The 'Abbasids had squandered their vast territorial and ideological resources with remarkable haste. Despite the appearances of sovereignty acquired from Persia, they lacked a consistent imperial strategy; they developed neither an imperial nor a state ideology. The Shi'i view of the Leader (on which they had partly risen to power), together with the monarchical traditions of the Iranian and Hellenistic worlds, could have provided a basis. But the 'Abbasids abandoned Shi'ism. In the emerging Sunni consensus, the standing of the Deputy was damagingly unclear. What made centralised imperial government finally impossible was that senior Judges in major cities, while appointed by the Deputy, had to be respected members of the 'ulama; and the substance of the Law they applied was beyond the control of any state (Crone 1980: 62). Perhaps it was impossible to reintroduce a centralised state into the Islamic thought-world; or too late to do so now.

The Iranian tradition of patrimonial monarchy was transmitted to all later Islamic dynasties via the 'Abbasid political culture expressed in these texts. This, as much as Islamic teaching, would determine how state officials and ordinary people regarded political authority and the ruler–ruled relationship.

NOTES

1. For what follows, see Hodgson (1974: vol. 1, pp. 241–305); *CH Iran* 4; Crone (1980); Crone and Hinds (1986); Lapidus (1975); Mottahedeh (1980); Michael G. Morony, *Iraq after the Muslim Conquest* (Princeton: Princeton University Press, 1984).
2. Max Weber, *Economy and Society*, ed. Günther Roth and Claus Wittich, 2 vols (Berkeley CA: University of California Press, 1968), pp. 231–6, 1013–15. In Michael Oakeshott's language, this kind of state is an enterprise association: *On Human Conduct* (Oxford: Clarendon Press, 1975), pp. 204–5.
3. Crone and Hinds (1986: 37); for similar views expressed in fourteenth-century Europe about the pope, see below, p. 48, n. 5.
4. I am grateful to Patricia Crone for helping me find my way through these tangled topics.
5. *Kalilah wa-Dimna*, tr. A. Miquel (Paris, 1957), p. 21.
6. Ed. and trans. Charles Pellat, *Ibn al-Muqaffa', mort vers 140/757, conseilleur du Calife* (Paris: Maisonneuve & Larose, 1976). See BL 64–73; Nagel (1981: vol. 2, pp. 159–83); E. Rosenthal (1958: 69–74); Richter (1932).

7. Abou Youssouf Ya'koub, *Le livre de l'impôt foncier (Kitab al-Kharaj)*, tr. E. Fagnan (Paris: Libraire orientaliste Paul Geuthner, 1921).

8. *EI* 4: 127b–8a; Kraemer (1992: 254).

9. *EI* 3: 1143b–4a and on Mu'tazila; Hodgson (1974: vol. 1, pp. 437–42); Fakhry (1983: 46–63); G. Hourani (1976).

10. Trans. in Jozef Bielawski and Marian Plezia (eds), *Lettre d'Aristote à Alexandre sur la politique envers les cités*, Archivum filol. 25 (Wroclaw: Polish Academy of Sciences, 1970), pp. 57–72. See *EI* 7: 985a; NL 842. The argument for the state is similar to that of Ibn Muqaffa' and of some Mu'tazilites.

11. *EI* on Djahiz; BL ch. 4; Pellat (1961, 1969); O. Rescher, *Exzerpte und Übersetzungen aus den Schriften des Philologen Gahiz*, part 1 (Stuttgart, 1931).

12. Marlow (1997: 39); *EI* on al-khassa wa 'l-'amma.

13. *Risala fi'l-Nabita*, trans. Charles Pellat, *Annales de l'Institut des études orientales de l'Université d'Alger* 10 (1952), p. 324.

14. Nabita, trans. Pellat, p. 317.

15. Compare Thomas Aquinas' conditions for a just war: *Aquinas: Selected Political Writings*, ed. A. P. D'Entrèves (Oxford: Blackwell, 1954), p. 159.

The Method of Tradition (sunna) 3

A completely different approach to politics was evolving among the Muslim Community. We will look first at the proto-Sunnis,[1] then at the branches of the Shi'a (Chapter 4).

The majority of Muslims belonged to what would become the Sunni community, sometimes known as 'the people of the Community and the Tradition (ahl al-kitab wa 'l-sunna)'. The foundations of their political thought were established during the late Umayyad and early 'Abbasid periods. It was based upon the development of Religious Jurisprudence (fiqh: lit. understanding). The first stage was the collection, sifting and writing down of Reports (sing. hadith) to form, together with the Qur'an, the source of authoritative data for Islamic praxis (chiefly c.720 to c.770). These were the purported sayings or actions of the Prophet and his Companions. Few can be reliably dated to before 730. Some were based on the administrative and popular practices of late Umayyad times.

These Report collections gave authoritative solutions to contemporary questions, showing 'that everything a Muslim was required to believe or do was founded on traditions purporting to prove that Muhammad, by example or precept, had so ruled' (Guillaume 1956: 92). Such Reports played a crucial role in the development of Shari'a and Sunna (Tradition: Sunna – lit. 'beaten path' – meant 'precedent', 'way of life', and finally 'the ideal or normative usage of the community' (Schacht 1953: 58)).

This was the work of scholar-teachers ('ulama) who, secure in a sense of intellectual superiority, moved with ease from city to city. A new type of religious leadership was emerging, based upon expertise in memorising and expounding Reports, at first circulated by word of mouth (and so potentially widely accessible), then written down, collected and interpreted by the 'ulama. This diffused mode of knowing, democratic in a way, gave rise to a new kind of meritocracy, those possessing the Knowledge ('ilm) required to understand and apply the revelation so defined.

The 'ulama, as they developed from the eighth to the tenth century, were 'a vaguely defined body of men'; there was no hierarchy. They held their position through their training and acknowledgement by followers and peers. 'A category with a self-conscious identity, ... their primary characteristic, their knowledge of [Reports], created an important bond between them' (Mottahedeh

1980: 140). As time went on, they became embedded in society at large, to such an extent that their 'other identities – as landlords, members of city factions, and so on – often overrode their common identification as 'ulama' (Mottahedeh 1980: 137); religious expertise was one, but only one, aspect of being a local notable. They often led, or expressed, public opinion.

The early 'ulama were often critical of the Umayyads on moral grounds, although they accepted the procedure by which they had come to power and continued to respect 'Uthman. The Reports, however, are mostly about ritual, law and personal morality; few address political topics directly. The crucial point was that authority was vested in 'the Book of God and the Sunna of the Prophet'; the Sunna meaning in effect the Qur'an plus the hadith, *as interpreted by the 'ulama*. This gave scope to a specific type of communal authority: the 'ulama were becoming the acknowledged moral and religious leaders of the majority of Muslims. And one point of appealing to the-Book-and-the-Sunna was that it 'deprived the Caliph of any say qua caliph in the definition of Islamic norms' (Crone and Hinds 1986: 58). Justice was defined independently of the political rulers or state authority. What was happening was that religious, social and economic legislation was being enacted from below. Thus a new and somewhat original view of religious and social authority was coming into being.

AL-SHAFI'I AND THE METHODOLOGY OF THE LAW

This undermined the project of monarchical authority and world government for the House of Islam. It undermined the project of forming political entities with the kind of moral and legal standing of the Greek polis, the Roman *respublica* and the European state.

Under the 'Abbasids, the proto-Sunnis were winning the battle for hearts and minds in Baghdad and other major cities. By the mid-ninth century they had persuaded the Deputies themselves to adopt their cause; and so the 'Abbasid dynasty, on losing actual power, began to become a symbol of religious unity, a champion of perceived orthodoxy. What alternative political ideology did these Learned have to offer?

The primary factor was the *method* by which the Right Way (Shar'ia: Code/Law, lit. 'the way to the watering-place') was being moulded by the Learned generally and the Legal Experts (fuqaha) in particular, in the religio-legal schools of Basra, Kufa and Medina. The methodology of law was as important for the history of mental life and political thought as its content. Jurisprudence developed its own discourse, technical vocabulary and procedures for correct interpretation. Eventually, four Law Schools (madhdhab) came to be recognised (they differed mainly on minor points): the Hanafi, following Abu Hanifa (d.767), who was based in Iraq; the Maliki, following Malik Ibn Annas (d.795), based at Medina; the Shafi'i, following al-Shafi'i (d.820); and the Hanbali, following Ibn Hanbal (d.855), based at Baghdad. Individuals and sometimes regions adhered to a particular school.

Al-Shafi'i's approach may be taken as a model of the kind of intellectual processes at work. It gives us a flavour of the Sunni mind at its best. Al-Shafi'i set out to synthesise the more literalist school of Medina, where he had studied, and the more rationalist Iraqi school of Abu Hanifa. At one time, he served as the Deputy's agent in Yemen; but he was dismissed, imprisoned and subsequently released by al-Rashid. He declined all further government posts, including a Judgeship offered to him by al-Ma'mun. In 814, he went to teach in Egypt. He was apparently knifed to death after a lecture by a Maliki, in which case he suffered for not being literalist enough.

Al-Shafi'i redefined Tradition to make it possible to identify what was and was not Law without the need for any external authority, or for codification by the Deputy (Schacht 1953: 59). He effectively reduced the four 'Roots of Jurisprudence' (usul al-fiqh) upon which an argument might be based from four – the Qur'an, the Reports, Consensus (ijma) and Analogy (qiyas) – to just two – the Qur'an and Reports. His basic premise was that the only authority was Muhammad himself. While in practice the 'ulama were deciding what the Consensus was, al-Shafi'i insisted that Consensus could only be appealed to as evidence of the mind of Muhammad himself, and only the Consensus of the People as a whole would indicate that an opinion was indeed Muhammad's own.

The problem which al-Shafi'i faced was that, while 'the divine revelation as expressed in Qur'an and Sunna provides for every possible eventuality' (Schacht 1953: 136), in the documents currently accepted there were both inconsistencies and gaps. Al-Shafi'i attempted to manage the problem by establishing, first, rules for distinguishing between authentic and inauthentic Reports, and, second, rules by which to determine which of two contradictory texts modified or abrogated the other. These were often of great subtlety.

First, only Reports which could be traced back by a sequence of authenticated transmitters to the Prophet himself should be accepted. Al-Shafi'i devised a complex but coherent method for determining which Reports qualified. His first criterion was the personal credentials of the transmitters in the 'chain'.[2] He drew a comparison between Tradition accumulated in this way and the Arab language: each scholar knows only part of it, 'yet what each may lack can be found among the others' (Risala, p. 89).

Second, in resolving potentially contradictory texts, al-Shafi'i insisted that one take into account the exact circumstances in which the Prophet had spoken or acted. (This was similar to the procedure which became known in Catholic Christianity from the twelfth century as 'concordance of discordant canons'. This formed the basis of Abelard's Yes and No (Sic et Non), and so kick-started European jurisprudence and philosophy. But, although al-Shafi'i developed it first, there is no evidence of influence.)

Third, some statements were intended to apply generally, others only to a particular category of cases. Analogy was the one Root in which al-Shafi'i accepted that reason could play a role. According to the Hanafi School, one may exercise personal reasoning (ra'y) by interpreting problematic texts in the light of such principles as maslaha (public welfare/utility) because one may assume these to have guided the Prophet's own thinking. Thus they appealed from the prima facie meaning of revealed texts to general guiding principles. Al-Shafi'i was unhappy with this. He sought to reduce individual reasoning to drawing quite limited analogies from a revealed text. Analogy is subordinate to the other three Roots, but 'obligatory': it

> is resorted to when there is no relevant text in the Qur'an, no [Tradition] and no consensus ... We hold concerning matters on which no binding explicit text exists that [the answers] should be sought by Independent Reason (ijtihad) – through Analogy – because we are under an obligation to arrive at the right answers. (in Schacht 1953: 122, 292)

What he actually had in mind was a very limited application of common sense. For example, if someone kills your animal, stipulate as compensation not cash (because prices fluctuate) but some other animal. All he would admit was that a Report from a Companion could be abrogated by an Analogy from a Report from the Prophet himself (*Risala*, p. 302–3). In other words, he reduced interpretation once again to a question of the *status* of *texts*. He did indeed praise 'reason' as God's gift to humans, but he gave personal Opinion (ra'y) no independent role. It cannot be used to discount or modify a revealed text, even if this appears incomprehensible or irrational: 'If a (Report) is authenticated as coming from the Prophet, we have to resign ourselves to it; your talk and the talk of others, about why and how, is a mistake' (in Schacht 1953: 13). Al-Shafi'i (like Nietzsche, whom he resembled in his tone of assertive righteousness) claimed no authority for himself (Schacht 1953: 6). The attitude adopted here profoundly affected the attitudes of the 'ulama and their followers towards the life of the mind in general.

Al-Shafi'i was ascribing to the entire body of the Law that absolute, unquestionable authority which Christians might give to the Bible or the Nicene Creed. His aspiration was to pluck the true Way out of the Qur'an and Reports without reference to any external reasoning. On the other hand, he gave authentic Reports the same juridical standing as the Qur'an itself. Whatever Muhammad had communicated, in the Qur'an or in Reports, was of equal authority. And, since the Prophet's opinions had developed over his own lifetime, later pronouncements overrode earlier ones. Thus Reports could on occasion modify the Qur'an.

This approach ring-fenced the literal meanings of sacred texts. The textual revelation was self-validating, coherent in its own terms once properly interpreted. No external mental procedure could validate or invalidate it. One implication was that gaps in the provisions of the Law could only be filled by new texts: an invitation, one would imagine, to the invention of Reports, or the unconscious acceptance of invented Reports. What Muhammad was deemed likely to have said or done was derived from 'the *figure* of Muhammad as this had been built up in pious circles' (Hodgson 1974: vol. 1, pp. 329–31).

Not surprisingly, there was something of a power struggle within the Traditional Community between the narrative and abstract modes of monotheism, which were being propounded by the hadith-collectors (Reporters: ahl al-hadith) and people like al-Shafi'i on the one hand, and by the exponents of theology (kalam: lit. discourse), especially Mu'tazilites, on the other. Partly in order to emphasise the literal authority of the texts, and to protect them from interpretation by the more rationally-minded, the Reporters, in the time of al-Rashid and al-Ma'mun – when the Caliphate appeared to be at its zenith – proclaimed that the Qur'an itself was 'uncreated' ('whatever is of God is eternal, and the Qur'an is of God'). (Eventually the Caliph al-Qadir declared (1029) that the doctrine of the created Qur'an was Unbelief, punishable by death.) This was a means of authorising the 'ulama to speak for the Community and interpret the Code. For them, the use of rational argument in religious questions was nothing short of heresy (bida', lit. innovation). The jurists were, on the whole, more inclined to the Reporters' position (some more so than others). Crucially, the Mu'tazilites, unlike the Reporters, had no popular support.

The process typified by al-Shafi'i took place between 100 and 200 years after the Prophet's death, and it did not gain general acceptance until the tenth and eleventh centuries. But in the long run, it determined the way that Muhammad's Message would be understood in Sunni Islam. Here, there were major differences between Sunni and Shi'a Jurisprudence. Doubtless the Message could have been understood in many different ways from those that became axiomatic within the Islamic communities.[3] The revelation and the means for transmitting it, defined in this way, were what from now on was to count as Knowledge ('ilm). In due course, this approach colonised every corner of mental life. This 'ilm affected the mental activity and the social order that became prevalent throughout the Sunni world. The 'ulama (lit. those with 'ilm) emerged as the most stable holders of social authority because of their hold on Knowledge. It was they who formed, and still form, the basic fabric of a society insofar as it claims to be Islamic. It was they who, once the imperial aspirations of the Deputyship had died away, held, and still hold, the House of Islam together. They are the authorities; others, sultans or presidents, merely hold power.

The Jurists had now established the terms in which transactions between persons were to be conducted and disputes settled. This, in the long run, would affect the way in which people thought about most things. Precise norms for moral, legal and ritual conduct, ranging from contracts to the mode of prayer, with varying penalties for different categories of people – free, slave, unmarried – had been revealed by God. This was apparently the strength of Islam in its competition with more 'spiritual' creeds.

Tradition and Law became fixed at a time of social flux but in forms which made it virtually impossible to change them ever after. Once a legal solution had been achieved by Consensus, it could not be undone, for Muhammad had said 'my Community will never agree on an error'.[4] Presumably the only justification for change would be the discovery of new Reports deriving from personal contact with the Prophet; but, given the origin of all Reports in oral tradition, how could anyone show that new ones existed if they had not previously been known? Even today, the scope for reinterpretation is limited, and the legitimacy of undertaking it contested, on the grounds that it would mean reopening questions already settled by the acknowledged criteria of Religious Jurisprudence which is alleged to be part of God's own revelation.

POLITICAL IMPLICATIONS

In the late eighth and early ninth centuries, this culture and these attitudes won over the Baghdad masses, fired mob politics and eventually made the Caliph think it prudent to ally himself with their champions (see below, Chapter 7). Presumably one attraction was the accessibility of Knowledge to wide strata of the population who had a narrative and, only quite recently, predominantly oral culture. (It was at this time that the manufacture of paper was introduced at Baghdad.) After al-Rashid's death (813), there were popular demands for greater conformity with 'the book of God and the sunna of the Prophet' in public life. The literalist Ibn Hanbal was denounced as '(head) of a sect which has gathered his commoners and riff-raff to proclaim in the streets that "Nothing which is of God is created and the Qur'an is of God"' (Lapidus 1975: 380). Vigilante groups took to the streets proclaiming that it was the duty of the Deputy to command the good and forbid the evil, that is, to enforce the Shari'a in public life. One popular leader said (813–14) that one should only obey rulers who observe the correct religious regulations (Lapidus 1975: 372). The political implications of the narrative outlook were beginning to show themselves.

There is hardly any *explicit* political theory in the Reports or early Jurists. The text in the Qur'an which might have invited political discourse was Q. 4:62 (see above, p. 14). In society at large, there was a tendency to include political rulers among 'those in authority'. But the Jurists did not discuss the Deputyship in any detail, though the title 'King of Kings' was condemned as usurping God's prerogative. They accepted the Deputy's right to designate his own successor as a form of choice by the Community, provided there was a formal allegiance-offer (ba'ya). This was, however, a personal covenant, not a constitutional law like primogeniture in Europe (Hodgson 1974: vol. 1, p. 299).

Reports exhort one to patience under unjust rule. This may have reflected the stand of the proto-Sunni opposition under the Umayyads. They also said that it is praiseworthy to say just things before unjust governors, though the Reporters themselves did not insist on the duty of commanding good and forbidding evil in public affairs. Ibn Hanbal taught that even a usurper could be Leader (Deputy), and that an unjust or impious Leader *must* be obeyed and served, unless he commits apostasy or fails to provide for communal prayer (*EI* 3: 1164b). But he said nothing about how such a Leader should be dealt with.

This suggests a certain indifference to constitutional procedures. Several Reports warned against having any dealings with political power (sultan); one Report (appropriately ascribed to al-Rashid) defined the happy man as him who has a fine house, wealth, a beautiful wife 'and does not know me and I do not know him'. Others highlighted the danger of accepting public office: 'of three Judges, two are in hell'.

Nevertheless, the mindset of the Reporters and 'ulama, justified by the methodology of the Jurists, laid the basis for how political questions would be discussed and determined and what criteria would count in political argument in Sunni Islam. What emerged was not principled or heartfelt support for the Deputyship, nor again principled resistance, but a critical distancing and mute toleration, based on an understanding among religious groups that nothing better was to be looked for. The 'ulama wanted a Deputy to be there, provided he left them alone (rather like the king in chess). It was a strange combination of obedience, indifference and resentment. This attitude was carried over to later regimes.

Thus the literalist-narrative method of the Reporters and Jurists did after all give rise to a certain approach to politics: non-resistance, disengagement, 'the characteristic rabbinic disjunction of piety and power' (Crone and Cook 1977: 124). One reason behind this was that the 'ulama were creating their own *non-state* structures. Al-Shafi'i insisted that Q. 4:62 referred not to 'the commanders of the Apostle's army' but to 'the ones whom the Apostle appointed, with conditional not absolute obedience, concerning their rights and duties' (*Risala*, pp. 112–13), which some later commentators understood to mean the 'ulama and Jurists.[5]

Those who moulded the Islamic religion opted for a Community based on a common Law and ritual, not on political institutions. And they were in fact successful in perpetuating their socio-religious identity, despite political instability, changes of dynasty and invasions, by these means. Institutions other than those specifically devoted to promoting Islamic Right were on the margins of thought.

The political decline of the Deputyship produced a *partial* split between religious and political power, between religio-moral-legal authority and politico-military power. The former became the domain of the Learned, the latter of the Sultan. The conduct of Holy War was separated from the pursuit of Knowledge; the Arabs were no longer a people in arms.

NOTES

1. For what follows, see Schacht (1953); Guillaume (1956: 93–105); Guillaume (1966); Hodgson (1974: vol. 1, pp. 317–22); Gibb (1962: 198–202); Makdisi (1990: 2–6).
2. 'He who relates a [Report] must merit confidence in his religion and be known as reliable … comprehending what he transmits, aware of any pronunciation that might change the meaning of the [Report]': Majid Khadduri (trans.), *Islamic Jurisprudence: Shafi'i's Risala* (Baltimore: Johns Hopkins University Press, 1961), p. 239.
3. Similarly, C. Wright Mills argued that Leninism was not the only possible development of Marxism, but it was one possible development: *The Marxists* (London: Penguin, 1962).
4. This is one of many points I am grateful to Patricia Crone for clarifying in a private letter.
5. Tabari in Khadduri, *Risala*, p. 112n.

Shi'ite Theories of Leadership (imama) 4

The doctrines that we know today as Twelver or Imami Shi'ism did not develop until the tenth and eleventh centuries. Early Shi'ism meant rejection of the Umayyads and 'Abbasids as legitimate Leaders of the Community on the grounds that they were notoriously impious and immoral, and that Leadership since the death of the Prophet should anyway have gone, and for true believers did go, to 'Ali and others. Different schools of Shi'ism held different opinions as to exactly who should be Leader at any particular time, and how the Leader should be chosen. What they had in common was a belief that the Imamate was absolutely central to Islamic belief and conduct.[1]

The Shi'ites were if anything more severely disappointed than the Sunnis by the 'Abbasids' blatant failure to deliver the hoped-for restoration of justice and the true Leadership (imama: Imamate). The main *political* aim of most Shi'ites was to have the true Leader recognised and obeyed. Until that happened, both the Leadership and the Islamic community were on hold. The most active opposition came from the Zaydis, who were committed to armed insurrection ('emergence: khuruj'), and believed that the true Leader is he who gains power in this way.[2]

THE IMAMI SHI'ITES

On the other hand, the proto-Imamis, under the guidance of their fifth and sixth Imams (r.713–65), rejected armed struggle and taught instead that one should await the installation of the true Leader by divine intervention. Jafar al-Sadiq, the sixth Imam, counselled patience, non-resistance and withdrawal from mainstream politics.

When Jafar died (765), a disputed succession produced a split between the Isma'ili (Sevener) and the Imami (Twelver) Shi'ites. The Isma'ilis claimed that Jafar had appointed his older son, Isma'il, as his successor; and that, since he predeceased Jafar, the rightful Imam was Isma'il's son, Muhammad Ibn Isma'il. He would return one day as Mahdi, the Rightly-guided one who would redress wrongs and fill the earth with justice.

The 'Abbasids kept the Imami Leaders under close surveillance and prevented them from communicating with their supporters. After their eleventh Imam died (873–4), the Imamis came to believe that *his* successor, Muhammad al-Mahdi – the twelfth Imam – had gone into hiding, and would from now on communicate with his followers through secret representatives. This 'lesser absence (ghayba)' lasted until 941. The Imamis then declared that he had gone into *permanent* hiding (the 'greater absence'). He would return at the end of time as Mahdi-Redresser-of-wrongs to establish justice and equality. Hence the belief in the Hidden Twelfth Imam, which has lasted to this day.

Sunni and Shi'ite views of religious Leadership, and hence of political authority, involved different conceptions of the nature of authority, and were based on somewhat different methods of argument. A rationalist theory of the Imamate appears first to have been stated by the Zaydi Shi'ite, al-Qasim ibn Ibrahim (785–Medina 860). It included the argument that political authority is necessary due to the imperfections of human nature:

> the desire for sex and food is implanted in men and, if there were not someone to limit and curb it, people would fight against each other to satisfy their desires, and consequently the world would be destroyed ... People need a guide to teach them these restrictions, and this guide is the Imam. Also the Imam punishes people if they disobey him, and rewards them if they obey him. In this manner people are kept safe.[3]

This argument was taken up by one thinker after another, and eventually it entered mainstream Sunni teaching on the origin and raison d'être of the state.

On the question of how the Imam is to be appointed, al-Qasim affirmed that both the Imamate and the individual Imam are gifts from God. He argued against elections in general on the grounds that human beings are intrinsically contentious; they will never agree on anything. An election would have to be carried out either by the elite or by the common people. But who would define the elite? Besides, these two groups would never cooperate (see al-Jahiz). Any election would have to be carried out by a shura (council), and its members 'must come from different and distant places, their aims will be different ... since every group of the council will claim the Leadership. Their controversy will bring about war, and war will lead to perdition.'[4]

Imami Shi'ite communities flourished in Iraq and Iran, especially in cities and among artisans. The Imamis developed their Jurisprudence, with its distinctive doctrine of the Leader, from the mid-ninth to the mid-eleventh centuries, especially in the writings of the Baghdad school: al-Mufid (d.1022), his pupil al-Murtada (d.1044), and his pupil al-Tusi (d.1067). They were writing under the Buyids (formerly Zaydi, now Imami Shi'ites); al-Tusi lived to see the staunchly Sunni Saljuks take over. The Shi'ites had their own Reports (hadith), the sayings of their Imams, which in many cases resembled Sunni Reports. In interpreting the Qur'an, the Shi'ites, and especially the Isma'ilis, distinguished between an outer (zahir: external) and an inner (batin: esoteric) meaning. According to the Imamis, the Imams have perfect knowledge of the Shari'a – the Qur'an and Reports – which they hand down from one Leader to the next. Hence only those taught by such a Leader, or his representative, have true Religious Knowledge. This authoritative teaching (ta'lim) of the Leaders and of those to whom they transmit their Knowledge, is indispensable in determining the Right (Shari'a). During the Greater Absence, the Imami jurists gave greater scope to reason ('aql) than the Sunni.

Recognition of, and devotion to, the succession of correctly designated Imams (Leaders) down to the present one was absolutely essential. The theology and political thought of the Imamis came to focus upon the Imam's status, characteristics and functions. In every age there must be a Leader; we may not know where he is, but he is somewhere. According to the doctrine apparently worked out by Jafar al-Sadiq and his pupil Hisham ibn al-Hakam, the Leader is the legatee (wasi) of the Prophet, whose role he inherits. He has intercessory powers. He is an ongoing embodiment of divine revelation. His moral and intellectual qualities are guaranteed by divine providence.

A THEORY OF LEADERSHIP

The twelve Imams themselves, and above all the present twelfth or Hidden Imam, were held to be necessary to the constitution of the universe and of true religion. The Imam is God's proof (hujja: guarantee); he is the pillar of the universe, the 'gate' through whom God is approached. Knowledge of revelation depends upon him. Al-Sadiq is reported as saying: 'it is by [the Leader's] blessing that God maintains the heavens, that they do not fall and destroy their inhabitants, and it is by our blessing that God sends the rain and shows forth His mercy ... If there were no Imam on earth to represent us, verily the earth itself would collapse' (in Lambton 1981: 237–8). This was a much stronger but purely spiritualised version of the high caliphate. In fourteenth-century Europe, the same kind of rhetoric was sometimes applied to the pope.[5]

The logic of the argument, as it was developed by al-Tusi and other Shi'i theologians, was as follows (in Halm's words):

> Since man is fallible and consequently in need of guidance, divine grace cannot but grant mankind the benefit of rightful guidance at all times by an Imam who is immune (ma'sum) from sin and error. Since the ruling caliphs are notoriously sinful and fallible and act tyrannically, there must be a Hidden Imam; without the latter's existence, mankind would be forsaken by God, man would indubitably go astray. (1991: 55–6)

Similarly, both Eastern Orthodox and Latin Catholic Christians held that the Christian revelation could only be sustained if there is an infallible decider of disputes; therefore God must have provided one. This was the ecumenical council of bishops. Under the influence of the papacy, the medieval Catholic church held that such a council must be recognised by the pope. Then the first Vatican Council (1870–1) asserted the infallibility (not moral purity) of the pope alone. This obviously brought Roman Catholic doctrine into line with Imami Shi'ism on one point. There remained a vast difference between the two theories of spiritual leadership: in the conception of the church, developed from the second century, as a public and visible institution, the papacy is anything but hidden.

Out of this emerged the remarkable Imami-Shi'ite approach to religious practice and organisation. During the absence of the true Imam, his religious functions are in abeyance; many of the public acts of the Islamic faith cannot be performed. There can be no legal taxes, no Legal Penalties and (according to some) no communal Friday prayers. Frontiers may be defended; apart from that Holy War is now a purely spiritual struggle, its main aim the conversion of other Muslims.

The Leader's role at present is not to aim at political power but to guide with Religious Knowledge. He is the true spiritual ruler; his rulings are known through his associates. Under the 'lesser Absence', he directs the community through a known representative; but now, during the 'Greater Absence', we do not even know who his representative is. Guidance therefore comes through Jurisprudence; consequently the Scholars ('ulama) and *especially the expert Jurists (fuqaha)* are for the present our spiritual guides. Here there was a parallel with the role of the 'ulama among the Sunnis; but the special role given to the Jurists was to be developed enormously and with dramatic results, especially under the Safavids and also today.

The Shi'ite 'ulama, and especially the fuqaha (legal experts), were not only moral-legal experts but also representatives of the Hidden Leader. 'The true [Leaders] have cast [the mantle of] judgment on the [Expert Jurists] of the Shi'a during such time as they themselves are not in a position to exercise it in person' (al-Tusi in Lambton 1981: 252). These, therefore, came to exercise an authority significantly greater than their Sunni counterparts. This approach gave rise to a remarkable attitude towards politics. The present authorities (the 'Abbasids and Sunni sultans) are usurpers. It is because of them that the true Leader has gone into hiding: 'so long as usurpers reign and true believers continue to be persecuted, the True Imam is prevented from exercising his rights and is threatened in life and limb; he not only may but must, therefore, remove himself from the clutches of the tyrannical false Imam' (Halm 1991: 55–6). This led to dissociation from the state and withdrawal into communal life. The realities of power, of which the Shi'a had much experience, make suspension of political activity the right option. Under an unjust (i.e., mainly, non-Shi'i) ruler, all engagement in public affairs is, in principle, forbidden. Their whole attitude was determined by the conviction – born of many bloody and unsuccessful attempts at revolution – that one must wait upon divine providence. This meant non-participation and resignation.

Until the return of the twelfth Imam, then, one must endure the tyranny and injustice of existing governments. But, if one's life, family or property are in danger, one is permitted to conceal one's true beliefs: taqiyya (precautionary dissimulation, Caution). Non-resistance and public conformism will protect the Shi'a community. One does not have to 'enjoin the good, forbid the evil' if doing so would harm oneself or the Shi'ite community. The Shi'a accommodated themselves wonderfully. Caution (al-Tusi argued) justifies cooperation with unjust rulers so long as they do not command anything contrary to Right. If one's *life* is threatened, one may even cooperate in actions contrary to Right, 'as long as the killing of anyone is not involved. In no circumstances is [Caution] to be adopted in the killing of anyone.'[6]

According to al-Murtada, however, certain conditions may make tenure of public office not only licit but obligatory: (1) if it enables you 'to support a right and to reject a false claim, or to order what is proper and to forbid what is reprehensible'; or (2) if it enables you to protect other Shi'ites; or (3) if you are threatened with death otherwise. Under such circumstances, one is actually holding office 'on behalf of the true Leaders', because one is following their guidelines on tenure of office (*Treatise*, pp. 25–7).

A Shi'ite Jurist may even, in cases when 'he fears for himself, his people or believers, or for their property', act as Religious Judge; he may even 'give judgements according to the Sunni Schools' (provided, once again, this does not involve killing) (al-Murtada). Al-Tusi, writing at the time of the Saljuks' takeover, argued that this was permissible insofar as it enabled one to implement the Shari'a: 'to apply the penalties of the law, enjoin the good and forbid the evil, divide (legal taxes) and (charitable welfare) among those entitled to them, and apportion favours to the brethren' (Lambton 1981: 255).

A category of ruler in between the true Leader and the usurper was also introduced: 'the just sultan', or 'the sultan of the time', one who 'orders what is proper, forbids what is reprehensible, and places things in their [proper] places' (al-Tusi).[7] A good Sunni ruler, and those Shi'ite rulers who acknowledge the true Imams, may be regarded as acting on their behalf, and so are approved by God. Thus, within the House of Islam, the Shi'ites identified the territory in which Shi'ism could be practised openly as the House of Faith (dar al-iman); this would presumably have included Buyid and Fatimid territory.

According to the Imamis, restoration of the true Leader is to be left to God. Only when the twelfth Imam returns will rebellion be justified; then it will be *obligatory*. 'None of the [twelfth Leader's] fathers was duty-bound to rise in armed revolt, proclaim the end of Caution and rally supporters around himself. But this is what the Leader of our age must do when he appears' (al-Mufid). '[The Leaders] publicly forbade [their followers] to draw the sword against [unjust rulers] and warned against inciting anyone to do so. Instead, they pointed toward the awaited one [mahdi] who would be descended from them and would come at the end of time. By him God would remove affliction from the community, revive and guide it' (al-Mufid in Lambton 1981: 262). Accordingly, neither the Buyids nor the Fatimids sought to impose Shi'ism on the Sunni majority.

THE ISMA'ILIS

The Isma'ilis developed a still more distinctive doctrine and organisation. From the late ninth century, they posed a serious revolutionary threat to both Sunni and Imami rulers, based on Gnostic and messianic ideas, which became interwoven with neo-Platonic Philosophy (see below, pp. 60–1). In their view, for each one of Muhammad's public (tanzil) teachings, 'Ali as his special agent (wasi: executor, trustee) had been given a corresponding secret allegorical interpretation (ta'wil). These embraced nature, numbers and astrology. The Isma'ilis emphasised the distinction, which the Imamis also made, between themselves as the elite (khassa) and the Sunnis as the common masses ('amma).

Alone among Muslims, they developed an idea of hierarchy. The universe was made up of seven emanations from God, the human world being the seventh; and there are seven major historical epochs, each with its own Prophet and 'executor'. We are living in the sixth, with a new age just round the corner. There are seven Imams (Leaders): 'Ali and his successors down to the disappeared Muhammad Ibn Isma'il. As trustee of Muhammad, the Imam was yet more elevated than in Imami Shi'ism: his person is the pivot of divine revelation. For salvation, it is necessary to be able to recognise, as only the initiated can, the true Imam, which now means the Hidden Seventh Imam.

To this metaphysical hierarchy there corresponded an actual political hierarchy. Knowledge of the secret teaching was entrusted only to the worthy few; the elements of a secret society were thus based on the most up-to-date understanding of the world order. True doctrine was disseminated by a missionary propaganda machine (da'wa) with a head of mission (da'i) in each region to supervise adherents, in 'a graded hierarchy of rank and knowledge' (Lewis 1967: 48). Members were strictly under oath not to reveal the doctrine or membership. In emergencies, a visible Leader acted as the true Leader's guardian, veiling and protecting him. This was an alternative political order in waiting.

FATIMID POLITICAL THEORY

The Isma'ilis were now the only ideological movement dedicated to putting the Islamic ideal into immediate practice by practical means. They expounded this strategy as an alternative to Imami quietism in the face of 'Abbasid corruption, and other governments based on force. In 909, the Fatimids proclaimed Ubaydallah 'al-Mahdi' (d.934) as Mahdi and true Imam (Tunis) and proceeded to conquer Sicily, North Africa and Egypt (969), and briefly Palestine and parts of Syria; they gained control over Mecca and Medina, to the dismay of the Sunni world. Most Isma'ilis in Iraq and Arabia, however, refused to recognise the Fatimid claim; some – the Qarmati – set up a tribal state in eastern Arabia (Bahrain), ruled, almost uniquely in Islam, by a council of elders. Their ambition too was universal: 'I will submit to my power all the peoples of the earth in east and west as far as the capitals of the Romans, Turks and Khazars' (in Canard 1942–7: 159).

Under three outstanding Imams, al-Mu'izz (953–75), al-Hakim (996–1021) – a brilliant fanatic, or madman – and al-Mustansir (1036–94), Egypt became a world power. The Fatimid state was the focal point of the east–west trade, linking Spain to India, and promoting commerce with the Italian city-states (the Fatimids built the only substantial Muslim navy of this period).

The arts and sciences, philosophy and religious Learning flourished in Fatimid Egypt. They had a policy of religious toleration; the majority of the population were Sunni and could practise their religion quite openly, except for a savage persecution under al-Hakim. Christians and Jews were on the whole well treated.[8] Yet the Fatimid Imam constituted a perceived, and at times real, threat to other Sunni and Imami governments, especially the neighbouring Buyids. Partly with them in mind, the Fatimids entered into friendly relations with Byzantium. Perceptions of the threat were magnified by the presence of secret Isma'ili organisations all over the Middle East, though many did not support the specific Fatimid doctrine and claims.

The Fatimids' eschatology, focusing again on the number seven, was expounded by al-Qadi al-Numan (d.974), an Isma'ili jurist who served under the first four Fatimid Deputies, became chief Religious Judge and founded the Isma'ili Law School; and by the neo-Platonic theologian al-Kirmani (d.after 1020). According to the Fatimid interpretation of historical cycles, astrology showed that their time in power (dawla) would now supplant all others and take over the world. 'The world is yours and your dynasty's ... Young is your empire, O Mahdi, and the time is its slave' (a poet addressing the Deputy Ubaidallah) (in Canard 1942–7: 184, 189). Fatimid rule was presented not as a return to the good old days of early Islam, but as the progressive unfolding of a new era in cosmic history.

The Fatimid Imams, no longer hidden but in the open, were accorded a status far loftier than that claimed for the Sunni Deputy. The Imam is the earthly form of the intellect emanating from God, the 'cause of the world which has been created by Him' (in Canard 1942–7: 161). He was conceived as an absolute ruler uniting religious and political authority, to whom complete obedience (taslim) is owed in everything. He controlled the religious and the political hierarchies through the chief religious teacher (da'i) and the vizier. Al-Qadi al-Numan added Holy War, and Faith (iman) or walaya (allegiance, devotion), to the traditional five pillars of Islam. Faith requires one 'to believe in the Imams, to know and acknowledge the Imam of the time and to submit to his will; to comply with God's commands and obey the Imam'.[9]

Abu l-Fawaris, a Fatimid Isma'ili writing in 996–1017, presented new *rational* arguments for the necessity of the Imamate, arguing (like others before him) from human needs, but including this time *epistemological* needs. Knowledge 'is the greatest and noblest of all things ... [and] is only comprehended by the purest of men'. Humans must possess knowledge if they are to reflect the perfection of their Creator. But evidence shows that knowledge requires a 'teacher elected and supported by God'. He concludes 'and this man is the Imam'.[10]

Further, we know that humans are in the nature of things unequal, and 'reason dictates that he who is superior should lead'. Without such inequality there would be no social order, no knowledge, because everyone would claim they knew everything. 'Disparity among us leads, therefore, to our advantage' (i.e. to the Imamate). These arguments suggest that the Imamate is necessary for humanity as a whole. In specifically Islamic terms, God's revelation has a hidden as well as an external meaning, and so it cannot be understood without 'a clarifier and an interpreter' (Makarem (ed.), pp. 25, 33–4).

The Prophet did not leave the method of appointment to be decided later, because he knew that would divide his community, like that of 'my brother

Jesus', into many sects. He 'set up a clear and definite law whereby a vicegerent would be clearly appointed and made known to the people' (Makarem (ed.), p. 26). And, because the Imam is Deputy of God and of the Prophet but not of the community, the method must be direct divine choice, that is by designation.

An Isma'ili work of the tenth century (of which there are two versions, one of them presented as a letter of 'Ali to the governor of Egypt)[11] demonstrates that Shi'ites could be quite positive about political activity and the state when writing about the rule of a legitimate Imam. The work is especially striking for its deeply pious and moral view of the relationship between ruler and ruled. The ruler should treat his subjects with love and kindness, for 'either they are your brothers in religion or your equals in creation'. Special respect is due to the common people, for they are the source of religion and Islamic solidarity (pp. 69–70). The poor should be received in audience and given a share of the treasury and conquered lands. Non-Shi'ite subjects have a claim to respect. All this will improve a ruler's reputation.

The author distinguishes *five* social groups in the polity: (1) soldiers, (2) officials, (3) 'payers of the poll-tax and the land-tax', both Muslim and non-Muslim – presumably mainly cultivators, (4) 'merchants and craftsmen', and (5) 'the lowest (group) – the needy' (pp. 71–2). What is remarkable about this version of Iranian status-group theory (below, p. 53) is the esteem given to each group. Farmers are singled out for attention: 'let your care for the prosperity of the earth be deeper than your care for the collecting of land-tax' (p. 75). It was very rare for non-Muslims to be given a recognised position, as they are in category (3), which groups all peasants together regardless of their faith. Merchants are valued because they bring goods 'from remote and inaccessible places'. The inclusion of the poor as a fifth group expresses the distinctively Islamic idea that they are worthy of specific attention.

This classification stresses the interdependence of the social groups. The sense of mutual esteem seems here to outweigh any inequality that might be implied by dividing society into groups. It also provides a prudential reason for justice; here there is an oblique reference to the Circle of Power (see below, p. 54): the polity depends upon the payers of land-tax (i.e., mainly, farmers); therefore, long-term prosperity will only be assured by fairness in tax-collection: 'the welfare of the taxpayers is the welfare of others' (p. 75). Here the author combined Islamic piety with the managerial approach of Iranian patrimonial monarchism. The political order is given a moral mandate and purpose.

THE NIZARIS AND VIOLENT REVOLUTION

A pro-Fatimid Isma'ili missionary leader in Iran, Hasan-i Sabbah (d.1124), stepped up the campaign to institute the reign of the true Imam, in response to Saljuk military campaigns designed to implement the Sunni policy of eliminating known Isma'ilis as apostates. Based in the remote fortress of Alamut (south of the Caspian: 1090), he sponsored a rebellion and initiated a plan to assassinate Sunni political and religious leaders. In 1092, the great Saljuk vizier Nizam al-Mulk (below, Chapter 8) was assassinated.[12]

When the Fatimid Imam-Caliph al-Mustansir died (1094), Sabbah backed Nizar, whom Mustansir had designated, against the man whom the Fatimid soldiery installed (they had Nizar killed). Sabbah himself claimed to be the hujja (proof/lieutenant) of Imam Nizar until Nizar should decide to reappear in person. He and his supporters proclaimed a new and purified version of the Isma'ili politico-religious programme, 'the new teaching'.

From their mountain redoubt, the Nizari 'assassins' set about implementing their new religio-political strategy by overturning local rulers and assassinating leaders of the Sunni community. Their aim was to inspire a spontaneous uprising in favour of the true Fatimid Imam Nizar. The Sunnis responded with a massacre of Isma'ilis (Nizari or not) in the cities of Iran (1096). Sabbah and his followers retained only a few strongholds, but they hung on in Alamut until the Mongols arrived.

This was a final attempt to achieve the consummation of history by force, to implement the Isma'ili programme whatever the costs here and now. According to surviving accounts of their teaching, Sabbah and the Nizaris put forward the argument that Prophecy and Imamate are necessary because, we can observe, humans cannot live without cooperation and coercive governance. Having proved that society in general requires leadership, they then argued that such leadership has divine sanction because people will only accept constraints and rules if they are from God (a presciently Durkheimian argument): 'the legislator must be that one whom God shall have appointed as his lieutenant' (i.e. a Prophet). Divine revelation, moreover, requires an authoritative exponent. It was even argued that 'Ali and his successors as Leaders were of higher status than Muhammad because it was they who reveal the *inner* and truer meaning of God's revelation.

The Nizari argument contained a further epistemological point. Reason alone cannot discover who the imam is; indeed (in Hodgson's words) 'the Imam cannot substantiate his claims by recourse to any proof beyond himself, or he ceases to claim ultimate authority ... [therefore] that Imam is true who *does not* allege extraneous proofs for his Imamate but *only his own existence*' (*CH Iran* 5: 436; my italics): and such is the Imam of the Nizaris (Nizar's grandson was alleged to be in hiding at Alamut). It was pure revelationism again, the same argument that has been used for the inerrancy of Scripture.

This hidden Imam is to be served by (1) someone who rules the Isma'ili community by ordinary coercive governance (siyasa) – 'the hand of power'; and (2) a spiritual guide – 'the tongue of knowledge'. The latter must obey the former. But both powers may, it seems, be vested in the same person, i.e. the present ruler of the Nizari community!

In 1164, the Nizari ruler announced the arrival of the new epoch of 'the Resurrection'. In a manner similar to some medieval Christian millenarians, he claimed that the Shari'a had been abrogated, and that he himself was the true Imam, the Redresser of wrongs. 'Men have been relieved', he said, 'of the duties imposed by the Shari'a, because in this period of the Resurrection they must turn in every sense to God' (in Lewis 1967: 73): the Shari'a was to be ritually violated. But forty years later, the new ruler at Alamut proclaimed himself a Sunni.

In the end, the Isma'ilis became a quietist sect. And all other Shi'ites now viewed the Leader's return and the final Redress of wrongs as events beyond human calculation. Islam as immediate *political* revolution had failed. From now on, there was the moral Code, with politics more or less as usual. Something of the distinctiveness of Islam had gone.

NOTES

1. For what follows, see *EI* 3: 1166a-9b, on Shi'a and Isma'iliyya; Halm (1991); Lambton (1981: 219–41, 288–306); Anon. (1970); Corbin (1964: 62–73, 110–15); Arjomand (1984: 27–65); Joseph Eliash, 'The Ithna 'Ashari-Shi'i Juristic Theory of Political and Legal Authority', *SI* 39 (1969), pp. 18–30; W. Madelung, 'Authority in Twelver Shiism in the Absence of the Imam', in Anon. (1982: 163–74).
2. Halm (1991: 206–7); Lambton (1981: 28–32); *CH Iran* 4: 487.
3. B. Abrahamov, 'Al-Kasim ibn Ibrahim's theory of the imamate', *Arabica* 34 (1987), pp. 80–105 at p. 86.
4. Abrahamov, 'Al-Kasim', pp. 91–2.
5. Walter Ullmann, *Medieval Papalism* (London: Methuen, 1949); Michael Wilks, *The Problem of Sovereignty in the Later Middle Ages* (Cambridge: Cambridge University Press, 1963).
6. Al-Tusi in Lambton (1981: 151–2); Wilferd Madelung, 'A Treatise of the Sharif al-Murtada on the Legality of Working for the Government', *BSOAS* 43 (1980), pp. 18–31 at p. 27.
7. Cited in Madelung, 'Treatise', p. 30.
8. Yaacov Lev, *State and Society in Fatimid Egypt* (Leiden: Brill, 1991), p. 10.
9. Sami Makarem, 'The Philosophical Significance of the Imam in Isma'ilism', *SI* 27 (1967), p. 41.
10. S. N. Makarem (ed. and trans.), *The Political Doctrine of the Isma'ilis (the Imamate): an edition and translation of Abu l-Fawaris ar-Risala fi l'Imama* (Delmar, NY: Caravan, 1977), pp. 23, 35.
11. ''Ali's Instructions to Malik al-Ashtar', in W. C. Chittick, *A Shi'ite Anthology* (London: Muhammadi Trust, 1980), pp. 68–82. The other is the political testament ('ahd) of al-Qadi al-Numan, an Isma'ili jurist who served under the first four Fatimid Deputies: trans. J. G. Salinger, 'A Muslim Mirror for Princes', *The Muslim World* 46 (1956), pp. 24–39. See W. al-Qadi, 'An Early Fatimid Political Document', *SI* 48 (1978). (I am grateful to Patricia Crone for guidance here.) The only significant difference is al-Qadi al-Numan's assertion that a disagreement between two Religious Judges should be resolved by the Leader; this would make sense under Fatimid rule.
12. See Lewis (1967); M. G. S. Hodgson, 'The Isma'ili State', in *CH Iran* 5: 422–82; Freya Stark, *The Valley of the Assassins and Other Persian Travels* (London: Century, 1936).

The Restoration of Persia c.850–1050   5

Out of the 'Abbasid debacle emerged smaller successor states in various regions.[1] By the end of the tenth century, three separate world powers, two of them Shi'ite, were established: the Ghaznavids to the east, the Buyids in the centre, and the Fatimids to the west. From now on, the House of Islam was an inter-state system with unstable components, fluid boundaries and powerful non-governmental, interstate movements. The main religious groupings – the Community-Traditionalists (Sunni), the Isma'ili Shi'a and the Imami Shi'a – were not territorially defined. Shi'ite dynasties, which played a major role in this period, ruled over predominantly Sunni populations. And each sect aspired to convert all the others to the true path.

There was little connection between boundaries and nationalities; most states were made up of a mixture of races and tribes. It was common for a region to be ruled by an ethnic – or tribal – minority, such as the Dailami Buyids or the Turkish Ghaznavids.

In the international system, the Shi'ite powers – the Buyids (western Iran, Iraq), Fatimids (Egypt), Hamdanids (Syria, Cappadocia) and Qarmati (north-eastern Arabia) – were balanced by the Sunni Samanids (eastern Iran), Ghaznavids (Afghanistan, north-western India) and Qarakhanids (or Ilek-khans: central Asia) to the East, and al-Andalus (Spain) to the West. Spain had never recognised the 'Abbasids; it was ruled by a branch of the Umayyads as Commanders (amirs) until 'Abd al-Rahman declared himself Deputy (929). The Ghaznavids and Qarakhanids began a Turkish tradition in adhering to the relatively relaxed Hanafi Law School. There was potential for religious conflict on both domestic and international fronts.

The Isma'ili Fatimids and Imami Buyids confronted one another along the Syria–Hijaz–Yemen line. The Buyids regarded Isma'ili groups as agents of a hostile power, although many of them did not recognise the Fatimid Leader. The Imami Shi'a, with scholarly centres at Baghdad and Qum, were sometimes a target of popular hatred among Sunnis. Mahmud of Ghazna (r.998–1030) championed Sunni orthodoxy with the encouragement of the 'Abbasid Deputy. He boasted that he had cleansed his territory of 'the Isma'ili cells and the Mu'tazilites and extremist Shi'i leaders, and the cause of the sunan (Tradition) has been helped to victory' (in Bosworth 1963: 53). Both Mahmud and the

Qarakhanid ruler Ibrahim (r.1052–68) came to be seen as Sunni heroes, exemplary righteous kings.

The Buyids, on the other hand, and the Fatimids mostly, were tolerant towards both Sunnis and other monotheists; this was partly because their own co-religionists were in a minority. The Fatimid regime was passionately Isma'ili but did not seek to convert by force; under the Buyids, religion was almost a private and communal affair. By providing political order without 'making windows into men's souls', these Shi'ite regimes, especially the Buyids, facilitated a surge in intellectual energy.

The power of the new states rested on a combination of tribal armies (the Fatimids used Berbers) and slave-soldiers (mamluks: mainly Turkish); these were migrants or prisoners who were converted and then trained in the lands where they were to serve. Sultans and dynasties controlled the levers of power through the personal fidelity of specific groups, often relying on ethnic minorities for their armies, while bureaucrats and merchants tended to come from religious minorities (the Fatimids had Christian generals and viziers). Mahmud's regime 'depended on combining the Muslim mountaineers as military power with the plainsmen of the Hindu Punjab as rich taxpayers' (Hodgson 1974: vol. 2, p. 41). It was a case of divide and rule. Slave-soldiers were obligated to the ruler by the special tie of patronage; their allegiance also depended on satisfactory emoluments, which in turn depended upon conquests to provide booty in land, slaves, wealth and sexual gratification (women and boys). Hence the constant pressure upon Islamic states to expand. The Turkic Ghaznavids were the first dynasty to originate from slave-soldiers. By relying on slaves and racial or religious minorities, a ruler could avoid being beholden to the majority population and its social networks, including the 'ulama. The result was a distancing between government with its court culture and the population at large.

A further sign of separation between state and society was that the landed aristocracy did not as a rule have military power or political influence. Theoretically, all the land belonged to the Sultan. It was often distributed in return for military service as iqta' ('fief': see below, p. 92). But such tenure was not hereditary; land could be redistributed upon the death or disgrace of the tenant, or a change of Sultan. There was, thus, no feudal system and no representation of landed interests as such. When hereditary local notables did emerge, they tended to be local powers tied into the religious network. Thus the European pathway to state formation and constitutional development simply did not exist.

DAWLA

Every effort was made to promote state power by ideological means. In the post-'Abbasid Islamic world, power gravitated towards a ruling clan and its chief, who assumed the title Sultan (lit. power). Behind the Sultan stood the dynastic clan, from which most regimes took their name. The ideology of power focused upon the idea of dawla (turn in power), applied to a particular clan dynasty. Dawla is the inexplicable outcome of cosmic forces. The Buyids 'cultivated a mystique of kingship, suggesting divine selection revealed in dreams, miracles and prophecies' (Lapidus 1988: 147). For both the clan as a whole and the individual Sultan, military conquest was the elemental legitimating factor: God made known the dawla through victory. A ruler needed to be perceived to be a good Muslim, observing the Religious Law and encouraging others to do so. The ruler's primary function was often said to be justice: 'Adud al-Daula, who ruled over Buyid territories from 950–83, styled himself 'the just amir', 'the just king'.

The clan's collective ownership of the regime was manifested whenever a sultan died. Most dynasties were disabled by succession struggles; it was difficult to establish any constitutional rule for succession in the face of Islamic Law and tribal custom, which divided a patrimony equally among all sons. This led to military and political contests which had a dissolving effect on whatever power even the ablest ruler could amass. A new ruler had to expend precious political capital merely on ensuring the succession. Thus Buyid power declined rapidly following the death of 'Adud al-Daula. Islamic dynasties tended to last for only 100 or 200 years (the Ottomans were the great exception); Ibn Khaldun suggests why (see below, Chapter 18). To gain the succession within a clan dynasty you needed, once again, to demonstrate that God was on your side. This meant acquiring support through a combination of military success and good repute.

The Sultan and ruling clan, whether Sunni, Isma'ili or Imami, relied on a common stock of royalist propaganda. The dynastic clan sought legitimacy by every means available in popular culture. Much was made of ancestors and genealogy – tribal, Islamic, royal-Iranian. The use of specifically Islamic ideas depended to some extent on the affiliation of the dynasty. A Sunni ruler, rather than claiming to be a religious leader in his own right, would seek endorsement from the 'Abbasid Deputy. The accompanying ceremonial was rich in symbolism and mutual exaltation. The Samanids, who ruled the east Iranian highlands and the Oxus basin from Bukhara (874/900–99), were content with the title *amir* (lit. military Commander). Mahmud of Ghazna was styled 'the right hand of the destined rule' (yamin al-dawla), that is, of the 'Abbasids (*CH Iran* 4: 169); he sent the Deputy detailed reports of his Holy War against the Hindus, which brought in massive treasure and looted idols. He was the secular arm of Sunnism in the east, long admired as a model Muslim ruler.

This situation gave rise to an embryonic distinction between government (dawla) and religion (din). According to a Persian secretary of the Ghaznavids, the two powers were separate and complementary:

> the Lord most high has given one power to the prophets and another power to kings, and he has made it incumbent upon the people of the earth that they should submit themselves to the two powers, and should acknowledge the true way laid down by God. (in Bosworth 1963: 63)

This was close to Pope Gelasius I (late fifth century) and paralleled subsequent statements within Latin Christendom.[2]

'Adud al-Daula, who as a Shi'ite needed to boost himself in the eyes of the Sunni majority among his subjects, sought to establish a special relationship with the 'Abbasid Deputyship. On his entry into Baghdad (977), he was invested by the Deputy; a distinction was formulated between government, which was assigned to 'Adud, and religion: 'it has pleased me (the Deputy announced) to transfer to you the affairs in government of the subjects, both in the east and in the west of the earth, except my own private possessions, wealth and palace' (*CH Iran* 4: 276).

The heritage of pre-Islamic Iran provided a language and images by which Islamic Commanders-cum-tribal chiefs could justify their ascent into absolute monarchy. The idea of a King (malik) became respectable again. According to the *Book of the Crown* (*Kitab al-Taj*: probably written for a regional dynasty in the mid-ninth century),[3] the king holds a position between God and men; the common people's way of life is different from his. 'The welfare of the people lies in their deference and submission' (in Pellat 1954: 27). The author was keen to impress upon his provincial patron the importance of court etiquette.

The Sultan's own person and qualities became a focus of legitimacy, and were exalted by every imaginable means. The Samanids in particular, who regarded themselves as a Persian dynasty, went further than the 'Abbasids in adopting Persian techniques in bureaucracy, language, style and etiquette. They were the first to use Persian as their language of government; this was part of a general revival of Iranian culture and manners. Their governmental tradition was taken over by the Ghaznavids and then became a model for the Saljuks. The Ghaznavids developed another Iranian instrument of social control, the postal-intelligence service (barid). This revival of Persian monarchism culminated under the Buyids. 'Adud al-Daula adopted the Persian title Shah-an-Shah (king of kings) – much to the disgust of his Sunni subjects.

FIRDAUSI ON THE ANCIENT KINGS

The need to transmit governmental skills from one dynasty to another inspired new works in the genre of Advice-for-Kings (see below, pp. 110–11). A vizier should 'be wise like a philosopher, put the land to use like a farmer, accumulate like a merchant, be brave like a soldier' (in Fouchécour 1986: 380). With *The Epic of Kings* (*Shah-nama*), composed (980–1010) by Firdausi (Tus c.940–1020s),[4] a Shi'i, for Mahmud of Ghazna, the rehabilitation of Iranian patrimonial monarchy was complete. Firdausi set out to 'revive ancient Iran (and) to do it in the Iranian tongue', to 'strengthen and consolidate an Iranian national consciousness'.[5] Into the mouth of the exemplary Iranian monarch Kay Khusraw, he put the idea of the special divine illumination granted to kings: 'praise be to God who granted me the Farr, this phase of the stars, my foothold and my power to give protection' (*Shah-nama*, pp. 174–5). Ardashir was the model of the good Sassanian king, whose modern counterpart is Mahmud. Ardashir's justice made the earth flourish. He encouraged agriculture and education, and remitted taxes. 'Each month distribute money to the poor', was his motto, for justice leads to prosperity. Khusraw Anushirvan ensured that 'he that had no seed or cattle ... was provided with them from the king's treasuries, and no ground was left ... untilled' (*Shah-nama*, p. 322). Thus patrimonial monarchy was justified, and at the same time regulated, by a pre-Islamic national narrative.

IBN QUTAIBA AND STATUS GROUPS

The age-old Iranian idea of social groups, derived from India, became current in the Islamic world. Early Islam had had an 'egalitarian potential' (Marlow 1997: 6) insofar as 'inequalities have no bearing on an individual's moral worth and ultimate fate in the next world' (Marlow 1997: 4–6). Nevertheless, the Qur'an sanctioned ranks: God has 'raised some above others in terms of rank, so that some may take others into servitude' (Q. 43:32). In al-Rashid's time, a vizier of old Iranian stock is reported as saying that society is divided into four strata: king, vizier, highly-placed men of wealth, the middle class (and the rest of humanity are scum interested only in food and sleep) (Marlow 1997: 37). *The Book of the Crown* adopted a modified version of the four distinct categories (or strata) current in India and pre-Islamic Iran (Marlow 1997: 175): (1) the high nobility and princes, (2) theologians and priests of the fire temple, (3) medics, secretaries and astrologers, (4) farmers and manual workers (Marlow 1997: 7, 66–90). The stability of society and government, the author argued, depends upon these distinctions being preserved. The moral is that everyone must keep to their station; in particular, the common people must not seek higher status.

From now on, this notion of social groups, usually four and with some variations in their composition, became widely accepted in the literature of the Islamic world. It was the current definition of social organisation. Unlike the organic analogy which played a similar role in European thought, it did not *necessarily* imply ranking and social stratification. Strictly speaking, it need not have contravened the Islamic ideal of legal equality among Muslims. It *could* refer simply to the division of labour in society. But ranking was generally implied. *The Book of the Crown* advised the king to avoid contact with the common people; their ways are not his ways. It became usual to divide society into the elite and the masses (al-khassa wa'l-'amma: lit. the special and the general), with the implication that the elite were superior people. Ottoman society was conceived in terms of 'askeri (lit. warriors) and re'aya (flock), thus connecting the elite/masses distinction with a division of labour.

The synthesis of Arabo-Islamic and Iranian ideas was consummated by Ibn Qutaiba (Marv 828–Baghdad 889).[6] This was the more remarkable because he was not a courtier by background but a Traditionalist, an admirer of Ibn Hanbal (see above, p. 37), not someone one would have expected to attempt any kind of synthesis, or to express agreement with monarchical ideas of non-Islamic origin. He had been Judge at Marv before moving to Baghdad, where he embarked upon a brilliant literary career. He more than anyone incorporated Persian ethics and historical lore into Islamic thought. His *Choice Narratives* ('*Uyun al-Akhbar*)[7] were a vast concoction of Islamic and Persian sayings, a synthesis between

Islamic piety and courtly culture. And this was deliberate: he justified the use of different moral cultures:

> There is not just one road to God, nor is all (that is) good ... confined to nightly prayer ... [Rather], the roads that lead to Him are legion, and the gates leading to the good are open wide. This book, although it does not treat of the Quran or [Tradition] ... yet shows the way to matters of high importance, gives guidance to noble virtues, restrains from moral [turpitude] and proscribes evil. (in Makdisi 1990: 171–2)

Ibn Qutaiba repeated the idea of four distinct social groups with their composition and relationships subtly changed: '(1) the learned who are the bearers of religion, (2) the horsemen who are the guards of the seat of power, (3) the writers who are the ornament of the kingdom, (4) the agriculturalists who make the lands prosperous' (in Horovitz 1930: 190–1). This emphasised the functional nature of the classification: each group has its own contribution to make. Cultivators, although the last in the sequence, get a category of their own. The importance of agriculture is recognised: 'act kindly towards the farmers, you will remain fat as long as they are fat' (in Horovitz 1930: 193).

This functional view of the social and political structure was reinforced by another ancient Iranian concept, which now made its first appearance in Islamic literature: the 'Circle of Power'.[8] 'There is no rule except through men, and men do not subsist except through property, and (there is) no property except through cultivation, and no cultivation except through justice and good government' (in Horovitz 1930: 193). Ibn Qutaiba also quoted a Report which made the same point: 'The relation between Islam, the ruler and the people is like that between tent, pole, ropes and pegs. The tent is Islam, the pole the ruler, the ropes and pegs the people. Every one ... of the[se] is dependent on the others for [its] well-being' (in Horovitz 1930: 185). Both these statements asserted interdependence and prescribed reciprocity. They were among the classic statements of agrarian patrimonialism.

On the state, Ibn Qutaiba inadvertently revealed the inconsistency between Persian and Arabo-Islamic culture. For the most part, he endorsed government as the partner of religion. The adage that 'kingdom and religion are two brothers; the one cannot do without the other' (in Horovitz 1930: 188, 197; see below, p. 94) also appears here. Government is a necessary part of social order: 'do not stay in a place where there are not five things: a powerful ruler, a just judge, a fixed market, a learned physician, a running river' (in Horovitz 1930: 190). On the other hand, Ibn Qutaiba quoted with respect the Reporters' pious aversion to government: people are naturally averse to government; government service is a dangerous undertaking, to be avoided if possible, for the sake of one's integrity (Horovitz 1930: 194, 336–7).

Much of Ibn Qutaiba's advice was about how to *manage* one's subjects. The ruler–ruled relationship is seen in both pragmatic and moral terms, mingling Iranian statecraft with Islamic ethics: gain the love of your subjects, use kindness rather than force; you can rule their bodies but you can only enter their hearts through kindness. As the Persians said, 'that king manages best who leads the bodies of the subjects to obedience through their hearts' (p. 191). The monarch should, like the good Deputy 'Umar, 'visit the sick of the Muslims, be present at their funerals, open their door for them, and busy himself with their affairs; because he is one of them, only God has made him the one whose burden is the heaviest' (p. 195). On the other hand, he quotes a Persian saying in the form of a hadith: 'Manage the best of the people by love, the common people by a mixture of love and fear, the low people by fear' (p. 192). Such juxtaposition of statecraft and piety became typical of the Advice genre (and rendered Machiavelli superfluous in the Islamic world).

Thus the political culture of the Islamic world was becoming half-Iranian. The idea of the fourfold division of society, based on people's different functions, remained current until the nineteenth century, when it was ousted as much by European ideas as by Islamic revival. Thus inequality lay at the core of much Muslim social philosophy: patrimonialism had ousted both tribalism and Islamic doctrine. It was a case of the conquered subduing their conquerors (as Horace had said of the Greeks and Romans). The idea of fixed ranks was new to Islamic society and contradicted the Qur'anic view that people's worth depends upon their piety and knowledge, and the neo-tribal belief in individual prowess whether in battle or spirituality. But no moralist, Sunni or Shi'ite, spoke against it.

The explanation, presumably, is that it was felt to be necessary to social order and, therefore, peace. The elite–masses distinction roughly paralleled the distinction in European society between those who fought and those who worked – the feudal relationship; the fourfold distinction included both warriors and cultivators. The Greco-European equivalent was the organic analogy, in which the separate parts of society *were* explicitly ranked. One could argue that such inequality was inherent in the existing agricultural mode of production. The warrior-landlord was a patrimonial monarch writ small.

States which succeeded the 'Abbasids in the sphere of the old Persian empire helped transmit the Iranian tradition of patrimonial monarchy to future Islamic states. They helped determine how state officials and ordinary people would regard political authority and, not least, the class system.

NOTES

1. See Hodgson (1974: vol. 2, pp. 12–61); *CH Iran* 4: 136–304; Bosworth (1963); C. E. Bosworth, 'The Heritage of Rulership in Early Islamic Iran and the Search for Dynastic Connections with the Past', *Journal of Persian Studies* 1 (1973), pp. 51–62; BL 31–47.
2. Joseph Canning, *A History of Medieval Political Thought 300–1450* (London: Routledge, 1996), pp. 35–6; Burns (1988: 288–300).
3. Trans. Pellat (1954); E. Rosenthal (1958: 75–7).
4. Ferdousi, *The Epic of Kings: Shah-nama, The National Epic of Persia*, trans. R. Levy (London: Routledge & Kegan Paul, 1967). See Grunebaum (1955: 168–84); Fouchécour (1986: 51–6).
5. *EI* 2: 920b; Grunebaum (1955: 176).

6. *EI* on Ibn Kutaiba; G. Lecomte, *Ibn Qutaiba: l'homme, son œuvre, ses idées* (Damascus, 1965); Lambton (1981: 49, 65–8).
7. Trans. Horovitz (1930, 1931).
8. J. R. Perry, 'Justice for the Underprivileged: The Ombudsman Tradition in Iran', *Journal of Near Eastern Studies* 37 (1978), pp. 204–15.

Knowledge and Power: Plato without the Polis 6

The decline of the Caliphate coincided with the golden age of Islamic humanism and philosophy.[1] Cultural and intellectual life benefited from the political and religious diversity of the House of Islam, just as it did later in Europe. Rulers became patrons of the arts and sciences. The fusion of Arabic, Iranian and Greek motifs produced an outburst of cultural vitality. In the sixth century, the Sassanians had given sanctuary to the philosophers of Athens and Alexandria fleeing Byzantine persecution, and philosophy now moved eastwards again. The Samanids set up a House of Wisdom at Bukhara, which became a centre for geography and astronomy. Out of Mahmud's looting came Biruni's (Khwarazm c.973–c.1051) informed accounts of India and Hinduism. Transoxania produced al-Farabi and Ibn Sina; central-eastern Iran produced Razi, Miskawayh, Balkhi and Amiri. Many gravitated to Baghdad, where the minority Shi'i dynasty, with its taste for toleration and pluralism, encouraged both Shi'i and Mu'tazilite theologians and Philosophers, and where 'Adud al-Daula founded a medical centre. The Fatimids founded the al-Azhar mosque-library-study centre and a House of Wisdom in Cairo.[2]

Under the influence of Greco-Arabic philosophy, the ruler could be presented as philosopher-king, or 'perfect individual'. The legend of Alexander, co-opted now into Islamic lore (see above, p. 26), flourished, especially in central Asia. A Tibetan king was made to tell Alexander that his victories 'proved to me that God guides you ... [that] whoever resists you resists the order of God and ... will be vanquished'.[3]

A new approach to politics and government was developed by the practitioners of Philosophy (falsafa) between the age of al-Ma'mun and the Saljuks. The East was intellectually superior to the West in jurisprudence, mathematics, medicine, astronomy and philosophy until around 1200. Early Islam was more open than pre-twelfth century Christendom to foreign and ancient ideas.

Contact between the new faith and the high culture of Mesopotamia, Iran and the late Greco-Roman world, whose philosophers had already fled from Byzantine persecution to Persia, ignited powerful charges. A young and self-confident culture conversed with ancient learning. By al-Farabi's time (c.870–950), most of Plato, Aristotle and their late Greek commentators had been translated (partly by Eastern Christians via Syriac). Aristotle's *Politics* was an exception; only its existence, and possibly a version of Books I and II, were known.[4] From the eighth to the eleventh centuries – the period when fundamental issues of politics were most widely discussed in Islam – interest in Hellenic philosophy was at its height. After that, it waned; Ibn Rushd and Ibn Khaldun were isolated figures.

And absorption only went so far. Philosophy was not allowed to question seriously the tenets of Islam. Soon it fell back upon itself, a spent wave. Philosophy in the Islamic world did not, as in the early Greek and modern European worlds, submit nature, ethics, existence itself to critical examination. 'The space which philosophy sought to occupy was *already* filled by theology, the theory of language and the well-developed jurisprudence' (Leaman 1985: 13). Moreover, Plato and Aristotle were mediated to the Arab world via the late Greco-Roman schools such as Alexandria.[5] What the Islamic world got was neo-Platonism; Plato and Aristotle were used as guides to understand the world and humanity within the framework of ethical monotheism.

The political indeterminacy of the post-tribal Islamic world meant that neo-Platonic ideas could have some influence on political discourse, on ideas about the purpose and structure of the polity. In political philosophy, the Arabo-Islamic thinkers showed originality by combining different political languages, using the Greco-Roman and the Judaeo-Islamic traditions to interpret one another. Islamic ideals of Imamate (Leadership) and Community (umma) could be read off on the template of neo-Platonism.

Al-Farabi and Ibn Sina seem to have regarded Philosophy as an alternative articulation of Islamic postulates, more promising than what they saw as the crass popular narrativism of the Reporters and, indeed, Jurists. Could this not make possible a more rationalist approach, reducing Religious Jurisprudence to just one possible articulation of the Qur'anic message?

But Greco-Arabic falsafa did not produce fundamentally new ideas. In its basic structure and reach, the Philosophers' vision remained bounded by their Islamic beliefs. For example, the moral aspect of the concept of humanity (insaniyya), prevalent in late antiquity, was not adopted – a clear sign of neo-tribalism. The Philosophers did have a concept of human nature that was for the most part Hobbesian. The proneness of human nature to greed, lust, conflict and competition was cited by Islamic moral and political theorists as proving the need for law and government. Common humanity as a basis for moral values, and therefore for political association, was discussed by a Christian faylasuf, Yahya Ibn 'Adi (893–974: pupil of al-Farabi and a translator of Aristotle). One ought to develop friendship (mahabba), he said, towards all human beings because 'men are one tribe (qabil) ... joined together by humanity. And the adornment of the divine power is in all and in each ... of them, it being a rational soul ... All men are really a single entity in many individuals' (in Kraemer 1992: 115). Al-Farabi, however, rejected the 'ignorant' opinion found in 'cities of peace' which seek to found polity on common humanity, though he found these the least reprehensible of deviant states, their supporters being 'free from everything unsound in their souls' (VC 315).

This had great consequences for moral and political thought. The Islamic Philosophers never adopted the idea of a universal, intercultural moral language for all humankind, or of rights and duties pertaining to human beings as such. Rather, all humans should adhere to the one true moral Code, the Muslim Shari'a; and their moral status depends in some respects upon their religious affiliation. They did, however, for the most part insist that right and wrong are subject to rational understanding and rational choice. Contrary to a developing consensus on predestination, they (like the Mu'tazilites) upheld freedom of the will.[6] But they do not seem to have thought that non-believers could attain true knowledge of the moral law; this was a crucial difference between them and Christian philosophers from Aquinas onwards.[7] What they did insist upon was that we can prove the validity of the Code – know right and wrong – from human experience and rational appraisal of the consequences of actions. They rejected the view that there is no perceptible rationality behind Prophetic morality, that we know right and wrong solely on the divine say-so.[8] One example of originality found in the Philosophers is their belief that true happiness and individual self-fulfilment come through rational understanding.

Philosophy could, on this basis, have been perceived as a road to the truth which non-Muslims too could travel. But only the Brethren of Purity (see below, p. 61) saw things this way. They thought that all prophets, despite differences in the laws they gave, shared the same basic opinions. Indeed, they argued that religious differences, far from being harmful, served a purpose by promoting discussion and knowledge (Marquet 1973: 429–30, 448). Different religious beliefs and codes could thus be seen as alternative determinations of the same universal monotheistic principles (although the Muslim one is always best). A kind of humanism is implied here; the Brethren of Purity also spoke of a universal human form or soul.

The idea of a rational basis for human action that was independent of divine revelation *was* proposed within the Islamic world but in terms of individual rational self-interest, and, once again, by a Christian, Ibn Zur'a (writing in Baghdad, 998). He distinguished between a 'law of nature' which 'impels us to acquire as many useful and pleasant things as we can', and a law of *reason* which 'restricts a man, among the things which nature puts before him as necessary, to that which is required by his needs with (additional) provision for difficult times'.[9]

The neo-tribal approach to human community also came out in a debate (Baghdad 932) about whether language or logic is the fundamental basis of human understanding. A Philosopher argued that logic provides the universal criterion of truth and falsehood valid for all peoples. His opponent argued that languages existed before logic, and all meaning is inextricably embedded in language. Understanding can only be achieved in a particular language; there can be no universal trans-linguistic canon of rationality. The champion of language was deemed to have won.[10]

The difference between the reception of Greek thought in ninth-century Islam and in twelfth-century Europe lay both in the *content* of what was received and in the *perception* of it. Islam and Europe knew different Hellases.

Very few Arabic Philosophers, for example, thought that reason and Prophecy contradicted one another. Unbelief hardly emerged as a problem. Islamic thinkers were on the whole more successful than Latin Christians in synthesising Greek philosophy with revelation to their own satisfaction. But this did not necessarily enhance their understanding of the originals.

Their attitude to Plato and Aristotle – and to philosophy in general – was encyclopaedic rather than critical or enquiring. They sought to understand and summarise the works of earlier philosophers rather than criticise or assess them; quotations from Plato and Aristotle were generally regarded as authoritative. This attitude also existed in medieval Europe but became less prevalent. Al-Farabi and his successors believed that Plato and Aristotle had founded the *philosophia perennis*, i.e. the neo-Platonism of the later Greek world. Al-Farabi was especially influenced by the Alexandrian school (although the extent of his debt in political thought has been disputed).[11] The Brethren, despite their rampant neo-Platonism, thought themselves devout followers of Aristotle (*EI* 3: 1,076a). Ibn Sina thought that the content of knowledge was fixed, contained in the intellectual 'spheres' of heaven. The job of philosophy is to 'actualise' it; Aristotle had already done most of this, and we have to fill in the gaps. It was al-Farabi's intention (in Walzer's words) to expound a civic philosophy 'universally valid and unambiguously true without reference to any special time or place' (Walzer in *VC* 36). This also had the effect of making him and others focus on abstract concepts rather than empirical data, which after all are transient.

Muslim Philosophers thought it was their task to restate and interpret the Platonic-Aristotelian body of knowledge and transmit it to the Islamic world for future generations. All that was needed was to fill it out at certain points, especially where the appearance of Islam had fundamentally changed things, as it clearly had in social moeurs and political organisation. This was how both al-Farabi and Ibn Sina saw their contribution to political theory. It severely circumscribed what they would say on the subject.

Philosophy in Islam lacked an institutional base. It had no place in an educational curriculum; most Philosophers were self-educated. The community of communicating intellectuals was small. This proved a fatal weakness. There was a degree of intellectual freedom and, in Baghdad and elsewhere, some prospect of patronage. But this did not compare with the means of transmission available to Religious Scholars.

AL-FARABI AND THE BRETHREN OF PURITY

There was some affinity between Philosophy and Shi'ism. The Imami Hamdanids established Houses of Wisdom in Mosul, Aleppo and Tripoli[12] and were patrons to al-Farabi. The Philosopher-ruler could double as Imam: for both Shi'ites and Philosophers, true authority comes from superior knowledge.

The affinity was especially marked with the Isma'ilis. This touched both metaphysics and politics. They shared a belief in intellectual intuitions which only an elite can fully attain, and which provide the premises from which reason can construct a true idea of the cosmos and human existence. For both Philosophy and the Isma'ilis the goal of creation is the development of the ideal human person, the true Adam, 'the perfect individual'.

The connection came out strongest in the 'Epistles of the Brethren of Purity (Ikhwan al-Safa')', an encyclopaedic work on philosophical theology, composed between 900 and 965, probably by the intellectual wing of the (non-Fatimid) Isma'ili underground at Basra, with the aim of 'arrang[ing] and fix[ing] the official doctrine of Isma'ilism'.[13] Their fifty-one epistles covered all the disciplines; they were designed for use as Isma'ili propaganda and instruction.

The Brethren held that both Philosophy and Prophecy are of divine origin and, with the aid of all the sciences, lead the human being to perfection as both believer and sage. According to their theory of history, each Prophet-legislator-Imam ushers in a new epoch, characterised by its own philosophy, religion, language and science. Each builds on the last: translation is therefore essential, and pre-Islamic belief-systems retain some significance. The Brethren's self-ascribed role was to pass on the accumulated wisdom of past humanity to the new age about to dawn; hence their encyclopaedic account of all the 'sciences and wisdom' of previous philosophers and Prophets, which they saw as the legitimate inheritance of the Isma'ili age. A government seeking to rule by 'philosophical knowledge' must have an understanding of astrology, from which we learn how the interactions of nations, evolving through spheres of Prophecy, correspond to astral conjunctions (Marquet 1973: 418, 420–6, 485). They enthusiastically adopted al-Farabi's political ideas.

Among the Philosophers of this period, al-Farabi and Ibn Sina were outstanding. Al-Farabi (Turkestan c.870–Syria 950) was probably an Imami Shi'ite, of Turkish origin, his father perhaps having moved to Baghdad as part of the Deputy's bodyguard. He was taught philosophy by a Christian (possibly of the Alexandrian school), and was friendly with the Christian Aristotelian and translator, Mata ibn Yunus. He lived in Baghdad, but did not belong to the court, bureaucracy or any literary group; he worked on his own. During this period, he touched on political matters in his *Survey of the Branches of Knowledge* (*Ihsa' al-'ulum*) and *The Achievement of Happiness* (*tahsil al sa'ada*), and composed a *Summary of Plato's Laws*. In 942, already quite old, he was invited to the Imami court of the Hamdanids (Aleppo). Here he did participate in court life, and it was from 942 to 950 that he produced his major works on politics: (1) *The Principles of the Opinions of the Inhabitants of the Best (Virtuous/Excellent/Perfect) State (al-Madina al-Fadila*: written 942–3, Baghdad and Damascus); (2) *The Governance of the State (al-Siyasa al-Madaniyya*: probably 948–9 in Egypt); (3) *Aphorisms of the Statesman (Fusul al-Madani*: 949–50; probably occasioned by his reading of Plato's *Statesman*).[14] This was a critical time for Imami Shi'ites; the Greater Absence (see above, p. 40) had just begun, an Imami dynasty, the Buyids, was taking over the 'Abbasid heartlands. Al-Farabi is said to have been killed by robbers while travelling.

Several other Philosophers discussed political topics, usually in connection with ethics, for example Miskawayh (Ray c.936–Isfahan 1030) in his *Treatise* on *Ethics* (*Tahdhib al-Akhlaq*);[15] he was secretary and librarian to a Buyid vizier, treasurer to 'Adud al-Daula, and a power-broker in Baghdad court and literary circles.

METHODS OF KNOWING

The Philosophers' view of the relationship between Philosophy and revelation (not quite reason and faith in Western language) was fundamental to their view of political knowledge and the enterprise of government. The project of al-Farabi and the Philosophers was (as we have seen) to unite two spheres of discourse: the Judaeo-Islamic and the Platonic-Hellenic. They did not question that God, the People and the Imam were the bedrock of cosmic and human existence. Neo-Platonism stated how God, humanity, the spiritual and material cosmos were related to each other and acted upon each other. Al-Farabi, the Brethren, Ibn Sina and others saw this as a means of understanding and interpreting the Prophet's Message. In politics, Philosophy was, above all, an attempt to illuminate the Islamic Law, Leadership (imama) and People through Hellenistic language. Here too, they sought to interpret the Judaeo-Islamic and Platonic-Hellenic discourses through each other; this was possible without doing violence to either because the Platonic tradition had already been developed as ethical monotheism, and had, in its Christian form, become related to aspirations for a universal community based on divine decree.

Al-Farabi and other Islamic philosophers do not seem to have been aware of other aspects of the Hellenic legacy in political thought, and, so far as they were, ignored them. As we have seen, Aristotle's *Politics*, which made the city-state the environment for human fulfilment, and proposed constitutional democracy, was never translated. What caught the attention of the Islamic Philosophers was the Greeks' treatment of the ideal society, of the legislator as origin of law, of the relationship between ruler and law, and of how to make people accept right opinions and conduct.

Islamic Religious Scholars regarded knowledge ('ilm) as the highest human attainment, and intelligence ('aql) as the supreme gift of God to humans; faith (iman) was of lower epistemological stature, thus reversing the Christian ranking. But their 'Knowledge' was not far removed from what Christians called faith, since it referred to what is known through the Qur'an and Reports, correctly understood through Jurisprudence. This may have facilitated the entry of philosophy into Islamdom. Islamic Philosophers could agree that reason was supreme ('make reason the Caliph of your soul', say the Brethren; Marquet 1973: 126–7); but they went on to say that with its help the best human intellects could unlock the truth without immediate reference to the Qur'an or Reports. Reason here meant syllogism and dialectic, and also the insights of the trained and purified mind. Islamic philosophers, like earlier neo-Platonists, held that they could deduce the First Cause and the regulated order of the cosmos from a rational examination of experience.

Ibn Sina (see below, p. 74) took the Philosophers' claim to inspired intuitive but rational knowledge to new heights, claiming that the human soul can, independently of sense perception, have a direct 'metaphysical apprehension of being'. Higher stages of knowledge are achieved through the Philosopher's reason coming into contact with the Active Intellect, which emanates from God.[16] The idea that we know being through inspired intuition was developed by Ibn Sina and others into mystical theology, the 'Eastern (ishraqi) philosophy' or 'philosophy of light' (*EI* 4: 120a). This trend led away from empirical knowledge into mysticism.

Philosophers claimed that they could attain by demonstrative proofs knowledge of the same truths which the Prophets taught by inspiration and rhetoric. Philosophy is 'true education' and the way to salvation (Miskawayh in Kraemer 1992: 231). There was no break between what was stated in the Qur'an and what was known by reason. Truth is the fundamental category, and it can be reached by different routes:

> The foremost and sublimest of [the pearls of wisdom] is contained in the Holy Quran, followed by the [Tradition: sc. Reports] of the Prophet ... The third source is ... reason ... Reason is the link between God and man, the stamp of God's word, the token of His Prophet ... Its law (Shari'a) is truthfulness ... The fourth [source] is experience, and I shall adduce something of the statecraft (siyasa) of the Persians and the philosophy (falsafa) of the Greeks; for wisdom is the goal of all believers and must be taken wherever it is found ... Wisdom is truth and truth needs no lineage, rather all things derive their lineage from truth.[17]

This held out the prospect of an alternative epistemology and therefore an alternative authority to that of the Jurists. Rational discourse, according to al-Farabi and most Philosophers, was an alternative way of perceiving, explaining and, above all, proving the truths of the Qur'an.

There were, however, differences of opinion among Philosophers. Abu Bakr al-Razi (Rayy?–Baghdad 925/32: a medic) was the only real sceptic. He called Socrates 'our Leader (imam)', and argued that, since one can know God by reason, revelation and Prophecy are unnecessary; indeed they are harmful because they retard knowledge and cause wars. They should therefore be rejected.[18] Abu Sulaiman al-Sijistani (Sistan 932–Baghdad 985, prominent in the Baghdad salons), on the other hand, agreed that the Philosophers' view of reason would indeed make revelation superfluous, and concluded that one should, therefore, acknowledge Prophecy alone as a true guide.[19]

For al-Farabi, Philosophy was not merely an alternative but a superior way of knowing the divine truths: 'Religion is an imitation of philosophy ... In everything of which philosophy gives an account based on intellectual perception or conception, religion gives an account based on imagination' (*Happiness*, 77). Philosophy demonstrates what religion symbolises. This resembles Hegel's view. Prophecy and Religion remain essential but only because so few can travel the path of Philosophy.

Al-Farabi explained this in greater detail in his discussion of the Best or Virtuous City and its Leadership. First, the excellence of this city resides in the *opinions* of its inhabitants ('the things ... which all the people of the excellent city ought to know are ... the first cause ... the natural bodies ... the first ruler and how the revelation is brought about').

> Now these things can be known in two ways, either by being impressed on their souls as they really are or by being impressed on them through affinity and symbolic representation ... The [P]hilosophers in the city are those who know these things through strict demonstrations and their own insight; those who are close to the philosophers know them as they really are through the insight of the [P]hilosophers, following them, assenting to their views and trusting them. But others know them through symbols which reproduce them by imitation ... Both are kinds of knowledge, but the knowledge of the philosophers is undoubtedly more excellent. (VC 277–9)
>
> The supreme ruler without qualification is he who does not need anyone to rule him in anything whatever, but has actually acquired the sciences and every kind of knowledge ... The men who are governed by the rule of this ruler are the virtuous, good and happy men. If they form a nation then that is the virtuous nation. (Governance, 36–7)

This was not, however, the distinction between theology and philosophy made in Latin Christendom. Al-Farabi's distinction was, rather, between religion (milla) and revelation (wahy); and al-Farabi aligned revelation with the supreme knowledge of the Philosophers. The person capable of knowing things as they are for himself is the true ruler and 'the one of whom it ought to be said that he receives revelation' (Walzer in VC 436, 441). Revelation comes via the Active Intellect. This implied that Muhammad and other Prophets were first and foremost high-class Philosophers.[20] It is clear that Philosophy-cum-revelation is here being presented as the superior way of knowing God and Islam. One can see why al-Farabi might not have been very happy in Baghdad, where the Hanbali version of Sunnism was in the ascendant.

The Philosophers followed Aristotle in distinguishing between speculative philosophy, which looks at things as they are in themselves, and practical philosophy, which looks at things 'from the perspective of what is base or noble ... (and) of what makes human beings happy or miserable'.[21] Ibn Sina, following Greek precedents, divided practical philosophy into (1) personal ethics, (2) household management or 'economics', and (3) political knowledge or science ('ilm al-madani). Through the last, 'one knows the kinds of political regimes, rulerships, and associations, both virtuous and bad ... [and] the way of preserving each, the reason for [their] disintegration and the manner of [their] transformation' (presumably referring to Plato's Republic, book 8) (LM 97). Political science shows one 'the necessity of prophecy, and the human species' need of the Law for its existence, preservation and future life ... the universal penalties that are common to all laws and ... the penalties pertaining to particular laws' (Ibn Sina in LM 97).

Al-Farabi took a lofty view of political science as the master-science of human conduct, embracing 'the types of voluntary action and conduct', 'the purposes which these should aim at', namely true happiness, and 'all those things by which a man achieves perfection' or which impede this: namely, virtues and vices.²² Political science requires 'knowledge of the soul as a whole'. It has a moral aspect and is a form of philosophy in the sense that it seeks knowledge of universals. It also has a practical aspect based on observation and experience, which is 'the faculty that man acquires through long experience in political deeds, dealing with the morals and the individuals existing in actual cities, and becoming practically wise through experience and long observation, as is the case in medicine' (LM 25). 'It is the power of deducing well the conditions by means of which the actions, ways of life and habits are determined.'²³ Al-Farabi tried to go into both aspects in *The Virtuous City*; like Plato, he defined the various good and deviant regimes as (Weberian) ideal types. But the Philosophers, like their counterparts in pre-Enlightenment Europe, made no empirical study of politics in this period. Factual detail remained the province of historians, who did sometimes use it for political instruction.

The objectives of political knowledge, al-Farabi went on, can only be achieved 'through rulership (ri'asa)', by means of 'siyasa (politics/government/ discipline)'. The 'kingly craft (al-mihma malakiyya)' is an 'art, habit or power'; ruling is a matter of both legislation and education. The idea of government as craft (sina'a) was also expounded by Abu Zayd al-Balkhi (c.850–934, a geographer who declined to work at the Samanid court). As medicine pursues health (he said), so political craft pursues 'the general welfare (maslaha)' as its 'form' to be made actual in the world. The sa'is (governor/politician) is concerned both to 'preserve the subjects' affairs that are (already) in good shape' and to 'improve' what has been 'affected by corruption and confusion'. This requires both incentives and intimidation.²⁴

KNOWLEDGE AND LEADERSHIP (IMAMA)

But the Philosophical path is open only to an intellectual elite. A critical consequence for social philosophy was the sharp distinction between those capable of philosophy and those needing religion. This was a development of Plato's views; it also paralleled Shi'ite views of spiritual enlightenment and Leadership. It massively reinforced the widespread distinction between elite and mob (al-khassa/al-'amma). According to the Brethren, 'Most of the words of God ... are the symbol of the mystery hidden from the wicked, known only to God and those grounded in knowledge'. One of the Brethren spoke of Philosophy as 'the medicine of the healthy', and the Religious Law as 'the medicine of the sick'.²⁵

Al-Farabi, like Plato and the Shi'ite theologians, based Leadership on Knowledge. Knowledge derived from 'certain demonstration ... is the superior science and the one with the most perfect (claim to rule or to) authority'.²⁶ The one who receives revelation from the Active Intellect is 'the true prince' (according to the ancients). Al-Farabi and the Brethren based the elite/mob distinction on the view that individuals are fundamentally different in their mental capacities. Thus al-Farabi's virtuous city is divided into a philosophical elite, which acquires knowledge by having it proved to them, and the common people who depend upon more graphic means of instruction. The Brethren divided the community into those able to understand the inner meaning of revelation and those only able to understand its outer meaning, with inter-mediate categories for those whose understanding lies 'between the open and the hidden' (*VC* 130). The elite are a companionship (walaya) close to God and act as intermediaries to the masses. But, whereas the Brethren sought actively to spread their ideas among the masses, the Philosophers never did so; indeed they often, partly to avoid misunderstanding or persecution, deliberately wrote in such a way that only the expert few could follow them. They were content that commoners should become virtuous by following the Islamic Law.

Al-Farabi made Knowledge and Leadership entirely interdependent. The perfect philosopher has to have 'the faculty for exploiting [the theoretical sciences] for the benefit of others' (*Happiness*, 76). Plato, he says, 'showed that the philosopher and king are one, that both are perfected by a single craft and faculty' (*Aphorisms*, 17). Without the perfect ruler, the perfect city 'will undoubtedly perish'. If, however, the philosopher-king is prevented from ruling by other people, his perfection is not impaired (possibly a reference to the Shi'ite Imams).

The main purpose of the political order, says al-Farabi (in his relatively early *Attainment of Happiness*), is the dissemination of knowledge and virtue. These are to be instilled in peoples (al-umam) and states (al mudun) by 'instruction and the formation of character'.[27] And 'instruction in the theo-retical sciences should be given either to the [Leaders] and the rulers, or else to those who should preserve the theoretical sciences'. These 'should be made to pursue a course of study and form the habits of character from their childhood … in accordance with the plan described by Plato' (sc. in *Republic*, Books 2–3: *Happiness*, 70). This shows that knowledge may come, initially, from the Philosophers; and indeed al-Farabi went on to observe that 'Philosophy is prior to Religion in time'.

The ruler must educate people according to their intellectual capacities, that is, by (1) demonstrative argument or (2) rhetorical persuasion or (3) narrative similitude. Further, the laws apply general truths to particular peoples. Again, some of the masses have their character formed willingly by oratory, others have to be coerced. This involves Holy War (jihad). The ruler's task is 'to prescribe the conditions that render possible' the implementation of morality, and to embody these in laws. Since some persons are naturally disposed to excel in virtue and deliberation, the legislator must be a Philosopher who 'occupies his place by nature and not merely by will'; and we arrive, by a Platonic route, at the proposition that 'the idea of Leader, Philosopher and Legislator is a single idea' (*Happiness*, 73, 78).

The legislator must therefore have good powers of persuasion. Since most people are non-philosophical, this means he must be good at forming like-nesses and images of the objects of knowledge. This combination of demon-strative knowledge and persuasive imagery, appropriate to particular audiences, marks out the true Prophet: Jesus, Muhammad and (according to the Brethren) Plato.

Such a person who 'knows every action by which felicity can be reached' and is 'a good orator able to rouse [other people's imagination] by well-chosen words' is 'the Leader ... the first sovereign of the excellent city' (*VC* 247). Al-Farabi listed, like a Jurist, the twelve 'natural qualities' which the Leader should have; five of them are qualities of mental perception. The Brethren followed him on this.

One function of religion and of 'the excellent city' is to apply the universal truths to *different* particular societies. Slowly but surely, one gains the impression that al-Farabi, probably a Shi'ite and writing now at a Shi'ite court, had *partly* in mind the Shi'ite People and its Leaders. Imami Shi'ism illuminates much of what he has to say about rulers, Prophecy and legislation; his more direct experience of Shi'ite government may well have stimulated his major political writings. 'The arguments on which he bases the necessity for the existence of prophets, the features which define the inner being of the prophet, the guide, the imam, correspond to those of Shi'ite prophetic theory' (Corbin 1964: 329). Some of al-Farabi's earlier works, on the other hand, suggest an almost relativist attitude to the different religious laws.

The skill of the Prophet-teacher-legislator lies in expressing truths in the way most likely to appeal to particular audiences. Thus different codes of conduct and some variations of religious opinion, in the sense of symbol and ritual, may be appropriate for different peoples.

> These things are expressed for each nation in symbols other than those used for another nation. Therefore, it is possible that excellent nations and excellent cities exist whose religions differ, although they all have as their goal one and the same felicity. (al-Farabi, *VC* 281; *Governance* 41)

The Brethren described the ideal person as 'Persian in origin, Arab in religion ... Hebrew in experience, Christian in behaviour ... Greek in science' (in Marquet 1962: 139).

Hence, to the functions of philosopher and king, is necessarily joined the function of *legislator*: here the merging of the Islamic, and especially Shi'ite, model with Plato is complete. 'The idea of Imam, Philosopher and Legislator is a single idea' (al-Farabi, *Happiness*, 78). But *only* the Leader-Prophet can make laws or change his predecessor's laws. The non-Prophetic ruler, who succeeds the Prophet as second-best ruler, should rule 'according to the written laws received from the past Imams' (*Governance*, 37). He will thus be 'king according to the (customary) law (malik as-sunna)'; this seems to translate Plato's 'political and royal' (i.e. non-absolute) ruler (*Aphorisms*, 17).

He will have six qualities, four of which refer to his soundness in Jurisprudence, and he

> will know and remember the laws and customs with which the first sovereigns [i.e. the original Leader-legislator(s)] had governed the city ... He will excel in deducing a new law by analogy where no law of his predecessors has been recorded, following, for his deductions, the principles laid down by the first (Leaders) ... and be powerful in his deductions to meet

new situations for which the first sovereigns could not have laid down any law. (*VC* 251)

And he must be capable of waging jihad. All this describes a degree of legal inventiveness beyond that allowed to the Deputy by Sunni Jurists. Legal interpretation is being understood as a classical Greek rational process. It may sound a bit like a combination of the Shi'ite 'just sultan' and the Shi'ite Jurist (faqih: Sachedina 1988); and, sure enough, al-Farabi proceeds to envisage the division of these qualities and functions between two or more individuals.

Al-Farabi's *Virtuous City* and his *Governance of the State* read, especially on the Imam, like an attempt to integrate two ideal types – Platonism and Imami Shi'ism (possibly with the Iranian tradition of the just king also in mind). This involved a high degree of abstraction from actual politics; and al-Farabi stays locked into abstraction, leaving out the practical detail which one finds in both Plato and Islamic Jurisprudence.

The Brethren of Purity put together the concepts of Leader, Philosopher and Legislator in a quite different overall vision. *Their* whole theory hinged upon six great world-Prophets, culminating in Muhammad, and the awaited deliverer (qa'im). Their Isma'ili faith is deeply coloured by their use of Hellenic language, but there is no attempt to come to terms with pre-Islamic ideas for their own sake. Hellenic notions are simply incorporated into their mystical system, which they then present as Philosophy (metaphysics) ('I am the Aristotle of this people', says their Prophet-Imam). Their Leader is directly inspired by the supreme intellect, the 'speaking universal human soul' (in Marquet 1962: 132). Their Knowledge is the esoteric lore of the Imams and their initiates (batini), who have 'preserved the hidden secrets of the book of God' so that they alone have 'the true meaning' and by their 'reception of ideas, of inspiration and revelation' can understand 'the secret interpretations'. There is no categorical difference between this Knowledge and Prophecy. The Leaders legislate on the basis of their direct knowledge of God. A great Prophet is succeeded by slightly lesser Leaders (such as the Isma'ili line), who are 'Deputies of the Legislator in the mysteries of the Law'. The Brethren often deliberately conflate Prophecy and Imamate, and use the term legislator (wadi' al-namus, wadi' al-shari'a) to mask the distinction.[28]

They regarded the 'Abbasids as anti-Caliphs. The Brethren's own Imams' functions as Deputies of *God* are to preserve the Shari'a, give life to the Sunna (Tradition), command the good and forbid the bad, apply the Legal Penalties, receive and distribute taxes, and guard the frontiers. But over and above these traditional functions, their Deputy exists to enable souls to reascend to the heavenly sphere by transmitting his inherited knowledge through himself and the missionary network.[29]

At the opposite end of the spectrum, the later Sunni idea of the *Sultan* as Deputy (see below, p. 143) was first hinted at by Abu l-Hasan al-'Amiri (d.992). Prophecy and Kingship are both necessary to society; but only Muhammad combined the two. Nevertheless, 'a person who makes good use of royal authority and political leadership and works hard at them' (could this be a reference to 'Adud al-Daula?) can 'achieve the noble Leadership'.[30] This could mean that any good and effective Muslim ruler may be accredited with the quality of Imamate. Later Sunni thought would take this to mean that such a person can perform the Legal and religious functions of Deputy.

THE POLITICAL COMMUNITY

Al-Farabi and Ibn Sina integrated their discussion of the Deputy or Imam into a wider discussion of human society and government. This was closely related to their epistemology and metaphysics. For them, the ruler (Imam) is the principal, indeed sole, political actor. Value attaches to the political community, but as the object, not the subject, of political action. This reflected the dynamic of human relationships implicit in the concept of Prophecy.

In his *Virtuous City*, chapters 15–19, and *Governance of the State*, al-Farabi presented the most systematic theory of the state that the Muslim world had so far produced. The *Virtuous City* is a wide-ranging treatise on metaphysics; we reach humanity in chapter 10, political society only in chapter 15. He looks first at the Imamate and other types of ruler, then at various types of community. These he classified according to the *opinions* of their inhabitants, his discussion of which is clearly derived from Plato's *Republic* (books 8–9) and *Laws*. ('Medina', though originally meaning city-state, is used to indicate the state in general, like civitas in Europe.) Thus he is back in the domain of beliefs and conduct, which are looked at mainly from a moral and spiritual perspective. In fact, al-Farabi never passes from the abstract to the practical or topical; and there are no references to regimes other than the monarchical. He located the differences between types of political society in social attitudes rather than in constitutions. *Governance of the State* is a reworking of the same material for a more general audience; it too starts with cosmology and proceeds to broadly similar political topics.

Al-Farabi's political works did, nonetheless, contain an at least implicit project for the reform of the religio-political world. He noted that Plato 'gave an account of how to abolish the ways of life of nations and the corrupt laws that prevail in the cities, how to move the cities and nations away from them and how to reform their ways of life'. Plato described 'the mode of government that ought to be applied in order to move them gradually to virtuous ways of life and correct laws'.[31]

Al-Farabi's discussion of social development and political organisation emerged (as did Plato's and, to a lesser extent, Aristotle's) out of discussion of knowledge, happiness and virtue. But in al-Farabi, political society is still more systematically tied into a cosmic, epistemological and ethical context. The main purpose of the political community is, as we have seen, to propagate knowledge and virtue. The Philosophers in general followed Plato and Aristotle in identifying happiness (sa'ada: eudaimonia) as the goal of human action, and of association, and of the craft of politics. This craft is both philosophical and royal in that it requires knowledge and power.[32] Happiness is 'the good without qualification'. Right conduct is what leads to happiness, wrong conduct is what prevents happiness. These Platonic ideas are Islamicised by saying that the aim is happiness in *both* this world *and* the next.

The Philosophers held that one achieves supreme happiness through development of the rational faculty, leading to full inner perception of the truth. Al-Farabi showed by *demonstrative* argument, based on empirical generalisations about human life, what the origin and purpose of political association is. First, the division of labour makes it necessary for human beings to live in society. 'Every human being is by his very nature in need of many things which he cannot provide for himself ... Therefore man cannot attain the perfection, for the sake of which his inborn nature has been given to him, unless many societies of people who co-operate come together' (*VC* 229). This argument came from Plato and Aristotle.

Al-Farabi produced a theory of the state based on a comparison between political society and the body, both of which contain different organic 'parts' and a ruler (ra'is: lit. chief). The state's parts (presumably the five categories based on the division of labour: see below) arise out of nature via the division of labour. But, he went on, people's 'dispositions and habits by which they perform their actions in the city are not natural but voluntary ... They are not parts of the city by their inborn nature alone but rather by the voluntary habits which they acquire such as the arts and their likes' (*VC* 233–5). Therefore, in human society, virtue and vice are the determining factors.[33]

Miskawayh, on the other hand, ascribed the human inclination to friendship and companionship (mahabba: philia) to natural sociability (uns): the Shari'a's preference for communal over individual prayer is one means of achieving this. This, he explained, is what we mean when we say 'man is political (madani) by nature': our full happiness requires madaniyya (civic community/urban civilisation).[34] Thus arguments developed by Aristotle to demonstrate the necessity of the *polis* and of citizenship therein were deflected into proving, rather, the necessity of communal life.

The Brethren argued that humans depend by nature for their happiness on (a) mutual aid with craft specialisation (see below, p. 73) and (b) submission to sunna (law/custom). Al-'Amiri argued that social order and the maintenance of law depend upon a ruler (sultan: lit. power); according to the Brethren they depend upon the Imam. But the Brethren also gave the Sultan (de facto ruler) a role, namely 'the protection of the law (al-namus)': 'were there no fear of the sultan, the majority of the followers of the laws of the prophets and philosophers would not attempt to place themselves under the ordinances and prohibitions of the law (al-namus)'.[35]

It was at this point in the argument that al-Farabi too introduced the Philosopher-Imam: 'the ruling organ in the body is by nature the most perfect ... of the organs'. Like the heart, 'the ruler of this state (madina) must [first come into existence], and will subsequently be the cause of the rise of the city and its parts, and the cause of the presence of the voluntary habits, and of their arrangement in the ranks proper to them' (*VC* 235). The way that al-Farabi made the ruler the cause of all the other parts, and indeed the first cause of the state, suggests that he may have had in mind the Prophet and the Shi'ite

Imams. And indeed there follows an account of the *intellectual* supremacy of the ruler and of his immediate receptivity to the Active Intellect. The Brethren saw the community of initiates itself, not just the Imam, as collective inheritors of the capacities of the Legislator, indeed as a kind of extension of the Legislator. In this they differed from both Plato and al-Farabi.

Al-Farabi followed Aristotle in distinguishing between self-sufficient ('perfect') and non-self-sufficient ('imperfect') communities; examples of the latter are the village, city-quarter, the street and the household (VC 229). These can only exist as parts of a perfect society. Al-Farabi's perfect society, which is capable of attaining the highest good for human beings, comes in three sizes: the whole habitable world (ma'mura: oikumene), nation (umma: ethnos), city (madina: polis).[36] He gave no specific consideration to any of these – an illustration of the abstract nature of his discourse.

Only some societies capable of self-sufficiency achieve true perfection, because 'good in its real sense is such as to be attainable through choice and will'. Human societies, unlike organisms, are a mixture of natural and voluntary elements. Perfection is achieved only in those societies 'in which people aim for association in co-operating for the things by which felicity in its real and true sense can be attained' (VC 231).

Al-Farabi's excellent (virtuous) city is a religio-political ideal which comes into existence because of the knowledge and virtue of its inhabitants: 'the men who are governed by the rule (riyasa) of this ruler are the virtuous, good and happy men'. We then discover that these may form an actual people, or they may be scattered as 'strangers' among non-virtuous people. 'Governed by rulerships other than this one ... these are virtuous men who are strangers in those dwelling-places' (Governance, 37). In ideal circumstances, one would attain knowledge and happiness in and through society. But this was not possible in contemporary societies, which al-Farabi and others (following Plato) saw as deviant because they were based on ignorance.

The Philosophers developed a distinctively pessimistic view about the role of the Philosopher in their own society. This reflected their estimation of the current chances of political success for the Philosophical programme. Plato had said of philosophers in imperfect societies: 'they have sprung up, like a self-sown plant, in spite of their country's institutions; no one has fostered their growth' (Leaman 1985: 115). Al-Farabi described the position of Philosophers in the deviant societies of his own time as 'strangers' (ghuraba') or 'weeds' (nawabit); the predicament which the Russians used to call 'internal exile'). The Philosophers' sense of isolation was acute and based on painful experiences. Al-'Amiri said (quoting Plato) that one should devote oneself to wisdom even at the cost of 'most of the things called good, like wealth ... feeling of kinship'. The Philosopher will be viewed as alien, inhuman, because people 'despise the non-conformist, and often seek him out so as to harm him ... even to the extent of beating and killing him' (in Kraemer 1992: 239–40). Ibn Sina portrayed this sentiment in an allegorical novel on the life of a solitary individual, who really belongs elsewhere and will only find fulfilment in 'the East' (EI 3: 941b). Even in the salons of Baghdad, falasifa had felt themselves an isolated minority. And, unlike the leaders of other intellectual movements, they had no intention of reaching out to the masses, whom they thought incapable of attaining their level of understanding. They saw little prospect for the reform of an 'ignorant city'.

One alternative was emigration. 'It is wrong for the virtuous man to remain in the corrupt polities and he must emigrate [do a hijra: the term for Muhammad's flight to Medina] to the ideal cities if such exist in fact in his time' (al-Farabi, *Aphorisms*, 72). In fact, al-Farabi did move from Baghdad to Aleppo. Philosophers thus put themselves in a similar position to the Shi'ite Imams and their followers. They were not to blame if society found no use for them; they could still practise Philosophy as a private way of life. It was a counsel of withdrawal. But, whereas Sunnis and Shi'ites withdrew only from politics, the Philosophers were also withdrawing from mainstream society.

Al-Farabi at least, however, still saw the virtuous as a community, albeit an invisible one, under the governance of their own supreme ruler – in this respect not unlike the Imami community. They even comprise 'a single soul' over many generations, united through their love for one another and 'because they agree in their endeavours, purposes, opinions and ways of life' (*Governance*, 37).

Similarly, the Brethren saw their community as a 'spiritual city' or mystical confraternity, a unity of hearts: brother aids brother materially and spiritually. This was a community of initiates, taught in seminars (sing. majlis), scattered throughout the world on their missions – 'the ascetics of different tribes scattered in the towns and countries but reunited by the same religion, teaching and opinion' (Marquet 1973: 378, 441). Like the inhabitants of al-Farabi's virtuous city, they are united throughout space and time. In these ways, both al-Farabi and the Brethren recycled Plato's ideal state as the community of the Shi'ites, whether Imami or Isma'ili.

Al-Farabi listed various types of city which fail to achieve perfection. This is based on Plato's account of deviant constitutions in the *Republic* (Book 8), to which he added examples from late antiquity. Once again, it is the state of knowledge which counts: all imperfect cities are sub-divisions of that ignorant city 'whose inhabitants do not know true felicity' (VC 255), and so pursue wealth, honour, power or freedom. Al-Farabi described 'the views of the cities which are ignorant of the true good' (VC 287); this included a résumé of 'ignorant' views held by ancient authors about human conduct and the origin of states.

First, there is the view that, because we observe animals destroying or overpowering one another, this is natural for humans and states (political Darwinism): 'Justice is to defeat by force every possible group of men which happens to be in one's way … The enslavement of the defeated by the victor is also just … Natural justice consists in all this' (VC 299–300). Others ascribed the origin of association to conquest, common ancestry, similarity of character, a common language or companionship. Al-Farabi blandly dismissed these views without discussion.

The *Governance of the State* followed the same line of argument (as if al-

Farabi were redrafting his ideas without having *The Virtuous City* in front of him). He inserted here a discussion of the causes of differences in language and national character, which he ascribed to celestial factors, causing differences in vapour, soil, air and water, and consequently in plants, animals and human diet (LM 32–3).

THE DIVISION OF LABOUR AND SOCIAL GROUPS

The division of labour and the consequent division of society into occupational groups are, according to al-Farabi, dictated by nature; but they have to be organised by the legislator. 'Everyone in the ideal city must have assigned to him a single art with which he busies himself solely' (al-Farabi, *Aphorisms*, 55). The argument that human beings depend on the division of labour and a variety of crafts was a special favourite of the Brethren. They had a pro-artisan mentality: in shaping matter into form, the craftsman mirrors the Creator's work; the humblest occupations, such as refuse-collection, are innately noble. In fact, craftsmen could rise to the top of the Isma'ili hierarchy. All the crafts (the Brethren went on) were legislated for by the Prophets and sages. And, in order to assign them to their proper rank, the Legislator must know each of the faithful's occupation and conduct.[37] Thus political economy was, as in Adam Smith, based on moral considerations. Miskawayh, again, in a passage based on Aristotle, stated that, since the goods exchanged by the carpenter and shoe-maker may not be equal in value, the division of labour requires not just law but also money as 'a middle term to realise justice'.[38]

Al-Farabi went into more detail. He divided the virtuous city into ranks (ajza', sing. juz'; or aqsam) derived from people's functions in society. These were: (1) the most virtuous, those with speculative and practical wisdom; (2) those who transmit such wisdom, such as religious teachers, poets and secretaries; (3) those who measure, thereby applying the teachings of (1) and (2), such as accountants, doctors, astrologers; (4) warriors; (5) property owners, such as farmers, herdsmen, merchants. This looks like Plato's threefold division of society, with Plato's first group of philosophers sub-divided into (1)–(3). It was an original classification of intellectual activities.[39]

The general view of al-Farabi and the Brethren thus appears to have been that one's profession (which European thinkers from Luther to Weber would call vocation: Beruf) is part of the good life. In these thinkers, for the first time, the division of society into occupational groups is made a requirement of the Religious Law. In these passages about the different crafts, there was no explicit ranking, and classes in the hierarchical sense may not have been intended. But the division of the ideal state into different *epistemological* categories was clearly based (as in Plato and pre-Islamic Iran) on the assumption that people are unequal in their mental capacities, which, especially for a Shi'ite, was all-important. Presumably (though al-Farabi is not explicit) his categories 1–4 comprise the elite, and the fifth the common people. Plato was, however, Islamicised to the extent that the parts 'are united and bound together by love'.[40]

IBN SINA (AVICENNA)

Ibn Sina (near Bukhara 980–Isfahan 1037)[41] was a genius whose work during a short and hectic life was to influence philosophy and medicine until the seventeenth century, and philosophy in Iran to this day. He was educated at Bukhara by his father, an Isma'ili sympathiser, but he himself remained a Sunni. He was adviser to various Samanid rulers, and so had more first-hand experience of politics than most philosophers of any period; some of his writings were, it is said, dictated from the saddle. At one time he was forced into hiding, and imprisoned, but he escaped and finally enjoyed fourteen peaceful years at Isfahan. In metaphysics, he was influenced by al-Farabi and the Brethren. His *Healing of the Soul* (*al-Shifa al-nafs*) is a vast encyclopaedia of Philosophy and science. His political writings are in Book 10. A *Book of Governance* (*Kitab al-siyasa*) deals with domestic and economic life.

Ibn Sina, like al-Farabi, based his theory of the state on the empirical generalisation that it is in the nature of human beings to complement one another: 'it is necessary for a man to find his sufficiency in another of his species who, in his turn, finds in the former and his like, his sufficiency' (*Healing*, 10: LM 99). Examples of the division of labour are when 'one man would provide another with vegetables, while the other would bake for him; one man would sew for another, while the other would provide him with needles' (LM 99). Collectively, human beings are self-sufficient; and thus they form cities and societies. Such partnerships require reciprocal transactions; these in turn require customary law (sunna) and justice; and these require a human lawgiver and law-enforcer, who is, therefore, essential for human survival.

Ibn Sina extended the argument using a Durkheimian theory of the social function of religion (see above, p. 16, n. 3) to prove that, to be successful, the lawgiver must also be a Prophet. Muhammad is presented as Philosopher and Prophet, combining 'theoretical wisdom', justice and Prophecy. This makes him 'the world's earthly king and God's Deputy in it' (LM 110). But people will obey laws only if the person making them is made to appear exceptional: therefore the Prophet must perform miracles. Secondly, in order to ensure obedience to 'the decrees put in the Prophet's mouth by the God', he must 'let men know that they have a [Creator] ... [and] that obedience is due to Him'. But only a *simple* religious doctrine will do here; too complicated a teaching (did he have Christianity in mind?) will make people 'fall into dissensions and ... disputations ... that stand in the way of their political duties' (LM 100).

Thirdly, religious practices remind people of God and of the rewards of the afterlife and, therefore, of the need to perform their moral duties: the Prophet, in order to secure 'the preservation of the legislation he enacts concerning man's welfare' (101), must ensure that God and the afterlife are constantly brought to people's minds through prayer, fasting, Holy War and pilgrimage. Thus religious observance 'perpetuat[es] ... adherence to civil law (namus) and Religious Law (Shari'a)' (LM 103).

The fact that the validity of all marriages and contracts depends upon the Leader also underpins political order. Thus Ibn Sina found in the basic facts of human life proof of the need not only for human government but also for the Islamic religious polity. Through political science, 'one knows the necessity of Prophecy, and that the human race needs the Shari'a for its existence, preservation and future life'.[42]

According to Ibn Sina, the Imam should be capable of exercising independent judgement in legal matters (ijtihad) (one feature of the high Caliphate); but, unlike the Prophet, he is not as a philosopher-king, someone of special intellectual gifts or in touch with the Active Intellect.

Ibn Sina also adopted a Sunni view on *succession* to the Prophet-Legislator. This can be either by testamentary designation – the 'Abbasid practice – or by 'consensus of the elders'. Ibn Sina recommended designation because it avoids strife. But, most unusually for the time, he accepted a right of rebellion. If a 'seceder' claims the Deputyship 'by virtue of power or wealth', 'then it becomes the duty of every citizen to fight and kill him ... Next to belief in the prophet, nothing brings one closer to God than the killing of such a usurper'. But the seceder might be able to prove that the ruling Deputy is unfit or seriously imperfect; what counted here was not Religious Knowledge, but 'practical judgment and excellence in political management' (LM 107–8) – a Sunni rather than Shi'ite view of the qualifications for the Imamate. And in this case the citizens should accept the seceder. This indicates the kind of influence Philosophy could have on political thought.

The *content* of the legislation needed for social order, in Ibn Sina's view, combined Platonic and Islamic norms, and included social and economic regulation. First, the legislator must establish social orders – three this time: administrators, craftsmen, guardians (i.e. soldiers). Here the Platonic division of labour ousts the Iranian. Thus Ibn Sina too gave social categories a basis in Religious Law. Both al-Farabi and Ibn Sina deduced, from the division of society into such groups, the government's function of redistributing wealth from producing groups (farmers, artisans, merchants) to non-producing ones: soldiers, civil servants, the poor and disabled.

The legislator, said Ibn Sina, must also get rid of idleness and unemployment. Occupations 'whereby properties and utilities are transferred without any benefit rendered in exchange' (LM 105), such as gambling and usury, are banned. According to al-Farabi, government must supervise weights and measures, commerce generally and public places: thus Plato underwrote the Islamic muhtasib (market regulator, supervisor of public morals) (*Aphorisms*, pp. 22, 24–5). Ibn Sina stressed (like Plato) that marriage and child-rearing should be regulated. Divorce should be permitted, but only by the man. Rules of the Shari'a were thus justified partly on grounds of rationality and social discipline.

The legal system must be flexible, with scope for revision. The legislator 'must relegate many questions, particularly those pertaining to transactions, to the exercise of the individual judgment (ijtihad) of the jurists; for different times and circumstances call for decisions that cannot be pre-determined'. While there must be penalties for all infringements of the law, 'acts that harm the individual himself' should only incur 'advice and warning' (LM 109) – a liberal touch.

While Ibn Sina retained most of the substance of the Shari'a, he placed it in a quite new epistemological context, and its functions are made explicitly to include the functions of ordinary civil law. His is a relatively open system, subject to adaptation; as one would expect, since it is based upon a rational understanding of the human predicament. Such a view was hardly compatible with Sunni Jurisprudence, but perhaps was with the Shi'ite. After al-Farabi's abstraction and the Brethren's mysticism, Ibn Sina is refreshingly concrete.

The Philosophers were the most articulate and original political theorists of this period. Most Islamic thinkers adopted their theory of the origin and raison d'être of political authority. Yet they opened up a vision of Islam without Jurisprudence, almost (one might say) of the Qur'an without the Reports. Of orthodox Jurists, al-'Amiri remarked: 'they have now made it their purpose to lord it over the common people, to curry favour with the authorities, to gain control over the property of the powerless';[43] though neither al-Farabi nor Ibn Sina seems to have criticised the 'ulama openly.[44] The point was that the Philosophers' whole approach to organising society and the legal system wrote the 'ulama out of the script. In any case, the Philosophers' fundamental strategy, their attempt to reinterpret the Islamic enterprise in terms of neo-Platonism, was drowned in the hubbub of Traditionalism, and eventually reviled by the populace.

The Islamic Philosophers took from Plato and Aristotle what they wanted. So did the Europeans in the thirteenth century. Law and order, social discipline, moral upbringing and philosopher-rulers were the familiar and 'relevant' topics. Al-Farabi and Ibn Sina were interested not in analysing the dynamics of contemporary institutions, but in their own versions of the ideal Caliphate. This may be related to the fact they never had Aristotle's *Politics*. The absence of an Arabic translation of this may also be related to the absence in Islamdom of city-states, indeed of cities qua unified, corporate legal entities. Self-government operated in sectarian not territorial groups; Islamic towns were aggregates of Shi'ites, Jews and others. There was thus no political civic culture, and this meant that the scope for political autonomy was limited: where else was it found except among tribespeople? And what kind of politics can you have without the polis?

NOTES

1. See *EI* on Falsafa; NL; LM; Badawi (1972); Corbin (1964); Leaman (1985); E. Rosenthal (1958); Fakhry (1983); Kraemer (1992); F. Rosenthal (1970); Makdisi (1981); Franz Rosenthal, *The Classical Heritage in Islam* (London: Routledge, 1975); F. E. Peters, *Aristotle and the Arabs: The Aristotelian Tradition in Islam* (New York: New York Press, 1968); Josef van Ess, 'The Logical Structure of Islamic Theology', in G. E. von Grunebaum (ed.), *Logic in Classical Islamic Culture* (Wiesbaden: Harrassowitz, 1970), pp. 21–50; S. Pines in *CH Islam* 2: 794–823.
2. Heinz Halm, *The Fatimids and their Tradition of Learning* (London: Tauris, 1997), p. 72.
3. Kodama ibn Dja'far, *Kitab al-Kharaj*, in M. J. de Goeje (ed.), *Biblioteca Geographorum Arabicorum*, vol. 6 (Leiden: Brill, 1889), pp. 204–5.

4. S. Pines, 'Aristotle's Politics in Arabic Philosophy', *Israel Oriental Studies* 5 (1975), pp. 150–60.

5. *EI* 2: 770; Leaman (1985: 20).

6. 'Choice (ikhtiyar) pertains specifically to man and not to all other animals ... and because of it there is reward and punishment' (al-Farabi, *Governance*, pp. 33–4; *VC* 231).

7. *Aquinas*, ed. D'Entrèves (see above, p. 31, n. 15), pp. 123–7; Janet Coleman, *A History of Political Thought from the Middle Ages to the Renaissance* (Oxford: Blackwell, 2000), pp. 182–5.

8. Philosophy could point to 'a universal truth and a universal morality which discarded the limitations of institutional dogma and law': Gerhard Endress, 'The limits to reason', *Akten d. VII Kongress f. Arab. u. Isl. Wiss* (Göttingen, 1976), p. 121; G. Hourani (1976: 61, 82–3); Goldziher (1981: 91).

9. S. Pines, 'La loi naturelle et la société: la doctrine politico-théologique d'Ibn Zur'a, philosophe chrétien de Baghdad', in U. Heyd (ed.), *Studies in Islamic History and Civilization* (Jerusalem: The Hebrew University, 1961), p. 173; Kraemer (1992: 116–23).

10. Kraemer (1992: 110–13). Al-Farabi had once tried 'to sketch a universal grammar which may be applied to every language': Walzer in *VC* 431.

11. Muhsin Mahdi, 'Al-Farabi's imperfect state', in *Journal of Oriental and African Studies* 110 (1990), pp. 691–726 (review of Walzer (ed.), *VC*).

12. *EI* 2: 774b; Peters, *Aristotle*, p. 73. Walzer sees Imami Shi'ism as 'the key to al-Farabi as a Muslim writer' (*VC* 315); Corbin remarks that 'The arguments on which he bases the necessity for the existence of prophets, the features which define the inner being of the prophet, the guide, the imam, correspond to those of Shi'ite prophetic theory' (1964: 329).

13. *EI* 3: 1072a. On the Brethren, see Marquet (1961, 1973); Kraemer (1992: 165–78); Lambton (1981: 289–95).

14. Thus we have: (1) *Survey of the Branches of Knowledge* (*Ihsa' al-'ulum*), ch. 5 trans. in LM 24–30; (2) *On the Achievement of Happiness* (*Tahsil al Sa'adah*), trans. in LM 58–82; (3) *Compendium legum Platonis* (*Summary of Plato's Laws*), ed. and trans. F. Gabrieli (London, 1952); (4) *On the Principles of the Views of the Inhabitants of the Excellent State*, ed. and trans. R. Walzer, *Al-Farabi on the Perfect State: Abu Nasr al-Farabi's al-madina al-fadila* (Oxford: Oxford University Press, 1985) = *Virtuous City* (*VC*); (5) *The Governance of the State* (*al-siyasa al-madaniyya*), trans. LM 31–57; (6) *Aphorisms of the Statesman* (*Fusul al-madani*), ed. and trans. D. M. Dunlop (Cambridge: Cambridge University Press, 1961). On al-Farabi, see *EI* s.v. al-Farabi; Miriam Galston, *Politics and Excellence: The Political Philosophy of Alfarabi* (Princeton: Princeton University Press, 1990); Walzer's introduction to *VC*; J. L. Kraemer, 'The Jihad of the Falasifa', *JSAI* 10 (1987), pp. 288–324.

15. M. Arkoun (trans.), *Miskawayh, Traité d'éthique* (Damascus: Institut français de Damas, 1969). On him, see *EI* 1: 328; Mohammed Arkoun, *Contribution à l'étude de l'humanisme arabe au IVe/Xe siècle: Miskawayh, philosophe et historien* (Paris: Vrin, 1970).

16. *EI* 3: 943a. The concept of the Active Intellect derived from Aristotle's idea of the formative aspect of human perception (nous poetikos, lit. making mind). This referred to the human mind's ability to construct concepts out of the sense-impressions received by the 'passive intellect'.

17. Al-Tawhidi (d. 1037), in Ashtiany et al. (eds) (1990: 117); compare Ibn Qutaiba (see above, p. 51)

18. Kraemer (1992: appendix, pp. 158–60; Fakhry (1983: 96–106).
19. Kraemer (1992: 139–64, 170); Endress, 'Limits', p. 123.
20. *Governance*, pp. 36–7. Al-Farabi equated 'the Platonic philosopher king with the Islamic prophetic law-giver and (Leader)' (Erwin Rosenthal 1958: 140).
21. Al-Farabi in Galston, *Politics*, p. 55.
22. In Badawi, *Philosophie*, vol. 2, p. 555.
23. Trans. L. V. Berman, 'Alfarabi on Religion, Jurisprudence and Political Science', in M. Mahdi (ed.), *Alfarabi, Book of Religion and Other Texts* (Beirut: al-Mackreq, 1968), p. 15.
24. In Franz Rosenthal, 'Abu Zayd al-Balkhi on Politics', in C. E. Bosworth (ed.), *The Islamic World from Classical to Modern* (Princeton: Princeton University Press, 1989), pp. 287–301 at p. 290. Cf. Aquinas in ed. D'Entrèves, pp. 78–80.
25. In Marquet (1973: 482) and Kraemer (1992: 171).
26. *Happiness*, 75; *Governance*, 37.
27. In *Happiness*, 69; see Badawi, *Philosophie*, vol. 2, pp. 557–8.
28. Marquet (1962: 49, 63–6); Marquet (1973: 375, 483, 497).
29. Marquet (1962: 50–2, 86–9); Marquet (1973: 442); Lambton (1981: 293).
30. Franz Rosenthal, 'State and Religion according to Abu l-Hasan al-'Amiri', *Islamic Quarterly* (1956), pp. 42–52 at p. 48; Nagel (1981: vol. 2, pp. 18–22).
31. Kraemer, 'Jihad', p. 320.
32. 'People aim through association at co-operating for those things by which felicity in its real and true sense can be attained': *VC* 231.
33. The organic analogy may have come from Plato's *Republic*; the idea of cities or states having 'parts' could have come from the way in which cities were arranged in al-Farabi's world.
34. Arkoun, *Contribution*, pp. 303, 305; Kraemer (1992: 232).
35. Lambton (1981: 295); Marquet (1973: 374, 377).
36. *VC* 229; he uses words presumably translated from the Greek.
37. Y. Marquet, 'La place du travail dans la hiérarchie Isma'ilienne d'après l'encyclique des Frères de la Pureté', *Arabica* 8 (1961), pp. 225–37 at pp. 232–3; Marquet (1973: 431, 586). Cf. Marsiglio on *Legislator humanus*.
38. Traité (see n. 15 above), pp. 180–1.
39. *Aphorisms*, p. 50; Walzer in *VC* 437.
40. *Aphorisms*, p. 53; Marlow (1997: 53–64).
41. His main work on politics was *Healing* (al-Shifa), Metaphysics X, chs 2–5, trans. LM 98–111 and G. C. Anawati, *Avicenne: la Métaphysique du Shifa*, vol. 2 (Paris: Vrin, 1985), pp. 173–89. On his practical philosophy, see *EI* s.v. Ibn Sina; D. Gutas, *Avicenna and the Aristotelian Tradition* (Leiden: Brill, 1988), pp. 219–25; S. M. Afnan, *Avicenna: His Life and Works* (London: Allen & Unwin, 1958), pp. 230–2.
42. LM 97; Erwin Rosenthal (1958: 145).
43. Franz Rosenthal, 'State and Religion', p. 48.
44. Al-Farabi's critique of false religion may be read as an attack on the Isma'ilis, especially perhaps the newly established Fatimids. Some satirical remarks on Religious Scholars may reflect his attitude towards the Sunni 'ulama; comments on the ruses and hypocrisies of piety (*VC* 305–6) seem to reproduce an ancient source.

Part II   Religion and State Power
(din wa dawla): Sunni Doctrine and the
State c.1000–1220

The Theory of the Caliphate

7

I n the central lands of Islam, a new power confronted Byzantium (Rum) and the Fatimids. The Saljuk tribe of Oghuz Turks had adopted Islam before they took over the Bukhara region (c.956). Under their leading clan, they crossed the Oxus, occupied Khurasan (1035–8), and then, led by Toghril (r.1055–63), western Iran and Iraq (1055); in the 1070s they became masters of Syria. For the first time since the early 'Abbasids, Iran, Iraq, Syria and the Caucasus were under the same ruler.

Inspired by frontier-warrior (ghazi) ideals, the Saljuks shattered the Byzantine army at Malazgirt (Manzikert, eastern Anatolia: 1071) and broke through into the Byzantine heartlands. The way was open for a Turkish-led Muslim takeover of Anatolia. This added huge material and human resources to the House of Islam, while East Rome lost its main source of manpower and agricultural produce. A new tranche of conversions followed. Manzikert also triggered the first crusade. Pope Gregory VII informed the western horsemen that Christian villagers were being pillaged, raped, massacred: one must intervene. Latin-Catholic ('Frankish') feudal levies marched across Anatolia and into Syria (1096); they captured Jerusalem (1099).

Under the Saljuks, the Islamic polity entered a new phase.[1] A dynasty of Sultans dedicated to Sunnism now ruled beside a Sunni Deputy over the central lands of Islam. A religio-political pattern emerged under which Islamic justice was administered by the 'ulama as Judges (sing. qadi), while military power became the basis of social order and legitimate political authority. This was a fairly significant development from the scepticism towards state power previously prevalent among Sunni 'ulama (see Chapter 3). Sunnism developed as the full partner of military-political power; socially dominant, it was integrated into public life and the socio-political order. Sultan and leading 'ulama cooperated and became interdependent. This found expression in the old Iranian idea of the Circle of Power.

The Saljuks, like the Samanids and Ghaznavids and most Turkish dynastic families, were adherents of the mild Hanafi Legal School. Their two most powerful rulers, Alp Arslan (r.1063–73) and Malikshah (r.1073–92) relied upon a military population that was predominantly Turkish, and a predominantly Iranian ('Tajik') civilian population from which the bulk of religious and government officials were drawn. The tribal army was reorganised into a partly professional force under Nizam al-Mulk (Grand Vizier 1063–92) on the basis of land distribution by iqta' – a new system of state finances.

SUNNI POLITICAL THEOLOGY

The theory behind all this was to some extent worked out by Sunni theorists before the Saljuk conquest transformed their prospects. The eleventh and twelfth centuries saw a proliferation of overtly political writings that was unique in Islamic history. This was probably because strategic political choices were now being made, and an influential audience was available. Community-Traditionalist (Sunni) Islam had been developing its cellular structures under the 'Abbasids and under the Shi'ite ascendancy of the Buyids. A wide-ranging religio-political strategy was submerged beneath legal niceties and acquiescence in existing regimes. We have seen how the fundamental particles of Religious Legalism (fiqh) were assembled, while the high-caliphal strategy was frustrated by the opposition of the People-of-Book-and-Tradition and by the rise to power of a mainly Turkish praetorian guard. The Sunnis evolved a strategy of radical disengagement between religious authority and official politics. The former permeated society at large and was the domain of the Scholars ('ulama); the latter was backed by military force (above, Chapter 3).

A certain kind of political mobilisation of the Sunni commoners (al 'amma: the generality), especially the urban masses, had been going on since the early ninth century. In Iraq, especially Baghdad, a spontaneous mass movement, 'well organised and strongly motivated', partly inspired by the learned and courageous Ibn Hanbal, had begun taking 'vigilante action to enforce morality, suppress alcohol and prostitution and attack rival sects'. The development of the Hanbali school of thought marked a new stage in the differentiation between religious and political institutions (Lapidus 1975: 383). The social and intellectual orientation of Hanbalism differed sharply from that of the Shi'a and the Philosophers. Unlike the Shi'a, it was explicitly anti-elitist, indeed populist. Unlike falsafa, the new Sunnism as a whole was well designed to survive the political confusion of the Deputyship after about 850, as well as the political ascendancy of Shi'ism.

As Buyid power declined, a more aggressive Sunni-restoration policy was undertaken under the combined leadership of the urban Scholars and two forceful Deputies, al-Qadir (lit. 'the one who decrees') (r.991–1031) and his son al-Qa'im (lit. 'the deliverer') (r.1031–75). Al-Qadir prohibited discussion of Shi'ite or Mu'tazilite teachings, and even banned theological disputation (kalam) itself from the madrasas (Religious Colleges). Mu'tazilites were deprived of positions of influence; pro-Mu'tazilite members of the Hanafi School were made to retract their views publicly. His political programme was to liberate the Deputyship from Shi'ite rule; and the chosen instrument were the Saljuk-led Turkish tribes to the East, with whom al-Qadir 'formed what amounted to an alliance' (Gibb 1962: 24).

The intellectual development of this type of Sunnism also came partly from the East, from Khurasan, 'the one important region of western Asia which had not fallen under Shi'ite government' (Gibb 1962:33). The theology of the movement derived especially from al-'Ash'ari (Basra 873/4–Baghdad 935).[2] He and his followers did not go as far as Hanbalism in rejecting 'rational speculation in any form' (Lapidus 1988: 222), but they nevertheless carried the pure revelationism and philosophical agnosticism of mainstream Shafi'i Legalism over into theology by denying the ability of human reason to translate the data of revelation into any language or set of postulates other than that in which it was set forth in the sacred texts. 'In 'Ash'arism it is the Law which defines the limits of reason and controls its activity'; 'the only dependable knowledge was historical knowledge'.[3] 'Ash'arites and Hanbalis both upheld the Uncreatedness of the Qur'an, a doctrine associated with the more textual approach to revelation.

The impact of 'Ash'arism on intellectual life in general was decisive. The 'Ash'aris endorsed the view that all events are caused directly by the all-powerful will of God, while secondary causes may operate but miracles do not require special explanation. Human actions themselves are directly caused by God; yet God is not responsible for evil. Intellectual coherence is not expected; 'ask not how' (bila kaifa) was the catchphrase. Such doctrines, flourishing first in the intellectual centre of Nishapur in eastern Iran, won increasing support in the Sunni world. 'Ash'arism ousted not only Philosophy but also the Mu'tazilites together with the whole trend towards rational discourse in theology. It was the final assertion of the concrete, particularist, linguistic and neo-tribal theory of knowledge.

Perhaps the most original theoretical justification of literalism was that of Ibn Hazm (Cordova 994–1064), who had been brought up in the palace harem where his father was the Caliph's vizier. Ibn Hazm himself became a vizier at the age of 29, was subsequently imprisoned, and spent the rest of his life thinking. His love story, *The Dove's Collar*, presented 'a ruthless analysis of ... motives, intentions and secret meanings' (*EI* 3: 793a). (One might see a psychological parallel with St Augustine.) Ibn Hazm believed it was impossible to understand anything which cannot be expressed in plain language, and was sceptical of the claims to inner spiritual enlightenment made by sufis and neo-Platonist falasifa, of allegorical interpretation, and even of reasoning by analogy.

Reason alone cannot establish anything; it can only work under the direction of revelation; right and wrong are defined by God. Language was instituted by God, and only what can be expressed in language can be known. Therefore, the only thing to be relied upon is the text itself of the Qur'an and of the Reports, taken in their straightforward (zahir) sense (*EI* 3:793). It was a peculiarity of Ibn Hazm's thought that this actually had the effect of *expanding* the area of what is permissible, since what is not explicitly stated in divine law cannot be forbidden.[4]

In general, the Shafi'ite-'Ash'arite approach to moral thought meant that right and wrong are prescribed by God through the sacred texts, and that the resulting moral code, the Shari'a, is not open to rational debate. It is, through the nature of its origins, superior to any other moral code; and it can only be known to Muslims. Therefore, to be moral one virtually must be Muslim. There is no rational or 'natural' law knowable by humans as humans through their own understanding. This was a '"command" theory of value', or theo-positivism.[5] It had and has a catastrophic effect on Islamic attitudes towards non-believers, or at least non-theists.

THE LEADERSHIP (IMAMA) OR CALIPHATE (KHILAFA)

An articulate Community-Traditionalist political theory was finally formulated in the first half of the eleventh century. Its doctrine of the Deputyship met the requirements of the emerging religious community by radically scaling down expectations placed on the Deputy, while retaining the legitimacy of the 'Abbasids as Leaders of the Muslims. The first four rightly-guided (rashidun) Deputies were now placed in a special category. The immediate motive was to safeguard the 'Abbasid Caliphate against alternatives – Imami Shi'ism or Isma'ili Shi'ism, especially in its Fatimid version – which might appear legitimate to Muslims.

The previous despoliation of 'Abbasid politico-military power made the Sunni apologists' task easier. For now the 'Abbasids could be asked to assert their religious authority without posing a threat to either the 'ulama or the actual rulers (sultans: lit. powers). The later 'Abbasids 'seem to have convinced most members of the religious class ... that in principle many Islamic institutions could function properly only if the reigning 'Abbasid caliph recognised them'. And, according to al-Biruni, 'the common people in the large cities had become accustomed to the 'Abbasid claim, and have been inclined to their rule, and obey them out of a sense of religion, and consider them possessed with the right to command' (CH Iran 4: 88).

It was now that the doctrine of non-resistance finally took root in Sunni Islam. Ibn Hanbal himself, true to his minimalist view of both politics and rationality, affirmed the duty of absolute obedience unless the Leader apostasised or failed to make provision for communal prayer. Otherwise even a usurper, if successful, must be acknowledged. Al-'Ash'ari himself denounced 'those who hold it right to rise against [the Leaders] whenever there may be apparent in them a falling away from right ... [W]e are against armed rebellion against [incumbent Deputies], and civil war' (in Lambton 1981: 70). Non-resistance became the most widely held view in Sunni Islam, stated for example by the Hanbali Ibn Qudama Muwaffaq al-Din (1146–1223), who taught that political opposition disrupts Muslim unity. One must never resist a ruler unless he command disobedience to God, meaning by this a blatant infringement of Religious Law. Any ruler in his right mind could avoid this.[6]

The 'Ash'arite reaction against the use of rational arguments was introduced into political theory by al-Baghdadi (d.1037), a contemporary of Ibn Sina, who worked at Nishapur. Humans may know 'by reason that subordination to [the Leadership] is admissible', but the Shari'a takes us further than human reason. It alone stipulates the essential socio-political functions which the Caliph-Imam and he alone can perform, namely enforcement of Legal

Penalties, giving women without guardians in marriage, trusteeship of the property of orphans and lunatics, sending troops to war, and 'many other functions which only the Leader, or the person appointed by the Leader, can perform' (Lambton 1981: 78). The true need for the Imamate can only be apprehended by revelation. Al-Baghdadi thus implicitly rejected the Philosophers' assimilation of the Leader to the philosopher-king and drew a distinction between the Imamate (Leadership) and ordinary human government (which, Ibn Sina had argued, might be said to perform similar functions on grounds of rationally perceived need).

Jurists discussed in particular the means of appointment, and grounds for dismissal, of a Deputy. According to al-Baqillani (d.1013, an 'Ash'arite), the Deputy's innate knowledge of a candidate's outstanding personal qualities did not justify designation of his successor (as the Shi'ites argued). But appointment could be made by testamentary designation ('ahd). Alternatively, the Imam could be elected by 'the people who loose and who bind (ahl al-hall wa'l-'aqd)' (that is, presumably, traditional community leaders, whoever they might be but surely including senior 'ulama). Such 'election (ikhtiyar)' is valid even if conducted by just *one* person provided that several Muslims witness it (Lambton 1981: 70–6). This again endorsed existing 'Abbasid practice. The same view, attributed to al-'Ash'ari himself, was given by al-Baghdadi.

To qualify as Imam, one does not, as Shi'ites said, have to be sinless or an exceptional character. One need only (according to al-Baqillani) 'have a sound view of war' and be competent to judge disputes. The grounds for deposing a Deputy are, therefore, dramatically reduced. Al-Baqillani said that allegiance may be revoked only on grounds of heresy, serious injustice (not accepted by most Sunni Jurists), physical incapacitation, or imprisonment (an important consideration given the Fatimid threat). A general and significant feature of Sunni thought was that there was no *procedure* for deposition. Their dry – and, of course, legalistic – approach was in contrast with the metaphysical theory of the Leadership held by the Shi'ites and some Philosophers.

AL-MAWARDI ON THE CALIPHATE AND POLITICAL POWER

The Community-Traditionalist view of the Deputyship was taken further by the Shafi'ite Abu l-Hasan 'Ali al-Mawardi (Basra 974–Baghdad 1058), who was Judge at Nishapur and later Chief Judge (qadi al-qudat) at Baghdad under the early Saljuks.[7] Contrary to the Hanbali tendency, he sought to overcome the radical disjuncture between religious leadership and coercive power by reconnecting the de facto rulers – Sultans and Amirs – with the 'Abbasid Caliphate. He sought to define their relationship in terms of Religious Law, so reabsorbing them into the religious system. This intellectual project arose directly out of the aspirations of the newly active Deputies, on whose behalf al-Mawardi negotiated with the Buyids and undertook various diplomatic missions in the 1030s and 1040s.

Al-Mawardi was a reforming jurist, willing to adapt the Law wherever possible to circumstances. He wrote on the Qur'an and on Prophecy, and, as part of al-Qa'im's efforts to restore Sunni Islam, he compiled manuals on the doctrines of all four Legal Schools. His output was (like that of all major Religious Scholars) voluminous: 4, 000 pages on the Shafi'i system alone. He wrote on courtly ethics (adab) (*On Conduct in Religion and in the World*: *Kitab Adab al-dunya wa 'l-din*).[8]

His main political work, *On the Principles (Ordinances/Rules) of Power* (*Kitab al-Ahkam al-Sultaniyya*)[9] was in the genre of Jurisprudence (fiqh), written between 1045 and 1058, just at the time when the Saljuks were coming to power in the 'Abbasid heartlands. Al-Mawardi says that he wrote it on the instructions of al-Qa'im, who wanted to 'know the views of the Jurists and those Principles which define his rights, that he may exact them in full, and his duties, that he may perform them in full, with the object of showing equity in his execution and judgment, and from a desire to respect the rights of others in his taking and giving'.[10] It was a defence of al-Qa'im's strategy in terms of Religious Jurisprudence; but it appears that al-Mawardi was expressing his own views.

In his *Conduct*, al-Mawardi summarised with remarkable insight the sources of social and political order ('salah al-dunya: worldly order'). Here he showed his familiarity with adab literature and the political theory of falsafa. These sources are: (1) 'an established religion, whereby man's passions are held in check', (2) 'A powerful ruler (sultan) ... for neither religion nor reason is by itself sufficient to bar people from wrongdoing or injustice, unless they are coerced by the superior authority of a strong ruler'; (3) 'justice, to ensure mutual love and submission to authority (and) ... the prosperity of the land'. This involves justice to subordinates, to superiors including God, and to equals. Following Miskawayh, he equated this with 'moderation or equilibrium (i'tidal) ... it is a mean between two extremes'. Next we need (4) 'law and order, resulting in a universal sense of security'; (5) 'general economic prosperity ... rooted in abundance of resources ... (and of) revenue'. This was an elaboration of the circle of power, to which al-Mawardi added lastly (6) 'vast hope, the pre-condition of any productive activity ... and of civilisation and continuous progress'. Religion, kinship and friendship are the bases of that 'mutual affinity (ulfah)' upon which social solidarity depends (in Fakhry 1991: 163–4). Thus al-Mawardi was here restating, with special emphasis on the values of contemporary Muslim society, the Iranian notion of the interdependence of polity, religion and justice (see above, p. 54).

But in the *Sultaniyya* (*Power*), he insisted that the Muslim religious polity both has, and in principle must have, a superior form of political organisation – the Leadership (Imamate or Caliphate) – which *cannot* be known by reason alone but only from revelation (the sacred texts as interpreted by orthodox Jurists). Here he seems fairly close to the Latin-Christian distinction between reason and faith.

Al-Mawardi did not hereby reject the Philosophers' view of the origins and raison d'être of political society, nor was he necessarily rejecting the rational basis of all public authority. What he was insisting on was that the special public authority *prescribed for Muslims* is known only through revelation:

Islamic Leadership cannot be deduced from reason. All that reason can tell us is that we should refrain from injustice and from 'severing the bonds of friendship' (Lambton 1981: 86); thus he had not abandoned the ideas expressed in *On Conduct*. But reason cannot tell us about the other important functions of the Leader (some of which a Westerner might describe as 'spiritual' or 'ecclesiastical', but most of which were at the same time patently social and political). These included: arrangements for communal prayer, the Pilgrimage, Alms and taxation, appointment of Religious Judges (Chapter 6), agriculture and irrigation, landownership, the bureaucracy (diwan), and public morality including economic conduct. Al-Mawardi thus arrived at a position similar to that later put forward by Thomas Aquinas, for whom the natural order of political society is brought to perfection through the divinely-revealed order. For Aquinas, too, 'secular' government is in principle separate from religious authority and nonetheless legitimate (Black 1992: 22–4). Al-Mawardi seems to have moved towards a distinction between secular and revealed powers which, for whatever reasons, was not developed further in the Muslim world as it was in the West.

In fact al-Mawardi's purpose was not to emphasise a distinction between worldly and divinely-revealed power, but rather to reclaim, in principle at least, socio-political authority for the Deputy. The Leadership is re-established as the instrument for the management of the Islamic people and the fulcrum of the political (to use Western language) as well as the religious dispensation of society. Al-Mawardi envisaged the Caliphate as the keystone of the system. On the basis of the divinely-appointed functions of the Caliph, al-Mawardi was in a position to assert his authority in 'political' as well as 'religious' matters. In this treatise devoted to *power* (sultaniyya), al-Mawardi now adopted the language of political reality, but only in order to reaffirm the Deputy's authority over the entire range of Muslim public life.

> God ... ordained for the People (al-umma) a Leader through whom He provided for the Deputyship of the Prophet and through whom He protected the Religious Association (al-milla); and he entrusted government (al-siyasa) to him, so that the management of affairs should proceed (on the basis of) right religion ... The Leadership became the principle upon which the bases of the Religious Association were established, by which the well-being of the People (masalih al-'umma) was regulated, and affairs of common interest (al-umur al-'amma) were made stable, and from which particular Public Functions (al-wilayat al-khassa) emanated. (in Lambton 1981: 85)

The principal public functions of the Islamic People are those of Judges, the Market Supervisor (muhtasib) and the Mazalim (Redress of Grievances) court. The Supervisor has the tasks of preventing fraud and regulating labour relations. (For example, he should prevent an employer from reducing an employee's salary or increasing his workload; and, if he does so, the Supervisor must inflict a proportionate penalty.) The crucial point is that al-siyasa (which may be translated as social discipline, governance and, in some contexts, government) is entrusted to the *Deputy*. It follows that all existing governments, if they are to be recognised as fulfilling legitimate public purposes within Islam, must derive from the Deputy. Only then can 'the Rules (ahkam) concerning Public Functions (al-wilayat) be arranged according to their proper categories' (in Lambton 1981: 85). Only if the Deputy ultimately controls all these things can right religion become the principle on which society runs.

Al-Mawardi used two concepts to formulate this relationship between the Deputy and existing rulers: wazir (vizier: government minister), and amir (Commander). He distinguished two types of wazir: (1) the vizier 'by delegation (tawhid)' to whom the Deputy delegates full powers, and (2) the vizier 'by execution (tanfih)', to whom he delegates powers for specific purposes only (Chapter 2). The wazirate can be acquired either (1) by express delegation by the Deputy, or (2) by de facto fulfilment of certain functions (that is, by the wazir taking power initially on his own initiative). The second confers more limited authority.

The Amirate is treated as 'a particular form of the wazirate' (chapters 3–4); that is, presumably, their territories are in principle no less under the Deputy's authority than those over which he had actual control and which he ruled through viziers. Two types of Amir are distinguished depending, again, on how office was acquired: (1) Imara freely conferred (by the Caliph) (al-istikfa'), (2) Imara by conquest (al-istila'). While the term Amir originally referred to a military office, under (1) al-Mawardi included judicial, financial and religious functions. That is – on the understanding that he is indeed the Deputy's recognised subordinate – the holder of the freely conferred Imara exercises in his own territory not only ordinary governmental powers but *also* the specific functions of Islamic authority: the appointment of Religious Judges, exacting the Legal Penalties, leading prayers, conducting jihad. Sunni rulers who recognised and were recognised by the 'Abbasids, such as the Samanids, Ghaznavids and Saljuks, were presumably in this category.

The second type of Imara is sub-divided into two categories. (2a) If a ruler who has achieved power by conquest recognises the Deputy, offers obedience, recognises existing religious officials, raises taxes in accordance with the Religious Law, implements Legal Penalties, and generally upholds the Shari'a and encourages others to do so, then the Deputy *must* recognise and invest him. And thereafter he has, presumably, the same authority as one whose Imara was freely conferred; thus most contemporary Sunni rulers would, it seems, fit into either category (1) or category (2a). (2b) If such conditions are not met, the Deputy *may* still recognise the Amir, but he must depute someone else to ensure that the necessary functions are in fact fulfilled.

> Although ... contrary to the principles of Shar'i government, ... this is permissible for two reasons: (i) necessity dispenses with conditions which are impossible to fulfil, and (ii) fear of injury to public interest justifies a relaxation of conditions which would not be justified in private matters. (in Lambton 1981: 101)

Was this an attempt to come to terms with non-Sunni rulers (such as the Fatimids and previously the Buyids) who nevertheless permitted Sunnis to practise, and under whom law-courts with Sunni Judges were able to function? In any case such an appointment of a Caliph's representative would have been revolutionary, and it never happened.

The moral and legal provisions of the Shari'a were to be complemented by the Redress of Grievances court and by custom ('urf). Al-Mawardi here signalled his acceptance of the early experience of Islam: the Shari'a needed to be supplemented by other forms of law. The Redress court is to ensure that decisions of Judges and Supervisors are enforced. Its special concern is redress of wrongs committed by government officials, or by over-mighty subjects. Compared with the Shari'a courts, its jurisdiction is 'wider and more unfettered, both in scope of action and in sentence'; it possesses 'greater power of intimidation' (von Grunebaum 1953: 164). The ruler's law and ruler's courts may be more effective political instruments than the Shari'a. Al-Mawardi coined the term 'the right of power (haqq al-sultana)' to indicate an area of public justice not covered by the existing concepts of 'the right of God' or 'the right of man', the point being that sometimes it was deemed necessary to apply *more rigorous* punishments than those prescribed by Religious Law (Heyd 1973: 205–6). He did not, however, clearly demarcate the competence of the mazalim court from that of the Religious Judges. The Redress court is kept within the religious framework insofar as it is established and operated by the Deputy or his authorised delegate.

Al-Mawardi's restatement of the Caliph–Sultan relationship allowed him to introduce a new way of getting rid of a bad ruler. If a usurper acts contrary to religion and to justice, the Caliph himself may 'call to his aid those who will restrain the usurper's hand and put an end to his domination' (in Gibb 1962: 160). This might have been a way of legitimising the Saljuk conquest. This made the position of the Caliph similar to that of the pope in the West; according to some, the pope could in emergency replace a wicked ruler.[11]

Al-Mawardi showed how the religious Code and the accepted Sunni theory of the Deputyship could be reinterpreted and developed so as to take account of existing power relationships. His theory made rulers technically dependent upon the Caliph's approval for their legitimacy. He laid an intellectual foundation for a revival of the 'Abbasid caliphate which might have gone further but for the Mongols. But in actual fact it remained a largely theoretical exercise; it was never put to the test, unlike similar papal claims in Europe, as events there in the later eleventh century were about to demonstrate. And indeed al-Mawardi does not give the Deputy the choice of refusing to recognise a ruler who is fulfilling his duties under Islamic law. It is not said who decides whether a ruler is failing in this respect; there is no indication that the Caliph should decide.

Rather, what happened was that Sultans steadily appropriated the religious functions of the Caliph, such as leadership in jihad. By establishing the legal conditions under which de facto rulers, as Commanders, might legitimately undertake religious functions previously ascribed to the Deputy alone, he gave a juristic basis for the phenomenon, soon to become widespread, of the 'Sultan-Caliph'.

Yet al-Mawardi's restatement of the relationship between the Deputy and de facto power gave his ideas importance in learned circles. His *Rules of Power* 'became widely accepted as an authoritative exposition of Sunni doctrine concerning the imamate'.[12] His views helped to legitimise subsequent practice, notably under the Ottomans, regarding the role of the Mazalim (Redress) court and of secular law in a Muslim state.

NOTES

1. On what follows, see *EI* 3: 158–60, 1164–5; Fakhry (1958); Lambton (1981: 69–102); Tyan (1954–6); Arnold (1924).
2. On what follows, see George Makdisi, *Ibn ʿAqil et la Résurgence de l'Islam traditionaliste au XIe siècle* (Damascus: Institut français, 1963), pp. 295–6; Leaman (1985: 75, 78, 140); Goldziher (1981: 111–15); Fakhry (1983: 209–11).
3. *EI* 3: 1146a; Hodgson (1974: vol. 1, p. 443).
4. *EI* s.v. Ibn Hazm; R. Arnaldez, *Grammaire et théologie chez Ibn Hazm de Cordoue* (Paris: Vrin, 1956); George F. Hourani, 'Reason and Revelation in Ibn Hazm's Ethical Thought', in P. Morewedge (ed.), *Islamic Philosophical Theology* (Albany NY: SUNY, 1986), pp. 142–60.
5. G. F. Hourani, 'Averroes on Good and Evil', *SI* 16 (1962), p. 33.
6. Henri Laoust, *Ibn Qudama Muwaffaq al-Din: le précis de droit* (Beirut, 1950).
7. On him, see Gibb (1962: 151–65); Henri Laoust, 'La pensée et l'action politique d'al-Mawardi', *REI* 36 (1968), pp. 11–92.
8. Trans. O. Rescher, *Das kitab adab ed-dunya wa'ddin' des Qadi Mawerdi* (Stuttgart, 1932–3); see M. Arkoun, 'L'éthique musulmane d'après Mawardi', *REI* 31 (1963), pp. 1–31.
9. Trans. E. Fagan, *Les status gouvernementaux* (Algiers, 1915), and Wafaa H. Wahba, *Al-Mawardi, The Ordinances of Government* (Reading: Garnet, 1996). There are three unedited political works: *EI* 6: 869b.
10. Preface in Gibb (1962: 152); trans. Wahba, p. 1.
11. Ullmann (1955: 52–7); Black (1992: 43–4).
12. *EI* 3: 1165a. Other important Sunni political thinkers of this period were Abu Yaʿla (990–1066), who wrote *al-Ahkam as-sultaniyya* (Makdisi, *Ibn ʿAqil*, pp. 342–8); and Ibn al-Farra (Laoust 1939: 380–458).

The Order of the Realm

8

The Saljuk ascendancy[1] was closely associated with two men, Nizam al-Mulk and al-Ghazali, perhaps the greatest statesman and the greatest theologian respectively of all time. Nizam al-Mulk (lit. 'Order of the Kingdom') (near Tus c.1018–1092) was the driving force behind the Saljuk regime at the height of its power. He helped shape Saljuk policies in every field and was the architect of much that was distinctive about the regime. The period became known as 'al-Dawla al-Nizamiyya (the destined reign of Nizam)'; his family held office under the Saljuks for two generations after him. Educated as a Shafi'i Jurist at Nishapur, Nizam followed family tradition in serving the Ghaznavids. He was appointed vizier by Alp Arslan (c.1055), and then given responsibility for Khurasan (1059–63), and finally appointed chief vizier. He accompanied Alp Arslan on his many travels and campaigns. By the time Alp Arslan was assassinated (1073), Nizam had already secured the succession of Malikshah as sole heir.

Nizam played a formative part in the establishment of judicial, fiscal and administrative structures which remained operative in Persia down to the nineteenth century, and in the development of the socio-economic infrastructure, including secure communications. Perhaps his most important political initiative was the provision of funds for the foundation and running costs of madrasas in every major city, including the Nizamiyya at Baghdad (built 1065–7); in which education was free. His aim here was to train secretarial staff and 'ulama capable of countering Isma'ili propaganda; indeed to bring about 'a Sunni political, cultural and intellectual revival'.[2] Many teachers were Nizam's own appointees.

In his *Rules for Kings* (*Siyar al-muluk*; also known as *Book of Government: siyasat-nama*),[3] written in Persian just before his assassination in October 1092, Nizam described his strategy and wrote down his thoughts on the art of ruling. He covered the Mazalim court (chapter 3), tax-collectors (chapter 4), the iqta' (lit. fief) and peasantry (chapter 5), Judges and preachers (chapter 6), the army (chapters 23–4, 31–2) and the secret intelligence network ('to enquire into the condition of the peasantry and the army') (chapter 13). He described the ruler's role as to advance civilisation by 'constructing underground channels, digging main canals, building bridges across great waters, rehabilitating villages and farms, raising fortifications, building new towns ... ; he will have inns built on the highways and schools for those who seek knowledge' (*Rules*, p. 10). In other words, he must look after both the economic and the religious infrastructure. Nizam appears consciously to have applied the praxis of the Circle of Power.

These institutional developments were made possible through taxation and the development of the iqta' system. The iqta' was a grant of land and the taxes due from it, made by the Sultan to an individual in return for, especially, military service. Iqta' grants involved some delegation of government responsibility, including religious patronage and Redress of Grievances. But, in contrast to European feudalism, there was no mutual oath, the grants being non-hereditary, indeed revocable at any time, though in practice they often became hereditary.[4]

Nizam stressed the need to supervise tax-collectors and ensure the security of the persons and property of cultivators. Iqta'-holders (sing. muqta') must take only 'the due amount which has been assigned to them from the peasants in a good way, and when they have done so the peasants shall be secure in their persons; and their money, wives, children, goods and farms shall be secure, and the muqta's have no claim over them'. He upheld the prevalent view that the Ruler is the ultimate owner of all land: 'the country and the subjects (ra'iyyat) all belong to the Sultan' (in *CH Iran* 5: 234). *Rules for Kings* was a classic statement of benevolent despotism.

The Saljuk phenomenon revived the dialectic between tribe and state. The Saljuks themselves had recently been tribesmen, led by a dynastic clan which, in Saljuk tradition, was primarily 'the guardian of the tribal confederacy' (*CH Iran* 5: 218). Much of their territory, such as the Arab amirates and Kurdish and Turkmen tribal areas along the Northern and Eastern frontiers, was governed indirectly through tribal families and chiefs. For such people, the Sultan was not 'an autocratic sovereign' but 'a supreme tribal khan'. Nizam, on the other hand, was 'the supreme exponent of the Iranian tradition of order and hierarchy in the state' (*CH Iran* 5: 79) handed down from Sassanian Iran. Mahmud of Ghazna and 'Adud al-Daula were his ideal rulers. He was driven by the ideal of a strong patrimonial monarchy that cares for its people just as it is sustained by them. Nizam strongly recommended the king to consult 'wise elders, loyal supporters and ministers of state' on all important questions; 'when they all hear one another's words and opinions and discuss them the right course will stand out clearly' (*Rules*, p. 92).

Despite Nizam's attempts to control local power-holders (sing. amir: 'notable'), the Saljuk domains were 'a series of political groupings rather than a unitary state' (*CH Iran* 5: 78). Absolute power, even when well intentioned, went against the grain of society. *Rules for Kings* was 'in a sense a survey of what [Nizam] had failed to accomplish'.[5] Nizam and Malikshah were both assassinated in the same year, the former (but probably not the latter) by agents of the Nizari Isma'ilis. Nizam had by then become estranged from the Sultan and had been unable to arrange the succession. The fissiparous nature of the polity reasserted itself.

Nizam's conception of patrimonial monarchy was to a significant degree inspired by Islamic norms. So far from there being, as historians are inclined to say of European state formation, a 'tension' between spiritual and secular, here the Iranian was fused with the Islamic so completely as to be conceptually inseparable and mutually reinforcing. This had much to do with the character of Islam in which coercive force, in the right hands, was always regarded as intrinsically beneficial, and not to be apologised for. The Machiavellian critique of Christianity as weakening state power would not apply to Islam.

NIZAM'S POLITICAL THEORY

Rules for Kings opens with a statement of dawla: God transfers sovereignty from one people to another through his inscrutable knowledge of their merits. A vizier of the Ghaznavids is quoted (via the Persian historian Bayhaqi: 995–1077) as saying that they made up for their lack of ancestry because

> God, since the creation of Adam, has decreed that kingship be transferred from one People (umma) to another ... God's removal of the shirt of kingship from one group and his putting it on another group is ... divine wisdom and for the commonweal of mankind (in Mottahedeh 1980: 88–9)

In restating this view, Nizam applied it to *individual* rulers as well. 'In every age and time God chooses one member of the human race and, having endowed him with goodly and kingly virtues, entrusts him with the interests of the world and the well-being of his servants' (*Rules*, p. 19).

Then comes the Islamic master-theme: religious observance and political success go hand in hand. 'Whenever there occurs any disobedience or disregard of divine laws ... kingship disappears altogether, opposing swords are drawn, blood is shed, and whoever has the stronger hand does whatever he wishes' (*Rules*, p. 19). On this subject, Nizam was fatalistic: 'at any time the state may be overtaken by some celestial accident, or influenced by the evil eye. Then the government will change and pass from one house to another, or the country will be thrown into disorder through seditions and tumults' (*Rules*, p. 139), after which monarchy is restored by divine decree. Another proverb, however, says 'a kingdom may last while there is irreligion, but it will not endure when there is oppression' (*Rules*, p. 12): Nizam was clearly not greatly concerned with intellectual consistency.

Malikshah is presented as someone to whom God has given merits 'lacking in the princes of the world before him', including 'true belief ... respect for religious authority ... doing good to the poor' (11). Therefore he has 'made all the world subject to him' (11). The king is accountable to God alone, in such a way as to instil terror into the king's heart. 'On the day of the resurrection, when anyone is brought forward who wielded power over God's creatures, his hands will be bound; if he has been just, his justice will loose his hands and send him to paradise; but if he has been unjust, his injustice will cast him into hell' (*Rules*, pp. 11–12). Nizam himself was both 'a pious Muslim with Sufi leanings' (Glassen 1981: 73) and someone who knew how to get power, keep it and use it.

Nizam masterminded Saljuk religious policy and left his mark on the religio-political order. He supported, and encouraged the Sultan to support, Sunni orthodoxy and the 'Abbasid Caliphate. This would, in his view, both promote true religion and underpin the authority of the Saljuks. A Saljuk–'Abbasid alliance had already been formed when Toghril sought the Deputy's recognition for his conquest of Nishapur and eastern Iran, for which he was rewarded with the title 'the mighty Ruler (al-sultan al-mu'azzam)'. When Toghril arrived in Baghdad (1055), he was acclaimed by the reformist Deputy al-Qa'im as 'King of East and West'. Alp Arslan was given the titles 'Trusted Son', 'Strong Arm of the Destined Rule ('Adud al-Daula)' and 'Light of Religion' (in *CH Iran* 5: 55, 78, 279). Nizam cemented good relations with al-Qa'im through the marriage of two of his daughters to the son of the Deputy's vizier. When relations between Malikshah and the Caliph deteriorated (1080–5), Nizam took matters in hand, went to Baghdad in person, and attended the wedding of the Deputy to Malikshah's daughter.[6] Nizam was very unusual in combining the roles of religious reformer and political manager.

Behind the religio-political strategy of Nizam and the Saljuks was the repeatedly stated assumption that 'religion and government (din wa dawla: lit. 'the way of God' and the 'providential reign' of state authorities) are twins'. That is, they need and support one another, their fortunes are intertwined. We have seen how al-Mawardi worked out an interpretation of this relationship in terms of orthodox Sunni Jurisprudence, which subordinated the Sultan to the Deputy, at least in principle. A different view emerges in non-Juristic literature, and in practice. Thus Bayhaqi implied that both Deputy and Ruling Power derived their positions directly from God:

> The Lord most high has given one power to the prophets and another power to kings; and he has made it incumbent upon the people of the earth that they should submit themselves to the two powers and should acknowledge the true way laid down by God. (in Lewis 1988: 134)

Similarly, in his *Advice to Kings*, al-Ghazali would say:

> God has singled out two groups of men and given them preference over others: one prophets, and the other kings. Prophets He sent to His servants to lead them to Him, and kings to restrain them from [aggression against] each other; and in His wisdom he [delegated to kings] the well-being of the lives of His servants, and He gave [kings] a high status. (in Lambton 1980: IV: 105)

This was virtually the dualist position of many European advocates of the autonomy of royal secular power.

If al-Ghazali referred to the 'high status' of kings, the Saljuks themselves went a stage further; for them 'there was one Sultan just as there was one Caliph, and the Sultan was the supreme military and political head of Islam' (Lewis 1988: 52). This had tremendous implications, which became clear in the Ottoman state (devlet: dawla), when the Sultan claimed to be, and was widely recognised as, the military leader of Sunni Islam; and then – the final twist – claimed to be Deputy as well. Whereas in Europe the issue of religious and worldly power was an occasion for church–state conflict over the centuries, in Islam it was sheathed within rhetoric and mutual accommodation. It arose in quite different actual relationships between the powers in question. In practice it was the 'ulama, not the Deputy, who wielded religious authority in the name of the Prophet; and they were in symbiosis with the Sultan.

Justice was the point where religious and worldly interests were perceived to meet.[7] The Shari'a courts run by the Judges (sing. qadi) were an absolutely essential part of social order. Speaking of qadis, Nizam said: 'In every age ... in every transaction ... men have practised equity, given justice ... and where this has been so dynasties have endured for generations' (*Rules*, p. 42). Judges should be paid a salary by the state. The position of the chief qadi, who was appointed by the Sultan, demonstrated the interdependence between sultan and 'ulama. Nizam stressed the sultan's duty to promote Religious Knowledge ('ilm) and support the 'ulama through education and patronage. Nizam's madrasas obviously increased government influence over religious leaders. In Transoxania, where the 'ulama had in fact become the local notables, Malikshah supported their cause against the Qarakhanid regime (1089). The 'ulama subsequently became the dominant force at Bukhara under Saljuk suzerainty.

Nizam also sought to develop the system of 'secular' sultanic justice, urging the Sultan to hold Mazalim courts throughout his kingdom and frequently (*Rules*, chapters 3 and 33). The principle behind this was that subjects should be able to address their ruler directly; 'the King should give judgment in person and hear the words of opposing parties with his own ears' (*Rules*, p. 44). It had been 'the custom of the Persian kings to give special audiences for the common people' twice a week. Unlike religious courts, they could apply customary law, inflict harsher penalties than those of the Shari'a, and enforce their own judgements. If the King is not well acquainted with the Shari'a, he may employ qadis in Mazalim courts. They would then be acting as deputies (sing. na'ib) at once of the King and of the Caliph. They would be appointed and dismissed by the King.

Rules for Kings was the most incisive and widely used manual of statecraft ever produced in the Islamic world. It came to be studied in Iran and Saljuq Anatolia, while in India it became 'the bible of Muslim administrators' (Qureshi 1942: 19). It was one inspiration behind the statist tradition of the Ottomans.

THE MIDDLE WAY

While as a pious Community-Traditionalist Nizam might perhaps have been expected to support the Hanbalis and the Sunni commoners in Baghdad and other major cities, his politico-religious complex was in fact of a different stamp. He 'sought to mitigate stresses by recognising pluralism within the Sunna' (Glassen 1981: 83, 87, 175–7). One of his principal allies in religious doctrine and policy was al-Juwayni (Nishapur 1028–Nishapur 1085), a prominent 'Ash'ari whom the Saljuks expelled for a while from Nishapur for his pro-Mu'tazilite views, but subsequently (1063) rehabilitated (Nagel 1988: 286–90). He was also al-Ghazali's teacher.

Nizam adopted a non-partisan policy towards the four Law Schools. He did not persecute the Mu'tazila, nor, more remarkably the Imami Shi'ites. To Hanbali protests against a curriculum that accommodated different theological traditions, Nizam is reputed to have replied:

> the Sultan's policy and the dictates of justice require us not to incline to any one [Legal School] to the exclusion of others; we aim at strengthening orthodox belief and practice [al-sunan] rather than at fanning sectarian strife. We have built [the Nizamiyya] madrasa only for the protection of scholars and in the public interest and not to cause controversy and dissension. (in *CH Iran* 5: 73)

The Isma'ilis, on the other hand, were avowed enemies of the Saljuk state: a pro-Fatimid uprising in Iraq (1090–1) and the Nizari policy of assassination (see above, p. 47) led to severe retaliatory measures, which in turn prompted the killing of Nizam himself.

It has been suggested that Nizam and, later, al-Ghazali (also a Khurasani from Tus) pursued a 'middle way' between the dogmatic extremes of Shi'ism and Hanbalism (Glassen 1981). Saljuk religious policy as developed under Nizam does appear to have been relatively tolerant. This may have been inspired by Nizam's own Sufi piety, as well as by statecraft. Nizam appears not to have seen religious opinions in themselves as a reasonable target for persecution. And indeed one alternative to legal and theological conformism as a way of engaging the masses – and in al-Ghazali's profounder thought as a way of approaching God – was the Sufi path towards which Nizam himself inclined. Nizam regarded the Sufis as 'indispensable' because of their popular appeal (Glassen 1981: 73), and he promoted the foundation of Sufi lodges (khanaqas: see below, p. 128). Nizam's tolerant and statesmanlike approach to religious politics appears to have left its mark on later Sunni regimes, particularly the Ottoman.

NOTES

1. On what follows, see *CH Iran* 5; Hodgson (1974: vol. 2, pp. 46–57, 63–9); Cahen (1968); Morgan (1988: 25–50).
2. *EI* 8: 71a–2a; Makdisi (1981).
3. Trans. H. Darke, *The Book of Government of Nizam al-Mulk*, 2nd edn (London: Routledge & Kegan Paul, 1978). See *EI* 7: 987b; *CH Iran* 5: 210–17; Fouchécour (1986: 381–9); Glassen (1981: 121–7).
4. *EI* s.v. Ikta'; Claude Cahen, 'L'évolution de l'iqta' du IXe au XIIIe siècle', *Annales, Économies – Sociétés – Civilisations* 8 (1953), pp. 25–52, repr. in Cahen (1977: 231–69).
5. Ed. Bosworth (1971).
6. George Makdisi, 'Les rapports entre Calife et Sultan à l'époque Saljuqide', *IJMES* 6 (1975), pp. 228–36 at p. 231.
7. 'Law was the point where life and logic met', Maitland said of medieval Europe.

Al-Ghazali's Balance

9

Abu-Hamid Muhammad al-Ghazali (Tus 1058–Tus 1111; Algazel) participated in religio-political life during Nizam's last years and became a pivotal figure thereafter. He defined the religious philosophy of Islam in a personal yet magisterial way that was deeply embedded in the needs of the time.[1]

After the early death of his father, al-Ghazali studied Shafi'i Jurisprudence at Nishapur (1080–5) under al-Juwayni. His exceptional ability attracted the attention of Nizam al-Mulk, who summoned him to Baghdad to teach at the Nizamiyya madrasa (1091). Here al-Ghazali found himself at the centre of the religio-political establishment, designated to play a part in the vindication of Sunni orthodoxy. The Nizari campaign of assassination (above, p. 47) was at its height; the following year it claimed the life of Nizam. One of al-Ghazali's first works was a defence of 'Abbasid against Fatimid claims, written (1094–5) at the request of the Deputy al-Mustazhir.

But in 1095 al-Ghazali suffered a physical and mental breakdown, associated (it is thought) with a crisis in his mental life; a 'phase of scepticism' seems to have stimulated him to reconsider his whole position and way of life.[2] He resigned his teaching post to his brother (a well-known Sufi), and disappeared into the Syrian desert. It is uncertain what part political circumstances – the Nizaris' assassination campaign against prominent Sunnis and the execution of his uncle and patron by the Sultan (1095) – played in this. It appears that al-Ghazali had turned away from formal academic life and involvement in the networks of power. In his autobiographical *Deliverance from Error* (written 1109–11), he explained:

> I turned to the way of the mystics ... I realised that what is most distinctive of [their principles] can be attained only by personal experience ['taste' – dhawq], ecstasy and a change of character ... I saw clearly that the mystics were men not of words but of personal experience, and that I had gone as far as I could by way of study and intellectual effort, so that only personal experience and walking in the mystic way were left. (in Watt 1963: 135)

He had come to feel that his teaching had been 'concerned with branches of knowledge which were unimportant and worthless'; he wanted to reject 'wealth and position' (in Watt 1963: 136).

Al-Ghazali had not in fact rejected Learning and Jurisprudence; rather, he sought to reinvigorate them. It was now (1096–1105) that he wrote his major work, *Revival of the Knowledge of the Religious Sciences* (Ihya' 'ulum al-din),[3] an encyclopaedic attempt to organise and re-examine the whole domain of Religious Knowledge, comparable with Thomas Aquinas' *Summa Theologiae* written nearly two centuries later. It was intended as a manual of the contemplative life and of social morality, covering, like the Shari'a itself, law, economics and politics. The focus was moral rather than speculative. To reach a wider audience, abridged versions were written by al-Ghazali in Persian, and by his brother in Arabic.

It was about the time of his departure from Baghdad that he wrote *The Incoherence* (or *Auto-destruction*) *of the Philosophers* (*Tahafat al-falasifa*: c.1095), a reassessment of the relationship between Islam and Philosophy. Al-Ghazali argued that reason cannot establish its own premises, and is therefore inferior to intuitive knowledge (gnosis). Once a premise has been established, however, syllogistic reasoning can be used. Falsafa and kalam are subordinate to revelation, providing explanations and apologetics (Leaman 1985: 78–85).

Eventually (1105), al-Ghazali was asked by the vizier of Khurasan (one of Nizam al-Mulk's sons) to return to public life. He began teaching at Nishapur. He dedicated a short *Counsel to Kings* to the new Saljuk Sultan, thus maintaining some connection with government and the public role of religion.[4] He finally retired (1109) to his home town of Tus, where he lived as a Sufi with a group of disciples.

RELIGIOUS KNOWLEDGE ('ILM) AND POLITICS

This was an astounding moment in intellectual history. The man chosen by the greatest power in Eurasia to champion its orthodoxy admitted the spiritual inadequacy of his own enterprise. Al-Ghazali believed Jurisprudence and theology to be incapable of inspiring true religion. He sought to 'revive' what he had been called upon to expound. He may have sensed the need for something more to carry conviction in the hearts of the masses. He chose a way that would take him deeper inside himself, and also closer to the pious masses in whose name the whole enterprise was undertaken. So, at the same time as he was writing the *Revival*, al-Ghazali turned to personal intuitive knowledge (ma'rifa) and the Sufi way. In the *Revival*, as his critique of the 'ulama's cooperation with political authorities shows, he was more concerned with getting religion right, with the Shari'a properly speaking, than with shoring up the emerging Sunni establishment.

For the Sufis, religion consists in the mystical knowledge of God through personal asceticism and intuition in a way that – typically for Islam – was accessible to the average person. They established networks of 'affiliated colleges and convents' across society and in all parts of Islam (Gibb 1962: 29).

To understand the political stance of al-Ghazali and of those who came to be influenced by him, one must uncover the link between the Sufi way and al-Ghazali's theory of knowledge, namely ma'rifa (gnosis): intuitive ecstatic knowledge, silent knowledge which does not know what it knows. Mystical awareness illuminates the soul and unites it with God, who is not however a mere object of knowledge. Upon this, al-Ghazali built his understanding of life. 'Knowledge ('ilm)' and 'intelligence ('aql)' remain the supreme religious values and pathways to the divine; the Reports say 'through his intellect, man becomes God's deputy'.[5] Knowing is the supreme religious act, 'the basis for happiness in this world and the next' (Revival 1, p. 26); it has priority over worship, prayer, legal observance and good works (as Aquinas also said). But the knowledge al-Ghazali had in mind here was the direct knowledge acquired by spiritual experience. In discussing the relative merits of engagement in the world and withdrawal from it, al-Ghazali argued that one could only understand the world by experiencing it. Knowledge is attained through 'taste (dhawq)'; it is personal experience which conveys absolute certainty.

> True knowledge is that in which the thing known reveals itself completely in such a way that no doubt remains about it and no error can tarnish it. It is a state in which the heart cannot admit or even imagine doubt. All knowledge which does not achieve this state of certainty is incomplete knowledge, subject to error. (in Corbin 1964: 254)

This cannot be communicated in words. Perhaps al-Ghazali's experience of religious doubt drove him to base his religion on something that was unassailably certain. By this means, we know the essence of things, independently of our perception of them through the senses as material objects, because the thinking soul receives 'the intelligible forms' directly from 'the universal soul' (in Corbin 1964: 254). Al-Ghazali held that we know right and wrong only by divine revelation, and also that things are right or wrong because God has willed it so.[6]

And true knowledge is knowledge which issues in action. Al-Ghazali insisted on the integration of knowing and doing, and of both with inner goodness. He attacked those 'ulama ('knowledgeable men') and Report-collectors who pursued knowledge without practising what they preached; they delude themselves. He also attacked those who put into practice their Religious Knowledge, but whose heart was not in it. In particular, he attacked envy, desire for power, hypocrisy and pride. (One can see why he found academic life unsatisfying.)

Al-Ghazali distinguished three radically different levels of knowledge, and three different sorts of human beings, depending on the knowledge of which they are capable. (1) True inner knowledge through personal experience is accessible only to the very few who have a 'natural gift' of 'penetrating intelligence and strong insight'. They pass this true inner knowledge on to others, but these others are still a select few. (2) Discursive reasoning is what Philosophers, Jurists and theologians are capable of; they sometimes use it to stir up trouble and disunity (Qur'an 3: 7). (3) The common people, absorbed by crafts and daily work, are capable only of faith (iman) or taqlid (following the authority of others); they should avoid all controversy.[7] Yet al-Ghazali condemned the taqlid advocated by the Hanbali Legalists and the Report folk, and the Shi'ite idea of knowledge as what is learned from the authoritative instruction (ta'lim) of a Leader. Only the Qur'an and Muhammad have that kind of authority. The distinction between this and the 'faith' which al-Ghazali accepted is, however, not clear.

Such an analysis of knowledge and of the radically unequal mental capacities of humans contained penetrating insights and had a certain realism. But it is a somewhat surpising view to find in an Abrahamic monotheist.

Al-Ghazali's adoption of ma'rifa as the basis of religious knowledge gave pure revelationism (or fundamentalism as one might as well call it) a kind of philosophical authority. For it validated the absolute distinction between religion and all other forms of knowledge, and the incomparable superiority of religious knowledge over all the others.[8] It meant that the attempt to ground knowledge on *a priori* reason or empirical evidence was more suspect than ever. (It was, perhaps, a further victory for Plato over Aristotle.)

Now religious knowledge is the sole basis of political knowledge. In al-Ghazali, the circle of power became a circle of knowledge: 'government educates the labourers; the prophets educate the 'ulama ... ; the 'ulama educate the rulers; and the angels educate the prophets' (in Othman 1960: 195).

> Be assured of this, O Sultan, that justice springs from perfection of the intellect and that perfection of the intellect means that you see things as they [really] are, and perceive the facts of their inner reality without being deceived by their outward appearance. (*Counsel*, p. 24)

But spiritual and physical knowledge, like mental and bodily activity, are intertwined: in order to understand mental discipline, we have to understand physical health. Plato has been made truly Islamic.

As usual in Islam, the religious and the worldly are interdependent. Al-Ghazali insisted that true Islam – and it alone – teaches a *middle way* between materialism and asceticism.

> This school does not teach the complete abandonment of 'this world' nor the eradication of appetites. The follower takes from 'this world' what is sufficient for provision. He suppresses those appetites that violate the law (shar') and reason.

The companions of the prophet 'did not take the world for its own sake but for the sake of religion. They did not ... renounce the present world; in their mode of living they did not go to extremes ... their mode of life struck a balance' (*Revival*, book 26, p. 213). Religion has priority over the world. Thus the traditional saying that religion and the world (or the state) are twins becomes 'religion (din) and kingship (mulk) are inseparable twins: religion is the root, power the protector'.[9] But the world (dunya) is important: it is the field where we sow the seed of the next life.

Again, al-Ghazali developed the theme of the interdependence of religion and government: 'no order exists in [the spiritual world] without existing in the material world' (*Revival* 1, p. 27). If religion is to flourish, this world must be properly organised so as to maximise the opportunities for paradise.

Religion is based upon socio-political order, knowledge (ma'rifa) of God, and the service (ibada) of God. The purpose of political society is to enable people to attain happiness in the next world. Social order is a fundamental value because without it we cannot serve God.

Legal understanding (fiqh) keeps its position as regulator of the infra-structure of society: 'the [making] of laws which regulate justice among people as well as guide them in their conduct (siyasa) is vested in the Jurists [sing. faqih]. The conditions for good health are the function of the physician' (in Othman 1960: 113–14). Fiqh is the norm of government (qanun al-siyasa); for the jurist 'acts as master (mu'allim) and director of conscience to sultan (political power), to administer and discipline men so that order and justice may rule in this world'.[10]

THE ORIGIN AND JUSTIFICATION OF THE STATE

But worldly order requires the satisfaction of basic human needs. This requires a social structure based on a division of labour between the necessary occu-pations, notably 'agriculture for raising foodstuffs, weaving for manufacturing clothes, architecture for building houses' (*Revival* 1, p. 27). Such basic occupations 'require tools and machines'; consequently 'the need for new craftsmen arises: [such as] carpenters, smiths and tanners, who are the makers of tools' (*Revival* 26, p. 202). Such essential occupations are (in the language of Islamic law) collective duties (fard kifaya) – tasks not everyone is obliged to perform but someone must. There is a remarkable interplay here between fiqh and Iranian (and to some extent Greek) social thought. Socially useful econo-mic callings, including commerce, provided they are carried out with equity and compassion, are given the status of jihad (Holy Striving). This is because they enable people to provide for their families and are necessary for society as a whole. Social organisation is also necessary because some are unable to earn a living due to sickness or old age.

Procreation, the education of children, and economic cooperation, all indicate that 'human beings were created [in such a way] that they may not live alone but are forced to flock together with others of their kind'. 'For the sake of fellowship and the exchange of knowledge, men have aggregated together and become bound to one another. They built cities and countries ... They laid down market places, inns ... ' (in Othman 1960: 194). Among human relationships, al-Ghazali valued spiritual brotherhood extremely highly; it is 'on the same footing as kinship', 'like the contract of marriage'. In its highest form, one puts one's brother before oneself.[11]

But 'whenever people live in houses and cities and carry out transactions between one another, frictions are bound to occur'. There are several reasons for this. (1) 'In the nature of man there is, besides love, hate, envy and competition. These qualities breed quarrelling and antagonisms' (in Othman 1960: 194–5). (2) 'Human association entails authoritative relationships', such as guardianships (wilayat), for example of husband over wife. And 'whenever authority is exercised over any rational human being it generates conflict'.

(3) 'Within the city conflict arises between the members in their business transactions for their respective needs. If they are left to themselves they will fight and extinguish one another' (*Revival* 26, p. 203). This is because, in the process of satisfying their basic needs, people sometimes 'forget themselves and their real objectives ... they eat to earn and earn to eat'. They may make wealth and power their aim (*Revival* 26, pp. 210–11).

The conflict caused by these factors in human nature means that, in additon to farming, weaving and building, a fourth activity and a fourth profession is also fundamental to human needs: siyasa (discipline/governance/government). As al-Ghazali puts it, the civil wars 'which occur at the death of sultans and imams' have to be restrained by a new ruling power obeyed by men (sultan muta'); otherwise people will starve and ignore God (Laoust 1970: 236–7). This function too is a 'collective duty'. Indeed, it is the highest profession because it unifies people and reforms society. Siyasa includes land-surveying, soldiering and adjudication. The inescapable need for these public tasks and professions arises from humans' proneness to conflict. This also makes taxation and bureaucracy necessary. So, at this stage of social development, one can see three broad social orders or categories among the people:

> first, the farmers, herdsmen and craftsmen; second, the soldiers ...; and, third, those who are the intermediary agents between these two classes in collecting taxes and allocating revenues. The last group are the governors, the tax collectors and their like. (*Revival* 26, p. 205)

This looks like some kind of restatement of Plato's three classes, but it is a rather original one because the economic producers, whom Plato put at the bottom of the social pile, are here given at least temporal primacy, and also a degree of logical primacy; and because the ruling class is conceived in purely instrumental terms – as the necessary means to social order – and not at all as philosophers.

Now enter commerce. This also acquires the status of a collective duty. Al-Ghazali's estimation of commerce reflected Islamic values and a greater awareness of the dynamics of political economy than that of the Greeks. 'All the wants of human beings are accommodated through [merchants] ... Every section in society requires all the rest; transportation of goods becomes essential, and merchants, whose function is this transportation, become necessary.' Merchants are unquestionably motivated by 'their desire to accumulate wealth' (though in fact they will probably lose it to a bandit or an unjust sultan). But such 'oversight and ignorance' on their part is one means by which God ensures 'the preservation of society and the welfare of mankind'. If it were not for 'the oversight and petty ambitions of men ... all the pious would perish' (*Revival* 26, p. 207). Al-Ghazali has introduced what looks like Adam Smith's 'unseen hand'. Al-Ghazali goes further. The economic interdependence of different regions makes (in Othman's words) 'the unity of mankind inevitable'; it is a means by which 'divine wisdom ... makes all peoples need one another' (in Othman 1960: 192). Here he seems to find a moral purpose in trade (which Hegel might have recognised).

Al-Ghazali rounded off his discourse on the division of labour by observing that every loaf of bread 'has been wrought by nearly 7, 000 kinds of "labourers", each one performing a fundamental job [in carrying out] the fundamental activities by which the welfare of mankind is accomplished' (in Othman 1960: 194). This was a telling development of the Iranian perception of political economy, and of the interdependence between the economy and government; it points the way to Ibn Khaldun. At the same time, the distinction between ranks is based not only on the division of labour but also (following Plato) on people's innate mental (epistomological) and, therefore, religious abilities – a surprising view for a Muslim. We have already encountered it in Shi'ism.

All this proved the necessity of government and law. Human quarrelsomeness makes necessary a ruling power (sultan); and a *single* monarch is needed to exercise constraint (shawka).

> If these various [governmental] functions were the responsibilities of many persons without any power to bind those persons together, order would disintegrate. Hence, a [king: malik] becomes indispensable. He should be a prince who commands obedience and who appoints for each office a person fitted for it. (*Revival* 26, p. 205)

Al-Ghazali distinguished four types of governance (siyasa): (1) Prophetic, (2) that of Deputies, Kings and Sultans, (3) that of of the learned ('ulama), (4) that of popular preachers. The first rules over the *internal* (batin) and *external* (zahir) lives of both elite (al-khassa) and common people (al-'amma); the second rules over the *external* lives of both these groups; the third over the *internal* lives of the elite; and the fourth over the *internal* lives of the masses. These are complementary and coexisting, not alternative or opposed, forms of governance. The noblest is the Prophetic, followed by the siyasa relating to knowledge and people's souls: namely, authoritative ta'lim. Types (2), (3) and (4) all share in this. It includes encouraging the good and forbidding the bad (hisba) by both persuasion and coercion. Such authority is essential to political order.[12] Thus religion and political authority once again cement one another. Consent is achieved through a shared understanding, albeit at different levels, of religious goals and duties. The Sultan must seek advice from devout 'ulama and mystics; Sufis and 'true souls' capable of ma'rifa have a part to play in the state.

CALIPH AND SULTAN

On the constitution of the Caliphate, al-Ghazali said that that the Deputy should be 'elected', even if only by a single person (rather than appointed by his predecessor), provided that person commanded military force and obedience. Election was to be followed by the contractual allegiance (bay'a) of the notables, those 'who loose and bind'. 'In concrete terms' (Lambton reminds us), '[this] meant the sultan, whose appointment of the Leader would then be recognised by the Saljuk Kings and Commanders and the chief officials of the bureaucracy, and would then, finally, be approved by the 'ulama. The constitutive process was thus a shar'i process but the constituent power was the sultan'. And indeed al-Ghazali concluded that the Deputy is he 'to whom the holder of military power professes his allegiance' (in Lambton 1981: 114, 117). Defending the young al-Mustazhir against the Shi'ites, al-Ghazali applied the Sunni argument that, while the Deputy must be sound in body and mind, he does not need to be infallible or an outstanding expert (mujtahid); rather, he can, and should, consult others more learned than himself – which is what the present Caliph does.

Regarding the relationship between the Deputy and other rulers, al-Ghazali recognised the status quo and defended it on grounds of public utility (maslaha), without recourse to the artifices of al-Mawardi. Public socio-political functions (wilaya), including the maintenance of order and Islamic justice, are formally bestowed by the Deputy, but nowadays, al-Ghazali acknowledged, 'the wilaya ... is a consequence solely of military power (shawka)'. The only condition is that the ruler show 'allegiance to the Deputy by mentioning his name in the Friday prayers and on the coinage'.[13]

For all practical purposes, even an unjust Sultan must be obeyed unconditionally. The principal reason for this is prudential, and also in line with Community-Traditional teaching, that anything (short of abandoning Islam) is preferable to civil war. In principle, a bad Sultan should indeed be deposed or obliged to resign; but

> an evil-doing and barbarous sultan, so long as he is supported by military force (shawka), so that he can only with difficulty be deposed, and that the attempt to depose him would create unendurable civil strife, must of necessity be left in possession, and obedience must be rendered to him.

The reasoning behind this was that, if power-holders were declared illegitimate, the entire edifice of public Islamic functions and social order would come tumbling down (in Lambton 1981: 116). So long as the de facto ruler ensures the conduct of Friday prayers and recognises the Deputy, who in turn underwrites the validity of contracts and legal punishments, he must not be opposed. (This resembles the Roman Catholic view that even a sinful priest may perform the sacraments; the argument in both instances being based upon the need for the stable conduct of the relevant functions.) On the other hand, hisba played a central role in al-Ghazali's view of religious life, and it may be exercised even against rulers. Only if hisba requires the use of collective force is sultanic authority required.

There are in effect no constitutional restraints upon the Sultan; the ability to exercise military control remained the overwhelming criterion of valid political authority. Al-Ghazali's whole argument here was based upon the fundamental moral and legal principle of public utility.

THE 'ULAMA

The 'ulama are 'the heirs of the Prophet'. Religious experts (sing. faqih), officials and students should, like soldiers, secretaries and administrators, be paid out of public funds. There should be a faqih in every tribe, village and city district. The 'ulama should regard the enactment of the prophetic Message as a missionary duty. This shows al-Ghazali's concern to counter the underground missionary activity of the Isma'ilis.

On some points, al-Ghazali did pursue his own religious agenda, giving first place to Right regardless of the interests of the state (or the Saljuk regime). This came out in his fierce attack on those 'ulama whose religion was based on the dictates of government; they 'deceive the ordinary people' with debating points and cheap rhetoric. Because of these, 'the science of the road of the world-to-come … [has] become rejected among men and completely forgotten' (in Watt 1963: 112).

The jostling of pro- and anti-establishment attitudes comes out most clearly in *Revival* book 14. Here he sought to confront the realities facing religious people. He discussed in detail whether one may accept gifts, patronage and money from 'the rulers of our time', concluding that this was reprehensible but not forbidden. His argument ran as follows. If one accepts gifts, one is expected to flatter in return, overlook injustices, give service and loyalty to the donor. One 'does not become a public sinner by the sole fact of accepting [such gifts]: but only if one puts oneself at the service of the prince … ; that is, if, most of the time, one does what is necessary in order to obtain the money' (p. 213). A further reason for not accepting gifts from rulers, he said, is that nowadays, in stark contrast to the time of the first four Caliphs, nearly all rulers' income comes from immoral sources. For the same reasons, it is preferable not to associate with unjust rulers; it is like visiting a house which has been stolen from someone else. 'Keep your distance, you don't see them, they don't see you'. The assumption seems to be that most present-day rulers are unjust.

Further still – and revealing the burning sense of religious Right behind al-Ghazali's political thought – he says it is *forbidden* to have dealings with religious Judges and functionaries appointed by such rulers; for they are paid with tainted money. The main reason for al-Ghazali's indignation was that such 'ulama deceive the masses in matters of religion. 'They look like men of Knowledge while … taking princes' money'; and yet people look to them as their model. 'In general, subjects are corrupted to the same extent as kings, and kings to the same extent as the 'ulama' (*Revival* 14, p. 247). Such a passage tells us much about al-Ghazali's attitude after 1095. To recommend a boycott of state-appointed Judges was a challenge to the ruler's power and to the existing social order.

It seems probable that al-Ghazali's religious beliefs went side by side with the desire to create a stable and strong Sunni establishment in the face of Shi'ism. But his views about the state and its relationship to Islam were the more convincing because they were obviously the result of personal striving and not mere ideology. The creation of a sound Sunni establishment required the integration of a regime based on military force (shawka) with the regime of pious wisdom (the 'ilm of the 'ulama); so too did Sunni principle.

THE BOOK AND THE BALANCE

Al-Ghazali frequently invoked the concept of the middle way, or balance, to define what is Right. The concept of balance (mizan: lit. weighing machine) came from Qur'an 57:25: 'We sent Our Messengers with the clear signs, and We sent down with them the Book and the Balance so that men might uphold justice. And We sent down iron, wherein is great might ... so that God might know who helps him, and his messengers, in the unseen'. Al-Ghazali quoted this in his treatise against the Shi'a, explaining that 'the scripture is for the common people, the balance for the elite'; and the iron for fomenters of discord, that is intelligent men who blindly follow partisan opinions (the Shi'a). Al-Ghazali called the Qur'an itself 'the Just Balance' because it reveals the 'rules' (mawazin, plural of mizan: balance) of thought through which we are able to attain truth.[14] Similarly, in his discussion of the respective merits of involvement and withdrawal from the world, the prophets' companions 'struck a balance' in their mode of life (*Revival* 26, p. 213).

Al-Ghazali called his treatise on ethics (mu'amala: moral relations between persons) *Mizan al-A'mal* (*The Balance of Actions*).[15] Here he discussed the traditional Hellenic virtues – wisdom, courage, temperance, justice – and he used wasat (just balance) to define justice between persons, that is giving and taking one's due.

In his *Counsel for Kings*, on the other hand, al-Ghazali presented a more straightforwardly Islamic view of justice. He summarised justice as to 'treat people in a way in which, if you were a subject and another were sultan, you would deem right that you yourself be treated' (p. 13) – a proto-Rawlsian view. Injustices towards fellow humans are less easily pardonable than those against God. In *Balance of Actions*, justice in government (siyasa), that is in relation to society as a whole, is said to consist in a praiseworthy or satisfying *harmonious relationship* between the King (malik) (who is served but does not serve), the army (which both serves and is served), and the people (re'aya) (who serve but are not served). It is the same harmony (tartib) as that found in the human organism and in the cosmos. As in Plato, justice is defined as not 'a part of the virtues but rather all of them together'. The implication seems to be (in Laoust's words) 'that good and bad qualities have been defined by the revealed law, and that the best way always lies in the middle way and in the spirit of proportion' (*Counsel*, p. 73). The influence of Greece, therefore, did penetrate into al-Ghazali's moral thought.

Al-Ghazali came to be regarded as 'not only the mujaddid (renewer) of his century, but as the great restorer of the faith'.[16] He combined concern for spiritual authenticity and concern for political order to an unusual degree. His social and political thought were more systematic and comprehensive than anything in Europe, where Plato and Aristotle were little known, though Roman law was being revived. Al-Ghazali played a pivotal role in Muslim thought, for Sunnis at least, because he downgraded Philosophy, and with it all non-revealed apprehensions of reality, on grounds that could carry genuine intellectual conviction – a post-modernist no doubt. His importance may be compared with that of Thomas Aquinas in European thought, though the philosophical effect was the exact opposite. By offering a new solution to the problem of knowledge, in which he answered the Isma'ili and the falasifa with his own doctrine of personal enlightenment, al-Ghazali may have done more to enhance the long-term prospects for a stable Sunni order than could have been achieved by religio-political strategy alone. Yet he did so by building in radical inequalities between the religious capabilities of different types of person. It is utterly remarkable that he endorsed a Platonic view of justice and of social status; and that these became embedded in Shari' orthodoxy.

NOTES

1. Laoust (1970) (a first-class study); Othman (1960); Lambton (1981: 107–28); Glassen (1981: 64–79, 131–5, 148–51, 156–67, 170–9); Watt (1963).
2. *EI* 2: 1039a; Watt (1963: 141–2); McCarthy (below, n. 3), *Freedom*, pp. xxxvi–xvi.
3. His works on politics are (1) *Revival*, of which parts are translated: book 1 as *The Book of Knowledge*, trans. N. A. Faris (Lahore: M. Ashraf, 1962); book 2, part 2 as *On the Duties of Brotherhood*, trans. M. Holland (London: Latimer, 1975); book 14 as Al-Ghazali, *Ihya: le livre du licite et de l'illicite*, trans. R. Morelon (Paris: Vrin, 1981); book 26 in Othman (1960: 199–213); and see G.-H. Bousquet, *Ghazali, Ihya ...: Analyse et index* (Paris: M. Besson, 1955). (2) *al-Mustazhiri*, trans. Victor Chelhot, 'al-Qistas al-Mustaqim', *Bulletin des Études Orientales* 15 (1955–7), pp. 20–52. (3) *Mizan al-A'mal* (*Criterion of Action*), trans. H. Hachem, *Al-Ghazali, Critère d'action* (Paris: Maisonneuve, 1945). (4) R. J. McCarthy, *Freedom and Fulfilment: an annotated translation of al-Ghazali's al-Mundiqh min al-Dalal and other relevant works* (Boston MA: Twayne, 1980).
4. *Counsel for Kings* (*Nasihat al-Muluk*), trans. F. R. C. Bagley (London: Oxford University Press, 1964). Only the first part is by al-Ghazali: Patricia Crone, 'Did al-Ghazali write a Mirror for Princes?', *JSAI* 10 (1987), pp. 167–91.
5. *Mizan* (see n. 3 above), p. 98.
6. Leaman (1985: 130–8); Othman (1960: 64–5).
7. *Revival*, book 1, pp. 231–5; *al-Mustanzhiri*, p. 75; Watt (1963: 164–5); Laoust (1970: 160).
8. Leaman (1985: 78–85); Othman (1960: 52–3).
9. *Revival*, book 1, ch. 16, in Laoust (1970: 197, 237).
10. Ibid., p. 197. 'The exercise of power implies constant recourse ... to the outstanding legal expert (mujtahid)': in Laoust (1970: 196).
11 *Revival*, book 2, part 2: *On Brotherhood*, pp. 21, 63.
12. *Revival*, book 1, p. 28; *Mizan*, p. 97; Laoust (1970: 193–4, 205, 378).
13. In Lambton (1981: 117); *Revival*, book 14, pp. 209–11; Laoust (1970: 127).
14. *Mizan* (see n. 3 above), pp. 12–13.
15. He also wrote a book called 'The golden mean in belief (al-Iqtisad fi'l-tiqal)': *EI* 2: 1040b; Laoust (1970: 86–90).
16. D. B. Macdonald in *Shorter Encyclopaedia of Islam* (Leiden: Brill, 1991), p. 112.

The Ethics of Power: Advice-to-Kings (nasihat al-muluk) 10

During the period c.1100 to 1220, between the Saljuk hegemony and the Mongol invasions, when the 'new Sunni internationalism' (Hodgson 1974: vol. 2, p. 255) was at its peak, political thought developed mainly in the more pragmatic Advice-to-Kings genre.[1] This reproduced and rounded off the ideology of the Sunni Sultanate. It disseminated Islamo-Iranian ideas to different parts of the world and to different peoples, and transmitted them from one dynasty to another. After the assassinations of Nizam al-Mulk and Malikshah (1092), the Saljuk empire began to disintegrate into regional chiefdoms. Branches of the Saljuks ruled Khurasan until 1157, Iraq and western Iran until 1194. Nevertheless, the political practice and ideology of the successor states demonstrated the solidity of the system conceived by al-Mawardi, Nizam and al-Ghazali.

THE RELIGIO-POLITICAL LEGACY OF THE SALJUKS

One vigorous successor state was the Saljuk sultanate of Rum (southern and eastern Asia Minor). Its ruler styled himself 'the Sultan of the land of Rum, of the Armenians, Franks and Syria', and adopted Iranian methods of government, using Nizam's *Book of Government* as a model. The Saljuks of Rum attracted scholars and Sufis from the east and were outstanding patrons of the arts. As ghazis (frontier-warriors), they took Holy War into central Anatolia, followed by waves of Turkish migrants. Christian communities, deprived of Byzantine leadership, dwindled, and agriculture gave way to nomadic pastoralism.[2]

In Syria and Palestine, minor Muslim rulers lost land to the Crusaders. But in the mid-twelfth century a new state was put together by Nur al-Din (r.1143–74), followed by Salah al-Din (r.1176–93: Saladin), founder of the Kurdish Ayyubid dynasty; they reunited Syria, drove the Franks into narrow enclaves and reconquered Jerusalem (1187). Nur al-Din achieved a triumph for Sunni Islam when he drove the Fatimids out of Egypt. From now on, Egypt became the dominant east-Mediterranean power and a focus for the expanding trade with the Italian city-states. Saladin, employing Turkish and Kurdish troops, cemented the relationship between Sultan and army. His civil servants came especially from the indigenous Coptic-speaking Christian community, which was well treated (*EI* 1: 796–807).

The first Saljuk empire left a lasting legacy. It established Community-Traditionalism as the political power in Islamdom from the Oxus to the Nile and beyond. The ability to impose order through coercive force based on military success was acknowledged as the basis of political legitimacy. Turks, who had long been militarily dominant, now became political masters as well. The Mamluks, Ottomans and Mughals – all dynasties of the Turco-Mongol genus – followed the same broad pattern of religious polity.[3]

The Saljuk phenomenon set the seal on Community-Traditionalism as the full partner of military-political power; from now on, Sunnism not only wielded social authority but was also integrated into political life. The moral and legal authority of the 'ulama was backed up by the coercive power of the Sultan – and vice versa. The religious establishment provided Judges, teachers and Muhtasibs (overseers of public morals); the Sultan's police (shurta) enforced their rulings.[4]

The Saljuks of Rum established a pro-active religious polity in Anatolia with Shari'a courts, madrasas, charitable foundations and funds for the free education of converts. Saladin founded madrasas in Syria and Egypt and encouraged the Sufi orders; and he abolished non-Shari'a taxes, which would have pleased al-Ghazali. The Ayyubids were devoted advocates of political Sunnism, and collaborated with the 'ulama. They followed Nizam al-Mulk's policy in giving equal recognition to the four Sunni Law Schools. Under Ghaznavid rule in the Punjab (1161–86) and the Sultanate of Delhi in the thirteenth and fourteenth centuries, 'Muslim political thought was largely based on the principles developed by Nizam al-Mulk, especially the close co-operation between the sultan and the ... 'ulama' (Ahmad 1962: 121).

This was replicated at the local level in the 'a'yan–amir system' (Hodgson 1974: vol. 2, pp. 46, 91–103), as power came to be shared between a local military leader (amir) and the 'ulama notables (a'yan). The 'ulama had social status and economic recources. Many amirs became more or less independent, their power resting partly on personal prestige. The tendency towards decentralisation gave renewed significance to the 'Abbasid Deputyship as 'the all-Muslim guarantor of every local authority' (Hodgson 1974: vol. 2, pp. 53, 131–3).

THE ADVICE GENRE: 'THE SEA OF PRECIOUS VIRTUE'

Royal documents under Sanjar (the last Great Saljuk, who ruled Khurasan from 1117 to 1157) expressed the Iranian concept of high monarchy. Sanjar, in imitation of the 'Abbasid Deputies, was 'the shadow of God upon earth'. At the same time, the Sultan was being conceived more and more in religious terms as an integral, and indeed pivotal, part of a Sunni order. A decree granting permission to teach in madrasas at Balkh reproduced the sentiments of Nizam and al-Ghazali.

> The foundation of the state (daulat) and the basis of dominion consist in the observation of the laws of God ... and in giving precedence to the raising of the banners of religion and the revivification of the signs and practices of the

Shari'a, and in respecting and honouring the sayyids [religious lords] and 'ulama, who are the heirs of the Prophet. (in *CH Iran* 5: 210)

The pre-eminence in Holy War was emphasised under Saladin and his successor al-'Adil: al-'Adil was 'the unifier of the word of belief, the subduer of the adorers of the idols ... killer of the unbelievers and polytheists, conqueror of the rebels and insubordinate'. He was 'the sword of the world and of religion, the Power (sultan) of Islam and of Muslims, the Lord (sayyid) of Kings and of noble Companions (salatin khalil)'. He was even called amir al-mu'minin (Commander of Believers), which was one of the Deputy's titles (letter to Pisa).[5]

The clearest instance of the application of Sunni ideas to politics is The *Sea of Precious Virtue* (*Bahr al-fava'id*, in Persian: 1159–62), which was written in Syria by a Sunni of the Shafi'i School.[6] Government should be conducted in accordance with the Shari'a. Kings must not take non-Shari'a taxes, they must dispense justice in open court and not, as some tell them, act on the principle 'rule as you please'. 'O amir, all the justice of kings is contained in one word: that in levying and dispensing, he respects the rights of each and acts according to the Shari'a' (in Fouchécour 1986: 294n.). 'Religion and the world are twins' is taken to mean that the 'ulama and the king must cooperate. The king should honour the 'ulama as heirs of the Prophet by consulting them regularly: even the kings of Rum and the Franks 'do whatever the monks command' (p. 215). The duties of kings and the rights of subjects consist in the protection of transport, punishment of crime, justice for the poor, promotion of prayer and Learning, and pursuit of Holy War. They have a special duty to promote the religious education of children (called 'children's rights').

The integration of religion and polity is tilted in favour of the 'ulama. The author supported some of his arguments by citing 'what the 'ulama have said' (rather than Reports and sayings of Persian kings). He quoted with approval the dictum that 'the worst kings are those who keep themselves distant from the 'ulama, and the worst 'ulama are those who seek closeness to kings' (p. 297). He was favourably disposed towards Sufis. On the whole, The *Sea of Precious Virtue* is closer to al-Ghazali than to Nizam al-Mulk.

The author even allowed rebellion against a king who commands bid'a or what is contrary to the Shari'a. He found a precedent for this in ancient Iran: 'when the Persians observed shamelessness ... in a king ... they would quickly depose him'.[7] Given that it was written in Syria, The *Sea of Precious Virtue* might have come to the attention of Nur al-Din, for whose policies of religious patronage the author expressed approval. He appears to have been influenced by the threatening proximity of the Christian world; the treatise begins with discussion of Holy War in its spiritual and physical aspects, and the ruler was told not to appoint Jews or Christians to office.

The Advice-to-Kings genre flourished now as never before or since, perhaps because it was such an important conduit of religious doctrine into ruling circles. Advice books were particularly useful in view of the rapid turnover of dynasties, passing on the tradition and experience of one regime to the next ('words of counsel are a legacy from the dead to the living').[8] The genre also taught social skills, personnel management, the art of conversation, how to deal with different categories of people, and often included discourses on friendship, polite culture (adab) and etiquette.

Advice Books contained Iranian and Greco-philosophical as well as Islamic material. Advice was proffered in a prudential and utilitarian spirit, but with regard to the other world as well as this one, as was typical in Islamic writing.[9] The burden of their teaching was certainly never un-Islamic; rather, Islamic ideas of justice and so on were depicted with a broad brush. There was nothing un-Islamic in the unscrupulous methods of government recommended, so long as the ruler's power was being used to support religion and Right.

Hence these were precisely not 'Mirrors for Princes' in the European sense;[10] the ideals to which the ruler was invited to conform were not those of Christianised Stoicism but of Islamo-Iranian Realpolitik. Their ethics were in part thoroughly worldly. Nor, on the other hand, were they 'Machiavellian'; their advice always combined morality with pragmatism, and political power was never a sufficient goal in itself. Here we find prudential ethics put into the context of monotheism and the doctrine of the resurrection of the dead: justice and virtue are advisable even if – just because – fortune is fickle and life short. Of course they were much concerned with a ruler's status and authority; after all, a secure and powerful Sultan was necessary for the defence of Islam, especially against the Crusades. Such Advice Books reaffirmed the values of the Sunni religious polity as they had developed under the Saljuks.

JUSTICE AND THE CIRCLE OF POWER

The Circle of Power was cited to emphasise the overriding duty of Sanjar's governors to practise justice.

> The foundation of kingship and the basis of rulership consist in making [the world] prosperous; and the world becomes prosperous only through justice and equity; and the justice and equity of a ruler are attainable only through efficient governors of good conduct and officials of praiseworthy beliefs and laudable ways of life, and only so does prosperity reach the people of the world.
>
> The stability of the empire (daulat) and the ordering of the affairs of the kingdom (mamlakat) are among the fruits of the spreading of justice and ... compassion. (CH Iran 5: 209–10)

One important aspect of this justice was seen as the maintenance of distinctions between status groups. 'Justice consists in ... keeping every one of the people of the world – the subjects (ra'aya), servants, officials and those charged with religious or worldly affairs – in their proper ranks and due stations' (CH Iran 5: 210). In a work influenced by Sufi ideas, Kai Kawus (1082–3, written in Tabaristan) rephrased the power circle:

> The king's survival depends on his forces and the prosperity of the countryside on the peasantry. Make it your constant endeavour to improve

cultivation and to govern well. For ... good government is secured by armed troops, armed troops are maintained with gold, gold is acquired through cultivation, and cultivation sustained through payment of what is due to the peasantry by just dealing and fairness. Be just and equitable, therefore.[11]

The vizier should take responsibility for the improvement of agriculture. Kai Kawus was especially concerned with the relationship between soldiers and peasantry, which was becoming a central topic in political thought as well as in real life. (This work circulated in five translations in the early Ottoman empire.)

Most Advice works written in Iran proclaimed the glories of kingship using a combination of Islamic and ancient Iranian languages and concepts. The king is said to be chosen by God to rule the world; to obey him is to obey God; the just king is God's shadow and, even if he is an Ethiopian black, Deputy. Thus the idea of the Sultan as Deputy (Caliph) was asserted. The mythology of kingship was enhanced by translations of the pseudo-Aristotelian *Letter to Alexander* into Persian; and there was a Persian version of the Alexander romance (*Sharaf-Nama*, c.1200).[12] The influence of pre-Islamic Iranian monarchical ideas was especially notable in a twelfth-century *Advice to Kings* written in Persian, which was once ascribed to al-Ghazali but was actually composed somewhat later by an unknown Sunni author.[13] This reintroduced the claim that a king possesses 'the divine effulgence' – 'a Persian concept of a manifestation of the sacred element of fire or light in the person of the rightful ruler, which had evidently endured from Sassanian times' (Bagley, p. xli). The Sassanian kings are held up as examples to Muslim rulers. Into this are thrown moral exhortations which, if taken seriously, would have led to the rule of law. The ruler must 'treat the unknown litigant ... and the well-known litigant of high worldly rank ... with complete impartiality'. Again, 'if a claim were lodged against the king by an influential person, the king should withdraw from the seat of sovereignty and submit the case to God's jurisdiction [a Religious Judge?] and then grant redress against himself'.[14]

'THE WISDOM OF ROYAL GLORY' AND TURKISH POLITICAL CULTURE

Perhaps significantly, the rule of law was most emphasised in a somewhat earlier work written in a Turkish tribal milieu, and in a recently Islamicised society as yet untouched by Saljuk religious policy. *Wisdom of Royal Glory* (*Kutadgu Bilig*: 1069, in Middle Turkish)[15] was distinctive in several ways. It was written by Yūsuf Khāṣṣ Ḥajib (in the form of a literary dialogue) in Transoxania under the rule of the Ilek-khans, a Turkish tribal confederation which had adopted Islam in the mid-tenth century; their ruler Ibrahim Tamghai Khan (c.1052–68) 'secured a leading place in the "Mirrors for Princes" and adab literature as the exemplar of a just and pious ruler' (*EI* 3: 1114b). They were soon to be ousted from Bukhara by 'ulama with Saljuk support, which may explain why this work was so little known.

Royal Glory too combined political morality and Irano-Islamic statecraft.

The both-worldly prudential element is obvious: for example, immortality is desirable if it brings lasting fame. But the main characteristic of this 'oldest monument of Islamo-Turkish literature' (p. 1) was that Turkish tribal ideas were expressed alongside Irano-Islamic ones. The author's aim was to show that the Turkish tradition of royalty and wisdom was comparable with, or superior to, the Arab or Iranian traditions, and equally suitable in an Islamic society ('the Turkish princes are the finest in the world').

Ḥajib was writing before Nizam al-Mulk, and there is little discussion of religion, though adherence to Islam is taken for granted. Referring to the need for prudence and pragmatism, he adapted the traditional saying to: 'the way of religion (din) and the way of the world (dunya) *diverge*' (p. 212). The 'ulama are there, but it is, rather, the *sage* who is 'the head of mankind', who, as partner to the king, 'grasps the pen and clears a beaten track' (p. 48).

Ḥajib's doctrine is unusual in the priority he gave to the rule of law, and not specifically the Shari'a. 'The kingdom stands on the law', 'The bond and lock of a land consists of two things: vigilance and law', 'By establishing just laws and applying them without partiality, a ruler can guard his rule for a long time', 'A kingdom is a good thing. But better is a toru (law), and it must be correctly applied.'[16] King 'Rising Sun' is made to say: 'It is on the basis of right alone that I decide a case, without regard to whether a man is a prince or a slave' (Ḥajib, p. 66). Some have seen this as an expression of pre-Islamic Turkish political ideas, much as Gierke on slender evidence saw similar ideas as inherently Germanic.[17] (Secular law (qanun) was to play a prominent role in the Ottoman empire.) The real issue was perhaps the sanctity of tribal law.

Kingship and fortune are linked to law and order because they enable one to rule for a long time and 'plant [one's] name firm and upright'. Political stability is based on (1) justice, (2) silver and (3) the sword: treasure, troops, a prosperous people, justice are all interdependent (the power circle again). So are the ruler and his people: virtue in the prince will make the people virtuous and prosperous.

The duties of a king are to 'keep the coinage pure ... give the people just laws and not allow them to do violence to one another ... [and] maintain the roads in security' (Ḥajib, p. 221). The duties of subjects are to obey, pay taxes and fight. The people must be kept well fed.[18] One may see in all this an attempt to bring together tribal and patrimonial-monarchical values.

One has the impression that the ruler is made somewhat more dependent than usual on the goodwill of his people, and therefore on their prosperity. Justice and prevention of oppression (that is, generally speaking, keeping royal administrators in check) will ensure an improved standard of living for all categories of commoners. (Ḥajib listed the status groups as the Learned, the Muhtasibs, royal servants and commoners; the last were divided in turn into poor, middling and wealthy.) 'If the poor are protected they will join the middle class; and if the middle class are left alone awhile, they will become wealthy. If your poor become middle class and your middle class become rich, all your realm will be full of wealth, the land will thrive and the people will be content' (pp. 220–1) – a Thatcherite sentiment. The king should cultivate good relations with farmers, for they are notable for being generous with what God has given, and with merchants, for they have a fine sense of profit and loss. The king's generosity will secure his reputation and ensure him a good name after death.

Such ethical ideals in the Advice-to-Kings literature were not developed or worked out in any detail; they were not integrated into the theory of kingship by divine right. European thought, similarly, is full of examples of how very different conclusions could be drawn from theocratic principles: only there the constitutionalist option was, over time, developed into a comprehensive praxis.

NOTES

1. Fouchécour (1986); *EI* s.v. Nasihat al-Muluk; Lambton (1980: V, VI); Richter (1932); Danishpazhouh (1988: 214–27); Marlow (1997: 128–39). As well as authors discussed below, see (1) al-Turtushi (Tortosa, Spain c.1060–Alexandria 1126), trans. T. Zachariae, 'Die Weisheitssprüche ...', *Vienna Oriental Journal* 28 (1914), pp. 182–210; Urvoy (1990: 90–3). (2) Zahiri of Samarqand (mid-twelfth century): Fouchécour (1986: 433–4). (3) Afzal al-Din Kermani (late twelfth century) and (4) Afzal al-Din Kasani (probably early thirteenth century): Fouchécour (1986: 433–5).
2. Cahen (1968); Speros Vryonis Jr, *The Decline of Medieval Hellenism in Asia Minor and the Process of Islamization from the 11th to the 15th centuries* (Berkeley CA: University of California Press, 1971).
3. 'The symbiosis which proved to be so fertile was that of Iranians and Turks': Cahen (1968: 369); Hodgson (1974: vol. 2, p. 399).
4. Cahen (1958–9: vol. 5, pp. 233–49).
5. S. M. Stern (ed.), *Documents from the Islamic Chanceries* (Oxford: Cassirer, 1965), pp. 19–23.
6. J. S. Meisami (ed. and trans.), *The Sea of Precious Virtue* (*Bahr al-Fava'id*): *A Medieval Islamic Mirror for Princes* (Salt Lake City: Utah University Press, 1991).
7. Ibid., p. 296. The idea of a right of resistance may conceivably be due to European influence.
8. Hajib (see below, n. 15), p. 48.
9. Also found in Pseudo-Aquinas, *Rule of Princes*, composed for the Frankish ruler of Cyprus in the late thirteenth century: ed. D'Entrèves (see above, p. 31, n. 15), pp. 37–41.
10. W. Berges, *Die Fürstenspiegl des hohen und späten Mittelalters* (Stuttgart: Hiersemann, 1938).
11. *Qabus Nama* (see below, p. 134, n. 4), p. 213 (adapted).
12. Danishpazhouh (1988: 214, 220); *EI* 4: 127b–8a.
13. Trans. Bagley (see above p. 107, n. 4); Fouchécour (1986: 396–412).
14. Bagley, p. 69. Compare the thirteenth-century English 'Bracton': Black (1992: 153).
15. Yūsuf Khāṣṣ Ḥajib, *Wisdom of Royal Glory* (*Kutadgu Bilig*): *A Turko-Islamic Mirror for Princes*, trans. R. Dankoff (Chicago: University of Chicago Press, 1983); Inalçik (1993).
16. In Inalçik (1993: 11–12).
17. Otto von Gierke, *Community in Historical Perspective*, ed. Antony Black (Cambridge: Cambridge University Press, 1990), pp. 4–5.
18. A pre-Islamic Turkish inscription says: 'I revived a people who had died, and nourished them. I clothed the naked, made the poor people rich and made the few people many' (Inalçik 1993: 14); the same sentiment was found in ancient Egypt and the New Testament.

Philosophy Goes West

11

In al-Andalus (Muslim Spain), there were similar developments in Sunnism. But the specific religio-political praxis associated with Nizam al-Mulk and the Saljuks did not develop, and the Iranian concept of patrimonial monarchy was absent.

A branch of the Umayyads had continued to rule Spain since early times. 'Abd al-Rahman V (r.912–61), a strong centralising ruler, declared himself Deputy (929); he campaigned in the Maghrib (north-west Africa) against the Fatimids. His successor, Al-Hakim II (r.961–76), was a patron of falsafa and science, and set up a library and university at Cordova, where Plato's *Republic* and *Laws* were studied. There was a revolt at Cordova (1031), the Caliphal dynasty was turned out, and al-Andalus disintegrated into separate regimes under local rulers (known as the 'Kings of the Parts': Muluk al-Tawa'if: Reyes de Taifas). Cordova and Seville became for a while self-governing quasi-republics. The Christians of the north, led by the kingdom of Castile, were making large territorial gains and captured Toledo (1086).[1]

In Spain, too, there were popular and intellectual movements in the later eleventh and twelfth centuries aimed at developing a more principled and effective Sunni religious polity. This programme was made more urgent by the Christian Reconquista. The first Community-Traditional reform movement, led by the Almoravid dynasty (al-Murabitun: lit. those who conduct Holy War in the correct Qur'anic manner), originated in Senegal. They formed a coalition of Berber tribes, then a delegation of 'ulama invited them to Spain, specifically in order to counter the Christians. The Almoravids halted the Reconquista and became masters of southern Spain (1106). They championed strict Sunni rectitude based on Jurisprudence and correct observance of the Religious Code, having affinities with Hanbali literalism. They tolerated neither falsafa nor Sufism, and al-Ghazali's works were publicly burned.

A generation later, the Almoravids themselves were overthrown by a Sunni reform movement of a different stamp, the Almohads (al-Muwahhidun: lit. devotees of divine unity). The Almohads emphasised morality and a straightforward theology rather than law; they were to preside over the great age of Spanish Muslim philosophy. Both these reformist regimes straddled the straits, drawing strength from Africa; the Almohads too had first dominated the tribal hinterland of the Maghrib, where they appointed as their leader Ibn Tumart (c.1080–c.1130), a Berber who had studied in Baghdad and conversed (it was said) with al-Ghazali. Anyway, he was an original religious thinker. Returning to North Africa (1117), he set about recreating the original People (umma) by close adherence to the example of Muhammad and his Companions. In 1145, the Almohads came to southern Spain which they conquered and ruled, with Seville as their capital, until 1224.

The Almohads believed that Ibn Tumart was the Mahdi (Awaited One) and that authority passed directly to such a person from the Prophet; they therefore repudiated the 'Abbasid Caliphate and declared their own chief as Deputy. In the early stages, the movement was led by a council of ten advised by tribal leaders. They were of the Shafi'i School and, while they were no less keen moral reformers, rejected the Almoravids' rigorous interpretation of the Shari'a. They gave scope to reasoning by analogy and to individual judgement in legal matters. They saw their mission as above all the proclamation of the 'unity (tawhid) of God', holding that God, since He is exclusively spiritual and abstract, must not be compared to any physical or human being; one must not interpret the Qur'an too literally. Ibn Tumart and his followers, influenced by al-Ghazali, supported the combination of legal rectitude with Sufism. Thus falsafa and science could be tolerated and even encouraged, as they especially were by Sultan Abu Ya'qub Yusuf (r.1163–84).

Thus military decline was accompanied by intellectual vitality. Ibn Hazm developed his textual authoritarianism (see above, p. 83) at the time of the fall of the Spanish Caliphate, and was critical of the city-state governments installed at Cordova and Seville. The first neo-Platonic Philosophers in Spain,[2] taking over a theme of earlier falsafa, focused their social thinking on the plight of the virtuous individual or true philosopher in an imperfect society (see above, p. 71). Ibn Bajja (Saragossa, late eleventh century–Fez, Morocco, 1139: Latin, Avempace),[3] a vizier under the Almoravids, who was imprisoned for alleged treachery and heresy before moving to Seville, could say with some authority that in imperfect states true philosophers live as 'weeds (nawabit)', a concept which came from Plato via al-Farabi. While philosophers must try to use their virtue to influence society and government (E. Rosenthal 1958: 161), in practice their intellectual journeying will make them internal exiles, estranged from society. Their main concern must be their own *self*-development. In *The Governance of the Solitary* (tadbir al-mutawahhid), Ibn Bajja said:

> The blessed ones, insofar as they can at all exist in these states, enjoy an isolated blessedness. For the just government is only the government of the isolated, be he one or be they more than one, whilst neither nation nor city-state are in agreement with their opinion … Though they live in their own countries and among their friends and neighbours, they are strangers in their opinions, they travel in their thoughts to other planes which are for them like homelands.[4]

With Ibn Bajja, intellectual solitude was raised to the level of doctrine. This was a spiritual vision, and it was not specifically Islamic.

Ibn Tufayl (southern Spain, early twelfth century–1185) took a similar view. He was court physician to the Almohad Sultan Abu Ya'qub Yusuf. In his philosophical novel *Hayy ibn Yaqzan* (*Alive, Son of Awake*), he recounted how 'an orphan child growing up in solitude finds means of realising man's highest development' (*EI* 1: 729a). (One wonders where Rousseau got his ideas from.)

IBN RUSHD (AVERROES): PHILOSOPHY AND RELIGIOUS KNOWLEDGE

Ibn Rushd (Cordova 1126–Marrakesh 1198: Latin, Averroes)[5] was one of the greatest Aristotelian philosophers of all time and one of the most original political minds in Islam. He came from a prominent family of 'ulama who had been active in politics. Cordova had shown unusual signs of European-style civic activity; it revolted against the Almoravids in 1121 when Ibn Rushd's grandfather led a successful delegation to get indemnity, and in 1145–6. This was partly in protest against the Almoravids' imposition of Ibn Rushd's father as Religious Judge.

Ibn Rushd himself supported the religious policy of the Almohads; he was Judge at Seville (1169 and 1179) and Cordova (1171), and Chief Judge at Cordova (1183). His early career was in law and medicine. His *Bidayah al-Mujtahid* (Urvoy 1991: 64) was a major work of Islamic Jurisprudence, and his even more celebrated medical encyclopaedia, *Kulliyat* (Latin: Colliget), was immensely influential in both the Arabic- and the Latin-speaking worlds. His late move into philosophy began through his friendship with Ibn Tufayl; this arose out of their shared interest in medicine. Sultan Abu Ya'qub Yusuf, to whom Ibn Rushd was introduced by Ibn Tufayl (c.1159), became his patron and protector, appointing him court physician in succession to Ibn Tufayl. This continued under Ya'qub al-Mansur (r.1184–99). But the renewal of war with the Christian states strengthened pressure from both public opinion and religious leaders for strict orthodoxy, and in 1195 Ibn Rushd was condemned for being a faylasuf, and therefore a heretic. He was banished to a Jewish settlement. When the Sultan's court moved to Marrakesh, Ibn Rushd moved with it for the last period of his life.

The short summer of philosophy in Almohad Spain was related to the regime's own beliefs. Ibn Tumart held that knowledge of God could be achieved by reason; it did not need to be based on mystical experience. Ibn Rushd's move into philosophy was in tune with the regime's theology; the sultan-Deputy himself declared: 'Would to God we could find someone willing to make a commentary upon the works [of Aristotle] and explain their meaning clearly, so as to render them accessible to men!' (in Urvoy 1991: 32).

His philosophy was based upon the Qur'anic esteem for knowledge ('ilm) and the Islamic tradition of Knowledge as the way to God. He argued that the Shari'a not only permits but obliges us to study and reflect on things with the intellect, by means of 'rational speculation ... whose method reaches perfection with demonstrative syllogism' (*EI* 3: 912a). Ibn Rushd defended the practice of falsafa against al-Ghazali in *The Incoherence of the Incoherence*. He affirmed, against al-Ghazali and others, that the discovery of *causes* is an intrinsic part of knowledge, that such causal explanation is valid, and that it underpins our knowledge of God himself, since he is 'the cause of the realisation of potential beings, in beings in actuality' (in Urvoy 1991: 87). Intuition and mysticism alone are not enough; al-Ghazali's reliance on personal experience as the starting point for knowledge of God leaves too much to prejudice and passion.

Ibn Rushd seems to have pursued an isolated quest demanding even greater courage than that of European philosophers. The place of philosophy in relation to Religious Knowledge was the central problem. On this, Ibn Rushd wrote *An Authoritative Treatise and Exposition of the Convergence which exists between the Religious Law and Philosophy* (LM 164–86). He saw no tension or contradiction such as experienced by European intellectuals; he was no 'Averroist' in the European sense. For Ibn Rushd solved the problem of faith and reason by distinguishing (like some of his Islamic predecessors in falsafa) between qualitatively different *methods* by which the *same* truths could be apprehended and transmitted: demonstration, dialectic and rhetoric. These were not only different but ranked: knowledge by demonstration is the best. It can be attained only by those of outstanding intellectual and morality, namely philosophers. Next came dialectic or rational explanation and advocacy of what is known. This is the domain of theology (in the Islamic sense: kalam); Ibn Rushd often criticised theologians (mutakallimun) for claiming to know more than they really did. Last came rhetoric and symbolism, the means by which knowledge is achieved by the masses, who must be content to accept others' interpretation (ta'wil) as authoritative, and therefore fall short of perfection.

But for Ibn Rushd all three methods teach the *same* truths: Religion (din) and Faith (milla) teach the same as philosophy; they differ only in the *means* by which they express themselves. Thus everyone can follow and be enlightened by the Shari'a, albeit in ways that are fairly fundamentally different. Religion is, therefore, absolutely necessary and obligatory precisely because it leads people 'towards wisdom in a way universal to all human beings' (in Leaman 1985: 177). Ibn Rushd exempted Jurists (fuqaha) from his criticisms (he was one himself), for the glory of the Shari'a is that it makes happiness available to *all*.

Yet only philosophy gives *complete* understanding of the divine truths and Religious Law. Human perfection is achievable only by going 'through all the stages of speculative science' (in Urvoy 1991: 57). Similarly, 'The human perfections are, in general, of four kinds: speculative, intellectual and ethical virtues, and practical conduct … All these perfections exist only for the sake of the speculative ones and as a preparation for them' (in Leaman 1985: 172). Thus Ibn Rushd, like many other Muslim intellectuals, differentiated between people on the basis of their intellectual abilities. This produced an epistemological theory of status groups, a Platonic rather than a Qur'anic view of human society.

It followed that philosophers with their superior mode of knowledge are the best qualified to interpret the Qur'an, the Sunna (Tradition) and the Religious Law. Aristotelian moral philosophy can and must be combined with the Shari'a; for the Law promotes justice and the other virtues defined and explained by Aristotle. Ibn Rushd rejected Shafi'i's view, long prevalent in Jurisprudence and widely established in Islamic discourse as a whole, that right and wrong are determined not by the nature of what they are but by divine command, so that they cannot be known by reason but only through the revealed divine law. He followed Aristotle in holding that 'good and evil, beneficial and harmful, beautiful and ugly are ... something that exists by nature not by convention' (in Leaman 1980: 172). He upheld Aristotle's application to moral thinking of a distinction between natural law, by which things are prescribed and forbidden because they are good or bad in themselves, and positive laws, by which things are prescribed and forbidden on the authority of a legislator. To understand Right, therefore, one must employ 'rational inference (qiyas 'aqli)' as well as analogy in the Jurisprudential sense (qiyas shar'i). It is indeed 'contrary to the law to forbid such an examination' (*EI* 3: 912a) by qualified persons. One must conclude, therefore, that the Deputy has a duty to protect philosophers and their writings.

Ibn Rushd's intellectual project was to elucidate and complete Aristotle's oeuvre. Aristotle was of supreme importance, first, because he relied exclusively on conceptual analysis and syllogistic demonstration: 'philosophy' meant the strict interpretation of Aristotle and adherence to his method shorn of neo-Platonic accretions. Second, Aristotle covered every aspect of what could be known. Ibn Rushd set out to realise his project in two ways. First, he sought by textual analysis to purge Aristotle's texts of neo-Platonic material. His achievements in this field are still admired by modern scholars; he was the first Muslim philosopher to recognise the importance of the differences between Plato and Aristotle. Second, like al-Farabi and Ibn Sina, he attempted to *complete* the Aristotelian oeuvre by adding knowledge gained in Islamic times. This especially concerned matters of law and social organisation. Ibn Rushd composed three different types of commentary on Aristotle, aimed at people's differing intellectual abilities: *Short Synopses*, written c.1160–70; *Intermediate Commentaries* written c.1168–77, in which he introduced some of his own opinions; and the *Great Commentaries* (1180–90). It was thus that he earned his reputation in Latin Europe as 'The Commentator'.

IBN RUSHD'S POLITICAL WRITINGS

Ibn Rushd dealt with government and politics in his 'intermediate' Commentary on Aristotle's *Nicomachaean Ethics* (1177, possibly dedicated to the Sultan; it survives only in a Latin translation, 1260),[6] and in an intermediate *Commentary on Plato's Republic*.[7] This was his last work (1194, probably addressed to Sultan al-Mansur; surviving in a Hebrew translation, c.1320). This was the only time he commented on Plato; and the reason he did so is worth noting.

Ibn Rushd thought that the *Ethics*, with its conceptual analysis of the virtues and moral character, comprised Aristotle's *theoretical* study of politics and legislation. For at the end of the *Ethics*, Aristotle did indeed discuss coercive law as one means by which most people achieve virtue, and by which social discipline is instilled; and Aristotle concluded by saying that this, therefore, was the prelude to the study of the polity. Ibn Rushd thought that here Aristotle was indicating a further work of his own, namely the *practical* study of politics and lawmaking; Ibn Rushd gave the title of this as *On Civil Government* (*De Regimine Civili*).[8] This would, he said, include 'practical character-formation (habitudo effectiva)'. But this book 'has not yet reached us in this island'. He hoped to find it; and if not, 'we will consider this matter according to the measure of our ability' (*On Ethics*, fol. 317v). That is, presumably, he would write something of his own to complete Aristotle's corpus on this subject. At the same time, Ibn Rushd noted that Plato's *Republic* dealt with 'how simple (types of) states are changed into one another'; but he thought that, from what Aristotle said, Plato's treatment was incomplete.

We may conclude that Ibn Rushd decided to write his *Commentary on Plato's Republic* after finally giving up hope of getting hold of Aristotle's own book on practical politics. The *Republic* is standing in for the lost politics of Aristotle.[9] This would explain why he deferred writing it for so long. It is an irony of intellectual history that Aquinas managed to get hold of Aristotle's *Politics* via Byzantium some sixty-five years later – at the very time when Ibn Rushd's *Commentary on the Ethics* was published in Latin.

The *Commentary on Plato's Republic* is in three parts: I and II are on the virtuous or ideal state, dealing respectively with the education of the young, and the philosopher-king; III is on non-virtuous states. Here, then, we have Ibn Rushd's promised discussion of the *practical* aspects of government. His intention was to elucidate Plato, show his relevance for an understanding of current events, and to interpret and restate Plato in the light of his own world. In fact, when he does deal with practical matters, Ibn Rushd's treatment is rather cursory. There is no remotely systematic or sustained discussion of actual events, just a few references, albeit important ones, to the politics of Ibn Rushd's time. But the work does contain a certain amount of what we would call political theory.

Ibn Rushd insisted, with Aristotle, that effective political action, by which he meant especially the ability to promote virtue through legislation, requires both theoretical and practical knowledge. As in all skills, one needs both knowledge of principles *and* experience (*experientia*). 'In music, medicine and the other active disciplines, a fine action is realised in two ways: it is discovered through cognitive science, and put into operation or proved through experience.' The masters in such fields are those who 'judge sensibly about what should be done on the basis of their experiences'.[10] Ibn Rushd in fact stressed the need for empirical experience a good deal more than Aristotle had, underscoring it by the analogy with medicine. 'Whichever of them is made the law-maker, he is appointed on account of his experience ... as happens in experimental medicine. Therefore it is necessary that those who wish to rule states should at least have experience' (*On Ethics*, fol. 317r). Although one undoubtedly does need the theoretical knowledge of general principles ('universals') that is contained in the *Ethics*, in practical arts, such as medicine and legislation, theoretical knowledge on its own is strictly useless, since the purpose 'is nothing other than action' (*On Republic*, p. 4). 'Hence it is said that the governance of cities is appropriate for the old, in whom knowledge of the theoretical sciences is combined with long experience' (p. 9). (Ibn Rushd was aged 68 when he wrote this.)

THE ORIGIN AND JUSTIFICATION OF THE STATE

Like Plato, Aristotle and earlier Islamic falasifa, Ibn Rushd analysed political society (madina, lit. city) in terms of its origins in the fundamental constitution of human beings. But he emphasised more than his predecessors the role of the state in the development of virtue.

> Either it is impossible for *one* man to attain all the (speculative, intellectual, ethical and practical) virtues; or, if this is possible, it is improbable that he will; whereas it is as a rule possible that all these virtues can be found among a multitude of individuals. It is also clear that no one man's substance can become realised through any of these virtues unless a number of humans help him, and that to acquire his virtue a man has need of other people. Hence, he is political by nature. (*On Republic*, pp. 5, 28)

Political society is also necessary because of what humans need 'for life itself, such as appropriating food, securing dwelling places and clothing, things which man in a certain way shares with the animals' (p. 5). Hence the division of labour. Here, Ibn Rushd re-entered common ground with the earlier falasifa. 'The individuals of this species are all different in natural disposition, corresponding to differences in their perfections ... the employment of a man in more than one art is either altogether impossible or, if it is possible, is not the best way ... every human in the city [should] do the work that is his by nature in the best way that he possibly can' (pp. 6–7). This is necessary if one is to attain intellectual and moral virtue; thus the two parts of Ibn Rushd's argument on the raison d'être of political society are connected.

This, and the need to gain a living, gives rise to distinct groups of individuals: the 'parts' of the state. Ibn Rushd also referred to occupational groups in his discussion of political justice: 'this state will be just because of the communities within it. For in it justice consists in every one of its citizens doing only that for which he is destined individually' (trans. E. Rosenthal, p. 160).

Here, Ibn Rushd was using the argument of complementarity: human beings are essentially interdependent, they need each other for their own fulfilment. He took this idea equally seriously in his view of philosophy itself: knowledge is achieved not by the individual but by the species. 'The process by which philosophy is carried out is ... the concern of humanity as a whole. Both are eternal, and philosophy must always be being enacted in one part of the world or another' (in Urvoy 1991: 110). (This was perhaps his way of responding to the problem of the philosopher's social isolation, which he himself certainly experienced as acutely as anyone.)

A happy society is one in which each of the three approaches to knowledge (demonstrative, argumentative and rhetorical) is in use. The philosophical elite 'does not exist and cannot attain happiness without the participation of the general populace' (in Urvoy 1991: 81); this was a significant departure from Ibn Bajja, whom Ibn Rushd looked on as his mentor. And of course the masses depend upon philosophers for good government and the just arrangement of society: a sound division of labour 'is only conceivable when the parts of the city are in submission to what theoretical science, and those who rule over it, decree' (On Republic, p. 7). The formation of society and the state is, therefore, driven by both epistomology and technology. In the 'perfect association' or virtuous state, all human perfections are realised.

For Ibn Rushd, the state is above all a moral agent. Its instrument is the division of labour, and this in turn requires (1) commutative and distributive justice, (2) education and (3) coercion (penal law). Ibn Rushd's first training was in the Religious Law, and he spent much of his mature life as a senior Judge. He clearly found extremely relevant Aristotle's and Plato's analyses of the role of law, the need for coercion in the formation of moral character and the development of virtue, and of the treatment of the less than virtuous. The idea that there exists an identifiable moral perfection for the individual, and that it is the primary function of the state to facilitate the development of this, gave such ideas a resonance for Islamic and Christian societies which they lack for modern liberal society. Here, both Plato and Aristotle reinforced the view of society upheld in ethical monotheism, suggesting how virtue could be achieved by as many as possible.

In restating and updating Aristotle's views, Ibn Rushd contributed some ideas of his own. In order to develop as a person, one needs to be taught to arrive at true opinions by whatever process one can manage – the demonstrative if possible. Knowledge of the virtues is enough to motivate the noble and the freeborn, but most men need 'fear and terror' as well. Hence the need to legislate for 'the behaviour of boys' (On Ethics, fol. 316v); some 'need laws all their lives'. Habit is important: good people are those who abstain from vice both deliberately and by habit. Again, virtue can be induced either by rhetoric and poetry, or by coercion and chastisement; similarly, Ibn Rushd observed, the Shari'a knows two ways to God: speech and war (On Republic, p. 12). A healthy moral education should be provided by the community ('provisio communis sana'); if it is not, everyone should look after their own children and friends (On Ethics, fol. 316v).

Ibn Rushd took Aristotelian thought in an authoritarian direction. Coercion is required to induce good behaviour even among 'those who inhabit cities of sound thinking' (presumably because not everyone in a good state is virtuous). And this requires strong absolute monarchy: good behaviour is found among people who 'are ruled by a strong man, and [abstention from bad behaviour] does not occur in cities except through the action of a strong ruler who coerces people to it'. Ibn Rushd drew the constitutional conclusion that 'coercive power to this end through the command of one man is not found unless the king is an absolute king (rex absolutus)' (*On Ethics*, fol. 316v). Though the text is obscure, this looks like a significant addition to Aristotle, based upon the model of Caliphal and Sultanic rule. In the *Commentary on Plato's Republic*, referring to non-virtuous cities, he noted that their rulers 'castigate their people by means of disgrace, occasional flogging with rods, and execution'.

> Nothing is more indicative of the citizens' evil dispositions and the baseness of their thoughts than their being in need of judges and physicians. This is because these citizens have no virtue at all of their own, but only attain it through compulsion. (*On Republic*, pp. 11, 31)

(This passage suggests an impatience with human weakness, no doubt influenced by Ibn Rushd's experience as a Judge.)

Ibn Rushd did not say much specifically about the Deputyship, which may reflect its declining importance in practical terms. 'Philosopher', 'king', 'legislator' and 'Imam' are 'as it were synonymous'. In contrast to al-Farabi, he did not say much about what this person was supposed to do. Did he need also to be a Prophet? 'Why, there is room here for penetrating investigation, and we shall investigate it' (p. 72); but he never did. From what he did say, we gather that a Prophet-legislator must also be a philosopher. This does not imply that philosophy is superior to prophecy because the Prophet as such has certain knowledge based on demonstration. What Ibn Rushd meant was, simply, that he who lays down any valid religious law (shari'a) – Muhammad above all, but also Jesus and Moses in their day – also qualifies as a philosopher-king. It is also possible for a philosopher-king to lay down a law (namus) which falls short of the best current religious law.

The qualities Ibn Rushd thought were needed in a philosopher-king included those prescribed by Plato and also some prescribed by Sunni writers for the Deputyship. He must have theoretical and practical knowledge; he must be able to teach not only by demonstration but also 'by persuasive and poetical arguments'; he must possess moral virtue, and the ability to bring to fruition in nations and cities 'those things that have been explained in practical science' (p. 71). In other words, he must be capable of implementing the teachings of Aristotle's Ethics.

CONTEMPORARY OBSERVATIONS

In the third part of the *Commentary on Plato's Republic*, Ibn Rushd discussed changes of regime and non-virtuous states, which he sometimes calls 'erring' (as in Plato), sometimes 'ignorant' (as in al-Farabi). The virtuous states are ruled by kingship or aristocracy. The omission of any mention of virtuous rule by the many is noticeable, especially when one compares Ibn Rushd with European commentators on Aristotle – it may be an example of what a difference Aristotle's *Politics* made. Non-virtuous states correspond to defective views about the purpose of life: timocracy is adopted by people who pursue honour, oligarchy by those who pursue wealth, democracy by those who pursue pleasure. Here, Ibn Rushd used examples from Islamic history and contemporary politics to illustrate what Plato had said. These are cursory, but suggest that he was seeking more seriously than other philosophers of this period, Islamic or European, to integrate new and contemporary political phenomena into the corpus of philosophical knowledge. The changeover from aristocracy to timocracy is illustrated by

> the case of the governance of the Arabs in early times, for they used to imitate the virtuous governance. Then they were transformed into timo-crats in the days of Mu'awiya. So seems to be the case in the governance now existing in these islands [sc. Spain]. (p. 121)

Under the first Almoravid, there was a Shari'a government, but his son changed to timocracy, and his grandson to heathenism. The Almohads under Ibn Tumart and his successor were a Shari'a regime, then they declined to timocracy, and 'these base things that they now have' (p. 145). In each case, the whole process of decline took about forty years. The transition from democracy to tyranny is illustrated by Cordova, which became 'democratic' in 1106, 'tyrannical' in 1145. Ibn Rushd was clearly pessimistic about his own polity and saw it as in a process of decline.

More significantly, he identified democracy as a regime in which 'the household is the primary intention and the city is only for its sake. Hence it is entirely domestic ... Every man, if he so wills, may have all goods in private ... the communities of many of the Muslim kings today are exclusively domestic communities'. In them, political society is an 'accident', merely tacked on. And indeed the role of the household had become of primary importance in Arabo-Islamic society and politics. Again, Ibn Rushd observed how widespread was the distinction between elite and common people: 'men are of two classes: one class designated [as] the multitude, and another class designated [as] the mighty. This was the case with the people in Persia, and is the case in many of these cities of ours' (pp. 111–12).

On two questions, Ibn Rushd recommended revision of the current Muslim code of practice. On Holy War, he looked to recent experiences, and concluded that Muslims had misunderstood 'the intention of the legislator' and turned an *ad hoc* recommendation to engage in war with unbelievers into a universal rule. War is 'useful, until the root of those who are different from (one's own) is extirpated'; even then, 'there are times in which peace is preferable to war'. But

> because the people of the [Muslims] held this precept of convenience for a necessary one (*pro necessario hoc praeceptum utile*), and because it was impossible to extirpate their enemies, many losses have followed from this; and these were on account of their ignorance of the intention of the legis-lator. Therefore one should say that sometimes peace is to be sought rather than war.[11]

Here, we get a glimpse of the role which a concept such as 'the intention of the legislator' could play in the Arabo-Islamic world; and of what might have developed if Greek ideas had been more widely accepted, as they were in Euro-Christian culture.

Ibn Rushd was at his most interesting and original on the subject of women. He expressed his own view as: 'we say that women, insofar as they are of one kind with men, necessarily share in the end of man'. Women may therefore practise crafts; they are 'weaker' at some, 'more diligent' at others. They may be warriors. They may be philosopher-rulers. This was surely influenced by Plato's admission of women as philosopher-rulers – in which case it is another instance of the potential importance of the influence of classical Greece. Ibn Rushd made it clear that the subordination of women in his own society was wrong, was based on ignorance, and contributed to economic backwardness.

> The competence of women is unknown, however, in these cities since they … are placed at the service of their husbands and confined to procreation, upbringing and suckling. This nullifies their [other] activities … Women in these cities are not prepared with respect to any of the human virtues … Their being a burden upon the men in these cities is one of the causes of the poverty of these cities. (*On Republic*, pp. 57–9)

At the end of the *Commentary on Plato's Republic*, Ibn Rushd made one important criticism of Plato. Social and political phenomena, he said, are 'voluntary' and not 'natural': changes of regime, therefore, may not follow the sequence predicted by Plato. And, since all the types of individual that have been discussed 'are to be found in all these cities, it is possible for any city among them to change into any other. We say that what Plato said undoubtedly is not necessary but it is [this way] as a rule' (p. 144). In other words, what Plato predicted should not be taken as a 'law' governing political societies; human behaviour is not subject to empirical generalisation. What might such a thinker have done if he had had Aristotle's *Politics*?

As it was, Ibn Rushd's works on politics were neglected in the Arabic-speaking world and never penetrated eastwards. Neither of them even survived in Arabic. Supporters of Sunni Legalism saw a clear contradiction between religion and philosophy, and they were now suppressing the practice of philosophy and persecuting philosophers, including Ibn Rushd himself. Something similar happened in Counter-Reformation Spain. Ibn Rushd was not the last philosopher to be dragged before a tribunal – in his case, despite his ruler's reluctance – to the accompaniment of a bibliographical act of faith (auto da fe).

A few years after Ibn Rushd's death, Cordova and Seville fell to the Christians, and Muslim Spain was reduced to the tiny kingdom of Granada. Ibn Rushd's intellectual progeny were Europeans. Not for the last time, Spanish political philosophy bore fruit in Northern lands.

FAKHR AL-DIN RAZI IN KHWARAZM AND THE CIRCLE OF POWER

Ibn Rushd and his eastern contemporary, Fakhr al-Din Razi (Ray 1149–Herat 1209),[12] the last significant Sunni Faylasuf, did not know one another. Razi was a Sunni teacher and missionary who propagated the established Sunni position on religion and polity in the new central Asian kingdom of Khwarazm. He did not buy into al-Ghazali's rejection of falsafa but tried to combine dialectical theology with a revised version of Ibn Sina's illuminationism.

His encyclopaedic *Collection of the Branches of Knowledge* (Jami' al-'ulum: written 1186–9 in Persian), dedicated to the Khwarazm emperor Tekesh (r.1172–1200), contained sections on 'knowledge of government ('ilm-i siyasat)' and 'the qualities of kings (adab al-muluk)'. But these are just a collection of previous ideas. Falsafa in the East was perhaps becoming less original.[13] Razi put forward what had now become the conventional argument on the origins of and need for government, following al-Ghazali. Human life depends upon the three elementary activities of providing nourishment, clothing and shelter, and, therefore, upon the three main crafts of agriculture, weaving and building. Because these functions interact with one another, they will inevitably lead to conflict unless someone ensures by means of regulation (siyasat: governance) that human beings do not oppress one another. Therefore 'the order of the world (nezam-e 'alam) is impossible without the existence of a king-emperor (padshah). From this, it is clear that the king is the representative (xalife: Deputy) of God' (in Fouchécour 1986: 426). The fourth of the arts is politics, the supreme art.

The ruler (sayes) should divide society into three status groups: those who exercise their judgement, those who exercise a skill, and those who guard the state (Fouchécour 1986: 427). There is no obvious connection with the skills previously identified as fundamental; this is an 'encyclopaedic' recitation of Plato.

This standard theory of the origins of society and government is used more blatantly than ever to justify royal authority. Razi repeated the injunction not to resist tyranny, holding that it was 'unlawful to speak evil of a tyrannical king ... The good which came from his existence was greater than the evil' (in Lambton 1981: 135).

He also justified cooperation between ruler and clergy. Governance relates to both the external or visible and the internal or invisible. The former is the concern of kings, the latter of the 'ulama. Prophets combine both roles, and the ideal (or absolute) ruler would be perfect in power *and* knowledge, and therefore worthy to represent (xelafat) the Prophet of Islam (Fouchécour 1986: 426). But for practical purposes, Razi restated the orthodox Sunni position: the Deputy need not be morally perfect. In another version of this passage, he identified the Deputy with the Sultan: 'the king (padshah) is the shadow of God and the representative (nayeb) of the prophet' (in Fouchécour 1986: 428).

There is also the most elaborate statement ever made of the Circle of Power, which may have been added by a later author:

> the world is a garden, irrigated by the state [dawlat: destined rule, good fortune, the dynasty]. The state is a power (sultan) whose guardian is the Shari'a. The Shari'a is the governing principle [discipline: siyasat] which safeguards the Kingdom (mulk). The Kingdom is the political society [city: madina] which the army brings into existence. The army is able to be

maintained through material resources. Material resources come from the subjects (ra'iyyat). The subjects are made into servants through justice. Justice is the axis of the well-being of the world.[14]

Here, as in a fine carpet, the threads of Iran, Islam and Greece make a joint impact; power is embedded in a web of relationships.

NOTES

1. Bernard F. Reilly, *The Medieval Spains* (Cambridge: Cambridge University Press, 1993); Urvoy (1990); Leaman (1985); L. P. Harvey, *Islamic Spain 1250 to 1500* (Chicago: University of Chicago Press, 1990); *EI* on Murabitun and Muwahhidun.

2. I have omitted the great Jewish theologian and philosopher, Moses Maimonides (1135–1204): see *EI* on Ibn Maymun; LM 191–226.

3. *EI* s.v. Ibn Badjdja; E. Rosenthal (1958: 158–74); Erwin Rosenthal, 'The Place of Politics in the Philosophy of Ibn Bajja', *IC* 25 (1951), pp. 187–295; Oliver Leaman, 'Ibn Bajja on Society and Philosophy', *Der Islam* 57 (1980), pp. 109–21.

4. In Rosenthal, 'The Place', p. 203. *The Solitary* is trans. in LM 122–33.

5. *EI* s.v. Ibn Rushd; Urvoy (1991); Leaman (1988); E. Rosenthal (1958: 175–209); E. I. J. Rosenthal, 'The Place of Politics in the Philosophy of Ibn Rushd', *BSOAS* 15 (1953), pp. 249–78; Charles E. Butterworth, 'New Light on the Political Philosophy of Averroes', in George F. Hourani (ed.), *Essays on Islamic Philosophy and Science* (Albany: SUNY, 1975), pp. 118–27.

6. Printed in Venice 1560, repr. Frankfurt 1962 (the text is somewhat corrupt); see Lawrence V. Berman, 'Ibn Rushd's Middle Commentary on the Nicomachaean Ethics in Medieval Hebrew Literatures', in Anon. (eds), *Multiple Averroes* (Paris: Les belles lettres, 1978), pp. 287–321; this contains a partial translation.

7. Ed. and trans. E. I. J. Rosenthal, *Averroes' Commentary on Plato's Republic* (Cambridge: Cambridge University Press, 1966); and trans. Ralph Lerner, *Averroes on Plato's Republic* (Ithaca NY: Cornell University Press, 1974) (I have used Lerner except where otherwise stated; I have occasionally slightly adapted his wording). See Charles E. Butterworth, 'Ethics and Classical Islamic Philosophy: A Study of Averroes' Commentary on Plato's Republic', in Hovannisian (1985: 17–45).

8. Reading *civili* for *vite*.

9. Oliver Leaman, 'Averroes' Commentary on Plato's Republic and the Missing Politics', in Dionisius Agius and Richard Netton (eds), *Across the Mediterranean Frontiers: Trade, Politics and Religion 650–1450* (Turnhout: Brepols, 1997), pp. 195–203.

10. *On Ethics*, 317v: 'electio actus nobilis in unaquaque artium non fit nisi per duas res: una quarum est scientia cognitionis illius rei, et altera experientia. Scientia namque est per quam invenitur actio, et experientia per quam dirigitur vel probatur, sicut se habet in art musica, et arte medicina, et ceteris artibus activis[.] [E]t domini experientiarum, per quos perficitur in hoc secundum perfectionem, sunt illi qui iudicant sane de operationibus per experientias.'

11. *On Ethics*, fol. 79r–v (text amended); he wrote on jihad in *Bidayah*: Peters (1977: 9–25).

12. *EI* s.v. Fakhr al-Din Razi; Lambton (1981: 132–7); Fouchécour (1986: 425–7).

13. His argument was 'not ... a demonstration but an attempt to give an appearance of logic to a description of accepted ideas': Fouchécour (1986: 426).

14. Lambton (1981: 137) and Fouchécour (1986: 437–8) (adapted).

The Politics of Sufism

12

Political thought in Islam was deeply affected by the growth of Sufism.[1] The intellectual history of Islam sometimes looks like that of Europe in reverse: an early 'renaissance' smothered by layer upon layer of pious sediment. Falsafa, unlike Jurisprudence and courtly adab, had no institutional or even social bases. One may contrast the social isolation and political impotence of Falsafa with the orchestrated social outreach of Sunni fiqh, Learned piety and Sufism. For these, the Sunni–Saljuk development acted as a kind of mortar. In addition to the social power of the 'ulama and the institutional structure of the madrasas, a third and perhaps decisive factor in spreading the religious mentality and winning over the masses to acceptance of the Sunni way was Sufism. This came to dominate the mental activity of both elites and commoners.

Falasifa themselves were inclined to take Sufi experiences very seriously. Many adopted illuminationism, a close ally of Sufi gnosis with a Platonic genealogy. Falsafa was condemned by Sunni Legalists but much less often by Sufis; neo-Platonism was akin to their reflective exploration of self and God, though no nearer to rational enquiry as understood by Aristotle or later Europeans. 'Whatever [the Philosopher] knows rationally, we sufis perceive intuitively' (in Rizvi 1978: vol. 1, p. 461). The Sufi philosopher Yahya Suhrawardi (north-west Iran 1155–Aleppo 1191), styled 'the master of the eastern light', taught neo-Platonic Falsafa as a necessary preparation for 'the unitive insights that mystical experience made possible' (Hodgson 1974: vol. 2, p. 237). He was executed for heresy. Ibn al-'Arabi (Murcia 1165–Anatolia ?1240) claimed that he possessed mystical knowledge through direct communication with the divine.[2] Yahya Suhrawardi became influential in Iran, and Ibn al-'Arabi in Anatolia. The tradition of Falsafa thus merged with religious intuitionism.

Sufism had enormous popular appeal. Its cognitive techniques became increasingly popular and were supported and diffused by elaborate social networks. Sufism developed institutional sinews with an entire parallel social organisation, the ta'ifa (sect, order) derived from a founding saint. Each ta'ifa had its own tariqa (spiritual path) and operated through a network of hospices (khanaqa, ribat, tekke) and teaching centres (zawiya). Crucially, Sufi teachings and practices penetrated the peasantry and the military. There were particularly strong social and spiritual alliances between Sufism and the urban crafts and futuwwa ('chivalry') clubs.[3] Sufi shrines and tombs of holy men became focal points for village, tribe, urban district and craft guild. Sufi masters were cultivated by rulers, bureaucrats and 'ulama. In northern Africa, ethnic and tribal groups reinvented themselves as Sufi brotherhoods or holy clans (Trimingham 1971: 35).

Sufi organisation combined informality with strict personal allegiance; the social ethos was both authoritative and fraternal. The internal organisation of orders had something in common with the familial and dynastic clan model prevalent throughout Islam. The spiritual master (shaykh, pir) was a new type of religious leader, to whom the disciple (murid) owed unquestioning obedience; the Sufi holy man was in turn the wali (protégé, favourite) of God. He was often called 'caliph', meaning truly representative of the divine to you. This was because the shaykh was thought to have achieved a personal mystical state that brought him into direct contact with God. Thus there was an element of spiritual elitism: 'God has an elite … conferring on them unique grace' (a Sufi pir in Trimingham 1971: 141). His authority was, therefore, absolute. A saint's baraka (grace) could be inherited. At the same time, Sufi organisations were relatively informal. They cultivated companionship (suhba) and spiritual brotherhood among themselves. A tariqa could resemble a tribe.

The significance of Sufism for political thought lay primarily in the doctrine of renunciation (zuhd): 'poverty, self-humiliation and complete surrender of personality became the highest values in life' (EI 1: 326a). Its initial role in the religious polity appears to have been to give religious meaning to social life under absolute rulers. It flooded into the space left by political disengagement. Once politics was off the religious agenda, as in different ways it frequently was for both Sunnis and Shi'ites, the way was open for the meaningful development of mysticism. Sufis understood the divine unity (tawhid) to mean 'loss of self and absorption in the divine being' (Lapidus 1988: 111). They focused on God's love and his relationship with the individual. Ibn al-'Arabi defined freedom as slavery to God. This also opened a way for syncretism with other religions, such as Christianity and Buddhism which were apolitical in character. Thus in the land of Islam these religions did not simply disappear.

But, although to begin with the Sufis' political stance was usually quietist, over time their social and political roles varied enormously. They became especially committed to helping the poor, and so they became spokesmen for popular grievances. They became 'a spiritual cement for the social order'. Sufi leadership became a pathway to power. Shaykhs often became de facto local leaders, 'pillars of society and established order' (Trimingham 1971: 239). In western Anatolia, religious leadership was exercised by Sufi preachers, Shamams and sorcerers (Lapidus 1988: 283). Elsewhere, Sufi leaders took their place alongside the 'ulama, and were sometimes merged with them.

Some branches of Sufism came to see themselves as having a role in government. Ghazi regimes in Anatolia looked for support to 'the wandering Turkish dervish' (Trimingham 1971: 68); one warrior-ruler received the shaykh's war-club at his installation and acknowledged him as 'lord'. A dervish led an unsuccessful revolt against the Saljuks of Konya (1240). Sometimes 'we find the leaders aspiring to political power, revolting against established authority, and sometimes actually successful in founding a dynasty' (Trimingham 1971: 239).

In the Sufi spiritual life, old political disputes and divisions changed or lost their meaning. Sufism crossed sectarian divides between different branches of Sunnism, and between Sunnis and Shi'ites. It appealed to Sunni commoners because it opened up a spiritual world beyond legal observance, and to Shi'ites wearied with revolutionary failure. Jihad became an inward endeavour. Sufism spiritualised the theory and praxis of Leadership and so provided a way by which Shi'ites might mutate into Sunnis without losing their spiritual identity. For them, a shaykh could appear 'like the shi'i imam, except that his position was defined without reference to historical disputes' (Hodgson 1974: vol. 2, p. 229). The inner light replaced the hidden imam.

> Increasingly the individual path to meaningfulness and salvation of the Sufis replaced the political way of the Shi'a among the alienated masses. The Sufi was concerned with the approach of the individual soul to God, not with collective salvation through revolt ... the Sufis were generally noted more for political quietism than for the activism found in the sects. (Keddie 1963: 50)

In fifteenth-century Iran and central Asia, 'the shaykh cult filled most of the gap between the Shi'i outlook and Sufism, thanks to the ever greater ideological affinity between imam and shaykh' (*CH Iran* 6: 613).

The combination of Sufism and Shi'ism sometimes led to a revolutionary millenarianism based on a mystical approach to politics. According to Ibn al-'Arabi, 'the Mahdi would impose the law of Islam with the sword, and Jesus would be one of his wazirs ... the Sufi saints would be his natural supporters' (*EI* 5: 1235b). Such ideas, in due course, became political dynamite in the highlands of eastern Anatolia and north-western Iran (see below, pp. 221).

Sufism was an unfathomable asset to a society bent on renewing itself. For the Sunni 'ulama and ruling classes, it opened up a way into the hearts of the people. It expanded dramatically during Saljuk times and was officially promoted by the most distinguished Sunni rulers. Nur al-Din and Salah al-Din set in train a 'parallel institutional development of madrasas and khanaqas' (Trimingham 1971: 9).

Sufism was of capital importance for intellectual and economic life. Its concept of knowing as direct intuition of the divine (ma'rifa: gnosis: see above, pp. 98–9), achievable by a few on their own and communicated to others by teaching, came to dominate mental life. This facilitated belief in mystical and magical phenomena, such as dreams and astrology, among both ordinary and educated people. 'Especially in its popular forms, [Sufism] came more and more to equate God's indwelling in the world with the animistic idea of divine powers ... inherent in material objects and persons' (Gibb 1962: 212). Paganism had not simply gone away.

Sufism was seen as complementary to the textual revelation and the Shari'a.

Combined, these socially accredited forms of knowledge left little, if any, space for philosophy and science; they were claimed to be the sole legitimate ways of knowing. Thus the realms of the unknown and the unknowable, both religiously fashionable, expanded: cosmic, natural and human affairs were under an inscrutable providence. To probe this was impious. While observatories were smashed, astrology was popular at court. Any innovation was heresy, the same word (bid'a) serving for both. Each event was supposedly a discrete expression of the divine wit, unaffected by causal laws. The effect was to narrow the scope for political philosophy and political science. Intellectual energy drained away.

All this affected political society, political economy and government. On the one hand, Sufism encouraged resignation, fatalism and quietism. Such attitudes fitted in with the concept of dawla, the keyword for 'kingdom' or 'state', signifying the divinely destined choice of a given house, on grounds of merit indeed, but of merit unknowable to humans. Advice literature was full of reminders that fortune is fickle, for individuals and for dynasties.

KAI KAWUS AND NAJM AL-DIN RAZI ON THE DIGNITY OF WORK

On the other hand, Sufism could also ascribe deep spiritual meaning to the workaday and to all human pursuits. This came out in the *Qabus Nama* (*Book of Qabus*, in Persian, written 1082–3), a discourse about the whole of life and society which Kai Kawus Ibn Iskandar, hereditary ruler of Gurgan and Tabaristan (south of the Caspian), wrote in old age for his son.[4] A deeply religious work, its piety combined traditional Sunnism with Sufi and neo-Platonic ideas. It circulated widely in the early Ottoman domains.

The *Qabus Nama* covered knowing God, gratitude to God, acts of piety required by an increase in wealth; gratitude to parents, the counsels of the Persian King Nurshirwan the Just to his son; age and youth, eating, wine, hospitality, games, romance, pleasure, baths, sleep, hunting, polo, battle; acquisition of wealth, buying slaves, buying a house and estates, buying horses, marrying a wife, rearing children, friendship, pardon and punishment; Religious Knowledge, merchants, medicine, astrology, poets, musicians, service to kings, boon companions, the secretariat, the vizier, the army, the conduct of kingship, agriculture and craftsmanship; and, finally, futuwwa (chivalry), the Sufi path and the codes of craftsmen. It ends with a section on Sufism and dervishes. There shines throughout a deep respect for the various crafts and professions, each of which has social and spiritual significance.

The work combined moral clichés with some sincere and original turns of thought. *Knowledge* is fundamental to Ibn Iskandar's concept of society and status groups. He made an interesting distinction between the professions, based on whether (1) science predominates with a craft-skill attached to it (e.g. medicine, surveying); (2) craft and science are combined (e.g. architecture, the construction of underground canals); (3) the craft exists on its own (no examples are given: he presumably means manual skills). Ibn Iskandar is unusual in employing the organic analogy, taken he says from 'the Philosophers', to classify groups. According to this, there are: (1) knights and soldiers: they are the body, and possess the virtue of nobility; (2) 'possessors of exoteric and esoteric knowledge and faqirs of the Sufi persuasion', who have fear of God and gnosis: they are body and soul; (3) 'philosophers, prophets and saints': they comprise body, soul and senses; and (4) 'spiritual men and the apostles', who represent 'body, soul, senses and ideas' (pp. 242–57).

The religious meaning of work and everyday things was also tellingly expressed in *The Path* (*Mirsad*: in Persian) by Najm al-Din Razi (Rayy 1177–Anatolia 1256), which he composed at Kayseri and Sivas (1221–3) for the Rum-Saljuk sultan Ibn Qilij Arslan.[5] The final section is on the 'wayfaring' of different status groups; here, Najm al-Din expounded a religious conception of the division of labour and of occupational ethics. The Qur'an is quoted as saying 'the best of what man eats is that which he earns with his own hand' (p. 482); so 'God has appointed everyone to a certain service or craft, which he practises for fifty or a hundred years without daring to engage in some other task for even a day'. Every labourer in the hospice of this world 'should form the following intent in the exercise of his craft and trade: "I perform this my task for the sake of God's servants; for my craft is necessary if the need of a Muslim is to be fulfilled"' (pp. 487–8). This obviously sanctified the division of labour and gave all work a religious meaning.

Agriculture is presented as the classic instance of stewardship on behalf of God, who in this case is most obviously the sole proprietor. It is the noblest occupation since it is quintessentially reliant upon God. Through it everyone shares in deputyship (khalifa, sc. of God); everyone engaged in it, from sharecropper to village headman, should function as 'the deputy of God in his capacity as the giver of daily bread' (in Lambton 1953: xxx). This and other productive crafts derive from a combination of skill and spiritual cognition, and therefore enable their practitioners to 'gaze on God's activity and work as maker' (p. 482).

The last chapter is on the 'wayfaring' of kings, written in the Advice-Book genre, and expounds the Sufi approach to government. Elsewhere, Najm al-Din cited 'Ali, Socrates, Plato, Alexander, Jesus and the Persian kings as political sages. Kingship is presented as a form of Sufi discipleship, one way of treading the mystical path. The king will earn divine favour if he acts justly, commands good and forbids evil (hisba), secures the roads, conquers the lands of unbelief, provides for the needy and the 'ulama, and respects ascetics. Kingship provides a unique opportunity for rejecting self-indulgence and seeking instead 'the nearness of God'. The king has a special opportunity to 'acquire the qualities of God' – the Sufi goal – because he is in a unique position to give generously. The ideal king is someone endowed with Learning and Prophecy; through him 'the dignity of religion is made manifest by the sword' (p. 400).

While agriculture remains central, this is very different in spirit from earlier writings on patrimonial monarchy. It shows how, in the Sufi way, religious eminence followed from the performance of duties, which could also include military and political duties. The Sufi goal is open to all, though achievable only by a very few. One could deduce from this that status depends upon performance. Sufi ethics could conceivably open the way to legitimising a change of ruler or of dynasty. But the concept of the state as composed of impersonal offices remains as remote as ever.

AN ATTEMPT TO RESTORE THE CALIPH AS POLITICAL LEADER

In the later twelfth century, the last days of the old East, the Khwarazmshahs, from their power base in Transoxania, expanded westwards and, in alliance with the 'Abbasid Deputy, wrested western Iran from the last Saljuk. The Mongols massing on the eastern frontier were ignored until it was too late.

Sufism became part of a religio-political programme undertaken by the last effective 'Abbasid Deputy, Nasir al-Din Allah (r.1180–1225).[6] During the decline of the Saljuks, the Deputies had been able to regain some political power as local rulers. Nasir appears to have been an ambitious and idealistic statesman; he attempted nothing less than to re-establish the political leadership of the Deputyship over the Sunni world. He consolidated his power in Iraq; then, allying with the Khwarazmshahs, destroyed Saljuk power in Iran. But the consequent advance of the Khwarazmshahs led to conflict between them and the Deputy.

Nasir now proceeded to work out what amounted to a new relationship between the Deputy and other rulers. He based this on a remarkable intellectual initiative which fed the Sufi notion of spiritual leadership into the ideology of the high Caliphate. The Sufi leader and theorist Umar al-Suhrawardi (Iran 1145–Baghdad 1254, acquainted with Najm al-Din) became Nasir's adviser. Together they seem to have evolved a strategy to reorganise Sunni Islam under Caliphal leadership, analogous to similar (and ultimately rather more successful) moves by the late-eleventh century pope, Gregory VII, and his successors. Suhrawardi enhanced the Deputy's role as religious leader by combining it with the status of a Sufi shaykh whose spiritual leadership people needed in order to return to God (Hartmann 1975: 112). Nasir also claimed to be an outstanding expert in Religious Jurisprudence. He gave all four Law Schools equal status and organised a College at Baghdad to propagate their teaching jointly; this emphasised the unity of the Sunni world. He also had himself recognised as a qualified expert in all four Schools, and produced his own collection of Reports.[7]

Nasir's vision went even further. He succeeded in converting the Imam of the Nizari Isma'ilis to Sunni Islam and he built bridges to the Imami Shi'ites, appointing Imamis as caliphal officials. Falasifa were excluded from the synthesis; their libraries were burned in the 1190s.

In 1207, Nasir proclaimed himself head of the Sufi-based futuwwa clubs and invited all other rulers to join a courtly version of the futuwwa.[8] This would make him their personal spiritual guide and bind them to him as disciples. To refuse might seem impious; the request was favourably received in Egypt, Syria and Anatolia. Nasir wanted all inter-Muslim disputes to be resolved through diplomacy by the Caliph, and he achieved certain successes in Ayyubid territory. Such an initiative underlined the role of Sufi groups at the heart of

Sunni Islam and increased the standing of the futuwwa. Had it taken root, it would have meant that the Deputy was 'the only one with the ability and the right to hold together the community of believers' (Hartmann 1975: 266). All this implied a concept of the People (umma) as a tighter organisational unity under the Deputy's leadership than had hitherto been conceived.

This could have been the final step in the consolidation of the Community-Traditional world. It was perhaps to some extent inspired by the need to create a unified bloc to counter the Christian world. Indeed, it is difficult not to see here a parallel with the papacy, which under Innocent III was entering a somewhat similar alliance with the new orders of Friars at this very time, and was also broadly sympathetic to the craft-guilds. But Nasir's edifice crumbled before the Mongol torrent. Umar Suhrawardi's general spiritual teaching lived on in Central Asia, India and Ottoman Anatolia. And Sufi groups were becoming part of the political, as well as social, infrastructure of Islam.

NOTES

1. *EI* on Tasawwuf; Trimingham (1971); Hodgson (1974: vol. 2, pp. 201–54); Gibb (1962: 28–32, 208–17); Zubaida (1995: 19–22); Ruthven (1984: 226–86).
2. NL 434–64, 497–528; Corbin (1964: 284–95); Fakhry (1983: 293–304); *EI* s.v. Ibn al-'Arabi.
3. *EI* on Futuwwa; Cahen (1958–9: 30–7, 233–9); Cahen (1968: 196–200); Hodgson (1974: vol. 2, pp. 221–3).
4. Kai Ka'us ibn Iskandar, *Prince of Gurgan, Qabus Nama, a Mirror for Princes*, trans. R. Levy (London: Cresset, 1951); Fouchécour (1986: 208–11).
5. Najm al-Din Razi, *The Path of God's Bondsmen from Origin to Return: A Sufi Compendium*, trans. H. Algar (Delmar NY: Caravan, 1982).
6. Hodgson (1974: vol. 2, pp. 279–85); *CH Iran* 5: 245; Hartmann (1975).
7. Hartmann (1975: 112, 115). Hartmann surely exaggerates when he suggests that Umar Suhrawardi's teaching implied adoption of the Shi'ite view that the Leader was 'a teaching authority for the divine law' (p. 115).
8. Chivalrous fraternity. Compare the knightly orders of Christendom.

Part III The Shari'a and the Sword

c.1220–1500

The Rape of Asia

13

Between 1219 and 1405, the Islamic world was torn apart. The Mongols under Chingiz (d.1227) devastated Transoxania and Khurasan (1219–31) and uprooted the Saljuks of Rum (1235–6).[1] Baghdad was razed and the last 'Abbasid Caliph was assassinated (1258). The Golden Horde, a federation of Mongol tribes, tore through the Ukraine, Russia and eastern Europe. The cultural and commercial cities of the Eurasian heartland, such as Balkh, Herat, Marv, Nishapur and Rayy, centres of Religious learning and Falsafa for half a millennium, underwent massacre and destruction on a scale not previously known (and not to be repeated until the twentieth century). 'Again and again, almost the entire populace of a city was massacred without regard to sex or age … Cities like Bukhara were heaps of rubble and of corpses. Some cities, like Tus, never were rebuilt' (Hodgson 1974: vol. 2, p. 288). The destruction of underground water channels turned agricultural areas into pasturage or desert.

The Mongol achievement was based on Chingiz's unification of nomadic tribes into a single 'people (ulus)' under an imperial ideology. To cement pan-Mongol unity, Chingiz wiped out traditional aristocrats and replaced them with his own kinsmen; tribal elites were broken up and reshuffled. An assembly of commanders and notables (qiriltai) 'elected' Chingiz as supreme ruler and thrashed out political and military strategy. The conquests and all their ruthlessness were stimulated and justified by profound religious beliefs: the supreme Sky-God gave Chingiz's clan-dynasty sovereignty over the whole world. Chingiz introduced, apparently from China, the idea of a supreme leader 'willed' by heaven: those who opposed him, or refused to surrender, deserved their fate.[2]

And yet within a generation, religious assimilation was proceeding apace. The Mongols, many of whom had adopted Buddhism, were especially attracted by the Sufi form of Islam. In 1295, Ghazan Khan, chief of the Ilkhan clan and ruler of Iran, became a Sunni Muslim. His conversion ruptured the unity of the Mongol people. The Golden Horde were the next to adopt Islam (1313). From now on, the Mongol states entered the power politics of the Islamic world. The Mamluks of Egypt had inflicted a decisive defeat on the Mongols at 'Ayn Jalut (Syria: 1260) which stopped their advance beyond the boundaries of the old Roman empire. But as Turks they regarded themselves as cousins of the

Mongols and made an alliance with the Golden Horde against Ilkhan Iran. The Ilkhans responded with overtures to European states. They finally made peace with the Mamluks in 1322. With the disappearance of the pan-Mongol ideal, the ideal of the Community of Believers (umma) resumed significance, albeit in a muted form. Chingiz achieved lasting renown in central Asia, unlike Hitler in Europe, regardless of his massacres; his dynasty 'established the basis for a common political culture throughout the Eurasian steppe and neighbouring settled lands' (Manz 1989: 5).

Ilkhan rule in Iran began as a continuation of plunder by arbitrary taxation.[3] Agriculture and commerce were severely damaged; the population declined. In religion and culture, the new rulers were at first relatively tolerant and favoured religious minorities; Imami Shi'ites and Nestorian Christians were admitted to government service. Some Imamis had welcomed the Mongol attack on the institutions of Sunni Islam: Nasir al-Din Tusi acted as their adviser on the campaign that led to the sack of Baghdad.

A REVIVAL OF IRANO-ISLAMIC POLITICAL CULTURE

Mongol regimes in Iran and elsewhere became assimilated in political structure, culture and style to those of their Irano-Islamic predecessors. Chingiz' method of governing through a detribalised personal following was not, in principle, very different from existing regimes; indeed, they all drew on the steppe tradition (Manz 1989: 3–4). Power rested, as before, with a central dynastic clan. In general, conventional methods, personnel and ideas continued to be used. Viziers and secretaries, recruited from the local population, managed the government and its finances. The main line of communication between regime and subjects was, as before, the Muslim religious leaders, now Sufi shaykhs as well as 'ulama. The same succession problems recurred; when the Ilkhan king died without heir (1335), Iran disintegrated into local dynasties. Thus social, religious and political regeneration was remarkably swift. After the initial conflagration there was, at least on the surface, much continuity in religious belief and political ideology.

In Persia, Ghazan (r. 1295–1304) said that he had achieved power 'only with my sword', thus asserting his independence from civil society. But he tried to persuade his Mongol military aristocracy to adopt a more clement and economically viable attitude towards their Persian subjects.

> I am not on the side of the Tazik ra'iyyat [Iranian populace]. If there is a purpose in pillaging them, there is no one with more power to do this than I. Let us rob them together. But if you wish to be certain of collecting grain and food for your tables in the future, ... you must be taught reason. If you insult the ra'iyyat, take their oxen and seed, and trample their crops into the ground, what will you do in the future? (in *CH Iran* 5: 494)

Such a statement reflected the tension between those who admired the Mongol tradition with its nomadic way of life, and the bureaucracy, 'ulama, large-scale merchants and landowners who looked to the agrarian and statist tradition of Persia. Reform of land tenure and taxation were pushed ahead by Rashid al-Din Fadl Allah Hamadani (1247–1318), a historian and vizier to Ghazan. He explained agrarian reform in terms of Irano-Islamic tradition and especially the Circle of Power:

> If the common people (ra'iyyat) are ruined, the king will have no revenue. The basis of administration is justice ... the government (saltanat) has no revenue but that paid by the army ... [there is] no tax that is not paid by the ra'iyyat ... and there are no ra'iyyat if there is no justice. (in *CH Iran* 5: 493)

In areas conquered by the Mongols, works of Advice-to-Kings provided continuity: what they had to say was unchanged from pre-Mongol days.[4] The Mongol ideology of divine authorisation of the ruler and of clan destiny was easily assimilated into current Irano-Islamic political thought. An exception was the way in which Ibn al-Tiqtaqa (a prominent Shi'ite, Baghdad 1262–?), in a history he wrote (1302) for the governor of Mosul under the Mongols,[5] recommended 'a secret pact unknown to others' between the ruler and God. This suggested a special relationship between the ruler and God, whom the ruler should address with 'special formulae appropriate for sovereigns but not for common mortals' (p. 59). This was alien to Islamic tradition. Otherwise, Ibn Tiqtaqa's advice followed convention. The Persian kings, he says, used belles lettres and history, while Muslim rulers used grammar, poetry and history: 'it is by intelligence that one leads kingdoms' (p. 25). But under the Mongols these have been abandoned for accountancy, medicine and astronomy (sc. for astrological use). He seems to have been trying to civilise his superiors. In general, there was a new emphasis on the ethnic-popular code of law known as 'the Great Yasa of Chingis Khan'.

THE BLACK DEATH AND TIMUR

The Black Death swept through the House of Islam from 1346 onwards and caused death rates similar to those in Europe.[6] Then came Timur Lenk ('the Lame', Tamerlane).[7] He smashed his way from Transoxania through Iran (1379) and Iraq, routed the Golden Horde on the steppes (1395), sacked Delhi (1398), penetrated deep into Anatolia and Syria, and died in 1405. Timur claimed to be heir to the Turco-Mongol empire of Chingiz, and claimed that his enemies were traitors to Islam; but his savagery had no parallel in Islamic history. Apart from that, his vision is obscure. He was an able military leader who used massacre and destruction as a means of political control. His aim was probably not world empire but personal dominion over Transoxania, Iran and Iraq. His power rested on a detribalised personal following, bypassing tribal limitations on a single ruler, and for this conquests were a prerequisite. He never designated an heir, and on his death his territories were divided up (Manz 1989: 150–3). Yet the tradition of authority conferred by military power was so strong that his rule was accepted, even admired; and his name, lineage and authority were invoked by succeeding dynasties in central Asia and by the Mughals in India. Here too, the tradition of the steppe coincided with existing

Islamic ways of legitimising government: both endorsed the personal power of the self-made man and saw 'a successful career of conquest and rule as proof of the favour of God', so that 'to resist such a man was to oppose the will of God' (Manz 1989: 15).

Such experiences changed intellectual life and attitudes. There was a resurgence of tribalism: the Mongol enterprise itself was the most dramatic example of the irruption of tribes from desert into settled life, the phenomenon explored by the youthful Ibn Khaldun, who later met and conversed with Timur. It was also the last.

The main impact on popular culture appears to have been a dramatic spread of Sufism, associated with mysticism and magic. In many places, Sufi brotherhood was 'the only form of social organisation left' (Gibb 1962: 31–2). Hospices sprang up all over Persia. Sufi attitudes and social action corresponded to the needs of the hundreds upon hundreds of thousands whose lives were devastated by the Mongol slaughters and the Black Death. Sufi missionaries were particularly successful in winning over the Mongols themselves to Islam. From one end of the House of Islam to the other, new Sufi orders were founded: the most important were the Mawlawiyya, founded by Jalal al-Din Rumi (Balkh 1207–Konya 1273) in Anatolia, and the Naqshbandi, founded by Baha al-Din Naqshbandi (Bukhara?–1389) in central Asia. Such orders spread in all directions; some of them later assumed political importance.

The institutions of religious Learning had been destroyed, their teachers killed or gone westwards. From now on, Islam would proceed without the mellowing influence of the old schools of central Asia. The centres of Islamic culture and thought were now in Asia Minor, Egypt, North Africa and India; it was from these that the next generation of original political thinkers came. Not until the seventeenth century did Persia recover its economic and cultural vitality; central Asia never has done. Can one find an original political theorist after Ibn Khaldun until the nineteenth century? In Europe too, there was actually a hiatus in original political philosophy between William of Ockham (d.1349) and Hobbes.

NOTES

1. Khazanov (1994: 234–48); Morgan (1988: 51–71); Thomas T. Allsen, *Mongol Imperialism: The Policies of the Grand Qan Möngke in China, Russia and the Islamic Lands, 1251–9* (Berkeley: University of California Press, 1987).
2. P. B. Golden, 'Imperial Ideology and the Sources of Political unity amongst the pre-Cinggisid Nomads of Western Eurasia', *Archivum Eurasiae Medii Aevi* 2 (1982), pp. 37–76; Igor de Rachewiltz, 'The Ideology of Chingis Khan's Empire', *Papers in Far Eastern History* 7 (1973), pp. 21–36.
3. *EI* s.v. Ilkhans; *CH Iran* 5: 483–97; Morgan (1988: 72–82).
4. Lambton (1980: II: 140–7); Fouchécour (1986: 437–9); Makdisi (1990: 167).
5. Ibn at-Tiqtaqa, *Al-Fakhri: Histoire des dynasties musulmanes*, trans. E. Amar (Paris: Leroux, 1910); also trans. G. E. J. Whitting (London: Luzac, 1947).
6. Michael W. Dols, *The Black Death in the Middle East* (Princeton, NJ: Princeton University Press, 1977).
7. Manz (1989); Morgan (1988: 83–93).

Mamluk Ideology and the Sultan-Caliph

14

INTEGRATION OF RELIGION AND POLITY

In Egypt and Syria, the regime of the Mamluks (lit. slave-soldiers: 1250–1517) established itself after their first great leader, Sultan Baybars (r.1260–77), had defeated the Franks (1249) and the Mongols (1260).[1] Protectors of Mecca and Medina, they became the foremost Sunni power and lasted longer than any previous effective Islamic government. This provided the political background for the last two towering geniuses of Islamic political thought: Ibn Taymiyya and Ibn Khaldun.

The Mamluks' political system was based not on the dynastic clan but on the households (tawa'if: lit. groups) of the military aristocracy. Each household was bound together by comradeship and personal loyalty to their master (ustadh) – a strong patron–client relationship. Power was centralised in Cairo; the provinces were ruled by Mamluk generals. The Mamluks were former infidels imported as slaves from the north and north-east borders of the House of Islam and married to imported slavegirls; this trade required good relations with Byzantium and the Golden Horde. The Mamluks formed a caste in the sense that they were distinguished from the rest of the population by their warrior profession, their rigorous training, their fair skin and non-Muslim names, their Turkish language, and conspicuous marks of social prestige such as dress and riding on horseback. Mamluk households exercised economic power through ownership of landed estates, held as iqta's, and their enormous consumptive capacity. This was called 'The Turkish State (dawlat al-Turk)', the Sultans 'the Kings (muluk) of the Turks'. Local notables, such as the 'ulama, were subordinate.

This accentuated the ethnic separation of military from civilian society; it was a further step towards basing state power on men with no familial or local ties (Lapidus 1988: 355). It sprang from the perceived need for a class devoted to a strict warrior ideal in order to defend Islam against the Christians and Mongols. Ibn Khaldun saw the Mamluks as the saviours of Islam.

After Sultan Baybars' victory over the Mongols at 'Ayn Jalut (1260), there followed a century of stability and prosperity for Egypt as the entrepot of east–west trade in spices, silks (exceptionally lucrative) and other commodities. Then came the Black Death, followed by depopulation. This hit the Mamluk class particularly hard because they refused to leave Cairo. In 1382, Circassian

Mamluks seized power from the Turks; there was civil war. Timur ravaged Syria. The economy declined; Egypt, producing few exports, had an unfavourable balance of trade with Europe. The response was price regulation and state monopolies; this made things worse, as did the appointment of state merchants (tujjar al-sultan), an 'extension of the bureaucratic apparatus to commerce'.[2] The Ottomans conquered Egypt in 1517, but continued to rule through the Mamluk aristocracy which, by Napoleon's time, had become virtually independent again.

The Mamluk Sultans were chosen, in theory, not by kinship ('kinship is sterile', they said), but by election. There was no defined procedure; personal prowess was supposed to be self-evident. There were crises of succession. The sultan's status was based on the oath of allegiance (bay'a) sworn 'to the ruler as sovereign ... to support him personally' (Holt 1975: 241). The Sultan, it was said, acquired his position as Deputy by the ba'ya of the 'Abbasid Caliph ('the Commander of the Faithful') and 'by agreement of the electors, the 'ulama and the great officials of the august state, and the consent of their lordships the amirs and the divinely assisted armies' (in Holt 1977: 45). But reciprocal obligations might be included in the sultanic oath, making him a bit more like a first among equals within the ruling class: this was a new development, and it paralleled features of European monarchy (and, possibly, Venice).

The Sultan's religio-political role was emphasised and expanded under the Mamluks. He was, above all, a warrior-king, and this made him a focal point of the religious enterprise. Baybars was told that

> by thee God has preserved the protection of Islam from decline ... Thy sword has made incurable wounds in the hearts of the unbelievers ... In the Holy War against the enemies of God be a leader, not a follower. Support the creed of unity. (in Holt 1977: 47)

The 'ulama were integrated into the regime more than ever before. They were indigenous moral leaders (Lapidus 1984: 134–42). Christian communities became victims of popular outbursts (the Crusades were still going on); Sufism remained a fringe movement on Mamluk territory. The 'ulama were connected with the ruling class through ties of patronage, kinship and intermarriage. Many earned their living as merchants. From their ranks came the Religious Judges, whose appointment the leading 'ulama families could influence through the religio-academic network. Judges depended on the government's police (shurta) for the enforcement of their rulings. The 'ulama knew the people and how to get things done; Sultans consulted them. During a rebellion or a succession crisis, their fatwas could make an important contribution to political stability. They dominated education and social welfare, which were funded by Mamluk nobles.

The Sultan himself played an extensive judicial role through the mazalim (redress of grievances) court; this was called simply 'the government (al-siyasa)'. Class entered into the administration of justice: for the mazalim court dealt specifically with affairs concerning Mamluks and petitions from iqta'-holders. In it, secular law played an important part; cases in which both parties were Mamluk were often 'judged not according to ... the Shari'a but according to the laws of the Mongol Yasa [folk law]' (Ayalon 1977: 324). When the Shari'a was ambiguous, the sultan could decide the issue by decree. Thus the scope of non-Islamic 'sultanic' or customary justice ('ada sultaniyya) tended to expand (to Ibn Taymiyya's disgust).

THE SULTAN-CALIPH

The relationship between Caliph (Deputy) and Sultan was transformed. Baybars installed a junior member of the 'Abbasid family as Deputy in Cairo (1261, three years after the extinction of the Baghdad caliphate). This Deputy was prevailed upon to proclaim Baybars Holy Warrior and to invest Baybars with all lands which he should conquer from the Christians and Mongols. The Deputy went on: 'I entrust to you the interests of all the Muslims and I invest you with all with which I am invested in the matters of religion' (in Tyan 1954–6: vol. 2, p. 200). This was repeated at the installation of later Sultans, for example in 1341 (Holt 1975: 244) and in 1412: '[I invest you with] all with which I have been invested by God, the interests of Islam and the Muslims ... so that you may ensure the observation of the fundamental laws of the right religion' (in Tyan 1954–6: vol. 2, p. 200). The Deputy thus transferred his religious and jurisdictional functions to the sultan. One aim was to boost the Mamluks' claim as pan-Islamic rulers. Above all, the sultan now came to be seen as the guarantor in his own territory of contracts, marriages and Shari'a Penalties – critical legal acts whose religious legitimacy formerly depended on the Deputy. The Sultan-Caliph had arrived.

There were similar developments in European Christian religio-political thought in this period, as national or regional churches under kings or dukes gained increasing independence from the papacy. This culminated in the Reformation; the ruler as 'head of the church' in his/her territory may look rather similar to the Sultan-Caliph. There was, however, no parallel between the powers claimed by the papacy and assumed by kings and those ascribed under Islam to a Caliph.

IBN JAMA'A AND THE JUSTIFICATION OF POWER BASED ON FORCE

The Sultan-Caliph was legitimised in the writings of Ibn Jama'a (Syria 1241– Egypt 1333; Chief Shafi'i Judge of Cairo) on fiqh (religious Legal theory). Ibn Jama'a was on good terms with the regime; he retired on a state pension (unlike his much more interesting contemporary, Ibn Taymiyya). In his *Tahrir al-Ahkam fi Tadbir ahl al-Islam* (*Summary of the Rules for the Governance of the People of Islam*),[3] he set forth 'the principles of sovereignty (al-ahkam al-sultaniyya)'. His most striking argument was the justification of power usurped by force as a form of vizierate by delegation, or general amirate. Whereas al-Mawardi had applied this terminology to the de facto power of provincial rulers, Ibn Jama'a used it to justify the occupation of the Imamate (Leadership, Caliphate) itself by force (see above, p. 88):

When there is no Imam and an unqualified person seeks the Leadership and compels the people by force and by his armies, without any ba'ya [oath of allegiance] or succession, then his ba'ya is validly contracted, and obedience to him is obligatory, so as to maintain the unity of the Muslims and preserve agreement among them. This is still true, even if he is barbarous or vicious, according to the best opinion. When the Leadership is thus contracted by force and violence to one [person], and then another arises who overcomes the first by his power and his armies, then the first is deposed and the second becomes Imam, for the welfare of the Muslims and the preservation of their unity, as we have stated.[4]

Ibn Jama'a surely did not intend this as a description of the existing Mamluk sultanate. But it could justify *any* ruler's assumption of the position of Deputy. This supported the assumption of caliphal powers by Sultans and would help to ensure their acceptance by orthodox 'ulama. It strongly reinforced the doctrine of non-resistance and a broadly Hobbesian view of religio-political authority. Modern Islamic thinkers have seen Ibn Jama'a as an example of the corruption of Islamic thought under adverse historical circumstances.

Not everyone agreed with Ibn Jama'a's view. A history of the Caliphate written by Suyuti (1445–1505)[5] emphasised the role of the Deputy as distinct from the Sultan throughout Islamic history, and in the present Mamluk state, arguing that there was direct continuity between the first Caliphs and the present 'Abbasid Deputy at Cairo. The present regime marked but one of many historical vicissitudes through which the Caliphate had passed. Suyuti insisted that the Deputy is the only fully legitimate ruler, and he alone can legitimise other rulers. Suyuti wanted to curb certain excesses of the Mamluk regime. He drew a favourable contrast between the piety of Saladin, the restorer of Sunnism in Egypt, and the present rulers. His praise went to Jurists, Religious Judges, Sufis and mystics; he highlighted the heroic resistance of a qadi to Baybars. Suyuti offers a glimpse of a Sunni 'pious opposition', at odds with the temper of the dawla and scornful of its power.

NOTES

1. *EI* s.v. Mamluk; Holt (1975, 1977); Ayalon (1977); David Ayalon, *The Mamluk Military Society* (London: Ashgate, 1979); Lapidus (1984).
2. Carl F. Petry, *The Civilian Elite of Cairo in the Later Middle Ages* (Princeton: Princeton University Press, 1981), p. 31; Lapidus (1984: 52–63); A. S. Atiya, 'A Mamluk "Magna Carta"', in George N. Atiya and Ibrahim M. Oweiss (eds), *Arab Civilization: Challenges and Responses* (Albany: SUNY, 1988), pp. 128–39.
3. Trans. Hans Kofler, 'Handbuch des islamischen Staats- und Verwaltungsrechts', *Islamica* 6 (1934), pp. 349–414 and 7(1935), pp. 1–64; Rosenthal (1958: 43–51); Lambton (1981: 138–43); Nagel (1981 vol. 1, pp. 436–40).
4. In Lewis (1988: 102). The sultan was also called 'proof' (that is authoritative witness) of the existence and unity of God.
5. J.-C. Garcin, *Espaces, pouvoirs et idéologies de l'Égypte mediévale* (London: Ashgate, 1987), vol. 6, pp. 33–89.

Nasir al-Din Tusi (1201–74): Social Philosophy and Status Groups

15

REVIVAL OF IMAMI SHI'ISM: THE AUTHORITY OF THE MUJTAHID (WELL-QUALIFIED JURIST)

The period following the Mongol invasions was one of revival and development for the Imami (Twelver) Shi'ites. The Mongols were in some ways their liberators, and gave Shi'ites prominent positions. Imamis were especially numerous in Iraq, north-western Iran and to the south of the Caspian; they had their own madrasas and leaders (sing. naqib: spokesman), and they were represented at the Mongol court by a chief spokesman.

Their intellectual revival was achieved by Nasir al-Din Tusi (Tus 1201–Baghdad 1274), al-Muhaqqiq al-Hilli (Hilla 1205–Baghdad 1277) and Ibn al-Mutahhir al-Hilli (called al-'Allama: The Most Learned; Hilla 1250–Tabriz 1325), who studied under Tusi and was greatly influenced by him. His father had led the surrender of Hilla to the Mongols and then joined the military entourage of Hülegü (the Mongol leader) at Baghdad; 'Allama himself held a post at the Ilkhan court at Tabriz, and helped convert the ruler to Twelver Shi'ism (1310). Al-Muhaqqiq and al-'Allama were Jurists based at Hilla (south of Baghdad), the main centre of Imami learning.[1]

Al-Muhaqqiq taught that Holy War was obligatory against all non-Imamis including fellow Muslims, but only when commanded by the Imam; which in practice limited Jihad to defensive war (Arjomand 1984: 62). Al-'Allama's contribution to Shi'ite thought was decisive in several ways. It was he who established the authoritative status of the legal rulings on previously undetermined issues made by a Mujtahid (an experienced scholar-Jurist), based on his individual 'effort (ijtihad)'. Such rulings are fallible, unlike those of the Prophet and the Imams, and can be revised ('someone who opposes a mujtahid is not an unbeliever': in Cooper, p. 243). This gave the Shi'ite legal system flexibility and dynamism; it enabled new questions to be taken seriously. Above all, it elevated *reason* ('aql) in the case of the qualified. Some modern writers have seen Shi'ite independent reasoning (ijtihad) as a move towards rational debate and hence democratic discourse (Enayat 1982: 44, 169–75).

This 'paved the way for the later – also political – role of the Shi'ite scholars, the mullahs ('ulama) and the ayatallahs' (lit. God's sign; al-'Allama was the first to hold this title) (Halm 1991: 68). Other believers, in al-'Allama's view, 'authorise' the qualified scholar to reason on their behalf, the process known as taqlid; thereafter they must accept his judgement. This is justified because 'if the vast majority were burdened with independent reasoning the world order would be disturbed, and everyone would be more concerned with discussing Legal problems than with his livelihood' (in Halm 1991: 70). Al-'Allama argued the necessity of the Imamate (Leadership) from common experience: 'the recourse which intelligent people have in all countries and towns to appointing leaders for the preservation of order shows that there is no other way than the Imamate' (in Cooper, p. 241).

NASIR AL-DIN TUSI: A SYNTHESIS OF JURISPRUDENCE, ARISTOTLE AND IRANIAN LORE

Original political thinkers in the post-Mongol world were rare, but those there were shone as persons of genius. Nasir al-Din Tusi was the last, and one of the most original, if disjointed, representatives of the old central Asian culture. He studied philosophy, theology and Jurisprudence at Nishapur, and was a highly original mathematician and astronomer. This carried a price: he was forced to work for some twenty years as an astrologer in the Nizari-Isma'ili fortress of Alamut (see above, pp. 46–7) This had a famous library, and he was able to continue his work as an astronomer. It was here, on the fringes of the Mongol torrents, that Tusi wrote (c.1235) The Nasirean Ethics (Akhlaq-i Nasiri: in Persian with much Arabic terminology; dedicated to the Quhistan prince Nasir Ibn Ali Mansur).[2] Tusi was never an Isma'ili but there are plenty of Isma'ili ideas in his work, which appear to have been partly edited out later. He was also probably the author of a summary of Nizari Isma'ili doctrines, Rawdat al-Taslim or Tasawwurat.[3]

The Isma'ilis believed that the world was governed by divine revolutions which could be traced in the stars, and apparently the Nizari Isma'ilis believed Tusi when he told them, during a Mongol assault on their forts (1255–6), that it was time to surrender. The capture of Alamut ended 150 years of Isma'ili power in the region. Tusi now became astrologer and adviser to the Mongol leader Hülegü, whom he encouraged in his expedition against Baghdad and the extinction of the Sunni Caliphate (Halm 1991: 64), after which he was made vizier and supervisor of religious Foundations to both Hülegü and his successor. He was thus able to promote the Imami cause in Iraq and Iran. Hülegü had an observatory built for Tusi, which enabled him to calculate new planetary tables.

Tusi wrote prolifically in the Twelver cause, including a work on the Imamate (Leadership). He composed The Rules and Customs of Ancient Kings (probably for a Mongol prince), which contained advice on finances.[4] He wrote on the mystical path and corresponded with the Sufi teacher Rumi.

In his religious thought, Tusi adopted the neo-Platonic teachings of Ibn Sina and Yahya Suhrawardi, to whom for tactical reasons he referred as 'wise men (hukama)' rather than 'Philosophers (falasifa)'. But, unlike Ibn Sina, he held that God's existence cannot be proved but has to be accepted 'like a basic axiom of logic'; and, as Shi'ites taught, humans need authoritative teaching (ta'lim) as well as philosophy. All this pointed towards mystical theology.

Tusi's political philosophy was a synthesis of Aristotelian and Iranian ideas. He combined Falsafa with the Advice genre, thus maintaining the connection beteeen Shi'ism and Falsafa. The *Ethics* is presented as a work of practical philosophy. It deals with the individual ('ethics': Part I), the family ('economics': Part II) and the community (jama'ati) of city, province, region or kingdom ('politics': Part III). Part I drew on Miskawayh's *Ethics*, Part II on Bryson and Ibn Sina, and Part III on al-Farabi, whom Tusi referred to as 'the second philosopher', after Aristotle (*Ethics*, p. 187).

Nasir al-Din Tusi set out to bring together philosophy (hikmat) and religious Jurisprudence (fiqh) on the grounds that good actions may be based either on nature or on convention. *Nature* presents us with unchanging principles, known to people of insight and sagacity. *Convention* refers either to community customs (adab) or, if taught by a prophet or Imam, to divine laws (nawamis-i ilahi); these are the subject of Jurisprudence (ilm-i fiqh). They are sub-divided into norms for (1) individuals, (2) families and (3) 'the inhabitants of cities or regions' (p. 29).

Philosophy deals only with unchanging truths. Divine laws, since they deal with types of action that are 'liable to change with revolutions and circumstances, with the pre-eminence of individual men, the prolongation of time, the disparity between epochs and the substitution of peoples and dynasties' (p. 29), are outside its scope. The Isma'ili perception of historical stages and of the relativity of revelations enabled Tusi to give more credit to the views of Plato and Aristotle on justice and political organisation than a Sunni writer. These belong to an earlier phase of human wisdom which, though superseded by Islam, may still have something to offer. Humanity moves through a series of divine dispensations; here the concept of state or dynasty as dawla is given an Isma'ili spin. New prophets may introduce new laws; there is scope for significant interpretation by expert jurists, and especially by Imams. Thus Tusi did not consider the present Shari'a to be as absolute as Sunnis did.

HUMANITY

Tusi's political thought was grounded on a view of humanity as midway between higher intellectual and spiritual ranks and lower physical and mortal ones. The human person may achieve eternal felicity, or disaster; that is up to him or her. This view of human freedom went with an elevated view of human nature. 'Man's perfection and the enabling of his virtue were entrusted to his reflection, reason, intelligence and will; and the key of felicity and affliction ... was given into the hand of his own competence' (p. 47). The human species, 'the noblest of existent things', is created by God, but its improvement and perfection 'are entrusted to its own independent judgement (ra'y)'.[5] This elevation of reason found an echo in the development of individual reasoning by Imami Jurists (see above, p. 145). There is greater diversity in humans than in any other species. This was the kind of view of human nature that one would find two centuries later in Italian renaissance thinkers;[6] they shared with Tusi the genealogy of neo-Platonic monotheism.

On humans' moral inclinations, Tusi considered the opinions of Stoics, that humans are good by nature; of Galen, that some are good, some bad, some could go either way; and of Aristotle, that 'evil men become good by instruction and discipline', or – as Tusi later put it – 'some men are good by nature while others are good by Religious Law (bi-shar')' (*Ethics*, p. 210). He concluded that human welfare requires first the organisation of the material world by reason, through the arts and crafts; and then instruction, discipline (tadbir) and leadership. Humans *may* attain perfection by their own effort and reason, but most of them need instruction, many need discipline, and some need coercion. 'Since man at the beginning of primal genesis was adapted to these two conditions [that is, the intellectual and the physical], there befell a need for Prophets and philosophers, Imams, guides, tutors and instructors' (p. 48). These would enable man to avoid disaster and attain felicity 'through leadership and direction, discipline and instruction (ta'lim)'. This emphasis to a certain extent reflected the Shi'ite (Imami or Isma'ili) view of the human predicament.

POLITICAL SOCIETY

The first element in Nasir al-Din Tusi's explanation of human cooperation and social organisation is political economy, especially the crafts. The necessities of life are provided by 'the organisation of techniques (tadbir-i sina'i) such as sowing, harvesting, cleaning, pounding, kneading and cooking' (p. 153). 'For this reason Divine Wisdom has required that there should be disparity of aspirations and opinions, so that each desires a different occupation, some noble and others base, in the practice of which they are cheerful and contented'.[7] And crafts depend upon *money*. This is 'the lesser law', 'a just mediator between men, but ... silently just'. Money is precisely an instrument of justice. For 'the just man is the one who gives proportion and equivalence to disproportionate and non-equivalent things'; and 'money, which is the equaliser of diversities, is required, for if there were not adjustment of diversities by diverse prices, then association and negotiation in ... taking and giving could not be determined'.[8] That is, money equates x amount of labour by a surveyor with y amount of labour by a bricklayer; it is the means of measurement. The result is equilibrium (i'tidal) and civic (we might say social) justice ('adl-i madani). This smacks of the labour theory of value; the common debt is to Aristotle.

The crafts depend upon social organisation. Because human beings have to cooperate, 'the human species is naturally in need of combination'; that is, 'civilised life (tamaddun)'. This term 'is derived from "city (madina)"', a city being a place of combination for individuals as they carry on, by their various trades and crafts, the co-operation which is the means of procuring a livelihood' (p. 190). The human being is, therefore, 'naturally a city-dweller (or citizen)'; Tusi condemned the solitary life as selfish, taking but not giving.

Finally such an association 'requires some type of management (tadbir)', that is siyasa (governance/government). Indeed, monetary exchange between people sometimes requires *arbitration*. So the second factor in Tusi's explanation of political society is justice. He followed Plato in seeing justice as 'all virtue', as harmony within diversity. Friendship, care for kin, and human fellowship are all species of justice. And 'the preservation of justice among men cannot be effected without three things: the Divine Commandment (namus-i ilahi), a human arbitrator (hakim), and money' (pp. 97, 190).

The ultimate factor in this explanation of human association is, surprisingly, love (mahabbat), which plays a more central part here than in any other Islamic social theory. Love engenders civilised life (tamaddun) and social synthesis (majmu') and is 'the connector of societies'. Love flows from human nature itself (this could have derived from neo-Platonism): the more purified we are, the more we become 'simple substances' which know 'no further disparity between using and forsaking the bodily nature', and achieve inward synthesis through 'the love of good men for one another'. Fellow feeling can arise by chance 'on shipboard or during journeys', yet 'the cause of this is a sense of fellowship which is rooted in the nature of man'. Love for one's own species is prompted not only by philosophy ('wisdom') but also by Religious Law: communal prayer is preferable to private prayer precisely because it encourages community (jam' iyat). And love is directed to fellow humans as such and so leads to an association of the human species. The reason why everyone should make the Pilgrimage once in their lives is so that 'the inhabitants of distant lands might come together, acquiring some share of that felicity which the inhabitants of cities [receive] ... and [display] that natural fellowship to be found in their innate disposition'. Indeed, Tusi sees all Muslims as comprising a single association (koinonia) in Aristotle's sense. And mutual help and co-operation point us also towards a community of the human species 'in order to attain perfection', a 'synthesis' which leads to the oneness of all in the 'Perfect Man' (of Isma'ili doctrine) (*Ethics*, pp. 199–200). Tusi seems here to have achieved a deeper integration between Aristotle and Shi'ite thought.

As for siyasa, Nasir al-Din Tusi, like all Islamic thinkers, focused on the nature and prerogatives of the ruler, whom he called malik (king). He seems to have had a better knowledge of Aristotle's political thought than most falasifa, because he notes that 'the philosophy of Aristotle' envisaged four types of government: kingship, domination, nobility, the community (jama'ati). What this means for Tusi is that all four coexist; the king is a 'government of governments' and organises the other three (p. 191).

While domination and nobility are non-virtuous forms of government, community government is the natural counterpart of kingly. Tusi seems to equate it with, or associate it with, the religious sphere of governance. Community government deals with 'enactments', for example 'contracts and transactions', and with 'intellectual judgments'. While he was presumably referring to Aristotle's 'rule by the many for the common good (politeia)', he did not interpret this as meaning government *by* the community. Rather, it requires 'a person distinguished from others by divine inspiration, in order that they should follow him': that is, the one whom the ancient Greeks called 'the possessor of the law (sahib-i namus)' and the modern Muslims call the religious law-giver (shari') (p. 191). This equation of the Hellenic legislator with the Abrahamic Prophet followed on from al-Farabi and Ibn Sina. So Tusi here seems to be equating Aristotle's rule by the people with the government of the Imams: presumably it is called 'community government' because it involves *consent* to the law. He was the only Islamic thinker who saw 'rule by the people' (as he interpreted it) as part of virtuous government. What he said would also fit in with rule by religious experts (mujtahids) such as was to be expounded by his pupil, al-'Allama. And so it may be viewed as part of the Imami Shi'ite development which led eventually to the first Islamic Republic (see below, pp. 333–5).

POLITICAL GROUPINGS

Again, groupings (or combinations: sing. ijtima') of individuals can be of the following types: (1) household, (2) locality (street, quarter), (3) city, (4) 'great communities (umam-i kibar)' – people, nation, and (5) 'the inhabitants of the world'. (This classification may have come from al-Farabi.) Since, due to the inevitable division of labour, each person does not produce his or her own food and other necessities on a daily basis, storage (accumulation) is required; for this we need households. Household management, Tusi noted with a brush of Islamic egalitarianism, is a branch of philosophy (hikmat) which *everyone* requires, because 'each person, in his own degree, is charged with assuming responsibility for the affairs of a community [sc. a household], so that he is their pastor (ra'i) and they are his flock (ra'iyyat)'. Each type of group has its own head (ra'is); the head of the household is subordinate to the head of the locality and so on, all being subordinate to 'the head of the world' or 'head of heads', who is the Absolute King or Leader. The survival and perfection of every human individual depends upon this ultimate community (p. 155).

This universal community in turn depends upon the *science of politics* (hikmat-i madani), the 'supreme craft' which oversees all the other crafts, being 'the study of universal laws (qawanin) producing the best interest of the generality inasmuch as they are directed, through co-operation, to true perfection' (p. 192). Knowledge, in the broad sense of wisdom, is fundamental to social order.

> The ordering of cities depends on kingship (mulk) and the ordering of king-ship on statecraft (siyasa) and that of statecraft on *wisdom*. When wisdom prevails and the true law (namus-e haqq) is followed, order (nizam) is obtained, as is the attention to the perfection of beings. But if wisdom departs, namus (law) is impaired, and when namus is impaired the adorn-ment of kingship disappears, and disorder (fitna) makes its appearance.[9]

The aim of political science, as of medicine, is equilibrium; the expert states-man is 'the world's physician'. Then comes a surprising statement: 'every person is compelled to study' the science of politics, in order that he may be capable of attaining virtue (p. 193). This is a remarkably egalitarian sentiment, and closer to the Sunni model of Religious Knowledge than to the Shi'ite. What it presumably means is that the aim of politics is virtue and that every person must learn for themselves how to achieve this.

Now the actual lawgiver (returning to what he said about types of government) is only needed once in a while. A king is needed all the time, to maintain the legal system: such a person is called 'Absolute King' by the ancients, Imam by the moderns; some, using Isma'ili terminology, refer to these two types of ruler as 'the speaker' and 'the foundation'. The 'king' in question may have no 'retinue or realm'; rather, he is 'one truly deserving of kingship, even though outwardly no-one pays him any attention' (p. 192). Again, rather like in al-Farabi, we are back with the ideal community, and, probably, the hidden Imam.

In fact, Tusi called the worldwide association, under the Imam, 'the virtuous city'. It is clear that he modelled the political part of his discourse fairly closely upon al-Farabi. By virtuous city, Tusi too seems to have meant the Shi'ite community (presumably Imami though it could also refer to the Isma'ilis). The virtuous city is described as a grouping of those who are in agreement about opinions and acts – a close-knit spiritual community. 'The people of the virtuous city, albeit diversified throughout the world, are in reality agreed … In their close-knit affection they are like one individual' (p. 215).

The types of non-virtuous city too are defined, again following al-Farabi, in terms of their aspirations towards 'necessity, affluence, pleasure, ennoblement, domination or freedom'; they too are based upon a common outlook (p. 225). Presumably Tusi conceived these types as coexisting in the actual world with the virtuous city. This would make sense of Shi'ite experience.

STATUS GROUPS

We now encounter social status. Within the virtuous city, people are graded according to their intellectual and spiritual ability. Thus we have (a) 'the most virtuous philosophers (afadil-i hukama)', who alone have true knowledge, and are very few; (b) 'people of faith (ahl-i iman)', who take on trust what the wise say: this seems to refer to the 'ulama and Religious Judges; it may also refer to the Shi'ite community as a whole; (c) those whose knowledge is based on imagination and rhetoric; (d) image-worshippers. He gave another grading of *five* status groups (rukhn: pillars): (1) the virtuous philosophers; (2) 'the community who bring the common people … to degrees of relative perfection' by transmitting the teaching of the philosophers through theology, Jurisprudence and poetry – the 'ulama again, presumably; (3) those who maintain justice and correct measurements by the crafts of accountancy, medicine and astrology; (4) warriors; (5) cultivators and tax-collectors (Ethics, pp. 212–16, 230). The first classification is based on religious criteria, especially as interpreted by al-Farabi and Ibn Sina. The second is based on the division of labour in society and, quite specifically, on al-Farabi's five status groups (see above, p. 73).

Mental diversity and inequality derive from birth and custom; they are the result of creation, and they are a 'cause of order'. The Legislator 'is designated to protect the whole community' and he speaks to people 'in the measure of their intelligences'. Moreover, members of the virtuous city, 'blundering along as they are on the road to perfection', may 'appear to differ in community and doctrine'; but these differences come only from 'different imprints of fancies and exemplars, all seeking the same end'. They 'are comparable to differences in foods and clothes' (p. 214). Does this suggest, as in the Isma'ili views of the Brethren of Purity, that different religious communities, including non-Muslim monotheists, are the result of accidental causes, and should therefore be tolerated?

Tusi also reproduced a version of the standard Irano-Islamic classification of status groups. There are: (1) 'men of the pen', those expert in knowledge, namely Jurists, Judges, secretaries, accountants, geometers, astronomers, physicians, poets, 'on whose existence depends the order of this world and the next'. This covered the first three categories in the previous classification of the Virtuous City. There follow (2) 'men of the sword'; (3) 'men of business', merchants, craftsmen and tax-collectors; (4) agriculturalists. He also divided people into five categories according to their moral nature (pp. 230–1).

Tusi then discussed the government of an *actual* state ruled by a 'supreme king (badshah)', in the Advice-to-Kings tradition. Here he used the same language as for the virtuous city, but to make the somewhat different point that, if kingdoms are to function successfully, they must have *spiritual* unity. For in general, states (dawlat-ha) depend upon 'the agreement of the opinions of a community who, in respect of co-operation and mutual assistance, are like the members belonging to one individual'. Their power depends upon many individuals becoming 'like one individual in synthesis and unity'; and this occurs only when their members have the same opinions. The degree of such spiritual unity determines the rise and fall of states (pp. 228–30). This would certainly not inspire toleration.

In actual states, the ruler's duty is 'to consider the state of his subjects and to devote himself to maintaining the laws of justice, for the order of the realm lies in justice'. This means, above all, maintaining equilibrium between the status groups. The ruler must avoid domination of one status group by another; he must determine 'the rank of each one in the measure of merited aptitude', and preserve 'equality between (the status groups) in the division of common goods' (pp. 230–2). So, while the groups are unequal in intellect, they should not be unequal in wealth (Plato would broadly have agreed). So Tusi made status, or class, a focal point of political governance. Status and occupational groups assume an importance unparalleled in any other pre-modern thinker, indeed in any thinker before Durkheim.

Tusi's *Nasirean Ethics* was widely read and imitated, especially in Persia and the Ottoman world. It provided a crucial link – almost the only one – between the pre-Mongol culture of Eurasia and the courtly-bureaucratic culture of early modern states. Nasir al-Din Tusi transmitted elements of classical Islamic political philosophy to the early modern world.

NOTES

1. Halm (1991: 63–71). See Henri Laoust, 'Les fondements de l'autorité dans le "Minhag" d'al-Hilli', in Anon. (1982: 175–207); S. Schmidtke, *The Theology of al-'Allama al-Hilli* (d.726/1325) (Berlin: K. Schwartz, 1991); John Cooper (trans. and ed.), "Allama al-Hilli on the Imamate and Ijtihad', in Arjomand (ed.) (1988: 240–9); al-Hilli ('Allama), *Al-Babu 'l-Hadi 'Ashar*, trans. W. E. Miller (London: Royal Asiatic Society, 1928).

2. *The Nasirean Ethics*, by Nasir al-Din Tusi, trans G. M. Wickens (London: Allen & Unwin, 1964). See Wilferd Madelung, 'Nasir ad-Din Tusi's Ethics: Between Philosophy, Shi'ism, and Sufism', in Hovannisian (1985: 85–101); Fakhry (1991: 131–41); S. J. H. Badakhchani (ed. and trans.), *Contemplation and Action: The Spiritual Autobiography of a Muslim Scholar: Nasir al-Din Tusi* (London: Tauris, 1998).

3. Ed. and trans. W. Ivanow (Leiden: Brill, 1950); Lambton (1981: 301–3).

4. Fouchécour (1986: 436–7); V. Minorsky, 'Nasir al-Din Tusi on Finance', in V. Minorsky, *Iranica* (Hartford CT: S. Austin, 1964).

5. *Ethics*, p. 78; *Tasawwurat*, p. 34.

6. Ed. Ernst Cassirer et al., *The Renaissance Philosophy of Man* (Chicago: University of Chicago Press, 1948).

7. *Ethics*, p. 189; compare Marsiglio of Padua: Black (1984: 89).

8. Pp. 97–8, 157; compare Miskawayh (see above, p. 73).

9. P. 233 and in Arjomand (1984: 97) (my italics).

Ibn Taymiyya (1263–1328): Shari'a Governance (al-siyasa al-shar'iyya)

16

At the opposite pole of Islamic political thought stood Ahmad Ibn Taymiyya (Harran, Syria 1263–Damascus 1328).[1] His career and his thought were an intense dialogue between the political context created by military pressure, embodied in the Mamluk sultanate, and Sunni textual correctness. A Mongol invasion made him a refugee at the age of six. He was educated in the Hanbali tradition and succeeded his father as director of a Damascus madrasa. Ibn Taymiyya spent his life as a religious critic in the Mamluk domains of Egypt and Syria. His mission was to propagate the correct meaning of the Religious Law. He was a bitter opponent of Sufism and Christianity, engaged in continuous controversy with the Shi'ites, especially al-'Allama al-Hilli (see above, p. 145), attacked anything innovatory (bid'a), and also turned on the laxity of his fellow-Sunni 'ulama.

Ibn Taymiyya gained a popular following, his outbursts threatened public order, and he had repeated spells in jail, on one occasion being interrogated by Ibn Jama'a himself. He thus achieved the rare privilege of persecution for Sunni loyalism. Yet once, appointed official preacher of Holy War, he personally rallied resistance to a Mongol invasion of Syria (1300–1). He spent his last two years in prison (1326–8), where he wrote an enormous amount, until his jailers deprived him of pens and paper.

Ibn Taymiyya adopted a restrictive stance on many legal questions (hashish is as bad as alcohol).[2] He was a tireless and uncompromising controversialist. His methodology was not rigidly Hanbali. He tuned in to al-Mawardi, Juwayni, al-Ghazali and Fakhr al-Din Razi, and he studied opponents with care, including the Imami al-'Allama and the Isma'ili Brethren of Purity. He would often cite Abu Hanifa, Ibn Hanbal and 'most Jurists' side by side as alternatives (Laoust 1939: 118). He did not advocate a purely literal interpretation of texts, but used Analogy and syllogism as means of relating particular instances to legal norms by rational argument. He endorsed the individual reasoning (ijtihad) of the qualified expert (mujtahid) as an aid to understanding the Consensus of believers. Most strikingly, he advocated a 'happy mean (wasat)' – or reconciliation – between reason (the method of theology), tradition (the method of hadith-Reporters), and free will (the method of the Sufis). Furthermore, the fundamental principles and values of the Shari'a must take account of new circumstances; the Religious Law as it stands might require considerable adaptation. The Shari'a could offer true guidance on every question only if one used all one's effort (ijtihad).

Ibn Taymiyya's main political work was *The Book on the Government of the Religious Law (al-Kitab al siyasa al-shar'iyya*: written 1311–15). His politics was inspired by the vision of a Shari'a which, to be true to its all-embracing mission, must be updated. He sought to achieve the moral purity of Hanbali tradition not, like his predecessors, by grudging abstention from high politics, but by applying the Shari'a to matters of government. This, he insisted, *was* the project of Islam. It had originally been achieved by the righteous caliphs; now it required other instruments. One may say that Ibn Taymiyya's horizons were opened up by the ending of the 'Abbasid Caliphate; for this cleared the way for more radical solutions to long-perceived problems. Thus he rejected the Mawardian view that the ruling Power (sultan), provided it was recognised by the Deputy and upheld the Shari'a, could be regarded as de facto independent and legitimate in Islamic terms. More stringent criteria must be applied.

The goal was Righteous Rule (siyasa shar'iyya). Ibn Taymiyya's treatise of this title began by recalling that God has joined 'knowledge and the pen, with their task of apostolate and persuasion, to power and the sword, with their task of victory and domination' (p. 1). It concluded by proclaiming the superiority of Islam over the other two revealed faiths on the ground that they proclaim religion without striving to achieve 'the conditions necessary for its existence: power, Holy War, material resources' (in Laoust 1939: 178). The trouble with the world today, he said, is that, on the one hand, rulers think they can achieve material ends by means of force, ambition and self-interest, while, on the other hand, religious people think that they can achieve spiritual ends by mere piety. 'Thus they abstain from all participation in political life and forbid it to others'. The right course is, once again, the happy mean (wasat): concern for 'the material and moral interests of the community – which are closely linked ... honesty joined with power' (in Laoust 1939: 55–7).

RELIGION REQUIRES STATE POWER

Ibn Taymiyya was particularly insistent that religion cannot be practised without state power. The religious duty of Commanding good and Forbidding evil (hisba) simply cannot be achieved 'except through the power and authority of a leader (imam)'. And 'all the other duties which God has decreed – namely Holy War, justice, pilgrimage, communal prayer ... assisting the oppressed, Legal Penalties and so on – cannot be fulfilled except through the power and authority of a ruler'. 'Religion without sultan (power), Holy War (jihad) and wealth, is as bad as sultan, wealth and conflict (harb) without religion.'[3]

Ibn Taymiyya proved this in Islamic terms by insisting that what we call 'political' offices and activities fall into the categories of 'Trusts (amanat)' and 'Public Functions (wilayat)' as understood by Religious Law (Laoust 1939: 3, 70–2). Thus the obligation to 'deliver trusts back to their owners' and to 'judge with justice' (Q. 4:61–2) – that is, to enforce Legal Penalties against the noble as well as the poor – falls fairly and squarely upon the political authorities. The Shari'a's principles of economic justice in exchange, restitution and distribution to the needy must be observed by public authorities as well as by private individuals (Laoust 1939: 2–3). (In general, Ibn Taymiyya sought to protect the rights of private ownership.) The purpose of all Public Functions is the material and spiritual welfare of human beings. But the material and spiritual welfare of human beings depends upon the (Prophetic) postulate of hisba: therefore, 'to Command the good and Forbid the bad is the supreme goal of every Public Function' (Laoust 1939: 70). No government can achieve this without adhering to Islamic norms. On the other hand, Commanding the good and Forbidding the bad cannot be effective without the threat of coercion.

This provided Ibn Taymiyya with the indissoluble link between religion and the state: 'It is, therefore, a duty to consider the Amirate as a form of Religion, as one of the acts by which one approaches God' (in Laoust 1939: 174). And conversely, the ruler's exercise of power is 'one of the most important duties of religion'. 'Since the aim assigned to dawla [state] and shawka [force] is to approach God, and to put his religion into practice, therefore when state and religion are wholly employed for this purpose, perfect spiritual and temporal prosperity is ensured' (in Laoust 1939: 177).

This was a radical development of al-Mawardi. It may be seen as going back to the original position of Islam, to what differentiated it most from Christianity: humans' material and spiritual welfare are inseparable. The theory of state origins corroborated this: if humans need association, and so are 'political by nature', and if their common purposes require 'obedience to one who commands them', then religion needs the state. In fact, religion and government need one another.[4] This thesis was to be explored empirically by Ibn Khaldun, whose study of history explored in detail the relationship between religion and other social forces.

One can thus say that rulership (sultan, mulk, amir) and the Shari'a are enfolded into one another as Righteous Government (siyasa shar'iyya). The Leadership (Imamate) is a special Function (wilaya), requiring force (shawka), kingship (mulk) and ruling power (sultan). The state is fully incorporated into Religious Thought (fiqh). At the same time, the distinction between Deputy (Caliph) and Sultan disappears for practical purposes. This of course reflected the contemporary situation. What Ibn Taymiyya meant here was that all good Islamic rulers perform the religious functions formerly ascribed to the Deputy. This brought further obligations: no ruler or 'representatives of authority', or their subjects, can 'dispense themselves from the government of God and the vicegerency of the Prophet' (in Laoust 1939: 172–3, 299). That is, they are all bound by the same religious obligation attaching to their office as the Deputies had been.

Within the Islamic community ('The People of Tradition and Community: ahl al-sunna wa-l-Jama'a') Ibn Taymiyya accepted the plurality of separate states. Within each state, the Leader-ruler is responsible for the application of Legal Punishments (hudud), the observation of fast and pilgrimage, the performance of public services, the application of social and economic norms and, above all, the conduct of prayer and Holy War (Laoust 1939: 253, 259).

THE RULER'S RESPONSIBILITIES

All this gave the Islamic ruler and public officials a high status, and it gave the people high expectations of them. Ibn Taymiyya expressed special admiration for the first four Deputies, and also for the Saljuks, Nur al-Din and Salah al-Din, and the first Mamluk sultans. Rulers do not define their own objectives; but they do have the authority to act and to be obeyed on the understanding that they are carrying out the objectives of Islam.

The dependence of legitimate power on the fulfilment of responsibilities was forcefully stated in the Qur'anic doctrine of trusteeship: those entrusted with power 'are but trustees, representatives, agents of authority, in no way proprietors'. *This* is what is meant by calling the ruler a shepherd; he is like the guardian of an orphan (Laoust 1939: 8, 299). The ancient Middle-Eastern and Iranian image of the absolute monarch was here fully Islamicised. All right, so the ruler's authority comes from God: but this means that the interests he is charged to serve are those of his subjects. The idea, now emerging in Europe, of the state as a trans-personal entity is not far away; and was probably not inconceivable within Ibn Taymiyya's mental universe. What is absent is any authority ascribed to, or ascribable to, the people.

Ibn Taymiyya allowed the ruler discretion over penalties not prescribed by the Law, for example for maladministration, financial malpractice and bribery – the traditional areas of secular law (qanun) and the Mazalim courts. Revenue sources beyond those stipulated by Religious Law, so long as they are not forbidden by the Juristic Consensus, may be permitted on the authority of individual reasoning. This was an extremely important concession to the Sultan. The ruler must choose as officials (governors, generals, prayer leaders, village chiefs) men suited to the task. Only in the case of Judges does he have to choose the *best* candidate. To choose someone *incapable*, however, is an abuse of trust (an attack on nepotism).

There is no mitigation of the strict Hanbali principle that *all* public authorities must be obeyed so long as their commands do not contradict the Shari'a. On the other hand, the ruler *is* morally-legally obliged to consult others; and all Muslims have the religio-legal duty to give good counsel (nasiha) as part of Commanding good and Forbidding evil. This is because the ruler or official may not possess in himself all the qualities necessary to carry out his functions. Such tendering of advice provides a happy mean (again) between acquiescence and armed rebellion. It is especially important that the Learned ('ulama) give advice. The term 'holders of authority' (Q. 4:61) —those to whom the Qur'an commands obedience – nowadays refers to the Lords (amirs) and the Learned (in Laoust 1939: 54, 68). In singling these out, Ibn Taymiyya was giving legal recognition to predominant social facts. One of the main reforms proposed by Ibn Taymiyya was that the 'ulama abandon their isolation from politics. Such obligatory consultation came as close as anything in Muslim political thought to a constitutional check upon those in authority.

This view of Righteous Government meant that all practical aspects of government fell within the moral universe of religion. Thus Ibn Taymiyya transported the prudential Advice-to-Kings material into Jurisprudence. His very undertaking was (in Laoust's words) to unite siyasa, 'the empirical and opportunistic art of government', with the Shari'a, thereby 'making the Shari'a more pliable through contact with ruling custom, and bringing together [current] custom with the general principles of religious Jurisprudence' (in Laoust 1939: 55). He achieved this, first, by applying independent reasoning to social and political questions; second, by liberal use of the religio-legal criterion of 'general welfare (maslaha)', as a justification for measures not strictly stipulated, or forbidden, by Law. Again, he reiterated the principle that God never requires the impossible or forbids the necessary.

What is required in a ruler or governor is not the ideal set of qualities listed by writers like al-Mawardi, but virtues which will enable him to achieve what he has to. These turn out to have been envisaged in the Qur'an. For war, the ruler needs courage and guile ('war is guile'); for adjudication, knowledge of justice and loyalty. But these are seldom all found in one person. So, choose the person with the abilities appropriate for the job in hand: a gentle leader should have a violent collaborator. 'God will strengthen this religion with the help of men without morality' (Report); 'I am the Prophet of Mercy, I am the Prophet of Carnage ... I am a bloody laugher'. The purposes of public office are achieved through terror and love alternately: 'in reality the two methods go together' (in Laoust 1939: 11, 14–16).

> One cannot govern men without generosity, which consists in giving, and without force of mind, which is a form of courage ... No spiritual or material life is possible without the existence of these two virtues. Whoever loses them will soon lose power. (in Laoust 1939: 53)

Ibn Taymiyya thus contributed to the concept of good government as necessarily including an element of severity. He insisted that, even if a criminal repents, the authorities must exact the full Legal Penalties without mitigation. This will stimulate obedience to God. 'Every governor must be inexorable in the application of the Legal Penalties and inaccessible to pity, because religion is at stake' (in Laoust 1939: 100). He was especially severe on brigands. He stressed the duty of Holy War as one of the chief acts of service to God, and ranked it above pilgrimage. Warriors top the list of those to be remunerated for serving the Muslim community. 'The supreme aim of Holy War' is punishment for the neglect of religious duties, or for forbidden acts (Laoust 1939: 73).

Ibn Taymiyya brought out with amazing clarity certain ideas which may plausibly be regarded as intrinsic to Islamic political thought. But he was perhaps the last original thinker in Sunni fiqh. For a long time, he had few followers and little influence (Laoust 1939: 477–505). A few Ottoman scholars studied him in the sixteenth century. Then in the eighteenth century he was adopted by the Wahhabi movement (see below, p. 256). He was in fact the only major political theorist to come from the fertile crescent for a very long time. From then on, his ideas have exercised increasing influence on Sunni political thought. How correctly his voluminous works are understood is another matter.

NOTES

1. *EI* s.v. Ibn Taymiyya; Laoust (1939) (a masterly survey, with translations); Lambton (1981: 143–51); Nagel (1981: vol. 2, pp. 109–40); E. Rosenthal (1958: 51–61).
2. Franz Rosenthal, *The Herb: Hashish versus Medieval Muslim Society* (Leiden: Brill, 1971), pp. 160–1.
3. In Laoust (1939: 172–3) and E. Rosenthal (1958: 54).
4. Lambton (1981: 146–7); Gibb (1962: 169).

The Dehli Sultanate and al-Barani: Statecraft and Morality

17

The Islamic lands of northern and central India were ruled by an Afghan and Turkic military elite of slave soldiers under the Delhi sultanate (1206–1526); under sultan Balban (r.1249–87), high office was restricted to Turks. The regime bore the marks of its origins in Sunni Central Asia and adhered to Community-Traditional orthodoxy. Although Sultan Mubarak Shah declared himself Deputy (1317), other sultans found it judicious to enhance their status in the eyes of the 'ulama by being recognised and invested by the 'Abbasid Caliph in Cairo.[1] Under the Tughluq dynasty (1320–1413), and especially under Muhammad Ibn Tughluq (1325–51), the area of Islamic control was extended southwards.

MUSLIMS AND HINDUS

Islam was spread by Sufi missionaries and Persian merchants; the Sufi form of Islam proved attractive in India. It accommodated syncretism between Islamic and Hindu practices and beliefs; 'Indian Islam seems to have been essentially a holy-man Islam'.[2] Urdu was a lingua franca. Islam offered relief from the caste system, but conversion was not all that widespread.

Below the dominant elite, society was pluralist. The conquests somewhat resembled a corporate takeover, in that 'the pre-Islamic political structure of India remained intact ... local lords and the Brahmin religious elite retained local political power under Muslim suzerainty', so long as taxes were paid (Lapidus 1988: 446). The traditional rural order remained under village headmen. Commerce and banking were dominated by upper-caste Hindus. Muhammad Ibn Tughluq appointed non-Muslims to high office and permitted Hindu temples to be built.

In political culture, syncretism was possible because both Muslims and Hindus agreed upon the absolute sovereignty of the divinely decreed sovereign. Moreover, 'the Muslim emphasis upon loyalty to the ruler, patron–client relations, and the virtues of service and honour were consistent with Hindu political ideals' (Lapidus 1988: 442). Sultans entered into a symbiotic relationship with Sufi leaders, to whom they looked for politico-religious support as their point of contact with the common people. The order deriving from Umar al-Suhrawardi (see above, p. 133) '[mediated] between the Delhi sultanate and the provincial provinces and tribes' (Lapidus 1988: 450). Sufi masters, for their part, were inclined to accept hierarchical order on religious grounds, advocated abstention from political activity and government service, and preached non-violence. Their power rested on their own communal organisation.

Islamic political thought in India was similar to elsewhere. Irano-Islamic ideas, especially in Nizam al-Mulk's version, were transmitted in Advice-to-Kings literature, for example in the thirteenth-century *Conduct of Kings* (*Adab ul-Muluk*) by Fakhr-i Mudabbir. Falsafa was absent.[3]

What was unusual was the prominence of the relationship between Muslims and non-Muslims; this became a contentious issue in religious policy among the Muslim elite. Some thought that Hindus qualified as monotheists and should therefore have the legal status of Protected People (dhimmi). Others disputed this; rather, Hindus should be fought and, if they refused conversion, killed as polytheists: Islam should in general be more rigorously enforced. According to Fakhr-i Mudabbir, Hindus were subordinate but they did have the status of a Protected People (Ahmad 1962: 121–3).

AL-BARANI (C.1285–C.1357)

The most reflective thinker of this period was Dhiya' al-Din Barani (Delhi before 1285–after 1357). He was the first Islamic theorist to expose and try to resolve the contradictions between Islamic and Iranian views of government. Earlier Islamic authors, whether or not they thought about them, never discussed them. Barani was a courtier's son; he probably wrote his *Fatawa-yi Jahandari* (in Persian) while in the service of Muhammad Ibn Tughluq.[4] This was an Advice Book in the form of sayings by Mahmud of Ghazna. The next sultan, Firuz Shah Tughluq (r.1351–88), had Barani exiled, probably due to the line he took in the succession dispute; Barani spent his last years composing books in the hope of a return to court. He dedicated *Ta'rikh-i Firuz Shahi* (*History of Shah Firuz*) to the new ruler. Here, he attempted to prove the advantages of following the advice he had given in his *Fatawa-yi*, in the light of the history of the Sultanate. As a historian Barani was unreliable, except for contemporary events. He died in poverty.

Barani's argument rotates around a clear distinction between state policy and personal morality: it is best that kings 'set the example of obeying the laws they impose on others', but the fact that they do not is 'irrelevant to the functioning of their governments'. What kings must do is enforce the Muslim Code severely. Barani placed the usual Islamic emphasis upon *justice*. It prevents oppression and protects the weak; without it there can be no religion. He adapted the slogan 'religion and the world are twins' to 'religion and justice are twins'. Justice is 'the real justification for the supremacy of kings'; human nature is so fierce that 'command and control over [humans] cannot be established without the terror and power of dominating kings'. Justice requires 'a strong ruler among the people' possessing 'force and authority' (*Fatawa-i*, pp. 3, 16, 34).

But then he innovates: justice requires strong government, in the pagan Iranian manner, and it cannot be achieved without departure from religious norms. He emphasised that the king must combine severity and mercy. These must be innate to him, they must be 'developed to perfection', so that he may exercise them whenever occasion requires. Such flexibility is 'a wonder of the wonders of creation'. A king with both these qualities is, indeed, God's Deputy and 'the axis of the earth (qutb-i 'alm), and in the next world [he] will find a place in the shadow of the divine throne'. If kingship is to succeed in enforcing laws and suppressing lawlessness, it must use 'terror, prestige and power'. The king must embody 'high resolve' (more or less the equivalent of Machiavelli's virtù) (*Fatawa-yi*, p. 86).

These latter points were in fact close to Islamic tradition. They were also stated by Lisan al-Din Ibn al-Khatib (1313–75),[5] a historian and vizier to the King of Granada, who became a close friend of Ibn Khaldun. Perhaps because of the European context in which he was writing, Ibn al-Khatib showed particular concern for the ruler–ruled relationship, but from a strictly pragmatic point of view. In a book on the conduct of viziers, presented as advice given by a sage to the Caliph Harun al-Rashid, Ibn al-Khatib said: 'the common people may be simple, but they are quite powerful, especially when they act collectively. If the king is faced by them as a rioting crowd, he should be diplomatic with them and stick firmly to his position until they disperse.' But then 'the king should strike hard at them and leave no room for mercy towards them' (p. 211). But Ibn al-Khatib took a markedly different line in a letter (1367) to Pedro the Cruel, the Christian King of Castile. This was in fact a unique instance of a Muslim Advice for a Euro-Christian ruler. Here he advised the King to respect the lives and property of subjects and the status of nobles, and to pardon his opponents: 'willing submissiveness is the only real submissiveness that can last'.[6] This reflected Euro-Christian rather than Islamic sentiment at this time.

Barani was unusual in seeing a direct clash between religion and politics. He set out to lay bare a contradiction between (on the one hand) Religious Jurisprudence and, still more, Sufi piety, and (on the other hand) Iranian teaching embodied in Advice-to-Kings literature: a contradiction which (we may say) Advice authors from Ibn Muqaffa' onwards had affected to ignore. The behaviour required in government, he believed, had only been clearly stated in the pagan Iranian tradition. A king can govern successfully only if he follows 'the policies of Khusraw Parvez and the great emperors of Iran'. But 'between the traditions (sunnah) of the Prophet Muhammad and his mode of living, and the customs of the Iranian emperors and their mode of living, there is a complete contradiction'. No king has ruled successfully 'while living according to the Prophet's traditions of poverty'. Rather, 'prophethood (the perfection of religion) and kingship (the perfection of worldly good fortune) … are opposed and contradictory to each other, and their combination is not within the bounds of possibility'. This, Mahmud of Ghazna is made to tell his sons, is 'known to all religious scholars' (*Fatawa-yi*, pp.39–40).

Such a view of religion and power was unprecedented in Islam. It may demonstrate the influence of Sufism; Barani was acquainted with Amir Khusraw, the Sufi poet at the Delhi court. What he had to say assumed a Sufi view of religion as requiring an attitude of helplessness and self-abnegation.

Kingship, on the other hand, requires 'luxurious living, self-glorification'. Only the first four Caliphs were able 'to combine poverty with kingship', due to a miracle from the Prophet – and three of them were martyred (*Fatawa-yi*, p. 39).

But Barani did seek to resolve the contradiction between kingship and Islam, by stating that the attributes ascribed to kingship are 'among the attributes of God'. And 'since kingship is the deputyship (niyabat) and vice-regency (khilafat) of God, it is not possible to be a king by adhering to the virtues of submission'. Here, we note, the Sultan already has Caliphal status, though probably in the spiritual-Sufi sense rather than the technical juristic one. Secondly, to follow 'the traditions of the pagan emperors of Iran' may be regarded, from a Shari' viewpoint, as permissible on grounds of necessity – like eating carrion (*Fatawa-yi*, p. 39).

SECULAR LAW

Barani strongly emphasised the need for sultanic (secular) laws (zawabit) in addition to the Religious Code – another way of resolving the contradiction between religion and practical politics. Such state laws may be customary, or they may be new laws made by the king in consultation with wise counsellors in response to 'change of time and circumstance'. These too are justified by the Juristic doctrine of necessity. Barani gave such new laws a higher status than that traditionally ascribed to non-religious law (qanun) in the Islamic tradition. For, he said, they are based on 'knowledge and reason'; they should be 'permanent', constituting '[rules] of action which the king has imposed as an obligatory duty upon himself for realising the welfare of the state, and from which he absolutely never deviates' (*Fatawa-yi*, p. 64).

The example he gave was honouring the well-born and degrading the low-born: he seemed to regard this as a kind of moral law of nature. Barani believed that political stability depended upon people staying in their own occupations. If profit lured soldiers into agriculture, or nobles into commerce, instability would follow. It is interesting that he chose social status as his example of such a 'natural' law. In fact, Barani wanted the king to impose upon himself a legal obligation 'to give the posts and offices of government to the noble and the free-born only' (*Fatawa-yi*, p. 64). In other words, he wanted the zawabit to be constitutional laws binding on the king. Both sultanic law and social immobility were to become central themes in Ottoman political thought, where they were linked: qanun was supposed to support the social hierarchy.

On practical questions, Barani urged policies that were not new in themselves but had original emphases. Kings should consult wise men (sing. hakim) 'for there is seldom a unanimity of opinion in an error' (*Fatawa-yi*, p.9). Such counsellors should have 'knowledge of the ancient kings' and practical experience; they should hold permanent positions. Discussion in the royal council must be frank and uninhibited. He argued that price control (which had been attempted by Muhammad Ibn Tughluq and earlier sultans) ought to be undertaken by the king 'according to the principle of production-cost' (*Fatawa-yi*, p. 35). Unless the prices of essential commodities are kept low, there will be instability in the army and among the people and consequently in the realm. Barani shows us an original mind grappling with a genuine problem – how to reconcile piety with political success – the very kind of problem which, at the opposite pole of the House of Islam, was preoccupying Ibn Khaldun.

NOTES

1. Hodgson (1974: vol. 2, p. 422). See Lapidus (1988: 437–50); Kulke and Rothermund (1998: 152–69); Ahmad (1964: 6–19); Qureshi (1942).
2. Trimingham (1971: 22); Lapidus (1988: 446).
3. *EI* 7: 88a; Ahmad (1962); Lambton (1980: VI: 438–9).
4. Translated in Mohammed Habib, *The Political Theory of the Delhi Sultanate* (Allahabad: Kitab Mahal, n.d.). See *EI* s.v. Barani; Ahmad (1962: 123–6).
5. Wada al-Qadi, 'Lisan al-Din al-Hatib on Politics', in *Union Européenne des Arabisants et Islamisants, Actes du 8me Congrès (1976): La Significance du bas moyen âge* (Aix-en-Provence: Edisud, n.d.), pp. 205–17.
6. Ibid., p. 211; Spanish version in Lopez de Ayala, *Cronicas de los Reyes de Castillo* (Madrid, 1776), vol. 1, pp. 484–93.

Ibn Khaldun (1332–1406): The Science of Civilisation and the Governance of Islam

18

ʿAbd al-Rahman Ibn Khaldun (Tunis 1332–Cairo 1406)[1] had a turbulent life even by the standards of Muslim intellectuals. Both his parents died from plague in 1349. But he had a conventional religious education and also studied philosophy extensively, reading Plato, Ibn Sina and Ibn Rushd, through whom he became acquainted with Aristotle. He knew works by Nasir al-Din Tusi and Fakhr al-Din Razi. For the enthusiastic youth, metaphysics was 'the noblest of sciences. He who knows it is superior in happiness ... The other sciences need it and it does not need them' (in Mahdi 1957: 33).

Ibn Khaldun went into government service with several minor rulers in the Maghrib and Granada; he served on a peace mission to Pedro the Cruel of Castile (1364) and so became acquainted with the politics of the Christian world. He formed a close friendship with Ibn al-Khatib, the vizier of Granada (see above, p. 162). Ibn Khaldun knew when to change allegiance; he had a special talent for understanding and negotiating with the nomad tribes of the interior. At this point, in Muhsin Mahdi's view, he saw himself engaged in 'reforming society through personal exercise of power or instructing a prince to become a wise ruler' (Mahdi 1957: 55).

But at the age of 36 he declared himself 'cured of the temptation of office. Furthermore, I have for too long neglected scholarly matters. I therefore ceased to involve myself in the affairs of kings and devoted all my energies to study and teaching' (in EI 826b–7a). It was to be seven years before he settled with his family near Oran and was finally able to enjoy four years of uninterrupted study (1375–9) – an unusual experience for a scholar of this period. It was here that he wrote much of his *Universal History* (*Kitab al-ʿIbar*), including the *Prolegomena (Muqaddima)*,[2] which he would continue revising for the rest of his life.

But then, quarrels going back to his time in politics forced him to move to Cairo (1382). The city made a deep impression on Ibn Khaldun; he saw the Mamluks as the saviours of Islam, their Sultanate as 'the paramount Muslim state' (Ayalon 1977 VII: 327). There he became a popular teacher of Jurisprudence, and sufficiently well regarded to be made Maliki Chief Judge (1384). But, as his family were on their way to join him, they were all shipwrecked off Alexandria. His local rivals had him dismissed as Religious Judge. He spent the next fourteen years as head of a Sufi hospice. He was reappointed Judge, then again dismissed (1399–1400).

After that, he was dragooned into accompanying the Sultan on an expedition to save Damascus from Timur. The Sultan abandoned the expedition, Ibn Khaldun was left to negotiate surrender, Damascus was sacked. Ibn Khaldun met Timur several times, and wrote a survey of the Maghrib at his request. He may even have seen him as the new leader of Islam. If so, it would say something about the kind of realist Ibn Khaldun was. In any case, it is wonderful that this apostle of primitive social energies engaged in conversation with the last major representative of warrior nomadism in world history. Back in Cairo, Ibn Khaldun was several times in and out of Judgeships (with Judgeship 'nothing else compares' in the eyes of God, he said [F. Rosenthal vol. 2, p. 149]).

Ibn Khaldun's political experiences were a good background for his understanding of political society and his use of historical sources. The *Prolegomena* uniquely combined the genres of Jurisprudence, Advice-for-Kings and Falsafa; though on one occasion he insisted that he was engaged, not in Jurisprudence or theology, but in an empirical analysis of historical data (*Muqaddima*, p. 190).

THE THEORY OF KNOWLEDGE

The inspiration of the *Prolegomena* is, as we shall see, unmistakably Aristotelian. Gibb somewhat exaggerates similarities between Ibn Khaldun and earlier Islamic thinkers. Ibn Khaldun's fundamental aim was to develop a new way of assessing the value of historical sources by applying the methods of philosophy to the study of history. His focus was the history of the Berbers and Arabs in the Maghrib. Historical understanding must not only take account of the vast variety of actual historical circumstances, but must above all be based on an analysis of *natural, universal human needs*. The *Prolegomena* was the ultimate response of Falsafa to Islamic Religious Knowledge (Hodgson 1974: vol. 2, p. 480); it embodied a unique synthesis between the analytical and the narrative.

Ibn Khaldun's intellectual life began in the field of philosophy. His analysis of knowledge itself was original. He distinguished three types of knowledge. First comes knowledge of essences, the realities behind phenomena. 'Speculative reason' produces 'the perception of existence as it is, with its various genera, differences, reasons and causes ... By thinking about these things, man achieves perfection in his reality and becomes pure intellect and perceptive soul. This is the meaning of human reality' (this summarised the programme of the Falasifa, combining knowledge and personal development). Secondly, there is knowledge of the material phenomena of the natural world and of human cultures, that is 'man's intellectual understanding of things that exist in the outside world, *whether by nature or by convention*, so that he may try to arrange these with the help of his own power. This kind of thinking mostly consists of perceptions. This is the "discerning intellect", with the help of which man obtains the things that are useful to him and his livelihood. ' Thirdly, there is moral knowledge. This is 'the ability to think which provides man with opinions [about] and rules [relative to] dealing with members of his own species, and governing them. Most of these are judgments gradually acquired through experience until their use is perfected. This is called "the experimental intellect".'[3]

This was in fact a strikingly original development of Aristotle's distinction between theoretical and practical knowledge. First, Ibn Khaldun has added to the clear distinction, within the theoretical, between metaphysics and knowledge of physical phenomena, a crucial further distinction within the latter, between knowledge of natural and knowledge of conventional or cultural phenomena, that is between natural and social science. Elsewhere, he also spoke of knowledge of natural phenomena of the kind which leads to action upon the natural environment: 'human actions control the whole world of things that come into being and all it contains'. He contrasted this with 'knowledge of civilisation ('ilm al-'umran)'. 'Civilisation' includes both technology and social and political relationships. Ibn Khaldun may have been indicating a distinction between knowing how to construct a shelter, and the specific architectural skills and styles developed in different cultures. He certainly here identified for the first time the field of knowledge which we call sociology. As he himself put it, 'the accidents involved in every manifestation of nature and intellect deserve study. Any topic that is understandable and real requires its own special science' (p. 39). He recognised social knowledge as a distinctive type of knowledge; no-one else recognised this until perhaps Vico. Knowledge of natural and of conventional phenomena is a *practical* form of knowledge in the sense that, in both cases, it is directed towards improvements in human living.

Ibn Khaldun's third category of knowledge referred to morality, law and politics; here, he emphasised the role of experience. This 'experimental intellect' covers everyday social skills, the ability to cooperate with others. These 'do not require very deep study. All of them are obtained through experience and derived from it'. Indeed, a ruler should not be too clever. But people are enabled to pick these up quicker than they otherwise could through experience alone by means of education and custom – if only they 'will follow the experience of their fathers, teachers and elders ... People can thus dispense with lengthy and meticulous first-hand study of events'. Hence the saying 'he who is not educated by his parents will be educated by time', which beautifully encapsulates the idea of tradition as stored experience (pp. 153–4, 336–7).

All of this shows Ibn Khaldun as someone who was prepared to take Aristotle as a basis from which new developments could be made. He thus marked a radical advance on the encyclopaedic approach of much earlier Falsafa. A similar development was taking place at just this time in European thought. Marsiglio of Padua (1275/80–1342/3) and William of Ockham (c. 1280–1349), in the fields of political philosophy and of logic respectively, were exploring what Aristotle had pioneered in quite new ways.

Reason and causal analysis are at the top of Ibn Khaldun's scale of values.

> The ability to think is the quality of man by which human beings are distinguished from other living beings. The degree to which a human being is able to establish an orderly causal chain determines his degree of humanity. (p. 335)

This set Ibn Khaldun apart from the established Islamic approach to cognition, that is from reliance on the sources of revelation for all fundamental knowledge of the world and of morality, and from seeing causal explanation as contradicting divine omnipotence. Some see Ibn Khaldun as a secular rationalist. He did set out to examine society and culture by rational means. And he may have evolved from his youthful enthusiasm for philosophy into a 'devout and austere old man',[4] a senior Religious Judge and respected Jurist. This would not be surprising in view of what he had gone through in his life. But he was probably all along a believing and practising Muslim. It is a mistake to think of non-belief as the alternative to conventional orthodoxy. Few if any Muslim intellectuals of this period took this path (so far as we can tell; of course the penalties of doing so in public were drastic); and it was rare enough among Christians. Therefore in the absence of unambiguous evidence we should not impute non-belief to the youthful Ibn Khaldun.

What was characteristic of Ibn Khaldun was an assertion of his ultimate independence from any tradition of thought: on the subject of historical knowledge, he claimed to be 'aware of these things with God's help and without the instruction of Aristotle' (p. 41). In the last analysis, he would use his own judgement. Nor did he claim to examine fundamental questions of human existence by 'purely' rational means. For the existence of causal relationships does not mean that reason by itself 'is able to comprehend all existing things and their causes and to know all the details of existence'. This view 'should be dismissed as stupid'. Human reason is, rather, a set of scales (a 'balance'), whose capacity for measurement is 'exact but limited'. 'The intellect should not be used to weigh such matters as the oneness of God, the other world, the truth of prophecy ... One might compare [this] with a man who sees a scale in which gold is being weighed, and wants to weigh mountains in it'.[5] For 'there exist things beyond the reach of man that can be learned only from God through the mediation of [inspired] individuals'; on such matters the Qur'an 'is its own proof. It requires no outside proof' (pp. 70, 73).

Later on in the *Prolegomena* he stated yet more unambiguously that Religious Knowledge, based on Prophecy ('revelation' in Christian language), was to be preferred to reason. Indeed revelation can override reason: 'When Muhammad guides us towards some perception, we must prefer that to our own perceptions ... even if rational intelligence contradicts it ... We must be silent with regard to things of this sort that we do not understand. We must leave them to Muhammad and keep the intellect out of it' (p. 390). He proceeded to a 'refutation of philosophy' with a devout warning against its dangers. Falsafa 'contains principles contrary to the divine law'. It can lead to pernicious results; no-one should study it without first being 'saturated with the Religious Law'. The errors of Falsafa consist precisely in an irrational overestimation of the capabilities of the human intellect; in thinking, as Aristotle, al-Farabi and Ibn Sina have done, that 'the essences and conditions of the whole of existence ... can be perceived by ... intellectual reasoning', that 'happiness consists in arriving [by reason] at perception of all existing things'. (This almost exactly contradicted what he had said earlier.) To think this way is wrong because 'existence is too vast to be completely encompassed or perceived' (pp. 335, 399, 404).

In demonstrating the rational limits of human knowledge, Ibn Khaldun used other arguments that could well have come from European nominalism (though there is no evidence that he was acquainted with this, and it is unlikely that he was). While 'the *existentia* of the outside world are individual in their substances', the mind can only 'conceive *general* concepts'. What philosophers do is to collect sense data and then strip them down to fit their abstract categories; all individual nuances are thereby lost, and with them a great deal of actual reality. Logic is 'too abstract and remote from *sensibilia*'. It does, none the less, have two uses: (1) in the physical sciences and mathematics it provides 'the soundest law ... that we know of'; (2) 'it sharpens the mind in the orderly presentation of proofs and arguments' (pp. 401, 405, 428). He had returned, it seems, to the position of al-Ghazali.

Ibn Khaldun thought that the errors of philosophy are particularly damaging in politics (siyasa). First, he rejected the view of earlier falasifa that Prophecy, being a necessary step to the formation of a sound political society, can be explained rationally. Ibn Khaldun's most original point here was that in politics the specific circumstances of the individual situation are, once again, all-important. 'It can happen that these matters contain *no* features which allow one to assimilate them to other instances [or: contain some element making it impossible to refer them to anything similar], and contradict the general principle which one wishes to apply to them [or: to which one would like them to conform]'.[6] This is a brilliant insight from which social theorists over the past 200 years could greatly have benefited. Nor can qiyas (Analogy) be used to compare cultural phenomena with one another: here the Jurists are mistaken.

Because they exaggerate the powers of human knowledge, philosophers often make mistakes in matters of government. The average person, on the other hand, 'restricts himself to considering every matter as it is, and to judging every kind of situation and every type of individual by its particular [circumstances]. His judgment is not infected with analogy and generalisation' (p. 428). Such people are less likely to make mistakes in politics; in fact, they 'conduct themselves with great judgment in their relations with other men (in Lacoste, p. 254).

These passages differ in both tone and content from earlier sections of the *Prolegomena*. One suspects they were written later, when Ibn Khaldun's thought ran along more orthodox lines. He did not explicitly reject his earlier approach; the *Prolegomena* contains layers of thought laid down in different periods of his life. He neither erased what he had written earlier, nor tried (like a European philosopher) to reconcile his divergent thoughts systematically.

At the end of his survey of human civilisation, Ibn Khaldun discussed knowledge ('ilm) and its branches: the religious disciplines, logic, mathematics, philosophy, Arabic, language in general and poetry – rather a traditional 'classification of the sciences'. Astrology and alchemy Ibn Khaldun regarded with contempt. There is an illuminating discussion of teaching, clearly of concern to Ibn Khaldun. The *Prolegomena* is a systematic book but, like other Arabo-Islamic works, has no conclusion.

HISTORICAL AND SOCIAL METHOD

The enterprise of the *Prolegomena* was fundamentally neo-Aristotelian. One wonders whether it could have been conceived in the spirit in which some of those later passages were written. It has been remarked that Ibn Khaldun failed to operationalise his critical principles in his actual historical writing.

Ibn Khaldun started off by saying that 'history ... is firmly rooted in philosophy. It deserves to be counted a branch of it' (p. 5). In setting out to write world history, he encountered the problem which lay at the core of Islamic learning, namely how to distinguish true from false reports about past events. What was needed was a reliable method of verification: something which would, among other things, distinguish what was possible from what was impossible under various circumstances. Aristotle had developed the analytical-empirical method of classifying things according to their common characteristics (the 'form' of, for example, horse), and proceeding to examine in minute detail the actual examples of such species so as to build up an accurate picture. In this process, the original definition may be refined. The formulation of concepts thus interacts with the study of facts to produce a full understanding of classes of phenomena and of things in themselves.

Aristotle had applied this method to the study of states. Ibn Khaldun knew that such a study existed, but he had not discovered the *Politics*. This is quite remarkable considering how well known it was now in Christendom. In any case, Ibn Khaldun applied this Aristotelian method to the study of human civilisation in a much wider sense than Arisotle or anyone else. Whereas Aristotle had confined his study to the Greek city-state, Ibn Khaldun would make world civilisation the subject of philosophical study (complementing perhaps the all-embracing claims of monotheism). Polis (madina: lit. city or city-state) had indeed been taken by the Islamic falasifa, and more recently by European thinkers, to mean civil society or state in general. According to Ibn Khaldun, history is nothing less than 'a narrative of human aggregation (ijtima') which is the organised habitation ['umran: civilization] of the world' (in al-Azmeh 1982: 48). Thus Ibn Khaldun's work was a continuation and large-scale extension to humanity as a whole, of Aristotle's study of humans as naturally social and political beings.

Much of the *Prolegomena* consists of generalisations about collective human behaviour, illustrated by examples. Such generalisations were the fruit of Ibn Khaldun's reflections on numerous case studies, on his own and other people's experiences ('observation'). Here, Ibn Khaldun added to Aristotle some more specifically historical insights. One 'should not reject data for which one finds no observable parallels in one's own time ... [For] conditions in the world and in civilisation are not [always] the same' (pp. 144, 148). Having assembled as much data as possible about past and present events, and having compared these, one must identify and define human culture, the fundamental subject-matter of history, and determine its basic characteristics. This is what the *science of civilisation* ('ilm al-'umran) consists in.

The criterion for distinguishing truth from falsehood in the study of historical reports according to their possibility and impossibility is to be found in our study of human society. We must distinguish between: (a) the modes pertaining to its essence and involved in its nature, (b) that which is accidental and need not be reckoned with, and (c) that which cannot possibly occur in it. When this is done we will have a criterion ... an infallible method of demonstration. (in Mahdi 1957: 156)

His argument will thus proceed from the 'necessity (darura) that proceeds from the nature of things' (in Lacoste, p. 255). Such knowledge of the *essence* of human culture would provide him with 'the fundamental facts of politics, the nature of civilisation, or the conditions governing human social organisation, ... the principles underlying historical situations' (*Muqaddimah*, p. 11). At this stage, he was clearly not concerned with nominalist objections to such a procedure; presumably he had not yet thought about them.

Thus Ibn Khaldun brought Aristotelian method to bear on what Islamic scholars cared about most: understanding the past. This produced, as he rapturously asserted, 'a science which may be described as independent, which is defined by its object: human civilisation and social facts as a whole' (in *EI* 829b). He would reveal history's inner (batin) workings. This would give Islam a new tool for self-analysis. And it would be extremely useful for statesmen.

This made verification and causal explanation possible. For such knowledge 'gives one possession of all the conditions which control historical information', so that one can proceed 'to the critique of transmitted reports. If these are compatible with the rules so identified, one accepts them as authentic; if not, one rejects them as false' (in Najjar, p. 116). In other words, is a report compatible with what we otherwise know about culture under the conditions of the time in which it is alleged to have taken place?

This method also enables one to know not only what happened but why it happened. The cognitive procedures of Greek philosophy and of Abrahamic revelation here achieved a productive fusion. The abstract and narrative modes of understanding could begin to inform one another. If philosophy could be criticised for neglecting the particular, Ibn Khaldun no less ruthlessly at this stage exposed the weaknesses of Islamic historiography, its 'incentive for inventing'; he condemned uncritical acceptance of reports as 'blind trust in tradition' (pp. 23, 527). His was Report (hadith)-analysis on a new scale. For Ibn Khaldun sought to understand Arabo-Islamic society in Aristotelian terms. If the method was a development of Aristotle, the purpose was to understand anew the stories of peoples and leaders – in other words, a continuation of the Bible and Qur'an by other means.

Ibn Khaldun's originality as a social investigator went further. He identified variations between peoples (nations: sing umma), and temporal changes in social organisation: these he called 'essential accidents' of human culture. The historian must

understand the character of things, the differences which exist between nations, regions and epochs regarding their behaviour, manners, habits, sects, doctrines and so on. He must understand all these things in the conditions of his own time, and recognise where this resembles the past and where it differs from the past; in order to proceed to an explanation of such resemblances and differences. (in Najjar, p. 116)

National characteristics and historical changes are not universal or permanent, but they do affect the essence of a culture. Temporal changes have, as we shall see, a distinctive pattern which recurs over and over again. Public offices may look the same and go by the same names, but they vary fundamentally over time. It is a mistake to think that a teacher, Judge or military Commander has the same social role today as long ago. This recognition of history went beyond anything in Aristotle.

THEORY OF SOCIAL CHANGE

But the most fundamental ideas of the *Prolegomena* are different again. Having discussed historiography and its errors, Ibn Khaldun began with the most general category: human association (al-ijtima' al-insani) or civilisation ('umran). This is 'necessary (daruri)': for 'man is "political" by nature. That is, he cannot do without the social organisation for which the philosophers use the technical term "city (polis: state)"'. Ibn Khaldun demonstrated this in a way similar to previous Islamic theorists but with some twists of his own: humans as individuals depend on each other for their livelihood, hence the division of labour. And they instinctively desire comradeship (suhba). But the resulting ijtima' al-'umran (association of culture) requires 'a Restraining influence' (wazi'), that is Kingship (mulk). Indeed, cooperation itself requires the use of force. Wazi' or mulk is, therefore, 'a natural (tabi'i) quality of man which is absolutely necessary (daruri) to mankind' (pp. 45–7).

   The use of the general term wazi' is important; for religion too can act as wazi', as an internalised constraint. Having religion rather than kingship as wazi' is, he thought, more conducive to a courageous attitude. We may see how religion here filled a space where some European thinkers of this period put the republic and its ethical values. The need for such strong restraint is peculiar to human beings.

   Ibn Khaldun used the same argument to explain ranks (or classes) in society. Rank means power to direct other people for one's own advantage; it 'affects people, in whatever way they make their living' (p. 306). Those seeking rank must be obsequious and use flattery.

   Ibn Khaldun's social theory sprang directly out of this Islamicised version of Aristotle's theory of the origins of political society. He proceeded next to discuss the inhabitable parts of the earth and the influence of climate and environment, including food, on human beings, in a way that anticipated Fernand Braudel. He then focused upon the means of production. 'Differences of condition among people are the result of the different ways in which they make their living ... Some people live by agriculture ... others by animal husbandry' (p. 91). Out of this recognition of the importance of what Marx would call the 'economic base (Bau)' sprang Ibn Khaldun's two fundamental social categories: badawa (wilderness life, primitive society, the wild) and hadara (cited life, civilised society). These are 'natural' and 'necessary'. To succeed, a wilderness or tribal society must possess Group Feeling ('asabiyya). This crucial quality is defined as 'the affection a man feels for a brother or a neighbour when one of them is treated unjustly or killed' (in F. Rosenthal, vol. 2, p. lxxix). It derives from kinship or its equivalent (for example clientage); and 'nothing can take it away'.

Ibn Khaldun isolated 'asabiyya as one driving force in history; whether a group has or does not have it determines that group's military strength and its potential as a political actor. 'Group Feeling produces the ability to defend oneself ... and to press one's claims. Whoever loses it is too weak to do any of these things' (p. 111). It was the natural force of 'asabiyya which gave rise to the community of clan or lineage. This in turn may develop into a 'house (bayt)', which tends to be characterised by nobility and prestige.

Out of these elements came Ibn Khaldun's theory of development, change and decline. The goal (destiny, telos) of 'asabiyya is Kingship (mulk). For, in any group with Group Feeling, one person will inevitably emerge as Restraining power; he will be able to 'force others to accept his rulings' (p. 108). And so, with the assistance of the collective Group Feeling, such a person will proceed from chieftainship (ri'asa) to Kingship (mulk: Dominion) 'as something to be desired'. In other words, he will create, or take over, the state.

But desert or wilderness people are 'rude, proud, ambitious and eager to be the leaders'. They will not take to royal government unless, through religion, they 'have some Restraining influence in themselves'; in that case, 'a complete transformation ... causes the bedouins to have a Restraining influence on themselves'. This is what happened in the case of the Arabs. Religion magnifies Group Feeling, for example in early Islam and under the Almoravids and the Almohads. But religious sentiment can only bring about change, whether by popular revolution or by moral-legal reform, if the movement is based upon 'asabiyya; people who fail to see this are insane, criminal or stupid. Ibn Khaldun concluded that 'royal authority and large-scale dynastic power (dawla) are attained only through a group and Group Feeling'; and that 'dynasties of wide power and large royal authority have their origin in religion, based either on prophethood or on truthful propaganda' (pp. 120-1, 123-5).

But with mulk come the factors which lead to its own decline. Once you introduce Kingship, the group undergoes profound sociological change. For such power needs to be concentrated in one man, and he will inevitably become proud and egoistic and claim all glory for himself. The regime indulges in luxury.

One feature of dominion is the development of cities, and it is at this point that Ibn Khaldun considered in detail cities and hadara (cited life, sedentary civilisation), the second category of social existence, which he contrasted with badawa (desert life). For 'towns and cities are secondary products of [Dominion]' (p. 263). Dynasty (dawla) and Kingship (mulk) are the final development ('form') of human civilisation, and cities are their material base ('matter'). In contrast to Aristotle, he did not see cities as necessary or natural to human beings in the sense that all humans 'desire them or feel compelled to have them'. No, they are built because kings force people to build them! This difference reflected the experiences of the Hellenic and Mesopotamian worlds respectively.

In the context of hadara, he discussed political economy (see below, p. 179). Problems in the political economy of Kingship and hadara bring him to the subject of *decline*, one cause of which is unjust confiscation and forced labour. Luxury and other forces limit the lifespan of a dynasty to approximately three generations.

MORAL AND IMMORAL FORMS OF AUTHORITY

During his analysis of royal-dynastic decline, Ibn Khaldun's discussion shifts rather abruptly to *moral and immoral* forms of authority; and so to the need for a divinely inspired Lawgiver or Prophet, who will lay down those religious laws which alone will guide humans to their true good in this world and the next. Prophets are succeeded by Deputies whose function is to ensure religious observance and good government. At this point the specifically Islamic institutions of the Caliph, Religious Judge, Market-Regulator and so on are described (pp. 154–60, 166–80). Observations on the historical fortunes of the Deputyship are mingled with conventional Sunni juristic statements, largely based on al-Mawardi.[7] Ibn Khaldun insisted that here he was not expounding Islamic Jurisprudence as such: he was introducing the religious functions of the Deputy only in order to distinguish these from royal government, which arises in the course of nature, and which is the subject of his work.

In fact, Ibn Khaldun's view of the relationship between Deputyship (khilafa) and Dominion (mulk), that is between Islamic and natural-political authorities and their functions, is fairly complex. It takes us into the dialectic between the 'science of culture' and religious revelation; between the natural forces of Dominion emerging from 'asabiyya, and divine justice.

There are three possible regimes (pp. 151–61, 171, 256–7): (1) 'natural Dominion' as it emerges out of an 'asabiyya (Group Feeling). Here, 'the people conform to the private ambitions and uncontrolled desires of the ruler' (in Lambton 1981: 166). This is a rationally organised polity, which aims primarily to secure 'the advantage of the ruler', and only secondarily the general welfare. Such a regime is liable to be tyrannical, unjust and unsustainable, because the people will be impoverished, disobedient and rebellious. (2) One may have government according to laws devised by 'men of intelligence and insight'. These are imposed on and accepted by the people, and they are aimed primarily at their general welfare. This is a 'polity based on reason (siyasat 'aqliyya)'; it was found among the Persians and others. But, if that is all it is, it will 'aim solely at apparent and worldly interests', and will, therefore, be 'blameworthy' (in Lambton 1981: 165). Next, (2a) Philosophers have described an 'ideal [virtuous] state (madina fadila)', in which people govern themselves and 'have no need of governors', as in Plato's *Republic* and al-Farabi's *Virtuous City*. (This was not an accurate description of Plato's or al-Farabi's ideal state: where has the anarchism come from?) But such a regime is 'unlikely to come into being, and [the falasifa] discuss it only hypothetically' (in E. Rosenthal 1958: 94).

(3) Finally, one may have a government according to laws which 'are laid down by God and promulgated by an inspired Lawgiver' (in Lambton 1981: 165): a 'polity based on religion (siyasat diniyya)'. This will be for the true good of the people in both this world and the next. Such a legislator will ensure that this world is arranged so as to be 'a vehicle for the world to come'; and he will, at the same time, pursue 'the common good of human culture'. This is the rule of the Prophets and their successors, the Caliphs. A recurring theme of the *Prolegomena* is that the laws of Islam were, among other things, intended by God, if not consciously by Muhammad, to sustain human culture. Even general human welfare in this world is better provided for by the Shari'a than by human philosophy.

But this dual role of the Prophets and Deputies poses problems for Ibn Khaldun. For, first, he has already described political society as arising out of the spontaneous forces of human nature. Now, having built a socio-political theory out of philosophy, he has decided to knock philosophy on the head. His response is:

> We have also mentioned that kingship and its power are sufficient for the realisation of this common good. Yes, it would be more perfect if [natural Dominion] were [in accordance] with the commands of the [Islamic] Law, since [the Law] knows best what this common good is. Thus kingship is below the Caliphate and becomes one of its subordinate [functions] if [the regime] were Islamic, but it may be separate if it were in another community. (in Mahdi 1957: 239)

Again, 'for us in [our] religious community (milla) and for the time of the first four Caliphs', God dispensed with the polity based on reason and aimed at the general welfare 'because the statutes of the Shari'a dispense with it in respect of the general and the particular welfare. The statutes of the mulk are included in the Shari'a' (in E. Rosenthal 1958: 95). In other words, natural polity may be quite good but it is not as good as Islamic polity.

A second problem arose out of the view that the Deputyship disappeared after the first four 'rightly-guided' Caliphs – a process which Ibn Khaldun analysed in a masterly way. At first, righteous Caliphal government was *combined* with Group Feeling and Kingship. True, Muhammad censured Group Feeling and Kingship, but only in their harmful aspects; Muhammad had condemned 'asabiyya on the grounds that it was likely to pervert the course of justice. Ibn Khaldun explained this away by distinguishing between Group Feeling used for 'worthless purposes', which makes a person proud, and Group Feeling used in support of truth and the divine law. The latter 'is not forbidden. On the contrary, it is something desirable and useful in connection with Holy War and propaganda for Islam' (in F. Rosenthal, vol. 1, p. lxxix). Similarly, when Muhammad censured Kingship, he

> did not mean rightful authority, sufficient compulsion of religion and concern for the general welfare, but he blamed useless subjugation ... For if

the king was sincere that his dominion over men were in the cause of God, and would charge them with service of God and Holy War against his enemies, it would not be blameworthy. (in E. Rosenthal 1958: 99)

Even the early Umayyads, although they were Kings, were not oppressors. But under them and the first 'Abbasids, 'asabiyya and the sword gradually replaced religion as wazi'. After that, 'the dawla (state/dynasty) became Dominion (mulk) pure and simple'.

> It is, therefore, evident that the khilafa at first existed without mulk, then their character became intermixed, and finally the mulk alone remained, isolated from the khilafa at the moment when its 'asabiyya became separated from that of the khilafa. (in E. Rosenthal 1958: 98)

Thus even the Caliphate established by the Prophet could not avoid the natural processes of socio-political decay.

What, then, is the situation for Muslims today? Ibn Khaldun says that we are back with natural Dominion, which is dependent upon 'asabiyya and aims at the *ruler's* advantage, 'except that Muslim kings act in accordance with the requirements of the Islamic Shari'a, as far as they can'. More precisely, 'their laws are composed of statutes of the Shari'a, rules of right conduct, regulations which are natural for political association, and necessary things concerning power and 'asabiyya'. In this combination, 'the requirements of the Shar' come first, then the philosophers with their rules of conduct, and after that the kings in their way of life' (in E. Rosenthal 1958: 95). In other words, Muslim rulers, ever since the early 'Abbasids down to today, rule with a combination of Shari'a and secular law (qanun). The latter includes some philosophical norms for the general welfare, based on reason ('the rules of right conduct') but also rules designed to promote the rulers' own power and the interests of those near them.

Ibn Khaldun now turned to Kingship; here he discussed bureaucracy and taxation (*Muqaddima*, pp. 188–221, 232–42). The offices of government are formally subordinate to the Caliph, but there is no Caliph. Once again, he differentiated what he was doing from religious Jurisprudence. Jurists, he said, have discussed the institutions of sultan, vizier and so on as falling under the Caliphate and the Religious Law. But in the *Prolegomena* the Caliphate has been discussed only in order to distinguish it from ordinary government. Ibn Khaldun was now, therefore, free to discuss Kingship (mulk) and Government (siyasa) 'only as the necessary result of the nature of civilisation and human existence. [They] will not be discussed under the aspect of particular religious laws' (p. 190).

This indicates that he distinguished very clearly, though not explicitly, between the historical fortunes of the Deputyship on the one hand, and of the Shari'a on the other: the one is tacitly defunct, the other of course very much alive. Ibn Khaldun spent much of his later life as a senior Religious Judge. He did not consider the Sultan to have become Caliph by default. Rather, the duty of sustaining the Shari'a falls primarily on specifically religious personnel, the 'ulama. The religious functions of the Deputyship are now performed by

Jurists and 'ulama. In his own life, and certainly after he went to Egypt, Ibn Khaldun seems, like most Sunni Jurists (but not Ibn Taymiyya), to have accepted the existing order in which the 'ulama presided over communal and personal ethics and rules as coming under the Shari'a, while leaving political power to the Sultan and his officials backed by coercion and military strength.

There are problems, and Ibn Khaldun is not only frank but also ironic. The 'ulama today are 'urban weaklings', characterised by 'sedentary culture, luxurious customs, tranquillity, and a lack of ability to take care of themselves' (p. 176). The government allows religious leaders to function because it respects the Shari'a and wishes to protect the Muslim community. It does not appear that he particularly approved of the current practice, notably in the Mamluk state, whereby the 'ulama were incorporated into the establishment or allied with it.

When some 'ulama complain about not being consulted on matters of state, they are mistaking the nature of royal government. For, first, political power 'belongs only to the person who controls the Group Feeling'; the 'ulama 'do not have Group Feeling, have no control over their own affairs, and cannot protect themselves'. They are 'dependent upon others'. Second, 'royal and governmental authority is conditioned by the natural requirements of civilisation', and this 'does not require that Jurists and 'ulama have any share in authority' (p. 177). This does not mean that the Shari'a is not in force; the rulers are, after all, Muslims. But Ibn Khaldun had no great expectations of the civil and military authorities of his time. He was also scornful about popular beliefs in a mahdi.

Ibn Khaldun was probably not being irreligious, but rather was determined to put both the rise of Islam and its present predicament into its proper social context, not letting religious belief cloud the observation of facts. One aim of Ibn Khaldun's sociology was to define the conditions under which a re-emergence of primitive piety and religious zeal might be possible. What his social theory does seem to rule out is the possibility of the traditional Deputyship persisting as a permanent institution (unless there were repeated divine interventions).

POLITICAL VALUES

Primitive and citied society are each associated with certain public moral values; the values of badawa are on the whole regarded more favourably by Ibn Khaldun than those of hadara. Political values are assessed above all for their impact on political success, on the rise to power, stability, instability and decay. The Shari'a, on the other hand, is to be observed for its own sake; its norms are to be aspired to under all circumstances. There is no suggestion that observance of the Shari'a might hinder dawla. In that respect, Ibn Khaldun's view of the historical process is Allah-centred, and not to be compared with, say, Machiavelli's.

Whereas Machiavelli thought that some religious values were an obstacle to political success, Ibn Khaldun saw religious values as a means to counteract disharmony and prevent decline in the natural course of empire. Religious devotion promotes manly badawa. Here, the differences between Christian and

Islamic values must, of course, be taken into account.

A good example of Ibn Khaldun's perception of the interaction between ethical norms and empirically observed phenomena is his description of the degrading effects of harsh treatment upon the character of pupils, servants or subjects.

> Students, slaves and servants who are brought up with injustice and tyrannical force are overwhelmed by it. It causes them to lose their energy. It makes them lazy and induces them to lie and be insincere. That is, their outward behaviour differs from what they are thinking because they are afraid that they will have to suffer tyrannical treatment [if they tell the truth]. Thus they are taught deceit and trickery. (p. 425)

'They lose the quality that goes with social and political organisation, and makes people human, namely the desire to protect and defend themselves and their homes; they become dependent on others.' In other words, they lose the capacity for socially responsible citizenship. Again,

> If the ruler is eager to mete out punishment and expose faults, … his subjects become fearful and depressed and seek to protect themselves against him through lies, ruses and deceit. This becomes a character-trait of theirs. Their mind and character become corrupted. (p. 153)

They become bad soldiers, and they may rebel. This identified what one may call 'the tyrannical personality', a contributory factor in the decline of the world Ibn Khaldun was describing.

There are a few explicit statements about political morality. Ibn Khaldun's moral thought is nearly always prudential, implying that proper behaviour will produce certain desired results. For example, natural kingship is said to be based on 'wrathfulness and animality'; its ruler is liable to act unjustly and oppressively. This will alienate the population and ruin the economy, and the subjects will be unwilling to fight. On the other hand, 'Kindliness and good treatment, care for [the subjects'] livelihood' and being friendly towards the subjects (in E. Rosenthal 1958: 93) will prolong the life of the dynasty.

There are only the merest hints of constitutional norms: a King cannot rule well by himself, he must 'have recourse to imposed laws, accepted and followed by the masses' (in Lambton 1981: 165), principally the Shari'a; and he must seek help from his fellows. Ibn Khaldun detailed the moral characteristics of kingship in accordance with Shari'a norms by quoting a letter supposedly written by one of al-Ma'mun's generals to his son. These norms include not acting as if 'I am in authority. I may do what I want to do' (in F. Rosenthal, vol. 2, p. 145). But restrictions on the ruler are, as usual, left completely informal. It is the ruler's attitude which is targeted; advice is on request.

POLITICAL ECONOMY AND THE DUTIES OF GOVERNMENT

In that same letter, the duties of public office were spelled out; these include caring for the poor, for 'people who have suffered accidents, and for their widows and orphans', and for 'Muslims who are ill' (in F. Rosenthal, vol. 2, p.

153). In general, every Muslim ruler must perform the standard functions of benevolent public authority: he must 'protect the community from its enemies', 'enforce restraining laws', prevent violence against persons and property, improve 'the safety of the roads' (p. 189).

One of the most important functions of government is to regulate and develop the economy. In discussing the political economy of cities, Ibn Khaldun launched into a general discussion of economics, 'the real meaning and explanation of sustenance and profit' (p. 297). The means of livelihood are agriculture, commerce and the crafts found in a developed city culture. Ibn Khaldun went into considerable detail. On the political aspect, the ruler must guarantee the subjects' livelihood and fairness in transactions between subjects (weights and measures, coinage) (p. 189). This is both morally right and sustains the civilisation on which the dynasty depends.

Ibn Khaldun's views on political economy were based on the Circle of Power. The version he quoted went:

> the world is a garden the fence of which is the dynasty (al-dawla). The dynasty is an authority (sultan) through which life is given to good conduct (al-Sunna). Good conduct is a policy (siyasa) directed by the ruler (al-malik). The ruler is an institution (nizam) supported by the soldiers. The soldiers are helpers who are maintained by money. Money is sustenance brought together by the subjects (al-ra'iyya). The subjects are servants who are protected by justice. Justice is something familiar and through it the world (al-'alam) persists. The world is a garden ... (in Lambton 1981: 137)

Thus a flourishing economy and civilisation depend upon secure property rights; these depend upon the enforcement of justice in economic transactions; there must be no arbitrary confiscation or forced labour. Ibn Khaldun developed this current wisdom somewhat in the direction of modern market beliefs: 'The equitable treatment of people with property' will give them 'the incentive to start making their capital bear fruit and grow', which in turn will generate increases in 'the ruler's revenue in taxes'. The ruler's revenues will be maximised by keeping taxes as low as possible, since confidence in 'making a profit' is an incentive to economic activity. Finally, 'profit is the value realised from labour', which suggests both the labour theory of value and surplus value (pp. 231, 234, 273, 297).

Here too, he drew on a contrast between badawa and hadara, between primitive and citied ('developed') moeurs. Tribal culture (badawa) goes with low taxation, and so promotes economic growth; in citied culture (hadara), the demands of the ruling class increase; this leads to a rise in taxes, and so to economic decline. Low taxation is both good morals and good policy.

A ruling dynasty has the ability to stimulate economic growth and so to promote civilisation and prolong its own lifespan, through the economic activity of the court itself. It should not, however, engage directly in commerce; its financial resources are so great that this would drive others out of business. Rather, since 'state and ruler are the largest market in the world' (in E. Rosenthal 1958: 90), the dynasty should stimulate economic activity by paying generous stipends: 'money must flow between ruler and subjects, from him to them and from them to him'. If a ruler holds money back, his subjects suffer loss. He hints that state expenditure on public works promotes the economy (F. Rosenthal 2, p. 146); these sound like invitations to demand management.

A CONCEPT OF THE STATE

A concept of the state is clearly present in Ibn Khaldun. As dawla, it is identified with the dynastic clan. There is a modicum of truth in al-Azmeh's argument that dawla rather than, as many have thought, 'asabiyya, is 'the primary object of study in the *Muqaddima*' (al-Azmeh 1982: 27): the state is the fulfilled 'form' of 'asabiyya. It is true that Ibn Khaldun emphasised the compelling force within a group with 'asabiyya to become dawla – a political power over others. On the other hand, it is 'asabiyya which makes dawla possible: the group, and especially its leading clan, depend wholly on their 'asabiyya for a successful bid for political power. (Does this offer some explanation of why republics so often become empires?) Once that 'asabiyya begins to drain away, through luxury and the other phenomena related to citied life, the rulers begin to lose political control, and eventually succumb to another group with a stronger 'asabiyya; as the Arabs lost power to the Turks. Thus it would seem that dawla and 'asabiyya are interdependent. As a causal factor, 'asabiyya is perhaps more powerful; dawla is not presented as an independent variable.

It is true, as al-Azmeh suggests, that dawla in the sense of *political success* was the focus of Ibn Khaldun's empirical historical interest. Here he may be compared with Machiavelli. Dawla in turn is valued because it sustains 'umran (truly civilised life); certain forms of conduct, such as kindliness to subjects and the ethics implied in the Circle of Power, are recommended because they promote dawla.

Ibn Khaldun did not conceive of the state as an order *separable* from the society in which it arose. It had no power apart from its 'asabiyya. Did he nonetheless see political authority (other than the Deputyship) as capable of being legitimised, of becoming something other than brute force? He did conceive of political order as the necessary outcome of the natural forces of human existence, and as a prerequisite for human civilisation. But Ibn Khaldun does not seem to have regarded this as a rational legitimation of state authority in the way that European political thinkers did. He did not recommend it as a reason why people should give their allegiance to a dawla. (He did say that philosophers regard the state based on reason in this way; but Ibn Khaldun dismissed such a state as somewhat defective in moral authority.) Subjects are only under an obligation to give their allegiance to a religious state operating the rule of the Shari'a. And it seems that in this case Ibn Khaldun thought the state legitimate even if its ruler held power by sheer force plus 'asabiyya, or by force alone. In other words, he adopted the mainstream view of Sunni Jurists like Ibn Jama'a.

Ibn Khaldun did detach the concept of the state from individual power-holders more than other Islamic thinkers; he occasionally implied that rulership (mulakah: Dominion) is a general category applicable to a variety of particular governments. For example, the Restraining authority that human society needs can be a person, or a social force such as religion. He even spoke of rulership as a relationship. 'The interest subjects have in their ruler is not interest in his person and body, in his good figure or acute mind. Their interest in him lies in his relation to them. Dominion (mulk) is something relative, a relationship between ruler and subjects' (pp. 152–3). Here he may conceivably have been influenced by Latin thought (see above, p. 162). But the idea of an abstract impersonal authority is taken no further.

HIS ACHIEVEMENT

The *Prolegomena* combined features of all genres of Islamic political thought. Its systematic argument from reason and evidence make it the crowning glory of Falsafa. It is a large-scale Advice-Book, about how to counteract decline, especially on the need for Group Feeling ('asabiyya) if one is to achieve social renewal. The discussion of offices in Islamic states picks up on the Juristic mode.

Ibn Khaldun constructed a general theory to explain social and political change using a wide range of historical and contemporary data from the Islamic world. His theory of history is neither cyclical nor evolutionary, but wavelike: the rise and decline of dynasties repeats itself again and again, driven by the same basic forces.

This fundamental distinction between primitive and civilised society is one that has been observed and dwelt upon by modern social theorists. But Ibn Khaldun's account of the development from badawa into dawla, mulk and hadara is unique. He presented it as a series of separate empirical histories with common systemic features, such as the role of lineage and the development of nobility. State and empire play a greater role in the transition from one kind of society to another than they do in modern social theory. Here, al-Azmeh's emphasis is right. Above all, Ibn Khaldun is unique in seeing *primitive* society as providing the driving force towards statehood and empire, and settled cities (civility) as part cause and part effect of decay. In other words, his perspective is more sympathetic than that of modern social theorists to the primitive. (One wonders whether there could be fruitful interaction between some of his ideas and those of Freud.) In fact, through personal contact and shared spirituality, he was closer than any other major theorist to people of badawa.

His social actors (badawa, dawla, hadara and so on) were constructed through analysis of empirical data, and perceived as social forces which under-lie, and therefore explain, events. They are natural forces; they come into being and pass away. In describing primitive society, he brought together a number of features, many of which he had observed at first hand among the Berbers, so as to construct an *ideal type*. Ibn Khaldun's ideal type of badawa still has significant explanatory power in tribal or quasi-tribal societies. The concept of 'asabiyya (Group Feeling) is perhaps Ibn Khaldun's greatest legacy to the study of society. It has been shamefully neglected. It is, in many contexts, preferable to modern concepts of 'tribalism' or 'Gemeinschaft' (with its cosy egalitarian assumptions). It might be fruitfully applied to phenomena outside Ibn Khaldun's experience, for example the Mafia or political parties.

His theory of the interaction between primitive and citied society throws light on important features of prehistoric, ancient and pre-modern history. On the other hand, the repeated successes of badawa in overturning established dynasties, and inheriting their civic culture, right through the millennia about which Ibn Khaldun was writing, was to some extent peculiar to the Islamic world. Persia, Rome, China and the Europeans succeeded in establishing longer-lasting states. Ibn Khaldun himself may have suggested a reason: the role which religious teaching plays in 'asabiyya, the driving force behind tribalism.

He was not, however, aware of the extent to which *his* world was exceptional in this way. In fact, badawa ceased to be operative when the reservoir of pre-urban peoples dried up, roughly speaking after the Mongols. Ibn Khaldun is another example of the owl of knowledge which sings only as dusk is falling.

He was unique both in his originality and in the oblivion which befell him. In terms of intellectual history, he came almost out of nowhere and went nowhere. There is 'no indication that the principles which he put forward were even studied, much less applied, by any of his successors' (Gibb 1962: 127). In the eighteenth century, Ottoman bureaucratic circles became interested for practical reasons in his treatment of the causes of decline (see below, pp. 268–9). But sociology had to be reinvented in eighteenth-century Europe. It is a privilege to walk the same earth as such a man.

NOTES

1. See *EI* s.v. Ibn Khaldun; Mahdi (1957); Y. Lacoste, *Ibn Khaldun: naissance de l'histoire passé du tiers-monde* (Paris: F. Maspero, 1966); Nassif Najjar, *La pensée réaliste d'Ibn Khaldun* (Paris: Presses Universitaires de France, 1967); E. Rosenthal (1958: 84–112); Lambton (1981: 152–77); Henri Laoust, 'La pensée politique d'Ibn Khaldun', *REI* 48 (1980), pp. 133–53; Gibb (1962: 166–75); M. Talbi, 'Ibn Khaldun et le sens d'histoire', *SI* 26 (1967), pp. 73–148; Fuad Baali, *Society, State and Urbanism: Ibn Khaldun's Sociological Thought* (Albany NY: SUNY, 1988); al-Azmeh (1982).
2. Ed. Quatremère, 3 vols (Paris, 1858); trans. Franz Rosenthal, *Ibn Khaldun: the Muqaddimah, an Introduction to History*, 3 vols, rev. edn (Princeton NJ: Princeton University Press, 1967); abridged by N. J. Dawood (London: Routledge and Kegan Paul, 1967) – all references are to this abridged translation unless otherwise stated. (For problems with the translation, see Hodgson (1974: vol. 2. p. 481n.) and review by H. A. R. Gibb in *Speculum* 35 (1960), pp. 139–42.)
3. Pp. 333–4 and in Mahdi 1957: 173–4 (adapted, my italics); see Mahdi (1957: 174–6).
4. Lacoste, *Ibn Khaldun*, pp. 246–7.
5. P. 350; Najjar, *La pensée*, p. 80.
6. In Lacoste, pp. 254, 427 (my italics).
7. Laoust, 'Pensée', pp. 138, 149–51.

The Decline of Classical Islamic Political Thought

19

I n central Asia, Timur's empire disintegrated on his death (1402).[1] The remains of his conquests were divided between his sons: Shah Rukh ruled Khurasan (1405–47), and Ulugh-Beg (r.1393–1449) Transoxania. In contrast to their father, they restored damaged irrigation systems and patronised the arts and sciences: from now date the spectacular relics of Bukhara and Samarqand. Shah Rukh was devotedly orthodox. He claimed to be a 'Restorer' of the Shari'a. To this he added the titles of Emperor (Padshah) and Lord of the Age (Sultan-ul zaman). He reduced the scope of the Mongol folk-law, and, following a revolt (1446), persecuted Shi'ites. Ulugh-Beg was more interested in philosophy and built an observatory. In their official documents, each of Timur's sons styled themselves Sultan-Caliph, the prophet's 'representative (wakil) with full power', a 'branch of the lotus tree of the Caliphate and of world dominion'. The ruler's mission, they said, was to ensure observance of the Shari'a, and to maintain true belief, peace and prosperity.[2]

TRIBALISM

All across the eastern and central Islamic lands, the ravages of Timur were followed by a revival in tribalism. Power gravitated to local clans and their leaders. In central Asia, this was a permanent obstacle to state development until, and in some cases beyond, the twentieth century. In parts of Iran, despite the centralising efforts of the Safavids, tribes exercised sporadic political control and were a force to be reckoned with until the later twentieth century.[3]

In western Iran, Azerbaijan and eastern Anatolia, the Oghuz-Turkish confederations of the Qaraqoyunlu ('black sheep') and Aqqoyunlu ('white sheep') battled for control. The Qaraqoyunlu leader Jahanshah (r.1438–67) ruled as Sultan and Turco-Mongol chief (khagan). But the Aqqoyonlu, under Uzun Hasan (r.1452–80), gained the upper hand. Political society was managed by the largely nomadic Turks in the army and the largely urban Tajiks (Persians) in the bureaucracy and religious judiciary. The link between rulers and ruled was, as usual, the 'ulama and Sufi masters. The Aqqoyunlu survived defeat by the Ottomans in 1473, but the area became a cockpit of inter-clan warfare in a political vacuum (Woods 1976).

Out of this turbulence and anarchy came a political explosion in the hill country of eastern Anatolia and north-western Iran. Here, folk-Shi'ite expectations of a Mahdi (Rightly-Guided One), whose reign of justice would prepare the way for the return of the Hidden Leader, fused with the well-organised Sufi orders, and became 'a tool for the mobilisation of the masses for political action' (Arjomand 1984: 69). The link between Shi'ite political idealism and Sufi organisation lay in the belief that 'sufi guides, like the imams, possess esoteric knowledge' (Trimingham 1971: 135); this empowered the shaykh (elder-leader-teacher) and the darwish (mystic: dervish). Individuals with mystical visions or other esoteric signs of authority gave exotic inter-pretations of religious symbols. Some laid claim to be the Mahdi; some, as self-styled 'lords of the sword' (Arjomand 1984: 73), proclaimed Holy War against Christian Georgia. The ultimate beneficiary of the implosion of the clan-based Aqqoyunlu power was to be the Shi'ite clan-dynasty of the Safavid Sufi order, the creators of modern Iran.

THE UZBEK STATE

In central Asia, the Shaybanis, a Mongol Uzbek clan under the influence of the Naqshbandi Sufi order, established a dynastic state from 1500 to 1598. This familial regime was ruled by a Great Khan; other members of the clan called 'sultans' ruled alongside him: 'in theory the entire eponymously related clan held collective title' to power.[4] Leading members of the Uzbek clans ruled their allotted lands by hereditary right and met together in a tribal assembly to elect the Great Khan. In 1567, this was replaced by primogeniture within the Khan's family. The Great Khan was called 'Deputy of the Merciful God (khalifat al-Rahman)' and 'Leader of the Age (imam al-zaman)' (Lapidus 1988: 425). But, within a century of the fall of Constantinople (1453), Christian Orthodoxy achieved a political revival as the Russians under Ivan 'the Terrible' (severe: grozny) launched upon the conquest of Eurasia. The Uzbek regime, hemmed into Transoxania by the Safavids and deprived of commercial outlets by the Russians, disintegrated into tribal and household units, an isolated outpost of Sunni Islam (Lapidus 1988: 426–30).

Central Asia remained renowned for its craftsmanship, literature and Sunni orthodoxy, nourished partly by émigré scholars from Shi'ite Iran. But, from c.1600 until, and in some cases beyond, the twentieth century, it remained a politically fragmented society in which clan patriarchs and tribal chiefs remained powerful. The 'ulama and Sufi orders held a 'practically unshakeable position' (CH Islam 1: 477).

DAWANI (1427–1502/3): A SIMPLIFIED PHILOSOPHY OF THE STATE

In the turbulent conditions of eastern Anatolia, Jalal al-Din Dawani wrote his *Jalalian Ethics* (*Akhlaq-i Jalali*: c.1475, in Persian).[5] Dawani was a Sunni (of the Shafi'i School) and was inclined to mystical illumination. He served the Qaraqoyunlu as Overseer of religious trusts (sadr); then he resigned and taught in College for a while; then he became qadi at Fars under the Aqqoyunlu. When the Safavids overran the area, he was prevailed upon to write a pro-Shi'ite tract in deference to the new regime. The Ethics followed very closely, often literally, Nasir al-Din Tusi's *Nasirean Ethics*; essentially it was an up-to-date popularisation, with a somewhat more otherworldly tone (not surprisingly). It bore little relationship to the turbulent events around him.

Dawani, like Tusi, had sections on the normative regulation of individual, household and state (tadbir-i mudun). He followed both Tusi and the Isma'ilis in exalting the human person as 'the abstract of all things, the model of models, and the quintessence of the world' (*Ethics*, p. 13), destined, as Sufis taught, to be God's Deputy (khalifa).

The state is derived as follows. Human nature requires division of labour; this requires cooperation which leads to civilisation (tamaddun); civilisation requires a means of restraint from violence. Such restraint is provided, first, by the person whom the ancients called lawgiver (sahib-i namus); that is, a Prophet or Shari' (giver-of-Religious-Law), whose law applies to this life and the next; secondly, by a 'personal ruler (hakim-i shakhsi)'. This ruler was called king by the philosophers, and, according to Dawani, 'world ruler' by Plato, 'statesman (insan madani)' by Aristotle; the moderns call him Leader (Imam). His duty is to uphold the Shari'a, to maintain equilibrium and the health of the world (*Ethics*, pp. 318–26). This was an almost farcically truncated account of classical Islamic political philosophy.

JUSTICE AND STATUS GROUPS

For Dawani, as for Tusi, the core value was *justice*. Justice means equilibrium or proportion (i'tidal). This requires some standard of measurement, which, Dawani said, following Tusi and partly, via him, Aristotle, is provided by (1) the Shari'a, (2) the Just Ruler and (3) money. Justice, equilibrium and harmony are maintained by love and friendship; therefore the king should behave as father and patron towards his subjects, and the subjects should give filial submission to the king. Dawani repeated Tusi's Kantian sentiment that, when the king administers justice in court, 'in every affair that comes before him he should suppose himself to be the subject and another the prince; and whatever he would hold impossible towards himself he should hold inadmissible towards his people' (*Ethics*, pp. 405, 144–5, 385).

A key component of justice was that status groups should be kept in their rightful positions with harmonious relations between them. To ensure this was a ruler's first duty. Dawani followed Tusi's classification of status groups exactly. First, in virtuous states, there are (1) those with true knowledge; (2) 'men of the tongue', those skilled in communication and the dissemination of knowledge ('the media'); (3) 'the measurers', who maintain balance by accountancy, medicine, astronomy; (4) warriors; (5) merchants and craftsmen – who are the taxpayers. In imperfect states, there are (1) men of the pen, including 'ulama, Judges and all branches of learning; (2) men of the sword; (3) merchants and craftsmen; (4) agriculturalists (*Ethics*, pp. 367–90). Thus in the second classification the 'ulama (the knowledgeable) are lumped together with the

Judges, while taxpayers-cum-producers (including manual workers) are divided into two groups, which might suggest a certain amount of importance attached to them. It was all very Platonic and Indo-Iranian.

Dawani's work was nothing more than a digest, presumably for rulers and civil servants, of Nasir al-Din Tusi's *Ethics*. It had a decisive influence on the political literature of the Ottoman, Safavid and Mughal empires, and in fact provided almost the only link between classical Falsafa and the early modern empire. It became the starting point for courtly political culture under the Ottomans and Mughals. The emphasis on status groups was perhaps the most notable feature.

KHUNJI (1455–1521) ON JURISPRUDENCE IN CENTRAL ASIA

Central Asia produced the best-known statement of this period in classical fiqh about the relationship between government and the Shari'a: *The Conduct of Kings* (*Suluk al-muluk*: 1512–14, in Persian) by Fadl Allah Ibn Ruzbihan Khunji (Shiraz 1455–?Bukhara 1521).[6] He wrote at the Shaybani court at Bukhara. Khunji, born into a family of wealthy 'ulama under Aqqoyonlu patronage, had studied under Dawani and began his career as secretary to the Aqqoyonlu. He joined the Naqshbandi Sufi order, and was involved with politically influential Naqshbandi leaders in Transoxania.

When the Shi'ite Safavids conquered his native Iran (1501), Khunji emigrated to the Uzbek court, and he devoted the rest of his life to the overthrow of the Safavids and the restoration of Sunnism in Iran. He addressed the Uzbek ruler as Holy Warrior, 'Imam of the Time' and 'merciful Caliph', and urged him to drive the Shi'ites out of Iran and restore Sunnism.[7] But Shaybani Khan was defeated and killed by the Safavids (1510); Khunji went into hiding for two years. He also supported the Ottomans, as champions of Sunni Islam, in their wars against his own country, and congratulated Selim I on his victory over the Safavids at Chaldiran (1514). Referring to himself as an 'unpatriotic Persian', he expressed the hope that Selim would imitate Alexander and annex Iran to the Ottoman empire ('Rum').[8] This demonstrated an underlying belief in the unity of the Sunni world; he obviously put religion before country.

When Shaybani's son, 'Ubayd Allah, recaptured Samarqand, Khunji was asked to promote the cause of Sunni orthodoxy, and it was to this end that he composed *The Conduct of Kings*. Khunji saw the Uzbeks as instruments of religious renewal in central Asia. In *The Conduct of Kings* he went through the usual fiqh topics (the appointment of Judges, distribution of Alms and so on) with special attention to jihad and the various categories of renegades and unbelievers. These were immediately relevant questions. Khunji based his reasoning on the Shafi'i and Hanafi Schools, sometimes combining them, sometimes stating them as legitimate alternatives; he used al-Mawardi and al-Ghazali a great deal.

Khunji set out to apply traditional Sunni Jurisprudence to the new politics of central Asia. He seems to have wanted not merely to expound the moral-legal code but also to provide as comprehensive and practical guide as he could for rulers of his time. Previous fiqh works had indeed spelled out how Shari'a norms should be applied to government, but with little or no attempt to argue that what was necessary in practice was, in religious terms, anything more than a pis aller. It was this 'disjunction between piety and power' which left Sunni regimes open to Shi'ite attack. The Advice literature, on the other hand, offered guidance that claimed to be at the same time practical and ethically normal. But, although this too was partly based on the Qur'an and Reports, it was not part of religious tradition in the strict sense. Such an approach stood little chance in a struggle for hearts and minds with the neo-Imami Safavids. Khunji wanted a credible Community-Traditional alternative to the Safavids' claim that they were establishing a holy polity on Shi'ite credentials (*Conduct*, pp. 4, 40).

The spirit of Khunji's enterprise was, therefore, to synthesise these two genres and, as his title implied, to provide Sunni rulers with a *practical* handbook on religious government but one *based on Jurisprudence*. It was necessary to demonstrate that Sunni fiqh could provide all the moral and legal guidance a regime needed in order to meet the requirements of religious righteousness; which was precisely what his patron wished to do.

Khunji introduced elements from rational political philosophy, which was not unusual in fiqh; he derived these from his teacher, Dawani. He justified royal authority on the ground that 'man is a political being by nature'; society requires 'a just man who will abate violence', that is, a man 'who has knowledge of "the mean"'; but 'that which defines the mean is the divine law ... Justice is, therefore, laid down by the Shari'a'. He concluded that 'such a person is the King' (padishah: emperor). The king, as Dawani and others had said, is an administrator (mudabbir) who operates a law laid down by a legislator (sahib-i shari'at). His authority is justified by the fact that 'he is obeyed' (in Lambton 1981: 187–8).

Khunji made the same point via Jurisprudence in a way which also underwrote the Sultan's assumption of the role of Deputy. The Sultan-Caliph's authority is justified on the grounds that he holds de facto power and he makes sure the Shari'a is applied. Khunji insisted, like Ibn Jama'a, that military force and not (as Imami Shi'ites claimed) lineage or character qualified a person to be Leader (Imam) or Deputy (Caliph). Khunji had previously referred to Shaybani Khan as 'Leader of the Age' and on one occasion called the Ottoman Selim I 'the Caliph of God and of Muhammad'.[9] His intention was, presumably, to give Sunni rulers a religious status as formidable as that claimed by the Safavids. On the other hand, the Sultan-Imam does not need to be a member of the fuqaha or even 'ulama himself, but he must follow the advice of the religiously Learned (*Conduct*, pp. 77–85). This was the Sunni response to the Shi'ite argument that a ruler only had religio-legal authority if he possessed certain outstanding spiritual qualities.

The responsibilities incumbent upon a Sultan-Caliph were strongly emphasised. As in previous Islamic authors, there were no constitutional checks, the general Sunni view being that a bad ruler could be got rid of only by spontaneous rebellion prompted by widespread disregard for the Shari'a: might itself was a crucial indicator of legitimacy (Lambton 1981: 186). And so it remained in Khunji.

Khunji sought further to safeguard observance of the Shari'a by means of a Shaykh-al-Islam, that is a religiously qualified official to oversee the institutions and practices of Islam. The Sultan, however, can appoint and dismiss the qadis (*Conduct*, pp. 139, 178). Thus *The Conduct of Kings* incorporated in fiqh the religio-political order that had developed in Sunni Islam by the time Khunji wrote.

Naturally, given the situation in Iran and the prospect of Sunni restoration there, Khunji considered the question of the religious status of non-Sunnis. Here he distinguished between the Safavids and their subjects. The Safavid 'red-heads (qizilbash)' were apostates, but in general there is 'no doubt that the Imami Shi'a is one of the sects of Islam'. Persia itself still belonged to 'the house of Islam', not to 'the house of conflict' (he justified this on the grounds that polytheism was not enforced, and Islamic practices were not forbidden). *Rebels*, however, may be treated as belonging to the house of conflict, and their property may be confiscated (*Conduct*, pp. 284–93). In a letter to Selim I, Khunji was less discriminating; he not only argued (like the Ottoman Shaykh-al-Islam Ibn Kemal Pasazade: 1468–1534) that war against Shi'ites counted as jihad, but also said that Holy War against them ought to take precedence over that against the Franks.[10] This was because the Franks were mere unbelievers, but the Shi'ites were renegades.

The Conduct of Kings is dry and uninspiring, much of it copied straight from earlier Jurists. One may ask whether the Sunna and its fiqh had the capacity to provide realistic, detailed guidance for an early modern state. The conception of government, which had been spelled out in fairly relevant detail for ninth-century Baghdad, was not seriously reconsidered. Khunji's list of royal duties was copied straight from al-Mawardi.

The problem lay not just in the content but in the underlying approach: the main questions have been resolved, to reopen them would be bid'a (heretical innovation). Thus Khunji's attitude to Falsafa was that, except for what has already been incorporated in religious studies, it is unnecessary. Contemporary Falsafa corrupts, and the teaching of it should not be permitted. He lamented the difficulty nowadays of finding a suitable Shaykh-al-Islam because 'most of the 'ulama in this era have become Falasifa'. Those skilled in Falsafa tend to get the best appointments through their slick arguments; but their knowledge is dangerous and 'does not benefit Muslims'.[11]

Khunji may have influenced 'Ubayd Allah. His work was studied in central Asia and perhaps Mughal India. It does not appear to have been known in Ottoman lands. Yet the picture he presented of the ruler's religious role would have fitted in quite well with the Ottoman system.

In general, Islamic political thought from the fifteenth to the nineteenth centuries is thin compared to what had gone before and what was to come after. There were few new ideas after Ibn Taymiyya and Ibn Khaldun, just as there was little development in philosophy or the natural sciences. Mental sclerosis[12] afflicted all genres of political thought, except Shi'ite Jurisprudence.

It was as if the devastations of the Mongols had deprived the mind too of irrigation. The life of the mind was increasingly dominated by mystical concerns; Sufism played a central role in Ottoman society, in the early Safavid polity, and above all in India. Not a single new idea or discovery in the sciences or even in technology was produced by the Islamic world in this period, or indeed since. Something of the same occurred in China.

NOTES

1. For this period, see *CH Iran* 6; Morgan (1988: 94–107); Arjomand (1984: 66–84); Brunschvig and von Grunebaum (eds) (1977).
2. In H. R. Römer, *Staatsschreiben der Timuridenzeit: das Saraf-nama des 'Abdallah Marwarid in kritischer Auswertung* (Wiesbaden: F. Steiner, 1952), pp. 35–6, 45, 53, 83–5.
3. Reid (1983); Lambton (1953).
4. Martin B. Dickson, 'Uzbek Dynastic Theory in the 16th Century', *Proceedings of the 25th International Congress of Orientalists* (Moscow, 1963), vol. 3, pp. 208–16 at p. 210.
5. Trans. W. F. Thompson, *The Practical Philosophy of the Muhammedan People* (London: W. H. Allen, 1839). See *EI* 2: 174; E. Rosenthal (1958: 210–23); Fakhry (1991: 143–7); Danishpazhouh (1988: 221–2).
6. Ed. M. Nizamuddin and M. Grouse (Hyderabad: Persian Manuscript Society, 1966); trans. Muhammad Aslam (M. Litt. Diss., Cambridge, 1962), to which I refer unless otherwise stated; I am grateful to Banafshe Lomas for translating some parts. See *EI* 5: 53–5; Lambton (1981: 178–200); Ulrich Haarmann, 'Staat und Religion in Transoxanien im frühen 16. Jahrhundert', *ZDMG* 124 (1974), pp. 332–72.
7. U. Ott, *Transoxiana und Turkestan zu Beginn des 16. Jahrhunderts* (Freiburg im Breisgau: Schwarz, 1974), p. 52.
8. V. Minorsky, *Persia in AD 1478–1490* (London: Royal Asiatic Society), pp. 4–5.
9. In Edward G. Browne, *A History of Persian Literature (AD 1500–1924)* (Cambridge: Cambridge University Press, 1924), p. 80. This is an example of the rhetorical use of the term 'caliph of God' (see above, p. 18) since he explicitly rejects the term in *Conduct*.
10. Haarmann, pp. 357–9.
11. Ed. Nizamuddin and Grouse, pp. 60–2.
12. See Brunschvig and von Grunebaum (eds) (1977: 247–62) on 'ankylose' in philosophy.

Part IV   The Early Modern Empires: Well-Protected Domains

International Relations

There followed a new phase in the political and intellectual history of Islam. The period from the fall of Persia (645) to the fall of Byzantium (1453) had in many ways been a single epoch, in which Muslim states and religious leaders were, and saw themselves to be, the dominant and expanding force in the world. In intellectual endeavour, this was 'classical Islam', corresponding chronologically with what in European history is called 'the Middle Ages'. In political thought, ideas forged under the Umayyads and early 'Abbasids continued throughout this time to be developed and rethought. Islam led the world in many fields of mental activity and technology. Now Islam ceased to be a world leader in either power or ideas. Yet Muslim states and religious leaders still saw themselves as the dominant world force until the early to mid-nineteenth century. This defines the 'Early Modern' period in Islam. There were developments in religious organisation, political culture, in political strategy and practice and political thought. But there was nothing new in the basics of Islamic political thinking, except for Wali-Allah of Delhi.

From c.1500 to c.1700, most of the Islamic world was divided up between three great powers (the 'gunpowder empires'): the Mughals in India, the Safavids in Iran, the Ottomans in the whole area from east of the Black Sea to the north African coast and from Hungary to the Hijaz. Under these powers, political and socio-intellectual divisions within the Islamic world were greater than ever before; though eventually, in the twentieth century, these proved not to be as permanent as they might have seemed (partly thanks to the meeting of minds on hajj). But, for a while, there were almost three separate Islamic thought-worlds, especially regarding government and social organisation. Each, in the struggle for survival and expansion, developed a praxis somewhat different from what had gone before, and strikingly different from the others. The differences between Sunnis and Shi'ites became entrenched in rival empires. There was some parallel with the confessional Protestant and Catholic states and the confessionalisation of interstate relations in Europe.

These states interacted with one other as parts of an international sub-system. Disputes between the Safavids and their neighbours were both religious and territorial. The Safavid empire was a missionary Shi'ite state, directed against Sunnism, which was championed by the Ottomans to the west and the Uzbeks to the east. War against Sunnis was Holy War. The

Ottomans posed as the champions of Sunnism against both Shiʿite Iran and Christian Europe. The rise of the Safavids threatened them with a domino effect on the restless Shiʿite tribes of eastern Anatolia. Hence Selim I ruthlessly persecuted the Shiʿites, and then (1514) inflicted a humiliating defeat on Ismaʿil, which seriously undermined the Shah's internal status. Selim proceeded to annex northern Mesopotamia, Kurdistan, Syria, Palestine and Egypt (1516). This confirmed the Ottomans as the undisputed superpower of the eastern Mediterranean. Süleyman I (r.1520–66: 'the Lawgiver (kanuni)'; known to Europeans as 'the Magnificent') extended Ottoman control to Azerbaijan and Iraq (Treaty of Amasya: 1555). Finally, the treaty of Kasr-i Sirin (1639) established a permanent border between the Ottomans and the Safavids on the understanding that the Safavids would cease destabilising eastern Anatolia.

There were trade wars too. Süleyman's conquests gave him control of the sea route to India; the Black Sea was for a while a Muslim lake. Shah ʿAbbas rerouted the invaluable silk trade through southern Russia so as to bypass the Ottoman empire. Asia and Europe became locked together in commerce.

On Iran's eastern frontier, it was a different story. Until the 1620s the Mughals had hardly any contact with the Ottomans. Relations between the Safavids and the Mughals were on the whole friendly. A pan-Sunni Mughal–Uzbek–Ottoman alliance against Iran was occasionally proposed by both Uzbeks and Ottomans, but for the Mughals it was never more than a pious sentiment, if that. It was definitively rejected by Akbar, who, in characteristically pacific manner, said he considered 'the relationship of [the Safavids] with the family of the Prophet' more important (in Farooqi 1989: 21). When Murad IV launched an attack on Persia, he urged Jahangir to join in, for 'if your majesty attacks them too, their kingdom will soon be destroyed' (in Farooqi 1989: 10). But Jahangir was on friendly terms with ʿAbbas and rejected the proposal. Shah Jehan proposed an anti-Shiʿite alliance to Murad in the hope of reconquering his central Asian homeland. Not until the devout Aurangzib was the project of a pan-Sunni alliance, with Bukhara in particular, taken seriously; by then Shiʿism was well established in Iran, and the Safavids were in decline. Thus confessionalisation played a very limited part in relations between Muslim states. In none of these cases was there any sense of rivalry arising out of differences of nationality.

The Muslim states were also being drawn into the Eurocentric world order, and even the European state system. This was especially so for the Ottomans with their at first apparently unstoppable Holy War. Murad II (r.1421–51) routed the Hungarians and their allies (1442) and ensured Muslim domination of south-eastern Europe. Mehmed II 'the Conqueror' (fatih: r.1451–81), partly in order to enhance his own domestic status, finally realised the old Muslim dream and took Constantinople (1453). He next drove far into the Balkans and Greece, brought Serbia under direct rule and made the Danube his frontier. Then Süleyman I shattered the Habsburg army (1526) and established direct rule over Hungary (1541). The military-political fulcrum of Islam shifted to the north-west and to Europe.

The Ottomans meanwhile became players in European diplomacy, allying themselves for example with France and the Lutheran Princes against the Habsburgs, to which Charles V responded by contacting Iran. They penetrated the European courts with spy networks (rivalled perhaps only by Florence); these told them what little they cared to know about Europe.

Each of the Muslim empires was strikingly successful in certain ways. Each had its peculiar institutions. The Safavids built a state dedicated to, and supported by, Twelver Shi'ism and watched over the rise of Shi'ite mujtahids to political power. The Mughals for a while presided over a new relationship between Muslims and Hindus. The Ottomans created a whole new kind of Islamic state, which lasted far longer than any before or since, and which for the first and only time invites some comparison in organisation, durability, allegiance and membership with the states of China, Russia and Europe.

All three have, since Weber, been classified as 'patrimonial' or (in Hodgson's phrase) 'military patronage' states (Hodgson 1974: vol. 3, p. 39). That is, they were in theory organised, insofar as they were organised at all, on the premise of a paternal or pastoral relationship between sovereign and subjects, and an identity of interests between them. There were no formal limits on the ruler's power, but it was assumed that his function was to look after his subjects, to protect them militarily and to support them economically; their function was to serve and revere him. The power of the state was still heavily dependent upon the ruling house. Military-political power was technically concentrated in the dynasty and the Sultan, who was held responsible for all aspects of public welfare and state management. Süleyman the Lawgiver, Akbar and 'Abbas I were monarchs of the same stature as Elizabeth I, Philip II and Louis XIV, and like them did much to build up the political identities of their states.

These remained distinctively Islamic states in the sense that religious personnel oversaw important aspects of social and moral life. Political and religious power remained, on the whole, in separate hands but in symbiosis with one another. The political importance and role of Islam varied considerably between them and between different periods within each state. Attempts to compare these states are contentious, the more so (it would seem) the closer people look.[1]

Culturally, the regions which these dynasties governed had much in common. In some respects, there was no cultural boundary between the Danube and the Ganges, just as in Europe high culture could cross confessional divides. But, as in Europe, *new* developments tended not to do so, and in terms of religious thought and political culture Shi'ite Iran effectively cut the eastern and the western branches of Sunnism off from each other for a while. The Mughals looked to Iran for models of political management, correct account-keeping, and understanding of Realpolitik. They considered themselves a central Asian dynasty, the rightful heirs of Timur, looking back nostalgically at Transoxania, 'the graveyard of our ancestors' (in Foltz 1998: xxviii): the Taj Mahal drew its inspiration from Samarqand. Poets, 'ulama and ambitious men migrated from Iran to the Mughal court, where Persian was spoken, and there they influenced moeurs, literature and the conduct and theory of state affairs.

NOTE

1. I. Metin Kunt, 'The Later Muslim Empires: Ottomans, Safavids, Mughals', in Marjorie Kelly (ed.), *Islam: The Religious and Political Life of a World Community* (New York: Praeger, 1984), pp. 113–36; Halil Berktay, 'Three Empires and the Societies They Governed: Iran, India and the Ottoman Empire', in Berktay and Faroqhi (eds) (1992: 247–63).

The State of the House of Osman (devlet-i al-i Osman)   21

The Ottoman dynasty (c.1290–1922) was unprecedented and unequalled in the Islamic world for its size and duration.[1] Virtually coextensive in time with the Habsburgs, it ended in the war which also brought down three Euro-Christian Empires. It extended from the Atlantic to the Euphrates, from the Russian steppe to the Sahara, including the core region of Islamdom from south-east of the Black Sea through Iraq to the Hijaz, taking in Syria, Palestine and Egypt. No other state before or since controlled this concatenation of regions. In the course of its lifespan, it undertook more than once programmes of both Islamicisation and modernisation.

On Islam's frontier in north-western Anatolia, the house of Osman seized the opportunity to expand across Byzantine territory and on into the disorganised areas of Thrace plus Macedonia, Bulgaria, Serbia and Bosnia. The Christian rulers proved incapable of coherent resistance. The early Ottomans appear to have ruled their territories partly on the basis of tribal and nomadic ideas; fictional genealogies gave outsiders equal status. 'The tribe was a useful device for pulling together such seemingly disparate groups as Turkish pastoralists and Byzantine settlers' (Lindner 1983: 33). They governed much of the Balkans and Anatolia as vassal principalities, allowing them to be ruled by their former lords in return for tribute and military service. In their relations with Christian rulers they were pragmatic, often allying themselves with local Christian lords. Sufis spread Islamic beliefs among the peasantry of Rumelia (Ottoman Europe), and they were generally willing to accommodate some aspects of Christian culture. In the revolt of 1416, a Sufi revolutionary, preaching economic equality and equality of status for Christians, could attract support from both Christians and Muslims (EI 1: 869).

When Timur routed the Ottomans at Ankara (1402), their fledgling state disintegrated. It took a fierce struggle to reunite Rumelia and Anatolia under Mehmed I (r.1413–21). Now began a golden age of expansion, development, liberality and state-building under a succession of unusually able Sultans. Mehmed II, Bayezid II, Selim I and Süleyman I between them ruled for over 120 years.

Political unification brought obvious commercial advantages. The Ottoman homelands of Rumelia with Anatolia were the natural pivot of Eurasian commerce. Ottoman foreign policy was influenced by strategic concern for long-distance trade routes, which were designed to converge on the major cities. The Europeans, especially the Italians, maintained a strong commercial presence in the Ottoman domains.

POLITICAL CULTURE AND THE ORGANISATION OF PUBLIC LIFE

From the mid-fourteenth to the mid-sixteenth centuries, the Ottoman Sultans and their servants were politically creative. In the organisation of their state, the Ottomans were pragmatic and inventive. They developed a new army and bureaucracy, based on recruitment of non-Muslim youths as loyal servants of the Sultan without social connections. The forced Levy (devşirme), instituted by Murad I (r.1362–89) and expanded under Bayezid I (r.1389–1402), was used to bring into the Sultan's service talented and attractive youths from the European dominions. These provided the Sultan's personal troops, known as ghulam (lit. young male slave), kapikulari (household troops) (*EI* 2: 1086–90), or Janissaries (yeni çeri: lit. new troops); and they staffed the central bureaucracy. Later, such people were among the foremost propagators of Ottoman ideology.

Here, the Ottomans displayed a genius for adapting and transforming an earlier practice – slave-soldiers; in this case, not untypically, with rather slight credentials in Religious Law. The Levy brought youths from the newly conquered parts of Europe – Thrace, Macedonia, Greece, Bulgaria, Serbia, Bosnia, Albania – into the heart of the Ottoman military and administrative system. It ensured that at least some senior posts were in the hands of dedicated personal servants of the Sultan with no independent power base. It gave the Ottoman elite a partly European component, in fact made this a genuinely *Eurasian* polity. It gave the bureaucracy a meritocratic character, reminiscent in some ways of the English public-school system. This made an impression on European visitors: 'in making his appointments, the Sultan pays no regard to any pretensions on the score of wealth or rank. It is by merit that men rise ... Among the Turks, honours, high posts and Judgeships are the rewards of great ability and good service' (in Zilfi 1998: 45).

The Turkish warrior-agrarian nobility ('askeri) had originated as frontier holy-warriors (ghazi). They held their land as a timar ('fief') and dominated the provincial armies and also the senior ranks of the 'ulama. The division between the native aristocracy and the slave-soldiers – a new and extended version of the Saljuk divide between military Turks and civilians Persians – was a fundamental source of tension in Ottoman politics (Lapidus 1988: 317). Sultans, in order to maintain their independence, tended to play the two off against each other, a new Sultan often supporting those neglected by his predecessor. Murad II and Mehmed II built up the Levy element in both the army and the administration. Mehmed II alienated the 'ulama and Turkish notables by policies of high taxation and confiscation of religious Trusts (sing. vakif) to finance his wars. After the capture of Constantinople, he felt strong enough to have his grand vizier, an aristocrat, imprisoned, and to appoint a Levy man as grand vizier. Bayezid II, on the contrary, favoured the 'ulama and promoted native Turks.

RELIGION AND THE STATE (DIN VE DEVLET)

The devlet-i al-i Osman was a religious polity. It was assumed that the *purpose* of the Sultan and his servants was to maintain and promote 'din ve devlet' (religion and dynasty, or regime: not quite church and state). But the relationship between the Learned leaders of religion ('ulama) and the executive power of the Sultan with his military and civil officers developed in a distinctive way and grew into a more complete symbiosis than under previous Islamic governments. The 'ulama were given, for the first time, a formal structure and a system of ranks. Well-qualified 'ulama could rise to the highest offices of state. The Sultans supervised the training of the 'ulama; they were anxious to improve and control education. Medreses (Colleges) were also ranked.

This symbiosis was based upon the Sultan himself since he was at once military commander, head of the Islamic People and supreme civil authority. His political and executive authority he delegated to viziers. These were headed by the grand vizier, who might be either a member of the 'ulama and Muslim-born Turk, or a Levy man; the other viziers usually came from the military-administrative, i.e. largely Levy, background. The grand vizier had considerable independence from the Sultan with almost unlimited powers of appointment, dismissal and supervision; when, in the later sixteenth century, Sultans became withdrawn from politics, he was often de facto head of state.

The organs of government were the Treasury, the Chancery, which dealt with administration and secular law, and the sphere of Religious Law (Shari'a: Turkish, Şeriat), which was now headed by the Şeykülislam (Shaykh-al-Islam). The heads of each department came from the religious career structure, so that the great offices of state were strongly influenced by the world of the medrese. The main day-to-day decision-making body was the Sultan's Council (divan-i humayun), consisting of the treasurer, chancellor and the two chief Religious Judges (kadiaskers).

The organisation of the treasury and chancery were more developed under the Ottomans than under any other Islamic government. The scribal bureaucracy (sometimes known as 'the men of the pen': secretariat) emerged as a distinct group. They were composed partly of highly-trained 'ulama, partly of Levy men educated at the palace. Later they became 'consolidated into a relatively discrete professional body' (Fleischer 1986: 215). By the mid-sixteenth century, 'the bureaucracy as a whole began ... to establish itself as a career path in its own right, independent of the religious career structure'. Many Levy men rose high in treasury and chancery. As confidential secretaries to viziers, 'well versed in the traditional principles of statecraft', they were 'really responsible for the success of several great Ottoman statesmen' (Inalçik 1973: 120). During the sixteenth and seventeenth centuries, the bureaucracy became increasingly autonomous.[2]

Ottoman political ideas, insofar as they were expressed at all, were expressed largely by this group. Their cultural background and position in government made them open to the Persianate Advice-to-Kings lore; they tended to promote adoption of European ideas, espcially in technical fields.

Their ideas were grounded in their administrative experience; Ottoman political thought was markedly pragmatic.

There were thus two 'parallel and separate systems of provincial administration', that of the military governors representing 'the Sultan's executive authority', and 'a legal-administrative one manned by graduates of the Religious Colleges', who represented 'the Sultan's (religious) legal authority'.[3] Much of the business of government and social control was conducted at the local level by the ümera (lit. 'Commanders': sing. emir): the governor-generals (beylerbeyi) of Rumelia and Anatolia, and under them the district-governors (sançakbeyi). These were appointed by the Sultan. Most were timar-holding knights, but some were slave-soldiers or senior 'ulama. They comprised a military elite: they had a separate law code (kanun-i sipayihan) and were under the special jurisdiction of two Chief Religious Judges (kadiaskers), another Ottoman innovation. Their households became centres of local power.

The timar (Persian for iqta': 'fief') was the key instrument of government and fiscal policy. This was assigned by the Sultan to cavalrymen (sipahi: 'Knights'). They were landowners in the sense that they were entitled to the taxes on the land; but the Sultan and the cultivators (re'aya: common people) 'retained rights over the land'.[4] The knight was traditionally responsible for local law and order; the Sultan's law-codes (sing. kanun) stipulated his duties to the cultivators and their rights. 'Fiefs' were not supposed to be hereditary: the timar could theoretically be reassigned at any time by the Sultan; the fief-holder was thus formally less independent than his European equivalent. This was the Ottoman version of the military-agricultural complex.

A parallel religious structure was headed by the Şeykülislam, an office which had precedents in earlier regimes but was considerably upgraded by the Ottomans. He was appointed, and could be dismissed, by the Sultan. The Şeykülislam's rulings on religious law (fetvas) were binding. Under him came the chief Judges, then the kadis (Religious Judges) of major cities: these were religious Experts (muftis), and they too could issue fetvas on points of law. Then came district kadis. All these were, to begin with, appointed by the Sultan on the recommendation of the grand vizier. Minor Judges were appointed by the chief Judges. The kadis were 'the backbone of the Ottoman administration'. The position of the Şeykülislam was strengthened in the mid-sixteenth century when he acquired power to appoint the chief Judges and other senior kadis; this effectively gave him 'control over the entire organisation of the ulama'.[5]

This gave the religious body greater independence; and it was a further step towards Islamicisation of the polity. The 'ulama were more free than other subjects from government action. Indeed, apart from the Sultan, they were the only self-authorising element in the polity. They were immune from execution or confiscation of property; unlike others, they could pass their landed wealth on to their children. Leading families came to monopolise the higher religious positions; the senior 'ulama were very much part of the ruling group.

Religion provided the strongest bond between government and subjects, between the ruling classes ('askeri) and the common people (re'aya) – that is, between those who lived off tax revenue and those who paid taxes. Symbiosis between government and religion did not take place only among the ruling and propertied classes.

The Ottoman state made allies of folk-Islam and the Sufi orders. This showed once again the multi-faceted strength of Islam as a religion of social control, as well as the skill of the Ottomans. Sufism had been the highway for ordinary people from Christianity to Islam. The Sufis' religious missions permeated rural and urban society and the army. The janissaries were devotees of the Bektashi order. The first Ottomans were invested with the sword of the gazi by a Sufi dervish. Sufi orders which preached against wealth and property and supported resistance to the Ottomans were suppressed. Orders devoted to mystical and humanitarian pursuits were generously patronised and took their place in the people's affections. The government and its adherents became patrons of dervish lodges, whose heads had to be approved by the Şeykülislam. Sufi orders quickly became part of the social cement, providing a welcome dose of political quietism.

Sufism enhanced social deference through its example of hierarchical order and unquestioning obedience to the master. It formed an integral part of social and spiritual life at the court, in the army, and among urban workers and the peasants. The mystical approach appealed to both learned and uneducated. Thus, 'relative harmony was achieved through toleration of three parallel religious strands: official Sunni legalism, the Sufi tekke (hospice) cult, and the folk cult' (Trimingham 1971: 69). This gave great strength to Ottoman political society.

The keystone of this interlocking of state and religion was the kadi (Religious Judge). They were religious magistrates, but they administered both the Shari'a and the 'secular' kanun, and they also supervised 'the execution of the Sultan's administrative and financial decrees' (Inalçik 1973: 118). This extension of the kadi's role into non-religious spheres was 'the main innovation of Ottoman public law' (Heyd 1973: 216). In applying the Shari'a itself, they had little discretion, since 'the entire body of law was perfectly known to the litigants; there were no secrets and no surprises'. The execution of judges' decisions was, as before, separate from the process of adjudication, with military governors enforcing court decisions. Recent research indicates that kadis' decisions did in fact have to be 'heeded by governors and police officials' (Gerber 1994: 177, 181). The Ottomans underwrote the Shari'a order of society by ensuring that kadis' decisions were acted upon.

This close integration of the 'ulama into the government brought benefits to both. It gave the 'ulama power and wealth. It gave the regime a ready-made legal and administrative framework with roots deeply embedded in popular belief, and it was the bedrock of the dynasty's legitimacy in the eyes of its Muslim subjects.

THE PATRIMONIAL SULTAN

The Sultan was the keystone of the whole Ottoman system. He held it together in his dual functions as religious and military leader, and he was also the focus of tribal, religious and patrimonial sentiment. The same had been true of other Islamic regimes, but the way in which the Ottoman polity developed made the role and person of the Sultan especially critical.

The Ottoman state began, like most pre-modern states in the Islamic world, as a clan dynasty; and, to the end, allegiance was focused on the family of Osman.[6] Like other regimes in Islamdom, it rested on its reputation for promoting religion, especially in this case through Holy War.[7] One indication of early Ottoman sentiment comes from the poet Ahmedi (d.1412), who dedicated a version of the Alexander epic, which he called 'a book of Holy War', to Bayezid I (r.1389–1402). Having praised 'the justice of the Mongol Sultans', Ahmedi asserted that the Ottomans are 'both Muslims and just rulers'. Those who call the Ottomans upstarts should remember that 'he who comes later, and remains, is better than his predecessors' (in Fleischer 1986: 290). But in the case of the Ottomans, the *patrimonial* factor came to the fore and for a while, during its greatest days c.1440–1580, was arguably the most important element. The dynastic regime of the House of Osman became a 'patrimonial' state, in the sense that monarchical authority was seen as the bastion of justice and agricultural wealth, and that power was the personal possession of the ruling Sultan. The Sultan's authority rested on the widespread conviction that 'the only way to realise [justice] was ... by means of an omnipotent ruler independent from all external influences, deciding and acting in absolute freedom, responsible only before God for his actions'.[8]

In this process, clan and tribal features gave way to the personal will of the Sultan. 'No longer was the state thought of as the joint property and inheritance of the dynasty. The padişah (emperor) was seen ... as the bearer of an absolute and abstract authority ... state and ruler [were] equated.' In foreign relations, military organisation, strategy and other affairs of state, 'every decision was expressed formally as deriving directly from the person of the Sultan' (Inalçik 1993: 60–1, 84). This meant that, in constitutional terms, patrimonialism meant absolutism.

The personal autocracy of the reigning Sultan was given a tremendous boost when Mehmed II finally captured Constantinople (Istanbul), for in the eyes of many, and perhaps especially of his recently converted or still Christian subjects, he had thereby tacitly inherited the status of Roman emperor. There are signs that this was how Mehmed II, in particular, perceived his own position. It was now that he issued a governmental law-code (kanunname), suggesting perhaps that the Sultan was laying claim not only to supreme executive power but to legislative power as well. Süleyman I was widely known as 'the Lawgiver (sahib-i kanun or kanuni)'. This was a unique development for a Muslim monarch.

Selim I asserted the Sultan's authority even over the Şeykülislam. When the Şeykülislam protested against a decision by Selim to have 150 treasury officials executed, the Sultan replied that this was 'a violation of the Sultan's authority ... No-one [has] the right or competence to question what the Sultan commands or forbids' (in Inalçik 1973: 94). The men were executed.

The Sultan's personal authority was further enhanced by his claim to be Deputy (see below, p. 206). As in the Byzantine empire, and in Middle Eastern tradition going back to ancient Egypt and Iran, religion supported the ruler's claim to an authority which it was sinful to question. As an educated reformer in the bureaucracy later put it, the Sultan has 'perfect wisdom and knowledge'.[9] It was popularly believed that he acted by 'divine impulse' (in Heyd 1973: 195n.).

In relation to kanun, the Sultan's position was absolute in the strict sense. Kanun rested solely on *his* authority. Uncertainties in its interpretation were to be referred 'to the capital' (sixteenth-century kanunname); and, whereas the Şeykülislam's fetvas were 'not legally binding on the kadis, the Sultan's firmans were' (Inalçik 1973: 73–5). The Sultan himself was not restricted by kanun; in acting for the sake of social discipline (siyasa), he could ignore it. This followed Turco-Islamic tradition; but the influence of the Byzantine world, from which many exponents of Sultanic ideology now came, should not be discounted.[10]

Of course, no Sultans could be all-powerful in practice. They all had to conciliate interest groups, such as the ʿulama, the timar-holding knights and the slave-soldiers (janissaries). The willingness of these to cooperate with the Sultan varied, partly with the fluctuating fortunes of the state finances. In the seventeenth century, the ʿulama and janissaries of Istanbul frequently challenged the Sultan's authority and severely restricted his room for manoeuvre, especially if he wanted to implement changes.

Behind this patrimonial absolutism lay the conviction that the Sultan's main duty was to implement justice (adalet). This involved his role as Deputy as well. He is the 'writer of justice on the pages of time'. Justice meant in particular protecting the common people (reʿaya: lit. flock), preventing oppression and abuse of power by landowners or officials. Both the land and the common people were deemed to be the Sultan's property and under his special protection (Inalçik 1973: 73). This was one reason given for the Sultan issuing his own law-codes and 'rescripts of justice (adaletname)'.

Special concern was expressed for the reʿaya qua cultivators upon whom the economy, and therefore the polity, depended. This meant keeping an eye on governors, military commanders and tax-collectors (Inalçik 1993: 73), and hearing complaints against them. Such people, as members of the ʿaskeri (ruling class), were especially subject to the ruler's immediate authority and disciplinary power (siyasa). They could be very severely punished for any dereliction of duty by instant dismissal, confiscation or execution. In popular opinion, 'as Allah's vicegerent in this world, the Sultan was regarded as a remote supreme power which punished the executive organs of his Government for their oppressive acts against the people' (Heyd 1973: 227).

Ordinary people seem to have looked with confidence to the Sultan as their main hope for the redress of grievances. In 1675, 'thousands of villages sent complaints to the far-away Sultan', implying that 'complaining was meaningful in achieving results' (Gerber 1994: 182). To achieve the goals of justice and order, the Sultan was entitled to exercise both severity and mercy; the people should be made to live 'between fear and hope' (Heyd 1973: 195).

Ottoman economic policy was largely patrimonial. The Ottomans in general tended to aim at imperial self-sufficiency, maximisation of government income, traditional justice and maintenance of the population's food supply. They regarded the economy as a dynastic resource; the government claimed control over land, water and agricultural labour,[11] while mining was regulated by the kadi courts. Economic policy was driven by the notion of the Sultan as provider for his people as well as by the military needs of the state. The Ottoman government sought to provide social and economic security. Economic management was an instrument of state policy. Exports were, on occasion, taxed more heavily than imports. Merchant capital was liable to exorbitant taxation or confiscation by the military authorities; farmers were regularly overtaxed. The accumulative activities of large notable households also played an important role.

Economic and social duties were also integral to the Sultan's role as religious leader and Deputy. He had to maintain and improve the infrastructure, endow mosques, medreses, caravanserais and hospitals, provide patronage for the 'ulama, and maintain a network of religio-charitable 'imarets'. These pious trusts typically comprised a 'mosque, medrese, hospital, traveller's hostel, water installations, roads and bridges'; they were supported by income from communal facilities such as 'an inn, market, caravanserai, bath-house, mill, dye-house, slaughter-house, or soup-kitchen' (Inalçik 1973: 142). The Sultan was responsible for consumer protection: his government supervised weights and measures and regulated prices to maintain a supply of cheap food for the army and large cities.

SULTANIC IDEOLOGY

These economic policies were justified by both Islamic ethics and Iranian patrimonialism. According to senior 'ulama, the Sultan's duty was to maintain 'the order of the world (nizam-i alem)', or (the same thing) 'the order of the country (nizam-i memleket)' (Heyd 1973: 194–6). The Circle of Power was invoked, though not until the mid-sixteenth century.

The Sultan's perceived status and potential for exercising power were enhanced by the very peculiarities of the Ottoman system. For he was also the protector and immediate overlord of religious minorities, and of tribal communities under indirect rule. There were no formal constraints on the Sultan's dealings with non-Muslim subjects. Tribal chiefs and others under indirect rule depended for their position on personal recognition by the Sultan.

Strictly speaking, Islam rejected the notion of absolute sovereignty, since all legitimate rulers are bound by the Holy Law. In theory, the Sultan's power was limited by the Şeriat and by the decisions of kadis; in cases of Religious Law, once a kadi had made a decision, it was binding even on the Sultan. But few rulers can have had greater opportunities for infringement of norms in private without public attention. Moreover, loyalty to the dynasty tended to be conflated with loyalty to Islam.

The Sultan was legitimised and glorified by exultant and effusive language which implied supreme status. This emanated from court circles, but much of the time it may have reflected popular feeling as well. Here, secular and Islamic language were used rather indiscriminately. The greatness of the Sultan as a world power, his successes in Holy War, and his position as religious leader all pointed in the same direction. The dynasty legitimised itself in tribal-Turkish terms; Osman, the founder, was placed in the lineage of Turkish Khans. The Ottomans were quick to take up the Persian titles 'emperor (hüdavendigar)' and 'the universal ruler who protects the world (padişah-i alempanah)'; foreign rulers frequently addressed the Ottoman Sultan as 'emperor'. The Ottoman Sultan was the heir of the great and beneficent Darius and Alexander. Murad I was styled 'the most high Sultan (sultan-i azam)', Murad II both 'king of kings (malik al-muluk)' and 'Sultan of Sultans (sultan al-salatin)'. Bayezid II was 'ashraf-i salatin (the most honoured (Muslim) ruler)'.[12] Thus Islamic and non-Islamic concepts were strung together.

Sultans used the language of world sovereignty. In the ancient imperial tradition, the ruler's domains constituted for all significant purposes the world. The Sultan's mother, writing to Queen Elizabeth I of England (1593), described her sovereign as 'the Khan of the seven climes at this auspicious time and the fortunate lord of the four corners of the earth' (in Stern 1965: 131). When Ottoman leaders spoke of 'the good order of society', the actual term used was 'the good order of the world' (nizam-i alem). In the words of a seventeenth-century reformer, may God grant that 'the shadow of your protection be the cause for the repose of the world and comfort for all mankind'.[13] The tribal leader had evolved into a world emperor for whom there are no outsiders.

The rhetoric of world-conquering empire reached a climax under Mehmed II and Süleyman I. Mehmed called himself 'the sovereign of the two lands and the two seas' (sc. Rumelia and Anatolia, the Mediterranean and the Black Sea). Italian observers reported Mehmed as saying he was advancing 'from east to west', reversing Alexander's route. Italy (he was claimed to have said) had once been strong under the Romans, but now 'you are 20 states ... you are in disagreement among yourselves ... There must be only one empire, one faith and one sovereignty in the world'.[14] This was doctrine inspired by ancient Rome; Mehmed could have been imitating the Euro-Christian ideology of empire. Süleyman I boasted: 'In Baghdad I am Shah, in Rum Caesar, in Egypt Sultan, who sends his fleets to the seas of Europe, the Maghrib and India' (1538: in Inalçik 1973: 41). Ebu's-Sü'ud, who was Şeykülislam under Süleyman, composed an inscription for Süleyman as 'Master of all lands and the shadow of God over all nations, Sultan over all the Sultans in the lands of Arabs and Persians' (1557: in Inalçik 1993: 78). The historian Mustafa 'Ali (see below, pp. 259–61), however, ascribed the status of 'world conqueror' only to Alexander, Chingiz and Timur (Selim I might have made it if had he lived longer). As it was, Mehmed II, Selim I and Süleyman were just 'succoured by God' (sc. undefeated in battle) (Fleischer 1986: 279–80).

RELIGIOUS LEADERSHIP

To all this was added the Sultan's claim to religious leadership. Like previous Turkish dynasties, the Ottomans had from the start been proudly ambitious on behalf of their adopted faith. The first Ottomans may have called themselves Frontier Warriors,[15] leaders in Holy War against unbelievers. This ideal was championed by Sufis, who were among the strongest supporters of the early Ottomans. Success in jihad was, once again, irrefutable proof of political legitimacy. Orkhan (r.1324–60) was called 'the great and magnificent Commander (emir), the warrior of the Holy War, Sultan of the ghazis ... hero of the world and the faith' (1337).[16] The Ottomans claimed to have received the sword of Osman ('Uthman, the third rightly-guided Deputy). The 'continued advance of Islam from east to west' was seen as 'clear proof that God aided them and that Islam was the true religion' (Inalçik 1973: 10). The Ottomans justified their campaigns against Muslim dynasties in Anatolia (1390s) because, by opposing the Ottomans, these had interfered with jihad. Süleyman had his wars against Iran justified by a fetva which declared it his duty to eradicate the Shi'ite heresy and restore the Shari'a.

In due course, the Ottomans claimed the title of Caliph (Deputy). The caliphal title 'Commander of the Faithful' (amir ul-mu'uminin) was used by Mehmed II. The belief that the Ottoman Sultans were Deputies rested especially upon their perceived military achievement. Whereas several regimes claimed Caliphal status for their Sultan, the Ottomans claimed this religious Imamate not just in their own territories but worldwide. They saw themselves as the world protagonists of Sunni Islam; no-one since Muhammad and the first four rightly-guided Caliphs had done more for the faith. The claim was sealed when Selim I became 'servitor of the two holy sanctuaries', Mecca and Medina (1516). Under Süleyman, who called himself 'the Caliph of the whole world' and 'the Caliph of all the Muslims in the world', it was taken for granted. Thus, 'by the grace of God I am head of Muhammad's Community. God's might and Muhammad's miracles are my companions. I am Süleyman in whose name the hutbe is read in Mecca and Medina' (inscription of 1538: Inalçik 1973: 41). Lutfi Paşa (see below, p. 213) argued that the universal Caliphate had been revived (in Inalçik's words) on the basis of 'Süleyman's ghazi power and protection of Islam in the world' (Inalçik 1993: 80). The Şeykülislam Ebu's-Sü'ud called both Süleyman and his successor, Selim II, 'Caliph to the Apostle of the Lord of the worlds' (that is, Muhammad's Deputy).[17] A posthumous edition of Ebu's-Sü'ud's work on Fiqh called Süleyman 'Sultan of the Time and of the earth, Deputy of the Lord of the worlds'; 'the garden of the Sultanate' and 'the pastures of the Caliphate' were assumed to be identical.[18]

The Ottomans' claim to be Muhammad's (or God's) Deputy (halife) on earth was more explicit than that of any other Sunni regime since the 'Abbasids. It was not just rhetoric. The Sultan-Caliph had responsibility to 'execute the decrees [of the Hidden Book] in all regions of the inhabited quarter' (as Ebu's-Sü'ud put it). The kadis administered justice on his behalf; 'authority to direct the kadis how to apply the law', both Shari'a and kanun, being 'theoretically reserved to the Sultan' (Heyd 1973: 187). In fact Ebu's-Sü'ud went so far as to claim that the Sultan 'makes manifest the Exalted Word of God' and 'expounds the signs of the luminous Shari'a', which implies an interpretative function as well (Imber 1997: 98, 104–6).

The obvious problem for such a regime was the liability of Sultans to die. In relation to the succession, tension emerged between the Sultan as supreme individual ruler and the state as joint property of the ruling clan. In both tribal and Islamic Law, all sons were equal heirs; primogeniture as practised in Europe was not permitted. The traditional view was that God made his will known through battle (Inalçik 1993: 60). 'You will confront each other and whoever then receives the devlet will also receive the fortress', said towns-people to two claimants in the early fifteenth century. There was also a view that God's will would be endorsed by all ranks of society. Thus, 'with God's help I have gained the Sultanate. On this date, with the perfect concurrence of the viziers, 'ulama and people of all stations high and low, I have ascended the throne of the Sultanate that has come down to me from my forefathers' (in Inalçik 1973: 62).

The Ottomans sought to improve on these traditions by a classic use of raison d'état. It became the practice for the victorious contestant to have his brothers executed on the grounds that they could destabilise the state. This was sanctioned in Mehmed II's law-code: 'that one of my sons to whom God grants the Sultanate, may lawfully put his brothers to death … for the sake of the order of the world' (in Inalçik 1973: 59; Heyd 1973: 194). Mehmed claimed that most of the 'ulama agreed with this. Medmed III (1595–1603) had his sons confined to a part of the harem known as the cage (kafes), thus depriving them of a power base and of political experience (Inalçik 1973: 60–1). Succession disputes continued; the politics of the harem now played a part.

That the Ottoman dynasty lasted so much longer than any other was partly due to their determination to overcome weaknesses inherent in a purely dynastic regime, by arranging the succession, by giving the grand vizier considerable independence, and by more elaborate bureaucratic structures. Whether it progressed to statehood in the Western sense of an 'abstract authority' detached from the individual power-holder seems very questionable.

It was generally assumed – probably rightly – that, if the Sultan's authority were removed, the polity would fall apart. This was presumably one reason why the Sultanate went virtually unchallenged for so long, and why reformers never considered an alternative until well into the nineteenth century. Rather, they staked their hopes on a strong reforming Sultan or ruthless Grand Vizier. The extent of this religious-patrimonial symbiosis may also explain why the Turkish Revolution produced a republic and the most secular regime in the House of Islam.

SELF-MANAGEMENT AND DIVERSITY

Contrary to the received image of absolutism, self-organisation flourished in certain sections of society. In town and countryside, the central 'despotism' was locked into symbiosis with secular and religious notables (ayan ve eshraf: the great and the good). There was a patchwork of local autonomies. By integrating the 'ulama and the kadis into the politico-legal system, 'the Ottomans in effect agreed to share power'. There was scope for 'bargaining and negotiating' in the administration of law and justice (Gerber 1994: 179, 181).

Self-government was widely exercised by ethnic and religious minorities. The incorporation of southern and eastern Europe, the Black Sea and the Caucasus regions gave the Ottoman domains a greater mix of ethnic groups than any other pre-modern polity. In outlying areas, the Ottomans favoured indirect rule through existing lords or tribal chiefs: Dubrovnik had its city council, Mecca its sharif, Kurdistan and the Tatar khanate of the Crimea their tribal chiefs. In the Danube basin, the Balkan mountains, eastern Anatolia and the southern Caucasus, nomads were grouped together under clan or tribal leadership and called a 'people (ulus)'. It was partly thanks to this that the Ottomans succeeded in bringing together such a remarkable variety of peoples with fundamentally different lifestyles, social structures and economies.

Such diversity was facilitated by the fact that this was a dynastic and not a racial regime: the rulers were conceived as Ottomans, and emphatically not as Turks. 'Turk' was a name given especially to the less cultivated semi-nomadic peoples of Anatolia (it was sometimes said that Turks were unsuitable for government). Here the Ottomans were closer to the Roman empire than to a modern polity.

This principle was carried into the very heart of government. The Levy brought successive generations of foreigners from all over south-eastern Europe into the army and the administration where they could attain the highest positions. Men of the Levy and of European birth were later prominent as reformers; some actually emphasised their ethnic background as a strength of the regime (see below, p. 264). Émigrés from Christian Europe also brought valued skills. Among Turkish writers, Mustafa 'Ali remarked that this mixture of races provided the regime with a wide range of talents; Katib Çelebi (see below, p. 265) ascribed the diversity of creeds and law-codes to the 'inner purpose' in God's plan.

There was also a remarkable religious diversity, and a degree of religious toleration not found in Christian Europe. In commerce and manufacture, there was even some cultural assimilation: 'Muslim and non-Muslim merchants and craftsmen belonged to the same class and enjoyed the same rights, while rich Jewish, Greek and Armenian merchants dressed and acted like Muslims' (Inalçik 1973: 151). The Ottomans developed the traditional system of self-management for non-Muslim monotheists by their own religious authorities within their confessional Community (millet). Jewish and Christian religious authorities, like tribal rulers, were given jurisdiction over their own people. The millet 'maintained its own institutions to care for ... education, religious justice and social security, [with] separate schools, hospitals and hotels, along with hospices for the poor and aged' (Shaw 1976: 151). The religious minorities were ruled by their own laws and were not subject to the 'ulama or kadis (unless they chose to go to a kadi court). The authority of the Patriarch of Constantinople was even enhanced, by making him religious superior of Orthodox Slavs as well as Greeks, and by giving him some civil powers as well. European merchants were slotted into the system via their consular representatives (Shaw 1976: 29).

Such ethnic and credal diversity was a continuation of the 'tribal' policy of the first Ottomans (and indeed the first Muslims), under which outsiders could acquire membership and its advantages. Qualified toleration for other mono-theists was rooted in Islamic tradition. Mehmed II (r.1451–81) in particular was something of an intellectual, presiding over what Westerners took for a renaissance court, and he appears to have been more tolerant than most of different points of view.

Ethnic diversity was legitimised by the Islamic emphasis upon creed rather than race. The Ottoman devlet could accommodate ethnic diversity precisely because ethnicity was not the determinant of political status; it was not an issue – a good Muslim tradition. It went relatively unremarked. The Ottomans tacitly encouraged peaceful cohabitation of races and creeds as never before or since, testifying to political skills which twentieth-century politicians might still admire, if they wished to emulate them.

Within the Muslim community, the government needed the support of popular religious leaders, including Sufi shaykhs and dervishes. Popular upris-ings were not uncommon and, especially in the capital, sometimes achieved their ends. The janissaries in particular grasped the possibility of collective political action during succession crises. They combined with the Istanbul 'ulama to frustrate reform at several junctures in the seventeenth and eight-eenth centuries (see below, pp. 257–8).

Socio-religious brotherhoods (akhi), influenced by Sufism, flourished in the army and among urban craft workers. City districts had their own leaders, an imam, priest or rabbi, and a warden as their contact with government. A warden acted for all the guilds and, together with the leading 'ulama and merchants, 'represented the town to the government' (Inalçik 1973: 153, 161). But he did not take part in the actual government of the city. Even cultivators organised themselves in response to the disorders of the 1590s.

Self-management was most developed in the craft guilds, which also originated partly as religious brotherhoods. Their aims were to control the number of workers, regulate the quality and price of goods, supervise employ-ment of labourers and purchase of materials, and resolve disputes. They tended to 'prevent competition'.[19] Master-craftsmen elected from among themselves a council of 'the six'; this was headed by a shaykh (spiritual leader) and a warden (kethuda), whose job it was to implment guild rules and maintain good relations with the authorities. Guild officials were confirmed by the kadi; guild regulations were inspected by the Sultan. Craftsmen could remove their warden; and they resisted government intervention in their elections (Inalçik

1973: 152). Here too, there was symbiosis between a spontaneous social movement and the authorities: the government tended to cooperate with the guilds in support of traditional working practices.

Kadis orchestrated one or two stirrings of actual local self-government. During the Anatolian crisis of 1596–1609, when commoners were summoned to arms, the kadi would convene the local notables, who would then elect one of themselves as chief (serdar). In the unusual event of taxes being raised collectively by local communities, the kadi might be ordered by the government to convene a council of the village Elders and to allocate taxes, as they put it, with the full consent of the ayan ve eshraf (Inalçik 1980: 336).

SHARI'A AND KANUN (SULTANIC LAW)

The greatest innovation of the Ottoman state was the development of non-religious law (kanun), also known as customary law (örf/'urf), the law of the Sultan, or Ottoman law (kanuni osmani). Here again the Ottomans regularised, extended and codified earlier practice. Most originally, they slotted it into the Shari'a system: both types of law were administered by the same courts. This was based partly on self-conscious respect for a Turco-Mongol tradition of popular law (yasa).[20] Ahmedi (see above, p. 202) said that the old Mongol rulers had been relatively lenient because Chingiz Khan's kanun prevented them from 'bathing their hands in the people's blood'. He declared that a just leader could actually *improve* the law: today 'there is little deficiency [in kanun]; let us now do away with any faults that remain' (in Fleischer 1986: 289–90). Kanun may also have owed something to the religious diversity of the empire: unlike the Shari'a, it applied to all Ottoman subjects.

The Sultans' promulgation of 'comprehensive and detailed regulations ... of secular criminal law and procedure' with 'orders to assemble them in the form of codes known as "kanunname"' (Heyd 1973: 2) was unprecedented in Islam. Kanunname were issued by Mehmed II immediately after the capture of Constantinople – just 900 years after the Digest and Codex of Roman Law had been promulgated from the same city. It is difficult to avoid the suspicion that some kind of precedent occurred to the Conqueror's mind. These kanunnames were updated in 1501, and later became known as 'Süleyman's law-code' (Inalçik 1993: 86). They were not in fact comparable with Roman Law: for 'unlike the Shari'a, the kanun generally does not define the legal terms used'. There was 'no attempt to elaborate general and basic principles of crime, punishment and evidence ... No systematic distinction is made between premeditated and accidental offenses. Mitigating circumstances are almost unknown' (Heyd 1973: 178). Provincial law-codes drew upon 'pre-conquest laws and customs of the area'; an Egyptian code stated that custom itself is 'one of the Shari'a proofs in matters on which there is no written authority'.[21]

Kanun dealt, first, with criminal law, especially for commoners. It was intended to supplement the Shari'a by specifying penalties, sometimes mitigating the Shari'a, more often stipulating harsher punishments. Second, it dealt with 'the collection of taxes in timars, the laws of land tenure and transfer, and the legal status and exemptions of cultivators (common people: re'aya)'. Kanun also covered 'mining, the circulation of coin, customs monopolies' (Inalçik 1973: 72–3). Finally, it dealt with state bodies, 'the form of government, its notables and their sphere of authority, their relationship with the Sultan, their ranks and degrees, promotion, salary, retirement and punishment' (*EI* 4: 564b). Thus it regularised the conduct and relationships of *status groups* within society. In fact, kanun was in part an attempt to control relations between landowners and cultivators from the top, that is to apply Iranian patrimonial principles and to protect the common people in accordance with the ethics of Islam.

The reasons given to explain and justify this development of secular law throw unique light on Ottoman political thinking. The aim seems to have been, on the one hand, to mitigate oppression, on the other to make more draconian the punishment of crime – both moves that favoured the common people. Kanun sought to prevent malpractice by tax-collectors and 'askeri by fixing the rates of taxes and fines; that is, to offer the common people justice and protection 'against the oppression of the authorities' (Heyd 1973: 3). At Erzurum (1540), it was said that 'the tribal communities, as well as merchants and other communities, could not bear the heavy load resulting from [the laws of the previous ruler] … They wanted the Rum [Ottoman] law to be put into force'. The Sultan agreed to give them 'the kanunname of Rum' out of 'feelings of compassion and justice in their favour' (preamble from Erzurum (1540) in Inalçik 1969: 128). Indeed, some historians think that kanun was fair, indeed liberal, in particular compared with the Christian-European feudal laws which preceded it. For example, Ottoman law forbade forced labour; and it introduced a simpler system of taxation.[22]

The penal supplements to the Shari'a were justified on the grounds that 'in the course of time, crimes have increased to such an extent that disputes and feuds can no longer be decided by "the sword of the tongue of the guardians of the Holy Law", i.e. the kadis, but require "the tongue of the sword of the authorities charged with inflicting severe punishment", i.e. the military' (Heyd 1973: 176). Severe corporal punishment and the death penalty were justified as legitimate discipline (siyasa). The Sultan might (to quote Heyd again) 'order the execution of certain offenders as an administrative punishment (siyasaten) within the framework of his discretionary power' (Heyd 1973: 196).

It was said that siyasa justified exemplary punishment by the Sultan as 'a deterrent example and warning to others' to deter criminality in general.[23] (Siyasa is here being used almost as a kind of raison d'état.) One example of such exemplary deterrent punishment was when, after the murder of a Muslim household, some 800 non-Muslim vagrants were rounded up and executed. The Chancellor, a distinguished 'alim, acknowledged that such action might give cause for moral concern, but upheld it on the grounds that people needed to be taught a lesson: 'for that reason the divine will became manifest; a warning example was given to the trouble-makers, and terror spread among the criminals. Since that time no similar atrocity has occurred. It is in the nature of the common people, so long as they have no fear of the sword, to dare to …

indulge in all kinds of wickedness' (in Heyd 1973: 195). This was an extreme instance of collective punishment, but by no means the only one.

The Şeykülislam and other muftis invoked 'the public interest (maslahat)' – a principle of Religious Law – and 'public order (nizam-i memleket)' as justifications for such measures. Severe punishments were required to protect 'the people'. In the same way, a new Sultan was permitted or even obliged to execute his own brothers 'for the sake of the order of the world (nizam-i alem)', that is, to prevent civil war (Heyd 1973: 194).

The most distinctive feature of the Ottoman system was the way in which it integrated kanun and Shari'a. In some respects, they were fused into a single legal system: this was unique in Islamic history. Thus the kadis implemented secular as well as religious law in Islamic courts. The kadis 'are not restricted to hearing Shari'a cases only, but are appointed and ordered to decide disputes and terminate litigation in regard to both Shari'a and örf (customary-law) matters. Therefore, just as on Shari'a questions Religious Jurisprudence (fiqh) is studied, so it is considered the kadi's duty in regard to örf matters to study the registers of the Sultan's kanuns' (as one early seventeenth-century court clerk put it: Heyd 1973: 216). The Şeykülislams even 'based some of their fetvas [on criminal matters] on the kanun' (Heyd 1973: 183).

The Şeykülislam and other leading 'ulama regarded the kanun as falling within their sphere of competence. Indeed, kanun was compiled not only by Chancery clerks but also by 'ulama who had been trained in Religious Jurisprudence, and who happened to be working for the Sultan in the Chancery. Ebu's-Sü'ud (1490–1574: Imber 1997), Süleyman's friend and confidant, Şeykülislam from 1545 to 1574, worked with Mustafa Celal-zade, the Chancellor (in office 1534–56), to promote kanun. In his work as Şeykülislam, Ebu 's-Sü'ud 'expounded the timar system as laid down in the kanun and applied its regulations to cases submitted to him' (Heyd 1973: 174). And after all, the overall aims of kanun were the same as those of the Shari'a: to give the common people a fair deal, to prevent as well as to punish crime, and to safeguard public order.

There was no question here of rival jurisdictions; it was simply that most people seem to have recognised that the Holy Law did not cover everything necessary for social order, the preservation of which was after all a basic postulate of Islam. There was for a while a conflation of religious and secular law. The term şer'an ('in accordance with Religious Law': the adverb corresponding to Shari'a) sometimes came to mean simply 'legally' in a general sense (Heyd 1973: 187). Kadis would be ordered to investigate a case 'according to the shari'a and the kanun', to 'pass sentence in accordance with the shari'a and the örf (custom)', to administer justice 'according to the noble Shari'a and the kanunnames deposited in the law courts' (in Heyd 1973: 216). Ebu's-Sü'ud called the Sultan 'the propagator of the Sultanic laws' as well as enforcer of 'the commands of the Quran ... all over the world' (in Inalçik 1993: 78). It was almost as if the Ottoman Sultans (like the first Caliphs) saw the Muslim ruler as someone authorised to continue the legislative activity of the Prophet, in order to meet the requirements of an early modern state.

Kanun and its relationship to the Shari'a was the one new development which did generate some theoretical discussion. After all, as Heyd observes, 'many basic features of kanun (e.g. inheritance regulations, taxes, fines etc) were in fact contrary to the Religious Law' (Heyd 1973: 174–5). The extended use of kanun could imply that the Shari'a was defective, or even perhaps that kanun had the same importance and authority, though of course nothing like this was ever said.

The practice of kanun was defended by state bureaucrats, especially, it seems, some with a Euro-Christian parentage or background. The Grand Vizier Lutfi Paşa (1488–1563),[24] a Levy man, probably Albanian, who was given (1539–41) the task of codifying and implementing kanun, said, in the first of many Ottoman Advice tracts, that his aims were to prevent arbitrary confiscation and imprisonment, enforce promotion on merit in government service, and balance the budget by limiting military expenditure. Many seventeenth-century reform tracts were to advocate revival and better implementation of kanun.

Ebu's-Sü'ud, Süleyman's Şeykülislam, was ambivalent. He does not appear to have held a consistent position, let alone a coherently worked-out theory of their relationship. When faced with a contradiction between kanun and the Shari'a, he either demonstrated their agreement or brought the kanun into line. He did once say that 'there can be no decree of the Sultan ordering something that is illegal according to the Shari'a'; presumably what he meant was that the Sultan's laws should be interpreted so as not to clash with the şeriat. On one occasion, however, he simply cited 'the rulings of both without making any further comment'.[25]

A slightly different attitude was indicated in the *Epistle on Shari'a Governance* (*Risalat al-siyasa al-shar'iyya*) by Dede Efendi (d.1565/8: Heyd 1973: 198–207), an otherwise obscure author. This work was fairly widely read, and may perhaps give us a better picture of public opinion. It was clearly inspired by the concerns of pious 'ulama. Without referring explicitly to Ottoman kanun, Dede Efendi reaffirmed siyasa in the traditional sense of the ruler's power to supplement the Shari'a in the public interest, especially by inflicting harsher penalties. He supported this by precedents from the Prophet and his Companions; and he quoted the saying 'God deters [people from transgression] more through the ruler than through the Qur'an'. He quoted Ibn Kayyim al-Jawziya, a fourteenth-century Hanbali Jurist, in defence of the kadi's right to apply non-religious Law, provided it is required by 'the usage and practice in a certain place and at a given time' (Heyd 1973: 200–1). Similarly, he justified what he called siyasa shar'iyya (Shari'a governance) on the ground that (in Heyd's words) 'penal justice has to conform to the public welfare (al-maslaha al-'amma), and since the latter varies at different places and in different times, criminal law and procedure must also change accordingly' (Heyd 1973: 200).

It seems as if Dede Efendi was using siyasa shar'iyya in a sense different from that of Ibn Taymiyya (whom he also quoted), to mean the Religious Law backed up by the ruler's penalties. He did not, unlike Ibn Taymiyya, mean an all-embracing public order derived exclusively from Shari'a principles. What Dede said could have implied justification for current Ottoman kanun, or at least for the participation of pious 'ulama in administering it. But of course it by no means described the actual Ottoman justice system. He was probably just trying to reconcile the position of the kadi in the Ottoman system with an orthodox, perhaps even a Hanbali, interpretation of Shari'a principles, to allay the conscience of 'ulama involved in the system. Like most Ottoman thinkers, he does not seem to have been working out general principles or applying them consistently.

The focus of writings on this subject was the perceived conflict between the way in which the religio-political system operated and the principles of the Shari'a. The development of kanun and its use alongside the Shari'a in the kadi courts do not appear to have been widely accepted by the 'ulama themselves. After Süleyman, the Şeykülislam became more ready to declare invalid any kanun which they thought contravened the Shari'a. Heyd surmises that 'many 'ulama most probably objected to the Kanun on principle' (Heyd 1973: 203).

The Ottomans' religio-political synthesis had developed in the days of continuous victory; it became subject to criticism in less propitious times. It was then that tension between the secular and Islamic aspects of the regime emerged, and there were calls for stricter adherence to Islam in order to improve performance on the field of battle. Thus one response to perceptions of the decline of Ottoman power was to advocate closer adherence to the Shari'a. Religious sentiments critical of kanun came from Syria, Egypt and north-west Africa. One writer warned against 'bad kings and amirs who have laid down statutes in contravention of the Shari'a, and called them siyasat and kanun': 'he who believes that the Sultan has the right to permit what is forbidden and to forbid what is permitted is an unbeliever [since] the law is God's' (in Heyd 1973: 204). Perhaps, despite widespread collaboration, pious disenchantment with power still worked under the surface. From the later sixteenth century, kanun came to be widely ignored.

One reason for this, and for the 'ulama's opposition to kanun, may have been that kanun was, as we have said, an attempt to regularise relations between landowners and cultivators from the top. As such, it could be expected to meet with resistance from those with an interest in tax-farming and the other means of feudal extraction; and local notables (a'yan) and 'ulama were often allies, if not the same individuals. Many enlightened reformers in the bureaucracy, on the other hand, men grounded in the patrimonial culture of the court, argued strongly the need *both* to improve the lot of the cultivators *and* to return to the good old kanun 'as it had been observed in Süleyman's time' (see below, p. 260).

Europe of course also had its conflicts between civil law and religious law (known as canon law, from the Greek word canon = rule, from which kanun also derived). In Europe, there were separate jurisdictions and, until the Reformation, two supreme courts of appeal. The striking difference, however, was that in the Ottoman empire theoretical discussion about the situation was almost completely absent. In Europe, this subject gave rise to massive paper controversies, and, significantly, helped to inspire theories of the secular state. In the Ottoman empire, Religious Law was based on well-known principles, but kanun had no theoretical basis, and this seems to have largely determined the outcome.

POLITICAL THEORY

The Ottoman devlet produced very little political theory, almost none before about 1580. This may have been due to its practical success and the pragmatic nature of the regime. Apart from the religious sciences, intellectual effort went into historiography, which was officially patronised and encouraged. Histories were composed in Turkish, designed to be listened to by large numbers of people, and they were read out and discussed in the salons of great men. Mustafa 'Ali (see below, p. 259) would insist that history be 'adorned with completeness' so that both the elite and the common people could understand it (Fleischer 1986: 246–7).

History assumed the role of 'the handmaid of theology', accorded to philosophy in the West. Kemal Pasha-zade (writing c. 1502) said the aim was that 'the glories and achievements of great rulers [should be] perpetuated for the ages to come'. It was also supposed to be 'the guide which will assist rulers in their duty of just Government'.[26] History played an important part in political discourse; among political theorists, 'Ali and Na'ima were historians, while Katib Celebi used history, past and present, as the tool of social analysis, and encouraged the Sultan to study it (below, Chapter 24).

This lack of theory was probably due partly to a progressive degradation of intellectual life (Inalçik 1973: 179–85). The fusion of religion and power had a catastrophic effect upon intellectual activity. Certainly Mehmed II encouraged mathematics, science and astronomy, and attracted eminent religious Scholars from central Asia and eastern Anatolia to his court. With his prestige as 'the Conqueror' he could afford to be tolerant and indulge intellectual curiosity. Even so, there was virtually no falsafa; al-Ghazali's criticism of the use of reason in religion retained its hold.

Mehmed's successor was manoeuvred into executing his father's librarian, an outstanding mathematician and encyclopaedist. Orthodox-minded 'ulama could charge anyone who showed independence of mind, especially if they criticised the 'ulama themselves, with heresy or unbelief. In such cases, the Sultan, if he were to maintain his status as religious Leader, had to be seen to act. Sufis were persecuted from time to time. Süleyman I ordered governors to build a mosque in every village, and to execute anyone who expressed doubts about the Qur'an. In 1580, an observatory as modern as any in Europe was destroyed, just three years after being built, on the orders of the Şeykülislam. It was symptomatic that Taşköprülüzade (d.1553), in a survey of all the branches of knowledge from calligraphy to politics, asserted not only that they were all connected, but also that they must be complemented by mystical contemplation (Inalçik 1973: 165–6). 'The narrow point of view progressively gained ground' (Lapidus 1988: 327).

This was one result of an increasing dependence of the Sultanate upon Sunni orthodoxy as its source of legitimacy (see below, p. 272). Scientific and philosophical personnel and institutions were almost on a level with taverns and prostitutes: they might or might not be tolerated. The pious strand in public opinion required that they be closed down from time to time; and it is easier to rebuild a brothel than an observatory.

Up to c.1600, there was nothing except a transmission of earlier ideas, and not all that many of them, and in a terribly simplified form. Tursun Beg (d. very old after 1491)[27] composed the first Ottoman essay in political thought. He had a medrese education and rose to be Treasurer; he had read Plato's *Republic*. He wrote a *History of Mehmed the Conqueror* in retirement at Bursa (1488–91). The introduction to this, apparently written in support of Bayezid II against a rival claimant to the Sultanate, gave a short summary of earlier Islamic views on the origin and purpose of government, and on the relationship between prophetic and philosophical rule, taken from Nasir al-Din Tusi.

Humans (Tursun Beg called them 'the sons of the species') have to live in groups such as towns, villages or nomadic tent-families in order to survive. These will be destroyed by disputes and war unless they have regulatory discipline (tadbir), so as to assign 'each to his proper place, so that each is content with his share and does not, through his activities, infringe upon the rights of others, but gives himself to whatever activity promotes the mutual aid of those of his kind' (in Nagel 1981: vol. 2, p. 148). This is also called governance (siyaset). This suggests that, as in most post-Mongol thinkers, status groups were perceived as prior to the state, and as an important reason for having a state.

Such regulation may be imposed 'by divine wisdom'; in this case it 'provides for happiness in the two worlds'. Or, it may be 'the product of reason [established] for the order of the visible world' (in Fleischer 1986: 291). Religious Jurists call the former the Shari'a, and its lawgiver (sari') Prophet; philosophers ('wise men'), who are (apparently) equally well acquainted with it, call it 'divine governance (siyaset-i ilahi)', and its institutor 'rational law (namus)' (in Heyd 1973: 169–70). Here, Tursun alluded to kanun: 'but, should the Regulation not be of this stature, but only a product of Reason established for the order of the visible world (such as, for example, the law of Chingiz Khan), then [the Jurists] attribute it to its proper cause, and call it Sultanic ordinance and imperial yasak (siyaset-i Sultani ve yasag-i padişahi), which in our usage is called örf (custom)' (in Fleischer 1986: 291–2). If such a statement had a contemporary bearing, it clearly subordinated kanun to the Shari'a.

In both types of regime, a *ruler* is absolutely essential. Divine law only needs one Prophet, but it also needs 'a sovereign at all times, for he has the full authority, in every era and age, to institute and implement these measures in accordance with the public interest. If his authority should be ended, men cannot live together as they should; indeed, all [people] may be destroyed, and that [divine] order too will perish' (in Fleischer 1986: 292). Tursun implied that those without divine law stand in even greater need of such a ruler. This was an eclectic repetition of earlier Falasifa. Tursun, nonetheless, did at least allude to a non-religious authorisation of the Sultanate, namely a regulation established on the basis of reason in order to ensure that everyone perform their proper task. The significance of this may be seen in the multi-confessional make-up of the empire.

The chief transmitter of Falsafa was Kinalizade (1510–72). He was a kadi, and eventually Chief Judge of Anatolia (1571). His *Ethics* (*Akhlaq-i 'Ala'-i*: in Ottoman Turkish) was finished in 1565.[28] It was little more than an expanded version of Dawani's *Jalalian Ethics*, written, as we have seen (above, pp. 184–5), under the Aqqoyonlu just after their defeat by the Ottomans. This in turn had followed very closely Tusi's *Nasirean Ethics*.

Although Kinalizade reproduced Dawani point by point, he adapted what he found to Ottoman circumstances. He seems to have identified Falsafa with the Sufi approach. He praised Süleyman as a philosopher-king who had managed to establish the Virtuous City (medine-i fazile). The just ruler both enforces the Shari'a and, with the help of the 'ulama, derives 'his own institutes from shari' principles'; thus Süleyman 'integrated rational and revealed law', that is Chingiz Khan's yasa and the Shari'a. This was clearly a reference to kanun; and it was a fair description of the Ottomans' achievement. Such government is the 'true Caliphate'. But in other passages, Kinalizade attacked deviations from the Shari'a in penal law: he said that Nur al-Din (see above, p. 108), whom he saw as a model ruler, had succeeded in suppressing crime precisely because he rejected 'false kanuns and novel siyaset'.[29] Thus, like Ebu's-Su'ud, he was ambivalent about kanun.

Kinalizade introduced the four status groups, the Circle of Power and the notion of equilibrium (see above, pp. 53–4) into Ottoman political thought. Human society, like the body, is composed of four elements, corresponding to water, fire, air, earth: 'men of the pen', 'men of the sword', traders and craftsmen, agriculturists. And:

> There can be no royal authority without the military; there can be no military without wealth; the subjects produce the wealth; justice preserves the subjects' loyalty to the sovereign; justice requires harmony in the world; the world is a garden, its walls are the state; the Holy Law orders the state; there is no support for the Holy Law expect through royal authority.[30]

The Circle of Power and the four status groups were thus related to one another. The elements of society are interdependent, they must be in equilibrium, and they must remain separate. If (for example) soldiers engage in trade, society will disintegrate; this clearly implied that status is hereditary. Justice is the special concern of men of the pen, that is the 'ulama and the scribal bureaucracy. The dependence of the Shari'a upon 'royal authority' implied in this version of the Circle of Power was clear enough under the Ottomans.

Kinalizade was the only link between classical Falsafa and Ottoman political thought. Thus Ottoman thinkers took their founding concepts from Tusi, the great Shi'ite who had helped in the destruction of the 'Abbasid Caliphate, via two lesser intermediaries. Their intellectual nourishment was classical Falsafa dried and reconstituted.

'THE ORDER OF THE WORLD' AND CLASSES

Perceptions of an underlying and ideal social order, often referred to as 'the right order of the world (nizam-i alem)', played a greater part under the Ottomans than hitherto. The idea of the four status groups had already appeared in a much earlier Advice work dedicated to Mehmed I (r.1403–21). In the seventeenth century, it would become part of the ideology of the educated.

> The concept of *had*, a carefully defined hierarchical station in life for all, the observation of which caused society to function harmoniously, and the transgression of which caused the unbalancing of the spheres, social unrest, loss of discipline and social disorder, is the central governing philosophy of the Ottomans formulated by the Sultan's Advisors belonging to the Professional Secretarial Class.[31]

And so a theory of caste became part of the ideology of the bureaucratic elite of Sunni Islam. In practice, of course, Ottoman society reflected this image only in a deeply fractured way.

A much more common conceptualisation was the simple distinction between the tax-receiving ruling class ('askeri: lit. warriors) and their tax-paying subjects (re'aya: lit. flock). The 'askeri were the special and immediate subjects of the Sultan; he only addressed the re'aya through them. The 'askeri were composed of the army (seifiye: those of the sword), both the timar-holding cavalry and the slave-soldiers; the religious establishment ('ilmiye: those of learning); and the secretaries or scribal bureaucracy (kelmiyye: those of the pen) (Fleischer 1986: 7). The re'aya were composed of all those who made their living through business and labour, members of subordinate communities – religious minorities and peoples under indirect rule. The principle behind this distinction was division of labour and harmonious collaboration, the 'askeri providing protection, the re'aya food.

Religious Jurists (fuqaha) seem to have made no contribution to political thought. Given public policy, the course of popular sentiment and the proliferation of medreses, it seems extraordinary that no works on politics or government were produced by Ottoman Jurists (unless research has so far failed to find them). Presumably Jurists saw their role as collecting, summarising and transmitting the Sunna, in particular for use by kadis.

They devoted much attention to minor points. Ebu's-Sü'ud examined in detail Alms, Holy War, Trusts, Judges and so on, but any discussion was about legal and ritual niceties. The judicial organisation of the empire, under which kadis appointed by the Sultan decided all legal disputes for Muslims, was not discussed, and it was anyway broadly in line with the prevailing view among Jurists. We have seen how some pious 'ulama attacked kanun and demanded stricter observance of the Shari'a in the state legal system.

This absence of political theory was one of the most striking features of the Ottoman empire. It may be contrasted with the wealth of ideas under the 'Abbasids and Saljuks, new theoretical developments under the Safavids and Mughals, and most of all with the take-off of political philosophy in Europe at this time. The fact that the political originality of the Ottomans was not reflected in ideas had an effect on the way they dealt with the crises that later hit the Empire. It left the way open for opposition by the religious establishment to any non-Shari' practices, especially secular law, and for the Islamicisation of the polity. We may say that political development withered for want of a conceptual framework. And, given the intellectual resources available, it is not *a priori* inconceivable that such a framework could have been constructed.

NOTES

1. For what follows, see *EI* 8: 190–209; Inalçik (1973, 1992); Shaw (1976); Cemal Kafadar, *Between Two Worlds: The Construction of the Ottoman State* (Berkeley CA: University of California Press, 1995); Lucette Valensi, 'The Making of a Political Paradigm: The Ottoman State and Oriental Despotism', in A. Grafton and A. Blair (eds), *The Transmission of Culture in the Middle East* (Philadelphia: University of Pennsylvania Press, 1990), pp. 173–203.
2. Kunt (1983); Inalçik (1992).
3. Kunt (1983: 9); Inalçik (1973: 104).
4. Inalçik (1973: 110); Nicoara Beldiçeanu, *Le timar dans l'état ottoman* (Wiesbaden: Harrassowitz, 1980).
5. Inalçik (1973: 96, 118); D. C. Repp, *The Mufti of Istanbul* (London: Ithaca, 1986).
6. Colin Imber, 'The Ottoman Dynastic Myth', *Turcica* 19 (1987), pp. 7–27; Halil Inalçik, 'The Rise of Ottoman Historiography', in Lewis and Holt (eds) (1962: 166).
7. But see now Colin Imber, 'What does ghazi actually mean?', in Çigdem Balim-Harding and Colin Imber (eds), *The Balance of Truth* (Istanbul: The Isis Press, 2000), pp. 165–78.
8. Inalçik (1993: 71–2); Inalçik (1992); Imber (1997: 73–6).
9. Ed. and trans. Rhoads Murphey, *Kanun-name-i sultani li Aziz Efendi* (Cambridge, MA: Harvard University Press, 1985), p. 3 (1632).
10. As it is by Inalçik (1973: 73). See Speros Vryonis Jr, 'Byzantine Legacy and Ottoman Forms', *Dumbarton Oaks Papers* 23–4 (Washington DC, 1969–70), pp. 253–308.
11. Halil Inalçik, 'Rice Cultivation in the Ottoman Empire', *Turcica* 14 (1982), p. 106; idem, 'The Ottoman Economic Mind and Aspects of the Ottoman Economy', in Michael A. Cook (ed.), *Studies on the Economic History of the Middle East* (London: Oxford University Press, 1970), pp. 208–18.
12. Inalçik (1973: 56); idem, 'Historiography', p. 166.
13. Aziz Efendi, p. 3.
14. In Franz Babinger, *Mehmed the Conqueror and his Time* (Princeton NJ: Princeton University Press, 1978), pp. 112, 182, 410; Inalçik (1973: 29).
15. Imber, 'Ghazi'.
16. In Lindner (1983: 3) (the authenticity of the inscription is disputed).
17. In Imber, 'Dynastic Myth', p. 25.
18. In Paul Horster, *Zur Anwendung des Islamischen Rechts im 16. Jahrhundert* (Stuttgart: Kohlhammer, 1935), p. 66.
19. Inalçik, 'Economic Mind', pp. 216–17.
20. Joseph Fletcher, 'Turco-Mongolian Monarchic Tradition in the Ottoman Empire', *Harvard Ukrainian Studies* 3 (1979), pp. 236–51; Isenbike Togan, 'Ottoman History by Inner Asian Norms', in Berktay and Faroqhi (eds) (1992: 185–210).

21. Heyd (1973: 182); Inalçik (1973: 73).
22. Inalçik (1973: 72–4). A Hungarian document of the mid-sixteenth century referred to evil innovations (bidat) such as forced labour and new taxes, which must be corrected: Inalçik (1969: 133–4).
23. In Heyd (1973: 312). See Imber (1997: 98).
24. *EI* 5: 837–8; Lewis (1954: 71–3).
25. Heyd (1973: 191–2); Imber (1997: viii, 269).
26. Inalçik, 'Historiography', p. 166; V. L. Menage, 'The Beginnings of Ottoman Historiography', in Lewis and Holt (eds) (1962: 177).
27. Inalçik (1993: 419–28); Fleischer (1986: 291–2).
28. Fleischer (1983: 218 n. 9) and (1986: 280). I am grateful to Dr Metin Kunt for help with this untranslated work.
29. Fleischer (1983: 219); Heyd (1973: 203–4).
30. In Fleischer (1983: 201); see Fleischer (1986: 291); Inalçik (1992: 54–5).
31. Murphey (see below, p. 275, n. 13), p. 556.

The Safavids

22

The Safavid dynasty (r.1501–1722)[1] reunited Iran for the first time since the first Muslim conquest as an independent great power. They established the first, and for a long time the only, nation-state in Islamdom.

The Safavid clan rose to power in the 'increasingly rootless and alienated tribal sector' (Woods 1976: 182) between the Caspian and the Black Sea. Turcoman tribes struggled to consolidate and expand their power in the political vacuum left by the Mongol invasions (see above, pp. 183–4). Safi al-Din (d.1334) founded a Sufi order and was enthusiastically supported by the Turcomans of eastern Anatolia and north-western Iran. By the mid-fifteenth century, the Safavid movement was changing from a typical Sufi order into a radical Shi'ite military group. Under Junaid, their leader from 1446 to 1460, these Turcomans, now known as qizilbash (lit. redheads), began to identify their Shaykh (master) as the mahdi or, alternatively, the precursor of the Twelfth Imam. They seem to have been inspired, as Ibn Khaldun more or less predicted, by a vision of dawla (destined statehood) through allegiance to a divinely appointed leader. They provided a tribal alternative to Ottoman government.

The young Shah Isma'il (1487–1524), Junaid's descendant, claimed leadership of the ruling Aqqoyunlu tribe, and, in a lightning campaign, captured Tabriz and then went on to expel the Turcoman rulers of western Iran (1501) and to defeat the Uzbeks in the east, reaching the Oxus by 1510. His authority was based on a combination of Aqqoyunlu dynastic claims, leadership of a Sufi order and his claim (or the claim which others made for him) that he represented the Twelfth Imam.[2] Thus out of the faith which had obliterated Zoroastrian Iran, in this battleground between steppe and sown, battered from east and west, grew the first Islamic nation-state, the progeny of radical Shi'ite spirituality and an Iranian identity.

The Safavid empire started as a missionary state, directed against the Sunni powers of the Ottomans to the west and the Uzbeks to the east. Isma'il made the revolutionary demand that all Muslims accept one version of Islam – a version hitherto noted mainly for its political quietism – under threat of force. He 'equated belief in the right religion with loyalty to the state'. Twelver Shi'ism was imposed as the official religion which all subjects of the empire were obliged to profess. When Isma'il was warned that 'The people may say they do not want a Shi'i sovereign; and if the people reject Shi'ism, what can we do about it?', he is said to have replied: 'If the people utter one word of protest, I will draw the sword and leave not one of them alive'.[3] Many Sunnis were executed. Rival Sufi orders were attacked. Never before in Islam had such piety gone with such intolerance. Thus was the first substantial Shi'ite state since Fatimid Egypt established. Shi'ite doctrine, which had evolved out of just such a military revolt, had gone underground; this new manifestation underlined the power of the original.

SACRED AND PATRIMONIAL MONARCHY

The early ideology of the Safavid monarchy combined Sufi, Shi'ite and patrimonial ideas. The Shah claimed a 'bedazzling array of unlimited worldly and supernatural powers' (Reid 1983: 27). He was the perfect spiritual director (murshid-i kamil), possessing the charisma (barakat) of the divinely authorised Sufi master. The Hidden Imam 'reveals his will to the Shah through the medium of dreams'. Some of these folk-Sufi ideas were repugnant to high Islam: Junaid was 'the living one, there is no God but he'. Shah Isma'il styled himself 'Jesus, son of Mary', 'the just, the perfect Imam (al-imam al-'adil al-kamil)', referring here 'both to a just secular ruler and, in Twelver terminology, to the hidden Imam himself'. He identified the Imam 'Ali with God, and claimed that he himself was 'of the same essence as 'Ali [for] a man can be a manifestation of Godhead; Isma'il is the Adam having put on new clothes'.[4] Defeat by the Ottomans at Chaldiran (1514) may have 'shattered the belief of the [redheads] in their leader as a divine or semi-divine figure who was invincible',[5] but it did not quench belief in the special religious status of the Shah.

He combined religious with political authority, but with a greater dose of religious authority than any major Islamic ruler had claimed since the Fatimids. Both the folk-Shi'ite belief that the Shah was the representative of the coming Twelfth Imam, and his position as master of the Safavid Sufi order, gave him unquestioned authority in spiritual and practical affairs. Among the Safavids' Turcoman followers, this Sufi view of social order was intertwined with tribal ideas of leadership. All of these pointed to the belief that spiritual and political leadership belonged to a particular bloodline. It was commonly thought that the Shah represented the Imam by virtue of his descent from the Prophet. At a coronation ceremony in 1667, according to Chardin, the Shaykh-al-Islam addressed the Shah as 'illustrious branch of the Imamic race [who is] according to the true law become the lieutenant of the monarch of all the earth, and [of the] lord of the world' (sc. of the Hidden Imam) (in Arjomand 1984: 178). Safavid rule was preparing the world for the return of the Twelfth Imam and his reign of true justice. As Halm puts it, as sole agent of the Awaited One, the Shah was 'the spiritual head of the Shia and indeed of the whole Islamic umma. The Safavids thus recreated a ruler's office with universal claims for the first time since the end of the Baghdad caliphate, combining both the highest secular and supreme spiritual power' (Halm 1991: 85).

Aspects of this royal ideology were persistently disputed by the orthodox Twelver Jurists (fuqaha). Shah Tahmasp (r.1525–76) rejected the title of Mahdi and persecuted those who gave it to him. But, despite Tahmasp's support for Twelver orthodoxy and the protests of high Shi'ism, these beliefs persisted as the basis of Safavid legitimacy. Eschatology remained in the air. People continued to regard the Shah as the representative of the Hidden Imam, who was himself 'the face of God insofar as this shows itself to man, and the face which man presents to God'. According to a tribal chief and historian, 'Abbas I possessed 'the power of controlling the revolutions of the world ... In relation to the twins of state and religion, he is overseer of the organisation of religion and government, being highest among those who are high ranking over the people'. Another author (1571) stated that, in the absence of the Hidden Imam, the Shah as 'the ruler of the age (sultan-e zaman), the lord of command (sahib-e amir) [should give] currency to the commandments of the Imam of the age'.[6] This stressed the Imam's title to political and military sovereignty and clearly implied that it is the *Shah* who is his Deputy. The Shah's claim to the Imamic quality of infallibility-sinlessness seems have been 'widely accepted' (Lambton 1981: 280). In the seventeenth century, the Persians still regarded their king 'as the vicar of the Twelfth Imam during his absence, and successor and vice-gerent of the Prophet; to whom belongs by right the universal government of the world, both spiritual and temporal, during the absence of the Imam'.[7]

Millenarianist belief in the ruler as representative of the absent Leader became intertwined with traditional Iranian devotion to the absolute ruler as shadow of God on earth and guarantor of world order. The line between rhetoric and doctrine was always thin.

Under Tahmasp and 'Abbas I (r.1587–1629), Iran became politically stable and prosperous, symbolised by the new capital at Isfahan with its super-bazaar and architectural magnificence. The arts flourished, and Falsafa struck roots again in the lands of Islam. Government as normal was resumed. The state began to lose its tribal and military character. Tahmasp, a pious individual, turned to the orthodox high Shi'ism of the Iraqi shrines in order to ensure that he had the correct version of the new national faith. This was accompanied by a restatement of Shi'ite political theology in a way that enabled Shi'ism to fulfil the role of social and political leadership. The Shah's court and the Shi'ite clergy cooperated to provide a workable foundation for political order.

At first, the Shah governed through tribal chiefs as provincial Commanders (amirs: a Qur'anic term). But the Shahs soon sought to free themselves from qizilbash domination. They employed the usual tactic of recruiting royal slaves from minority ethnic groups, especially Armenians and others from the Caucasus. The mainly Turcoman military were balanced by the mainly Iranian civil bureaucracy. Military, religious and civilian functions, fused together in the tribal-Sufi polity, were once again separated. 'Abbas created a standing army owing direct allegiance to himself. Administration became 'centralised in the hands of the Shah to an extent previously unparalleled' (Morgan 1988: 136). Tribalism was undermined by shifting power from chiefs to lesser families. The standing army was paid for by taking lands from redhead

Commanders into royal ownership as crown lands (khassa). More land was allocated as 'fiefs' (sing. iqta') or given to royal tax-farmers. The influence of pastoralism and the steppe declined; the ancient order of agrarian patrimonial monarchy re-emerged.

The state was known as the dawlat-i qizilbash, 'the ordained rule of the redheads', as mamlika (domain) and, like the Ottoman empire, as 'the protected domains (mamalik-i mahrusa)'. The sacred and wonderful concept of the ruler bequeathed by folk-Shi'ite eschatology was not, however, completely abandoned. Rather, it was accompanied by more traditional assertions of absolute dynastic and personal power. The conquest of Iran had made the Safavid ruler an Emperor (padishah: king of kings) as well. 'Abbas preferred to appeal to 'love of the king' rather than 'Sufi probity' (Arjomand 1984: 111). The Safavids' religious genealogy made their monarchy more absolute, in theory, than any other. The peculiar religious sentiments of Safavid Shi'ism were now used to accentuate the theory of absolute kingship. They underpinned the doctrine of non-resistance and unconditional obedience. Chardin acutely noted how belief in the Shah's spiritual and temporal authority as representative of the Absent Leader went side by side with the belief that 'kings are naturally violent and unjust, one must regard them in this light; and nevertheless, however unjust and violent their orders may be, one is obliged to obey them' (vol. 5, p. 219). People accepted this as the way of their world.

Traditional Irano-Islamic views of kingship were transmitted in the Advice Genre. The literate community were familiar with the covenant of Ardashir (see above, p. 21); commentaries were written on it. The writings of Nasir al-Din Tusi were available. But, in contrast to the Ottoman elite's articulation of political society, neither the four orders nor the circle of power became current. The four orders would certainly have been at odds with human equality as preached in millenarianist and orthodox Islamic thought.

Patrimonial ideology was coloured, not for the first time, by Shi'ite ethics; this emphasised kindness and equal treatment for all subjects. ''Ali's letter' (see above, p. 46) was translated several times in the late seventeenth century. Tahmasp addressed ministers, provincial governors, generals, tribal chiefs and other public functionaries on 'the law of political power (saltanat)', emphasising their responsibility for secure road networks, the promotion of agriculture and farmers' welfare, the dissemination of 'knowledge and art and education, so that talent from [all] classes of people is not wasted'. In administering justice, Tahmasp went on, everyone's problems must be handled with good will and an open heart, regardless of 'friendship or enmity, kinship or otherness'. Punishment may, nonetheless, depend on a person's class: 'with a person of high nature, a sharp look is the equivalent of killing; with the lowly, even mutilation is of no avail'.[8]

Governors and tribal chiefs (khans) were regarded as state servants and could be dismissed at will. Jean Chardin, a Huguenot jeweller who wrote eyewitness accounts of Iranian politics and society during visits in 1666–7 and 1672–7, described the regime as 'monarchical, despotic and absolute', and indeed the most absolute in the world because government was 'entirely in the hands of a single man, the sovereign head' (vol. 5, p. 229). What he meant was that the Shah could issue whatever orders he liked and they would be put into effect, regardless of precedent, justice or common sense: the Shah could decide everything on the basis of raison d'état (situational ethics). There was, Chardin went on, no 'conseil d'état' as in European states (or, he could have added, the Ottoman empire). Tahmasp advised officials to 'consult a person wiser than themselves', but 'not many' (vol. 5, p. 258).

In practice, however (Chardin observed), the Shah usually acted on the advice of the vizier and other chief officials; in case of war, he 'assembles the principal officers of all his orders' (vol. 5, p. 238). The political reality was indeed that the Shah needed the support of local power-holders, with whom he sustained a patron–client relationship.

'Abbas and his governors exercised some control over the legal system. Tribunals administering the customary law ('urf) functioned alongside the Shari'a courts. Religious Judges depended, as was usual, 'on temporal power for the execution of their verdict'. 'Abbas commissioned a leading Jurist to compile a handbook on the Shari'a, and this became 'the officially recognised guide for the religious courts of the realm' (Arjomand 1984: 175, 195). This included recent developments in law made by Mujtahids using independent reasoning (see below, p. 230). Chardin said the Shah was 'master pure and simple (à pur et à plein) of the lives and goods of his subjects'; but, while the Shah is 'above natural law', he is 'below divine law', and, 'except in extraordinary cases, the Persian government regulates itself by the laws of civil right (the Shari'a) and observes its customs, to which the subjects claim that the ruler holds himself firmly attached' (vol. 5, pp. 233, 236–7).

Chardin observed that in practice the absolute power of the monarch was used mainly over 'the people of the court and the great ones (les grands)'; for these are slaves rather than subjects, and the Shah 'does not feel obliged to use ordinary methods in dealing with them'. Chardin's conclusion is interesting: 'in Persia, as in no other country in the world, the condition of the great is the most perilous, their fate the most uncertain, and often deadly. On the other hand, the condition of the [common] people is much more secure and more pleasant than in some Christian countries'. The Persians, Chardin went on, 'know the value of liberty'; for, when nobles were informed about the rule of law (sc. in Europe) which 'protects the life and property of each against every sort of violence, they admire and envy the happiness of that land' (vol. 5, pp. 232, 236–7).

The Safavid Shahs sought to apply traditional Islamo-patrimonial principles to the management of the economy for the benefit of the state and its subjects. Tahmasp made governors and headmen responsible for the welfare of orphans; he insisted that prices be kept down and there be no hoarding. There were hospitals and food distribution centres for the poor. 'Abbas sponsored commerce by developing bazaars, notably the great bazaar of Isfahan, and by measures designed to free agriculture and craft production from tribal control. In international trade, he relied on Jews, Indians and above all Armenians. He obtained English help in freeing the Gulf from the Portuguese. He encouraged trade with the Europeans on his own terms, doing his best to ensure that domestic crafts remained competitive.

Some groups exercised independent social power and a degree of self-government. In upland regions, tribal communities remained semi-autonomous. The Armenian community in Isfahan was granted virtual autonomy. Villages and urban districts appointed their own representative (kadkhuda) to administer the common law ('urf). Many ordinary people entered futuwwa groups directed by Sufi shaykhs. In guilds, the heads (bashi) were, apparently, chosen by the community and appointed by the king. By far the most powerful and independent group was of course the clergy ('ulama or mollas: lit. masters).

IDEOLOGICAL CONTROVERSY

From the 1530s to the 1690s two fundamentally different conceptions of religious and political leadership coexisted in Iran. Beneath the glittering edifice of Safavid cultural and economic achievement, a social and intellectual power struggle was going on between rival Shi'ite schools, and also between dynastic and clerical notions of authority. Of the two Shi'ite schools of thought, the akhbaris (Traditionists) adhered to the tradition of quietism which went back to the ninth century. They could live with patrimonial monarchy and even its leadership in religious matters. The other school – the usuli (the Principled) – could not.

Support for the Traditionists was entrenched in a 'powerful estate of indigenous clerical notables', including sayyids (claimants to descent from 'Ali). These served in the judicial and educational organs of the regime, which they dominated until the later seventeenth century. Wealthy 'ulama converts from Sunnism also did well. Hereditary sayyids based their claim on 'the chain of filiation to the House of Prophecy and Imamate'. Thus a link between the Traditionists and the monarchy was the belief that religious authority was passed down in bloodlines. The Traditionists on the whole believed in 'the charisma of lineage of the ruling dynasty' and also of the sayyids, and above all saw the function of religious leaders as to uphold the basic traditions as they stood. They rejected the exercise of independent reasoning and the consequent authority of the Well-Qualified Jurist (see below); connection with the Prophet's House could not, they claimed, be achieved 'through effort and endeavour' but is 'a bounty from God' (Arjomand 1984: 107, 146, 151). In Christian language, theirs was a doctrine of grace rather than works.

Falsafa appeared fleetingly in Safavid political theory under 'Abbas I and 'Abbas II (r.1642–66). The latter patronised falasifa and Sufis. Mir Damad (1543–1631) and Molla Sadra (Shiraz 1571–Basra (on pilgrimage) 1640) developed a doctrine of reason as the inner light.[9] They combined the neo-Platonic philosophy of 'absolute being', Sufi belief in intuition (Gnosis: irfan) and the Shi'ite esoteric (batin) method of interpreting the sacred texts. They saw these as complementary methods of reaching the same truth. As Mulla Muhsin Fayd Kashani (c.1598–1680), Molla Sadra's pupil and son-in-law and the founder of a Sufi convent, put it, 'intellect is a revealed law within man, just as the revealed law is an intellect outside of man'.[10] Their emphasis was upon the mystical vision achieved by 'the eye of the heart'. Philosophy was not so much enquiry as an inward journey to a predetermined goal: 'the script of doubt and uncertainty I destroyed' (Mir Damad in NL 605, 625). In a case of conflict, religion takes precedence: 'if a person finds the Law in conflict with his own intellect, he must consider his own intellect mistaken, and not criticise the revealed Law' (Kashani, p. 279).

Mir Damad and Molla Sadra showed no interest in politics; earthly government had little value in their spiritual and intellectual enterprise. Molla Sadra noted that there were 'many and famous ... Traditions in derogation of the world, of the seeking of fame among men, and sociability with men' (in Arjomand 1984: 155). However, their philosophical views brought them into conflict with the orthodox Jurists. They were well connected and had links with the court, where they served as physicians and astronomers; the court gave them what support it could. Mir Damad was Shaykh-al-Islam of Isfahan; he performed the coronation rite for Shah Safi (1629). Their political quietism was in line with both Sufi and patrimonial attitudes.

A Philosophical view of politics was, however, articulated by Kashani in his *Kingly Mirror* which he wrote (1650) at the request of 'Abbas II. It was in simple Persian, aimed at a wide audience; Kashani was a notable populariser of religious teachings. He combined Sufi ideas of authority with traces of the Philosophers' justification for the state. Kashani looked on kingship and political power (saltanat) from a Sufi viewpoint, as just one of five senses in which there may be a 'ruler' or 'commander' (hakim) over human beings (see above, p. 132). These were: (1) intellect and (2) nature or caprice – these rule from within the person; (3) the revealed Law (shar') and (4) common law ('urf) – these issue commands from outside the person; and finally (5) habit, which is 'nature from the outside'. Now 'these commanders are always at war with each other inside man'. The intellect and revealed law teach the same things; so do nature and habit. When common law includes coercion, it is called sovereignty (saltanat). Now 'intellect and the revealed law are nobler and more excellent than the other commanders' (Kashani, pp. 276–7); and common law is the lowest commander. The aim of life is, therefore, to enable intellect to overcome nature; the outcome of this struggle determines one's final status. Thus Sufism brought Muhammad and Plato once more together.

Now, although common law is the lowest commander, 'it commands all of them, dominating and overpowering them in most people'. For 'every society (ijtima') must have sovereignty in order for the collectivity to be put in order (nizam) and the means for the people's livelihood to be arranged'. But common law deals only with this world and only with individuals. Religious Law, by contrast, 'sets aright the whole collectivity and puts in order both this world and the next' (pp. 274, 277). Therefore earthly rule is incomplete without Islam; whereas divine revelation could, in principle, stand on its own. The king is necessary to enforce the Shari'a.

This is certainly *not* intended as a statement of the relationship between the Shah and the 'ulama. Kashani's only practical conclusion was the traditional one that, if the state law commands something contrary to Right, 'it must be avoided, unless by reason of self-protecting dissimulation (taqiyya) or the fear of loss'. Otherwise, he concluded on a metaphysical plane, 'whenever the sovereign obeys the revealed law and follows its commands, the outward appearance of the cosmos known as the kingdom (mulk) follows the inward reality of the cosmos known as dominion (malakut)' (pp. 274–5, 278). Arjomand calls this 'a radical devaluation not only of political domination but also of the political sphere in general and of political action' (1984: 174). There was, however, nothing new in this.

Qadi Sa'id Qumi (d.1691) made another connection between Sufi spirituality and monarchical authority: Muhammad had been given the choice between being a servant and being a ruler (saltanat). He had chosen to be 'a servant-prophet, not a king-prophet' (in Anon. 1970: 167).

AL-KARAKI (C.1466–1534) AND THE RELIGIO-POLITICAL AUTHORITY OF THE MUJTAHID

The Principled school had its immediate roots in the religio-political predicament of the Safavid state, in the way Shi'ism was imposed on the Persian population and made the basis of a new patrimonial empire. For the Safavids were imposing alien beliefs on a predominately Sunni population; Shi'ite Learning was not strong in Iran; and Isma'il promptly had to turn to the eminent Jurists (fuqaha) of Iraq and the Lebanon to galvanise his project. Tahmasp was a pious adherent of Twelver orthodoxy who rejected folk-Sufi millenarianism. But in a society in which the dominant thought-pattern was Islamic, the alternative to mahdist legitimacy had to be legitimacy in terms of shari' orthodoxy, with the ruler as enforcer of religious rectitude. This opportunity to engage in the religious management of a new Shi'ite *dawla* produced a seismic upheaval in Shi'ism itself. Shi'ite thought took off in a new direction. It moved away from quietism and the long-suffering deferment of the hope for a just political society, towards a political theology of clerical activism.

The person primarily responsible for this new theoretical development was al-Karaki (c.1466–Najaf 1534) (Arjomand 1984: 133–42), whom Isma'il had invited to mastermind the propagation of Shi'ism in eastern Iran. For centuries, orthodox Twelver Shi'ites had held congregational prayer and other communal activities to be suspended during the absence of the Twelfth Imam; their practice was forbidden until the return of the true Leader. In politics, they were committed to quietism, caution and dissimulation (taqiyya). All this arose out of their experience of persecution and repression. But it had made it much more difficult for the Shi'ites, in urban centres for example, to undertake the sort of collective action which had given Sunnism a public face since the ninth century. Al-Karaki now taught that congregational prayer *was* legal, indeed obligatory, provided a Well-Qualified Jurist (Mujtahid) was present. He taught that a Shi'ite sultan could legitimately impose the land-tax (kharaj), at a rate to be determined by custom, and that Shi'ite 'ulama could accept payment from this source as their remuneration: for the land-tax belongs to the Shi'a as a whole. In other words, he made it possible for the Shi'ite 'ulama to become state employees. Finally, while the old Twelver view allowed only the Imam himself to use coercive force, al-Karaki extended this to the Mujtahid, qua Deputy, when he was delivering judgement and imposing Legal Penalties. Al-Karaki's 'affirmative, world-embracing' (Arjomand 1984: 134) teaching ensured the weekly assembly of the male population and gave the Jurists a salient role as corporate prayer leaders. It greatly enhanced their potential, and that of the 'ulama (in Iran, mollas) in general, as social and political actors. In fact, Tahmasp recognised al-Karaki as the Imam's Deputy; al-Karaki promptly 'ordered the removal of Sunni 'ulama and [appointed] Shi'i imams to lead the prayers and instruct the public everywhere', and he 'instructed the governors concerning the assessment of the land tax' (EI 4: 610).

In making such radical departures from long-standing Shi'ite tradition, al-Karaki claimed to be speaking on behalf of the absent Imam himself, as his Deputy. This was a claim to the highest possible authority, which no orthodox Twelver teacher had made before. He was supported by Tahmasp, who addressed al-Karaki (1533) as 'the Jurist who has all the qualifications for giving authoritative opinion ... the highly positioned seal of the mujtahids ... the exemplar of expert ulama, the proof of Islam ... who is obeyed by the great governors in all times, the clarifier of the permissible and the forbidden, the Deputy of the Imam (na'ib al-imam) who has clarified the difficulties of the rules of the Community of believers and the rightful laws' (in Arjomand (ed.) 1988: 251, 253). The title 'Deputy of the Imam' was, however, personal to al-Karaki; his successors were called more modestly 'Mujtahid of the age'. Predictably, al-Karaki's views sparked an enormous controversy among Shi'ite scholars. Some were genuinely shocked at his claim to be the Imam's Deputy.

This marked the most significant development in political thought under the Safavids. It revolutionised the attitude of those Jurists and mollas who followed al-Karaki – the Principled – towards public life and government. Whereas traditional Shi'ism strongly discouraged participation in Government or even contact with rulers, al-Karaki and his colleagues eagerly collaborated with Tahmasp and claimed doctrinal support for doing so. Tahmasp endorsed the adage that 'the best of the acts of worship is the ordering of the affairs of the people' (in Arjomand (ed.) 1988: 257) – thus bringing Shi'ism into line with a strand in Sunni thought. The insistence upon a pious distance from political establishments was, in the face of much criticism, abandoned. The Well-Qualified Jurist was now not merely permitted but expected to play a full part in applying the Shari'a in the Shah's religious courts. According to the collection of Shi'ite Law promulgated by 'Abbas I, the Judgeship is a collective duty (you have to undertake it if no-one else does); on occasion it may be the duty of a specific individual. Shi'ites were held to be obliged 'to assist [the mujtahid] in the administration of [Legal Penalties] and [decisions] among the people' (al-Karaki in Sachedina 1988: 196).

Al-Karaki's most remarkable development of doctrine, and the one with the greatest long-term repercussions, was his elevation of the Well-qualified Jurist (Mujtahid). Al-Karaki and the Principled school argued that a Mujtahid could use his reason and expertise (ijtihad) to interpret tradition and determine the correct religio-legal praxis. And in doing so, the Mujtahid acted as *Deputy for the Hidden Imam*: the Imams 'have appointed [the Jurists] Deputy in a general manner' (in Arjomand 1984: 141). The Mujtahid could, therefore, 'undertake many practical activities [previously] reserved for the Imam' (*EI* 8: 777b). He was given the status of 'just Leader (al-imam al-'adil)' and 'just Ruler (Sultan al-'adil)', titles previously assigned to the Imam.

This of course made the Mujtahids the immediate representatives of the highest authority in Shi'ite Islam; it gave them unchallengeable personal authority. The rank of Mujtahid was given only to very few. But the 'ulama generally shared in their enhanced status as persons possessing a degree of knowledge not shared by ordinary people. The new Shi'ite doctrine encouraged people to see the 'ulama as lesser links with the Hidden Leader, as 'the doors of heaven' (in Arjomand 1984: 138). The concept of ijtihad mutlaq ('the general competence of the person of the Mujtahid in all fields of sacred law') allowed the Mujtahid not only the traditional right to answer the questions of a puzzled believer, but also the right to define the scope of his own authority.

This theory greatly extended the scope of independent judgement, and therefore in a sense of rational judgement, in religio-legal matters, for the few. It allowed living experts to override deceased predecessors; earlier Mujtahids, since they were using their own reason, could have made mistakes. A living Mujtahid is, however, exempt from correction. This gave them more spiritual authority than the Sunni 'ulama. Of course it carried a price if expectations ran too far ahead of actuality (as with the clergy in Christendom). In the late seventeenth century, some credited Mujtahids with infallibility-sinlessness ('isma).

The masses ('ammi: unschooled believers; or muqallid: followers) were supposed to exercise taqlid (unqualified submission) towards a Well-Qualified Jurist. Al-Hilli in the late thirteenth century had authorised taqlid towards a Mujtahid on the ground that ordinary believers do not have time to go into legal niceties. But submission was now being demanded over a wider range of more fundamental issues concerning doctrine and practice within the community, and on behalf of a more explicitly authorised clerical group. This theory of the Mujtahid was in effect a new version of the philosopher-king. Once again, a distinction, this time an intellectual one, between elite and masses was made central to religious thought (see above, p. 151).

This theory was strongly disputed by the Akhbaris. Al-Qatifi ruled that congregational prayer was impermissible without the Twelfth Imam, that mollas should accept neither land nor salaries from a king, and that so far as possible they should avoid all contact with him. Kings were tyrants. Above all, Traditionists 'disputed the Jurists' ability to reach independent legal decisions and their claim to represent the hidden Imam, and they awarded sole authority to the transmitted word of the Prophet and the Imams' (Halm 1991: 98). Not everyone agreed wholeheartedly with one side or the other in this dispute. Al-Ardabili (d.1585) opposed al-Karaki but nevertheless affirmed 'submission' to a Mujtahid as a fundamental moral obligation; though he insisted that it was obligatory only 'when the follower knows that the model is rightly-guided', and provided that 'a proof for it has been established, such as the Mujtahid's ability to derive legal judgements'.[11]

These doctrinal changes worked at the core of Islamic discourse. They transformed the relationship between the unseen and the seen. Henceforth, the Hidden Imam would function through clearly-designated Deputies; he would be officially represented. The moral authority thereby created was considerable. As the first major Twelver state, the Safavid dawla had prompted a radical readjustment of doctrine. This was the opportunism of conviction. It gave rise to one of very few genuinely *constitutional* conflicts in Islamic history, a conflict about what category of persons was entitled to hold authority, and the respective powers of different agencies.

These changes in the Shi'ite understanding of the revealed Code had the potential to transform the authority of the religious leaders, and also the relationship between them and the state. The steady conversion of the Iranian masses to Shi'ism was orchestrated by the Shah and implemented by the mollas; coercion was sometimes used. The institutions of religion were developed. The Mujtahids provided the nucleus of a professional clerical hierarchy. The Shi'ite 'ulama had 'social and soon also political influence' as prayer-leaders, Judges and managers of pious endowments (Halm 1991: 94). A Shaykh-al-Islam was appointed for every major city. The Shaykh-al-Islam of Isfahan was especially prestigious, and performed the coronation ritual and other major ceremonies.

The Principled, as we have seen, had the support of Tahmasp. With the decline of millenarianism, the dynasty was impelled towards alliance with the mollas in order to maintain its own credibility, that is its authority in shari' terms. There was a certain parallel here with the increased emphasis on religious rectitude by the Ottomans (see below, p. 272). The Shah accepted al-Karaki's teachings on religion, community and the state and his claim to be the Hidden Imam's Deputy. Tahmasp gave practical effect to al-Karaki's claim by authorising him to appoint and depose religious officials throughout the Empire. All ranks, including top dignitaries and state officials, were ordered to obey him. This was a more extensive authority than that of sadr or Shaykh-al-Islam. It marked a great step towards victory for the Principled party within Iran.

MONARCHY VERSUS CLERGY

But, when it summoned up the resources of Shi'i orthodoxy, the Safavid regime entered into a relationship of which it was not to be the main beneficiary. As time went on, the Principled version of Twelver political theory challenged the Safavid claim to charismatic leadership in both religion and politics. Tahmasp boasted how the Safavid dawla had enabled the Shari'a to make 'the marks of oppression and ignorance ... removable'. But, when he recognised al-Karaki as the Imam's Deputy, he was implicitly divesting himself of his own claim to religious leadership. In this 'bounteous and privileged age', Tahmasp went on, guidance of the Shi'a – 'the people of submission (ahl-e taqlid)' – is reserved for the Imams and for al-Karaki himself. 'The path for reaching this goal [the return of the Hidden Imam as Time Lord] is undoubtedly the following of and obedience to the religiously Learned' (in Arjomand (ed.) 1988: 253).

Tahmasp's course suggested a separation of religious from political authority. But, as in medieval Christendom, it could be argued that *in extremis* the former must always override the latter. The coronation ritual implied that the Mujtahid of the age (or the Shaykh-al-Islam of Isfahan) authorised the Shah. Isma'il II is quoted as saying to the supreme Mujtahid (at his coronation, 1576): 'this power (saltanat) in truth belongs to the [Hidden] Imam, the Lord of the Age, and *you are the Deputy appointed in his place* to put into operation the decrees of Islam and the Shari'a. You spread the carpet for me and seat me on the throne, so that I may sit on the throne of government and *rule by your decision and will*' (in Lambton 1981: 277; my italics). There was a clear parallel with the much earlier, and now effectively discarded, claims of the Roman papacy over secular rulers. Certainly there was an element of rhetoric here, but what was actually said reflected Principled doctrine.

It was a century and a half after al-Karaki's death before the doctrines of the Principled triumphed in Iran. The argument between Principled and Traditionists became entangled in social tensions among the Clergy. Mollas in general were gaining control of a significant amount of land as pious endowments and were becoming particularly close to the landowner class. They formed an alliance with 'the artisan middle-classes of the towns, the bazaaris, whose interests they represented against the remote central authority and its tax officials' (Halm 1991: 97). They were becoming embedded in civil society.

There was rivalry between the Principled mollas, often from abroad, and the local clerical notables. The native clerical estate favoured political quietism. They rejected the incomers' doctrinal innovations and the discretionary power of the Well-Qualified Jurist. They preferred the Traditionists' view that one should rely solely upon the teachings of the Prophet and the first Imams.

Falsafa and Sufism became involved in the conflict. The philosophical 'school of Isfahan' was closer in spirit to the native clerical estate and the Traditionists. Mir Damad's son wrote in support of the sayyids. Falsafa was intellectually close to the high-Sufi approach but shared with the mollas in general, and especially the Principled, a strong hostility towards superstitious practices associated with folk-Sufi cults. On the other hand, Philosophers, as of old, had little time for legal precision as the road to salvation, and they resisted the doctrine of the Well-Qualified Jurist. The Philosophers and Sufi gnostics regarded the Jurists as literal-minded and opinionated power-seekers, 'animals on two legs', learned only 'in the eyes of the ignorant and the masses' (in Arjomand 1984: 150–1). The Jurists for their part were ready to pounce on anything that could be regarded as deviating from strict orthodoxy; in their eyes, Philosophers and Sufis were heretics. Like their Sunni predecessors in ninth-century Baghdad, they would not accept that one could approach God or measure justice by any methodology other than their own. This was one reason why the Falasifa adopted an 'abstruse and convoluted' style (NL 598); the Sufi convent founded by the Philosopher Kashani was destroyed by mollas.

Qumi indicated a possible compromise between the parties, by trying to reaffirm the separation between the religious and political spheres. He argued that the Imams are Deputies for the Prophet in matters of religion (khilafa diniya); their purpose is to facilitate 'the passage from this world and the return to the other world' (Anon. 1970: 167). But everyone has a duty to obey the Shah.

The court itself, as we have seen, especially under Tahmasp, at first allied itself with the Principled. Among the population at large and especially the tribesmen, however, the old view of Safavid leadership lived on. 'Abbas I's assault on the power of tribal chiefs unwittingly removed one obstacle to the spread of the new ideas. Philosophy, along with high Sufism, received support from 'Abbas II (r.1642–66); it seems that for a while they provided an intellectual focus for those wishing to prevent the Jurists from extending their power in the legal and political system. Both 'Abbas I and 'Abbas II knew that they had to come to terms with the mollas. They incorporated senior mollas into the court. 'Abbas I tried to subordinate the clergy to the sadr (Overseer), a state appointee. 'Abbas II had a molla as grand vizier and a council made up of civil servants and royal slaves.

From the 1530s to the 1660s, those who supported the Mujtahids' rather the Shah's Deputyship of the Twelfth Imam steadily extended their control over the intellectual life of Iran. The Principled, like the Jesuits, seem to have set out to win the hearts and minds of the court, the clerical intelligentsia and the population at large. They were winning the intellectual debate among Shi'ite scholars themselves, both in Iran and at the Iraqi shrines, the spiritual and intellectual headquarters of the Shi'a. The crux was the Mujtahid's authority to interpret tradition. When the Ottomans conquered Iraq (1638), Shi'ite scholars there were able to assert their religious independence from the Iranian monarchy.

By the 1670s, the conflict between (in Chardin's words) 'the ruling House' and 'church people' had became remarkably public. Chardin expressed it as an argument about the claims of 'biological descent from 'Ali', on the one hand, and learning and piety, on the other, as qualifications for authority. The Mujtahids' argument was that 'the supreme throne of the universe belongs only to a Mujtahid ... If the Muslims are to be guided by divine decree then Allah must make his will known to a mortal'. But this can only be 'a totally spiritualised person who, having renounced all worldly desires, devotes himself entirely to the contemplation of God': that is, the Imams 'and in these days exclusively ... their successors, the Mujtahids'. They pulled no punches: 'how can these infamous kings who drink wine, are driven by passion', and who can hardly read, possibly be God's representatives? How can they 'communicate with Heaven' or 'solve matters of conscience and doubts concerning the faith' (vol. 5, p. 219 and in Halm 1991: 95)? (Chardin here seems to have been putting the debate in rather Euro-Christian language.) A contemporary Iranian reported the same controversy, among the 'ulama, between the sayyids, who based their claim on 'the chain of filiation to the house of Prophecy and Imamate', and the Principled, who based theirs on 'knowledge and practice' (Arjomand 1984: 151). It was a conflict between charisma plus tradition and a more rationalist approach to religion and government.

THE MAJLISI REVOLUTION: THE CLERICAL ASCENT TO POWER

The dynasty was in any case in trouble. Too much, as in all patrimonial states, depended on the qualities of the individual emperor. Succession was a major problem. 'Abbas I was so afraid of rebellion that he had one son assassinated and another two blinded, and thereby deprived the dynasty of capable heirs. From then on, heirs to the throne were, as in the Ottoman empire, confined to the harem and so had no political training. By the later seventeenth century, the economy was stagnant and the army weakened.

Shah Sulayman (1666–94) transferred his support to the Jurists. Sultan Husayn (1694–1722) was 'under the influence of the [clergy] to such an extent that he was derided as "Molla Husayn"' (Halm 1991: 97). The last Safavid Shahs allowed an accumulation of clerical power, presumably out of piety and in the belief that, by getting the active backing of the Jurists, they could regain popular support and shore up the authority of the dynasty. But now a revolution took place in the structure of religious power itself. This was especially the work of Muhammad Baqir Majlisi 'the Younger' (1627–1700), who was appointed Shaykh-al-Islam of Isfahan in 1686. On Sultan Husayn's accession, he was given the title 'head molla (molla bashi)', and thereafter he practically ran the country. In 1712, Husayn appointed a new chief molla as 'the head (ra'is) of all 'ulama' (in Halm 1991: 99). As if to symbolise the turn of events, Majlisi's father had been a man of broad learning and an adherent of the gnostic-mystical way; Majlisi the Younger 'dramatically changed his alliance to the opposing camp' (Arjomand 1984: 152). He appears to have been a man of genuine convictions. He was a dedicated and energetic spiritual leader, combining political and administrative talent with skills of communication – clever if not original.

Majlisi used his position to take out Sufism, Falsafa and 'alien' creeds (Christianity and Judaism), and to establish the Principled version of Twelver orthodoxy as the sole legitimate religious way. He himself undertook a vast amount of religious controversy and propaganda; he wrote in Persian to enable, he said, 'the masses of believers and the common Shi'a' (EI 6: 1087a) to know the Reports at first hand; he launched an intellectual crusade against Sufism and Philosophy.

Majlisi brought the religious establishment under the central direction of the Jurists, and especially of the senior Mujtahid. They produced popular versions of essential juristic texts. They appealed to the religious sentiments of the masses by sanctioning the ritual commemoration of the sufferings of Imam Husayn, and by appropriating other themes of popular devotion. This undercut support for the Traditionist-sayyid party. From now on, Shi'ism in Iran would mean adherence to the revealed texts as interpreted by Twelver tradition up to and including the Well-Qualified Jurists of the present day.

Arjomand interprets Majlisi's religious teaching as a 'definitive change in the direction of other-worldliness' on the grounds that he played down reason, God and justice and emphasised the afterlife 'in lurid detail' and the ritual cursing of the first three caliphs (Arjomand 1984: 168). This seems slightly to miss the point. Majlisi was no political quietist: his own programme, based on al-Karaki's teaching, shows that. His attitude towards political activity should be seen in the light of the role prescribed for Mujtahids: activism for the Well-Qualified few, resignation and otherworldliness for everyone else. Majlisi adapted the Report, 'If two groups in my community are righteous ... my community will also be righteous; and if they are corrupt my community will also be corrupt', to make the two groups refer to 'the *Jurists* and the amirs' rather than 'the 'ulama and the amirs' as in the traditional version.[12] This was a version of the ideal of the philosopher-rulers; it was more Islamic than the Falasifa's view of philosopher-rulers because, although there are in effect two separate politico-intellectual classes, what is known and how it is known are the same for everybody. Majlisi's life's work was aimed at giving everybody access to the textual sources of religious revelation.

Arjomand sees the 'urge to legitimate hierocratic authority' as a 'a theological substitute for political theory' (1984: 141, 143). It certainly was, and was intended to be. Arjomand's critical tone implies categories alien to the participants, and assumes that theology and political theory ought to be separate. It might be better just to see all this as a non-European transition to modernity.

Majlisi wrote a brief discourse on governmental power (saltanat); he also wrote about justice in a religious work intended for popular consumption ('*Ayn al-Kayat*), and translated ''Ali's Letter'. An interesting view of the relationship between king and subjects emerges. Majlisi remarked that everyone possesses saltanat in some form: the householder over his servants, every human being over animals and his own body, behaviour and religious acts. While subjects have moral rights against kings, kings 'of the right religion' 'have many rights over their subjects'. Majlisi emphasised the authority of kings over their subjects, who 'must pray for the Kings and recognise their rights' (in Arjomand 1984: 176). Yet all this is said about kings 'of the right religion', and it may be seen in relation to Majlisi's drive for conformity throughout the whole country.

Majlisi stressed the king's duty to act justly; as a Report put it, 'a king will remain while he is an unbeliever, but not while he is a wrong-doer'. The reason why kings 'have many rights over their subjects' is that their subjects' 'religion, life, property and honour is secured through the protection of the kings', who 'repel the enemies of religion from them'. Thus Majlisi based kings' power on their ability to protect their subjects' 'religion, life, property and honour' (in Arjomand (ed.) 1988: 291). There is a very slight parallel here with the (also theological) theory of John Locke; it is just possible that Majlisi had come into contact with Western ideas through Europeans in Iran. Regarding the relationship between clergy and monarchy, on the other hand, what was happening resembled, rather, the Gregorian Revolution of the eleventh century in Europe (Ullmann 1955: 262–309). Once again, Islamic history looks like European history in reverse.

Majlisi's revolution established the modern Iranian version of the Shi'ite religious polity. In Iran, Majlisi's writings 'enjoyed tremendous popularity through the nineteenth century down to the present time'. Practically every aspect of modern Shi'ism is 'fully depicted or presaged in [Majlisi's] writings'. This development massively enhanced the social power of mollas generally; 'the Shi'ite lawyer caste' had become 'a clergy'.[13] It meant a fundamental shift in the relationship between clerical and royal authority. Both the Learned and the common people now believed that 'according to divine law the Mujtahid, as the highest spiritual leader, is entitled to rule the Muslims, while the Shah is only required to observe and implement Reports of the supreme pastor' (according to Kaempfer, in Iran 1684–5: in Halm 1991: 96). Chardin put this point in terms of medieval Catholic papalism, with the king as the clergy's instrument: 'as the Mujtahid is a holy man, and consequently a man of peace (homme pacifique), there has to be a king who carries the sword for the implementation of justice'. The king should act only as the Mujtahid's 'minister'; he is 'dependent upon him' (vol. 5, p. 216). This interpretation seems to be borne out by Kaempfer: 'without [the Mujtahid's] advice, no matters of importance can be undertaken in governing the believers' (in Halm 1991: 96). The Mujtahids had cashed the cheque of Shi'ite political theology.

TRIBALISM AND POLITICAL DECLINE

The increased power of the clergy did not save the Safavid dynasty; in fact, it hastened its demise. In drawing attention to immoral and impious behaviour at court, it helped to undermine the authority and political effectiveness of the dynasty and (therefore) of the state.[14] In 1722, the Safavids lost control; the country was overrun by Afghan tribes. The Khaldunian cycle had moved on. In the short term, power passed not to the Shi'ite clergy but to tribal amirs.[15] The 'ulama may not have cared. With their popular power base, they no longer needed the Safavids.

The next effective ruler of Iran was Nadir Khan (r.1729–47), a Redhead tribesman. Having seized power, he had a serious legitimacy problem; he 'tried to revive the pre-Safavid Turkman tribal principles of legitimacy', and to justify himself on the grounds of descent from Timur and his manifest military exploits. At a Mongol-style assembly (1736), Iranian chiefs 'elected our august majesty to kingship and sovereignty which are the hereditary prerogatives of the noble Turkman tribe' (in Arjomand 1984: 221). His attempt to reintegrate the Shi'a into the Sunni Community by declaring Shi'ism a fifth law-school (madhdhab) did not make him popular in Iran. Notoriously cruel, he was killed by fellow-tribesmen.[16]

Karim Khan Zand (r.1750–79) ruled through a coalition of tribal chiefs. In his attempt to restore economic stability and law and order, he invoked traditional Islamo-patrimonial ideals: the aims of government are (in Lambton's words) 'the ordering of agricultural affairs, making the province populous ... the restraining of the hands of the unjust from the weak and poor, the good treatment of the peasants (re'aya)'. His rule was perceived as beneficent and just. His title 'representative of the people (vakil al-ra'aya)' probably referred to the 'centuries-old tradition of a provincial ombudsman in Iran'.[17]

Rule by a 'king of kings (shahanshah)' was re-established by the Turkish-speaking Qajar dynasty (1779–1925).[18] But Iran remained 'fragmented into innumerable tribal, ethnic and local factions headed by their own chieftains' (Lapidus 1988: 571). The Qajars 'never established an effective central army or national bureaucracy', and hardly qualify as a patrimonial monarchy.[19] Fath 'Ali Shah (r.1797–1834) seemed to Fraser, a British traveller, to govern his country 'as a property of which he has a lease ... like a conquered nation' (1825). A Persian (writing 1784–1836) described his country as 'in a state of decay, in which there is no proper accounting practice or accountability, where good customs and desirable laws are not found, and which is always disturbed by tyranny and oppression'. Fraser made the same point in his own way: 'The principal direct check to improvement and prosperity ... is the insecurity of life, limb and property, arising from the nature of the government.'[20]

NOTES

1. What follows is based on *CH Iran*, vols 6–7; *EI* on Safavids; Halm (1991: 84–111); Arjomand (1984, 1988); Reid (1983); Lambton (1981: 264–87) and (1953: 105–40); Kathryn Babayan, 'The Waning of the Qizilbash: The Spiritual and Temporal in Seventeenth-century Iran' (Ph.D. thesis, Princeton, 1993); Kohlberg (1991). To these should be added C. Melville (ed.), *Safavid Persia* (London: Tauris, 1999); and K. Babayan, 'The Safavid Synthesis: From Qizilbash Islam to Imami Shi'ism', *Iranian Studies* 27 (1994), pp. 135–61.

2. I am extremely grateful to Charles Melville for clarifying points in this and the preceding paragraph.

3. In Roger Savory, *Iran under the Safavids* (Cambridge: Cambridge University Press, 1980), pp. 29–30.

4. In Arjomand (1984: 81); see also Woods (1976: 27); Michel M. Mazzoui, *The Origins of the Safavids* (Wiesbaden: F. Steiner, 1972), p. 85; *EI* 8: 777b.

5. Savory, *Iran*, p. 46.

6. In Arjomand (1984: 182); Anon. (1971: 171); Reid (1983: 6).

7. Jean Chardin, *Voyages en Perse*, ed. L. Langlès, 10 vols (Paris: Le Normant, 1811), vol. 5, p. 229; Lambton (1981: 281–2).

8. 'Two Decrees of Shah Tahmasp', ed. and trans. S. A. Arjomand in idem (ed.) (1988: 257).

9. NL 597–662; Arjomand (1984: 150).

10. William C. Chittick (trans. and ed.), 'Two Seventeenth-century Persian Tracts on Kingship', in Arjomand (ed.) (1988: 269–84) at p. 277.

11. 'The Muqaddas al-Ardabili on Taqlid', trans. and ed. John Cooper in Arjomand (ed.) (1988: 264).

12. Trans. and ed. Chittick in Arjomand (ed.) (1988: 286–304) at p. 286.

13. Arjomand (1984: 154, 158); Halm (1991: 99).

14. I am grateful to Charles Melville here.

15. Jos Gommans, *The Rise of the Indo-Afghan Empire c.1710–1780* (Leiden: Brill, 1995).

16. *EI* 7: 354; Arjomand (1984: 221–9); Ernest Tucker, 'Religion and Politics in the Era of Nadir Shah' (Ph.D. thesis, Chicago, 1992).

17. *CH Iran* 7: 97–8; Lambton (1953: 133).
18. *EI* on Kadjar; Algar (1969).
19. Ed. Keddie (1972a: 213).
20. In Lambton (1953: 135–6); Lambton (1974: 107).

India and the Mughals

23

The Mughal (sc. Mongol) dynasty[1] began as another central Asian invasion of northern India, this time under the Mongol clan leader Babur (d.1530) after they had been pushed out of central Asia by the Safavids and Uzbeks. His claim to leadership rested on his supposed descent from Timur and Chingiz; the Mughals looked back on Afghanistan and Transoxania as their dynastic homeland. Akbar (r.1556–1605) made extensive conquests to the west, east and south and transformed the dynasty into a world power. Under Aurangzib (r.1658–1707), their rule extended over most of India except the far south, creating the largest Indian state since Ashoka in the third century BCE. Akbar set out to create a multi-credal empire. From the mid-seventeenth century, the polity reverted to orthodox Sunnism. Mughal power declined rapidly in the eighteenth century.

This was another example of the Turco-Mongol ability to seize power and govern. Babur called himself padshah (world ruler) and, after his victory at Panipat (1526), he called his new capital, Agra, in the Ganges plain, 'the seat of the caliphate (darul khilafat)' (Farooqi 1989: 188). The culture of the court was influenced by Persian moeurs, literature and architecture; Persian poets, scholars and men of ambition were attracted to it, and Persian was the court language.

AKBAR (R.1556–1605), THE ENLIGHTENING MONARCH

Akbar and his government displayed a remarkable capacity for adaptation and innovation. Their project was to bring Muslims and Hindus, Sunnis as well as Shi'ites, into a single political community, by granting religious toleration and equality of status to the different creeds. This gave the early Mughal empire its distinctive political identity. It owed much to the Indian environment. The majority of the Mughals' subjects were Hindus; they formed a larger proportion than in any previous Muslim state. A policy of religious toleration had been initiated by Babur. He counselled his son, Humayun, to 'ignore the disputations of the Shi'a and Sunnis; for therein is the weakness of Islam'. He pointed out that

> The realm of Hindustan is full of diverse creeds ... It is but proper that thou, with heart cleansed of all religious bigotry, should dispense justice according to the tenets of each Community ... And the temples and abodes

of worship of every Community under the imperial sway, you should not damage ... The progress of Islam is better with the sword of kindness, not with the sword of oppression. And bring together subjects with different beliefs in the manner of the four elements, so that the body politic may be immune from the various ailments.[2]

Under the Mughals, as under many Islamic regimes, monotheistic religious communities dispensed their own laws in civil matters such as marriage. Criminal law remained the same for all.[3] But here something more was being suggested, that groups with different religious beliefs should each play their role 'in the manner of the four elements' (a simile also used of occupational groups), that is as interdependent parts of the socio-political system.

A significant body of religious opinion in India, both Muslim and Hindu, had already entered on a path of symbiosis. Crucial to this was the fact that Sufi masters, rather than 'ulama, provided much of the religious leadership for Muslim communities in both central Asia and India.[4] Sufi mysticism had developed close affinities in praxis and doctrine with the yogic strand in Hinduism. Members of both faiths could agree that God was everywhere and was to be reached through the heart. Many Muslims accepted Hinduism as a fundamentally monotheistic creed, despite appearances to the contrary.

Akbar's governmental strategy seems to have been based on a remarkable open-mindedness in religious and philosophical matters. He realised early on that he could only rule effectively with the cooperation of the conquered Hindu princes now coopted into the empire, and of the Hindus in society at large. But he was also a man of 'widely-noted mystical affinities' (AS 132) and an enquiring mind: 'how I wish for the coming of some pious man who will resolve the distraction of my heart' (he is reported to have said). This led him to seek out Hindu as well as both Muslim teachers and ascetics. He apparently came to believe that 'each person according to his own understanding gives the Supreme Being a name, but in reality to name the Unknowable is vain' (in Rizvi 1975: 283, 383).

In the mid-1570s, he found a close friend and adviser in Abu'l-Fadl (1551–1602; EI 1: 117–18). Abu'l-Fadl had been given a spiritual and philosophical education by his father, who held that 'there is no creed that may not be mistaken in some particular, nor any that is entirely false' (in Vanina 1996: 64). Abu'l-Fadl reflected, stimulated and articulated Akbar's ideas and political goals. His A'in-i Akbari (Regulations of Akbar: part of his Akbar-Name (Book of Akbar), a history of the reign) embodied their views on kingship interspersed in narratives of Akbar's exploits. Abu'l-Fadl 'presents Akbar as he wished to be understood, and probably as he understood himself'.[5] The A'in was divided into sections on household, army, empire; it included a discourse on land-taxes and also an explanation of Hinduism. His purpose was that 'hostility towards [the Hindus] might abate and the temporal sword be stayed awhile from the shedding of blood; that dissensions within and without be turned to peace and the thornbrake of strife and enmity bloom into a garden of concord' (in Vanina 1996: 63).

Here, religious and philosophical developments within the court, building on wider intellectual currents in Indian society, coincided with the perceived need of the dynasty for cooperation among all its subjects in the common cause of the new empire. 'It has been our disposition from the beginning not to pay attention to the differences of religion and to regard all the tribes of mankind as God's servants. It must be considered that divine mercy attaches itself to every form of creed' (in Vanina 1996: 34).

Then Abu'l-Fadl recorded how in, 1578, Akbar 'experienced "the sublime joy" of the "attraction of the cognition of God"'; a hostile witness described this as 'a strange state and strong frenzy' (AS 133). Empire (padshahi), Abu'l-Fadl now said,

> is a refulgence from the Incomparable Distributor of justice ... a ray from the sun, the illuminator of the universe and the receptacle of all virtues. The contemporary language calls it farr-i izidi [the divine effulgence] and the tongue of antiquity [sc. Middle Persian] calls it kiyan khura [the sublime halo] ... Without a mediator it appears as a holy form to the holders of power and at the sight of it everyone bends the forehead of praise to the ground of submission.[6]

Such status is bestowed upon the king as a spiritual gift from God. Humayun (Akbar's father and predecessor) also believed that he 'received his inspiration and intuition directly from God' (Farooqi 1989: 188).

Remarkably, Akbar's illumination prescribed philosophical enquiry. Religious statements and rules, he now said (1578), must be subjected to critical scrutiny: 'Now that the light of truth has taken possession of our soul, it has become clear that ... not a single step can be taken without the torch of proof, and that that creed is profitable which is adopted with the approval of wisdom' (Rizvi 1975: 380). Such an approach, Abu'l-Fadl went on, means that one can learn something from all religions. Abu'l-Fadl felt himself 'drawn to the sages of Mongolia, and to the hermits of Lebanon; I longed for interviews with the lamas of Tibet or with the padris of Portugal, and I would gladly sit with the priests of the Parsis and the learned of the Zendavesta [sc. brahmins]' (in Vanina 1996: 159). In a 'Letter to the Learned of the West' written on Akbar's behalf (1582), Abu'l-Fadl expressed a belief that people of all faiths, once they adopt 'the searching spirit – the best among the creations of reason', can communicate and learn from each other. Abu'l-Fadl himself drew upon the ancient Indian *Laws of Manu* and the *Mahabharata*, of which he commissioned a translation into Persian, as well as on Nasir al-Din Tusi and Dawani, whose ideas were widely disseminated under Akbar.[7]

At the same time, Akbar's 'religious experience' authorised infallible monarchical authority. (The same kind of contradiction has been noted in Plato.) This was a fresh articulation of patrimonialism, combining the personal illumination of the new religions with a revival of the ancient Iranian and Egyptian royal cult, in which the monarch was the source of light. As such, it was a new theory of monarchical sovereignty and was applied to kingship in general. The ruler (in Blake's words) 'acquires the qualities and virtues needed to govern successfully' (p. 20). Akbar merited supreme power because of his personal illumination. He himself was the 'perfect man (insan-i kamil)' – an originally Isma'ili concept since adopted by the Sufis; it meant the rare individual who has achieved moral and intellectual perfection.

Akbar was credited with being able to induce spiritual awakening in others (*A'in* 1: 164). The keystone of Akbar's revolution was the combination of the role of king with that of spiritual teacher. People who are enlightened will recognise such a king as their spiritual leader because 'a king possesses, independent of men, the ray of divine wisdom' (in Streusand 1989: 150). Thus 'what really changed the emotional climate, and gained increasing solidarity and strength for the Mughal throne, was the Sufic ideology of the Perfect Man propounded by Abu'l-Fadl which appealed both to Hindus and Muslims' (Rizvi 1975: 361). Such a monarch combines spiritual and temporal authority; the distinction between din (religion) and dunya (world) no longer applies here.

The difference between Akbar's philosophy and the later European 'enlightenment' was of course that in the former philosophical openness was sanctioned by mystical experience. (Rousseau would say 'my rule to abandon myself to feeling rather than reason is confirmed by reason itself'.) Abu'l-Fadl developed the perspective of the Sufi philosopher Ibn al-'Arabi: by a combination of dialectical reason and spiritual exercise, one could attain through direct experience inner knowledge of the divine (see above, p. 128).

RELIGIOUS TOLERATION

Observance of the Shari'a was not, therefore, the principal path to God. Akbar and his followers deplored the authority of religious tradition, including and especially the Islamic tradition because it involved the 'slavish following' (taqlid) of others: one ought not to submit to any human being as a moral and intellectual authority, especially when it is 'not possible to know which of his sayings are correctly his own' – a clear reference to Muhammad (in Vanina 1996: 65). Akbar became ashamed of having converted people by force.

All this provided Akbar with a new approach to religio-political authority. It enabled him to tackle the crucial problem of how to gain legitimacy in the eyes of his subjects, and so to extend central control over his governors and the army. It was part of a strategy to develop imperial values in place of tribal ones, and to make his domains less segmented.

It clearly involved a fairly radical departure from Islam, at least as hitherto conceived. Akbar's policy of religious toleration went much further even than the extremely liberal version of Islam suggested by Babur. First, he repealed those aspects of Islamic Right that discriminated against other religions. Hindus were allowed to repair their temples and to build new ones. Conversion to Islam by force was prohibited; those previously converted by force were permitted to return to Hinduism without the prescribed death penalty for apostasy. Next, after an inspection (1578) of land-grants to religious foundations, Akbar revoked grants to Muslim institutions which were found to be invalid, and extended the donation of land for charitable purposes to yogis, brahmins and parsis. Finally, he abolished (1579) the discriminatory poll-tax (jizya), so ending a long-standing religious tradition basic to Muslim privilege.

Thus Akbar gave Hindus the same social status as Muslims. These moves struck at the core of the regime in which the 'ulama achieved social dominance. 'Members of all religions joined [Akbar's] service as if they were of the same religion'; many Hindus rose to high positions.[8] For a time, Hindus and Muslims lived together in a situation of virtual social and political equality, beyond anything which Jews or Christians acquired under the Ottomans. The Mughals seem to have achieved their goal of bringing their subjects together under a single imperial allegiance regardless of differences based on religious faith and community.

For the same reasons, Akbar sought to reconcile the sects within Islam. This too was an original move, and one which marked a complete contrast with the religious posture of the Ottomans, Safavids and Uzbeks. But his strategy involved an extraordinary reassertion and aggrandisement of his own religio-legal authority as a ruler of Muslims, in terms calculated to appeal to both Sunnis and Shi'ites. In an attempt to make both communities see the emperor himself as the ultimate authority in religious matters, Akbar issued (1579) the so-called 'infallibility decree' (Mahzar). This stated that

> Should in future a religious question arise, regarding which the opinions of the highly-qualified religious jurists (Mujtahids) differ, and His Majesty in his penetrating intellect and clear wisdom be inclined to adopt, for the benefit of the people and for the betterment of the administration of the country, any of the conflicting opinions which exist on that point, he should issue an order to that effect. We do hereby agree that such a decree shall be binding on us and on the whole community.

The ultimate right of interpretation (ijtihad) was given to Akbar as Timurid emperor and 'true king'. The decree went on: 'should His Majesty think fit to issue a new order, all shall likewise be bound by it, provided always that such [an] order shall not be in opposition to the injunctions of the Qur'an and be also of real benefit to the people'. Akbar got several senior 'ulama to sign this decree.[9]

What the first passage meant was not that he could give his own opinion ('legislate' on Shari'a matters), but that he could decide which of the Mujtahids' opinion was correct and should be followed. This meant that Akbar himself was to be the supreme religious authority within the Islamic community. The second passage obviously did give scope for imperial legislation, at least in the sense of issuing new rules, like kanun, to supplement the existing Shari'a in response to the needs of the time. This was presumably how the 'ulama who agreed to sign the decree understood it. Akbar himself, however, may not have intended his legislative power to be restricted by the Shari'a, for he proceeded to legislate on marriage, and to prohibit certain Muslim and Hindu customs which he considered undesirable. He seems to have been claiming the kind of authority which Ibn Muqaffa' (see above, pp. 22–3) had urged upon the 'Abbasid caliph centuries earlier.

One justification for the status given to the emperor in the Mahzar was that 'the rank of a just sultan (sultan-i adil) is higher in the eyes of God than that of a mujtahid' (AS 141). 'Just sultan' was the title given by Shi'ites to a good king who, in the absence of the true Leader, upheld religious values. Akbar also assumed the title 'lord of the age (sahib-i zaman)', the ruler chosen by God to govern the Muslim community at a particular moment in its history. Akbar's supporters took this to mean that he would 'remove all differences of opinion among the seventy-two sects of Islam and the Hindus'. Akbar claimed to be the Sunni Deputy ('commander of the faithful (amir al-mu'minin)'), to be 'Imam of Islam and of the Muslims', a title presumably intended to claim leadership of the Shi'ites as well as the Sunnis. The claim of the Ottoman Sultan to the Caliphate was dismissed; he was merely Caesar of Rome (Qaiser-i Rum). Even Akbar's orthodox Muslim opponents were prepared to accept him as 'Caliph of the age', 'Caliph of God'. He was given the title Badshah-i Islam ('emperor of Islam'), and said to be an even greater Islamic hero than Saladin, because he was reconciling Shi'ites and Sunnis, and because he made sure that 'unbelievers are shouldering the burdens of Islam' – a reference to the military role of Hindus.[10]

A SPIRITUAL EMPEROR

In Akbar's view, then, the emperor was empowered to oversee the religious life of his subjects and in particular to remove religious discord among them. In short, it was more important for the ruler to achieve social peace than to enforce the Shari'a. Here, Akbar and Abu'l-Fadl were extending the traditional Irano-Islamic view, that the role of the king is to bring peace to an otherwise strife-torn human world, by seeing sectarian strife itself as specifically 'a basic cause of human misfortune' (in Streusand 1989: 137). This was precisely the point from which Marsiglio of Padua had set out to construct the first European theory of the modern state, when he said that the one cause of discord which Aristotle had not been aware of was the pope's claim to temporal authority (Black 1992: 58). Abu'l-Fadl regarded the preoccupations of the 'ulama as small-minded but also pernicious in their effects on human relations. The king (shah) as emperor (padshah) ensures stability and possession (pad). The abolition of religious conflict and of the divisive attitudes that go with it was an essential part of the functions of kingship (Rizvi 1975: 354, 364).

Akbar's view of religion enabled him to develop a new ideology of kingship for the Islamic world – an 'enlightened' approach, in the eighteenth-century European sense that the ruler may get rid of undesirable practices, even if they have religious sanction, in the light of a higher, philosophical view of morality. This was summed up as 'universal peace (sulh-i kull)', 'universal concord', and 'love for all men'. This comes into existence, Abu'l-Fadl said, in a 'time of reflection [when] men shake off the prejudices of their education; the threads of the web of religious blindness break; and the eye sees the glory of harmoniousness' (A'in 1: 163). Spiritual insight creates harmony among humans. Abu'l-Fadl saw this universal peace as 'the foundation of the arrangement of mankind' (in Streusand 1989: 137). Akbar told Philip II of Spain that international alliances were important for 'establishing peace and harmony on earth' (in Farooqi 1989: 20) (Akbar proposed an anti-Ottoman alliance with the Portuguese.) Abu'l-Fadl urged (1582) kings to 'establish among themselves the bonds of friendship and cooperation, so that the peoples, for God's glory, may enter into good and worthy relations among themselves' (in Vanina 1996: 160). This cosmopolitanism is reminiscent of Stoic thought under the Hellenistic and Roman empires.

From the mid-1580s, Akbar and Abu'l-Fadl went further and presented not just a revised form of Islam but a new religion, the 'religion of God (din-i illahi)'. Akbar was to be the spiritual master (pir) of a new religious order in the Sufi mode, with his senior officials and army officers as his disciples. Pre-Abrahamic forms of the cult of royalty were revived in rituals involving fire and light. Akbar bowed before the sun: 'a special grace proceeds from the sun, the exalted, in favour of kings' (Akbar, quoted by Abu'l-Fadl in Streusand 1989: 136). To denote this new 'divine (illahi)' era, a new solar calendar was introduced.

Akbar's religio-political order was designed, above all, to create a new bond between ruler and subject. He cast his senior officials (mansabdars) as Sufi-yogi disciples, with an elaborate initiation ceremony. This now included a rejection of traditional Islam: 'I liberate and dissociate myself from the traditional and imitative Islam which I have seen my fathers practise ... and join the religion of God of King Akbar, accepting the four degrees of devotion, which are sacrifice of property, life, honour and religion' (in Streusand 1989: 150). Thus Akbar emphasised the bond of unconditional loyalty between ruler and subjects. Senior officials were now related to the emperor by a unique tie of *spiritual* patronage. This relationship was extended in principle to his subjects in general: 'he is a guru, other people are all his chelas [disciples]' (a Sufi poet said). Thus people of all classes would mill together at dawn under the emperor's special balcony for darshan (lit. seeing, part of 'the interaction between Hindu spiritual teachers and their disciples': Streusand 1989: 124). This was one climax of the ideology of patrimonial monarchy.

To most orthodox Muslims, Akbar's ideology was of course apostasy. But it had several pedigrees in political culture. It obviously revived some Sassanian and Zoroastrian notions. It had parallels with the Islamic philosophers' view of government, in particular al-Farabi's ideal ruler. It was reminiscent of Ibn Muqaffa''s idea of a religious monarchy independent of the 'ulama. Abu'l-Fadl in fact shared Ibn Muqaffa''s fate of death by assassination, in an unrelated incident, and Akbar died of grief soon after. Nearer to home, the religious philosophy behind Akbar's project was clearly inspired by spiritual ideas that had been developing in India. It coincided with Hindu ideas of kingship; Akbar was presented as an incarnation of Krishna. And the new religion was invented just before the Muslim millennium (1591–2) when some were expecting a Mahdi, or 'just king'.[11]

But above all, Akbarism resonated with Mongol ideas.[12] This may provide the key. For the Mughals prided themselves on their Mongol heritage and descent, seeing themselves as Turanis – central Asians. Above all, they prided themselves on their descent from Timur, the world-conqueror, and from Chingiz Khan. Akbar's successors took the title 'world conqueror (Jahangir)' and 'king of the world (Shahjahan)'. Akbar was 'the lamp of the tribe of Timur'. Abu'l-Fadl went to great lengths to present a sacred lineage from Adam to Timur: he claimed that the divine light had been transmitted to Akbar from Adam through fifty-two generations. In one mythical ancestor, it 'took shape without human instrumentality or a father's loins'. Akbarism made sense in terms of the origins and perceived homeland of the dynasty in central Asia: were not the pre-Islamic Mongol courts of central Asia renowned for their religious liberty and free debate between faiths? Akbar's legitimacy in ethnic and dynastic terms perhaps made him toy with abandoning the Islamic credentials of his regime. But (in this respect like twentieth-century political religions) Akbarism did not last long.

On a more practical plane, the royal cult gave credibility to the move away from clan kingship, in which several family members shared political power and could claim the succession, to absolute sovereignty located in the individual ruler. The right of succession was confined to Akbar's direct descendants. The new tie of unconditional loyalty through religious discipleship created a relationship not unlike military slavery. Whereas before recruits to the armies of Muslim rulers had been expected to adopt Islam, the new system justified employing Hindus because they too were royal disciples.

It was part of an attempt to centralise government. Akbar systematised the bureaucracy and classified officials into distinct ranks. But centralisation never progressed very far. The attempt to make the senior officials more subordinate to the king succeeded only insofar as it made them more easily moveable from one province to another. Within their provinces, they retained much autonomy; in many provinces, 'segmentary' tribal rule persisted and imperial rule made little difference.

ORTHODOX SUNNI POLITICAL THOUGHT

Akbar's religio-political policies were continued under Jahangir (r.1605–27) and Shah Jahan (r.1628–58). The circle of 'disciples' was widened to include much of the nobility, Muslim and Hindu. Even some Muslim reformers endorsed the policy of 'Hinduism wielding the sword of Islam'.

But the *ideological* enterprise of Akbar and Abu'l-Fadl did not last. Some of Akbar's ideas continued to be expressed among Hindus and Sufis; justice meant the universal peace established by Akbar, 'the just ruler, who united the faiths of the Hindus and Muslims' (a Sufi poet in Vanina 1996: 61). Jahangir continued Akbar's practice of seeking counsel from Hindu holy men; he was called 'master of both faiths'; and an orthodox Advice book referred to the divine glow of enlightenment that came to him from his ancestors (Adam to Timur). But the attempt to replace, or supplement, traditional Islam with a royal 'religion of God' met with much disapproval and was abandoned. On the other hand, Jahangir refused to revoke the infallibility decree.

The orthodox observance of the religio-legal Tradition (sunna) remained relatively weak in the face of alternative forms of piety, such as Sufism. It was typical of Indian Islam that it was someone with a Sufi understanding of religious life who initiated the intellectual revival of Sunnism. Shaykh Ahmad Sirhindi (1564–1624, a Naqshbandi) was deeply opposed to Akbarism and urged a return to Islamic values in public life. But he accepted that it was the corruption of the 'ulama that had made Akbarism possible. He led a 'jihad by persuasion' to get Jahangir to appoint 'a pious and honest 'alim to be the final arbiter for the interpretation of the Shari'a' in place of the infallibility decree (Rizvi 1978: vol. 2, p. 365). Jahangir had him imprisoned.

Sirhindi's programme was based on an original interpretation of Islamic history and the role of the Prophet. In the 1,000 years since the Prophet's death, Sirhindi argued, his human or worldly aspect had been declining, while his spiritual aspect had been 'steadily gaining strength'.[13] In other words, what was needed was a restoration of Islamic values in public and political life. Sirhindi saw himself as someone who would bring about a return to the ideal conditions of the Prophet's lifetime by restoring the public aspect of the Shari'a, so that what was now practised spiritually would once again be practised in public life. He was to be a Renewer (mujaddid) for the new Muslim millennium; he even put himself on a par with the Prophet's Companions and claimed that he shared Muhammad's prophetic qualities.

Yet his aim was to restore the Shari'a not as understood by the orthodox jurists but in the 'essential' sense of Sufi piety. He sought to recover the Sufi tradition from its association with Hinduism and to maintain its ascendancy within Islam. He wanted to change the prevailing Sufi attitude towards non-Muslims: 'the humiliation of infidels is for the Muslims life itself' (he remarked after an execution).

In general, mainstream Islamic thought drew on traditional fiqh and the Advice-for-Kings genre without saying anything new. An orthodox view of religious polity was put forward by Hasan 'Ali bin Ashraf Munshi al-Khaqani (in his *Akhlaq-i Hakimi*, written 1579–80); by his grandson Nur al-Din Qazi al-Khaqani, whose *Akhlaq-i Jahangiri* (1620–2) included a chapter on siyasa shar'iyya (the governance of the Religious Law); and by Shaykh 'Abd al-Haqq of Delhi (1551–1642), who 'stressed the precedence of religious law over the mystic path'. In his *Risalah-i Nuriyyah-i Sultaniyya*, al-Haqq rejected the emperor's claim to religious authority, and praised the king who, with the assistance of the Learned, upholds the Shari'a. Military and political matters were discussed in *Malfuzat-i Timuri* (1637–8), compiled by Abu Talib.[14] (It would be interesting to know how much influence Khunji (see above, pp. 186–8) had on these writers, given the contacts between northern India and central Asia.)

Works of Advice-to-Kings written under Akbar and Jahangir reproduced conventional ideas on ethics and state management with hardly a trace of Akbarism. Dawani remained a model; Jahangir also commissioned a translation of Miskawayh (see above, p. 61–2). The orthodox Sunni Islamo-Iranian approach to government was reformulated by Muhammad Baqir Najm-i Sani (d.1637), a Persian 'alim in Mughal service, in his *Mau'izah-i Jahangiri* (1612–

13).[15] Baqir restated the traditional justification for the state. 'To maintain order in the affairs of the world and to carry out the business of the human race, law is needed'; this has been provided by the Prophet; what is required now, therefore, is 'a prudent and powerful ruler with exalted authority, maintaining order and strengthening the pillars of the true religion ... and achieving the blessings of peace and security'. Once again, religion and political power are interdependent: 'without the ruler's regulation of control, the decrees of the Shari'a will not be promulgated'. Baqir reiterated the Hobbesian view that 'to have a [condition] like paradise, peace and security must be assured by the sword of the emperors ... The loftiest heaven is indebted to the swords of just rulers' (pp. 41–2, 47–8).

Above all, the emperor must mould his life and government on the Shari'a. Abu'l-Fadl had recommended the ruler to consult 'a sage (hakim)', but Baqir urged that, as 'head of the [Muslim] community (millat)', the emperor should 'pattern [his] policies after the advice, counsel and judgment of the 'ulama' (p. 42). Baqir quoted 'sages' and 'philosophers' as his authorities, suggesting a role for non-Islamic, or at least non-Juristic, teachers. This would make his subjects prosperous and therefore loyal. In order that he may 'solve and resolve problems' in the interests of social welfare and security, the emperor must have wide-ranging powers 'over people's lives and possessions' (pp. 42, 46).

Justice remained the focus of Muslim political morality. As Baqir said, 'governmental justice (siyasah 'adalah) and equity [are] the means to survival of [kings'] rule, the permanence of their fame, and their reward in the hereafter. To them, nothing should be more binding than pursuit of the people's welfare' (p. 46). Justice 'is the basis of the functioning of the world and the races of men' (Shah Jehan is reported to have said: in Kulke 1995: 271).

Nur al-Din al-Khaqani equated justice with universal tolerance. For most Muslim writers, however, justice meant what it had always meant in the Muslim world: impartiality in judgement; protection of the weak; redress of grievances for the poor, especially cultivators, against oppressors. 'The king should so award punishments that the cruel cannot oppress their victims, and [the nobles] may treat the poor mildly, and the garden of the world flourish, owing to the removal of the thorns of cruelty' (official chronicle in Kulke 1995: 271). Nobles and commoners, landowners and peasants must be treated equally. As Abu'l-Fadl said, 'it is a prerequisite of ... sovereignty that justice be administered to the oppressed, without distinguishing between friend and foe, relative and stranger ... so that ... those attached to the court may not make their relationship a means of oppression' (in Rizvi 1975: 364). The emperor should listen attentively to the complaints of ordinary farmers.

The division of society into four occupational groups was taken seriously by Mughal writers; these groups were analogous to the four elements. Abu'l-Fadl derived this from Dawani and Nasir al-Din Tusi, and like them based it on the division of labour; but he put the groups in a different order. Warriors come first; craftsmen and merchants next: for 'from their labours and travels, God's gifts become universal' (compare al-Ghazali, above, p. 102). Men of the pen drop from first to third place, presumably to downgrade the 'ulama; and among the men of the pen Abu'l-Fadl put first 'the sage' with a philosophical training and Sufi enlightenment; he did not mention Jurists or Religious Judges. Farmers remain last. Abu'l-Fadl emphasised that the parts are interdependent as in an organism; and there should be 'equilibrium ... unanimity and concord, a multitude of people ... fused into one body'.[16] 'Abd al-Haqq compared the relationship between the king and social groups ('the pillars of the world and mankind') to that between body and soul (Rizvi 1978: vol. 2, p. 363). Mughal authors classified officials into four groups or 'pillars of the empire', reflecting Akbar's systematisation of ranks. In Baqir's version, the third such group consisted of a magistrate (hakim) whose job it was to punish the powerful on behalf of the weak.

Abu'l-Fadl insisted that it is the ruler who allocates individuals to their social group: for 'by uniting personal ability with due respect for others', he would 'cause the world to flourish' (Rizvi 1975: 368). Baqir and 'Abd al-Haqq said that the ruler should support 'the distinction of ranks' by not allowing the low-born to claim equality with others. This echoed Barani, and resembled the programme of some Ottoman reformers. It was in line with the interests of the magnates and 'ulama.

The Circle of Power (see above, p. 54) does not seem to have featured much, but it was invoked by a Sufi master in conversation with Shah Jahan. He stressed the importance of agriculture: the emperor's priority should be to promote 'the prosperity of his subjects, by seeking to populate new areas and bringing them under cultivation'; this would make 'the soldiery contented and the treasury full' (in Rizvi 1965: 341).

Stricter enforcement of the religious Code was implemented under Shah Jahan, who was called 'the pillar of the Shari'a', 'deserving to hold the rank of Deputyship (Khilafat) and niyabat [vicegerency] of God on earth', 'Deputy of God in both worlds' (in Farooqi 1989: 194), Renewer (sc. of the millennium). He forbade the construction of non-Islamic places of worship. In the succession struggle between his sons Dara Shukoh and Aurangzib, the Islamicisation of the polity and in particular the relationship between Muslims and Hindus became an issue. Dara Shukoh, supported by many Sufis, championed partnership, 'the confluence of the two oceans'; was not Muhammad 'a blessing to all the worlds and not only to Muslims'? (in Rizvi 1965: 341) Aurangzib (r.1650–1707) won. He embarked upon jihad against Hindu rulers and extended the Mughal Empire over southern India. He reintroduced Sunni orthodoxy into public life and tried to establish a unified legal system, based on Hanafi jurisprudence (of which a major collection, *Fatawa-i 'Alamgiri*, was published). And he finally reimposed the poll-tax on non-Muslims.

After Aurangzib, with its original praxis gone, the Mughal empire fell apart. Governors such as the nawab of Bengal gained independence; Sikhs set up their own state; Hindu princes such as the Marathas regained power in southern India. Afghan tribes invaded, first led by Nadir Shah (1739), the new ruler of Persia, then by Ahmad Shah Durrani (1757–61). Wali Allah hoped that Durrani would save India from the infidels. Delhi was looted on both occasions. The Mughals still claimed that they occupied 'the throne of khilafat and sovereignty', maintaining until the end (1857) the fiction that other rulers in India, including the British, were their delegates.[17]

WALI ALLAH OF DELHI (1703–62): HUMAN NATURE AND CIVILISATION

In these unfavourable times, Shah Wali Allah al-Dihlawi (Delhi 1703–Delhi 1762)[18] initiated a fresh approach to Islamic social and political thought, based on an original view of social evolution. A member of the Naqshbandi order, he had succeeded his father as head of a madrasa; he then went on pilgrimage to Mecca (1730–2) and returned with a resolve to establish a reformed Shari'a Community. Together with his sons, he translated the Qur'an into Persian and Urdu. Wali Allah criticised Sufis for making so much of their personal authority, the 'ulama for their pedantry, and the 'ulama and the soldiery for taking income from public funds without working for it. This, he said, combined with the oppressive taxation of producers – farmers, merchants, artisans – is what causes states to decline.

Wali Allah developed two important theoretical initiatives. The first was to extend the use of ijtihad (individual rational judgement). This was related to a revolutionary and modern idea, that the Shari'a should be interpreted in the light of the circumstances under which it was formulated, and that it must be adapted to changing needs in the present-day world. It must respond to the human condition which may differ from time to time and from place to place. This was formulated in his *Conclusive Argument from God (Hujjat Allah al-Baligha)*,[19] which is still on the curriculum at the al-Azhar in Cairo, and in the Sudan.

Secondly, Wali Allah set out to resolve the differences between the 'ulama's juristic and the Sufis' mystical approaches to religion. He advocated 'down with all systems', and put forward an approach based on reconciliation (tatbik). For it is 'God's express will that we should refrain from disagreement and sectarianism'. This too followed from his revolutionary approach to history: in considering doctrinal differences, 'one should take into account that all of them were adapted to the spirit of the time' (Baljon 1986: 202). Merely ritual variations should be tolerated.

Wali Allah (like al-Ghazali) advocated *balance* (tawazun). For example, one may say that 'a life of ease and comfort is good'; or, again, that it is bad 'due to its requiring conflict, competition, hard labour … a neglect of planning for the next life' (Hujjat, p. 304). But in fact 'what is pleasing to God is the middle way, maintaining the supports of civilisation while including with them the remembrances of God'. He recommended balance (tawazun) in economic relationships as well.[20]

But toleration was for Muslims only. Wali Allah's attitude towards unbelievers, and especially Hindus, was harsh: unbelievers should be kept down, they should remain agricultural labourers, and they should pay a hefty poll-tax. This was in line with Aurangzib's reaction against the inter-communal partnership. Perhaps it too reflected the insecurity of a ruling group that was in a minority.

Wali Allah's idea that the Religious Law would vary with the times was developed in the context of a general theory of human social development. Humans have three qualities in their nature that are not found among other animals: (1) a 'universal outlook (al ra'y al-kulli)'; (2) an aesthetic sense; and (3) among 'people of intelligence and awareness', the ability to 'discover the appropriate supports of civilisation (irtifaqat)', that is 'stages of increasingly refined order and elaboration of arts of civilised life'. Other humans, being 'motivated by the same concerns', 'accept wholeheartedly' what the more intelligent people tell them because the irtifaqat are 'in agreement with what they know' (pp. xix, 115–16).

There are four irtifaqat or stages ('moments' in Hegel's language). The first stage consists of language, agriculture, pasturing, building, clothing, female monogamy and tools. This is achieved by *all* peoples, including the bedouin and 'small societies such as inhabitants of deserts, high mountains and regions far away from temperate zones' (in Baljon 1986: 193).

The second stage is the science (hikma) of testing and refining conduct in these spheres 'by correct experience in every field'; of selecting 'those attitudes which are further from harm and closer to benefit ... on the basis of friendly interaction among people and proper association with them'. This stage gave rise to 'the proper manner of eating ... defecating, sexual intercourse, clothing, dwellings ...'. It arises among 'communities of sedentary people and townsmen flourishing in temperate zones'. It includes household management and economic transations arising out of the necessary division of labour, roughly speaking what Hegel would call 'civil society'. This irtifaqat 'establishes exchanges, cooperation, the means of earning' and the various professions. For there cannot be cooperation without contracts and conventions (sing. al-rusum) on matters such as 'share-cropping, hire and lease, partnership, power of attorney ... borrowing and keeping in trust ... witnessing, writing up documents, mortgages, guarantees and bills of exchange'. People should be tied to their profession and place of residence.[21]

In this sphere, different conventions arise among different peoples, due to royal decrees or popular sentiment. Some conventions are bad and should be suppressed, by force if necessary. People often don't know why they are following a convention; but having conventions is what differentiates humans from animals (pp. 142–3).

The third irtifaqat is the science of ruling a city or state (madina), that is 'a group living in close proximity to one another who have dealings with one another and who dwell in separate houses'. This is necessary because disagreements force people 'to set up a king to judge among them with justice, restrain the rebellious ... and collect taxes to spend as they should be spent' (pp. 117, 129). Therefore one needs a 'strong and powerful personality, a leader (imam) in the fullest sense' (as Baljon puts it: p. 194).

Fourthly, kings of such states quarrel. Therefore 'they are forced to appoint a Caliph ... who has an army and equipment which make it clearly impossible for someone else to usurp his domain' (*Hujjat*, p. 137). Enter Alexander and, more successfully, Muhammad. Wali Allah sees such Caliphs as ruling not the whole world, but large parts of it.

It appears that in Wali Allah we have a theory of natural law, which had so far been so conspicuously absent from Islamic thought. He said that humans, like all species, have 'a law (shari'a) infused into the breasts of its individuals by means of the specific form'. He saw moral obligations and social rules as necessarily arising out of the human condition. 'In every topic there are issues collectively agreed on among the people of all countries, even if they are far from each other'. For Wali Allah, 'the universal beneficial purposes for the human species (are) embodied in its ideal natural constitution (fitra)'. This 'substratum of beliefs and practices suited to the basic constitutions of all peoples' Wali Allah called the madhdhab tabi'i (lit. nature's law-school). All this is most obviously true for the first stage of civilisation, but he also said that human beings are 'naturally predisposed' to the second and third stages of civilisation (pp. xix, 122, 303). Here again, we may find the influence of the Indian environment, perhaps even of Mughal religio-political policy, in which different moral-legal-religious systems coexisted side by side. In this discussion of the relationship between nature and convention, there are parallels with Montesquieu.

All human societies are compelled to make rules on certain matters, although the content of these rules may vary from one society to another. Actual legal systems differ, but these differences are legitimate, being based upon the same human needs and having the same 'beneficial' purposes. 'Every nation has a style and set of manners which distinguish it, as required by variations in temperaments, habits and so on.' Differences between religions, according to Wali Allah, arise because prophets, while remaining as close to the 'natural way' as possible, respect existing cultural norms and conventions so long as these accord with the universal outlook, that is, aim at the common good (compare the Brethren of Purity: above, p. 61). They only introduce changes which people can recognise as reasonable and can be persuaded to adopt. In some matters, a rule has to be made, but it does not matter what the rule is, for example serving water from the right (pp. xxi, 122, 126, 132, 309).

What is most remarkable is that Wali Allah's account of human nature leading to social organisation and thence to polity (first on a small scale, then on a large scale), while clearly drawn from experience of the Islamic world, is basically naturalistic. That is, morality, law, society and polity were considered to be derived from human need and human nature. He was thus the only Muslim to conceive of a natural moral law of the kind which transformed moral ideas in Europe between the thirteenth and the eighteenth centuries.

Wali Allah's first two stages resembled Ibn Khaldun's badawa and hadara (see above, p. 173), but he did not use Ibn Khaldun's terminology, nor did he refer to 'asabiyya. He followed traditional Islamic Falsafa in seeing the state as the outcome of conflict in a complex society, rather than, as Ibn Khaldun saw it, as the instigator of complex hadara.

People also need an infallible prophet, who has absolute knowledge directly from God, and upon whose authority 'the consensus of all agrees, whether he is present among them or his report is preserved among them' (pp. 247–8). Religious Right is based on, first, human nature, and, second, the conventions of a particular time and place. Wali Allah's theory of the Deputyship was remarkable for the way in which it reconciled Sufi and juristic views by distinguishing between a spiritual (batini) Caliphate for religious instruction, and a political (zahiri) Caliphate for promoting public religious observance.

Wali Allah also made an unprecedented distinction between Caliphate in a 'special (khass)' sense and in a 'general ('amm)' sense. The special Deputyship was held only by Muhammad and the first two rightly-guided caliphs who had been (he said) designated by Muhammad. (This view was conciliatory in the sense that it accorded neither with the Shi'ite nor with the Sunni view.)

All other Caliphs are (just) good Muslim rulers; they are elected by the people and they should consult others. Their aim is 'the enforcement of religion by means of a revival of the religious discipline, undertaking Holy War ... taking charge of the judicature, and so on' (in Baljon 1986: 125). They are to be obeyed unless they reject Islam; then there is a duty to use force against them. An example of Caliphs in this general sense was the 'Abbasids, and the best of all such Caliphs was Mahmud of Ghazna. Here, he lowered traditional expectations of the Deputyship, enabling it to be applied to any ruler who observed the Shari'a, and endorsing the Sultan-Caliph.

The Caliphate in this sense was held by pre-Muslim empires. This was a remarkable extension of the religious vocabulary. The decline of the Persians and Byzantines was caused, Wali Allah thought, by their excessive wealth, which they acquired by 'multiplying the taxes on the peasantry, merchants and their like, and oppressing them'. (The 'Abbasids and Turks also ruled like this.) And God 'cured this illness by cutting off its material aspect' through 'an unlettered Prophet' (pp. 306, 308).

Wali Allah was a dedicated advocate of Islamic reform and of the establishment of a traditional Islamic state. His teachings led to a revival of Islamic thought in India. His son 'Abd al-'Aziz (Delhi 1746–Delhi 1824) declared areas under British rule to have reverted to 'the land of conflict'; therefore people living there needed to elect their own imams, who would lead congregational prayers and supervise Legal transactions.[22] One of his son's disciples, Sayyid Ahmad Barelwi (1786–1831) (Hardy 1972: 51–9), made a final attempt to liberate Muslims from infidel rule by declaring Holy War against the Sikhs, and possibly also the British.

Wali Allah's ideas, and above all the approach which he used to justify his views and explain the present predicament of Islam, were new. He was a purist, like Ibn Taymiyya whom he greatly admired, but unlike him a conciliator. With his notion of the use of ijtihad and the relativity of religio-legal practice, he was indeed 'the founder of Islamic modernism' (EI 2: 254b). His conception of human nature *could* have opened the way for a reorientation of Islamic thought, whether or not in response to European rationalism (EI 3: 430b); but this did not in fact happen. His theory of the 'general' Deputy laid a basis for political thought in the twentieth century, as did his reference to election and consultation. In his partial secularisation of the Caliphate, and therefore of Islamic statehood, he appears in fact more modernist than any other Islamic thinker. Nevertheless, he retained the notion of an intellectual elite.

NOTES

1. For what follows, see especially *EI* on Mughals and 3: 429–40; *CH India* I. 5 and III. 4; Kulke and Rothermund (1998: 184–223); AS; Streusand (1989); Kulke (1995); Subrahmanyam (1992); Ahmad (1964, 1967, 1969); Vanina (1996).

2. In N. C. Mehta, 'An Unpublished Testament of Babur', *The Twentieth Century* (Jan. 1936), pp. 339–44 at p. 340.

3. Sajida S. Alvi, 'Religion and State during the reign of Jahangir', *SI* 69 (1989), p. 105.

4. K. A. Nizami, 'Naqshbandi Influence on Mughal Rulers and Politics', *IC* 39 (1965), pp. 41–52; Foltz (1998: 94–7).

5. Streusand (1989: 148n.). The *Akbar-name* is trans. H. Beveridge (Calcutta, 1903–10, repr. 1927–49); and (the version I have used) H. Blockmann (vol. 1 containing the *A'in*) and H. Jarrett (vols 2–3) (Calcutta 1873–94, repr. Delhi 1977–8). It was originally edited by Sayyid Ahmad Khan (see below, p. 300) in 1855 (Ahmad 1967: 39). See Rizvi (1975) and F. W. Buckler, 'A New Interpretation of Akbar's "Infallibility" Decree of 1579', in M. N. Pearson (ed.), *Legitimacy and Symbols: The South Asian Writings of F. W. Buckler* (University of Michigan, 1985), pp. 131–48.

6. *A'in* in Streusand (1989: 130); Stephen P. Blake, *Shahjahanabad* (Cambridge: Cambridge University Press, 1991), p. 20.

7. Vanina (1996: 63); Rizvi (1975: 353); Ahmad (1962: 128).

8. Streusand (1989: 137); Alvi, 'Religion and State', p. 107.

9. In Sri Ram Sharma, *The Religious Policy of the Mughal Emperors* (London, 1962), p. 32; and Vanina (1996: 33).

10. In Subrahmanyam (1992: 305); Streusand (1989: 132); Farooqi (1989: 193).

11. In Vanina (1996: 33); Rizvi (1975: 353, 357, 362).

12. For what follows, see Foltz (1998: xxix); AS 17; Subrahmanyam (1992: 304); Farooqi (1989: 23, 98); Streusand (1989: 131).

13. Y. Friedmann, *Shaykh Ahmad Sirhindi* (Montreal: McGill-Queen's University Press, 1971), p. 15.

14. AS 23; Ahmad (1969: 2) and (1962: 130); Rizvi (1978: vol. 2, p. 363).

15. Ed. and trans. Sajida Sultana Alvi, *Advice on the Art of Governance, Mau'izah-i Jahangiri of Muhammad Baqir Najm-i Sani* (Albany: SUNY, 1989).

16. In Vanina (1996: 36); Rizvi (1975: 367–8).

17. Buckler, above, n. 5.

18. *EI* 2: 254–5; A. A. Rizvi, *Shah Wali-Allah and His Times* (Canberra: Ma'rifat, 1980); Baljon (1986).

19. Trans. M. K. Hermansen (Leiden: Brill, 1996).

20. Nizami (above, n. 4), p. 51.

21. Hujjat, pp. 121, 127–8; Baljon (1986: 194); Rizvi, *Shah*, p. 310.

22. A. A. Rizvi, *Shah 'Abd al-'Aziz: Puritanism, Sectarianism, Polemics and Jihad* (Canberra: Ma'rifat, 1982).

The Decline and Reform of the Ottoman Empire

24

The subject of the decline of the Ottoman empire from the late sixteenth century onwards has been debated among both contemporaries and historians.[1] It was the starting point for Ottoman political thought from the later sixteenth to the early twentieth century. Historians have contested the very idea of decline: did the empire become less stable and powerful in comparison with what it had been, or only in comparison with contemporary Europe? Were the causes of 'decline' internal or external? If one compares the Ottoman state with other states in the Islamic world, decline is not so evident. Insofar as it is, the wonder is not that it declined but that it lasted so long.

The Ottomans suffered their first military reverse at the battle of Lepanto (1571), 'the greatest battle ever fought on the Mediterranean' (Inalçik 1973: 41), and (however one looks at it) the one with the most consequences since Actium or Salamis. This was followed by military stalemate in the Balkans (1596–1606: 'the long Turkish war'). The Ottomans became locked in conflict on several fronts, with the Habsburgs and Iran, and, later in the seventeenth century, with Russia, Poland and Venice. Against Iran, Murad IV (r.1623–40) achieved some success, resulting in the treaty of Kasr-i Sirin (1639), which established a permanent border between the Ottoman empire and Safavid Persia. In the later seventeenth century, they suffered disastrous defeats on land, following their failure to take Vienna (1683). They were forced to cede Hungary, Transylvania, Dalmatia and southern Greece (Treaty of Carlowitz, 1699). Attempts to reverse this led to further defeats with the loss of much of Serbia (Treaty of Passarowitz: 1718).

The economic condition of the empire in particular occasioned debate then and now. Commerce was moving from the Mediterranean to the Atlantic and the Cape; Russia gained control of the route from central Asia. Trade between the Ottoman empire and the outside world was handled mostly by Europeans. Inflation in Europe sucked raw materials out of the empire. Capital investment and the development of manufacturing industry in Europe led to an unfavourable balance of trade. It also meant a continuous struggle to keep abreast in military technology.

Military reverses inflicted psychological wounds. The Ottoman empire was a warrior state. Ottoman political culture centred upon the images of Holy

War and the Sultan as the sword of Islam. The Ottoman economy, the sense of collective purpose and social cohesion itself depended upon continual conquest and expansion. Ottoman society flourished so long as its morale was boosted by victories, its leaders rewarded by the spoils of war. Belief in their own religious supremacy and the policy of jihad made Ottoman ruling circles unwilling to accept territorial losses and eager to renew war on any occasion. This kept them locked in conflict and reinforced a dysfunctional militarisation of society and state, and the dominance of a military caste.

The government's attempts to improve the army's capability led to changes in society and polity. The experiences of the Austrian Wars (1596–1606) proved the importance of musket and cannon. The government proceeded to run down their cavalry, recruit more infantry and train them in the use of firearms; this greatly increased the number of professional slave-soldiers (janissaries). In order to increase the numbers and efficiency of the infantry and artillery, and to provide them with up-to-date equipment, the Sultans and their advisers deprived the timar-holding cavalry of land and income, and redistributed this to the 'new troops' and tax-farmers, who developed into a new elite. Mercenaries were recruited from among the farmers of Anatolia and landless vagrants. When not required by the state, these formed semi-tribal armed bands (sekbans) which roamed the countryside and preyed upon the agricultural producers. This led to the Celali rebellions in Anatolia (1596–1607), named after a pro-Safavid Sufi who claimed to be the Mahdi. There followed a 'great flight' from the land. In 1687–9, military failure in Europe sparked off another round of revolts; for a while, 'all Anatolia was in the hands of the sekbans' (Inalçik 1980: 299–301). Agricultural production was disrupted.

The despatch by the government of janissaries into the provinces to quell these disorders contributed to the development of a new and semi-independent ruling stratum, based largely on military force. Slave soldiers formed part of 'a new upper class' (Inalçik 1973: 51), which alongside the 'ulama and merchants controlled the land and commerce. This became part of the government's problem. Deprived of the spoils of war, the regime turned to tax-farming (iltizam) and exploitation of the peasantry to reward its elites and servants. Political reformers were quick to identify these as a principal cause of military decline as well as of social disorder. Hereditary 'aristocracies' were crystallising. In the provinces, governors became a focus of independent power with 'vast economic resources' (Kunt 1983: 92–3), and capable of defying the central government. Landed property, legal-administrative power, religious leadership and commerce became concentrated in the hands of dynasties of local notables (ayan). North Africa, Syria and Iraq achieved de facto autonomy under former Ottoman paşas, Egypt under the Mamluks. In the eighteenth century, Arabia fell into the hands of tribal leaders, among whom the Wahhabi Sa'udis became prominent. Even in Anatolia, local lords acquired some autonomy as 'genuine local dynasties with strong loyalties' (Lewis 1968: 38).

At the centre, the meritocratic career structure based on the Levy was giving way to promotion by means of 'family and household connections'. The religious establishment too was becoming subject to 'ascriptive criteria and hereditary recruitment'. Above all, the army became 'an immense corporation whose purpose was the exploitation of the country through the administrative and fiscal organisation of the state ... The concentration of an immense army in the environs of the capital, without the counter-balance of the [traditional feudal] cavalry, constituted a permanent danger to the security of the state'.[2] Slave-soldiers were influential in the vizierate and the treasury. The political centre showed signs of disintegration: some Sultans took little interest in government. Thus 'in the period between 1617 and 1656, state affairs were decided primarily by a coalition of the household of the Sultan, dominated by the mothers of the Sultans and by palace officials ... the higher 'ulama ... and the high officers of the janissary corps' (Inalçik 1980: 289).

These developments generated the political literature of decline and reform. The primary aim of reform was to restore military superiority and thus the religious credibility of the polity. In the first attempt at political reform, Osman II (r.1618–22) tried to replace foreigners in the army and government by Turks, and to reduce the power of the 'ulama. But the janissaries and 'ulama rebelled; Osman was deposed and assassinated. Murad IV wanted to restore the 'good old traditions', eliminate corruption and balance state finances. He ruthlessly suppressed rebels and real or imagined opponents, including a Şeykülislam. The severity of his measures provoked another backlash from an alliance of janissaries, the palace harem and the 'ulama – the military, political and religious conservatives. They were supported by the Şeykülislam and the populace of Istanbul.

The most effective reform programme was that of the Köprülü family, begun by Mehmed Köprülü (grand vizier 1656–61) (EI 5: 257–61). He was of Christian origin, one of the last Levy recruits, probably from Albania. He secured a guarantee of non-intervention from the Sultan. He resumed Murad's programme of appointment by merit and the dismissal of incompetent and corrupt officials. He resumed the policy of reducing state expenditure and increasing state income by reassigning timars ('fiefs'). He too dealt severely with dissidents; he brought to an end (1658) a long period of 'rebellious governors' in Anatolia. He also attempted to re-establish the social boundaries between the 'askeri and the re'aya. He won plaudits from the political literati.

These policies were continued in a milder form by his son, Ahmed Köprülü (grand vizier 1661–76). The interplay between foreign and domestic politics, and between both and the issue of reform, was intensified by the military defeats of the 1680s and consequent economic collapse. These resulted in the deposition of the Sultan by a combination (once again) of soldiers, notables and 'ulama. One of the leaders was Mehmed Köprülü's younger son, Fazil Mustafa Paşa; appointed grand vizier in 1689, he at once renewed efforts to stamp out bribery as the means to high office and to make tenure of timars dependent upon military ability. His efforts were frustrated by political changes after the death of Süleyman II (1691). Another Köprülü, Amca zade Huseyin Paşa (1644–1702), who was appointed grand vizier to represent the Sultan at the peace negotiations of Carlowitz (1699), initiated another reform programme. This focused upon measures to promote the economy: reduction of sales taxes, stabilisation of the currency, development of domestic manufactures. He was frustrated by a powerful Şeykülislam; the Sultan was deposed by a revolt of the 'ulama and the Istanbul guilds.

There were, broadly speaking, two separate reactions to the problems facing the dynasty. One was to emphasise the religious basis of government and insist on a stricter application of the Islamic Code. The other was to emphasise the authority of the Sultan or grand vizier, and to demand stricter application of kanun. Both strategies were rooted in the same formal values of justice and the well-being of the common people. Advocates of both were aware of decline and disorder; and they agreed in ascribing them primarily to moral failings and their social consequences. Fundamental values and ways of thinking did not change.

Each group had its own agenda. Religious reformers or Islamisers strove for the proclamation of Sunni orthodoxy, for social observance of the moral and ritual precepts of the Shari'a. They were aligned with trends towards decentralisation and the weakening of central authority, towards a kind of feudalism based on local notables. Political reformers, on the other hand, stressed appointment by merit and (paradoxically perhaps) maintenance of social distinctions and purity of rank. They developed the theory of the four social orders (see above, p. 185). They were in essence advocating the reimposition of patrimonial ideals; sometimes they came close to enunciating a modern theory of dictatorship. These two strategies represented two distinct trends in the politics of the region, and of Islamicate societies generally. They persisted, with various mutations, down to the end of the Empire, and beyond.

THE DECLINE AND REFORM SCHOOL

The one genre of political writing that flourished and became distinctive under the Ottomans was that of Advice-to-Kings.[3] Earlier authors in this genre, including Nizam al-Mulk, al-Ghazali and Pseudo-Ghazali, were available in Ottoman Turkish (Kai Ka'us was translated five times). Süleyman I expressed interest in them. Almost all the Ottoman authors of Advices on reform either worked in, or were closely connected with, the central state apparatus. A large number were of European descent. They were sincerely devoted to the Ottoman House. They set out to enquire why the Ottoman armies were so much less successful than before. Their answers included social criticism and programmes for social as well as political reform.

These works were written by people experienced in the workings of government but without power to initiate policy; they were familiar with chancery and treasury; several used the language of kanun; one used 'sample imperial decrees as a literary device' (Howard 1988: 67). Their recommendations are practical and detailed and show an intimate knowledge of the workings of government, its procedures and linguistic style. Their compositions were intended for the immediate and urgent attention of those in power, and for circulation among top civil servants and like-minded people. They were designed to shape policy: *The Approved Book* (*Kitab-i Müstetab*: 1620)[4] may have influenced the reforms of the ill-fated Osman II, to whom it was addressed; Koçi Beg presented his *Epistle* to Murad IV; Katib Çelebi laid out a programme for Mehmed Köprülü just before he became grand vizier. It cannot be assumed that they represented the views of any wider public. Perhaps on some points they did, but in many cases they probably represented the views of a small minority inside the central government.

The first work on government reform was by Lutfi Pasha (1488–1563).[5] His proposed reforms covered social relationships and economic needs as well as managerial aspects of government. Writing at the zenith of Ottoman power, he spoke of the empire as already in decline.

MUSTAFA 'ALI (1541–1600)

In complete contrast was Mustafa 'Ali (Gallipoli 1541–Istanbul 1600),[6] a poet and literateur who ended up as virtually a freelance author. 'Ali had a medrese education; Kinalizade, the Ottoman master in falsafa, was his teacher and mentor. The high point of his chequered bureaucratic career was when he was secretary to the tutor of the future Selim II. 'Ali accompanied him to Cyprus and Persia (1570), where he composed a collection of customs and legends. He eventually decided to write a world history (*Kunh al-akbar: The Essence of History*), of which he also produced an abbreviated version (*Fusul*) just before he died. Cairo was the best place for sources, and he went there from 1592 to 1597.

None of this quite prepares us for the *Counsel for Sultans* (*Nüshat üs-selatin*: 1581, in Turkish).[7] This was a new and modern essay in the Advice genre, full of personal observations, flowing rhetoric and some rather daring invective. It was addressed personally to the Sultan Murad III, and the tone throughout is that of a personal confidant, which 'Ali wasn't. He took great pains to write in an appealing style, littering his argument with moral anecdotes, mostly based on the Qur'an, and with his own verses. Perhaps it was a bid for attention and employment; this would fit in with 'Ali's self-confident naïveté. The final chapter on injustices done to himself detracted somewhat from the impact of his reform proposals.

'Ali's intention was to promote 'empire and nation', 'the orderly state of the inhabitants of the country', 'faith and fatherland', to 'hold together the essential points of Sultanate and Caliphate' (*Counsel* 1: 115). The Sultan must be made aware of the injustices committed in his name by the viziers. He must remember the difference between courtiers and friends. What he should do is appoint someone of high mind and rank, an 'eloquent, educated companion of rare qualities', someone 'magnanimous' and 'severed from the ties of an office', expert in both Jurisprudence and astronomy (so that he could give counsel on astrology – perhaps he did not have himself in mind here), to 'enable him to see what is out of sight' and to give 'advice, secretly and openly' (1: 24, 41–2).

Kings need above all the love of their subjects. What has brought about 'the decline of certain kingdoms' is 'the viziers' tendency towards tyranny'; 'the ruin of the weak and helpless is caused in times of peace by the negligence of the grand vizier' (1: 22, 41; 2: 29). Therefore, great care must be taken when appointing viziers, and they must be personally supervised by the Sultan. The quality most needed in a Sultan is justice, and this means personal supervision of the viziers to ensure that acts of oppression are remedied. 'Ali lamented the interference of the harem women in the Sultan's government (1: 45). He reasserted the Sultan's duty to rule in person. He criticised the Sultan with amazing frankness for withdrawing from public affairs, 'preferring isolation' and 'putting the state of hiddenness before the personal management of affairs so as to remain an object of awe and veneration to the people' (1: 21).

'Ali highlighted the 'disruption [caused by] disregard of kanun'. By this he meant especially the intrusion of low-born, unworthy people into those offices and careers which should be kept for an elite of well-bred and intellectual people. Here too, 'the evil innovation that the high persons are left out and low people are given priority springs entirely from the wickedness of the viziers and from the unawareness of the land-conquering Sultan' (1: 37, 40). Appointment on merit is the primary duty required by the Sultan's required commitment to justice. 'Entry of unauthorised people into the military' leads to destruction of kingdom and state. God made Adam his Deputy (caliph) because of his 'sweet skill of speech and awareness of God'; rulers should not, therefore, 'promote inferior persons over the qualified'. In the selection of government officials, 'the complete superiority of the Learned (ulema) and the precedence of the wise must be respected'.[8]

'Ali enumerated the 'illicit practices' of senior officials; and he turned to wider social problems which lay behind the decline in military standards. The provision of material goods is ultimately the responsibility of the grand vizier; he must 'provide for the life necessities of the country's population in general and of the inhabitants of the capital in particular' (1: 19). The main reason for the inadequate supply of food to the army and for the soldiers' inadequate pay is the flight of peasants from the land. 'Ali blamed price rises on the appointment of unworthy muhtasibs (market regulators). Prices must be controlled so that merchants do not enrich themselves at the expense of soldiers and other state servants. Thus 'Ali endorsed the patrimonial view of the state as economic provider and, therefore, manager.

He looked to the Sultan and to kanun as the main remedies. Justice is embodied in kanun as well as in the Shari'a, of which kanun is a natural and necessary extension. 'Ali called the chancellor 'the mufti [sc. authorised exponent] of kanun', just as the Şeykülislam was of the Shari'a. The law-codes of Mehmed and Süleyman had been 'the guiding documents of the Ottoman system' (Fleischer 1986: 228). It was kanun which specified the rules, based on merit and service, for government appointments. According to his *Fusul*, Mehmed the Conqueror 'planned well for the future by establishing a venerable law (Kanun-i qadim)'; 'once this law is observed,' Mehmed had asked his vizier, 'how can the State be destroyed?'; to which the vizier replied: 'There is no path surer or firmer than this kanun we have established'. There are, nevertheless (the vizier went on), 'two ways in which the kingdom and state could be destroyed': first, if a Sultan fails to observe kanun and says 'Kanun is whatever [the Sultan] decrees' (in Fleischer 1986: 178). (This rejection, in principle, of legal absolutism, presumably meant that the law should not be changed without good reason.) The other way a state could be destroyed was the 'entry of unauthorised persons into the army'.

The institutions which 'Ali most valued were the House of Osman and the Sultan. The Sultan is 'the emperor of the world, God's shadow on earth, the heir to the heroes of old times ... the bright star in the sky of piety and rectitude ... the lord of the world': he is 'God's Deputy (Caliph)'.⁹ As for the Ottomans, God 'has given to this matchless, august race such perfect luck and all-embracing happiness ... The depth of the sea of their majesty is beyond the reach of the diving thought'; their 'august lineage' is the most stable of all. Kings of the House of Osman are 'of the stature of Alexander the Great', 'pillars reminding [one] of Alexander the Great', 'in violence and fierceness each one [is] a Tamerlane' (in Fleischer 1986: 37–8).

'Ali picked up on the Turco-Mongol identity of the regime, devoting one of the four sections of his world history to Mongol and Turkish dynasties. Mongols earned the right to rule through the universal justice of their common law (yasa). Timur's conquests of Anatolia were justified because he restored the justice of the Shari'a. Ottoman subjects (Rumis) who are linked to the Turkish and Tatar tribes are 'a select community, and pure, pleasing people'; while other subjects are 'of confused ethnic origins' (in Fleischer 1986: 254). This was the most explicit statement so far in the Islamic world of an ethnic basis for the state. Osman II's unsuccessful reforms were in line with such a view.

This emphasis on the Sultan, kanun and nationality did not make 'Ali a 'secular' thinker. He actually condemned the Levy as contrary to the Shari'a. 'Religion and state (din ve devlet)' are distinguished, but not opposed; the sovereign is 'lord of prayer and coin' (hutbe ve sikke sahibi) (in Fleischer 1986: 279). 'Ali saw religion and the medrese system as the moral and intellectual bases of the state: piety, competence and expertise among the 'ulama are no less essential to the well-being of the polity. The Sultan is responsible for maintaining such qualities by, once again, appointing the right people to senior posts.

'Ali ascribed 'power and sovereignty (mulk ve saltanat)' to 'the destined rule of the Ottomans (devlet-i Osmaniyye)'. Here, he seems to be approaching a less personal and slightly more abstract notion of the state. Ottoman subjects are Rumi (lit. Romans) and their domains 'the land of Rum', 'the protected lands' (rather than, perhaps, the Sultan's personal possessions). Indeed, 'king and subjects, especially army leaders and statesmen, all constitute one organism'; 'Ali quoted with approval the saying that 'the head of a tribe is its servant'. On the other hand, generals and officials are still described as the Sultan's 'seeing eyes, his grasping hands, his speaking tongue'; and 'Ali's whole argument implied that the integrity of the system depended upon the character of the Sultan. In this respect, the state is identified with the Sultan; although, as a pious Muslim, 'Ali believed that there is no duty to obey Sultans if 'the purport of their orders turns out to be ... a veritable sin'.¹⁰

AL-AQHISARI AND STATUS GROUPS

The military setbacks of the 1590s brought the issue of governance to the forefront of public attention. A mutiny of senior officers in Transylvania and Wallachia (1596) shocked the Bosnian Hasan Kafi al-Aqhisari (1544–1616) so much that he gave up his position as kadi, so that, at the prompting of Allah, he could (as he put it) write a short, sharp, little book on governmental reform. His *Sources of Wisdom in the World Order* professed to draw on 'the old scholars of Islam and the books of the wise and great', that is the traditions of Jurisprudence and falsafa.[11] Al-Aqhisari's career was a complete contrast to 'Ali's; but his educational background and message were not dissimilar. He compared Austria's improvements in discipline and weapons to the Ottomans' indiscipline and lack of training. He identified the causes of deterioration as negligence in the administration of justice, appointment of incompetent officials, bribery and corruption.

Al-Aqhisari was the first writer of the decline-and-reform school to introduce the age-old idea of the division of society into four status groups based on occupation; this, he said, was of divine ordinance. The four orders were: (1) men of the sword – emperor (padishah), viziers, governors, commanders, soldiers; (2) men of the pen – religious scholars and those engaged in works of piety and knowledge, whose duty it is to write books, teach the Shari'a, and give advice that will lead both Sultan and people towards the good; (3) farmers, both Christian and Muslim, who rear cattle and produce cereals, fruit and wine: their work 'is the most necessary of all'; and (4) artisans and merchants, whose businesses are extremely varied (*Sources*, p. 146). The usual order had been (2), (1), (4), (3); it is possible that al-Aqhisari wanted to give encouragement to the soldiers and the farmers. He was unusual in giving Christians a place and accepting viniculture as normal. These groups are the basis of the order of the world (society).

Everyone must stay in the group to which they belong: it is especially harmful to draft farmers and artisans into the army, as has recently been happening in Croatia and Bosnia. This harms agriculture and leads to price rises. Everyone must belong to one of these groups; those who will not work 'are useless and should be killed'; this was what made Rome great (p. 147).

The foundations of government are justice, counsel, weapons and piety. Both the Prophet and Ardashir (Artaxerxes: the Persian emperor-sage) established the primacy of justice; the former when he said 'justice is a greater force in the hand of the emperor than religion itself', and the latter with his doctrine of the Circle of Power, that is the interdependence of all the parts of society: 'the emperor exists only ... because of soldiers; one can only maintain soldiers with money; money comes only from a rich, flourishing countryside; a rich, flourishing countryside comes only through a just and good government' (p. 147).

Regarding counsel, 'even the cleverest man needs the advice of others just as the best horse needs the whip, and the gentlest woman cannot survive without her husband. People see the things nearest and furthest away with their own eyes, but themselves they cannot see except with the help of a mirror.' Al-

Aqhisari also quoted Hindu proverbs and the saying that 'in war a clever person counts more than a thousand horsemen'. As for piety, this demands that we get rid of those 'new-fangled, so-called coffee-houses'.[12]

From this al-Aqhisari deduced the duties of the emperor. He must behave kindly towards all the four groups which make up society. Justice requires that he appoint viziers for their intelligence and experience, 'ulama for their piety and uprightness. As for piety, the emperor can inspire awe in his subjects only if (once again) he promotes the outstanding, is merciful to the weak, helps orphans, wards off enemies, and makes the roads secure for travellers (pp. 149–50).

Al-Aqhisari concluded on international relations, with an appeal for peace and the observance of treaties: 'it is a great sin to conduct war against those who want peace', and 'God gives over into the power of their enemy a people who break a treaty' (the Prophet said: p. 157). This was a radical adjustment to the ideology of jihad; a century would pass before the Ottoman government accepted it. Al-Aqhisari combined Iranian with Islamic ideas. He deduced what should be done from an Irano-Islamic view of government.

Other works written between c.1600 and 1630 discussed specific legal and administrative reforms. They identified the neglect of kanun as the cause of decline and looked back to the happier times of Süleyman, 'the lord of kanun (sahib-i kanun)'. For example, 'Ayn 'Ali Efendi summarised (1609) the kanun on timars and criminal jurisdiction, and wrote on the janissaries.[13] *The Laws of the Janissaries* attempted to systematise the rules for those who are 'the arm and the wing of the House of Osman' (in Fodor 1986: 229). It attacked the innovation of recruiting 'Turks-Murks [sic]' instead of men of the Levy.

WHY IS THE STATE IN DECLINE?

The next development was a more detailed consideration of the social dynamics behind the troubles; this was undertaken by Koçi Beg (d.c.1650), who wrote his *Epistle (Risale)* in 1630.[14] Koçi was born in Macedonia into a family of Albanian origin (his brother escaped to Russia and became a Christian). He had come to Istanbul as a young man and was educated at the Palace school. He served under Ahmad I (r.1603–17) and became an especially close adviser and confidant of the reforming Sultan Murad IV (r.1623–40). Koçi's primary concern was reform of the army; but he recognised that the failures of the army and the government had their roots in social problems. His perception of more deep-seated causes made his plea for reform more urgent, at times desperate.

Why is the state in such trouble? Why are our inhabitants worse off than they were? Koçi gave two main reasons: bad appointments, and misallocation of military fiefs. There has been unrest in the provinces for the past fifty years, some provinces have been lost, all because of the appointment of unworthy governors. Koçi's main remedies were to abolish bribery, appoint only worthy men as 'ulama, give state officials a reliable income, and draw up rules for the assignment of timars. He was particularly insistent about the need to give political and military posts only to people of a certain background and training;

even the 'satanic' Shah 'Abbas of Iran knows that men of the sword must be upright, well organised and hereditary, and must avoid luxury (*Epistle*, pp. 289–93, 307).

Military status should pass from father to son, whereas nowadays 'Turks' (that is, peasants and nomads from Anatolia), gypsies, Jews and townspeople are allowed in. Janissaries and elite troops should only be recruited from the Levy; Albanians, Bosnians, Greeks, Bulgarians and Armenians are especially suitable. In the good old days, he said, there was a core of government ministers who were either slaves of former viziers or recruits from border provinces such as Bosnia and Albania; they were all slaves (i.e. state servants), and all had a Palace training. They were therefore well disposed and faithful to the dynasty.[15] As Aziz Efendi (above, p. 219, n. 9) also put it, such persons 'recognise, each one of them, that willingness to sacrifice life and soul in the service of the state and the Sultanate is the way to earn admission to paradise' (p. 6). Once again we have the devshirme view of ethnic superiority, and a certain concept of the state.

According to Koçi Beg, good order in empire and religion and restoration of military power depend upon observance of the Shari'a. This in turn depends upon religious learning and, therefore, the appointment of worthy 'ulama. A reform of the system of religious appointments, especially of the Şeykülislam, is urgently needed. The quality of the 'ulama would be improved by giving them greater security of tenure (pp. 289–93).

Koçi came back again and again to the need to reform the timar system. Timars are nowadays no longer allotted to Holy Warriors for their military exploits or ability, but to venal officials, and even to commoners who are no use at fighting. Small timar-holders, once the core of the Islamic army, are reduced to wage labour. Due to this elevation of mercenaries and depression of timariots, 'the order of the world is taken away and the bond of human society in the state is broken'. 'If it is the earnest will of the padishah to organise the army, the most important thing is to restore to order the great and small timars, and to give villages and cornfields to men of the sword'. Justice must be restored and the peasantry well treated (pp. 306, 310, 317). God entrusted the common people to the Sultan-Caliph. Thus Koçi championed the cavalry (sipahi) class and was against relying on mercenaries.

These reforms are to be achieved by the personal authority of the Sultan and grand vizier, who should be empowered to act independently and without interference, and should not be subject to dismissal except for extremely serious reasons (pp. 276, 285, 325). In protest against harem politics, Koçi was insistent that no-one should be allowed to intervene between the Sultan and the grand vizier. The Sultan must rule in person, as Süleyman I did, not by delegation; he must keep an eye on the provinces for himself. He must be prepared to use force. Desperate as things are, if only the Sultan himself would take the right action immediately, the army could be restored and the dynasty saved (pp. 275, 306–12).

The most penetrating reform tract was *The Code of Action for the Rectification of Defects* (*Destur ul-Amel li-Islah il-Halel*: c.1653, in Turkish) by Katib Çelebi (Istanbul 1609–57: also known as Hajji Khalifa).[16] The reforms he proposed were yet more far-reaching, his tone yet more urgent. For the first time, Katib expressed actual pessimism about the prospects of reform. He had been born into a military family and educated as a secretary and accountant. After spending his early years in the army, he entered the treasury, but failed to gain promotion. A legacy enabled him to devote himself to research in history and geography. He was the first Ottoman author to use European sources; he wrote a brief description of religion and government in Europe.[17] His *Code of Action* was inspired by Sultan Mehmed IV's request to have the public deficit explained to him; Katib was apparently present when this was discussed by senior officials. It was written on the eve of the rise to power of Mehmed Köprülü, on whom reformers now pinned their hopes.

Katib redefined Ottoman problems by a general analysis of political society. 'Let it be known that the state (devlet), which means kingdom (mulk) and power (saltanat), consists of human society organised in a particular form or manner.' He made an elaborate comparison between society and body; he restated the principle of the four orders or 'pillars' of society (arkan (sing. rukn: lit. pillars) was used both of social groups and of humours of the body). Katib indulged in medical rhetoric. Society, like an individual, goes through stages of growth, maturity or stagnation, and decline. If we recognise these, we will understand better what is going on. Our problems are 'caused by the normal course of the world ordained by God and brought about by the nature of civilisation and human society'.[18]

Katib was the first modern author to be influenced by Ibn Khaldun.[19] He did not develop Ibn Khaldun's social analysis or use it as an investigative tool. He held to traditional monarchical theory, and he reiterated the doctrine of the four orders and the interdependence between government, army, money and peasantry. 'The human social body, which is made up of four chief members (arkan), and held together by the guide-rope of its leadership and government by means of the great men of the state (a'yan-i devlet) who correspond to the (body's) heart and natural vigour, is made secure by the sure hand of the all-high Sultan, who represents the rational soul. ' The four pillars are: (1) the 'ulama, (2) the 'askeri (warriors), (3) the merchants (tijjar), (4) the peasantry (re'aya). These correspond to the four liquids of life: (1) the 'ulama to blood, for 'knowledge is the cause of the social body's existence and preservation'; (2) warriors to phlegm – the insult may be intentional; (3) merchants to yellow gall; (4) farmers to black gall (*Code*, p. 120: derived from Galen).

This medical analogy is used to illustrate the factors leading to decline, and the drastic nature of the remedies needed. For health depends upon balance between the four life-liquids. Katib described the, in his view, unwarranted increase in military personnel to the detriment of agriculture as too much phlegm, a characteristic of old age, and harmful to the body. He used statistics to demonstrate the extent of the increase in military personnel and the consequent huge rises in state expenditure. Rather than increasing taxation, which would further denude the tax base, agriculture, the state budget should be balanced by reducing the armed forces (pp. 116, 125–8).

Katib painted the bleakest picture yet of social conditions. Corruption appears no longer as something which can be singled out and punished; rather, it is driving the system. Bad appointments are contrary to both the Shari'a and reason; even unbelievers like the European Christians forbid this. He perceived the main problem to be the poverty of the peasantry. Katib had seen for himself the depopulation of Anatolia; in the old days, emperors ensured that no village was left unoccupied. If undernourished, the peasantry like black gall turns poisonous. The root of the peasants' plight was excessive taxation. The army, on the other hand, was now seen as part of this problem. Katib was the first political writer anywhere to make systematic use of statistics, for which he used government sources (*Code*, pp. 121–4).

How can reform be brought about? Katib made the usual points of administrative morality. Corrupt officials must be removed. The great men of the empire and leaders of the army must devote themselves wholeheartedly to the devlet (state, dynasty). Soldiers should only perform their proper military functions. But he admits to some doubt: his proposals are 'at this time partly possible, partly impossible'. For the army is best equipped to root out extravagance, but it is at present incapable of doing so because so many of its members are given over to sensual pleasure, enjoying what they should be destroying, and so few are devoted to duty. Reduction of expenditure requires coercive measures in the form of sultanic decrees. Katib's solution here was not revival of kanun but rather 'a man of the sword (sahib-i seyf)', a strong and determined ruler (pp. 128–9). He means military dictatorship; he may well have had Mehmed Köprülü in mind. This was one possible outcome of Irano-Islamic ideology.

After the defeats by Habsburgs and Poles in 1683–1713, some of the Ottoman elite began to look more searchingly to the West and to support a more extensive adoption of European techniques and even the import of European culture, rather than restoration of an ideal past. The treaty of Carlowitz (1699) made a serious impact upon elite opinion. The process was at first tentative. Ahmed III (r.1703–30) and his grand vizier, Damat Ibrahim, developed a policy of openness to Europe, the 'tulip period' (1718–30). For the first time, Ottoman ambassadors were despatched to European courts. The first Ottoman printing-press was established (1727), and the government encouraged translation of European (especially French) works on military technology, tactics and organisation, and also on geography and history. The press was also intended to revive Muslim learning. There was still no change in basic outlook, and no adoption of Western social and political ideas. Amazingly, it was only in 1725–30 that even Ibn Khaldun was translated into Turkish and his approach to history and society became generally known (Lewis 1986: 529). And even this limited process of Westernisation was abruptly reversed when, following defeat on the eastern front by Nadir Shah (1730), a revolt of janissaries, supported by the 'ulama in the name of Islamic purity, led to the deposition of Ahmed III and the dismissal of Damat Ibrahim (1730). Their cultural policies were overturned; military reform was abandoned, the old ways resumed.

These defeats and social crises produced no new ideas. Şari Mehmed Paşa (Istanbul?–1717), who wrote an Advice-book for viziers and governors(1703),[20] and Na'ima (Aleppo 1655–1716), who reflected on contemporary politics in the introduction (c.1704)[21] to his official history of the Ottomans, are indicative rather of a drying-up of Irano-Islamic tradition. Şari, a grocer's son, became treasurer, was demoted, and was later executed for criticising a decision of the Sultan. Na'ima was a janissary's son, educated at the palace and sympathetic to the reform policies and pro-active leadership of Huseyn Köprülü: his writing may reflect discussions in the households of Ottoman leaders. His approach was conventional; he followed Katib Çelebi, often word for word, and did not look beyond the borders of Islam. Şari's and Na'ima's only idea of learning from Europe was espionage.

Both recited the power circle, but they had no new ideas about what should be done. Na'ima discussed the role of the 'ulama in the polity, perhaps because the current Şeykülislam, Feyzullah, a close confidant of the new Sultan Ahmed III, was an ardent opponent of reform. The two parallel hierarchies, he said, of the 'ulama under the Şeykülislam, and the bureaucracy under the grand vizier, should balance and check one another. The 'ulama's role was to give moral guidance. Citing the example of Muhammad, who used 'those practical everyday means which were and are at hand', Na'ima supported the policy of making 'peace with the Christians of the whole earth, so that [the Ottoman state] may be put into order and [the Ottomans] may have respite' (pp. 70–1).

It is interesting that both Şari and Na'ima repeated earlier pleas for strong personal government by Sultan or grand vizier. Na'ima admired Murad IV's approach: 'it was absolutely indispensable to terrify the general populace with the well-tempered sword'; Murad was right to shut down coffee-houses and barbers' shops, because that was where people met to criticise the government (p. 94). Şari said the grand vizier should be 'a religious and upright man', 'like Aristotle in sagacity', and should be given complete freedom of action (pp. 64–5).

Ibrahim Müteferrika (1674–1745) wrote *Rational Bases for the Polities of Nations (Usul al-hikam fi nizam al-umam)* in 1731–2 for the new Sultan Mahmud I (r.1730–54).[22] A Hungarian convert to Islam, he founded the first Ottoman printing-press and was special adviser to Ahmed III, then a diplomat; he promoted anti-Habsburg movements among Hungarians. His writing was in the Advice mode; the emphasis, however, was not so much on reviving Islamic or patrimonial practices as on adopting European ones. He gave Peter the Great as the example of what could be achieved by military reforms on the European model. He was aware that people would only accept change if it was proposed in terms of Islamic orthodoxy. In this respect, he was the first in a long line of apostles of modernisation in the Islamic world (see below, Chapter 25).

Islam would triumph because of the inherent superiority of its Religious Law and its commitment to Holy War; their religion gave the Ottomans greater courage. 'Our failure is not due to the inadequacy of … our political laws and of the Şeriat.'[23] Müteferrika maintained the theory of four social groups and the Circle of Power, in which he gave the military a key role; people should stay in their own class (Aksan 1995: 187). Ottoman decline was due to neglect of the Şeriat, unsuitable appointments and bribery.

But above all, it was due 'to our ignorance of the new methods of the Europeans'. Here, he appealed to the Islamic taste for knowledge in general, and at the same time urged recognition of the fact that others had some knowledge which Muslims (at present) lacked. Also, 'it is of the utmost importance to understand the malicious behaviour, the power, the populations, and the general condition of neighbouring states'. Müteferrika introduced an argument that would much later become part of modern Muslims' intellectual response to Western hegemony: Europeans had developed rationality because their religion did so little to help them solve real-life problems. 'The Christian nations are not ruled by divine mandates ... and, having no Şeriat to settle their conflicts, their orders are based on ... rules invented by reason' (in Berkes 1964: 43–5). This in turn had enabled the Europeans to develop military methods superior to those of the Ottomans. It was perfectly legitimate to use the tactics of unbelievers against themselves. Such tactics would in fact then be put to higher use. For example, knowledge of geography would promote 'unity among the Muslim countries which are [at present] unaware of each other' (in Berkes 1964: 44). Here was an implicit distinction between the knowledge needed to solve practical problems, in which it may be admitted that unbelievers are superior, and religious knowledge.[24] Müteferrika accepted the paradox that Muslim knowledge of reality is inherently superior, but European ideas have proved more successful in practical life.

In political theory, Müteferrika introduced a slightly more up-to-date classification of types of government. These are: (1) monarchy; here 'the people obey a just and wise sovereign and follow his opinions'; (2) aristocracy; here notables elect one of themselves as head but he remains 'dependent upon the rest in counsel and decision, lest he ... deviate from ... justice' (an allusion to Venice?); and (3) democracy; here 'sovereignty belongs to the people'. He gave a brief description of parliamentary representation and ministerial accountability, with the Netherlands and England as examples (in Berkes 1964: 42). Müteferrika was thus the first Muslim to show any real awareness of European politics; the reason was presumably personal experience and increased contact through diplomacy.

THE USE OF HISTORY AND OF IBN KHALDUN

The only glimmer of innovation in the Ottoman school as a whole was the use of history and of Ibn Khaldun. Katib Çelebi, a man of independent means, was the only original theorist of the decline-and-reform school. He believed that history and contemporary experience were the tools of social analysis, and he encouraged the Sultan to read history. He sponsored the translation of Latin chronicles and composed a 'Guide for the Perplexed on the History of the Greeks, Byzantines, and Christians'.[25]

Ibn Khaldun's *Muqaddima* was first rediscovered by the Ottomans only in the mid-seventeenth century; Na'ima described him as 'the greatest of all historians' and his *Muqaddima* as embracing 'the whole of knowledge' (in Lewis 1986: 529). He mentioned without comment some of Ibn Khaldun's criteria for assessing historical evidence. For Ibn Khaldun, the formulation of general social laws was essential to historical knowledge. Inferences from his theory could have been applied to Ottoman experience. Katib Çelebi used the terms 'civilisation ('umran)' and 'human society (ijtima')' (see above, p. 172), and thought that Ottoman society would pass through the stages of maturity or stagnation and decline as established by Ibn Khaldun's theory. Ibn Khaldun may have been responsible for the fact that appeals for the restoration of the good old kanun now dropped out of Ottoman writing. Huseyn Hezarfenn said (1669) that one should not try to restore the customary law of earlier times because society changes and 'every age has its örf ... The desire to adapt the örf of these days to that of the past is a false and stupid idea which is borne of ignorance'.[26]

Na'ima quoted Ibn Khaldun's statement that history can teach one 'what are the causes and the springs of action ... which bring decay and decline to the civilisation of mankind'. In order to understand events, one has to grasp the 'inherent qualities' of a particular state, its roots and principles of action (Thomas, pp. 111–13). Na'ima applied Ibn Khaldun's theory of the stages of development to his own society. The Ottomans were now in the stage of 'contentment or surfeit'; people shy away from public office; government expenditure exceeds its revenues. Na'ima concluded from this that financial reforms were necessary and government appointments must be carefully monitored; people must be roused by sermons and songs (p. 80). He recommended astrology, which Ibn Khaldun had dismissed. Thus Ibn Khaldun was used merely to justify what was already familiar. Rather than developing Ibn Khaldun's use of observation and empirical generalisation, Na'ima drew the somewhat mystical conclusion that 'many secrets are concealed in that divine necessity which causes the epochs to change' (pp. 110–11).

In general, the Ottoman Advice school addressed the Sultan with conventional flattery, but they were nonetheless frank and personal in drawing attention to the problems confronting the state. Please excuse my boldness, Aziz Efendi said, but you must be told how bad things really are. The Sultan is asked please to keep this 'reality-encapsulating report' to himself (only one copy survives). These authors did experience intellectual freedom within a very closed circle. They relied upon the discretion of those whom they advised. There was no repetition of the fate of Ibn Muqaffa'. Al-Aqhisari, on the other hand, set the tone of moral urgency and translated his Advice into Turkish (1597) so that 'army officers, the religiously learned, the Sultan's officials and advisers might read it and understand its clear, simple message' (*Sources*, pp. 143–4).

The decline-and-reform authors were motivated by a profound commitment to the state, this state, and the Sultan: the attitude of slave or personal follower was evolving into one of civic self-sacrifice among some Levy men: 'order and command belong to our Sultan; we stand ready to sacrifice our bodies and our souls on behalf of our Sultan' (Aziz Efendi, p. 9). They stand for the antithesis of familial or corporate self-interest which they see as corruption.

What these authors also had in common was their disgust at the gulf between theory and practice in Ottoman politics and society. In their view, failure in battle was the result of moral and social decay – a characteristically but not exclusively Islamic sentiment. According to the norms expressed in the Şeriat and kanun, offices should be allocated on merit, timars for military service; whereas government posts are now being given to favourites in return for bribes, and timars to tax-farmers. The peasantry are exploited, agriculture wrecked; state coffers run dry. The soldiers are badly paid, badly trained, indisciplined and lacking modern equipment. The underlying reason is that the socio-economic system designed to support them has fallen into disrepair.

The Ottoman theorists' response to crises was to invoke elements of the Irano-Islamic tradition, emphasising especially the Iranian ideology of patrimonial government and the social orders. The Sultan's function is to uphold 'the good order of the world (nizam-i 'alem)', defined as the Circle of Power and the four pillars: it is as simple as that. This is coupled with reminders of the Sultan's moral duties in Islamic language. And beneath references to the Sultan's wisdom, justice and divine inspiration, lay a moral sub-text: God be praised, our Sultan is so wise, 'he enquires into the affairs of the governors and knows the righteous among them, he diligently concerns himself with the protection and preservation of all his most humble subjects' (Aziz Efendi, p. 3).

Throughout their writings, they implicitly assumed that a Sultan or grand vizier with sufficient good will and strength of character could accomplish all their goals and restore Ottoman greatness. He could remove even the most deep-rooted social evils, punish exploiters, rescue the peasantry and re-establish the fourfold order of society. The Sultan, if he would only get round to it, could remould society from the top. This unquestioning faith in monarchy or dictatorship was both Islamic and Iranian.

The Şeriat and kanun were inviolable, but apart from this the theorists expressed no constitutional opinions. It never occurred to them to consider alternative forms of government, far less to discuss the premises of state authority.

Religion is not prominent in their works. But this is not to say that secular attitudes were replacing religious ones. State and religion remained inseparable; religion dominated public discourse. It enjoined good citizenship: in appealing for good conduct in government, Lutfi Pasha bade the grand vizier put away all private interests: 'everything he does should be for God and in God and for the sake of God' (in Lewis 1954: 71). God is the public interest.

Some political reformers criticised the conservatism and narrow-mindedness of some of the 'ulama; 'Ali with his mystical leanings was scathing about religious standards. He attacked lower-class 'ulama for refusing 'to consider that new insights or new works are possible' (in Fleischer 1986: 259). In his *Balance of Truth* (*Mizan al-Haqq*: 1656), Katib Çelebi attacked the populism and anti-intellectualism of the neo-orthodox Kadizadeler (see below, p. 272), and 'that denial of science which is so prevalent among the people'.[27] When Mehmed Köprülü took office later that year, he dealt severely with the Kadizadeler. Katib argued that the educational curriculum should be opened up to include once again the 'rational' disciplines of mathematics, astronomy, medicine and natural science – that is to say, an element of secular learning. In the good old days of Süleyman I, 'scholars who combined the study of the sacred sciences with philosophy were held in high renown'. And Katib found a nice precedent in early Islam: although the first Imams banned Greek learning, once religion was securely established, 'the prevailing view was that it was important for Muslims to know the science of the truth of things. Hence they translated the books of the ancient peoples into Arabic' (*Balance*, pp. 25–6). Na'ima wanted Huseyn Köprülü's policy (siyaset) to combine human rationality with the Şeriat (Thomas, p. 76). Thus some reformers, and especially Katib, did recognise an intellectual problem behind Ottoman decline.

ADVOCATES OF STRICTER RELIGIOUS OBSERVANCE

Others saw neglect of religion as the primary cause of decline and therefore wanted the polity to become more strictly Islamic. In fact, the most common response to crisis and perceived decline was to demand the cranking-up of religious observances. This could also be in the interests of the dynasty. As jihad brought diminishing or negative returns, conspicuous adherence to the Islamic Code became an increasingly important factor in the Sultan's and the dynasty's credibility. Thus one response of the dynasty to military defeats was to turn up the volume of internal religious transmissions. The Ottomans had always been proud of their Islamic credentials; but they had accepted non-religious elements in their polity, such as kanun, the Levy and religious minorities. Ottoman ideology oscillated between the concept of the Sultan as emperor ruling over diverse peoples and faiths and the concept of him as Caliph of Muslims. The Safavids, by contrast, began with great religious fervour and adopted patrimonial tendencies as they went along. Here, the Ottomans possessed a certain advantage because they could claim that the stricter development of true religion would show how wonderful the regime really was, and restore it to its pristine vigour. They had not yet exhausted the potential of religious ideology.

In response to Shi'ite disturbances in eastern Anatolia, Süleyman I emphasised Sunni orthodoxy as the state norm.[28] Islamicisation appealed to all strata in Muslim society. In the seventeenth century, public sentiment seems to have turned to the roots of Islam as the bastion of order and the best hope for the resuscitation of the state. Increasing attention was paid to the religious qualities of the Ottoman ruler and the Ottoman armies. Fewer and fewer non-Muslims were recruited into the military-administrative elite. The dividing line between 'askeri (upper, military class) and re'aya (lower, taxpaying class) was to some extent replaced by that between Muslim and non-Muslim.[29] The 'ulama were elevated in the public mind as 'pillars of the throne-hall of faith and kingship, the firmly-rooted legs of the structure of empire and community' (in Zilfi 1988: 233). There was a payoff: the 'ulama were 'expected to be a unifying force in society, both legitimating and mediating the sovereign authority' (Zilfi 1988: 231).

In the 1630s, a group of strictly observant 'ulama (known as the Kadizadeler: followers of Kadizadi Mehmet Efendi, d. 1635) made a bid for the moral high ground in public life with a campaign against the moral laxity of the upper classes. Their catechism was 'probably the most widely read document of the century' (Zilfi 1988: 202), and it condemned everything that could be seen as a departure from the strict interpretation of the Code (including drinking coffee and dancing). They used direct public exhortation and demonstrations as a form of hisba to enforce their purism.

An Advice work of 1640 emphasised the common interests of 'religion, dynasty and Muslim Community (din, devlet, jama'a)', and of 'Shari'a, din, devlet'.[30] It urged the new Sultan to employ only good, pious Muslims; this was part of a conservative reaction against Murad IV's reforms.

Non-Islamic features were in fact steadily extruded from public life. The Levy was discontinued. Non-religious schools were converted into medreses. Members of the 'ulama attacked kanun for provisions which were contrary to the Shari'a, or for its very existence: the Shari'a alone suffices. In practice, the scope of kanun contracted, while that of the Shari'a expanded. Kadis 'tended to assume more and more administrative and financial duties ... to the point where, in many areas, they were in fact the local government'.[31] The Şeykülislams, who under Süleyman I had acquired power to appoint and dismiss senior Judges and medrese Professors, in the seventeenth century intervened increasingly in politics; they were especially prominent in opposing reforms, which were portrayed as irreligious innovation (bida').

The defeats of 1683–1718 created a legitimacy crisis for the Sultans. They sometimes turned to religious orthodoxy and pious observance as the ultimate bases of their title to govern. And indeed in the later seventeenth century there was an 'upsurge in Muslim orthodoxy'. A decree was issued (1696) to the effect that 'all the public and private affairs are completely and exclusively regulated by the Quran and the Shari'a' (Heyd 1973: 154–5): from now on, the Sultan went on, actions must be justified on the authority of the Shari'a alone without reference to kanun. Denied success in jihad, Sultans presented themselves as pre-eminent in ritual and observance.

THE BEGINNINGS OF WESTERNISATION

It was especially in the Ottoman domains from c.1700 onwards that a new relationship between Islam and the West, based upon a perception of the technical, military and economic superiority of the West, manifested in loss of territory, reconquests by Christian states, and the economic and (in certain fields) cultural hegemony of Western powers, first developed. This evoked diverse responses from intellectuals in the Muslim world, culminating in the twin movements of modernism and fundamentalism.

The process of Westernisation was slow in starting (Aksan 1993). During the eighteenth century, interaction with Europeans and their ways of thought remained limited; Ottoman political society maintained its traditional Irano-Islamic thought-patterns and practices. There appears to have been little or no change in Religious Jurisprudence. Several members of the scribal bureau-cracy, which dominated the administration, were open to European practices and ideas; but the ayan and the ulema were the dominant powers in society, and they remained opposed to any shake-up of the system. Sultans themselves, when they wanted reform, had little freedom of action. 'Here it's not like in France where the king is sole master; you have to persuade the ulema, the men of the law, the ministers in office and those no longer in office' (a French observer, 1786: in Heyd 1961: 77).

Some advances were made in military technology and organisation, inspired by European models, but all attempts to overhaul public finances and reform public life drained away in the diffuse solidarities of Ottoman public life. Resistance to systemic change was rooted in existing structures and backed by the ulema and their version of Islamic orthodoxy.

Russia was now as great a threat as the Habsburgs. The Russian empire, like the Ottomans, was an autocratic land power deriving its political legitimacy from religion and dynasty, and also in the Russian case from nationalism. Their relationships with the European world were in some ways parallel. For the Russians as for the Ottomans, political legitimacy derived from belief in the religious mission of their state. The Russians based their claim to rule and their imperial mission on nationhood, the Ottomans on dynasty. The Russians, due no doubt to religious similarities, found it easier to learn from the West.

Ottoman political thought was dominated, even more than before, by their decline in relation to the West and Russia. The treaty of Kücük Kaynarca (1774) made the Russian Tsar protector of Orthodox Christians throughout the Ottoman empire. This was an unprecedented intrusion into the sovereignty of a great Islamic power, though the Sultan was reciprocally recognised as reli-gious leader (Caliph) of the Crimean Tatars, now under Russian rule. Pregnant as pretexts for intervention, these moves signalled a developing interplay between religious communalism and international politics.

Ahmed Resmi Efendi (Ottoman diplomat: 1700–83) used the theory of decline to justify the policy of negotiation and peace in place of Holy War, following defeats by the Russians in 1769–74. States in decline ought not to expand but to be content with their boundaries and seek peace. 'War is not always the best thing ... Prosperity and power ... are dependent upon peace and reconciliation with the enemy when circumstances so require.' The division of the earth into separate peoples with natural boundaries may even be God's will (on the basis of Q. 7:128).[32] Resmi did not deny the principle of Holy War, but, like Ibn Rushd in twelfth-century Spain, thought it impractical under present circumstances.

The French Revolution of 1789 provoked some typically conservative comment. The head of the civil bureaucracy criticised (1798) its attack on religion: 'it is well known that the ultimate basis of the cohesion and order of every state is a firm grasp of the roots and branches of holy law [and] religion ... [t]he control of the subjects cannot be encompassed by political means alone'. Social stability depends on the fear of God. His severest criticism was of people who 'set their hearts on equality and freedom, through which they hoped to attain perfect bliss in this world, in accordance with the lying teachings ... ' (in Lewis 1968: 66). De Maistre would have liked this.

On the other hand, revolutionary tracts were translated into Turkish. Above all, the ease with which Bonaparte conquered Egypt (1798) showed the helplessness of Muslim forces before a modern European army. Selim III's reform programme of 1789–1807 was, once again, a response to military failures. He set up a new type of military and fiscal organisation (the New Order: Nizam-i Cedid – a term also used to describe the French Revolution).[33] He justified reforms on the basis of the Circle of Power and the traditional principle of using 'the enemies' tricks to overcome them' (Inalçik 1964: 49). In the end, Selim III's reforms, like so many before them, fell foul of the janissaries and the ulema. Reaction was initiated by a group of Balkan notables (ayan); a fetwa from the Şeykülislam declared Selim III unfit for the Caliphate, and he was deposed.

But on this occasion, the rebels went further: they extracted a pledge from the new Sultan that no action would be taken against them. The chronicler records that this was unprecedented (Inalçik 1964: 51–2). And the ayan of Rumelia and Anatolia now combined to take power away from the janissaries. They signed a 'covenant of union (Sened-i Ittifak)', in the form of a Shari'a contract, with Mahmud II (r.1808–39). In it, the vezirs, ulema and provincial ayan dynasties, in return for protection for notables against government intrusion, promised 'always to respect the sovereign authority of the Sultan and the orders of the grand vezir ... and to take action against any rebellion'. The ayan also swore to protect the common people and adhere to tax regulations. This entrenchment of the position of the notables was reminiscent of feudal contracts between king and barons in medieval Europe. Utterly conservative in intent, this was also, in the context of patrimonial monarchy, a revolutionary document. There were no provisions to enforce it.

The overriding concern was to preserve the dynastic state (Aksan 1995: 184). Some senior ulema were also coming to the view that adoption of Western military techniques was permissible as an example of fighting the enemy with his own weapons; they argued that the Europeans had taken the idea of a salaried bureaucracy from the Şeriat. Some were now prepared to adapt the Religious Code and justify alliances with unbelievers and even recognition of the independence of former Muslim territory. Modernisation could thus be defended as part of the obligation to obey the Sultan in anything not contrary to the Şeriat (Heyd 1961: 74–6, 88).

The next reform movement was again initiated from the top, by Mahmud II (1826). This time, the janissaries' revolt against military reorganisation was anticipated and vigorously suppressed; the janissaries were finally disbanded ('the Beneficent Event'). This removed the main obstacle to military reform. Mahmud abolished timars (1831) and brought the finances of Religious Trusts under the Sultan. He thus set out, as Moltke (writing 1835–9) put it, 'to unite the whole plenitude of power in his own hand' (Lewis 1968: 89, 126) – in other words, a radical centralisation of political power along European absolutist lines, and also in accordance with earlier calls for dictatorship. The balance of power within the government was shifting towards Westernising bureaucrats.

NOTES

1. Howard (1988). On what follows, see Shaw (1976), Gerber (1994), Kunt (1983), Inalçik (1980), Heyd (1973), Zilfi (1988), Şerif Mardin, 'Power, Civil Society and Culture in the Ottoman Empire', *Comparative Studies in Society and History* 11 (1969), pp. 258–81.

2. Ömer Lütfi Barkan, 'The Price Revolution of the Sixteenth Century', *Journal of Middle Eastern Studies* 6 (1975), pp. 23–4; Kunt (1983: 56); Zilfi (1988: 214).

3. See in general Fleischer (1983); Fodor (1986); Howard (1988). Many of these writings remain unedited and unsatisfactorily translated.

4. Inalçik (1969: 106); I am grateful to Dr Metin Kunt for information about this work.

5. See above, p. 213. His *Asafname* is ed. and trans. R. Tschudi (Berlin: Mayer & Müller, 1910).

6. Fleischer (1986), reviewed by Rhoads Murphey in *IJMES* 21 (1989), pp. 243–55.

7. Trans. Andreas Tietze, *Mustafa 'Ali's Counsel for Sultans of 1581*, 2 vols (Vienna: Verlag der österreichischen Akademie der Wissenschaften, 1979–82).

8. *Counsel* 2: 93; Fleischer (1986: 206).

9. *Counsel* 2: 110; Fleischer (1986: 96).

10. *Counsel* 1: 17, 20, 25; 2: 103; Fleischer (1986: 208).

11. Trans. E. von Thalloczy-Karacson, 'Eine Staatschrift des Molla Hassan Elkjafi', *Archiv für slavische Philologie* 32 (1910), pp. 139–58 at p. 145; Nagel (1981: vol. 2, pp. 156–61).

12. Pp. 152, 155. In renaissance Italy, it had been remarked that one letter by the famous humanist Salutati was worth 1,000 Florentine horse.

13. Fodor (1986); Howard (1988); Rhoads Murphey, 'The Veliyyuddin Telhis: notes on sources and interrelationships between Koçi Beg and contemporary writers of Advice to Kings', *Belleten* 43 (1979), pp. 547–71.

14. Trans. W. F. A. Bernhauer, 'Kogabeg's Abhandlung', *ZDMG* 15 (1861), pp. 272–332. See *EI* 5: 248–9; E. Rosenthal (1958: 226–8); Nagel (1981: vol. 2, pp. 153–5); Lewis (1954: 76–7).

15. *Epistle*, pp. 279, 285, 325–6; Lewis (1954: 76).

16. Trans. W. F. A. Bernhauer, 'Hagi Chalfa's Dustür', *ZDMG* 11 (1857), pp. 110–32. See E. Rosenthal (1958: 228–33); Lewis (1986: 78–81); *EI* 4: 760b–2a. I am grateful to Dr Metin Kunt for helping me to understand the translation in the light of the original.

17. V. L. Ménage, 'Three Ottoman Treatises on Europe', in Bosworth (ed.) (1971: 421–32).

18. *Code*, p. 118; E. Rosenthal (1958: 228).

19. Fleischer (1983: 199); Lewis (1986: 528–30).

20. Ed. and trans. W. L. Wright, *Ottoman Statecraft: The Books of Counsel for Vezirs and Governors of Şari Mehmed Pasha, the Defterdar* (Princeton NJ: Princeton University Press, 1935).

21. Trans. Lewis V. Thomas, *A Study of Naima* (New York: New York Press, 1972).

22. *EI* 7: 996b–8a; Mardin (1960: 416–17); Berkes (1964: 42–5); Aksan (1995: 186–8); Ménage, 'Ottoman Treatises', pp. 424–9.

23. In Berkes (1964: 45); see Aksan (1993: 56).

24. Compare the distinction between practical and theoretical knowledge expounded by the Falasifa, derived from Plato and Aristotle: see above, p. 64.

25. Ménage, 'Ottoman Treatises', pp. 421–3.

26. In Heyd (1973: 170–1); see Lewis (1954: 81–2, 86).

27. Trans. G. L. Lewis (London: Allen & Unwin, 1957), p. 24.
28. Elke Eberhard, *Osmanische Polemik gegen die Safaviden im 16. Jahrhundert* (Freiburg im Breisgau: Schwarz, 1970).
29. I. Metin Kunt, 'Transformation of Zimmi into Askeri', in Benjamin Braude and Bernard Lewis, *Christians and Jews in the Ottoman Empire: The Functioning of a Plural Society* (New York: Holmes & Meyers, 1982), vol. 1, pp. 55–67.
30. W. F. A. Bernhauer, 'Das Nasihatname', *ZDMG* 18 (1864), p. 721. This work is sometimes ascribed to Koçi Beg, a view upheld by Rhoads Murphey (personal communication).
31. Shaw (1976: 136); Gerber (1994: 181).
32. Berkes (1964: 57); Aksan (1995: 196); R. A. Abou-El-Haj, 'Ottoman Attitudes toward Peace-making: The Karlowitz case', *Der Islam* 51 (1974), pp. 131–7.
33. Lewis (1968: 57); Shaw (1971).

Part V Islam and the West

The Age of Modernism
c.1830–1920

25

The nineteenth and twentieth centuries saw little change or development in the *basics* of Islamic political thought.[1] Despite the aspirations of some intellectuals, there was to be no Islamic Thomas Aquinas or Martin Luther. The great thinkers of earlier times have up to now had no successor. Rather, there have been adaptations, and new strategies. The main characteristic of this period has been that political thought was dominated by the West, either as a model of how societies could and should develop, or as an 'other' and enemy. The one exception is Shi'ite political theology; this developed in new ways under its own momentum.

Islamic intellectuals reacted to the West either, on the one hand, by syncretism, justified by seeing certain Western ideas as expressions of true Islam; or, on the other hand, by revivalism, going back to the sources of revelation. Modernism and fundamentalism were driven by the experience of Europe's technical and military superiority and its economic penetration and exploitation. They may be defined, and to a large extent they defined themselves, by their relationship to the West. Modernism was an adaptation of religious ideas and practices to take account of what the West had achieved, and to improve upon it. Fundamentalism was a return to a supposedly original core Islamic praxis as a way of overcoming the West. Fundamentalism came after modernism but has not replaced it. Today, both movements are alive and thriving.

Each involved analysis and reappraisal of Islamic and European cultural histories. The underlying aspiration common to both was the desire to revive Islam by going back to its first principles as set out in the Qur'an and parts of the sunna. The ultimate objective for both was to get rid of Western hegemony. Where they differed was that modernism identified some of Islam's basic principles as identical to the political values of European parliamentary liberalism; values which had become submerged in Islamic countries due to despotism – the Mu'awiya phenomenon (see above, p. 15) – and which, it was alleged, Europe had borrowed from Islam.

The decline of the Islamic empire-states and the experiences of Western colonialism, together with the improved communications which this brought with it, served to reunite the dar al-Islam. There has been cross-fertilisation between Sunni and Shi'ite reformers. Awareness of what is going on in different parts of the House of Islam has been greater than before.

THE OTTOMAN TANZIMAT (REFORM) (1839–71)

Between the Crimean War (1854–6), which found the Ottomans allied to two liberal powers and on the winning side, and the 1914–18 war, which found them allied to two Euro-Christian monarchies and on the losing side, a romance blossomed between Islamic intellectuals and the European phenomenon.[2] This was at a time when Christian and post-Christian states were spreading their tentacles all over the globe. During the mid- to late–nineteenth century, France consolidated its hold on north-western Africa; the British gained control of Egypt and Sudan; the Dutch ruled what is now Indonesia; the British ruled Malaya. Russia conquered vast tracts of Eurasia, including the old Muslim heartland of Transoxania. The French Revolution had made a strong impact on Christian minorities in the Ottoman empire; the Serbs and Greeks took to heart the ideal of national self-determination. Greece had become the first of several European-style nation-states on former Ottoman territory (1829). Partly due to Russian support for the liberation of her fellow-Orthodox, Romania, Bulgaria and Serbia gained independence (1878).

Barely half of the dar al-Islam remained under Islamic rule. The remaining Islamic polities were virtually powerless in world politics. The shrinking Ottoman devlet looked to Germany for support. Britain and Russia competed for economic control of Iran, which was weakened by the self-serving Qajar dynasty, as part of 'the great game' of central Asia.

Modernism began in the Ottoman empire as part of its programme of Westernising reforms, to which it devoted more energy than any other Islamic state. The later Ottoman state thus formed a bridge between traditional patrimonial government and the modern state. The setbacks of the late eighteenth and early nineteenth centuries, culminating in the loss of Egypt and Greece, had an increasing impact on domestic politics, and made a deep impression on intellectuals. Europe's successes in war, technology and economic development began to be attributed more specifically to the European legal and political system. Ebubekir, for example, a diplomat in Vienna (1792–3), had noted admiringly how 'the laws ... and taxes laid down by their kings are observed properly by high and low persons' (Shaw 1971: 96). In Europe there was, he went on, freedom of speech and trade, freedom in daily life generally. 'They have no religious law', he added perceptively (except that marriage is subject to religious rules, and not always that in the case of monarchs). Ottoman reformers looked above all to France as a model (Shaw 1976: 266).

The Tanzimat (reform, reorganisation, regulation) edict of 1839, issued in the name of the new Sultan Abdulmecit I (r.1839–76) and published simultaneously in Turkish and French, went beyond earlier administrative reforms. For the first time, an official decree in the House of Islam, indeed issued by the premier Islamic state, adopted the language of European political thought. It initiated a series of far-reaching institutional reforms during the Tanzimat period (1839–71). It was also partly aimed at securing British and French support against Muhammad 'Ali, the first ruler of fully independent Egypt (r.1805–48), in Syria, by demonstrating the liberalising intentions of the

Ottoman government, especially towards its Christian subjects.

Muhammad 'Ali himself had responded to the European example by constructing a centralised bureaucratic state in the European mode with a national army. He undertook economic development, creating through monopolies an updated version of patrimonial monarchy. His response to a translation of Machiavelli's *Prince* shows that he did not think Europe could teach him much about the art of ruling: 'I did not find much that was new in the first ten pages, but I hoped that it might improve; but the next ten pages were not better, and the last are mere commonplace. I see clearly that I have nothing to learn from Machiavelli. I know many more tricks than he knew' (in A. Hourani 1983: 52). Tahtawi (1801–73), writing in Egypt in the late 1860s, owed his intellectual formation to his stay in Paris (1826–31), where he had drunk at the well of Montesquieu and Rousseau; he combined the Middle Eastern tradition of strong central authority and the four social orders with an urgent plea for education, civic virtue and patriotism.[3]

A further Ottoman reform decree, issued during the Crimean war (1856), was aimed even more specifically at improving the position of religious minorities, and it too was designed partly for European consumption. But these measures were also based on 'a genuine belief that the only way to save the empire was to introduce European-style reforms' (Zürcher 1998: 59); and they were justified on the grounds that this was at the same time a fuller implementation of Islamic norms ('countries not governed by the şeriat cannot prevail': Tanzimat decree, in Deringil 1998: 9). The ideals of 'justice égale pour tous' and 'protection des faibles' (proclaimed on a medallion, 1850: in Deringil 1998: 27) could equally well come from Islamic tradition or the European Enlightenment.

A new Supreme Council of Reforms was set up to undertake legislation aimed at restoring Islam and the state; the Sultan promised to obey its laws. The Ottoman central government was reorganised, with new ministries, consultative assemblies, and 'a complete hierarchical system of provinces and subdivisions ... largely based on French practice' (1864). A new penal code (1843) was to apply equally to Muslims and non-Muslims, with special courts to hear cases between Muslims and non-Muslims. A new civil code (Mejelle: 1870), based on the Shari'a but modified by the Sultan's officials, was administered through state courts;[4] the Shari'a itself was thus reduced to a family law for Muslims.

The most noticeable change in official political language was the introduction of the word 'subject' (teb'a: a neologism: Mardin 1960: 425) to refer to inhabitants of the empire – as distinct from categories based on religion or occupation which had been current up to now (Muslim, peasant and so on). The Tanzimat edict stated that there must be 'guarantees insuring to our subjects perfect security for life, honour and fortune' (in A. Hourani 1983: 46). The Sultan declared that 'the difference of religion and sect among the subjects is something concerning only their persons and not affecting their rights of citizenship. As we are living all in the same country under the same government, it is wrong to make discriminations among us' (Abdulmecit I, 1846 in Inalçik 1964: 57–8). The 1856 decree was stronger:

Every distinction or designation tending to make any class whatsoever of the subjects of my Empire inferior to another because of their religion, language or race, shall be for ever effaced from the laws ... of the empire ... As all forms of religion are and shall be freely professed in my dominions, no subject of the empire shall be in any way annoyed on this account and no-one shall be forced to change his religion.

Appointments are 'wholly dependent on my sovereign will, all subjects of my empire, without distinction of nationality [sc. or religion], shall be admissible to public employment ... according to their ... merit' (in Shaw 1976: 125). This introduced, at least in theory, a striking amount of religious toleration, similar to that found in the more liberal states of Europe.

Another important innovation was that tax-farming was replaced by central collection of taxes through paid agents: all subjects were to be taxed on the same basis. The Tanzimat measures were decreed by the Sultan and implemented by his officers. They greatly increased the scope of the central government (as their opponents pointed out).

All this certainly did not mean that religious, occupational or hereditary status became much less important in practice (any more than in European countries), although the age-old theory of four hereditary status groups based upon occupation did now disappear. The conceptual implications of these moves were, however, considerable. 'Subject' implied a civil agent with rights and duties as a member of the state. It implied a closer and more direct relationship between the Sultan and his subjects; it implicitly strengthened the Sultan's position by ignoring intermediaries between ruler and subject. Such a relationship had been one of the bases of modern statehood in Europe, going back to the later Middle Ages but still in the process of implementation. It was in line with previous Ottoman reform programmes, and was surely just what was intended. One of the first undertakings of the reformers was to end the quasi-servile status of Balkan peasants. Subjects now became, in theory, a uniform category as 'Ottomans (Osmanli)'. Only as Caliph did the Sultan remain in a special relationship to Muslims. Thus, as in Europe, dynasty was providing a conceptual path from a society based on status to one based on citizenship.

Religious toleration had a precedent in the Islamic law regarding dhimmi (protected people), but what was enunciated here went far beyond that; it was clearly based on current Western, especially French, ideology. There was also a clear precedent in earlier Ottoman praxis for the elevation of the Sultan in relation to all the peoples of his empire; the role given to civil law had a precedent in kanun. Thus, probably due to its earlier history, the Ottoman empire found it easier than most to go in for a *degree* of secularisation. Here, for the first time, ideas and practices from outside the Islamic world were explicitly applied to a Muslim state. The Ottoman domain, under pressure from its rivals, was moving towards assimilation with the Euro-Christian empire-states, as well as incorporation into the European states system.

That these accommodations of European liberal sentiment could be seen as actually strengthening the Sultanate is reflected in the absence of any move towards representative government. The plan was to strengthen the dynasty and to make the people contented by means of efficient, that is bureaucratic, government. The model being followed here was Habsburg or Prussian rather than French or British. 'Life and honour [are] the most precious gifts to mankind'; and, if a person 'enjoys in that respect perfect security, he will not depart from the ways of loyalty, and ... will contribute to the good of the government and [of] his brothers' (Tanzimat edict 1839 in A. Hourani 1983: 46). It was, as Deringil points out, an Enlightenment agenda. Indeed, some religious thinkers argued against the Reforms on the constitutionalist grounds that they led to tyranny by reducing the traditional role of the ulema and the Shari'a, which had formerly limited the Sultan's power, and protected the security and prosperity of individuals. Such people argued that it was religion that created political order; if it is ignored, the state will decline.[5]

There was not much political theory behind these reforms. Ahmed Cevdet Paşa (1822–95), 'one of the most prominent statesmen of the nineteenth century' (Deringil 1998: 69), who played a decisive part in the codification of civil law, justified the introduction of secular courts by arguments taken from Dawani and Kinalizade; the latter was still widely read in the nineteenth-century Ottoman domains.[6] The most articulate thinker was Sadik Rifat Paşa (1807–56), a colleague of the minister who composed the 1839 edict; he expounded 'something that may be called the theory of the Tanzimat reforms' (Mardin 1960: 425). Writing while ambassador in Vienna (1837), he reflected the combination of liberalism and étatisme: social development requires a strong state. He used the term vatan, connoting territory and *patrie*, alongside devlet (dynasty). Europe's prosperity was due to the security and liberty provided by their sovereigns who thought it their duty 'to protect and safeguard the welfare and prosperity of countries'. The state, he thought, should encourage, but not control, agriculture and commerce.[7]

Reşid Paşa ('in many ways the real architect of the nineteenth-century Ottoman reforms': Lewis 1968: 105) was more conservative. He described the 'pillars of the state' (rükn-ü devlet: see above, p. 265) as, first, the Islamic Community, the Turkish devlet, the Ottoman Sultan, and the capital Istanbul; and, second, as Islam, Sultanate and Caliphate.[8] Cevdet Paşa was one of the first to suggest Turkish nationhood as the basis of the state. Such political nationalism was another European import, and perhaps the one destined for the greatest influence in the long term. What held together the 'various peoples and strata [sinuf: also, guilds]' was 'the unity of Islam'; but the Turks had set up the state before it became a Caliphate, and therefore 'in reality it is a Turkish state ... The real strength of the Sublime State lies with the Turks. It is an obligation of their national character and religion to sacrifice their lives for the House of Osman until the last one is destroyed. Therefore it is natural that they be accorded more worth than other peoples of the Sublime State' (in Deringil 1998: 169–70).

The Tanzimat reforms may have been inspired by Ottoman pragmatism (see above, p. 200), forcefully expressed by a one-time Minister of Education when he said (1879) that 'to accept the civilization of Europe in its entirety' was the only way to prevent foreign intervention and even the loss of 'Turkish' independence (in Berkes 1964: 185). The reforms were given religious sanction: Westernisation was said to be justified by the Juristic doctrine that 'necessity permits what is prohibited', especially when it enables the ruler to undertake such fundamental duties as Jihad and the protection of Islamic territory. Religion does not teach fatalism but encourages human beings to be active on their own behalf.[9]

IRAN: THE SOCIO-RELIGIOUS STATUS OF THE MUJTAHIDS

In Iran modernism and Westernisation started in the mid-nineteenth century.[10] Here, the political situation could hardly have been more different. A state in the modern sense hardly existed. The main development in political thought was in Shi'ite political theology. We have seen how the political situation in the eighteenth century had left a vacuum in moral leadership which was filled by the Shi'ite 'ulama (mollas), and that at this time 'the Shi'ite clergy in Iran acquired the form in which they have since been known' (Halm 1991: 100). The organisation and doctrine of the Shi'ite hierarchy became of critical importance in the nineteenth and twentieth centuries (see above, p. 236).

The mollas had economic resources, social prestige, religious status and continuity, and a worked-out ideological perspective. They ran most schools and hospitals. They decided questions of personal law, mediated in disputes, including some between government and subjects; they were the defenders of local and communal interests, the champions of those with grievances against state officials. As in most Islamic regimes, 'the administration of justice was divided between Islamic Shari'a courts, run by the 'ulama, and the courts of customary law, presided over by the Shah and his officials' (CH Iran 7: 178).

The Mujtahids (Well-Qualified Jurists: see above, p. 229) in particular were regarded by their fellow-countrymen, in the words of an English traveller, as 'their guides in religion, and their protectors against their rulers; and they receive a respect and duty which lead the proudest kings to join the popular voice, and to pretend, if they do not feel, a veneration for them'.[11] They wielded local power; their judicial decisions were implemented by their own strongmen. As recipients of khums (a fifth of all income) on behalf of the absent Imam (Leader), the Mujtahids' economic resources were secure from government intervention. They had 'close ties with bazaar merchants and artisans' (CH Iran 7: 178). Some of them amassed great wealth. The safe haven of the Iraqi shrines gave them immunity from government persecution. The mollas resisted all attempts by government officials to extend secular jurisdiction.

The usuli (Principled) doctrine, that any well-qualified Jurist may exercise independent reason (ijtihad), and that every believer should take such a Mujtahid as his/her religious guide, gave the Mujtahids a special status, based on their capacity for creative interpretation of the revealed divine Law (ijtihad).[12] The status of Mujtahid depended on recognition by other Mujtahids; his actual power on the number and position of his followers. Each individual believer had to make his/her own choice of a Mujtahid, based on his learning, justice and godliness, as their 'absolute spiritual guide' (marja'-i taqlid: lit. source of imitation).[13] In the eighteenth century, this doctrine finally triumphed at the Iraqi shrines, the nerve centre of the Shi'ite international community. In Iran, 'a handful of eminent Mujtahids' became de facto leaders of 'an autonomous Shi'ite hierocracy' (Arjomand 1984: 230).

The organisation of the 'ulama including Mujtahids remained informal. They 'fill no office, receive no appointment, have no specific duties, but are called upon, from their superior learning, piety and virtue, by the silent but unanimous suffrage of their countrymen' (Malcolm in Lambton 1970: 248). Among Mujtahids, differences of opinion were allowed on matters of legal interpretation. But the divide between Mujtahids and the rest stratified the religious community into those with the authority to offer guidance, and all other believers.

Sometimes a particularly eminent Mujtahid emerged in a position of religious headship (riyasat shari'yya), or universal juristic authority (marja'iyat-i tamm), within the whole Shi'ite umma.[14] This universal headship developed partly out of 'the need for arbitration by a superior authority in cases of disputes between the Mujtahids and their chief clients, the merchants', out of 'the mechanics of the madrasa–bazaar interaction'. This too was an informal process, a development of patron–client relationships. Such a person was chosen not by fellow-Mujtahids but 'at the discretion of the emulators – more the laity than the lower-rank 'ulama' (Arjomand (ed.) 1988: 118, 123–4). This position was bestowed on Shaikh Murtaza Ansari (d. 1865), and later on Mirza Muhammad Hasan Shirazi (d. 1895). After Shirazi's death, they reverted again to diffuse 'collective' leadership with different Mujtahids sometimes taking different lines. During the great constitutional crisis of 1905–11, not only was there no single religious leader; the Mujtahids became sharply divided among themselves over fundamental political issues.

The Mujtahids' religious status was crystallised in the doctrine that they held the collective vicariate/vicegerency (niyabat-i 'ammah) or collective vilaya (delegated authority, guardianship, trusteeship of the twelfth Imam, sometimes referred to as 'the concilium [qatiba-yi: assemblage] of the 'ulama of the time'. (Ansari remained unconvinced that the collective vicariate could be deduced from the Legal Sources.)[15] Ja'far al-Najafi (d.1848/9) defined vilaya as 'holding office for administering justice, organising the order of society (al-nizam), exercising coercive discipline (al-siyasa), collecting taxes ... on behalf of the Just Ruler [sc. the Hidden Leader]' (in Sachedina 1988: 208, adapted). This was conceived as an open-ended delegation of authority covering the entire range of functions needed for the guidance of the Islamic Community. These functions were derived from the general obligation to 'command the good', which in this respect was specialised in the Mujtahids.

According to the theory of the collective vicariate, Mujtahids could exercise functions previously reserved to the Hidden Leader and therefore held in abeyance: these included corporal punishment (hudud), declaration of jihad and excommunication. It also entitled Mujtahids to the Imam's share of religious donations. In this way, they acquired the ability to order society and to exercise de facto political leadership.

In nineteenth-century Iran, the 'ulama were the only national institution. When Iran became prey to Russian expansion and British capitalism, they had the potential to represent national interests. During wars with Russia (1808–13, 1826–8), the Shah relied on the Mujtahids to declare Holy War, which they agreed to do, declaring this jihad to be 'individually incumbent' not only on volunteers but on every Shi'ite (Arjomand 1984: 242). Jihad was a prerogative of the Hidden Imam, so the Mujtahids were here putting into practice their belief in their collective vicariate, a doctrine which they were careful to explain on this occasion.[16]

The 'ulama were the only effective opposition to the Qajar shahs, 'the only group who could act as a restraint on the government and who could put openly to the Shah and his advisers the dangers of a particular policy' (Lambton 1970: 249). They incited 'communal action through the mobilisation of the masses'. The first thing they did was to demand persecution of Sufis, Baha'i (babis) and non-Muslims generally. This indicated their view of the Iranian Shi'ite state; they had 'no conception of a secular society' (Arjomand 1984: 250–2).

On some political questions, opinion among the Mujtahids was divided. Aqa Muhammad Baqir Bihbahani (1705–91), one of the Mujtahids who had been instrumental in the triumph of the Principled in Iraq, is reported to have said: 'If the Mujtahid who is appointed by the Imam on the basis of general permission is appointed sultan or ruler (hakim) for the people of Islam, there will be no unjust rulers, as was the case with the children of Israel. This is so because the enforcer[s] (hakim) of the Holy Law (al-shar') and of secular law (al-'urf) are in such a case both appointed by the divine will (al-shar')' (quoted by Najafi, in Sachedina 1988: 208, adapted). This presumably meant that a Mujtahid could be appointed ruler; certainly, that he could supervise those who were rulers.

On the other hand, Shi'ite political thought was driven as much by traditional Jurisprudence as by circumstances, and thus also retained 'the attitude of pious antipathy to temporal power and of political indifferentism' (Arjomand 1984: 236). Conspicuous disengagement from the world of power had indeed been the basis of their popular following (Malcolm in Lambton 1970: 248). There was thus a division of opinion between, on the one hand, those religious leaders who became involved in politics, either because (in Lambton's words) 'they believed that they could exercise a restraining influence', or because 'they saw participation … as the road to wealth and influence'; and, on the other hand, those who took the view that 'sultans and governors cause all their writs and orders to run by tyranny' (early nineteenth-century Mujtahid). One Mujtahid who declined to participate observed that, if his advice were taken, 'the affairs of kingship will be held up', and if not 'I shall suffer contempt' (in Lambton 1970: 249). Thus Bihbahani's view was not widely accepted. Najafi himself demurred; he supported the doctrine of the general vicariate, but criticised some who shared this view out of 'love of leadership (riyasa) and power (saltana)' (in Arjomand 1984: 236, adapted). Ansari was opposed to involvement in politics and even to what he saw as excessive judicial activity by Mujtahids; he sought to 'depoliticize the clerical community' (Arjomand (ed.) 1988: 112) – out of respect for the Legal Sources.

There was no development of the theory of patrimonial monarchy during the nineteenth century. The few works written in the Advice-to-Kings genre lack all originality.[17] But some Mujtahids did express views in line with the Irano-Islamic conception of monarchy. They developed a *dualist* theory of the vicariate of the Hidden Imam, according to which the 'ulama on the one hand and kings on the other each have a 'specified vicariate (niyabat-e khassa)'. That is, each acts on behalf of the true Leader in their own special field. This was an exact equivalent of the 'two-sword' theory held by some in medieval Europe. 'The Mujtahids and the rulers both hold the same office of Imamate, transferred to them from the Imam through vicegerency, and consisting of two pillars (rukn): knowledge of ... religion; and the implementation of this in ... imposing order on the world, called kingship or sovereignty' (Kashfi, d. 1850, in Arjomand 1984: 226). Or, as Ja'far (d.1812–13) put it in language even more reminiscent of medieval Europe: '"Knowledge" and the "sword" have become separated', so that norms 'which relate to the organ of the sword and the affairs of sovereignty and politics ... (relate to) the king and rulers'.[18] Kashfi's, on the other hand, was not quite a 'two-sword' theory: for what he meant was that, ideally, there should only be one Deputy, as there was only one Imam; the 'ulama have only 'abandoned sovereignty' because of 'the contention of the rulers with the 'ulama, leading to sedition and anarchy'. On the other hand, it is due to their 'inclination toward the baser world, that is mere worldly sovereignty' that rulers have abandoned religious Knowledge and 'made do with the science of politics only' (in Arjomand 1984: 226). This implied that the 'ulama are really superior. Kashfi did not, however, claim authority for them over kings under present circumstances. His ideal was, rather, cooperation: if they become 'mutually antagonistic', the 'ilm of the 'ulama stagnates, and rulers resort to brute force. In such a case, 'both groups [fall] short of discharging the office of vicegerency'. This was dualism of a sort.

The dualist view was reaffirmed by the Jurist 'Ali Kani (d.1888) in a letter to the Shah (1873) at the time of the Reuters controversy (see below, p. 291). Shirazi, when as chief Mujtahid he was asked to intervene in a dispute about imported sugar, took a similar line: 'originally government (dawlat) and Religious Community (millat) were established in one place ... [and] political duties regarding this kind of general affairs (umur 'amma) were entrusted to the same person'. Shirazi ascribed their separation to 'the requirements of divine wisdom'. Once again, the ideal was cooperation: it is up to 'both these powers to aid each other in protecting the religion and worldly interests (din va dunya) of the servants of God'. But Shirazi seems to have thought that, if the government (in Arjomand's words) 'fails to carry out its duty of protection of religion and the interests of subjects, the millat will, under hierocratic leadership, do whatever is necessary, because it is responsible to the Lord of Time' (1984: 252). The 'ulama can override the ruler in an emergency (subsidiarity).

Thus, under the pressure of commercial problems affecting the national economy, some Mujtahids moved from dualism to hierocracy, giving themselves the ultimate authority. The language of this debate is reminiscent of medieval Europe and had no counterpart at this time anywhere else in the world.

WESTERN IDEAS: MALKOM KHAN (1833–1908)

Western political ideas entered public discourse in Iran when the government was attempting to codify and reform the legal system in the late 1850s. This was partly in order to limit the scope of the 'ulama (Lambton 1970: 259). As in the Ottoman empire, Westernisers in Iran were at this stage supporters of the monarchy. But, unlike most Ottoman reformers at this time, they were concerned to define and limit the powers of the Shah.

Mirza Malkom Khan (1833–1908)[19] was an Armenian whose father had adopted Islam, possibly because of his career. Malkom had been educated in Paris, where he developed an interest in humanism, freemasonry and Auguste Comte, although he did not explicitly reject Islam now or later; tactical reasons may have come into play here too. Malkom drafted a *Book of Reform* (*Daftar-i Tanzimat*: 1858) for the Shah, and founded a secret society, the Faramushkhaneh (House of Oblivion), to spread his ideas. He believed that Europe's progress was not simply a matter of technical and economic achievement but was due above all to the 'customs of their civilisation' and their political system. At this stage in his career, Malkom held that the government of Persia should be 'based on absolute monarchy', and that 'constitutional monarchy (saltanat-e mo'tadel) has no application to the condition of Iran'. He looked to Austria, Russia and the Ottoman empire as models for modernisation. The main function of government, monarchical or republican, is to implement the rule of law.[20]

But he advocated significant constitutional and administrative changes in order to strengthen Iran against foreign intervention. Malkom's constitutional proposals were based upon the separation of powers. Only in this way would reforms be implemented as well as decreed: 'enforcing such laws is impossible … except through that wondrous system that the states of Europe have invented for these laws of theirs'. Power must be divided between two state councils, one for legislation, in which there was to be freedom of expression, the other to supervise the executive. Both were to be appointed by the Shah. The legislative council was to codify the existing shari'a and 'urf, together with some elements of European law, into a single system, which he denominated qanun (secular law, a new term in Iran). This should include a bill of rights and a code of conduct for the government; it would express 'the will of the Shah and … the interests of the general public'.[21]

Another advocate of a thorough overhaul of Iran's legal system, Mirza Yusef Khan, had been chargé d'affaires in Paris. Writing about 1862, just when or perhaps before the Young Ottomans came on the scene (see below, p. 292), he was one of the first Muslim authors wholeheartedly to adopt the principles of French republicanism. Yusef argued not only for the adoption of the 'essential principles' of French law but also for 'government by the will of the people and through elected representatives' (Bakhash 1978: 39–40).

Above all, while up to now Westernisation had been seen as a process justified by necessity but essentially extrinsic to Islam, Yusef seems to have been the first to see Western and Islamic principles as in agreement. In an essay with the significant sub-title 'The spirit of Islam', he argued that, while the French legal system had advantages over the shari'a in its organisation, and in being based on the will of the people, 'if you study the contents of the codes of France and other civilised states, you will see how the evolution of the ideas of nations and the experiences of the peoples of the world *confirm the Shari'a of Islam* ... Whatever good laws there are in Europe ... your Prophet set down and established for the people of Islam 1,280 years ago' (in Bakhash 1978: 39–40, my italics). It is significant that, both here and in the Young Ottomans, it was the proponents of parliamentary democracy who developed this line of thought.

Some Iranian reformers were definitely anti-Islamic. Akhundzade (also writing about 1862) argued that, as Bakhash puts it, 'Islam, with its discrimination against women and non-Muslims, and its claim to dictate to men what they must believe, could not be made to appear compatible with equality and liberty' (1978: 41); at the very least, it needed to be radically reformed.

These first Iranian attempts at reform petered out. The Shah was at first sympathetic to Malkom's proposals, but they were condemned by the religious leaders, and Malkom was exiled (1861). Westernisation and reform got going again briefly in the early 1870s, when Malkom was recalled as a special adviser. One of his ideas was to attract foreign investment; he thought that European commerce was bound to spread to less developed countries, and it would bring benefits. 'The peoples of Europe have no aim and business in foreign lands other than the expansion of trade and the increase of prosperity' (in Algar 1973: 111) – a benign view of economic imperialism. But Malkom also sought personal gain, and, once this came out, he was exiled again (1873), this time as ambassador to London. There he came into contact with Afghani (see below, pp. 301–2) whose general approach in many ways he now came to adopt. In 1889, Malkom was dismissed from his post for further financial impropriety. This further changed his views, turning him into 'a radical journalist presenting the ideas of modern Europe'.[22]

In order to spread European ideas as widely as possible in Iran itself, Malkom started a crusading newspaper, *Qanun* (*Law*). This was quite influential. He still saw the main need as 'law and more law'. He was not alone in thinking that Persia's social and economic problems stemmed from fundamental uncertainty in the administration of justice.[23] Mirza Aqa Khan Kermani (Malkom's contact with al-Afghani, executed in Persia in 1896) believed that, 'In a country where there is law ... famine and scarcity will be abolished ... the treasuries of the nation will be built up ... the rights of all men will be well-protected'.[24]

Malkom's ideas now developed along lines similar to the Young Ottomans (see below, pp. 293–4): he argued that such laws should be formulated by 'the great national consultative assembly (majlis-e shawra-ye kobra-ye melli)' (in Bakhash 1978: 337). Qanun advocated a parliament with two chambers: 'one, the assembly of representatives of the people, elected by the people themselves; and the other, the assembly of notables, consisting of the accomplished and learned ones of the realm'. This would accommodate both the preference for democracy and a role for the 'ulama and other intellectuals. At one point, Malkom also suggested that a national assembly should consist of 'one hundred Mujtahids and other learned persons of the country'.[25]

And indeed, Malkom's view of religion and of the 'ulama was also developing, probably under Afghani's influence. Western-orientated intellectuals were few and isolated, and they could only hope to achieve their aims through alliance with other leaders of public opinion; there was a general awareness among them that 'only the 'ulama could lead a popular movement' (Bakhash 1978: 343). They also knew that, to win over the Iranian masses, they must base their argument on religious principles. Thus Malkom presented his European-derived ideas as an articulation of fundamental Islamic values. 'I assert with the deepest conviction that in all the new institutions which Europe offers us there is nothing, absolutely nothing, which is contrary to the spirit of our religion.'[26] 'Whatever good laws the Europeans have they have taken them from the sacred books of Islam', said another Iranian reformer (in Bakhash 1978: 356).

This was used as an argument to persuade the 'ulama to support a liberal-parliamentary programme. Surely, 'the 'ulama know that the [secular] law (qanun) is nothing else but the implementation of the commands of the Shari'a; the Shari'a is the basis of the law, the meaning of both words [shari'a and qanun] is the implementation of justice on the basis of equality' (Maragheh-i, in Bakhash 1978: 355–6, adapted). Malkom and other reformers incorporated specifically Shi'ite ideas into their arguments for constitutionalism. 'The present monarchy of Persia' was, they said, 'contrary to the principles of Islam' because it was 'imposed by force'; the Shi'ite view of the Imamate meant that in Iran the Sultan could not be absolute. Indeed, Malkom seems to have believed more strongly than did the Mujtahids themselves that they were an alternative government-in-waiting. 'There are in Iran today two governments: one [legitimate] belonging to the 'ulama, the other usurped and [tyrannical]' (in Bakhash 1978: 340). Even the secular-minded Kermani urged Shirazi, the senior Mujtahid, to take a more active political role: 'Why should the spiritual leader of sixty million Shi'is sit trembling and hidden in the corner of some outlandish village?' (in Algar 1973: 212). Reformers like Malkom argued that European-style reforms were an application to Iran of the 'immutable' principles of good government; the Europeans just happened to have got there first. The alternative to following Europe would be 3,000 years of painful historical development. It was as easy to adopt their system of government as their technology (Bakhash 1978: 13–4, 17).

It is not certain how clearly Malkom thought through this equivalence between Islamic and European ideas, or how sincere he was. He once told a British friend: 'I was determined to clothe my [reform proposals] in a garb which my people would understand, the garb of religion' (in Bakhash 1978: 18). There was an element of speculative adventure: 'I conceived a plan which should incorporate the practical wisdom of Europe with the religious wisdom of Asia.' He may have been freewheeling rather than insincere (in Algar 1969: 186, 188). Like Afghani, he argued that Islamic prophecy and the Shi'ite Imamate were a basis for good government. They underpinned Malkom's favourite principle, the rule of law: 'All that the Prophets proclaimed was for the sake of the strengthening and execution of law ... All the Immaculate Imams ... inwardly and outwardly have propagated the principles of just government' (in Algar 1973: 207). But *Qanun* also argued for a radical reform of Islam itself along lines suggested by, in particular, Afghani: we need 'the Islam of learning, not the Islam of ignorance; the Islam of love, not the Islam of persecution ... the Islam of unity, not the Islam of division ... the Islam of reason ('aql), not the Islam of imitation (naql); the Islam of man, not the Islam of things' (Malkom, in Bakhash 1978: 343).

Secular beliefs surfaced more often in Iran than elsewhere (Keddie 1980: 22, 25, 35). Religious alternatives to Islam, such as the Baha'i movement, had already won considerable support, and there was some acquaintance with Western philosophy. Malkom himself, influenced by St Simon and Comte, urged belief in humanity (adamiyyat); he called his network of groups the League of Humanity. *Qanun* urged its readers to become human beings (sing. adam) by fulfilling the duties that were incumbent upon the whole species. Nevertheless, Malkom insisted that 'the principles of adamiyyat are so much in accordance with Islam ... that every intelligent Muslim, as soon as he perceives its truths, instinctively joins the society ... Some think this World of Humanity was established by the prophets and saints of Islam' (in Algar 1969: 191). Even so, this was the first expression of humanism in the Islamic world.

A few wholeheartedly secular-minded people rejected, or ignored, Islam and appealed instead to Iranian national values and the glories of a pre-Islamic past. Kermani blamed his country's decrepit state on the Arab legacy and religious principles like 'imitation (taqlid)' and 'precautionary dissimulation (taqiyya)'.[27]

THE CONSTITUTIONAL REVOLUTION (1905–11)

In the 1890s, an alliance was forged between the Shi'ite religious leadership and the Westernising constitutionalists. The Mujtahids had previously faced down attempts by the Shah's government to introduce judicial reforms that would have curtailed their jurisdiction and undermined their economic independence. In 1871–2 and again in 1890–2, they stood up for the interests of local merchants against both the Shah and foreign capitalism. To many, they seemed to embody both economic justice and the national interest. A monopoly of tobacco sales and exports granted to a British firm (1890) threatened the livelihood of bazaari merchants, a major constituency of the 'ulama. Shirazi, the supreme Mujtahid, issued a fatwa declaring the consumption of tobacco irreligious; the Shah was forced to cancel the monopoly. Thus was formed a secularist–'ulama alliance that was indeed 'unusual in world history'; this 'coordinated movement ... [of] 'ulama, modernists, merchants and towns-people' was 'the first successful mass protest in modern Iran' (*CH Iran* 7: 193, 196). It suggested that modernism and traditional religious authority might go hand in hand. It was a sign that this specifically Shi'ite form of political Islam could mobilise opposition to Western capitalism.

The Constitutional Revolution of 1905–6 began with widespread opposition to foreign, especially Russian, influence. It was led by the 'ulama and culminated in the demand for a 'place of justice' to ensure the application of the Shari'a. Once again, 'major leaders of the 'ulama were in alliance with merchants, guildsmen [and] secular intellectuals' (Keddie 1980: 7). A national assembly was convened (1906) and a constitution drawn up, modelled on Belgium (1831), but with a provision that all laws must be ratified by a committee of Mujtahids.[28]

The principle of equivalence between the Shari'a and constitutionalist ideals was now widely propagated: 'government according to the law of Islam, justice and equality, or according to science and civilisation ... are one and the same' (in Algar 1969: 253). There was overwhelming support in the country for the view that the Shah was under an obligation to observe the Shari'a, and for the rule of law generally. But the Mujtahids and 'ulama became bitterly divided over the relative merits of parliament and monarchy. Some Mujtahids pronounced approval for constitutionalism in principle on the basis of Islamic Right.[29] One pro-constitutionalist 'alim, declaring that 'the eyes of the Iranians have been opened ... they now have become a "people of loosening and binding"' (meaning something akin to sovereign), took the view that 'the Europeans have taken their laws and constitutions from the Qur'an and the words of the Imams'. He saw a connection between constitutional monarchy and expansion, between 'world conquest' and 'wealth', and between absolute monarchy and decline. On the other hand, the leader of the anti-constitutionalist 'ulama declared that 'the foundation of Islam is obedience, not freedom; and the basis of its commandments is the differentiation of collectivities ... and not equality'. Those 'ulama who did support the parliament wanted to limit its authority to 'matters of livelihood'.[30] The parliament was finally suppressed in 1911.

PARLIAMENTARY LIBERALISM AND ISLAMIC VALUES: THE YOUNG OTTOMANS

It was in fact once again Ottoman society that produced the first large-scale and, as it turned out, enduring movement for a reformist ideology combining the Western principles of individual liberty, constitutional government and representative democracy with Islamic idealism. With the Young Ottomans (Yeni Osmanlilar),[31] the interaction between Islamic and Western political thought became systematic and intense.

In the 1850s, a number of reforming bureaucrats, protégés of the Tanzimat statesman Reşid Paşa, became disenchanted with the progress of reform, and turned to journalism. Ibrahim Şinasi (1826–71), a poet who had studied in

France during the 1848 revolution, started his own newspaper, *Tasvir-i Efkar* (*Illustration of Opinion*: 1862). Fearing political reprisals, he returned to France in 1865. The most systematic thinker of the group was Namik Kemal (1840–88), son of the court astronomer, also a poet and literary critic. He now took over as editor and gave the paper a more radical turn. Then he too, along with others, fled to Europe (1867). This group intensified their efforts to spread their ideas in print; the popular journal *Hürriyet* (*Freedom*) was started in 1868. They believed that 'the expression of one's ideas by word and pen concerning the interests of one's country must assuredly be reckoned one of the acquired rights', and that political newspapers were the way to empower people through knowledge, as happens in 'the civilized nations' (Şinasi, 1860: in Lewis 1968: 147). The Young Ottomans were 'the first who … consciously tried to create and influence public opinion' (Zürcher 1998: 74). They were bankrolled by Mustafa Fazil, an Egyptian crown prince who had been excluded from the succession.

For this generation, liberty became a fundamental value. As a Turkish visitor to the Paris Exhibition of 1878 put it, European technological achievements were 'the work of freedom': 'without freedom, there can be no security; without security, no endeavour; without endeavour, no prosperity; without prosperity, no happiness' (*EI* 3: 592b). (This was a new expression of the traditional Irano-Islamic connection between politics and economics: see above, p. 54.) The Young Ottomans gave liberty the political meaning it had acquired in Europe since 1789. They argued, as had some ulema, that the Tanzimat had led to a one-sided development of the 'Mongolian' features of bureaucratic despotism; it had abandoned the checks and balances provided by the Religious Law and the ulema. So the Young Ottomans wanted to take the Tanzimat project a stage further. Their political ideals were summed up by Namik Kemal as 'the sovereignty of the nation, the separation of powers, the responsibility of officials, personal freedom, equality, freedom of thought, freedom of the press, freedom of association, enjoyment of property, sanctity of the home' (in Lewis 1968: 143). Namik Kemal especially admired the constitution of the French Third Republic. Crucially for the story of Islamic political ideas, this group of activists for the first time explicitly combined Westernisation with Islamic idealism. And they gave coherent reasons for doing so.

The Young Ottomans equated the political language of Islam with that of modern liberal-parliamentary democracy. 'For them ümmet meant nation, icma social contract, bîat … the delegation of sovereignty to the ruler by the people, içtihâd meant parliamentary legislation, meşveret democracy' (Berkes 1964: 261). They developed the technique of reinterpreting texts from the Qur'an and Hadith as arguments for constitutional democracy; for example, Q. 3:153 ('So pardon [your brothers] … and take counsel with them in the affair') and the hadith 'difference of opinion within my community is an act of divine mercy' were presented as arguments for parliamentary government. So was the traditional juristic principle of 'consensus (icma) of the community (ümmet)'.[32] The Ottoman dynasty holds power on the basis of Islamic contract (bîat). All this meant in fact transforming the meanings of old Islamic words. It was a distinctive and original development in Islamic political thought. It would lead to a rethinking of political values, past and present.

The European ideals of parliamentary liberalism were, in their opinion, both good in themselves and in accordance with the essential tenets of Islam. They were morally superior to the norms and institutions which for many centuries had counted as Islamic tradition because these had departed radically from the Islamic ideal. Thus Namik Kemal observed that the sovereignty of the people 'in the technical language of the Şeriat is called Baya (contract)'. It is also 'a right necessarily arising from the personal independence that each individual by nature possesses' (in Lewis 1968: 143). For the first time in Islamic political thought, popular sovereignty was based upon the liberty of the individual, and indeed upon human nature.

What was needed, then, was a return to what had been prescribed by true, original Islam, namely constitutional and parliamentary government, based on the sovereignty of the people. This was what was currently practised in European states. By adopting Western ways of thinking and political ideals in the name of a return to the first principles of Islam, the Young Ottomans became the first true Islamic modernists. What now took place was an exercise in cultural exhange comparable to the transfer of Arabo-Aristotelian philosophy and science to Latin Europe in twelfth-century Spain.

But the Young Ottomans were not simply proposing the age-old ideal of return to the purity of original Islam. They were also arguing that, as Berkes puts it, 'the provisions (ahkam) of the Şeriat were capable of alteration in accordance with the requirements of the time' (1964: 213). In other words, they distinguished between a core or essence of Islamic ideals and the way these had been spelled out under specific historical circumstances. They were thus able to argue that, rather than taking over Western legal systems, one should apply the spirit of the Shari'a to modern conditions. In this way, it was the Young Ottomans, rather than the flamboyant al-Afghani, who reopened the gates of rational interpretation (ijtihad). Similarly, they insisted that not everything is predetermined by God; some things are dependent upon human action (Mardin 1962: 407).

This juxtaposition and fusion of Islamic and European ideals, reading each in the light of the other, produced original thought on the relationship between popular sovereignty and justice. The decisions of a democratic majority have to be reconciled with the abstract Right laid down by God in nature. For 'in Islam the good and the bad are determined by the Şeriat which is the expression of the abstract good and the ultimate criterion of truth'. Namik Kemal equated this with the idea of natural law as developed by the West 'through philosophical deductions ... because they did not have a Şeriat' (in Berkes 1964: 212, 216). (He had read about this in Montesquieu.) Here he established a fundamental premise of Islamic modernism: that in the moral sphere Islam already has all that the West has to offer. The advantage of Western modernity lies in its material and technical achievements, which (not helping his argument, perhaps, but quite accurately) Namik saw as the product of Western philosophy (Mardin 1962: 405).

The Young Ottomans thus distanced themselves from secularism in the European sense. But they did not believe in the traditional or revivalist religious polity either; they supported full civil rights for non-Muslims. Some, like Mustafa Fazil, asserted (1867) the separation of religion from politics: 'religion rules over the spirit and promises other-worldly benefits. But that which determines ... the laws of the nation is not religion. If religion ... descends into interference with worldly affairs, it becomes a destroyer of all as well as of itself' (in Berkes 1964: 208–9). But, for most Young Ottomans, religion provided the moral basis for politics.

Their degree of secularism may be defined by their principled adherence to the principle of state sovereignty and of loyalty to the fatherland. For the Young Ottomans 'identified closely with the state they wanted to save through liberal reforms'. They were patriots, devoted to vatan (patrie) and millet (people) (Zürcher 1998: 72–3). 'The Fatherland', said Namik Kemal, 'is a sacred idea, sprung from the union of the many lofty sentiments, such as nation, freedom, welfare, brotherhood, property, sovereignty, respect for ancestors, love of family, memory of youth' (in Lewis 1968: 337). But this did not refer to an ethnic or racial community in the European sense, but rather to a multi-ethnic 'community' in the Islamic sense – precisely, the Ottoman fatherland (Shaw and Shaw 1977: 132).

The problem they, like everyone else, faced here was that, once you transfer sovereignty from dynasty to people, political loyalty tends to be determined by social identity, which, especially in the European parts of the Ottoman domain, consisted in explosive combinations of nationality and religion. Hence the fear that (as Namik Kemal perceptively put it) 'the differences of race and religion among our countrymen might bring total dissolution to our country'. Namik responded by pointing out that in the Ottoman empire such groups did not occupy distinct territories but were intermingled, and that the Ottoman government was more tolerant than most; like Mustafa 'Ali in the sixteenth century (see above, p. 208), he saw advantages in diversity (Lewis 1968: 338–9). Unfortunately, he was being too optimistic on both counts.

Namik Kemal also – inconsistently – looked to Islam as the basis of Ottoman political identity. Indeed, fearing the cultural hegemony of the West, he became an advocate of unity among the people of Islam, 'not in political aims or doctrinal disputes, but in the presence of preachers, in the pages of books'. He wanted to counter 'the balance of the West' by 'the balance of the East'. Namik went on to say that, in view of the Caliphate and their 'nearness to Europe, the present home of civilization', it was in the Ottoman domains that 'this union of which we speak will surely have its centre' (in Lewis 1968: 341). This may have been a call for cultural rather than political unity (as Bernard Lewis suggests), but it coincided with early versions of pan-Islamism.

KHAYR AL-DIN AL-TUNISI (1822/3–90)

The most systematic statement of the relationship between Islamic and European civilisation came not from Turkey but from Tunisia. Khayr al-Din al-

Tunisi (1822/3–90),[33] an Ottoman slave-soldier from the Caucasus in the service of the reformer Ahmad Bey (ruler of Tunisia, 1837–55), rose to become president of the Grand Council (a consultative body of notables set up under the new constitution of 1861). He had been influenced by his visit to Paris on government business in 1853–6. He resigned his post because he was opposed to a loan from European funds. During 1862–9 when he was away from Tunisia, he wrote *The Surest Path to Know the Conditions of the State* (*Aqwam al-masalik fi ma'rifat ahwal al-mamalik*: publ. 1868, authorised French translation, 1869). Khayr al-Din was the flower of the modernists, largely forgotten today, a man of piety and principle with an open mind. It must be a coincidence that, like his spiritual successor al-Fasi (see below, p. 339), his main association was with the land that produced Ibn Khaldun.

Khayr al-Din's aim throughout his life was to restore 'what was taken from our hands' (*Surest Path*, p. 73), and the independence and strength of the Islamic world community. There was a remarkable coherence between his thought and his actions. Like the Young Ottomans, he saw the adoption of European political ideas and institutions as both desirable in itself and in line with original Islam; but he went further than the Young Ottomans because he also saw this as the first step in a geo-political strategy to regain world ascendancy for Islam. He supported closer ties among the peoples formally subject to the Ottoman Caliphate, 'le centre moderne de l'Islamisme' (p. 134).

In *The Surest Path*, Khayr al-Din set out to analyse 'the causes of the progress and backwardness of nations, generation after generation', by combining empirical evidence ('which experience has decreed should be accepted') (p. 71) from both European and Islamic history. His Introduction (*Muqaddima*) is followed by a comparative study of twenty-one European states. Khayr al-Din went further than the Young Ottomans in his analysis of the causes of European greatness. He frequently referred to Ibn Khaldun, and it seems that he was trying to adopt his method. His originality lay in his awareness of historical changes and the need to bring the historical experience of Europe into the frame. Above all, he systematically justified learning from non-Muslims.

International competititon, the 'keen rivalry' between great nations, meant that Muslim society could only thrive by acquiring 'knowledge of those outside our own group'. Therefore, 'with God's help I have collected all possible information about European inventions related to economic and administrative policies', and shown how Europeans have progressed in politics and how this has enabled them to acquire 'the utmost prosperity for their countries' (pp. 71–3). He was concerned to justify learning from others as a sound Islamic principle and as necessary for the promotion of the present-day interests of Islam. This message was aimed especially at the 'ulama. The public interest can only be served when Learned and ruler work together, and they in turn can only administer the Shari'a in an informed way if they have political experience (pp. 73, 61, 124, 129).

It is 'a mistake under any circumstances' to reject 'all [the] behaviour and organisations of non-Muslims ... [and] their books'. One has to learn from outside Islam because nowadays many factors 'bring men and ideas closer together'; today the whole world may be conceived 'as a single united country peopled by various nations who surely need each other. The general benefit to be derived from the experience of each nation, even when it is pursuing its own interests, suffices to make it sought after by the rest of mankind' – cultural globalisation. The French, in particular, have 'attained the sound organisation of their affairs in this world' by 'ceaselessly emulating what they deem good in the work of others' (pp. 72–5).

There is a more fundamental reason why borrowing is justified: all humans live in the same sphere of knowledge, the discoveries of reason are in principle common to all, and the fact that non-believers make discoveries first is neither here nor there (p. 75). This may sound simple enough. But at the time it was an entirely new idea for the Muslim intellectual. Here, Khayr al-Din was, unusually for a modern Muslim, at one with the Muslim and Christian Aristotelians of earlier times. There was an implicit cosmopolitanism in his statement that the Shari'a includes 'the protection of the rights of mankind whether Muslim or not' (p. 82). He argued, further, that the political principles we are talking about are ones which Muslims once had, and have been 'taken from us'.

Khayr al-Din declared that his purpose in examining European states was to take from them 'what is suitable to our own circumstances [and what] at the same time supports and is in accordance with our Shari'a' (p. 73). The Shari'a, he insisted, is 'applicable to both religious and secular matters'. One may legitimately borrow from non-Muslims anything that will promote the prosperity and well-being (maslaha: public interest) of the Islamic Community and that is not explicitly contrary to the Shari'a. Put another way, Europe can teach us the means by which we may attain the goals of the Holy Law.[34] Such was the relationship between European politics and the Shari'a.

The reason for the present political weakness of the umma is its economic backwardness, which leads to an adverse balance of payments, and hence an inability to buy even the military equipment needed in time of war. This is due to Europe's 'technical progress'. The crux of Khayr al-Din's argument was that this in turn was the product of the European 'constitution [tanzimat: regime]', which is 'based on justice and liberty' (p. 78). Here, one may see Ibn Khaldun being used creatively. Liberty and tanzimat produce prosperity ('umran: Ibn Khaldun's term for 'civilisation' (see above, p. 172) (p. 164). And they are in fact the very bases of our own Holy Law. Khayr al-Din rightly observed that Islam had long recognised the principle that justice and good administration are 'the causes of an increase in wealth, peoples and property' (pp. 79, 81).

Liberty for Europeans, he pointed out, had two aspects, personal and political. What they call personal liberty involves 'the individual's complete freedom of action over himself and his property, and the protection of his person, his honor and his wealth', so that he cannot 'be prosecuted for anything not provided for in the laws of the land duly determined before the courts'. This gave people 'complete control over the conduct of commerce' (pp. 160, 163–4).

Both personal liberty and justice are achieved by the rule of law, which for Khayr al-Din, as for most Ottoman and Iranian reformers of the time, was the most important constitutional principle. Khayr al-Din's reflections on constitutional law have a partly Khaldunian flavour: 'oppression foreshadows the ruin of civilization' (p. 82). Government cannot be beneficial unless the ruler himself, who is the necessary restraint (Ibn Khaldun's term) upon the behaviour of the human species, is likewise subject to restraint. For the well-being of kingdoms without the rule of law depends entirely upon the personal qualities of kings; this one may see from the history of European kingdoms 'before the establishment of laws', at a time when Islamic rulers observed justice and the umma was at the height of its power.[35] It is therefore 'essential that the restrainer should have *his* restrainer to check him, either in the form of a heavenly Shari'a or a policy based on reason'. In other words, constitutional law may be based either on revelation or on reason; here he quotes Ibn Khaldun's *Muqaddima*.[36] Legal and constitutional restraints require enforcement. For this reason, 'the Europeans have established councils and ... the freedom of the press', while among us 'it is incumbent upon the 'ulama and notables of the umma to resist evil' (sc. hisba) (p. 84).

'European progress in the sciences, industry and agriculture' stems 'from the consensus of the ruler and the ruled'. This in turn derives from 'laws providing the basic requirement of liberty for preserving the rights of the individual in his person, honor and wealth' (p. 175). Thus personal and political liberty are linked by Khayr al-Din, as in the European republican tradition.[37] He noted that what Europeans mean by political liberty is participation by the subjects in politics. This principle, he said, was recognised by the Caliph 'Umar (pp. 160–1). Khayr al-Din equated constitutional democracy with Islamic shura (consultation) (pp. 82, 85–6). This, he observed, may be applied either to 'general policy matters' (through parliamentary legislation), or to 'all executive acts' through ministerial accountability; and he described how this worked in France (pp. 90, 172–3).

While Khayr al-Din expressed cautious support for the Young Ottomans' programme of democratisation, he pointed out the difficulties facing a representative assembly in a polity containing so many races, religions and languages as the Ottoman empire (pp. 116–18). He thought that the functions of a European 'Chamber of General Deputies' could be fulfilled by 'those qualified to loose and bind' (sc. an assembly of notables: see above, p. 85) 'even though [these] are not elected by the people' (p. 161). He thus saw consultation as mandatory, but not democracy – a fairly common Muslim standpoint (see Mawdudi, below, p. 320). He made allowance for temporary autocratic rule by a 'dictator' in an emergency (p. 176) – following European and Roman tradition.

Khayr al-Din was the first Muslim political analyst to use his study of European systems as the basis for a geo-religious strategy not only to prevent the further decline of Islamic power, but also to restore Islam's former greatness, and once again to surpass Europe. This Islam was well able to do, because the 'Muslim masses are superior in intelligence to the masses in other nations' (note the 'racist' attitude); and 'freedom and human resolution', which others have achieved only through political reform, are inculcated into Muslims by their education and the Shari'a (p. 130). He thus anticipated the ideological initiatives usually credited to al-Afghani.

Tunisia's foreign loans and financial mismanagement led to the imposition of an Anglo-French commission to supervise the country's finances (1869). Khayr al-Din returned as its president and became chief vizier (prime minister) from 1872 to 1877. He struggled to put the country's finances on a sound footing, to reform the administration and to improve the status of farmers. But he was forced out of office in 1877 – and then invited to serve a new Ottoman Sultan.

ISLAMIC CONSERVATISM AND PAN-ISLAMISM

When Abdulhamid II (r.1876–1909) came to the throne, the Ottoman constitutionalists seemed on the verge of success. A constitution was drafted, partly under Young Ottoman influence. But the Sultan insisted that it should be issued solely on his own authority, and the powers of the parliament were severely curtailed. The constitution did reaffirm individual liberty, especially in religious matters, and equality between people of different faiths. The one success of the Young Ottomans was the statement of a new conception of citizenship: 'All subjects of the Empire are, without distinction, called Ottomans whatever religion they profess ... All Ottomans enjoy individual liberty on condition that they do not interfere with the liberty of others ... All Ottomans are equal in the eyes of the law. They have the same rights and duties towards the country without prejudice regarding religion.'[38]

Abdulhamid soon prorogued parliament and suspended the constitution (1878). 'I now understand', he said, 'that it is only by force that one can move the people with whose protection God has entrusted me' (in Shaw and Shaw 1977: 213). Khayr al-Din served briefly as Grand Vizier, an experience which turned him 'into a belated Young Ottoman' and confirmed his constitutionalist and parliamentary beliefs (*EI* 4: 1154b). Autocracy was now part of Abdulhamid's official ideology; he published hadiths on the authority of the emperor (padishah). The Young Ottomans' ideals of individual liberty and parliamentary representation were discarded.

The Ottoman government, in an attempt to gain the committed support of at least the majority of its subjects, turned to Islamism. This was partly a response to new setbacks in the international arena: the Treaty of Berlin (1878) gave independence to Romania, Bulgaria and Serbia. This was an apparent victory for the Russian empire, the Ottomans' arch-rival and the champion of pan-Orthodoxy and pan-Slavism. So the Ottoman regime decided to base the loyalty of subjects on Islamic solidarity, and to emphasise the role of the Sultan as Caliph of Sunni Muslims. Sunnism of the Hanafi school became the official faith; there was 'a systematic policy of conversion' aimed especially at Shi'ites and other non-Sunni Muslims (Deringil 1998: 47, 68, 91). The version of Islam invoked by the Sultan was conservative, emphasising the Caliphate and other traditional institutions, and tying religion and state closely together. The office of Şeikhülislam was expanded to include responsibility for the Religious Judiciary and the upkeep of mosques. The ulema were awarded increased salaries from Religious Trusts. Such an approach was justified by an Ottoman prince (1918) on the grounds that 'There is no need for democracy in

Islam. The West needed it because there was no equality there ... The internal class struggles of Western society do not exist in Islam ... The West seeks justice through laws whereas Islam finds it in faith' (in Berkes 1964: 370, 372): a sentiment that would find especial favour in the new century.

Abdulhamid also asserted his position as Caliph of Muslims living outside the Ottoman empire, and his the right to appoint Religious Judges in Egypt and the independent Balkans. The papacy had responded in a not dissimilar way to the loss of the papal states when it had the pope declared infallible in doctrine (1871). These policies coincided with Pan-Islamism, an attempt on the part of some Muslim leaders to encourage concerted action and a feeling of common identity among Muslims across state boundaries – in other words, to revive the umma.[39] (Some Arab nationalists suggested that, if there was to be a universal Caliphate, the Arabs should have it, an idea originally floated by the English romantic Wilfrid Blunt (1882).)[40] At the outbreak of the First World War (1914), the Ottoman Caliph issued 'a universal proclamation to all the people of Islam', which called upon Muslims everywhere to 'rise up as the rising of one man, in one hand the sword in the other the gun, and in his pockets balls of fire and annihilating missiles, and in his heart the light of faith' against 'the English, the Russians and the French' as oppressors of Islam: 'India for the Muslim Indians ... Algeria for the Algerians ... Caucasus for the Caucasians' (Landau 1994: 353, 357). This, if anything, was political Islam. The Mahdist state in the Sudan (1881–98)[41] showed that such a call to political awakening was not only the last resort of a state in decline.

INDIA: BRITISH RULE AND THE MUSLIM–HINDU QUESTION

Pan-Islamism had a special resonance in India,[42] where the situation for Muslims was dramatically different from elsewhere – and unusual in all Islamic experience – and where the sense of religious Leadership (Imamate) was numbed by British rule. After the failure of the Mutiny of 1857, Muslims were under British rule in lands previously ruled by their own Caliph-emperor but with a non-Muslim majority. A sense of Islamic solidarity and even of loyalty to the Ottoman Caliphate provoked demonstrations following the Ottoman military reverses in the Balkans in the 1870s. Indian Muslims con-tributed generously to the construction of the Hijaz railway by the Sultan as protector of the Holy Places.[43]

Modernism in India was a response to the need to come to terms with infidel rule in a country where democracy would have meant more infidel rule. Sometimes it was also the product of admiration of British administration. Sayyid Ahmad Khan (1817–98) in particular was very favourably impressed by a trip to England (1869–70) and called British rule 'the most wonderful phenomenon the world has ever seen'. He professed loyalty 'not from servile submission to a foreign rule, but from genuine appreciation of the blessings of good government' (in Ahmad 1967: 33). Ahmad Khan responded to those who now looked to the Ottoman Sultan as Caliph by saying: 'His sovereignty does not extend over us. We are residents of India and subjects of the British

Government, which has guaranteed us religious freedom. Our life and property are protected and our personal affairs – marriage, divorce, inheritance – ... are administered according to the Shari'a.'[44]

Muslim intellectuals and activists such as Ahmad Khan and Chiragh Ali (1844–95) asserted as a matter of principle the distinction between the ethical essentials of Islam, which they reduced to the explicit commandments of the Qur'an, and everything else in the Muslim religio-legal tradition (Shari'a), which they saw as expedients produced by historical circumstances. Most of the Law and virtually everything to do with politics fell into this latter category. In politics, one should adopt the best arrangements available in a given time and place. Indian modernists were among the pioneers of equality between the sexes among Muslims.[45]

The most contentious issue, as always, was the Muslims' relationship with the Hindu majority. From now on, this was to dominate Muslim politics in India. British rule had provided an unexpected and novel solution. The modernists went a long way towards developing a new attitude. Chiragh Ali rejected legal discrimination between Muslims and non-Muslims. Ahmad Khan regarded Hindus and Muslims, since they inhabited the same territory, as fellow-citizens of the same 'nation (qawm)'. He was willing to 'designate both the nationalities that inhabit India by the term "Hindu" [sc. Indian]' (in Malik 1980: 244–5).

But the prospect of independence or even limited self-government pitted the modernists' admiration for British parliamentary institutions against their dread of being ruled by the Hindus, their old rivals and 'polytheists'. Even Ahmad Khan's perception of Hindu–Muslim relations led him to reject the elections proposed for local government in India (1883). He accepted that 'representation by election' was 'no doubt the best system that can be adopted ... where the population is composed of one race and creed'. But, in areas of mixed faith, representative government would mean 'the representation of the views and interests of the majority of the population', so that 'the larger community would totally override the interests of the smaller'. This 'might make the differences of race and creed more violent than ever'. 'In India peace cannot be maintained if either Hindus or Muslims rule the country. It is therefore inevitable that another nation should rule over us.'[46] This was not a position which either more orthodox Muslims or the democratising modernists would sustain. But both Ahmad Khan and Khayr al-Din showed insight into the problems facing democracy in areas of mixed race and faith.

AL-AFGHANI (1837–97): RATIONALISM, REPUBLICANISM AND THE RELIGIO-POLITICAL REVIVAL OF ISLAM

Sayyid Jamal ad-Din 'al-Afghani' (Asterabad? 1837–Istanbul 1897)[47] moulded these separate but parallel movements into a single universal programme. He took the idea of a return to the first principles of Islam from India; the demand for charismatic leadership and revolutionary action from Shi'ism; and he shared with Sayyid Ahmad Khan and Khayr al-Din the positive attitude towards Western science. But he was the first philosopher who came to see the position of Islam and the West in truly pan-Islamic terms. For him, Islam was an infinitely rich cultural unit, a great Community which had allowed itself to become degraded and was now threatened on all sides by a sophisticated infidel. He conceived Shi'ites and Sunnis as members of the same Community, and drew on both traditions in order to combat the common enemy. He was not only a teacher and pamphleteer but also in some ways, in the circumstances in which he wrote, an original thinker.

His programme was, in the classical Islamic mould, at once intellectual, spiritual and political. Educated in Iran, he spent his early twenties in post-Mutiny India; there he learned to admire European science and detest British rule. He took part in Afghan tribal resistance to the British (1866–8). He arrived in Cairo in 1871 and became the great fringe teacher (1871–9); he combined reappropriation of the Islamic philosophical and mystical tradition with the call to restore Islam to political ascendancy.

He was quite open to new ideas. Some suspected him of atheism. '[His] originality consisted in this, that he sought to convert the religious intellect of the countries where he preached, to the necessity of reconsidering the whole Islamic position, and, instead of clinging to the past, of making an onward intellectual movement in harmony with modern knowledge', as one of his Egyptian students put it. Keddie goes somewhat further: 'Afghani, at least with his most intimate disciples, tended rather to lead men away from traditional beliefs toward an open-mindedness and rationalism that had an indigenous pedigree' (Keddie 1972b: 30–1, 86, 126). He used Shi'ite dissimulation (taqiyya) in tailoring his ideas to suit different audiences.

Al-Afghani began to espouse the Pan-Islamic cause in the wake of the Treaty of Berlin and Abdulhamid II's move towards political Islam. He conceived of a kind of international league: Muslims 'from Edirne to Peshawar … should … agree between themselves on defense and attack' (1884) (in Landau 1994: 320). This, he said, rather than alliance with Germany, should be Ottoman policy. He returned to India (1879–82), then went to Paris and London (1883–?6). He became a focus for émigré Muslim intellectuals such as the Persian, Malkom, met Europeans interested in Islam, and engaged the post-Christian Renan in discussion about the role of religion in society. Everywhere he looked for opportunities to stiffen resistance to Western culture and power. He counselled the constitutionalist intellectuals of Iran, and during the tobacco protest of 1891–2 urged the supreme Mujtahid to use his religious authority to quash the foreign monopoly. He pleaded with the Iranian 'ulama to depose the Shah, who in the end was assassinated by one of his disciples. He aspired to become the mentor of the Ottoman Sultan-Caliph; but Abdulhamid found him a difficult customer, and al-Afghani spent his last years a virtual prisoner. Everywhere he set about converting fellow-Muslims to his new vision of Islam and urging political leaders to undertake whatever action they could against the Europeans.

Al-Afghani's thought tapped into the view, found in Ibn Sina and some Shi'ites, that prophecy, mysticism and philosophy are essentially one: truth is reached through revelation, intuition and reason. 'There was, is, and will be no ruler in the world but science', he said; European science was of course the development of an originally Islamic heritage. And the overarching science was falsafa: without 'the spirit of philosophy' the other sciences wither (Keddie 1972b: 69, 86, 161). All this was a political statement: it was through their science that the Europeans were dominating the world.

Al-Afghani shared with other modernists an 'idealist' view that mind and character are the motor of historical change. What Islam needed first of all, therefore, was spiritual and intellectual revival. A radical change in outlook was required, reversing the trend of the whole preceding epoch. What al-Afghani had in mind here was, in particular, a re-evaluation of the relationship between religion and science. Renan had ascribed the backwardness of Eastern countries to the anti-scientific attitude of Islam, and al-Afghani went a long way towards endorsing this. 'As long as humanity exists, the struggle will not cease between dogma and free investigation ... a desperate struggle in which, I fear, the triumph will not be free thought, because the masses dislike reason'.[48] Thus, whereas some earlier Falasifa had seen religion as the way of teaching the common people truths they were unable to attain by philosophy, al-Afghani took a more pessimistic view.

But for al-Afghani there was more to it than this. In an argument more akin to twentieth-century social analysis, he insisted that part of the cause of the relative decline of the Islamic world was political authoritarianism. Science and philosophy had been stifled by 'our ... fanaticism and tyranny', by religion *and* despotism.[49]

But al-Afghani did not, as many others did, deduce from this critique that religion was passé. One can be scientific *and* religious. To take on board the latest European developments was tantamount to a return to true Islamic principles in both philosophy and politics. We must abandon the superstition and inertia which he, like Europeans, saw as characteristic of present-day Islam, and return to true Islam, that is to a religion which did accord with the spirit of modern science. Members of religious traditions 'must shun submission to conjectures and not be content with mere imitation (taqlid) of their ancestors'. What Islam needed now, therefore, was something like the European Reformation; al-Afghani saw himself as a kind of Luther, or 'secular Messiah' (in Keddie 1972b: 95, 142, 178, 359).

This was the intellectual basis for his programme of strengthening Islam as a people and culture against the West. His critical religious analysis was, in a manner charateristic of Islamic thinking, designed to support the political project of revivifying the Islamic Community (milla), and re-establishing it as a political power (Keddie 1972b: 62, 126, 133, 141). In his *Refutation of the Materialists* (written from India in Persian), he defended religion because it promoted social stability, honesty in international relations, and peace between social classes. He thus gave sharper edge to the Islamic tenet that law and order depend on religious belief, and applied it very explicitly to the contemporary world.[50]

The revival of Islam in both the political and religious spheres depended, he thought, upon the adoption of constitutional or republican government and an active civic spirit. Here he spoke, perhaps unconsciously, with the voice of the European Renaissance. We need patriotic zeal, citizens 'who know that their honour is only in their race (jins), their power is only in their community (umma), and their glory is only in their fatherland (watan)'. We need 'parliamentary rule' (in Keddie 1972b: 108–10). Al-Afghani was willing to combine this appeal to nationalism with an appeal to Islamic identity because both would help rouse Muslim peoples to resist foreign encroachment. He wanted to 'breathe ... the new spirit of nationality' into the Ottoman 'ulama and notables, to incite the Turcomans of central Asia with 'the pride of their Turkish race' so that they would 'carry the banner of Unity of Islam' (in Keddie 1972b: 135–7). In India, he advocated an Urdu rather than a Muslim nationalism, for 'there is no happiness except in nationality, and ... no nationality except in language' (in Keddie 1972b: 157). This suggests that opposition to European domination was his overriding motive.

Al-Afghani saw such political activism, inspired by nationalism, as the way to galvanise people's energies, to overcome the lethargy of traditional Islamic moeurs, and to motivate people to advance themselves in all departments of life. Political activism is the engine of civilisation, the spring that will drive Islamic society forwards. 'The desire to protect fatherland and nationality (vatan va jins) and the wish to defend religion and coreligionists, that is, patriotic zeal, national zeal, and religious zeal, arouse men to compete in the arena of virtues and accomplishments' (in Keddie 1972b: 166). Again, he was echoing Renaissance humanism.

Al-Afghani was the catalyst of modernism, which he imbued with a spirit that would become fundamentalism. In al-Afghani, the currents of modernism were fused into a more wide-ranging internationalist and aggressive political project. While he embraced European philosophy and science, he took a confrontational political stance towards the West. He was the pinnacle of the modernists and the foundation of the fundamentalists – a genius of a kind.

His influence went everywhere. From Egypt to Afghanistan, he 'has become almost a mythical hero'. To the Muslim Brethren, al-Afghani was 'the announcer'. In India, where his works became popular from the 1880s, many regarded him with 'something like worship';[51] the Caliphate movement of the 1920s and the poet-philosopher Muhammad Iqbal used his ideas. The special relationship between Shi'ite political theology and Western constitutionalism in Iran also reflected his approach.

'ABDUH AND LEGAL REFORM

Muhammad 'Abduh (Lower Egypt 1849–Cairo 1905)[52] was the most effective of al-Afghani's followers. He adopted al-Afghani as spiritual guide, and under his influence combined journalism and politics with his early interest in mystical spirituality. Banished from Egypt (1882–9), he co-published with al-Afghani a successful reformist journal (Paris, 1884); back in Cairo, he worked to reform the Shari'a, and was appointed official mufti (senior religious Judge: 1899–1905). He was a member of the representative legislative council.

'Abduh's contribution to reformism lay partly in his role as a Jurist and senior Religious Judge. He greatly expanded the scope of ijtihad (individual reasoning), teaching that morality and law must be adapted to modern conditions in the interests of the common good (maslaha). He argued that humans can in principle know good and evil by reason alone (Kerr 1966: 125–32). But (like the Falasifa) he thought that most failed to do so; moreover, humans can only be *motivated* to do good by religion. Indeed, the actual obligation to *do* what is right is known only by revelation. Thus, while he could have been on the brink of a significant change in moral philosophy, reversing a Juristic tradition going back to the beginnings of Islam (see above, Chapter 3), his moral rationalism did not in fact go as far as Aquinas' or Locke's.

In politics, 'Abduh was more moderate than al-Afghani. He thought that 'political organisation is not a matter determined by Islamic doctrine but is rather determined from time to time according to circumstances, by general consultation within the Community' (in Kerr 1966: 148). He took an approach similar to the Young Ottomans'; under his influence, 'the maslaha of the Maliki jurists and Ibn Taymiyya [gradually turned] into the "utility" of John Stuart Mill, the ijma' of Islamic jurisprudence into the "public opinion" of democratic theory, and "those who bind and loose" into members of parliament' (A. Hourani 1983: 344).

Clearly he was thinking of his own society when he said that a moral social order can arise when people who have been living under an unrestricted strong man, and only considering their own interests, 'learn something of the conduct of other nations ... [and] recall that they once had rights as a group ... [and] a prosperous life ... Then they will resolve to redress their society in accordance with those principles that its nature demands'. Then public opinion (ar-ra'y al-'amm) will emerge, and people will recognise that they do indeed have common interests (a somewhat Rousseauist sentiment). They will be 'unwilling to confide the task of instituting this law to a single (person), since a single individual is unable to interpret the [seemingly] divergent interests of all' (in Kerr 1966: 132–3). Education would bring about the necessary improvements in social outlook.

But later he came to believe that 'a just dictator' was needed to bring progress to 'the East', before representative institutions could be made to work. Islam, nevertheless, knows only 'a civil ruler (hakim madani)', one who is bound by a law which is not under his control, and installed in office by 'the nation', which supervises him, and may depose him (in Kerr 1966: 135, 149).

'Abduh promoted the salafiyya ('pious-forefathers') movement in northern Africa, and established modernist reformism as a force in Egypt. He helped to spread al-Afghani's ideas in Egypt, Syria, northern Africa and Indonesia (*EI* 8: 902a; Choueiri 1997: 36).

NOTES

1. The best overall studies are A. Hourani (1983) and Enayat (1982); see also Landau (1994).
2. In general, see Lewis (1968); Zürcher (1998); Shaw and Shaw (1977); Berkes (1964); Mardin (1960, 1962); Inalçik (1964).
3. A. Hourani (1983: 75); Vatikiotis (1991: 112–18).
4. Lapidus (1988: 598–9); Shaw (1976: 119).
5. Berkes (1964: 214); Mardin (1962: 199–200).
6. Mardin (1962: 198, 202); Berkes (1964: 165, 168). See above, p. 217.
7. Lewis (1968: 132); Mardin (1960: 425–6).
8. Lewis (1968: 347); Deringil (1998: 29).
9. A. Hourani (1983: 76, 89); Mardin (1960: 426).
10. For what follows, see Algar (1969); Bakhash (1978); Keddie (1980); Lambton (1970); Helm (1991: 103–17); Arjomand (1984: 221–57); Arjomand (ed.) (1988); Sachedina (1988: 226–36); *CH Iran* 7: 174–97, 732–9; Lapidus (1988: 571–9).
11. Malcolm (1829) in Lambton (1970: 248–9).
12. Halm (1991: 101–2); Keddie (1972a: 225n.). See above, pp. 228–9.
13. Arjomand (ed.) (1988: 100); Morgan (1988: 160); Lapidus (1988: 572).
14. Arjomand (ed.) (1988: 111, 119); see above, p. 234.
15. Halm (1991: 104); Arjomand (1984: 232, 237); Arjomand (ed.) (1988: 108).
16. Arjomand (1984: 224, 242); Kohlberg (1991: 82–3); Halm (1991: 107–8); Algar (1969: 87–90).
17. Lambton (1974); Danishpazhouh (1988: 225–31).
18. In Arjomand (1984: 227); see Keddie (ed.) (1972a: 226).
19. *EI* 6: 291–2; Algar (1973).
20. Algar (1973: 28–9); Bakhash (1978: 10–11).
21. Bakhash (1978: 8–12); Algar (1973: 29).
22. Ervand Abrahamian, 'The Causes of the Constitutional Revolution in Iran', *IJMES* 10 (1979), pp. 381–414 at p. 397.
23. In Abrahamian, p. 399; see Algar (1973: 235); Bakhash (1978: 306–11, 354).
24. In Bakhash (1978: 336); see *CH Iran* 7: 184; Keddie (1980: 34).
25. In Algar (1973: 237) and Abrahamian, p. 399.
26. In Algar (1973: 75); Bakhash (1978: 15).
27. Bakhash (1978: 345); Keddie (1980: 37, 94).
28. *EI* 2: 650–3 and 4: 398; *CH Iran* 7: 202–7; Keddie (1980: 66–79); Halm (1991: 115–16); Abrahamian (see above, n. 22); Arjomand (ed.) (1988, chs 8, 16).
29. *CH Iran* 7: 733–4; Enayat (1982: 164, 174).
30. In Arjomand (ed.) (1988: 181–2, 339–40, 346, 357).
31. See especially Mardin (1962); Lewis (1968: 138–74); Berkes (1964: 208–61); Zürcher (1998: 70–4).
32. Berkes (1964: 213); Lewis (1968: 140).
33. Khayr al-Din al-Tunisi, *The Surest Path: The Political Treatise of a Nineteenth-century Muslim Statesman*, trans. Leon Carlos Brown (Cambridge, MA: Harvard University Press, 1967), with intro.; A. Hourani (1983: 84–94); *EI* 4: 1153–5.
34. 'Les moyens pour y parvenir peuvent être de nature différente et varier indéfiniment, selon les temps et l'état des mœurs; et lorsque notre loi ne les indique pas formellement, comme elle ne les interdit pas non plus, la saine interprétation de cette loi indique qu'il faut les prendre en considération, les adopter et en favoriser l'application': p. 123.
35. Pp. 82, 88, 97. He explains the meaning of the rule of law on p. 170.

36. P. 84; see above, p. 172.
37. Quentin Skinner, *Liberty before Liberalism* (Cambridge: Cambridge University Press, 1998), pp. 66–77.
38. In Shaw and Shaw (1977: 177); see *EI* 2: 642 and 3: 592b.
39. *EI* 8: 248; Landau (1994: 5–6).
40. A. Hourani (1983: 268–73); Berkes (1964: 268).
41. P. M. Holt, *The Mahdist State in the Sudan 1881–1898* (Oxford: Oxford University Press, 1958).
42. For what follows, see especially Ahmad (1967); Hardy (1972); Ahmad and von Grunebaum (eds) (1970).
43. Landau (1994: 186–9); Ahmad (1964: 63).
44. In Malik (1980: 237); see *EI* 9: 287–8.
45. Ahmad (1967: 60–1, 72–8); Hardy (1972: 100, 113); Malik (1980: 240).
46. In Hardy (1972: 137) and Ahmad (1967: 34).
47. On his much-disputed life story, see the masterly study by Keddie (1972b); A. Hourani (1983: 103–29).
48. In Keddie (1972b: 193); see Keddie (1980: 30–2).
49. Keddie (1972b: 62, 109); Keddie (1980: 30); Jamal ad-Din Afghani, *Réfutation des Matérialistes*, trans. A. M. Goichon (Paris: P. Geuthner, (1942), pp. 178, 184.
50. Keddie (1972b: 172); see above, p. 74 (Ibn Sina).
51. Ahmad (1964: 61); Keddie (1972b: 422); Mitchell (1969: 321).
52. Kerr (1966); A. Hourani (1983: 130–60).

The Age of Fundamentalism
C.1920–2000

26

The First World War punctured the myth of the superiority of the West in political and social organisation. Muslim intellectuals no longer felt inferior to a Europe which had sacrificed millions on the altar of political rationality. Many continued to believe in liberalism and democracy (as representative government was now called), and to strive to introduce them into the Islamic world. Others looked to critiques by Europeans of European culture and society, to moral revivalists and theorists of Western decadence. Some political thinkers and activists in Muslim countries were attracted by aspects of Fascism, others by aspects of Marxism. Marxism made particular sense of the colonial experience and offered a radical and up-to-date solution. Marxist theories of economic exploitation and revolution by the oppressed could be amalgamated with traditional Islamic views about justice and the means to achieve it. All the leading so-called fundamentalist theorists took something from this. Sunni radicals also adopted Fascist or Leninist methods of party organisation, leadership and social mobilisation. The Iranian Shi'ites already had their own method.

The Ottoman empire left behind it a power vacuum and a loose bundle of ethnic, religious and territorial political identities. The French and British mandates in Syria, Palestine and Iraq were blows to the perceived ability of Muslim peoples to govern themselves in their original heartlands. The final blow was the recognition by the United Nations, after the civil war of 1948, of the state of Israel.

But from now on the political fortunes of Muslim states began to revive. This was initiated mainly not by religious leaders but by secular politicians. In Pakistan, Jinna sought to create a modern secular state in which religious identities would be relegated to private life. Arab leaders defined their mission as anti-colonialism, nationalism and socialism.[1]

The post-Christian West had one more card to play: Marxism could explain the failure of secular liberal democracy without conceding the moral superiority of religion. In the 1950s and 1960s, states legitimised by a theory of the sovereignty of the people and the pursuit of social and economic justice, and defined by some form of nationhood, enjoyed widespread support in the struggle against the colonial powers. Political parties or leaders who saw their vocation and legitimacy in secular terms gained power in Egypt, Syria and Iraq;

the Pahlavi monarchy retained power in Iran. In the 'radical revolution' of 1958–61, Gamal Abdul Nasser of Egypt (r.1953–71) and the Ba'th parties in Syria and Iraq appealed to Arab nationhood and Arab socialism. Islam seemed to be becoming irrelevant to politics.

The Marxist and secularist card was trumped by the Israelis when they destroyed the Soviet tanks of the new Arab regimes in the Six-Day War (1967). Political Islam now became 'the one idiom which remains available and untarnished after the fall of their former idols'.[2] This, it could now be hoped, would rise up against the forces of post-Christian secularism: Western capitalism and atheist Communism. Had not Islam begun as a simultaneous triumph over two exploiting empires? The new mood borrowed from the Marxism it was supplanting; it was most of all defined by opposition to 'the West'.

States do not live by ideology alone, and the varied ideologies of the new states of the Muslim world were a cloak for a variety of personal, factional and class interests. Twentieth-century states in the Muslim world differ, broadly speaking, from Western states in the strength of traditional networks throughout the 'civil society' over which they rule. Social membership and obligation run in family clans, sects large and small, Muslim and non-Muslim, local districts and tribes. In the heyday of secular ideology, 'the categories of political action, whether observed in Syria, Iraq or the Yemen, remained the traditional ones of jama'at (groups), kutal (factions) and fi'at (cliques)'.[3] Political parties serve as the instruments of such units, or of the state or the ruler. Politics and social life in general depend upon a patronage system, in which people are grouped 'into families, quarters, villages, sects and tribes', which have even 'stifled the emergence of class and interest groups' (Choueiri 1997: 47–8, 71). Familial and hereditary factors operate at the pinnacle of state authority in Saudi Arabia, the Gulf sheikhdoms ('no more than the private property of individual families'),[4] and the hereditary monarchies of Jordan and Morocco. Militias belonging to clans, religious groups or terrorists often deny the state the monopoly of the legitimate means of coercion; these 'reassert, at the expense of the military, the function of the warrior in Arab societies' (Charnay 1986: 265).

Such traditional units constitute the power base of governments. Nationhood can create some sense of common membership in states such as Turkey, Iran, Egypt and Uzbekistan. But usually the sense of membership adheres to smaller units. In the case of Arabs, nationhood itself has created a supra-state allegiance. Some national groups, such as the Kurds, are sub-units within different states with a supra-state allegiance of their own.

In states in the Muslim world, there is usually a close relationship between the military and the government, either because the ruler is at the same time the personal commander of the armed forces (as in Islamic tradition); or because military leaders take over the government (e.g. Pakistan, Nigeria). In Turkey, the most secular state in the Islamic world, the army holds a permanent veto over the political process, as it also does in Indonesia. Iran, Saudi Arabia and to some extent Morocco, Tunisia and Yemen are exceptions. And Iran is under the supervision of the Shi'ite 'ulama, Saudi Arabia a family fief.

There is usually a symbiotic relationship between the state and economic resources; modern states in the Islamic world perpetuate some of the ways of patrimonial monarchy. Membership in the ruling clan or network becomes one of the chief means of acquiring wealth. Such arrangements can also be presented as state socialism. Compared with previous dynasties, however, modern states are more 'intrusive and directive in many spheres of social and even domestic life' (Zubaida 1993: 162). Thus there tends not to be an independent bourgeoisie; 'civil society' is here so different that it should perhaps be called something else.

These distinguishing features are especially noticeable in cases when the military head of state rules through his own network, for example in the 'republics' of Syria and Iraq. Such rulers are often called dictators, but their style and methods are in some ways those of a traditional sultan, for example in perpetuating their power through their own offspring. These factors prevent the development of democratic parties and impersonal institutions of government. Succession remains a major cause of instability, as it always has been in Muslim states. Thus a 'tribal' element remains relatively strong in many Muslim states (see above, pp. 10–11).

The organism which, if any, holds a 'monopoly of the legitimate means of coercion' is not Weber's impersonal bureaucratic state but a network led by an individual – what Ibn Khaldun called an 'asabiyya (see above, p. 173) ('the modern state in the Middle East ... is a successful 'asabiyya': Roy 1994: 15, 18). Some have gone so far as to argue that one cannot create the state as an independent order in the Islamic world (Vatikiotis 1971: 5–8). But post-Atatürk Turkey, post-Khomeini Iran and perhaps Tunisia under Bourguiba[5] may be exceptions. In any case, it is for such reasons that democratic politics in the European sense, based on freedom of expression and association, is virtually unknown.

All of this builds upon certain features in the traditional political cultures of the Islamic world. The recognised function of the coercive power of the state (lit. sultan) is above all to enforce the law and maintain social peace, between groups as much as between individuals. So long as the ruler or state is capable of doing that, he or it ought to be obeyed. Secondly, it is assumed, however tacitly, that such power acts on behalf of religious values of which other, religiously qualified persons, notably the 'ulama, are the official custodians. It has also for the most part been tacitly accepted that the ruler and his servants are for practical purposes independent of the religious leaders (they worship Allah and do what they want, to adapt St Augustine). One of the notable recent changes is the increasing number of exceptions to this.

Ideology becomes important only when other means of securing control – coercive force, ties of family or sect, distribution of wealth – are weakened. This is especially likely when a ruler dies. Secular ideologies were widely discredited by the Six-Day War and the failure of secular governments to deliver the promised economic goods. Hence Islamic political thought has come back onto the agenda. As under earlier regimes, when dynastic bonds or Jihad failed to deliver, the government in a Muslim society is likely look to religious solidarity for support, or else becomes threatened by religiously-inspired alternatives. It is this which has given spokespersons for religious correctness power beyond their numbers. Fundamentalism can make its mark by setting the agenda and defining what carries weight in public discourse. It does so because it can plausibly claim to represent 'true' Islam. Modernists, as we have seen, looked to original Islam chiefly as a basis for religious reform, and took their political norms from Europe. Fundamentalists look to original Islam for their political norms as well; not only and perhaps not mainly the sayings of Muhammad, which are relatively few and obscure on this topic, but also his praxis at Medina.

Hence the incremental Islamicisation of the legal and social agenda in countries as diverse as Egypt, Pakistan and even Turkey. The cost of refusing to listen to Islamicists is being borne in Algeria. Afghanistan has gone through another familiar sequence of events: the monarchy held the tribes together, and once that went, they fell apart. Not for the first time, different tribes have espoused their own religious causes. A group under an Imam with its own version of religious rectitude – the Taliban – has for the time being come out on top (Choueiri 1997: 175; Roy 1994: 158–61).

THE CALIPHATE AND POPULAR SOVEREIGNTY: SEPARATION OF POLITICS FROM RELIGION?

The Turkish revolution of 1920–4[6] was as momentous as the Russian one of 1917–21, but Western historians and social scientists have given it much less attention. For it was a defining moment in the relationship between Islam and the state. It brought into being the first avowedly secular state in the Muslim world, and it forced former subject peoples of the Ottoman empire, the Arabs in particular, to rebuild their political identity.

Opposition to autocracy had continued in the Ottoman empire under Abdul-hamid II, as in Russia under Nicholas II. Partly because of the Sultan's alliance with Islamic tradition, opposition now took a more secular turn. The Ottoman Society for Union and Progress was formed in 1889. Both they and the Young Turks advocated parliamentary liberalism. The Young Turks, like the Young Ottomans, continued to cherish the Ottoman dynasty as the basis of the state.

But, around 1900, nationalist movements in the Balkans finally provoked Turkish-speakers to seek a new form of identity in their own nationality. Meanwhile, pan-Turkism was developing among the Turkic peoples of Russia and central Asia (Lewis 1968: 343, 348–51); it was to resurface after the fall of the Soviet Union (1989). Various Turkish-speaking groups had long regarded themselves, and been regarded by others, as a distinctive element within the Islamic umma, and had frequently appropriated military and political power in multi-ethnic societies, for example in the Saljuk and Mamluk regimes. During the long decline of the Ottoman empire, not just Muslims but Turks specifically had begun to claim a privileged position in state and society, on the grounds of their ethnic affiliation with the ruling house, or their supposed innate qualities. Now the special qualities and history of the Turkish people and, finally, their right to their own nation-state, as other nations were claiming, became increasingly popular ideas.

The Young Turks, in the wake of the Russian and Iranian revolutions (1905–6), gathered enough support in the army to force Abdulhamid to restore the constitution of 1876 and recall parliament (1907–8), a move generally supported by Islamic reformers and modernists. This takeover of the Ottoman government by the Young Turks stimulated Turkish scholars and publicists to renewed study and glorification of the Turkish past, just like their nineteenth-century counterparts in Europe.

Young Turks like Ahmet Riza (1859–1930) continued to popularise their ideas in the Islamic idiom.[7] Others, including Abdulhamid II himself, argued that parliamentary liberalism owed nothing to Europe, and could be justified purely on the basis of Islamic values.[8] But on the whole there was a strong correlation between nationalism and secularism. Turkish nationalism was attractive to the more secular-minded supporters of the Ottoman constitution. After the Balkan wars of 1912–13 had reduced the Ottoman hold on Rumelia to a fragment north-west of Istanbul, 'official and popular opinion moved strongly toward Turkish nationalism' (Shaw and Shaw 1977: 289, 309). Under the government led by the Young Turks during the First World War, the ulema were brought under state control, and so were religious properties, the Shari'a judicial system and religious education (Shaw and Shaw 1977: 306–7). These measures of secularisation extended into private law with the incorporation of Shari'a regulations for Muslims in a new Code of Family Law (November 1917) promulgated by the state itself.

The rationale for secular nationalism in an Islamic society was set out by Ziya Gökalp (1876–1924). He argued for the separation of religion from the state on the basis of Durkheim's theory of social evolution. In the primitive form of solidarity, the different aspects of society – religion, polity, culture and law – do indeed go together. But it is an essential feature of organic solidarity, which exists in a developed society, that these should be separated out. He also argued that people form many different kinds of groups, from the family to international society, but that the most important of these is the nation. Just as Durkheim taught that morals spring out of group interaction, so 'patriotism should be the most important area of morality for the Turks'.[9] Gökalp was not a complete secularist: religion still has a part to play because this is what creates patriotism by uniting men 'through common sentiments and beliefs'. Gökalp took the modernist view that, while 'the divine part' of the Shari'a does not need to be changed, social rules can and should evolve along with society (E. Rosenthal 1965: 52–3). During the 1910s, Gökalp drafted proposals for secularisation that were more thoroughgoing than those adopted.

Defeat in the war which the Sultan-Caliph had declared a Holy War was, as for Russia and other imperial states, a catalyst for change in the very grounds of political legitimacy. It resulted in the transfer of sovereignty from the Sultan-Caliph to the elected representatives of the Turkish nation. It was to a special degree due to the military prowess of Mustafa Kemal (later called Atatürk: 'father of the Turks'), the hero of Gallipoli and 'the only remaining victorious general in Turkey' (Lewis 1968: 245), that political legitimacy passed from Sultan to Assembly. We may see the role of successful military leadership (imara: amir) carried over from Islamic tradition into the secular regime that succeeded it. A Grand National Assembly of delegates met at Ankara (April 1920) under Kemal's leadership. Sultan Mehmet VI signed (August 1920) a treaty with the victors that 'would have left Turkey helpless and mutilated'. Greece took advantage of the situation, and her armies drove deep into Anatolia (1920–2). Kemal routed them and also regained eastern Thrace. He thus ensured that 'Turkey, alone among the defeated powers, ... secured the acceptance of her own terms' (Lewis 1968: 247, 254).

At home, Kemal and his supporters faced a unique constitutional situation. They wanted to base the new state unequivocally on the sovereignty of the Turkish people. But Mehmet VI, though powerless and known to be incompetent, was Caliph and widely recognised in the Ottoman empire and other parts of the Islamic world both as the legitimate head of the Ottoman state and as the religious leader of Muslims. He was also a focus for a powerful group of religious conservatives who wanted to avoid the 'republican form of government' (in Berkes 1964: 449).

The Assembly declared (January 1921) that 'sovereignty belongs without reservation or condition to the nation'; and that it, as 'the only real representative of the people', is 'the holder of both legislative and executive power' (in Lewis 1968: 256). Kemal also based his actions partly on the principle that legitimacy ultimately depends upon de facto power. Here, Sunni Jurisprudence and European revolutionary doctrine coincided. 'Sovereignty has never been given to any nation by scholarly disputation. It has always been taken by force ... The Turkish nation has now taken back its usurped sovereignty by rebellion ... This is a fact' (Mustafa Kemal in Berkes 1964: 450).

Kemal now decided to separate the Sultanate from the Caliphate. The Assembly abolished the Sultanate, declaring (October 1923) that 'the form of government of the state of Turkey is a Republic' (in Lewis 1968: 261). The Caliph retained his religious status. But the 'ulama looked to the Caliph to oppose further moves towards a secular state and society, and they found support from the international Muslim community, especially in Egypt and India. For many, the removal of the Caliph's political functions and the separation of religious from political authority constituted heresy (bid'a) or even apostasy: for 'the Caliphate is a general headship (ri'asa) in matters of religion and of this world' (Egyptian ulema in Berkes 1964: 453). This led Kemal, now President, and the Grand National Assembly to decree the deposition of the Caliph and the abolition of the Caliphate (March 1924).

These measures were defended in a tract published by the National Assembly (1922). They argued that the Caliphate had not been established by the Prophet, but derived only from (as they put it) 'the "law of ijtihad [individual judgement]", on which there is little consensus'. The form of government was a pragmatic device for 'avoiding anarchy' (a view of the state's role consonant with Muslim tradition). It was therefore something for Muslims to decide for themselves in the light of contemporary circumstances: 'the question of the Caliphate is not a religious one ... The means for this should vary with the times'. Further, the Caliph, as an ordinary human ruler, is subject to election and deposition.

> The community alone can confer authority. The contract of the Caliphate is essentially one of agency, which consists, in the words of (the Ottoman civil code), of 'one person empowering some other person to perform some act for him'. As the nation's mandatory, the Caliph is always subject to recall for the abuse of power. (in Kerr 1966: 181–2)

Exactly the same argument, incidentally, had been used by supporters of the authority of general councils of the church against the papacy in fifteenth-century Europe (Black 1979: 163–4). These arguments suggest that Kemal's supporters were trying to redefine the relationship between the religious and the political within Islam, rather than to destroy Islam as a religion. It was an extreme version of the political programme of Islamic modernists, and was subsequently defended by at least one distinguished 'alim.

Measures were now undertaken to put into practice the decisively secular character of the Republic. Religious jurisdiction, religious colleges and the office of Şeikhülislam were all abolished. The Şeriat itself was replaced with a civil code based on Swiss (and thus partly Roman) law; this established the right to change one's faith, and equality in marriage between female and male. The use of religion for political ends was targeted in the new criminal code (1926), which forbade the use of religion for political purposes, and outlawed political associations based upon religion.[10] This appeared to take Turkey 'right out of the Islamic world and radically into Western civilization' (E. Rosenthal 1965: 54). But, although Kemalism has outlasted Bolshevism, it is only with great difficulty and the threat of overwhelming military force that an Islamic party has been prevented from leading a coalition government in Turkey today.

RASHID RIDA (1922–3)

The abolition of the Caliphate caused protests but no serious reaction.[11] But it had important long-term consequences for Islamic political thought because it cleared the way for new Islamic political initiatives; some welcomed it as 'the final fruition of purely Islamic ideas' (in Ahmad 1967: 139). It also facilitated a greater plurality of Muslim states and a new approach to international relations. It opened the way for extensive rethinking of how Islam should be expressed politically and of the political role for Muslims, which was not slow in coming.

The process began with the 'alim Rashid Rida (near Tripoli, Lebanon 1865–Cairo 1935) in On the Caliphate (Al-khilafa),[12] written (1922–3) after the abolition of the Sultanate while the question of the Caliphate was still under consideration. Rida started out as a disciple of 'Abduh; he travelled widely. At first, he pinned his hopes for religious reform on the Young Turks. Disappointed with them, he turned to pan-Arabism (1911–12); he supported the Arab Revolt and, when the Sharif of Mecca declared himself Caliph (1916), Rida supported him. He welcomed the first stages of the Turkish revolution: whereas Western civilisation 'is in our time doomed to ruin' – the lesson of 1914–18 had been learned – the Islamic (sic) government in Turkey, 'which has shown the most brilliant gifts in the arts of war', could achieve something positive 'if [it] wants to promote a Muslim reform'. He was, once again, disillusioned by the abolition of the Caliph's political powers.

This and the prospect of the abolition of the Caliphate itself prompted his *Al-khilafa*. Here, he reopened the question of the institutional structure of Islam. Rida had adopted the approach of al-Afghani and 'Abduh that the 'gates of individual judgment (ijtihad)' should be reopened; that we should 'return to sources' (Gardet 1981: 352). Like modernists from Khayr al-Din to Gökalp, he distinguished between those parts of the Shari'a that deal with what is divine and unchanging, and those parts that deal with social conduct: these may be adapted according to the utility principle (maslaha) (A. Hourani 1983: 344). The ulema, he had said, instead of upholding 'tyrannical autocracy', should have embraced parliamentary constitutionalism long ago (in Choueiri 1997: 46).

But now events made him wary of relinquishing the priority of the Sunna: in *al-Khilafa* he cautioned that redevelopment of social morality must be based exclusively on the Shari'a 'which is the basis for all human legislation'. The Caliphate, he argued, certainly is necessary, and it certainly does cater for the worldly as well as the religious interests of Muslims. Indeed, in true Sunni fashion, he insisted that the Caliph is specifically not a religious leader in the sense that he cannot decide questions of Religious Law. He is a worldwide leader, but in the modern world he would not supplant existing states. He is to preside over Muslim states and Muslims living under 'foreign rule' in a kind of confederation or 'commonwealth'. So the Caliph's political powers are also practically non-existent. The sort of thing he could do was to look after those concerns in which existing governments (he claimed) 'exercise no control': such as 'the organisation of religious education ... and laws of personal status'. Rida cited the papacy as a model for what he had in mind (Kerr 1966: 184–5). While the Caliph was not himself a judicial, far less a legislative authority, he might 'in political and judicial matters pertaining to government ... give prefer-ence to certain conclusions of ijtihad over others, after consulting the Learned ('ulama) among the "people who bind and loose" [sc. leaders of the Islamic community], particularly if he himself is not a qualified mujtahid'. Above all, he should take on the task of supervising the redevelopment of the Shari'a on social questions.[13] In other words, he gave the Caliph an updated role of moral leadership, religious guidance and exhortation.

On the question of the constitution of the Caliphate, Rida's debt to modernism came out but, once again, he diluted modernism with a strong dose of Muslim constitutional tradition. Election and consultation are basic principles of original Islam only abandoned by the Umayyads; for 'true obedi-ence is due only to God, and coercive power has been entrusted [sc. by God] to *the social body of the community*'.[14] Rida took the view that 'all that the [European] laws possess that is good and just has long since been laid down by our shari'a'.[15] This enabled him to decide on grounds of traditional Muslim criteria just how far he wanted to go towards popular sovereignty in the

Western sense. In Kerr's words, shura (consultation) became 'the hallmark of [Rida's] political theory ... in the fields of election, constitutional interpretation, administration, and legislation' (1966: 163, 172).

Now, as it turned out, Rida assigned all of these functions to 'the people who bind and loose (ahl al-hall wa 'l-'aqd)'. These notables or prominent citizens are not elected, just recognised. Rida equated them with 'the people (umma)' (Kerr 1966: 163) in the sense that their choices and decisions constitute the choices and decisions of the people. It was, once again, partly by such an equivalence between a self-selected representative body and the whole community that representative constitutionalism had started in Europe (Black 1979: 184–7). But here Rida was obviously watering down the theory of popular sovereignty as stated by Islamic modernists, presumably because of the secularising tendencies of the Turkish National Assembly.

Whom exactly he meant by 'the people who bind and loose' is problematic. Perhaps he meant acknowledged leaders of local communities whose decisions would automatically command respect (Kerr 1966: 161–3); that was one traditional meaning of the term. Sometimes he seems to be referring to 'ulama capable of exercising individual judgement (ijtihad) – in other words, Mujtahids. It is tempting here to see a parallel with Shi'ite thought: the 'reopening of ijtihad' could have given Sunni 'ulama the same status as Shi'ite Mujtahids. One of Rida's ambitions was to found a college for the training of such new religious scholars. In other words, he wanted to update religious structures and practices in order to implement traditional values more effectively in the modern world. And his constitutional views left open the possibility of direct participation by the 'ulama, or at least the better educated among them, in social and political leadership.

What was different about Rida seems to have been the revised relative weight given to European and Islamic traditions, namely his appeal to Islamic sources excluding, or at least ignoring, Western influence. Once again, Islamic theory had something in common with Plato: Rida was advocating constitutional rather than representative government. It is not surprising that he was read by 'the traditional elite and the educated or half-educated Muslim public' more than in governmental and Westernised circles (Gardet 1981: 350–1).

'ABD AL-RAZIQ (1924–5)

In 1925 Shaykh 'Ali 'Abd al-Raziq (1888–1966) published a response to Rida: *Islam and the Bases of Government (al-Islam wa usul al-hukm)*.[16] Its appearance set the tone for ensuing political debate in Egypt, the Arab world and Islam as a whole. 'Abd al-Raziq was also a disciple of 'Abduh; but he had studied at Oxford. He was, unlike Rida, a senior member of al-Azhar University, an authoritative centre of Sunni Learning.

'Abd al-Raziq's book was 'in a sense a justification of the Turkish Revolution', defending the Turkish National Assembly's approach to the separation of religious and political authority, and the secular origin of the Caliphate.[17] He sought to argue on the basis of Islamic texts that Muhammad did not set out to establish a state and that Islam did not lay down any particular political system. Here 'we meet for the first time a consistent, unequivocal theoretical assertion of the purely and exclusively religious character of Islam' (E. Rosenthal 1965: 86). In this, he was following the spirit of Western Biblical criticism, in the sense that he was prepared to countenance the possibility that prevailing tradition had radically misinterpreted its own sources. 'Abd al-Raziq's reply to Rida was that 'Islam has nothing to do with the Caliphate as the Muslims understand it'. The rules which the Prophet did lay down concerned only such things as prayer and fasting; and they were in fact rules appropriate for his particular culture, for people 'in a simple state with a natural government' (in E. Rosenthal 1965: 96, 98). He thus took the modernist argument – that the social norms of the Shari'a could be changed because they derived from specific historical circumstances – an important stage further. The Caliphate itself was the product of history, an institution of human rather than divine origin, a temporary convenience; and therefore a purely political office with no religious meaning or function. The universality of Islam lay not in its political structure but in its faith and religious guidance.'Abd al-Raziq's aim was, nonetheless, like that of all modernists and most reformers, to enable Islamic countries to develop politically so that they could 'compete with other nations' on equal terms (E. Rosenthal 1965: 98–9).

The conclusion is that constitutional forms can be remoulded from top to bottom. In political matters, we should be guided by reason and experience. 'All political functions are left to us, our reason, its judgments and political principles. Religion ... neither commands nor forbids [such things], it simply leaves them to us so that in respect of them we have recourse to the laws of reason, the experience of nations and the rules of politics' (in E. Rosenthal 1965: 98). Muslims have 'absolute freedom to organize the state in accordance with [existing] intellectual, social and economic conditions' (in Binder 1988: 131). 'Abd al-Raziq invoked again what we may call the 'autocratic' theory of Islamic history: despite their knowledge of Plato and Aristotle, Muslims had hitherto failed to develop political science, because the study of different constitutions would have constituted a threat to the power of their kings.

'Abd al-Raziq's argument was interesting, and he made some remarkable observations about original Islam. He argued that the Prophet did have a special 'force (quwwa)' in order to enable him to carry out what was a unique mission. This force was, however, peculiar to Muhammad; and – the crucial point – it was fundamentally different from the political power (hukm al-salatin) of a governor, king or sultan.[18] In Muhammad's case, it was not so much that politics was separate but that it was subsumed under a 'higher', 'wider' power to 'rule over the affairs of body and spirit ... [and] the administration of this world and the hereafter' (in E. Rosenthal 1965: 100). This unique power of the Prophet was more effective than ordinary governmental power because it involved voluntary leadership rather than coercion. The rulings which he did make were not in the same category as the functions of a modern government. Political authority in the ordinary sense did appear in the Islamic community, but only after Muhammad, and it was not part of God's revelation.

This was astute and also very original. 'Abd al-Raziq did not commit the obvious heresy of saying that the Prophet's power was limited to the spiritual. Western readers may be struck by the similarity between what 'Abd al-Raziq was saying here and the usual Christian view of religion and politics. The kind of leadership he attributed to the Prophet resembled the kind which Christian theologians usually attribute to Christ. The restriction of the scope of revelation, and the extension of the role of reason, were exactly the sort of moves made by Thomas Aquinas for Christianity in the thirteenth century. These had opened the way for the scientific and political development of the West. Was 'Abd al-Raziq, then, influenced here by Euro-Christian perspectives?

The crucial question for all students of Islamic political thought is whether 'Abd al-Raziq's interpretation of the Prophet's mission is a plausible one. Or, does it entail a break, not only from traditional Islam, but from the very enterprise of Muhammad himself and his first followers, so far as anyone today can ascertain this? It is not difficult to criticise 'Abd al-Raziq's interpretation of early Islam on scholarly grounds (Gardet 1981: 357). In Chapter 1, it was argued that it was their design specifically to include political and social matters in the divinely-revealed order of things; I know of no modern scholar who would disagree.

What 'Abd al-Raziq did was to articulate clearly for the first time the virtual and de facto separation between religion and politics, and between religious and political authority, which had actually been experienced during most of Islamic history, and as it was tacitly understood by most of his contemporaries. Still more, he justified this on grounds of religious science.

Thus, we may say, the needs of modern states seemed to make separation between politics and religion more imperative than ever. The challenges of European science and material development, the tremors these had set off across the Islamic world, were forcing people to reconsider their fundamental perspectives. Most politicians in the Islamic world in the twentieth century have certainly conducted their affairs as if politics were separate from religion. But no-one had previously said this in so many words, still less that the Prophet was not a political leader. Traditional jurisprudence, notably in al-Mawardi and Ibn Taymiyya, vigorously proclaimed the unity between the religious and the political; and this was the stuff of rhetoric.

Al-Azhar immediately condemned 'Abd al-Raziq's book; he was thrown out of the University, and dismissed from his position as Religious Judge. His views received no support in religious circles. Gökalp could preach the separation of religion from politics as a sociologist and be ignored by the spokesmen of religion, despite his not inconsiderable influence on Turkish political thought. But 'Abd al-Raziq was writing as a religious specialist. His thesis would have freed up political institutions and much of social, legal and political practice once and for all from the restrictions of the Shari'a; precisely what modernist reformers had been arguing for. But religious theory refused to bow down to practice.

'Abd al-Raziq had, like Machiavelli in Europe, sought to close the gap between rhetoric and practice. But the spokesmen of Islam refused to accept, or even tolerate, this way of closing the gap. The only other way to close it was by a renewal of political Islam; unless of course one chose not to close it at all, which had long been the preferred option of practical men. In the context of Islam, one might see 'Abd al-Raziq as the real revolutionary, perhaps the 'Luther' looked for by al-Afghani.

FUNDAMENTALISM: THE MUSLIM BRETHREN, AL-MAWDUDI, SAYYID QUTB

The opposite view was put forward, also in Egypt, a few years later in a different context. In 1928, Hasan al-Banna, also a zealous disciple of al-Afghani and 'Abduh, founded the Society of Muslim Brethren (Jam'iyyat al-Ikhwan al-Muslimin).[19] His aim was to educate people, raise their standard of living and spread the message of an 'Islamic order (al-nizam al-islami)'. Al-Banna and his followers reaffirmed the all-embracing vision of Islam covering political, social and economic life: 'Islam is a faith and a ritual, a nation (watan) and a nationality, a religion and a state, spirituality and action, Qur'an and sword' (in Mitchell 1969: 233). At the same time, they reaffirmed as their ideal the Caliphate as head of the universal Islamic Community; until that could be achieved, they would be content with the modernist view of constitutional democracy for separate Islamic states (Mitchell 1969: 235–48). Al-Banna saw patriotism as a sacred duty, and assigned Egypt pride of place among the nations. The nation of Palestine also came onto their agenda.

Here was a new self-confidence, self-assertiveness, coupled with a determination to reject Western cultural, political and economic intrusion. Al-Banna nevertheless, in the spirit of al-Afghani, still distinguished between the humane advances of the West, and also of Communism, and their degenerative 'materialism'. This more aggressive attitude towards the non-Islamic world was extended to people within Muslim society, especially Egypt, who adopted Western ways – the internal enemy. This outlook was developed in Muhammad Ghazali's denunciation (1948) of 'domestic imperialists' (Mitchell 1969: 220–1, 224–9). Rhetoric turned to action; the Muslim Brethren collaborated, albeit briefly, with the Free Officers' movement to overthrow the pro-British Egyptian monarchy (1952).

The Brethren were also something new, a new *type* of Islamic community. They were 'the first mass-supported and organized, essentially urban-oriented, effort to cope with the plight of Islam in the modern world' (Mitchell 1969: 321, 326–7). Members had to swear an oath of loyalty to the leader. There was a new mood abroad. The Brethren were fundamentalist in the sense that they wanted to rebuild the Muslim Community. They were not particularly dedicated to violent methods: al-Banna acknowledged that it would only be possible to organise an Islamic society and an Islamic state when the Brethren's message had become widely accepted (Mitchell 1969: 308, 312).

A broadly similar approach was adopted, independently and about the same time, by Abu'l-A'la al-Mawdudi (Hyderabad 1903–Pakistan 1979)[20] in India. During the debates about what sort of post-colonial state Muslims should work for, he asserted the integrity of Islam and the impossibility of separating religious from political life. Like the Muslim Brethren, he was determined to 'break the hold which Western culture and ideas [have] come to acquire over the Muslim intelligentsia' (in *EI* 6: 872b). In his analysis of Western capitalism, fascism, socialism and Communism (1947), Al-Mawdudi distinguished consistently between what he thought was good and bad in each of these, showing how in each instance Islam adopted the right, middle way. In one respect, al-Mawdudi went further than the Brethren: he was the first major Islamic thinker to reject explicitly and wholeheartedly the modernist programme of al-Afghani and others, the strategy of adapting the Shari'a to the modern world through a renewal of ijtihad. He returned to the literalist view of revelation: the Shari'a is unchangeable. He was thus a second founder of fundamentalism.

In order to achieve an Islamic society modelled on the values revealed by God to Muhammad, one has to get hold of political power. For 'among the factors that influence human morality and civilization the strongest ... is government ... What ultimately determines human advance or decline is the identity of those who exercise control' (1948). Again, 'the nature of [the Islamic] faith itself requires that [the Muslim] should concentrate all his effort upon wresting leadership from unbelieving and corrupt men to entrust it to the righteous' (in Ahmad and von Grunebaum (eds) 1970: 157–8, 160).

Like the Muslim Brethren, al-Mawdudi developed a new type of political organisation, the Jama'at-i Islami (Islamic Association: 1941). Achieving power has to be a collective effort: 'there must exist a righteous community ... devoted to the sole purpose of ... realizing the system of truth'. But al-Mawdudi's organization was different from the Brethren's: it was not a mass organisation but a moral and intellectual elite. Its members are to be dedicated to jihad 'against unbelief and immorality in every field of life' (in Ahmad and von Grunebaum (eds) 1970: 166). On the other hand, the Association was, like the Brethren, subordinate to its leader. In his mode of organisation, al-Mawdudi was partly influenced by the examples of Fascism and Leninism. He himself, like several reformers inspired by religion in this period, condemned political parties (Ahmed 1987: 100). In some respects, the Jama'at resembled the Opus Dei, a contemporary movement in the Catholic Church dedicated to the reform of public and private life through political involvement and also dominated by its founder-leader.

Al-Mawdudi held that Indian Muslims must establish their own separate state; but this must not be a nation-state à la Europe, but rather an 'Islamic state' with a religious rather than an ethnic identity, and based on Islamic rather than European political principles. Al-Mawdudi reiterated the view that consultation (shura) as practised in early Islam indicated parliamentarianism for the modern state. Thus there would be an elected ruler (amir) and an elected legislature (majlis-i shura); this was to legislate only on matters not already dealt with by the Shari'a.

After independence, al-Mawdudi and the Jama'at mobilised opinion against Jinnah's idea of a secular state. They were successful insofar as the 1956 constitution expressed the aspiration to establish a 'Muslim society on a truly Islamic basis and [to revise] all existing laws in the light of the Qur'an and

Sunna' (in *EI* 6: 873a). The first ruler endorsed by al-Mawdudi was General Zia al-Haqq (1977).

Thus al-Mawdudi broke with modernism. With his literalist view of divine revelation and his assertion of the necessarily political nature of the Islamic project, he as much as anyone established what has come to be known as fundamentalism. His influence reached all parts of the Islamic world, not least Egypt.[21]

Sayyid Qutb (Asyut, Egypt 1906–Cairo 1966)[22] was inspired by al-Mawdudi, but his theory of Islam was distinctive and very much his own. Qutb was a poet and a teacher. He never married, and all his life he suffered from ill health. A job in the Education Ministry led to him being sent to the USA (1948–50). There he was shocked by the racism and sexual permissiveness; in *The America That I Saw*, he described American virtues as 'those of production, organization, reason and work' but not those of 'social and human leadership … manners and emotions' (Moussalli 1992: 25–9).

Qutb joined the Muslim Brethren; he was a leading cultural adviser to the Free Officers movement during the 1952 revolution in Egypt. His Islamic political priorities soon led him to fall out with Nasser. He became editor of the Brethren's newspaper (1953), but the following year the Muslim Brethren were outlawed by the government, and Qutb was arrested with other leaders (1954); Nasser kept Qutb behind bars until 1964. His treatment in prison, including apparently torture, exacerbated his cardiac weakness and arthritis (Moussalli 1992: 34); he was in prison when a number of Muslim Brethren prisoners were massacred (1957). It was while in prison that, in 1959–60, Qutb came upon *L'homme, cet inconnu* (1935) by Alexis Carrel (1873–1944), a French anatomist and author who ended up in the service of the Vichy government. Carrel had outlined the demoralising effects of material progress; what was required was a new ascetic and mystical elite to rescue humankind from the degrading effects of democracy. On reading this book, Qutb apparently 'felt as if all the pieces of the puzzle had begun to fall into place' (Choueiri 1997: 149–55). Thus elements of the West's self-critique significantly influenced Islamic fundamentalism.

During his prison years, Qutb revised his multi-volume Qur'an commentary. His most original work, *Milestones* (*Ma'alim fi'l tariq*, lit. *Signposts along the Way*)[23] was published just after his release. Qutb held the view that those who opposed the Islamisation of society and the state, above all supposedly Muslim rulers, were to be regarded and treated as jahili (pagan, unbelieving, apostate), that violence against a jahili regime was justified, and that 'the Egyptian regime was definitely un-Islamic and jahili and consequently could be overthrown legitimately'. He was rearrested (1965) on a charge of armed revolt and terrorism, and executed in 1966 (Moussalli 1992: 36–7).

Qutb may be counted among the most original thinkers of the twentieth century; he took a new approach to Islam. First, the Qur'an contains all anybody needs to know. Qutb is anti-modernist in his denial of the need to learn anything from the West about society and politics, and of any equivalence between Islamic and Western values.

Islam altogether presents to mankind an example of a political system, the like of which has never been found in any of the other systems known to the world either before or after the 7th century. Islam does not seek, and never has sought, to imitate any other system, or to find connections or similarities between itself and others. On the contrary, it has chosen its own characteristic path ...

Islam proposes independent solutions to human problems ... We must be careful not to relate it to other principles and theories in order to explain it by means of them ... Islam is a comprehensive philosophy and a homogeneous unity, and to introduce into it any foreign element would mean ruining it. It is like a delicate piece of machinery which may be completely ruined by the presence of a foreign body. (1949)[24]

On the other hand, Islam's teachings about human relationships and social order are not fixed in the ancient Jurisprudence; they are adaptable. The point is, by whom and how? Here, Qutb is radical. The Qur'an, he says, should be read as poetry; the unique methodology (manhaj) of Islam is 'characterised by vitality, tone, direct touch, and allusion. It is allusion to the great truths which are not represented by words but alluded to by words' (in Moussalli 1992: 78, 162). One is reminded here of al-Ghazali's concept of 'taste (dhawq)' (see above, p. 99), a word which Qutb uses (Moussalli 1992: 178). Islam (as Binder puts it) 'is a tasawwur, a conception, an idea, an intuition, a vision, or something depicted or imagined. The form [of the word tasawwur] is actually participial, so that it could be translated as a conceiving, a visioning, or an imagining' (1988: 189, 191–5). The touchstone of correct understanding is the sensibility of the individual.

Thus Qutb is in the tradition of pure revelationism (see above, p. 83). But he gives it a new meaning; for what he advocates is 'direct, personal and intuitive understanding of revelation ... If man is left alone to his own conscience and soul with the help of religion, he will be able to acquire an adequate understanding of the universe' (Moussalli 1992: 86). Similarly, 'political theory in Islam stands on the foundation of conscience rather than on that of the law' (*Social Justice*, p. 99). This approach marks him off sharply not just from al-Mawdudi but from traditional Islam as a whole.

Knowledge is also linked to playing an active part, to participation in the Islamic movement. The Islamic conception and order (nizam), he says, 'will profit those to whom [it] is presented ... only if they are actually engaged in an actual Islamic movement'; Qutb's Qur'an commentary is 'activist exegesis'.[25] There is thus an analogy between Qutb and both Nietzschean and Marxist thought (Binder 1988: 178).

Qutb's theory of knowledge left the reinterpretation of social and political Islam wide open; in a sense, anything goes. When it comes to the actual organisation of an Islamic society and state, Qutb advocates 'the government of umma', and shura,[26] using exclusively Islamic language to describe a form of representative democracy. But, like all fundamentalists, he is little concerned with the exact form of the constitution; once the heart is freed from human subjection and subjected to the governance (hakimiyya) of God alone, everything will be all right.[27] He is more specific about social welfare: everyone, including the unborn, has a right to health care, and everyone should have the same educational opportunities. If the community does not provide these, the state should (Moussalli 1992: 180, 189).

For Qutb and those who think like him, 'religion' overrides 'politics': in *Signposts* there is no 'affirmation of an ordered and predictable social world' (Binder 1988: 199). Again, 'Qutbian discourse is political only in a rather unusual sense. It tends to influence people's thoughts and actions in a psychologically tense way that creates in the individual not the ability to reconstruct reality, but rather the dream of breaking with that reality'.[28]

There is thus in Qutb something of the Western individualist and existentialist; this has not been explored (but see Binder 1988: 194–5, 201). His approach makes the interpretation of Islam highly subjective. Truth and therefore authority derive from personal aesthetic vision. Moreover, action does not have to be related to consequences. As Binder puts it: 'the true believer will do what he must without concern for the consequences. The overriding conception is complete subservience to God marked by the extremes of jihad and martyrdom' (Binder 1988: 199). His is, obviously, one type of mystical approach; has Sufism finally captured the citadel of Jurisprudence (this was not quite Qutb's intention)? There is, again, an obvious analogy with Luther's idea of the authority of the original revealed text as grasped intuitively by himself. But Qutb takes for granted 'the equality of all Muslims in terms of their capacity to understand revelation' (Moussalli 1992: 82, 224). He did not make a special claim to religious leadership for himself.

On the means of achieving an Islamic society and state, Qutb took a nuanced and interesting position, which accords with much in Islamic practice and doctrine. First, the world is perceived in sharply dualist terms reminiscent of St Augustine: there is 'the party of God (hizb Allah)' (which follows God's teachings) and 'the party of the devil' (which does not) (Moussalli 1992: 168). Islam is engaged in an age-old struggle against Jews, Christians, Zionism and Communism (the Jews are planning to take over the world) (Esposito (ed.) 1983: 80; Choueiri 1997: 122, 157). This may take the form of a 'struggle over land, produce or military bases', but it is in reality a battle of ideas. For Qutb (as for all fundamentalists), 'the liberating struggle of jihad does not cease until all religion belongs to God' (in Esposito (ed.) 1983: 80, 82); this Qutb describes as 'revolution (al-thawra)'.

The means to be used depend on circumstances, and on what the jahili enemy is doing. The principal tactic is missionary teaching (da'wa); only when the masses are converted to correct Islamic views can an Islamic state be set up (Moussalli 1992: 37, 201, 211). So long as freedom of speech is not threatened, peaceful methods are to be used. Only when it is denied is physical jihad required (Binder 1988: 181; Moussalli 1992: 227). Qutb, like Lenin, advocated a clandestine armed vanguard; *Signposts* was dedicated to such a group. He has become the theoretical inspiration of Islamic groups prepared to use violent means to achieve their ends in the Middle East (such as the Society of Muslims, Jama'at al-Muslimin).[29]

ISLAMIC SOCIALISM

In the 1950s and 1960s, Arab socialism was the official ideology in Egypt, Syria and Iraq under regimes that were eager to assert the secular identity of the state and which persecuted the Muslim Brethren. It also became the official ideology in Algeria (1962), South Yemen, and somewhat later Sudan and Libya (1969).[30] Qaddafi (r.1969–) later made his own socialist interpretation of Islam the official doctrine of the state in Libya (Esposito (ed.) 1983: 140–5). Arab socialism adopted the Marxist theory of imperialism and the Marxist programme of state ownership and redistribution of wealth. The conception of the state as economic provider with a monopoly of key resources, centrally managed on behalf of the population, brought it into line with the tradition of patrimonial monarchy.

Its exponents also claimed the mantle of 'Islamic socialism', presenting Islam as 'the religion of justice and equality', and Muhammad as 'the first socialist' (al-Azhar mosque-college).[31] Here was the high-point of modernism, with Islam being the shell, modern social and economic ideals the content, of political belief, and socialism itself being harnessed to both local and Arab nationalism. In India, a sincere attempt was made to develop a theory of Islamic socialism that would combine the social programme of Marxism with Islamic principles. Looking to Shah Wali-Allah (see above, p. 250) for inspiration, Sihwarwi (c.1942) justified limits on private ownership and regulation of industrial relations by the state (Ahmad 1967: 198–204).

Arab socialism shared with fundamentalism a fierce antipathy towards the West as imperialist. On the other hand, whereas Arab-socialist regimes tended to look to the USSR for international support (especially over the Israeli question), fundamentalists were equally opposed to Western capitalism and Soviet Communism.

In domestic social and economic policy, there were differences in principle between Arab socialism and religious revivalist groups such as the Muslim Brethren, who also sometimes called themselves 'Islamic socialists'. For they insisted, in accordance with long-standing Muslim tradition, on the inviolability of the rights of private property (though everything really belongs to God). Social welfare, which they strongly emphasised, was seen as an up-to-date way of practising zakat – quite like what in the West is now called 'the third way'. The most important practical consequence was that traditional landowners and religious Trusts (sing. waqf) were unlikely to lose out under 'Islamic socialism'. This could strengthen the political constituency of revivalism, notably in Pakistan. When in the 1970s Bhutto tried to introduce his more statist version of Islamic socialism in Pakistan, many 'ulama condemned it as anti-Islamic (Ahmed 1987: 217).

THE IRANIAN REVOLUTION OF 1979

The collapse of the brief attempt at introducing a parliament in Iran (1905–11) was followed by a period of anarchy.[32] In 1923, Reza Khan (r.1923–41) assumed power. He first tried to found a secular republic like Atatürk's Turkey. Opposition from the 'ulama persuaded him, rather, to establish a new dynasty, the Pahlavi. He became in effect a military dictator. But he still pursued a policy of centralisation and modernisation. This included cutting back the power of the 'ulama and their role in public life. He introduced a civil code modelled on France, replaced religious with lay courts, and developed and partly secularised education. He propagated a nationalist ideology which emphasised the glories of pre-Islamic Iran, but its appeal was confined to the upper classes.

The 'ulama returned to traditional Shi'i quietism and kept out of politics, a policy endorsed by the supreme Mujtahid Burujirdi (1875–1962), though Burujirdi and other leading Mujtahids succeeded in frustrating an attempt by Mosaddeq (Prime Minister 1951–3) to give women the vote. The 'ulama were relieved when Mosaddeq's left-liberal government was overthrown with the help of the CIA. Reza Khan's son, Muhammad Reza (r. 1941–51, 1953–79), continued his father's policies of centralisation and modernisation. Measures aimed at land reform and equal rights for women brought him into conflict with the religious leaders, as did increasing American influence within Iran and the Shah's pro-Israeli foreign policy.

As in the period c.1890–1910, a rapprochement now took place between secular and religious intellectuals. A remarkable example of this alignment was the lectures and writings of Dr 'Ali Shari'ati (Khurasan 1933–Damascus 1977),[33] who had studied in Paris under the eminent Islamicist Louis Massignon (1959–64), and absorbed Sartre and modern sociology. He was especially drawn to the Algerian theorist of Third World revolution, Franz Fanon, whose *Wretched of the Earth*, along with Che Guevara's *Guerrilla Warfare*, Shari'ati translated into Persian.

Back in Iran, Shari'ati became the star lecturer in a Tehran institute aimed at winning young people with a secular background over to Islam. His views on Islam and democratic leadership posed a threat not only to the Westernising regime of the Shah but also to the ayatollahs and the Shi'ite religious establishment. He had already been imprisoned when he was a student at Mashhad for his activities as a member of a group called 'the God-worshipping Socialists' (1959). He was now arrested again (1972), then eventually (1977) allowed to leave Iran. He died on his way to England in 'circumstances that aroused immediate suspicions of foul play and earned him, in the eyes of many, the rank of martyr' (*CH Iran* 7: 757).

Shari'ati brought together the strands of modernism and Islamic revivalism in an original synthesis. One has the impression that for him European ideas were not an afterthought, they became part of him. He denounced Western capitalism and imperialism with its consumerist culture which threatened to become hegemonic in the world. At the same time, he denounced as decadent the current teaching and practice of Islam. Islam's original mission, he said, had been to liberate the 'oppressed' (mostaz'afin: a Qur'anic term, Watt 1988: 134), which nowadays meant the poor and exploited in Iran and in the Third World. He 'saw in Islamic humanism the sole ideology that could save Iran and all oppressed peoples' (Keddie 1981: 217). But Islam in its present form needed to be changed if it was achieve this goal.

So Shari'ati was revolutionary, first, in his attitude towards the West; here he followed in the steps of Marxism and Franz Fanon. But his main originality lay in his attempt to set in motion a revolution within Islam itself, and in the way that he linked these two projects. Shari'ati distinguished between, on the one hand, 'the corrupt role which, at present, religion plays among the masses', its 'abstract spirit fossilized inside traditional forms ... ceremonies and rituals'; and, on the other hand, Islam as it once was, 'a profound ... dynamic religious spirit ... equipped with the most current logic, philosophy, science, art'. This kind of Islam 'invites people to submit themselves to God, and urges revolt against oppression [and] injustice'. In the Qur'anic perspective, the pursuit of knowledge and the victory of the oppressed are one and the same project. Here, Shari'ati, again like the modernists, identified the cause of Islamic decadence as the abandoning of independent reasoning (ijtihad); 'ijtihad guarantees permanent revolution' (*What is to be Done*, pp. 21, 44, 99–100, 109–12). He had 'a distinct hostility towards the clergy and their role in society' (Choueiri 1977: 166).

But Shari'ati, unlike the modernists, did not think that Islamic values could be recovered by learning from modern Europe; rather, the true Islamic project is to be rediscovered from within Islam itself by what he called 'the intellectual enlightener (rawshan-fikr)' (Halm 1991: 124), that is someone capable of taking a critical but positive view of their own cultural heritage. Such enlightenment did, however, owe a great deal to interaction with European philosophy. Zubaida observes that the views he derived from sociological analysis of history 'are in all respects modern and Western' (Zubaida 1993: 22).

Shari'ati's most ambitious move was to assimilate the Islamic philosophy of history with the Marxist. The Qur'anic view is precisely that the *people* should be empowered through an understanding of 'the laws (sunan) of history, the laws of social change'.[34] In fact, 'Islam is the first school of social thought that recognizes the masses (al-Jamahir) as ... the fundamental and conscious factor in determining history and society'. Islam itself possesses 'a scientific philosophy of history', which combines 'general scientific determinism' with 'humanistic and historical optimism' to predict 'the inevitable victory of the weak and the oppressed classes'. In his *The Philosophy of History: Cain and Abel*, Shari'ati explained the Biblical and Qur'anic story as indicating how society has become divided into a property-owning minority and a majority who 'possessed only hunger and the ability to work' (*Sociology*, pp. 48–9, 54, 101–9).

Shari'ati adopted neither the doctrine nor the spirit of fundamentalism. To be sure, 'the city of the Prophet, al-Madina ... reveal[s] the Prophet's style and method in setting up a society, its ... infrastructure, classes ... the role of government in society' (*What is to be Done*, p. 126). But Shari'ati did not seek to use a purified vision of original Islam as his model for future society. Rather, his approach to Islam was that of critical theory. Here, Shari'ati adopted a rational approach similar to that of the modernists and of the falasifa, whose works were available in Iran.

Shari'ati took a yet more hostile view of Western culture. Like fundamentalists, he viewed the world as a battleground between Western materialism and

Islam; and he drew the parallel between the present predicament of Islam, caught between the rival and equally corrupt superpowers of the capitalist West and the Communist Soviet Union, and Muhammad's Mecca, which stood midway between the Byzantine and Sassanid empires. He was extremely critical of people in the Islamic world who adopted Western ways. They need 'to replace their hollowness of soul ... their collapse of originality, their self-alienation, their other-worshipping ... with the spirit of faith'. The Westernised bourgeoisie who reject religion are 'hirelings of the philosophy of consumerism'. Such people are happy to see the masses taking to a corrupt version of Islam 'so that (Islam) could not be used as a means of resistance ... but instead would function as a narcotizing and benumbing agent'. The most dangerous enemy is the 'slave merchant who has put on the makeup of a devout saint'. In fact, 'the ridiculous war of modernity versus traditionalism' is ultimately a distraction from 'the real war between the East and the West, producer and consumer, colonizer and colonized' (*What is to be Done*, pp. 31, 36, 47, 83–92, 116).

True Islam, for Shari'ati, is a faith which concerns itself at once with the material and the spiritual. It is

> based on constant striving (jihad) and justice ('adalat). Islam pays attention to bread, its eschatology is based on active life in the world, its God respects human dignity and its messenger is armed ... The Prophet of Islam was the only one who simultaneously carried the sword of Caesar in his hand and the heart of Jesus in his chest[35] ... [This is] the religion whose founder is an 'armed messenger' and whose follower is 'Ali [sc. the holy warrior]; the religion whose history began amidst politics and struggle (jihad); the religion whose taxation is on a par with praying; the religion which ... has built societies, political and economic systems. (*What is to be Done*, pp. 23, 43, 79)

Religion and politics obviously go together. However, Shari'ati wanted to update radically the social and political programme of Islam, as the modernists had; he championed, for example, the rights of women.[36]

Shari'ati's view of the political organisation of Islam, the role of the umma (Community) and leadership (imama) was also original, especially for a Shi'ite. During the period of the Absence of the Hidden Imam, 'the mission of the prophets and imams [falls] upon the people themselves'. The people may elect a group to guide them, and they can also 'elect from among themselves someone in the place of the Imam' (in Keddie 1981: 224). He thus reaffirmed popular sovereignty in a Shi'ite context. He reconciled devout Shi'ism with a democratic point of view.

> The power of sovereignty (hakemiyat) originates from ... the Community ... The responsibility of Leadership lies with those who hail from the people and are elected by the masses of the people. The leadership of society ... is based upon the principles of study, designation, election and consensus (ijma) of the people. (in Akhavi: Keddie 1983: 138)

The leader and guides he has in mind here are not a Mujtahid or the 'ulama, but the 'intellectual enlighteners'. Such persons, like himself of course, are the natural leaders for Muslim society today. 'Although not a prophet, an enlightened soul should play the role of the prophet for his society' as 'the vanguard of the caravan of humanity'. Again, such 'enlightened souls' have the same 'responsibility and role ... [as] the prophets and the founders of the great religions', who in their own day were 'revolutionary leaders who promoted fundamental structural changes'. The enlightened soul, it emerges, is one who has a particular type of *knowledge*, neither traditional religious 'ilm nor modern science, but 'an awareness unique to man, a divine light and a source of consciousness to the social conscience' (*What is to be Done*, p. 5).

What is needed is someone who combines deep Islamic commitment with knowledge of the modern social sciences. 'A new breed of Muslim [experts] will take over, who feel Islam in their hearts and minds ... [and] who know scientific research methodology, know the progress of sciences in the contemporary world, and in short *know both cultures*'. The enlightened soul must use social science to 'identify the real causes of the backwardness of his society ... [and] the rational solutions which would enable his people to emancipate themselves from the status quo' (*What is to be Done*, pp. 16–17, 114; my italics).

He also has to be someone 'who can generate responsibility and awareness, and give intellectual and social direction to the masses', his mission being 'to assist them in saving themselves from ignorance, polytheism and oppression' (*What is to be Done*, pp. 4–6, 56–9). This was the way the Falasifa described the prophet, one who combines rational knowledge with the moral quality of leadership (see above, p. 67). As an example, Shari'ati suggested Muhammad Iqbal (1875–1938),[37] the Indian Sunni philosopher and poet who had absorbed Nietzsche, and who eventually gave his support to the Muslim League's programme of a separate state for Indian Muslims. Iqbal, says Shari'ati, refused to confine himself to academic philosophy; 'he sought neither escape nor isolation. He realised he had been sent on a mission to his people.' Such a theory of Leadership was in complete contrast to Khomeini's 'mandate of the jurist'.

The revolutionary movement of 1978–9 was a coalition between the bazaar trading classes, the 'ulama and secular intellectuals. It relied less on arms and more on popular demonstrations than perhaps any other modern revolution.[38] Popular sentiment had for a century been fuelled by resentment at foreign exploitation of national resources, personified now by the Shah's increasingly autocratic and repressive regime which was backed by the capitalist powers. The revolution was a patriotic movement rooted in a feeling of Iranian grandeur and hurt national pride. The USA fulfilled the expectations of both Islamic and Marxist demonology. The revolution combined the Shi'ite tradition of religious protest and leadership with the nationalist and liberal ideology of 1905–11, plus a Marxist-socialist programme of social justice and popular revolution. This special combination of forces was facilitated by the extent to which Islamic and Marxist ideas had for some time been merging, notably in Shari'ati, whose ideas caught on in the late 1960s and were now, after his death, widely disseminated.[39]

But the Shi'ite Mujtahids regained the initiative, and from now on it was they, and especially Khomeini, who 'formulated the constitutive values of the movement' (Arjomand 1988: 98). They had their own well-thought-out theory of both the aims and the organisation of the movement. Theirs was a pro-gramme rooted, to a degree unique among modern revolutions, in age-old popular beliefs.

Ruhullah Khomeini (south-western Iran 1902–Tehran 1989)[40] had lost his father in his infancy. At madrasa, he went in for falsafa and mystical know-ledge (irfan) as well as traditional Jurisprudence. He taught at Qum (1944–62), where he had a large following of students, many of whom were recruited into positions of power after 1979. In 1962–3, he took the unusual step of publicly denouncing the Shah's reform proposals and his 'tyranny (zulm)'. He was imprisoned, then exiled (1964). He went to Iraq; there he developed 'close con-tacts with the Palestinian movement'.[41]

Khomeini gave the fullest statement of his political principles in lectures delivered at Najaf (Iraq) in 1970 (published as *Islamic Government: Hukumat-i Islami*), just at the time when Shari'ati was lecturing in Tehran. To what extent did the two know of each other? Did they see each other as competitors or, perhaps, as distant allies, in opposing the Shah and formulating an alter-native to the Pahlavi monarchy?

Khomeini, like Shari'ati, denounced the current ethos of Islam, though largely for different reasons; they both agreed, however, that one of the shortcomings of contemporary Islam was that it did not apply religious principles to politics. Khomeini held that one must establish an Islamic government, and that the example of the Prophet showed this quite clearly: 'he sent out governors to different regions; both sat in judgment himself and appointed judges; dispatched emissaries to foreign states ... and took command in battle. In short, he ful-filled all the functions of government ... The ratio of Qur'anic verses con-cerned with the affairs of society to those concerned with ritual worship is greater than a hundred to one' (*Islamic Government*, pp. 29, 41, 134).

Khomeini too ascribed the depoliticisation of Islam to the influence of Western imperialism as part of 'the overall plan of the imperialists to prevent the Muslims from becoming involved in political activity and establishing an Islamic government' (pp. 36, 141). Muslims had become alienated from their true revolutionary identity by 'Westoxication'. Actually, of course, non-participation was recommended by traditional Shi'ism, and for that reason practised at this time by almost the entire Shi'ite establishment. Khomeini was one of very few Mujtahids to insist that religion demanded political involvement, and he was almost the only one ever to assert that Jurists should actually rule.

Khomeini, like Shari'ati, spoke of economic imperialism, and used Islamic language to express the polarisation between oppressors and oppressed. But his emphasis was more specifically on the plight of Iran; it was the *Iranian* 'people' he had in mind. 'Our public funds are being embezzled; our oil is being plundered; and our country is being turned into a market for expensive, un-necessary goods by the representatives of foreign companies, which makes it possible for foreign capitalists and their local agents to pocket the people's money.' This was rather more succinct than Lenin. It seems that he was thinking, at least before 1979, of revolution in Iran rather than of world revolution. His primary purpose was to discredit the Shah; he always reminded his audience that it was through its local 'political agents' that 'the imperialists have imposed on us an unjust economic order'. Khomeini also denounced Iran's close ties with Israel (*Islamic Government*, pp. 49, 115, 120).

But Khomeini's political thought was quite different from that of other revolutionaries and perhaps unique in the modern world, in that he insisted most of all upon rule by the right persons, or the right person; *Islamic Government* was sub-titled *The Mandate of the Jurist*. Discrediting the Shah as an agent of foreign imperialism was a means to this end. We have seen how in the eighteenth and nineteenth centuries Mujtahids (well-qualified Jurists, the more eminent of whom were now called ayatollahs) had emerged as an informal group of authoritative religious guides for other Muslims (see above, p. 284). In Iran, the 'ulama, and especially the Mujtahids, had become the effective leaders of the community, and had provided the most significant effective opposition to the Qajar government. This had been justified by saying that they held, on behalf of the twelfth Imam, a collective vilaya (Mandate, delegated authority, guardianship, trusteeship).[42] Such a Mandate could, in the words of one nineteenth-century Jurist, embrace a wide range of social functions, including some quasi-governmental ones (see above, p. 285). The Mujtahids' informal social powers were thus based on an articulate religious doctrine. The tradition of non-participation in politics was, nevertheless, still prevalent among Shi'ites.

In the late 1960s and early 1970s, Khomeini, together with a few others, came to the view that 'when government is in practice in the hands of usurpers and oppressors ... the Just Jurist and mujtahid must, if possible, take over the reins of Islamic government and establish order and justice among Muslims' (Gulpaygani, in Arjomand (ed.) 1988: 191). The reason for coming to this view at this particular time was their perception of the Shah's regime as anti-Islamic. Khomeini drew the conclusion that monarchy itself was non-Islamic – a highly original opinion given the enthusiastic Shi'ism of the Safavids, and the principled, albeit grudging, acceptance of dynastic monarchy by Shi'ites high and low from 'Abbasid times onwards. The participation of so many 'ulama in the constitutional revolution of 1906 did provide some precedent.

But the point was that the Pahlavis were Westernisers. Muhammad Reza's vision of a modernised Iran clearly included reforms that offended both the material and the spiritual interests of the 'ulama. That too had occasionally been true of the Qajars. But the present Shah went about it in a particularly tactless way. At the Persepolis 'party' (1971), he trumpeted 2,500 years of Persian monarchy, elevating national tradition as part of an attempt to celebrate secular political identity. It misfired badly. From Khomeini, it drew a particularly interesting response: having repeated the early Muslim view that 'the title of King of Kings ... is the most hated of all titles in the sight of God', he went on: 'Islam is fundamentally opposed to the whole notion of monarchy'.[43]

The main argument of Khomeini and others for removing the Shah and all he stood for was that this was a prerequisite for the implementation of the

Shari'a. This was the main, indeed the only purpose of government. Put the Shari'a into practice, and all the present-day evils of society and of the whole world will be sorted out. For the Shari'a is God-given, and it was precisely God's intention to cover the whole of human life with His Law. The Holy Law 'amounts to a complete social system' with 'regulations concerning war and peace and intercourse with other nations; penal and commercial law; and regulations pertaining to trade and agriculture'. Islam itself demanded fundamental social reforms, such as universal health care and education. 'Islam has solved the problem of poverty and inscribed it at the top of its program: "Sadaqat (alms) is for the poor"' (pp. 30, 43, 120). In saying this, Khomeini was in agreement with Sunni fundamentalists like al-Mawdudi and Qutb (both of whom had been translated into Persian).[44]

Since the Shari'a is God-given and all-embracing, there can be no such thing as human legislation properly speaking – a view also shared by Sunni revivalists. The scope of all political institutions is confined, therefore, to supervising the executive and laying down rules about things like town planning and traffic (January 1979).[45] This was not quite reflected in the Constitution of 1979; the legislative Assembly was, however, subject to scrutiny by the Guardian Council.

Khomeini asserted, in accordance with Islamic Philosophy as it drew on Plato and Aristotle, that the aim of the Law is 'to produce integrated and virtuous human beings who are walking embodiments of the law, or, to put it differently, the law's voluntary and instinctive executors': good laws engender good habits. So the purpose of Islamic government is to create 'conditions conducive to the production of morally upright and virtuous human beings'.[46] He gave a slightly jumbled version of the argument that the Shari'a, like all law, requires a government to implement it (see above, p. 70).

Above all, Khomeini took the revolutionary view that *only an Islamic government can be relied upon to implement the Shari'a.*[47] The traditional view had been that a government is legitimate so long as it promotes, or at least does not prevent, the application of the Religious Code. Only if a government prevents Muslims from practising their faith, or fails to enable them to do so, should an attempt be made to get rid of it. For Khomeini this was clearly not enough. He had a certain amount of experience on his side. To many, especially the poor, in Iran and the rest of the Muslim world his arguments carried some conviction because the rulers who promoted Westernisation and neglected the Shari'a were the very ones who oppressed the poor. The view that only an Islamic government could be relied upon to implement the Shari'a was shared by Sunni revivalists, though what or whom they meant by an Islamic government differed widely. The focus of Khomeini's political theory was precisely the question, what constitutes Islamic government: who rules? His answer was the Jurist's Mandate (vilayat al-faqih): when there is an individual Jurist sufficiently outstanding in the qualities of learning and justice, the Hidden Imam's Trusteeship falls upon him. Hitherto, the 'general vicegerency' exercised by senior Jurists on behalf of the Imam was a specifically *collective* trust, held by the Mujtahids at large.[48] In 1970, Khomeini himself was still sometimes saying that it was the *Jurists* (in the plural) who were designated by the Hidden Imam 'to exercise the functions of both government and judgeship'. He insisted that 'it is the duty of all Muslims to obey this decree of the Imam'. But he was also proposing a new doctrine that the Mandate could be attributed to an individual: 'if a worthy individual possessing [the qualities of legal expertise and justice] arises and establishes a government, he will possess the same authority as [Muhammad himself] in the administration of society, and it will be the duty of all peoples to obey him' (*Islamic Government*, pp. 62, 64, 96). He promptly qualified this extraordinary claim by saying that such authority is strictly confined to the 'rational and extrinsic' matters of government (p. 63); the mandate of the individual Jurist would not apply to religious affairs. It was still some claim.

Restating this view the following year, Khomeini argued that government was a collective duty in the legal sense that *someone* must carry it out, and that this could be either an individual or a group of Jurists. 'Undertaking a government and laying the foundation of the Islamic state (al-dawla al-islamiyya) is a [collective] duty incumbent on just Jurists.' But, 'if *one such* succeeds in forming a government it is incumbent on the others to follow him' (my italics). If, on the other hand, the task requires collective action, 'they must unite to undertake it' (1971) (in Arjomand 1988: 179).

Khomeini based his case partly on pragmatic grounds, from the perceived need of the Shiʿite Community for good government. Under circumstances like the present, he said, it is for the Jurist to use what has been entrusted to him for the salvation of his country: 'But as for the supervision and supreme administration of the country, the dispensing of justice ... – these are precisely the subjects that the [Jurist] has studied. Whatever is needed to preserve national independence and liberty is precisely what the [Jurist] has to offer' (p. 137). Similarly, after 1979, Khomeini and his supporters justified their theory partly on the grounds that it is necessary for 'the maintenance of order in society' (in Arjomand (ed.) 1988: 198). Thus Khomeini, like Lenin, developed a theory to meet the present-day needs of his country, which also looks as if it was designed to impel him to power.

As a thinker, Khomeini was as revolutionary in the religious as he was in the political field.[49] Shiʿite religious thinkers had traditionally emphasised the gulf between the absolute authority of God, the Prophet and the Hidden Imam, on the one hand, and all other religious leaders, on the other. Some had ruled out the possibility of anyone, apart from the Prophet and the Hidden Imam, exercising 'wilaya [guardianship] over others' (for example, the supreme Mujtahid Ansari, in Arjomand (ed.) 1988: 193). Yet this was precisely what Khomeini was claiming for the just Jurist.

This doctrine was new, but it had roots in Shiʿite thought and could fairly plausibly be claimed as a legitimate development of it. Sometimes in the past a single Mujtahid had been recognised by consensus as the supreme *religious* guide of all Shiʿites; this was a personal status which lapsed with the death of the individual. Thus Baqer as-Sadr (1935–80, executed by Saddam Husein), a leading Jurist writing in Iraq independently of Khomeini, could also say (1979) that 'public deputyship (an-nibaya al-'amma) pertains to the supreme jurist (al-mujtahid al-mutlaq)'.[50] The idea of the specially gifted individual was part of the gnostic tradition with which Khomeini was familiar. It reflected the importance which Shi'ism had always attached to the status of particular divinely authorised *individuals*.

But Khomeini went further: he included in the authority bestowed by the Mandate *political as well as religious authority*. The reason for this was his conviction that the purposes of religion could not be achieved without holding political power. The common Shi'ite view had for centuries been that politics was so morally contaminating that one should avoid any involvement in it whatsoever. Certainly this doctrine had led to many difficulties. It had created special anomalies when, under the Safavids, Shi'ites took power and Iran became a Shi'ite nation. The question had been disputed in the later eighteenth and nineteenth centuries (see above, p. 286), and 'ulama had played a prominent part in the Constitutional Revolution of 1906–11. But the doctrine of non-involvement in politics had remained widely prevalent; indeed it had regained ascendancy after the failure of the Constitutional Revolution.

Khomeini clearly thought that only his view, that religion required political activity, would make it possible for Muslims to carry out the original mission of Islam. Here, he and his supporters saw themselves as overcoming the defects of the past: 'with this revolution [the Mandate of the Jurist] reached perfection in practice and occupied its true station' (in Arjomand 1988: 181). And one of his students interpreted Husain's martyrdom as 'a political uprising against an unjust and impious government, and thus the model for Shi'ite political activism' (Arjomand in idem (ed.) 1988: 201).

In his general orientation and his desire to revive Islam as a world power, as indeed *the* world power, based on Islamic justice, Khomeini was at one with Sunni fundamentalists. Like Sunni fundamentalists such as Qutb, he was prepared to go back to what he perceived as first principles and interpret the Law very radically in the light of the basic, original goals of Islam. Unlike Qutb, he did not explicitly say that this was what he was doing. But political Islamists of all persuasions soon recognised in Khomeini a kindred spirit and a model.

THE CONSTITUTION OF 1979

After the overthrow of the Shah, the Constitutional Law of the Islamic Republic of Iran (qanun-i asasi-yi Jumhurii-yi Islami-yi Iran: ratified by referendum December 1979) 'translated [Khomeini's] concept of a purely Islamic government into reality'.[51] It reflected the role which those who had emerged on top in the revolutionary struggles wished to ascribe to the Mandated Jurist. The Constitution stated that 'During the Occultation of the [Hidden Imam], the Mandate (vilayat) and Leadership (imamat) of the Community devolve upon the just and pious Jurist (faqih)' (art. 5). Ayatollah Khomeini is named as the present occupant of this position (art. 107). The language of article 5 'inevitably awakens associations with the rule of the Twelfth Imam' (Halm

1991: 128); but Khomeini eventually let it be known that he claimed for himself the more modest title of Forerunner of the Mahdi. If no-one is deemed to qualify as the just and pious Jurist, the Constitution goes on, a Leadership Council is to function in his place (art. 5). The wide-ranging powers of the Leader, or Leadership Council, include supreme military command and declaration of war and peace (art. 110).

The Constitution also reflected some attempt to synthesise this doctrine with democracy. The Just Jurist, as well as possessing the requisite personal qualities, must be 'recognised and accepted as Leader by the majority of the people'. But this is qualified: the Leader, or Leadership Council, is to be chosen by 'experts elected by the people' (arts 5, 107). So long as Khomeini was alive, the democratic principle was entirely subordinate to that of the Mandate of the Jurist. President Khamene'i stated (1988) that the Constitution derives its legitimacy not from 'the majority of [the] people' but from 'the ruling Jurist'; 'the Mandate of the Jurist is like the soul in the body of the regime' (in Arjomand 1988: 183). But since his death, the democratic element has been reasserted. While the vilayat-i faqih has parallels in the Roman Catholic theory of the pope, Khomeini's status, unlike that of a Christian bishop, derived from his personal qualities. He could have no successor. Today, the Islamic-Platonic and the liberal-democratic elements are locked in a contest of which the outcome is wholly uncertain.

A National Consultative Assembly (majlis), and also provincial and other local councils, are to be elected, following the practice of shura (art. 6, 7).[52] Legislation by the majlis is subject to scrutiny by the Guardian Council, which consists of six Religious Jurists, selected by the Leader or Leadership Council, and six other jurists elected 'from among the Muslim jurists nominated by the Supreme Judicial Council' (arts 91, 94, 96, 98).

The Constitution is unique in Islamic history and in world history. Seeking to balance expertise and accountability, it combined (in theory) the three types of rule in classical Greco-European constitutional theory: rule by one, by a few wise, and by the people. Certainly it is dominated by the ideas of Shi'ite Islam as interpreted by Khomeini; but personal Leadership and the expert Jurists are to some extent balanced by checks on power and elected assemblies; the Leader or Leadership Council can be dismissed (art. 111). Thus it owed something to European models and the modernist tradition. Shura is understood in the modernist sense, meaning election as well as consultation. The role of the Guardian Council is particularly striking; it places the Constitution in the Platonic tradition. So does the emphasis on knowledge and piety as qualifications for rule.

The word chosen to express Republic was Jumhuri, meaning not *la chose publique* but the crowd or generality of people. The concept itself was new to Islamic Jurisprudence.[53] In one respect, Republic was a new expression for the traditional Islamic view that a just government is by definition limited by law: it must operate within the Religious Code ('Islamic government [is] ... the rule of divine law over men': Khomeini, *Islamic Government*, pp. 55, 79). Iqbal had said, in the context of the Turkish Republic in the 1920s, that 'the republican form of government is ... thoroughly consistent with the spirit of Islam' (in Enayat 1982:60). Khomeini expressed the hope that oppressed Muslims everywhere would establish 'independent and free republics' (*Last Counsel*, published 1989).[54] Jumhuri can also refer to the Islamic Community (jama'a) in a general sense.[55]

The Constitution obviously did achieve, on paper, the aim of integrating religion and politics. But there have been considerable gaps between theory and practice. Since 1979, state and society in Iran have been dominated by the ayatollahs and the 'ulama. 'The open political field has been entirely Islamicized', but in the sense that religious status and allegiance have become qualifications for office rather than in the application of new Islamic administrative principles: 'the most Islamic element ... is not so much in the administration, as in ... [the] personnel'. The clergy have appropriated the bureaucracy.[56] The Friday sermon has been made the main instrument of propaganda and control ('The secret of victory is unity of expression', as Khomeini put it in 1979).[57] But the Shari'a has been applied only fitfully, and with considerable adaptation, including artfully concealed borrowings from Western legal practice.[58]

The main development in Iranian Shi'ite political thought since 1979 was the further elevation of Khomeini as holder of the Mandate of the Jurist. Phrases were used which appeared to put him on a level with the Twelve Imams (1983) (in Arjomand (ed.) 1988: 197), though these were not of course endorsed by Khomeini himself. The theory of the vilayat-i faqih has been systematically propagated in mosques and taught in schools. And the duty of obedience to the mandated Jurist and the 'ulama has been preached as a religious obligation. Political participation and voting have been made obligatory as a shar'i duty, an act of religious devotion ('ibadat) (Arjomand (ed.) 1988: 197, 202).

On the other hand, Khomeini's theory of the vilayat-i faqih has not been generally accepted among Shi'ites. Even in Iran, it has been quietly opposed by some ayatollahs, for example Rouhani (1919–97). Unusual steps were taken to 'demote' the grand ayatollah Shari'at-madani for his known criticism of the Mandate; other 'ulama who disagreed with it have been purged (1982).[59]

The disappearance of any theoretical separation between politics and religion has led to the subjection of other Mujtahids, even those with the status of 'sources of imitation (marja'-i taqlid)' (see above, p. 285), to the Mandated Jurist as constitutional Leader ('with the establishment of Islamic government marja'iyyat, in practice and officially, took the form of leadership and rule over society', it was said: in Arjomand 1988: 181). This would have been unthinkable before. In other words, religious and political power have been collapsed into one, but here it seems to be the demands of the political order that are setting the tone. The achievement of political power by the Mandated Jurist has transformed the structure of purely *religious* authority.

The most remarkable such development was when, in January 1988, President Khamene'i said that Islamic government must remain within the framework of the Shari'a. Khomeini took him to task, and declared that the Jurist's Mandate is 'the most important of the divine commandments ... [it is] one of the primary commandments of Islam and has priority over all derivative commandments, even over prayer, fasting and pilgrimage to Mecca' (in Arjomand 1988: 182). It is difficult to accommodate such a statement within the framework of orthodox Islam; it smacks of the millenarianist strand which held that the Shari'a was superceded (see above, p. 47). Was the logic behind it an extreme concern for personal authority?

After coming to power, Khomeini developed the Islamic version of the theory of imperialism, or dependency theory, and he refined his view of the significance of the Iranian revolution for the world at large, especially the Muslim world. The rest of the world, he said, including the Muslim peoples, remain under the control of 'the world-eating big powers' and their local puppets. Many Muslims are still 'blind imitators of the East [sc. Communism] or the West' (Last Counsel, pp. 87, 112–13).

Khomeini reaffirmed the age-old promise of Shi'ism that the time will come when 'brotherhood and equality' are realised through God and the Twelfth Imam. He thought that the Islamic revolution in Iran had hastened the day when 'governments of the meek will be established; the way will be open for the world government of the Imam Mahdi'.[60] In his Last Counsel, Khomeini appealed to Muslims everywhere to 'stand firm' and 'sever the chains of dependence upon others'. They should 'put up with hardship to realize an honourable life free of domination of foreigners', presumably practising economic self-sufficiency at the price of austerity. The revolution in Iran should be exported by example and propaganda, not by force. Other countries should not expect help from outside (pp. 89, 97).

Throughout the Islamic world, the Iranian revolution has been seen as an example of what political Islam might achieve. This was the first time that Islamic leaders, or religious leaders of any kind, had taken power in a major modern state. It became an inspiration for political Islamists everywhere. Yet what can be forged out of Iranian monarchism is surely different from what can be forged out of Arab or Afghan tribalism.

Patrimonial monarchy in Iran, which had survived Arab-Muslim and Mongol invasions, collapsed in the twentieth century. After 1,300 years of cohabitation, Islam finally replaced it with its own religio-political order. The Islamic Republic of Iran is a unique phenomenon. How it will develop is impossible to predict. It seems unlikely that, given the long history of the Shi'ite clergy's ascent to power, they will lose it easily.

FUNDAMENTALISM TODAY

In the Sunni world, President Numeiri, under pressure from the Sudanese Muslim Brethren, declared *his* country an Islamic Republic (1983). The programme and ideology of the Sudanese Brethren was shaped by Hasan al-Turabi (Sudan 1932–),[61] who had studied in Paris and London. Following a coup in 1989, Turabi became 'the regime's supreme ideologue and Sudan's de facto ruler'. He has worked out his own approach, which combines elements of both modernism and fundamentalism: the legal and social programme of Islam must be interpreted anew in the light of a few basic principles. Islam must find new solutions to modern problems with help from the social sciences. Ijtihad should be undertaken, not by one inspired individual (such as a Mahdi), but collectively, and, he goes on (reminiscent of Shari'ati), *by intellectuals*. 'Because all knowledge is divine and religious, a chemist, an engineer, an economist or a jurist are all 'ulama'. Such 'ulama, 'public opinion leaders or philosophers, should enlighten society' (Esposito (ed.) 1983: 245). He has proclaimed freedom and equality for women, including equal rights in marriage and equal political rights and liberties (*The Woman in Islamic Teachings* (1973): in Osman, pp. 416–7).

The Muslim Brethren, al-Mawdudi, Qutb and Khomeini are grouped together as 'fundamentalists' (or 'radicals'), along with various groups which justify political violence in the name of Islam. Such groups are sometimes supported by people who do not themselves want to practise violence, but who sympathise with their aim, the 'restoration' of the Shari'a, and who think that only such groups are likely to achieve this (compare the IRA in Irish politics). Indeed (with the exception of Qutb), these theorists do not themselves advocate violence in domestic or international politics. On the other hand, of course, many groups that have nothing to do with Islam have adopted terrorist tactics and principles (nineteenth-century anarchists, some Marxists, several nationalist groups). It has been observed that some members of Islamic fundamentalist groups are not particularly knowledgeable about their own religion.[62]

As we have seen, Qutb and the other fundamentalist thinkers each hold distinctive views, and it is probably not helpful to group them into one 'school'. Fundamentalism has sprung up in different localities (Dekmejian 1995: 3–4); but ideas have also spread from one place to another. Fundamentalism is as much a tactical and organisational stance, a mood and spirit, as a body of doctrine.

Islamic fundamentalist groups have adopted a variety of organisational forms, ranging from pressure groups engaged in missionary and welfare activity (such as the Muslim Brethren) to tightly disciplined elite groups (Jama'at Islami). The Iranian Shi'a, in this as in many respects, are obviously in a category apart. Some groups aim first and foremost at raising consciousness; they see this as a prerequisite for influence over government policy (the Brethren, Jama'at Islami). Others aim to take over the state themselves. They all believe in the legitimacy of violence under certain circumstances (as does most traditional Islamic and European thought) but differ in their judgements as to when those circumstances exist.

Fundamentalism constitutes a specific reaction to modern social and economic conditions, rapid urbanisation, the dislocation of traditional communities and crafts, unemployment and anomie. Its more articulate followers include 'small merchants, middle traders, artisans, students, teachers and state employees'.[63] They have flourished on the disappointment of hopes held out by secular ideologies. The approach of a theorist like Qutb, in particular, seems likely to strike a chord with the enquiring, the socially dislocated, and those looking for a role in life. Fundamentalism represents a return to what in British politics might be called 'basics', and to cultural roots; in this they resemble European Fascists, with whom they sometimes express sympathy.

The question the historian must ask is: to what extent is their ideology new within Islam, and not, as they themselves think it to be, a revival of ancient virtue? Zubaida interprets fundamentalism as a specifically modern product: '"fundamentalism" is modern, and can best be understood in terms of the concepts and assumptions of modern political ideas associated with ... the nation and the nation state'. He discerns the influence, however unconscious, of the West, for example in the conception of 'the people' as a political entity and in Leninist party structures (Zubaida 1993: ix, 18, 33, 155). Ayubi goes further and argues that the very belief 'that Islam is by its very nature a "political" religion' is of recent origin. The frequent earlier symbioses between religion and politics occurred 'by way of the State appropriating religion' (Ayubi 1991: 3–5).

These interpretations need to be re-examined. First, the idea of going back to sources (sc. 'fundamentals', usul), of reviving a Golden Age, is almost as old as Islam itself. Second, appeals for mass political action, resting on the concept of the umma, have been made time and again, from at least the ninth century onwards (see above, pp. 37, 82). Third, while it is true that a separation between religion and government took place, and that many Muslim groups practised disengagement from politics, not many translated this into a *principle*. Rather, many Muslims have throughout history seen political power as a necessary part of their religious project. What else were the early Shi'a, the 'Abbasids, the Almohads, the Safavids engaged upon? This was what al-Mawardi and Ibn Taymiyya taught.

What has changed is that today political action takes place in the context not of tribe and dynasty but of nation and state. The disintegration of tribal and traditional ties has given new meaning to the umma – though not perhaps in Afghanistan. On the other hand, fundamentalists are united in their opposition to nationalism as a principle and to the nation-state.

What does characterise fundamentalism, and distinguishes it from modernism, is, first, rejection of the West and all it is supposed to stand for, including Communism and Zionism. This arises from a perception that 'the West' poses a threat to Islam that is new in both power and scope. Second, there is a new emphasis on the obligation of jihad (lit. effort) in the military sense of struggle against unbelievers; Sadat's assassins called it 'the neglected duty'.[64] Still more, the *individual* act of political violence is sometimes viewed and undertaken as a religious act of self-sacrificing martyrdom, to be pursued as a glorious end in itself regardless of the consequences. It is sincerely believed that God disposes, so that such acts are not really meaningless; God will reward the individual in paradise and His people on earth. We find this also in the millenarianist sects of other monotheistic religions, and in hard-core Nazis at the end of the Second World War. Within Islam itself, such inconsequentialism actually goes back as far as the assassins of 'Uthman and 'Ali. These two features are combined in a neo-tribal division between Us and Them as a way of perceiving believers and unbelievers. This bodes ill for any non-Muslims in a revivalist state.

Most Muslims, intellectuals and community leaders as well as ordinary people, are not fundamentalists. Like members of other religions, they adopt a variety of political attitudes. From North Africa to East Asia, the modernist tradition lives on as attempts continue to be made to combine Western politics and economics with Islamic values. In North Africa, the legacy of Khayr al-Din, reinforced by 'Abduh, has been strong. Al-Fasi (writing in Morocco in the 1950s), for example, is a statesman and scholar deeply read in European culture, and equally deeply committed to political development and Islamic values.[65] A number of Egyptian writers have been making the case for an open society; some reassert the liberal position of 'Abd al-Raziq that in Islam (as in Christianity) politics is and should remain separate in principle from religion. Some see advocates of stricter enforcement of the Shari'a as 'judaising' Islam.[66] These authors tend to be widely read in the Arab world.

QUESTIONS FACING ISLAMIC POLITICAL THOUGHT TODAY

For most Westerners, the main issues today are Islam's relationship to liberal democracy and international order. Many Muslims might see the implementation of justice, including specific precepts of the Shari'a, as more important. Many Christians and Marxists might take a similar view, substituting for the Shari'a specific precepts of the Bible, or social and economic rights.

The principles of popular sovereignty and the rule of law are supported by the great majority of Islamic thinkers, fundamentalist as well as modernist; but only in very general terms. What precisely they mean by these, and how they would see them being implemented, is often less clear. This is precisely the crux of the matter.

Behind these general observations lies the simple but basic fact that Muslims *as Muslims* have a different starting point from Western liberals. Basically they are non-humanist: that is, for all but the most radically liberal and Westernised Muslims, people only become legitimate persons by being Muslims, or adherents of some other revealed monotheistic faith with a revealed moral code. Until a century or two ago, much the same was true for inhabitants of the Christian West, if you substitute the priority of Christianity for that of Islam. This, to start with, fundamentally alters one's perception of citizenship.

Secondly, what is above all else important to a Muslim *as a Muslim* is that the law of God should be observed, by oneself and, so far as possible, others. How this is achieved is of secondary importance. This gives a very different set of political priorities. It means that human rights, liberties, the rule of law and democratic procedures, however important they may be, are of secondary worth. So far as democratic procedures are concerned, the same might also have been said of inhabitants of the Christian West up to a couple of centuries ago (one might be tempted to say, until it ceased being in a full sense the Christian West). But human rights, liberties and the rule of law have become fundamental and incontrovertible principles in Western society (however often they are neglected in practice, particularly with regard to outsiders). This, I would contend, is due not so much to Christianity but to ancient classical Stoicism and similar philosophies which have for centuries permeated Western culture.

One must see these points together with a third point, which strikes anyone who has studied the history of Islamic political thought, namely the overwhelming tradition, in practice and in theory, of dynastic monarchical government, limited (only) by the Shari'a. Alternative forms and practices have only come onto the agenda in the Islamic world since, and one is forced to conclude because, it became subject to Western influence. (Of course, something broadly similar might be said about other non-European political cultures today.) What this means is that the tendency towards one-man rule, whether in the form of hereditary monarchy or of 'dictatorship' (meaning government by one person in the name of some principle or common interest), is not accidental but written into the political culture of many if not all parts of the Islamic world (though Iran and Turkey now provide exceptions). In other words, such regimes are held to be legitimate because they exist, provide some form of 'law and order', and encourage or sanction the implementation of Islamic justice (the Shari'a). It seems to me, quite surprisingly in view of much recent American propaganda, that the only serious exception is Iran.

Having said that, let us make the following further observations. First, among Muslims generally, everyone including rulers is held to be subject to the rule of law; but this may only mean that they must adhere to the Shari'a. It is generally assumed that a ruler should be elected, or, if he is not, that there should be clear evidence of his popular support. In most predominantly Muslim countries, there is an elected representative assembly. This can be legitimised by the Islamic norms of shura (consultation) and ijma (consensus).[67] Few would oppose democracy itself in the name of Islam (but see Enayat 1982: 137–8). For example, 'political power ... is neither valid nor exercisable except by and on behalf of the community through the process of [shura]. No-one is authorised to ... rule by personal discretion' (Islamic Council of Europe 1980 and 1981).[68] The Islamic Council of Europe also made political participation a right and a duty, based on hisba.[69]

Putting this in the context of what was said above, the point is that a variety of forms of dictatorship are not ruled out by the values dominant in much Muslim political culture (although they may nowadays be considered imperfect and disapproved of by many) so long as they do not infringe the fundamental values of Islam (belief in God, the prophecy of Muhammad, the Shari'a). Here, let us also note that, quite apart from mainstream political culture, fundamentalists, in particular, emphasise *leadership* alongside shura. There is an 'incessant quest for a charismatic chief' (amir), who would rule by virtue of his personal qualities: 'in general, the more radical the party, the more central is the figure of the amir'. Such a person would be a religious as well as a political leader (Roy 1994: 43–4). This springs out of another monarchical element in Islamic culture, namely the belief that certain individuals (analogous to Muhammad himself, albeit acknowledged to be of lower status) are from time to time inspired, or chosen, by God to lead the community. Such persons are recognised not by popular vote but by the religious criteria of piety, virtue, personal presence and the like.

Fundamentalists explicitly qualify popular sovereignty, and the authority of elected representatives, by the sovereignty (al-hakimiyya: absolute rulership) of God (Ayubi 1991: 66). In theory, again, all theists would agree. But Islamic fundamentalists employ the theory of divine sovereignty in a special way. First, they emphasise the need for representatives to be properly qualified, that is to have certain moral and intellectual qualities that are regarded as desirable on religious grounds.[70] One finds a broadly similar idea in John Stuart Mill and T. S. Eliot.[71] In practice, it easily leads to the subordination of elected governments to a self-appointed religious elite, as in the case of Iran.

Second, the legislative scope of parliament is limited by the Shari'a for the obvious reason that this is a divinely legislated code (for example, al-Mawdudi in EI 6: 873b). For example, Turabi believes that 'an Islamic order of government is essentially a form of representative democracy', but he qualifies this in a remarkable way: 'an Islamic government is not strictly speaking a direct government of and by the people; it is a government of the Shari'a'. But (he goes on) 'in a substantial sense, it is popular government since the Shari'a represents the convictions of the people and, therefore, their direct will. This limitation on what a representative body can do is a guarantee of the supremacy of the religious will of the community' (in Esposito (ed.) 1983: 244). This is a fairly typical statement. It obviously has the effect of removing real authority from democratic elections. It reinterprets the Western idea of democracy in an interestingly Rousseauist way, and so reunites it with the Islamic ideal.

The question of course is, how and by whom is the Shari'a to be interpreted? How are we to know what 'the religious will of the community' is? This is, characteristically, left unanswered. A Christian might hold similar views, but he/she would be more likely to leave the interpretation of religious Right, at least in a political context, to the individual voter. An issue like abortion, however, provides an exception in some countries.

Finally, on constitutional matters, Islamic political thought as a whole, both modernist and fundamentalist, is characterised by a remarkable lack of detail. The Muslim Brethren said that they would leave the 'specifics' to 'time, place and the needs of the people' (in Mitchell 1969: 245). For Qutb, it may be said, 'the form of government … based on the principles of Islam is not of vital importance. In theory, it is a matter of indifference … whether the Islamic state has a republican or other form of government'. For him, 'the goodness of the state does not depend on its institutions but … on its underlying principles' (Moussalli 1992: 162–3). Fundamentalists tend to dismiss the details of constitutions and governmental procedures – the stuff of practical politics – as 'futile arguments about mere technicalities'. Choueiri comments that 'this aversion to discuss concrete politics … has become the hallmark of contemporary Islamic radicalism. The role played by Qutb's negative approach in this respect was undoubtedly the most decisive factor' (p. 154). V. S. Naipaul captures this in his record of interviews in the Islamic world, conducted just after the 1979 revolution, when expectations were at their highest and the fundamentalist project at its peak:

This late twentieth-century Islam appeared to raise political issues. But it had the flaw of its origins – the flaw that ran right through Islamic history:

to the political issues it raised it offered no political or practical solution. It offered only the faith. It offered only the Prophet, who would settle everything – but who had ceased to exist. This political Islam was rage, anarchy.[72]

Similarly, Ayubi comments, 'one may search the manifestoes of the Muslim Brethren or the Iranian clerics for a detailed description of what an Islamic *state* or an Islamic *economy* should look like, but such a search will be in vain' (p. 42). This is partly due to an implicit belief that moral principles and the virtue of those in power are what really matter; that, once these are settled, everything else will fall into place (see Roy 1994: ix, 45, 62). The result is that, when people speak of popular sovereignty and the rule of law, one cannot always be clear whether it is a serious proposition or a rhetorical device.

LIBERTY, EQUALITY, THE POSITION OF WOMEN AND NON-MUSLIMS

Liberty as a social and political norm[73] has entered Islamic political thought only during the last 150 years or so and in response to European influence. The progress of liberal values in general depends, partly though not wholly, upon a separation between religion and the polity. But, for both traditional Islamic thinkers and fundamentalists, the function of the state must include enforcement of religious values in public life; this is stated time after time as the state's most serious, indeed its only, duty. Fundamentalist manifestoes regularly 'include, a priori, a detailed account of the moral precepts that the public is to obereve collectively and that are to be overseen authoritatively, especially in the area of sex, women and the family' (Ayubi 1991: 42) (on this last point compare Roman Catholicism). Al-Mawdudi provides an example: 'a state which does not take interest in establishing virtue and eradicating vice and in which adultery, drinking ... obscene literature, indecent films ... immoral display of beauty, promiscuous mingling of men and women, co-education, etc., flourish without let or hindrance cannot be called an Islamic State' (in Ahmed 1987: 93; see also Khomeini, above, p. 000). It is all Devlin and no Hart. For liberty in the Western sense to exist, one would have to change, or ignore, aspects of traditional Islamic teaching.

Equality, on the other hand, has been emphasised in Islam, past and present, more than it has in Christian or humanist thought (for a recent example, see Ahmed 1987: 158). In social and economic policy, modern writers, including fundamentalists, usually identify Islam as a middle way between the erroneous extremes of capitalism and state socialism (or Communism).[74] Thus Islam, it is said, upholds the right to private property, but only as a trust from God, the ultimate owner; Islam emphasises the duty to provide for all members of society, especially the poor. The Muslim Brethren call this Islamic socialism.[75] Muhammad Iqbal, writing in India in the 1930s, pointed out that the main problem that would face a new Muslim state would be poverty, and that 'for Islam the acceptance of social democracy in some suitable form and consistent with the legal principles of Islam is not a revolution but a return to the original purity of Islam' (in Ahmad 1967: 163). The Prime Minister of Pakistan said (1949): 'Islamic socialism ... means that every person in this land has equal rights to be provided with food, shelter, clothing, education and medical facilities' (in Choueiri 1997: 52). This combination of social welfare and private property brings mainstream Islamic thought close to the views of Aristotle, John Locke, the modern Roman Catholic Church and much recent Western political philosophy.[76]

But of course what has traditionally been meant by equality is equality among male Muslims. This raises the question of human rights in an Islamic state or in a state with a Muslim majority. Zubaida observes that 'Islam has no specific doctrine of human rights', but that Muslims have endorsed the Universal Declaration on Human Rights (1948) and found it fully compatible with Islamic doctrine; indeed, they have claimed that Islam got there first.[77] One strength of Islamic moral culture has certainly been the *informal* exercise of moral duties regardless of the state. But, once again, the real issue is how rights are applied *in detail*; and, of course, *to whom.*

On the whole, the greater the influence of traditional Islam, or of fundamentalism, the more restricted women are, and the more difficult is the situation of non-Muslims, especially non-theists. Many modernists, but among fundamentalists only Turabi, have championed equality for women in marriage, including monogamy and an equal right to divorce, and equality for women in education.[78] (One should remember that in many European countries until recently, neither men nor women were at liberty to divorce.) A pupil of 'Abduh argued (1899), along the same lines as Ibn Rushd, that Muslim civilisation had declined because of the servile status of women, who were consequently unable to fulfil their role of forming 'the morals of the nation'. Oppression in the home, this writer said, is the basis of oppression in the state: 'freedom and respect for personal rights' are found where 'the status of women has been raised to a high degree of respect and freedom of thought and action'.[79]

Rashid Rida, on the other hand, defended traditional Muslim Law on relationships between the sexes (E. Rosenthal 1965: 72–3). The Muslim Brethren envisaged greater equality: women could be educated and go out to work; but women's political rights 'should be left in abeyance until both men and women are more educated' (Mitchell 1969: 257). Al-Mawdudi strongly reaffirmed the traditional segregation and subordination of women, and their exclusion from political life; he defended four wives and child marriages.[80] Qutb's defence of differential treatment was more moderate and less specific (*Social Justice*, p. 50). Shari'ati seems to have found this a difficult topic: he wanted women to be separate but equal; he favoured their participation in public life (Keddie 1981: 220–1). Turabi has gone further in giving women equal political rights (Osman, p. 416).

Current Islamic views about the rights of non-Muslims have received less attention in the West, for obvious reasons of political correctness. But this is no less serious a matter; it can be a matter of life or death. The prospects for political, or even legal, equality for non-Muslims are tied in with people's perception of their political and social identity. For Pakistan, al-Mawdudi upheld the traditional Legal view that non-Muslims should be given protection on payment of jizya, but no political role; and that anyone who abandoned

Islam was liable to the death penalty.[81] Jinnah, on the contrary, in his famous address to the Constituent Assembly on the eve of independence (1948), endorsed the separation of religion from citizenship: 'You are free to go to your ... places of worship in this State of Pakistan. You may belong to any religion ... ; that has got nothing to do with the business of the State ... We are starting with this fundamental principle that we are all equal citizens of one state. ' He believed that 'You will find that in the course of time Hindus would cease to be Hindus and Muslims would cease to be Muslims, not in the religious sense, because that is the personal faith of each individual, but in the political sense as citizens of the State' (in Ahmed 1987: 79). It was one of the most candid public statements of the separation of religion from politics, and of a secular political identity, from the Muslim world. In fact, the very opposite happened in Pakistan. Al-Mawdudi's view has triumphed.

It seems more difficult for a Muslim than for a Christian or humanist to detach citizenship from religious affiliation. This goes back to historical origins and first principles (see above, p. 10): Christianity started in an alien society and detached itself from the state; Islam took over political society. The authoritative texts of the two faiths, to which believers in divine revelation are morally bound to refer, reflect this difference. Within Islam, probably only an intellectual revolution of the kind attempted by 'Abd al-Raziq could change things.

ISLAM AND NATIONALISM

The alternative to religion as a basis of civic identity has generally speaking, especially in Europe, been nationhood. Muslims have always recognised nationality; people of different race, colour, language and customs coexist within the overarching religious Community. But until the late nineteenth century, nationhood has never been seen as a basis for statehood (although Iran was a de facto nation-state, its identity was Shi'ite).

The idea of the nation-state entered the Islamic world along with other European political ideas. Love of one's homeland or country (watan: *patrie*) began to be preached by some Egyptian and Turkish writers as a positive virtue.[82] Tahtawi (1801–73) held that people of the same homeland had the same obligations towards one other as people of the same religion (A. Hourani 1983: 79). Lutfi al-Sayyid (1872–1963, also an Egyptian) associated universalism (the idea that 'the land of Islam is the watan (homeland) of all Muslims') with Islamic (that is, Ottoman) imperialism; it was out of date and should be replaced 'by the one faith consonant with the ambition of every Eastern nation that has a defined watan ... the faith of nationalism (wataniyya)'.[83] The question of the nation-state was immensely complicated by Arab nationalism,[84] because there was never a practical prospect of a pan-Arab state.

Many modernists, however, saw nationalism as divisive and 'incompatible with Islamic universalism'.[85] The fundamentalists go further: nationalism is the product of jahiliyya (pre-Islamic ignorance: Qutb), 'the satan of racist and national fanaticism' (al-Mawdudi in Choueiri 1997: 102). Qutb was scathing about Arab nationalism, so dear to his tormentors, saying that it glorified 'the inferior and brutish bonds' of race (in Choueiri 1997: 104). The ideal of a home-land (watan) was appropriated for the Islamic umma (Enayat 1982: 115). It is perhaps no coincidence that Christians were prominent in the development of the ideology of Arab nationalism (Vatikiotis 1971: 165).

On international relations, there have been frequent calls for closer economic cooperation between Muslim states, and also for a Muslim World Court.[86] AbuSulayman (a Malaysian academic, writing in 1987) has sought to update the application of Islamic principles to international order; he argues for the abandonment of military jihad and a new world order based on tawhid – the unity and equality of humankind.[87] But no serious attempt has yet been made to put any of this into practice. The original transnational ideals of Islam, and of late–nineteenth century Pan-Islamism, seem to have been replaced (like the multi-national empires which embodied them) by the state system.[88] Many Muslim states have a tenuous sense of national identity, and this is further undermined by those who argue that the nation-state itself is un-Islamic. What we seem to find is that, the more self-consciously Islamic one becomes, the less inclined one is to endow the nation-state with any moral authority.

Therefore, insofar as nationhood is the only available alternative to a religious definition of community and citizenship, the prospects for a non-sectarian view of citizenship in the Islamic world are not good.[89] This means that the prospects for liberty and human rights are not good either. But the West cannot claim moral superiority: far worse atrocities were committed in the twentieth century in the name of the nation than in the name of Islam.

NOTES

1. On this period in general, see Enayat (1982); Ayubi (1991); Choueiri (1997); Zubaida (1993); Roy (1994).
2. Zubaida (1993: xvii); Ayubi (1991: 59).
3. Vatikiotis (1971: 12, 109); *The Economist* 17 October 1998, p. 90, 'A matter of health in Uzbekistan'.
4. Robert Fisk in *The Independent*, 28 January 1999.
5. Choueiri (1997: 70); *EI* 2: 638–40.
6. For what follows, see especially Lewis (1968: 234–74); Berkes (1964: 368–455); Zürcher (1998: 132–7).
7. Lewis (1968: 326–7, 345); Shaw and Shaw (1977: 262); Zürcher (1998: 136).
8. Lewis (1968: 145); Berkes (1964: 369).
9. N. Berkes (ed.), *Turkish Nationalism and Western Civilization: Selected Writings by Ziya Gökalp* (London: Allen & Unwin, 1959), p. 302.
10. Lewis (1968: 265, 272–3, 412); but see Lewis (1968: 357). See Ayçe Güneş-Ayata, 'Pluralism versus Authoritarianism: Political Ideas in Two Islamic Publications', in Richard Tapper (ed.), *Islam in Modern Turkey: Religion, Politics and Literature in a Secular State* (London: Tauris, 1982), pp. 254–79.
11. Landau (1994: 211); Ahmad (1967: 138 and 1964: 65–6).
12. On him, see Kerr (1966: 159–85); E. Rosenthal (1965: 66–84); Enayat (1982: 69–83); A. Hourani (1983: 222–44); Gardet (1981: 350–5); *EI* 8: 446–7.
13. Gardet (1981: 353–5); Kerr (1966: 165); Lewis (1968: 159).

14. In Gardet (1981: 353). Compare the views expressed by the Turkish National Assembly (1922): Kerr (1966: 181–2).
15. In Gardet (1981: 352); a similar approach was taken by some early Christian thinkers to pagan philosophy ('Whatever things were rightly said among all men, are the property of us Christians': Justin Martyr, second century, in Étienne Gilson, *History of Christian Philosophy in the Middle Ages* (London: Sheed & Ward, 1955), p. 13).
16. On him, see Binder (1988: 131–60); A. Hourani (1983: 183–91); Enayat (1982: 62–8); Gardet (1981: 355–7); especially good is E. Rosenthal (1965: 85–101).
17. E. Rosenthal (1965: 85–6); Binder (1988: 135).
18. E. Rosenthal (1965: 92–3, 96). He used Ibn Khaldun when discussing early Islam: Binder (1988: 132–4); E. Rosenthal (1965: 88–97).
19. Mitchell (1969); Enayat (1982: 85–92); Choueiri (1997: 39–43); Ayubi (1991: 130–3); Zubaida (1993: 48–50); EI 3: 1068–71.
20. On him, see Ahmad (1967: 208–22); E. Rosenthal (1965: 138–53); Choueiri (1997: 102–6, 118–20); on Mawdudi and Pakistan, see Ahmed (1987).
21. Binder (1988: 174); E. Rosenthal (1965: 112); Moussalli (1992: 36).
22. On him, see Choueiri (1997: 93–143); Ayubi (1991: 134–42); EI 9: 117–18; outstandingly good are Moussalli (1992); Binder (1988: 173–205).
23. Trans. International Islamic Federation of Student Organizations (Beirut, (1978).
24. Sayed Kotb (Qutb), *Social Justice in Islam*, trans. John B. Hardie (Washington DC: The American Company of Learned Societies, 1953), pp. 88–91.
25. Binder (1988: 198); EI 9: 118a.
26. Moussalli (1992: 157, 166–8); Choueiri (1997: 115–17).
27. Moussalli (1992: 163, 200); Binder (1988: 177).
28. Ayubi (1991: 141); Zubaida (1993: 55).
29. Roy (1994: 69–70); Zubaida (1993: 54); Choueiri (1997: 158–60); Ayubi (1991: 78, 142–3); Moussalli (1992: 244).
30. Gardet (1981: 382–7); Ahmad (1967: 197–205); EI 4: 123–6.
31. Choueiri (1997: 78); EI 4: 125a).
32. On what follows, see Halm (1991: 117–30); CH Iran 7: 228–96, 735–50); Keddie (1980: 77–111); Keddie (1981); Keddie (ed.) (1983); Arjomand (ed.) (198); Arjomand (1988); Shaul Bakhash, *The Reign of the Ayatollahs: Iran and the Islamic Revolution* (London: Tauris, 1985).
33. Keddie (1981: 215–24); Watt (1988: 132–5); Shahrough Akhavi, 'Shariati's Social Thought', in Keddie (ed.) (1983: 125–44). Some of his writings are trans. in Dr 'Ali Shari'ati, *What Is to be Done: The Enlightened Thinkers and an Islamic Renaissance*, F. Rajaee (ed.) (Houston TX: IRIS, (1986); and in *On the Sociology of Islam*, trans. Hamid Algar (Berkeley CA: Mizan Press, 1979).
34. *What Is to be Done*, pp. 99–100, 128; Zubaida (1993: 21–3). He does not refer to Ibn Khaldun.
35. Note the parallel with Machiavelli's 'prophet armed' (*The Prince*, ch. 6), and with Ibn Taymiyya (see above, p. 158).
36. *What Is to be Done*, p. 145; Keddie (1981: 220–1).
37. Ahmad (1967: 139–65); EI 3: 1057–9.
38. Fred Halliday, 'Iranian Foreign Policy since 1979', in Juan R. I. Cole and Nikki R. Keddie (eds), *Shi'ism and Social Protest* (Newhaven CT: Yale University Press, 1986), p. 89.
39. Keddie (1980: 76–7 and 1981: 103, 223); Arjomand 1988: 97, 149); Ayubi (1991: 146).
40. As well as the works cited in n. 32 above, see Gregory Rose, 'Velayat-e Faqih and the Recovery of Islamic Identity in the Thought of Ayatollah Khomeini', in Keddie

(ed.) (1983: 166–88). Khomeini's *Islamic Government* and other writings are trans. Hamid Algar, *Islam and Revolution: Writings and Declarations of Imam Khomeini* (Berkeley CA: Mizan Press, (1981).

41. Rose, p. 188; *CH Iran* 7: 751–3.
42. Sachedina (1988 passim); Arjomand (1984: 232); Halm (1991: 104).
43. In *CH Iran* 7: 285; *Islamic Government*, pp. 47–8.
44. Arjomand (1988: 97); Moussalli (1992: 46–8).
45. In Arjomand (1988: 148–9); *Islamic Government*, p. 55.
46. In Rose, pp. 183, 187 n. 102.
47. P. 43; Rose, p. 180.
48. Ed. Arjomand (1988: 191, 193); see above, p. 285.
49. His was 'an original, creative enterprise': Rose, pp. 176, 188; see Arjomand (ed.) (1988: 124, 192).
50. Chibli Mallat, *The Renewal of Islamic Law: Muhammad Baqer as-Sadr, Najaf and the Shi'i International* (Cambridge: Cambridge University Press, 1993), p. 70; Dekmejian (1995: 125).
51. Halm (1991: 128); text in Arjomand (ed.) (1988: 272–83).
52. See also Baqer as-Sadr in Mallat, p. 70.
53. It first appeared in Turkey in the late eighteenth century; see *EI* 2: 594a.
54. 'The Testament of the Islamic Revolution: Imam Khumayni's *Last Counsel*', *Al-Tawhid* 6 (1989), pp. 69–118 at p. 113.
55. Khomeini in Arjomand (1988: 183).
56. Zubaida (1993: 176); Bakhash, 'Ayatollahs', pp. 242–3; Arjomand (1988: 164).
57. In Rose, p. 186; see Arjomand (ed.) (1988: 199); Arjomand (1988: 169).
58. Arjomand (1988: 183–8); Bakhash, p. 247; Roy (1994: 178).
59. Zubaida (1993: 176); Arjomand (ed.) (1988: 196).
60. Ramazani, 'Khumayni's Islam in Iran's Foreign Policy', in Adeed Dawisha (ed.), *Islam in Foreign Policy* (Cambridge: Cambridge University Press, 1983), p. 26.
61. A. A. Osman, 'The Ideological Development of the Sudanese Ikhwan Movement', *Proceedings of the 1988 International Conference on Middle-Eastern Studies* (Leeds, 1988), pp. 387–430; Ayubi (1991: 105–7); Dekmejian (1995: 186–9); extract from his writings in Esposito (ed.) (1983: 241–51).
62. On the concept of fundamentalism, see especially Ayubi (1991: 42–4, 80–1); Choueiri (1997: xvi–xix); Roy (1994: 11).
63. Choueiri (1997: xv, 64); Zubaida (1993: ix); Roy (1994: 3).
64. *EI* 7: 291; Choueiri (1997: 143–6, 160); Roy (1994: 152–8).
65. E. Rosenthal (1965: 154–78); *EI* 8: 901–2.
66. Ayubi (1991: 202–11); Alexander Flores, 'Secularism, Integralism and Political Islam: The Egyptian Debate', in Beinin and Stork (eds) (1987: 83–94; D. Sagiv, 'Judge Ashmawi and Militant Islam in Egypt', *Middle Eastern Studies* 28 (1992), pp. 532–46; E. Rosenthal (1965); John Cooper et al. (eds), *Islam and Modernity: Muslim Intellectuals Respond* (London: Tauris, 1998); Carolyn Fluehr-Lobban (ed.), *Against Islamic Extremism: The Writings of Muhammad Sa'id Al-'Ashmawy* (Gainesville FL: Florida University Press, 1998).
67. Enayat (1982: 131); Ahmed (1987: 151).
68. Salem Azzam (ed.), *Islam and Contemporary Society* (London: Longman, 1982), p. 260; Bruno Étienne, *L'Islamisme radicale* (Paris: Hachette, 1987), pp. 355, 358.
69. Azzam (ed.), p. 260; Étienne, p. 359. On Islam and democracy, see Gudrun Kraemer, 'Islamist Notions of Democracy', in Beinin and Stork (eds) (1997: 71–82); Fazlur Rahman, 'The Principle of Shura and the Role of the Umma in Islam', *American*

Journal of Islamic Studies 1 (1984), pp. 1–9; Enayat (1982: 129–38); Gardet (1981: 331–43).

70. See Rashid Rida in Gardet (1981: 128–31); Enayat (1982: 136); and The Muslim Brethren in *EI* 3: 1070b.

71. J. S. Mill, *Representative Government*, ch. 7; T. S. Eliot, *The Idea of a Christian Society* (London: Faber & Faber, 1939).

72. *Among the Believers* (London: Penguin, 1981), pp. 89, 331.

73. *EI* on Hurriyya; F. Rosenthal (1960).

74. For example, Mawdudi: M. A. A. Maudoodi (sic), *Capitalism, Socialism and Islam*, 2nd edn (Kuwait: Islamic Book Publications, 1987); Azzam (ed.), pp. 259–60. See Choueiri (1997: 118–22); Enayat (1982: 139–58).

75. *EI* 3: 1070a–b; Choueiri (1997: 50–1).

76. See for example James Tully, *A Discourse on Property* (Cambridge: Cambridge University Press, 1980).

77. Sami Zubaida, 'Human Rights and Cultural Difference: Middle Eastern Perspectives', *New Perspectives on Turkey* 10 (1994), p. 8; Enayat (1982: 132).

78. Osman, pp. 416–17; Ahmad (1967: 72–5); Ahmad and von Grunebaum (eds) (1970: 57).

79. A. Hourani (1983: 164–8); see above, p. 125.

80. Ahmad (1967: 213, 219); Ahmed (1987: 108–9).

81. Ahmed (1987: 103–4); Choueiri (1997: 111–12); Ahmad (1967: 220).

82. Lewis (1988: 40–1); A. Hourani (1983: 70–1); Choueiri (1997: 31, 177); E. Rosenthal (1965: 171).

83. In E. Rosenthal (1965: 122–3); see A. Hourani (1983: 178, 206).

84. On this, see A. Hourani (1983: ch. 11); E. Rosenthal (1965: chs 5, 7); Choueiri (1997: 53).

85. Enayat (1982: 115); 'Abduh in Kerr (1966: 139).

86. For example, Azzam (ed.), pp. 264–5.

87. AbdulHamid A. AbuSulayman, *The Islamic Theory of International Relations: New Directions for Islamic Methodology and Thought* (Herndon VA: International Institute of Islamic Thought, 1987). I am grateful to a paper by David George (1994) for this reference. See Khadduri and Liebesny (eds) (1955: 350–72).

88. James P. Piscatori, *Islam in a World of Nation-States* (Cambridge: Cambridge University Press, 1986).

89. Vatikiotis (1971: 204–5 and 1987: 38, 55).

Conclusion

The history of Islamic political thought shows us a unique intellectual tradition. What first leaps to our eyes is the relationship between religion and politics. Islam started out as a faith determined to conquer and convert the world. 'Politics' and 'the state' were subsumed into its mission: Islamic communities and rulers raised taxes through zakat and the poll-tax, their armies were devoted to jihad.

But from around 850 things changed somewhat. Power came to be divided between a Sultan, who managed military affairs and enforced law and order, and the 'ulama who managed social, family and commercial affairs. The religio-political project of the Prophet and early Imams was replaced, among Sunnis and Imami Shi'ites, by political quietism. In this respect, Islam moved in the opposite direction to Christianity, which had started out opposed to political participation, but became politicised under the late Roman empire and beyond. This detachment of the political order from religion was most marked under the Ottomans. But the military aspect of Islam was never lost sight of; quietist 'ulama did not question external aggression.

This was a change in practice, but not so much in theory, though it reveals what people found acceptable. There was now a considerable gap between theory and practice (Keddie 1963). The political dimension of Islam continued to be expressed in Jurisprudence and political rhetoric. It was reasserted in an updated form by al-Mawardi. Under the Saljuks and their successors, it was understood that public authorities must uphold and enforce the Shari'a, and use their power and patronage to promote Islamic teaching.

There was a specific relationship between 'knowledge' and power in Islamdom (Chamberlain 1994), as there also was in Christendom. The ideal of Prophet and Caliph brought together 'true' knowledge ('ilm in the religious sense) and power. The mode of knowledge that eventually acquired sole legitimacy in the Islamic world (F. Rosenthal 1970) reinforced the social authority of the 'ulama (knowledgeable ones), because they alone could claim to know what is right. The 'ulama, like the medieval Christian clergy, could wield a veto over what could be done. In medieval Christendom, knowledge (scientia, meaning revealed truth) was for a time associated with the offices endowed by Christ – the bishops and the Roman church (Tierney 1972: 39–45). The power that knowledge attracted to the 'ulama was more diffuse and implicit than that of the clergy in

Europe, but it proved far more enduring.

The founding texts of Islam, to which conscientious believers were obliged to refer, made it always possible that some, in the attempt to practise their faith, would reassert in stronger form a necessary link between political power and religious authority. Thus, al-Mawardi on the Caliphate, Ibn Taymiyya on the Sultanate. In the same way, Christianity's founding texts, such as 'Render unto Caesar the things that are Caesar's, and unto God the things that are God's' (*Matthew* 22:21), made its political role always contestable. No new Islamic dynasty could afford not to insist upon its superior religious rectitude and zeal. Some dynasties, relatively relaxed about religion to start with, later turned to Islamic orthodoxy for support. Time and again, the virtues of a patrimonial system, which had enabled different cultural groups to coexist peaceably, were lost in an attempt to enforce Islamic rectitude – the programme of Ibn Taymiyya, Majlisi, Aurangzib and Abdulhamid II. Still more, many religious movements within Islam saw the capture of political power as essential to their mission (the Almohads, for example); some were explicitly revolutionary (the Safavids). The present-day fundamentalists stand in this tradition.

A second striking feature in the history of Islamic political thought is the continuous dialectic between neo-tribalism and patrimonialism. This persists today. To some extent, it drives the relationship between religion and politics, 'ulama and sultan. Neo-tribalism emerged in an exclusive attitude towards (religiously-defined) outsiders, an emphasis on personal relationships, including those involved in the transmission of religious knowledge and insight, belief in the responsibility and worth of the achieving individual (see above, p. 11), and the narrative theory of knowledge. Neo-tribalism and patrimonialism went together in the belief in heredity as an indicator of religious worth and social status; in the priority given to family, clan, dynastic and tribal connections; and in the institution of patronage–clientage (wala'). The households of notables – 'ulama, landowners, merchants, whose status rested on acquired and inherited qualities – were the cells of political society (Chamberlain 1994). (This was compatible with large-scale commerce, but probably not with industrial society.) Patrimonialism on its own was manifested in the theory of the Circle of Power and in the ideal of social hierarchy expressed in the Four Orders, and in the universal distinction between elite and masses. Patrimonial and indeed originally Hindu values could override the Islamic and tribal value of social equality (Marlow 1997). Cultivators made up one of the four orders; the common people appear in the patrimonial model as ones to be cared for, sheep to be protected in return for tax.

Both patrimonialism and neo-tribalism lie behind what most of all differentiated Islamic from European political thought: the absence of the concept of public office, of the state as separate from individual rulers, and of a distinction between private and public.[1] The notion of the state, being abstract, was alien to narrative thinking. The idea of an explicitly secular political authority could not take hold because political language had been determined by religious 'ilm.

This had far-reaching consequences. Islamic rulers might wield great power, but most dynasties lasted only for a relatively short time (the Ottomans were, as often, an exception). This was precisely because they could not attach their personal authority to an abstract, impersonal state. Moreover, the very idea of a constitution, the rule of law, procedures which precisely define legitimate tenure of power, presupposes a separation of authority from the individual. In the Islamic world, authority remained tied to the outstanding individual and dynasty. This reflected both the tribal view that it is personal qualities that count, and the mode of divine revelation through the chosen individual.

In Europe, by contrast, constitutional rules were embedded in the 'feudal' order and survived even under the 'divine right of kings'. The absence of rules such as primogeniture made succession problematic under Islam. This affects political culture and practice today, making a peaceful transfer of power and the introduction of new blood through elections very difficult. Electoral democracy *presupposes* the authority of offices rather than individuals. In Islamic society, there was no attempt, prior to sustained Western influence, to replace Imamate or Sultanate with constitutional monarchy or a republic.

This is the more surprising because, from early on, there *was* a theory of state origins, of the raison d'être and legitimacy of state power as such: namely, that human beings have to cohabit and cooperate in order to survive; we are quarrelsome and disagreements are bound to arise; therefore there must be a law; law needs an enforcer. In other words, political authority was seen to derive from human nature. In this common Irano-Islamic theory, law actually *precedes* rulership; and it was indeed universally acknowledged that the ruler was under a law which he could not change – the Holy Law.

This proto-Marsilian or proto-Hobbesian theory of sovereignty was constantly reiterated. It was precisely the kind of argument that in Europe was used to justify the extension of royal authority, and, partly under its aegis, the development of state authority.[2] But it was not developed in the Islamic world. No-one suggested that someone other than a monarch should do the ruling. It was assumed that the enforcer must be a monarch without whose sovereignty people would be at each other's throats.

The argument from law and order produced a conception of political authority as imposed on society from outside, not an expression of the will of society. Authority did not come from the people but 'from God and the sword' (as a sixteenth-century Frenchman put it), soldiers and religious leaders frequently acting as power-brokers. The resulting system operated relatively benignly in a multi-cultural society, in which groups such as Islamic sects, Christians and Jews orchestrated their own internal affairs. These (as the theory said and subsequent experience has lamentably demonstrated) could not coexist peacefully without a sovereign who was independent of them all. There were thus advantages in the prevalent system. Once you derive sovereignty from the people, a new problem of minorities arises, as both de Tocqueville and Sayyid Ahmed Khan were aware: compare the Balkans and the Levant now and under the Ottomans.

The domination of neo-tribal and patrimonial mentalities may also partly explain the absence of a notion of corporate bodies, such as cities, business corporations or voluntary associations, which played such a decisive role in European political development (Black 1984). The religious waqf (trust) never became a general category. But there must be other reasons why city-states and even semi-autonomous cities did not appear in areas where they had once flourished and in the midst of a mercantile economy.

The greatest number of original thinkers were active between about 800 and 1100, at a time when Islam was the most creative culture in the world. In its springtime, Islamic political thought and culture looked more promising than the West's. The idea of the Circle of Power suggests a sophisticated understanding of political society.

But then things went static – or stable; political thought has remained in many respects unaltered since the eleventh century. This was certainly the intention of its exponents. Religio-political thought became impermeable: new facts or experiences were not allowed to penetrate a system regarded as perfect and all-embracing. Thus the genres of Jurisprudence and Royal Advice remained unchanged, the same statements recurring again and again down to the twentieth century. Only the impact of the West made some Muslims consider new political ideas and forms of government.

This turn of events was exemplified by the misfortunes of Falsafa. Never a popular subject, always liable to attack by populist religious leaders, it depended largely on court patronage. Several philosophers led extremely hazardous lives and showed remarkable courage in the face of persecution, political disaster and personal tragedy. Of the founding fathers of other intellectual genres, Ibn Muqaffa' was officially murdered, Shafi'i knifed to death (probably) by a student after a lecture. Yet in the great days of Islamic intellectual life, several thinkers played a prominent part in public affairs: Ibn Sina, Nizam al-Mulk (who was assassinated), Ibn Rushd and Ibn Khaldun. Al-Ghazali was the most symptomatic: public figure, recluse and possibly refugee from Nizari assassins; the one who, by exposing the 'incoherence' of philosophy, legitimised its exclusion.

The philosophers' approach was systematically rejected as impious innovation. Doubt was frowned upon as unbelief (F. Rosenthal 1970); what we need to know, what we need to do, is already encapsulated in the Shari'a. The very possibility of original thought was steadily extruded like a foreign body from Islamic culture. Real knowledge was the divinely-revealed Law defined by the Consensus and upheld by the 'ulama – the opposite of Plato's view. Religion also sanctioned physical violence in the divine interest and so promoted conformism and discouraged new ideas.

In Islam, a narrative approach to mental activity, embodied in linguistics, story-telling, poetry and historiography, ousted the abstract approach of philosophy. What is real is what has happened, and this we know from the mouths of our pious forefathers. This was typifed in the way Islamic Jurisprudence was formulated by stringing together Narratives (hadith) about the Prophet's life and teaching. Genealogy and history were dominant means of expressing individual or collective self-esteem.

This went with a sceptical attitude towards causal explanation and laws of nature as instrusions upon divine omnipotence. Phenomena are unmediated acts of God, to be understood only as the inscrutable will of God. 'Occasionalism' (Fakhry 1958) drowned the possibility of natural or social science.

The closed intellectual approach developed at a time when the economy of citied agrarian society in Iran and the Middle East was fatally disrupted by the Mongol invasions. The prospect of an independent bourgeoisie was suppressed by '"military patronage states". in which the steppe principle of nomad patronage of urban culture was generalised' (Hodgson 1974: vol. 2, p. 204). There was a shift towards pastoral nomadism with its values of kinship and clientage, especially evident in post-Safavid Iran and Afghanistan.

Resignation was a functional response to the catastrophes of the thirteenth to the fifteenth centuries and to an often unpredictable social environment. God re-emerged as fortune or fate, unknowable and arbitrary. Belief in magic, dreams and astrology became widespread among all classes. The highest expression of this was the mysticism of the Sufis.

Perhaps all this is another way of saying that Islamic political thought did not undergo the process of secularisation – the translation of religious concepts and norms into secular equivalents – that we find in Aquinas, Locke, Rousseau and others in Europe. Secularisation was successfully ruled out by the religious authorities.

The Sultan had presided over a military-agricultural complex as effective as that of 'feudal' Europe. In the twelfth century, Islamic society and Latin-Catholic Europe both still shared fundamentals of material culture and social organisation going back to the time of Plato, Jesus and Muhammad. Islamdom was producing thinkers as original and subtle, as worth reading today, as many in the Western 'canon': Nizam al-Mulk, al-Ghazali, Ibn Rushd, Nasir al-Din Tusi, Ibn Taymiyya and Ibn Khaldun. The two cultures shared some ideas, sometimes put in startlingly similar language, due to the shared heritage of Abrahamic monotheism and Greek philosophy. But these were expressed within very different overall social and intellectual contexts and with very different meanings. Islam knew nothing of the Roman political tradition, while Europe knew nothing of the Indo-Iranian. Then after about 1200, Islamdom and Christendom diverged much more sharply, as Latin Europe developed new types of polity and new political notions.

What does Islamic political thought have to offer today? First, in the Royal Advice literature, it offers a tradition of prudential ethics, political realism and managerial know-how going back to Ibn Muqaffa'. This is valuable because it contains practical insights analogous to those of Machiavelli without a pathological rejection of humanitarian values.

Second, it offers us the concept of mizan (lit. balance) or equilibrium (i'tidal) as a guide to rational calculation in practical affairs. The verse of the Qur'an, 'We sent aforetime our apostles with clear signs, and sent down with them the Book and the Balance (kitab wa mizan) that men may uphold justice' (57: 25), was taken to mean that right must be interpreted and applied through human intelligence. Mizan referred to the merchant's scales; it was the method for calculating the balance of justice. The idea of Mizan was related to a middle way between extremes, held to be characteristic of the wisdom of Islam. This was exemplified above all by al-Ghazali. It is the opposite of the spirit of fundamentalism.

And lastly, Ibn Khaldun should be read by every modern social scientist for his understanding of the kind of society that existed in the Islamic world from the seventh to the seventeenth century, and to some extent beyond.

NOTES

1. For the way in which this developed in Europe, see Skinner (1978: vol. 2, pp. 352–8); Black (1992: 186–91).
2. Antony Black, *Monarchy and Community* (Cambridge: Cambridge University Press, 1970).

Glossary

Glossary of words used frequently, and their usual English equivalents (shown by capital letter).

adab	polite culture
'ālim	*see* 'ulamā'
amīr	military Commander; ruler
amīr al-mu'minīn	'commander of the faithful' (Caliphal title)
'askeri	warriors, Ottoman upper class
bay'a	(from bā'a, to sell) contract, homage, Election
bid'a	innovation connoting impiety
dawla, devlet	(from d-w-l, to alternate) political success, turn in power, Dynasty, State
devlet	*see* dawla
devşirme	forced levy of youths
dhimmī	(those of the covenant) non-Muslim monotheists protected under Muslim rule
dīn	Religion
falāsifa	(sing. faylasūf) Philosophers, those engaged in falsafa q.v.
falsafa	Philosophy or metaphysics in the Platonic and Aristotelian tradition
faqīh	*see* fuqahā'
fatwā (fetva)	authorised legal opinion
faylasūf	*see* falāsifa
fiqh	(understanding) Religious Jurisprudence
fuqahā'	(sing. faqīh) Religious Jurists
futuwwa	chivalry, guild fraternity
ghazi	frontier warrior
ḥadīth	Report or narrative of what the Prophet said or did (usually translated Tradition, but see Hodgson 1974: vol. 2, pp. 93–4)
ḥisba	overseeing of public morals, especially in trade
hudūd	Legal penalties (of the Sharī'a)
ijmā'	Consensus (of believers) (especially on points of Law)
ijtihād	(lit. self-exertion) independent reasoning (especially in Law)
'ilm	knowledge or learning, especially Religious Knowledge

imāra	the office of amīr q.v.
imām	(*see also* khalīfa) Leader of the Muslim community (also leader of congregational prayer); (modern) head of state
imāma	the office of imām
Imāmī Shī'ism	the branch which recognises twelve imams, of whom the last went into hiding and will emerge to restore true religion and justice (also called Twelver)
iqtā'	'fief' (see p. 92)
jamā'a	assembly, Community
jihād	Holy War, personal striving
jizya	poll-tax levied on non-Muslims
kādī	*see* qādī
kānūn	*see* qānūn
khalīfa	(*see also* imām) Caliph, Deputy/successor (of Muhammad), Leader of the Muslim community
al-khaṣṣa wa'l-'āmma	elite and commoners
khilāfa	Caliphate, Deputyship, the office of khalīfa q.v.
madrasa	Religious College
mahdī	the rightly guided one, an expected ruler who will restore justice
malik	King (*see* mulk)
maṣlaḥa	Public or social Welfare
maẓālim	grievances (court for redress of)
medrese	*see* madrasa
milla (millet)	religious community; (modern) nation
mīzān	balance (*see* p. 106)
molla	*see* 'ālim
muftī	expert authorised to issue fatwā q.v.
muḥtasib	Overseer of public morals (*see* ḥisba)
mujtahid	one entitled to use ijtihad (especially in Shi'ite law); senior Jurist
mulk	possession, whence Kingship, Dominion (cf. Latin dominium)
mulla	see 'ālim
örf	see 'urf
qādī (kādī)	(Religious) Judge
qānūn (kānūn)	(from Greek canon) non-religious law
qiyās	reasoning by Analogy (in Law)
ra'īyya (re'ayat)	common people
sayyid	lord, descendant of 'Ali
Şeriat	*see* Shari'a
şeykülislām	*see* shaykh-al-islām
shah	king (Persian)
Sharī'a	Religious Law, Right, Rectitude, Code (see p. 33) ('the whole body of rules guiding the life of a Muslim in law, ethics and etiquette': Hodgson 1974: vol. 2, p. 585)
sharīf	noble; descendant of the Prophet

shaykh	elder, chief of tribe, sufi teacher
shaykh-al-islām	chief official of the religious judiciary and administration in a state
shūrā	consultation
siyāsa	discipline, Governance, government[1]
sulṭān	power, ruler, sovereign
sunna	custom, Religious Tradition (*see* p. 32)
Sunnī	those 'Traditional' Muslims, in fact the large majority, who proclaim adherence to the Sunna as defined in their four law-schools (see Chapter 3)
taqīyya	precautionary dissimulation
timar	*see* iqtāʿ
ʿulamāʾ, ʿulema	(sing. ʿālim) those with knowledge (ʿilm q.v.), the Learned, Religious Experts
umma	the People or Community (of Islam); (modern) nation
ʿurf	non-religious customary law
vatan	*see* waṭan
vilayet	*see* wilāya
walī	protector, patron, companion
waṭan (vatan)	homeland, nation
wilāya (vilayet)	legal competence, guardianship, Mandate
waqf (vakif)	pious foundation, religious Trust
zakāt	alms-tax due by law from Muslims

NOTE

1. Bernard Lewis, 'Siyasa', in A. H. Green (ed.), *In Quest of an Islamic Humanism* (Cairo, 1984), pp. 3–14; Fauzi M. Najjar, 'Siyasa in Islamic Political Philosophy', in M. E. Marmura (ed.), *Islamic Theology and Philosophy* (Albany, New York: SUNY Press, 1984), pp. 92–110.

Bibliography

Primary sources are given in a note at the start of the relevant sections, indicated in **bold** in the Index under the author's name.

Ahmad, Aziz (1962), 'Trends in the Political Thought of Medieval Muslim India', *SI* 17, pp. 121–30.
—— (1964), *Studies in Islamic Culture in the Indian Environment*, Oxford, Oxford University Press.
—— (1967), *Islamic Modernism in India and Pakistan, 1857–1964*, Oxford, Oxford University Press.
—— (1969), *An Intellectual History of Islam in India*, Edinburgh, Edinburgh University Press.
Ahmad, Aziz and G. E. von Grunebaum (eds) (1970), *Muslim Self-statement in India and Pakistan, 1857–1968*, Wiesbaden, Harrassowitz.
Ahmed, Ishtiaq (1987), *The Concept of an Islamic State: An Analysis of the Ideological Controversy in Pakistan*, London, Pinter.
Aksan, Virginia H. (1993), 'Ottoman Political Writing, 1768–1808', *IJMES* 25, pp. 53–69.
—— (1995), *An Ottoman Statesman in War and Peace: Ahmed Resmi Efendi, 1700–83*, Leiden, Brill.
Alam, Muzaffar and Sanjay Subrahmanyam (eds) (1998), *The Mughal State 1526–1750*, Delhi, Oxford University Press. = AS
Algar, Hamid (1969), *Religion and State in Iran 1785–1906: The Role of the Ulema in the Qajar Period*, Berkeley CA, University of California Press.
(1973), *Mirza Malkum Khan: A Study in the History of Iranian Modernism*, Berkeley, CA, University of California Press.
Amanat, Abbas (1988), 'In between the Madrasa and the Marketplace', in Arjomand (ed.), pp. 198–127.
Arjomand, Said Amir (1984), *The Shadow of God and the Hidden Imam: Religion, Political Order and Societal Change in Shi'ite Iran from the Beginning to 1890*, Chicago, Chicago University Press.
—— (1988), *The Turban for the Crown: The Islamic Revolution in Iran*, New York, Oxford University Press.
—— (ed.) (1988), *Authority and Political Culture in Shi'ism*, Albany NY, SUNY.
Arnold, Thomas W. (1924), *The Caliphate*, Oxford, The Clarendon Press.
Ashtiany, Julia et al. (eds) (1990), *'Abbasid Belles Lettres*, Cambridge, Cambridge University Press. = BL
Anon. (1970), *Le Shiisme Imamite* (1970), Colloque de Strasbourg 1968, Paris, Presses Universitaires de France.

Anon. (1982), *La notion de l'autorité au moyen âge: Islam, Byzance, Occident* (1982), colloques internationales de la Naipaule, Paris, Presses Universitaires de France.

Anon. (1985), *La notion de la liberté au moyen âge: Islam, Byzance, Occident* (1985), Paris, 'Les belles lettres'.

Ayalon, David (1977), *Studies on the Mamluks of Egypt*, London, Ashgate.

Ayubi, Nazih (1991), *Political Islam: Religion and Politics in the Arab World*, London, Routledge.

al-Azmeh, Aziz (1982), *Ibn Khaldun*, London, Routledge.

Badawi, A. (1972), *Histoire de la philosophie en Islam*, vol. 2: *Les philosophes purs*, Paris, Vrin.

Bakhash, Shaul (1978), *Iran: Monarchy, Bureaucracy and Reform under the Qajars, 1858–1896*, London, Ithaca.

Baljon, J. M. S. (1986), *The Religion and Thought of Shah Wali Allah Dihlavi*, Leiden, Brill.

Beinin, Joel and Joe Stork (eds) (1997), *Political Islam: Essays from Middle Eastern Reports*, London, Tauris.

Berkes, Niyazi (1964), *The Development of Secularism in Turkey*, Montreal, McGill University Press.

Berktay, Halil and Suraiya Faroqhi (eds) (1992), *New Approaches to Middle-Eastern History*, London, Frank Cass.

Binder, Leonard (1988), *Islamic Liberalism: A Critique of Development Ideologies*, Chicago, Chicago University Press.

Black, Antony (1979), *Council and Commune*, London, Burns & Oates.

—— (1984), *Guilds and Civil Society in European Political Thought*, London, Methuen.

—— (1992) *Political Thought in Europe, 1250–1450*, Cambridge, Cambridge University Press.

Bosworth, C. E. (1963), *The Ghaznavids: Their Empire in Afghanistan and Eastern Iran, 994–1040*, Edinburgh, Edinburgh University Press.

—— (ed.) (1971), *Iran and Islam*, Edinburgh, Edinburgh University Press.

Brunschvig, R. and G. E. von Grunebaum (eds) (1977), *Classicisme et déclin culturelle dans l'histoire d'Islam*, Paris, Maisonneuve & Larose.

Bulliet, Richard W. (1994), *Islam: The View from the Edge*, New York, Columbia University Press.

Burns, J. H. (ed.) 1988, *The Cambridge History of Medieval Political Thought, c.350-c.1450*, Cambridge, Cambridge University Press.

Cahen, Claude (1958), 'Zur Geschichte der städtischen Gesellschaft im islamischen Orient des Mittelalters', *Saeculum* 9, pp. 59–76.

—— (1958–9) 'Mouvements populaires et autonomies urbaines dans l'Asie musulmane du moyen âge', *Arabica* 5, pp. 225–50 and 6, pp. 25–56, 233–65.

—— (1968), *Pre-Ottoman Turkey: A General Survey of the Material and Spiritual Culture and History, c.1071–1330*, London, Sidgwick & Jackson.

—— (1977), *Les peuples musulmans dans l'histoire médiévale*, Damascus.

Cambridge History of India, The New, vol. 1, part v (1993), *The Mughal Empire* by John F. Richards, Cambridge, Cambridge University Press.

—— vol.3, part iv (1994), *Ideologies of the Raj* by Thomas Metcalf, Cambridge, Cambridge University Press. = *CH India*

Cambridge History of Iran, The, vol 4: *From the Arab Invasions to the Saljuqs* (1975), ed. R. N. Frye, Cambridge, Cambridge University Press.

—— vol. 5: *The Saljuq and Mongol Periods* (1968), ed. J. A. Boyle, Cambridge, Cambridge University Press.

—— vol. 6: *The Timurid and Safavid Periods* (1986), ed. P. Jackson and L. Lockhart, Cambridge, Cambridge University Press.

—— vol. 7: *From Nadir Shah to the Islamic Republic* (1991), ed. Peter Avery et al., Cambridge, Cambridge University Press. = CH Iran

Cambridge History of Islam, The (1970), 2 vols, ed. P. M. Holt, Ann K. S. Lambton, Bernard Lewis, Cambridge, Cambridge University Press. = CH Islam

Canard, M. (1942–7), 'L'Impérialisme des Fatimids et leur propagande', *Annales de l'Institut orientale de l'Université d'Alger*, pp. 156–200.

Chamberlain, Michael (1994), *Knowledge and Social Practice in Medieval Damascus, 1190–1350*, Cambridge, Cambridge University Press.

Charnay, J.-P. (1986), *L'Islam et la Guerre: de la guerre juste à la révolution sainte*, Paris, Fayard.

Choueiri, Youssef M. (1997), *Islamic Fundamentalism*, rev. edn, London, Pinter.

Corbin, H. (1964), *Histoire de la philosophie islamique des origines jusqu'au mort d'Averroes (1198)*, Paris, Gallimard.

Crone, Patricia (1980), *Slaves on Horses: The Evolution of the Islamic Polity*, Cambridge, Cambridge University Press.

Crone, Patricia and Michael Cook (1977), *Hagarism: The Making of the Islamic World*, Cambridge, Cambridge University Press.

Crone, Patricia and Martin Hinds (1986), *God's Caliph: Religious Authority in the First Centuries of Islam*, Cambridge, Cambridge University Press.

Danishpazhouh, Mohammed-Taqi (1988), 'An Annotated Bibliography on Government and Statecraft', in Arjomand (ed.), pp. 213–35.

Dekmejian, R. Hrair (1995), *Islam in Revolution: Fundamentalism in the Arab World*, rev. edn, Syracuse NY, Syracuse University Press.

Deringil, Selim (1998), *The Well-Protected Domains: Ideology and the Legitimation of Power in the Ottoman Empire, 1876–1909*, London, Tauris.

Enayat, Hamid (1982), *Modern Islamic Political Thought*, London, Macmillan.

Encyclopaedia of Islam, 2nd edn, ed. H. A. R. Gibb et al. (1960–), Leiden, Brill. = EI

Esposito, John (ed.) (1983), *Voices of Resurgent Islam*, Oxford, Oxford University Press.

Fakhry, Majid (1958), *Islamic Occasionalism*, London.

—— (1983), *A History of Islamic Philosophy*, 2nd edn, London, Longman.

—— (1991), *Ethical Theories in Islam*, Leiden, Brill.

Farooqi, N. R. (1989), *Mughal–Ottoman Relations (1556–1748)*, Delhi, Idarah-i Adabiyat-i Delhi.

Fleischer, Cornell H. (1983), 'Royal Authority, Dynastic Cyclism, and "Ibn Khaldun-ism" in Sixteenth-century Ottoman Letters', *Journal of Asian and African Studies* 3–4, pp. 198–220.

—— (1986), *Bureaucrat and Intellectual in the Ottoman Empire: The Historian Mustafa 'Ali (1541–1600)*, Princeton, Princeton University Press.

Fodor, Pal (1986), 'State and Society, Crisis and Reform, in 15th–17th Century Ottoman Mirrors for Princes', *Acta Orientalia Academiae Scientiarum Hungariae* 40 , pp. 217–40.

Foltz, Richard C. (1998), *Mughal India and Central Asia*, Oxford, Oxford University Press.

Fouchécour, C.-H. de (1986), *Moralia: les notions morales dans la littérature persane du 3e/9e au 7e/13e siècles*, Paris, Éditions recherche sur les civilisations.

Gardet, Louis (1981), *La Cité Musulmane: vie sociale et politique*, Paris, Vrin.

Gerber, Haim (1994), *State, Society and Law in Islam: Ottoman Law in Historical Perspective*, Albany NY, SUNY.

Gibb, H. A. R. (1962), *Studies on the Civilization of Islam*, Princeton, Princeton University Press.

Glassen, E. (1981), *Der mittlere Weg: Studien zur Religionspolitik und Religiosität der späteren 'Abbasiden-Zeit*, Wiesbaden, F. Steiner.

Goitein, S. D. (1966), *Studies in Islamic History and Institutions*, Leiden, Brill.

Goldziher, Ignaz (1971), *Muslim Studies*, ed. S. M. Stern, vol. 2, Chicago, Aldine and Atherton.

—— (1981), *Introduction to Islamic Theology and Law*, Princeton, Princeton University Press.

Grunebaum, G. E. von (1953), *Medieval Islam: A Study in Cultural Orientation*, 2nd edn, Chicago, Chicago University Press.

Guichard, P. (1977), *Structures sociales 'orientales' et 'occidentales' dans l'Espagne musulmane*, Paris, Mouton & École des hautes études en sciences sociales.

Guillaume, Alfred (1956), *Islam*, 2nd edn, London, Penguin.

—— (1966), *The Traditions of Islam: An Introduction to the Study of the Hadith Literature*, Beirut, Khayali.

Halm, Heinz (1991), *Shiism*, Edinburgh, Edinburgh University Press.

Hardy, P. (1972), *The Muslims of British India*, Cambridge, Cambridge University Press.

Hartmann, A. (1975), *An-Nasr ad-Din Allah (1180–1225): Politik, Religion, Kultur in der späteren 'Abbasidenzeit*, Berlin, de Gruyter.

Heyd, Uriel (1961), 'The Ottoman Ulema and Westernization in the Time of Selim III and Mahmud II', *Scripta Hierosolymitana* 9, pp. 63–96.

—— (1973), *Studies in Old Ottoman Criminal Law*, ed. V. L. Ménage, Oxford, The Clarendon Press.

Hodgson, Marshall G. S. (1974), *The Venture of Islam: Conscience and History in a World Civilization*, 3 vols, Chicago, Chicago University Press.

Holt, P. M. (1975), 'The Position and Power of the Mamluk Sultan', *BSOAS* 38, pp. 237–49.

—— (1977), 'The Structure of Government in the Mamluk Sultanate', in P. M. Holt (ed.), *The Eastern Mediterranean Lands in the Period of the Crusades*, Warminster, Aris & Phillips, pp. 44–61.

Horovitz, J. (1930), 'Ibn Qutaiba's 'Uyun al-Akhbar', *IC* 4, pp. 171–98, 331–62, 488–530.

—— (1931), op. cit., *IC* 5, pp. 1–27, 194–224.

Hourani, Albert (1983), *Arabic Thought in the Liberal Age, 1798–1939*, 2nd edn, Cambridge, Cambridge University Press.

Hourani, George F. (1976), 'The Islamic and Non-Islamic Origins of Mu'tazilite Ethical Rationalism', *IJMES* 7, pp. 59–87.

Hovannisian, R. G. (ed.) (1985), *Ethics in Islam*, Malibu CA, Undena.

Howard, Douglas A. (1988), 'Ottoman Historiography and the Literature of "Decline" of the Sixteenth and Seventeenth Centuries', *Journal of Asian History* 22, pp. 52–77.

Imber, Colin (1997), *Ebu 's-Su'ud: The Islamic Legal Tradition*, Edinburgh, Edinburgh University Press.

Inalçik, Halil (1964) 'The Nature of Traditional Society', in Robert E. Ward and D. A. Rustow (eds), *Political Modernization in Japan and Turkey*, Princeton, Princeton University Press, pp. 42–63.

—— (1969), 'Suleiman the Lawgiver and Ottoman Law', *Archivum Ottomanicum* 1, pp. 105–36.

—— (1973), *The Ottoman Empire: The Classical Age, 1300–1600*, London, Weidenfeld & Nicolson.

—— (1980) 'Military and Fiscal Transformation in the Ottoman Empire, 1600–1700', *Archivum Ottomanicum* 6, pp. 283–337.

—— (1992), 'Comments on "Sultanism": Max Weber's Typification of the Ottoman Polity', *Princeton Papers in Near Eastern Studies* 1, pp. 49–72.

—— (1993), *The Middle East and the Balkans under the Ottoman Empire*, Bloomington IN, Indiana University Press.

Itzkowitz, Norman (1972), *Ottoman Empire and Islamic Tradition*, Chicago, University of Chicago Press.

Izutsu, T. (1966), *Ethico-Religious Concepts in the Quran*, Montreal, McGill University Press.

Keddie, N. R. (1963), 'Symbol and Sincerity in Islam', *SI* 19, pp. 27–64.

—— (ed.) (1972a), *Scholars, Saints and Sufis*, Berkeley CA, University of California Press.

—— (1972b), *Sayyid Jamal ad-Din 'al-Afghani': A Political Biography*, Berkeley CA, University of California Press.

—— (1980), *Iran: Religion, Politics and Society: Collected Essays*, London, Cass.

—— (1981), *Roots of Revolution: An Interpretative History of Modern Iran*, New Haven CT, Yale University Press.

—— (ed.) (1983), *Religion and Politics in Iran: Shi'ism from Quietism to Revolution*, New Haven CT, Yale University Press.

Kerr, Malcolm H. (1966), *Islamic Reform: The Political and Legal Theories of Muhammad 'Abduh and Rashid Rida*, Berkeley CA, University of California Press.

Khadduri, M. (1984), *The Islamic Conception of Justice*, Baltimore MD, Johns Hopkins University Press.

Khadduri, M. and H. J. Liebesny (eds) (1955), *Law in the Middle East*, Washington DC, Middle Eastern Institute.

Khazanov, Anatoly M. (1994), *Nomads and the Outside World*, 2nd edn, Madison WI, University of Wisconsin Press.

Kohlberg, Etan (1991), *Belief and Law in Imami Shi'ism*, London, Ashgate.

Kraemer, Joel L. (1992), *Humanism in the Renaissance of Islam*, 2nd edn, Leiden, Brill.

Kulke, Hermann (ed.) (1995), *The State in India, 1000–1700*, Delhi, Oxford University Press.

Kulke, Hermann and Dietmar Rothermund (1998), *A History of India*, 3rd edn, London, Routledge.

Kunt, I. Metin (1983), *The Sultan's Servants: The Transformations of Ottoman Provincial Government, 1550–1650*, New York, Columbia University Press.

Lambton, Ann K. S. (1953), *Landlord and Peasant in Persia: A Study of Land Tenure and Land Revenue Administration*, Oxford, Oxford University Press.

—— (1970), 'The Persian 'Ulama and Constitutional Reform', in Anon. (1970), pp. 245–70.

—— (1974), 'Some New Trends in Islamic Political Thought in Late 18th and Early 19th century Persia', *SI* 39, pp. 95–128.

—— (1980), *Theory and Practice in Medieval Persian Government*, London, Ashgate.

—— (1981), *State and Government in Medieval Islam: An Introduction to the Study of Islamic Political Thought: The Jurists*, Oxford, Oxford University Press.

—— (1988) *Continuity and Change in Medieval Persia: Aspects of Administrative, Economic and Social History, 11th to 14th Centuries*, London, Tauris.

Landau, Jacob M. (1994), *The Politics of Pan-Islam: Ideology and Organisation*, rev. edn, Oxford, Oxford University Press.

Laoust, Henri (1939), *Essai sur les doctrines sociales et politiques d'Ibn Taymiyya*, Cairo, Institut français d'archéologie orientale.

—— (1970), *La Politique de Gazali*, Paris, Librarie orientaliste.

Lapidus, Ira M. (1975), 'Separation of State and Religion in Early Islamic Society', *IJMES* 6, pp. 363–85.

—— (1984), *Muslim Cities in the Later Middle Ages*, 2nd edn, Cambridge, Cambridge University Press.

—— (1988), *A History of Islamic Societies*, Cambridge, Cambridge University Press.

Leaman, Oliver (1985), *An Introduction to Medieval Islamic Philosophy*, Cambridge, Cambridge University Press.

—— (1988), *Averroes and his Philosophy*, Oxford, Oxford University Press.

Lerner, Ralph and Muhsin Mahdi (eds) (1963), *Medieval Political Philosophy: A Source-book*, Toronto, Free Press of Glencoe. = LM

Levy, R. (1957), *The Social Structure of Islam*, Cambridge, Cambridge University Press.

Lewis, Bernard (1954), 'Ottoman Observers of Ottoman Decline', *IS* 2, pp. 71–84.

—— (1967), *The Assassins: A Radical Sect in Islam*, London, Weidenfeld & Nicolson.

—— (1968), *The Emergence of Modern Turkey*, 2nd edn, Oxford, Oxford University Press.

—— (1986), 'Ibn Khaldun in Turkey, ' in M. Sharon (ed.), *Studies in Islamic History and Civilization*, Leiden, Brill, pp. 519–30.

—— (1988), *The Political Language of Islam*, Chicago, University of Chicago Press.

Lewis, Bernard and P. M. Holt (eds) (1962), *Historians in the Middle East*, London, Oxford University Press.

Lindner, Rudi P.(1983), *Nomads and Ottomans in Medieval Anatolia*, Bloomington IN, Research Institute for Inner Asian Studies.

Mahdi, Muhsin (1957), *Ibn Khaldun's Philosophy of History*, London, Allen & Unwin.

Makdisi, George (1981), *The Rise of Colleges: Institutions of Learning in Islam and the West*, Edinburgh, Edinburgh University Press.

—— (1990), *The Rise of Humanism in Classical Islam and the Christian West*, Edinburgh, Edinburgh University Press.

Malik, Hafeez (1980), *Sir Sayyid Ahmad Khan and Muslim Modernization in India and Pakistan*, New York, Columbia University Press.

Manz, B. F. (1989), *The Rise of Tamerlane*, Cambridge, Cambridge University Press.

Mardin Şerif (1960), 'The Mind of the Turkish Reformer, 1700–1900', *The Western Humanities Review* 14, pp. 413–36.

—— (1962), *The Genesis of Young Ottoman Thought: A Study in the Modernization of Turkish Political Ideas*, Princeton, Princeton University Press.

Marlow, Louise (1997), *Hierarchy and Egalitarianism in Islamic Thought*, Cambridge, Cambridge University Press.

Marquet, Y. (1961), 'Imamat, résurrection et hiérarchie selon les Ihwan al-Safa', *REI* 30, pp. 49–142.

—— (1973), *La Philosophie des Ihwan al-Safa*, Algiers, Études et documents.

Mitchell, Richard P. (1969), *The Society of Muslim Brothers*, Oxford, Oxford University Press.

Morgan, David (1988), *Medieval Persia 1040–1797*, London, Longman.

Mottahedeh, Roy P. (1980), *Loyalty and Leadership in Early Islamic Society*, Princeton, Princeton University Press.

Moussalli, Ahmad S. (1992), *Radical Islamic Fundamentalism: The Ideological and Political Discourse of Sayyid Qutb*, Beirut, American University of Beirut.

Nagel, Tilman (1981), *Staat und Glaubengemeinschaft im Islam: Geschichte der politischen Ordnungsvorstellungen der Muslime*, 2 vols, Zurich and Munich, Artemis.

——(1988), *Die Festung des Glaubens: Triumph und Scheitern des islamischen Rationalismus im 11. Jahrhundert*, Munich, Beck.

Nasr, S. H. and O. Leaman (eds) (1996), *History of Islamic Philosophy*, 2 vols, London, Routledge. = NL

Othman, A. I. (1960), *The Concept of Man in the Writings of al-Ghazali*, Cairo.

Pellat, Charles (tr.) (1954), *Le Livre de la Couronne: Kitab al-Taj attribué à Gahiz*, Paris, Les belles lettres.

——(1969), *The Life and Works of Jahiz: Translations of Selected Texts*, Berkeley CA, University of California Press.

Peters, R. (1977), *Jihad in Medieval and Modern Islam*, Leiden, Brill.

Qureshi, I. H. (1942), *The Administration of the Delhi Sultanate*, Lahore, M. Ashraf.

Reid, James J. (1983), *Tribalism and Society in Islamic Iran 1500–1629*, Malibu CA, Undena.

Richter, Gustav (1932), *Studien zur Geschichte der älteren Arabischen Fürstenspiegel*, Leipzig, Hinrichs.

Rizvi, A. A. (1965), *Muslim Revivalist Movements in Northern India in the Sixteenth and Seventeenth Centuries*, Agra, Agra University.

——(1975), *The Religious and Intellectual History of Muslims in Akbar's Reign with special reference to Abu 'l Fazl (1556–1605)*, New Delhi, Munshiram Manoharlal.

——(1978), *A History of Sufism in India*, 2 vols, New Delhi, M. Manoharlal.

Rosenthal, Erwin I. J. (1958), *Political Thought in Medieval Islam: An Introductory Outline*, Cambridge, Cambridge University Press.

——(1965), *Islam in the Modern Nation State*, Cambridge, Cambridge University Press.

Rosenthal, Franz (1960), *The Muslim Concept of Freedom Prior to the 19th Century*, Leiden, Brill.

——(1968), *A History of Muslim Historiography*, 2nd edn, Leiden, Brill.

——(1970), *Knowledge Triumphant: The Concept of Knowledge in Medieval Islam*, Leiden, Brill.

Roy, Olivier (1994), *The Failure of Political Islam*, tr. C. Volk (1992), London, Tauris.

Ruthven, Malise (1984), *Islam and the World*, Harmondsworth, Penguin.

Sachedina, A. A. (1988), *The Just Ruler (al-sultan al-'adil) in Shi'ite Islam: The Comprehensive Authority of the Jurist in Imamate Jurisprudence*, New York, Oxford University Press.

Schacht, Joseph (1953), *The Origins of Muhammedan Jurisprudence*, rev. edn, Oxford, Oxford University Press.

Shaw, Stanford J. (1971), *Between the Old and New: The Ottoman Empire under Sultan Selim III, 1789–1807*, Cambridge MA, Harvard University Press.

——(1976), *History of the Ottoman Empire and Modern Turkey*, vol. 1: *Empire of the Ghazis: The Rise and Decline of the Ottoman Empire 1280–1808*, Cambridge, Cambridge University Press.

Shaw, Stanford J. and E. K. Shaw (1977), *History of the Ottoman Empire and Modern Turkey*, vol. 2: *Reform, Revolution and Republic: The Rise of Modern Turkey 1808–1975*, Cambridge, Cambridge University Press.

Skinner, Quentin (1978), *The Foundations of Modern Political Thought*, 2 vols, Cambridge, Cambridge University Press.

Stern, S. M. (ed.) (1965), *Documents from Islamic Chanceries*, Oxford, Cassirer.

Streusand, Douglas E. (1989), *The Formation of the Mughal Polity*, New Delhi, Oxford University Press.

Subrahmanyam, Sanjay (1992), 'The Mughal State: Structure or Process? Reflections on Recent Western Historiography', *Indian Economic and Social History Review* 29, pp. 291–321.

Tierney, Brian (1972), *Origins of Papal Infallibility*, Leiden, Brill.

Trimingham, J. S. (1971), *The Sufi Orders in Islam*, Oxford, Oxford University Press.

Tyan, E. (1954–6), *Institutions du droit public musulman*, vol. 1: *Le Califat*, vol. 2: *Sultanat et Califat*, Paris, Sirey.

Ullmann, Walter (1955), *The Growth of Papal Government in the Middle Ages*, London, Methuen.

Urvoy, Dominique (1990), *Pensers d'al-Andalus: la vie intellectuelle à Cordoue et Seville au temps des empires Berbères (fin XIe siècle au debut XIIIe siècle)*, Paris, Éditions du CNRS.

—— (1991), *Ibn Rushd (Averroes)*, London, Routledge.

Vanina, Eugenia (1996), *Ideas and Society in India from the Sixteenth to the Eighteenth Centuries*, Delhi, Oxford University Press.

Vatikiotis, P. J. (1971), *Conflict in the Middle East*, London, Allen & Unwin.

—— (1987), *Islam and the State*, London, Croom Helm.

—— (1991), *The History of Modern Egypt from Muhammad Ali to Mubarak*, 4th edn, London, Weidenfeld & Nicolson.

Watt, W. Montgomery (1963), *The Muslim Intellectual: The Struggle and Achievement of al-Ghazali*, Edinburgh, Edinburgh University Press.

—— (1968), *Islamic Political Thought*, Edinburgh, Edinburgh University Press.

—— (1988), *Islamic Fundamentalism and Modernity*, London, Routledge.

Wensinck, A. J. (1971), *A Handbook of Early Muhammedan Tradition*, Leiden, Brill.

Woods, John E. (1976), *The Aqquyunlu: Clan, Confederation, Empire*, Minneapolis MN, Bibliotheca Islamica.

Zilfi, Maddine C. (1988), *The Politics of Piety: The Ottoman ulema in the Postclassical Age (1600–1800)*, Minneapolis MN, Bibliotheca Islamica.

Zubaida, Sami (1993), *Islam: The People and the State: Political Ideas and Movements in the Middle East*, London, Tauris.

—— (1995), 'Is there a Muslim Society? Ernest Gellner's Sociology of Islam', *Economy and Society* 24, pp. 151–88.

Zürcher, Erik J. (1998), *Turkey: A Modern History*, rev. edn, London, Tauris.

Index

Index (main entries shown in **bold**)